Seventy-Five Years in California

Also from Westphalia Press
westphaliapress.org

The Idea of the Digital University

France and New England Volumes 1, 2, & 3

Treasures of London

The History of Photography

L'Enfant and the Freemasons

Baronial Bedrooms

Making Trouble for Muslims

Material History and Ritual Objects

Paddle Your Own Canoe

Opportunity and Horatio Alger

Careers in the Face of Challenge

Bookplates of the Kings

Collecting American Presidential Autographs

Freemasonry in Old Buffalo

Young Freemasons?

Social Satire and the Modern Novel

The Essence of Harvard

Ivanhoe Masonic Quartettes

A Definitive Commentary on Bookplates

James Martineau and Rebuilding Theology

No Bird Lacks Feathers

Gilded Play

Earthworms, Horses, and Living Things

The Man Who Killed President Garfield

Anti-Masonry and the Murder of Morgan

Understanding Art

Homeopathy

Fishing the Florida Keys

Collecting Old Books

Masonic Secret Signs and Passwords

The Thomas Starr King Dispute

Earl Warren's Masonic Lodge

Lariats and Lassos

Mr. Garfield of Ohio

The Wisdom of Thomas Starr King

The French Foreign Legion

War in Syria

Naturism Comes to the United States

New Sources on Women and Freemasonry

Designing, Adapting, Strategizing in Online Education

Gunboat and Gun-runner

Meeting Minutes of Naval Lodge No. 4 F.A.A.M

Seventy-Five Years in California

A History of Events and 19th Century Life

by William Heath Davis

WESTPHALIA PRESS
An imprint of Policy Studies Organization

Seventy-Five Years in California: A History of Events and 19th Century Life
All Rights Reserved © 2015 by Policy Studies Organization

Westphalia Press
An imprint of Policy Studies Organization
1527 New Hampshire Ave., NW
Washington, D.C. 20036
info@ipsonet.org

ISBN-13: 978-1-63391-161-1
ISBN-10: 1633911616

Cover design by Taillefer Long at Illuminated Stories:
www.illuminatedstories.com

Daniel Gutierrez-Sandoval, Executive Director
PSO and Westphalia Press

Rahima Schwenkbeck, Director of Media and Marketing
PSO and Westphalia Press

Updated material and comments on this edition
can be found at the Westphalia Press website:
www.westphaliapress.org

SEVENTY-FIVE YEARS
IN CALIFORNIA

SAN FRANCISCO
1849

DRAWN ON THE SPOT BY HENRY FIRKS

LATEST EDITION CORRECTED BY A COMMITTEE OF
PIONEERS CONSISTING OF
RICHARD M. SHERMAN   WILLIAM HEATH DAVIS
FERDINAND VASSAULT

1 Am. Sh. Huntress
2 Br. B. Asenath
3 Dan. B. Neptunas
4 Fr. B. Staveuil
5 Fr. Schr. Chateaubriand
6 Mer. Sch. Victoria
7 Am. Sh. Forrester
8 Am. B. Oberon
9 Am. B. Superior
10 Am. Sh. Philadelphia
   (Burned June 24)
11 Ch. B. Carmen
12 Haw. B. Mary Frances
13 Am. Sh. Edwin
14 Fr. Sh. Ronald
15 Dan. Sh. Adelia
16 Am. Sh. Grey Eagle
17 Br. B. John Ritson
18 Am. B. Col. Fremont
19 Ch. Sh. Virginia
20 Am. Sh. Sea Queen
21 Ch. B. Maria Louisa
22 Ch. B. Romano
23 Am. Scr. Thomas
24 Am. B. Quito
25 Am. B. Louisiana
26 Am. Sh. Greyhound
27 Ch. Sh. California Dorado
28 Am. Steamer Panama
29 Am. B. Col. Benton
30 Am. Sh. Massachusetts
31 Am. B. Lucy Penniman
32 Fr. B. Limanienne
33 Ch. Sh. Gen. Ferrias
34 Am. Sh. Honolulu
35 Fr. B. Olympe
36 Am. Sh. Herber
37 Am. Steamer Oregon
38 U. S. S. Warren
39 U. S. S. Southampton
40 Quarm. P. Invincible
41 H. B. M. Inconstant
42 Launch for Stockton
43 Customhouse (Emily & Jane)
44 Golden Gate
45 Parkers Hotel
46 P. M. S. S. Cos. Office
47 S. H. Williams & Cos. Store
48 F. Vassault & Cos. Store
49 Leisdorff's Residence
50 Cross, Hobson & Cos. Store
51 Starkey, Janion & Cos. Ware Ho.
52 City Hotel
53 Sherman & Ruckel
54 Mellus & Howard
55 Burling & Hill
56 Wm. H. Davis
57 Macondray & Co.
58 Wm. S. Clark
59 Catholic Church
60 Marsh & Simonton
61 Ward & Smith
62 Isld. Yerba Buena

𝔖𝔢𝔳𝔢𝔫𝔱𝔶=𝔣𝔦𝔳𝔢 𝔜𝔢𝔞𝔯𝔰
IN CALIFORNIA

A HISTORY OF EVENTS AND LIFE IN CALIFORNIA: *Personal, Political and Military;* Under the Mexican Regime; During the Quasi-Military Government of the Territory by the United States, and after the admission of the State to the Union:

Being a compilation by a witness of the events described; a reissue and enlarged illustrated edition of "Sixty Years in California," to which much new matter by its author has been added which he contemplated publishing under the present title at the time of his death; edited and with an historical foreword and index by DOUGLAS S. WATSON—

BY

WILLIAM HEATH DAVIS

TO
HERBERT HOOVER
EXEMPLIFIER OF AMERICAN IDEALS

AND FOREMOST CALIFORNIAN

The permission granted to inscribe "Seventy-five Years in California" to you permits the linking of your name with the vital chronicle William Heath Davis has left us of the early days of California, the State of your adoption, and in which you have shown such profound interest.

J. H.

WILLIAM HEATH DAVIS
1822–1909

Portrait of the author by an unknown artist, painted in 1850 when Mr. Davis was twenty eight.

PUBLISHER'S PREFACE

"SEVENTY-FIVE Years in California" would have been published by its author William Heath Davis before his death in 1909 but for the great San Francisco Fire in 1906. His manuscript was ready for the printer. All the new material which he contemplated adding to his book "Sixty Years in California"—San Francisco 1889—in order to bring out a new and enlarged edition under the title which this work bears, was contained in two dispatch boxes upon his desk in his office in the Montgomery Block. Mr. Davis endeavored to enter and save the matter upon which he had labored for years, but was prevented from doing so by United States Marines, and although the building escaped destruction, when he returned after the conflagration, the two boxes containing his papers had disappeared.

At his home, however, he had preserved fragments and notes from which his finished manuscript had been prepared. At eighty-four one does not possess the vigor to attack a task of doing over again what has taken years to accomplish. Upon his death three years later, his papers passed from his heirs into other hands, eventually coming into possession of the Huntington Library. Due to the hearty co-operation of this institution, the publication of Mr. Davis' book under the title he had chosen has been made possible.

William Heath Davis lived through California's Pastoral Period, when the Missions were disintegrating and their lands were passing into the hands of the great rancheros; he welcomed the American Invasion which resulted in the Conquest under Sloat, Stockton and Frémont; he took a prominent part in the up-building of San Francisco after the Discovery of Gold; and more than all, his intimates were those foremost men, natives of California and Americans alike, whose lives of heroic pattern are woven into the historical background of the Golden State.

"Seventy-five Years in California" is not a simple narrative. It is rather an encyclopædia of episodes and personal portraits. No book written by a contemporary dealing with California has been so widely quoted as the volume of which the present work is the outgrowth. It is the acknowledged source book for the period which it covers.

William Heath Davis came from a Boston sea-faring, ship-owning family, although born in Honolulu in 1822. His father, Wm. Heath Davis, senior, married a daughter of Oliver Holmes, another Boston ship-master and a relative of Doctor Oliver Wendell Holmes. It is interesting to note that the shipping trade to the Coast and to Hawaii was almost exclusively in the hands of Boston firms from its beginnings to the days of the Gold Rush. Davis' grandmother on his mother's side was a native of Hawaii, and her husband, Oliver Holmes, in addition to his trading operations, was at one time Governor of Oahu.

Another of Oliver Holmes' daughters married Nathan Spear, one of that trio of first merchants to settle in San Francisco; William Sturgis Hinckley and Jacob Primer Leese being the other partners.

Davis first visited California as a small boy in 1831. He came a second time in 1833, and at length, in 1838, he arrived aboard the "Don Quixote" to enter the service of his uncle Nathan Spear as a clerk in the latter's store in Monterey.

For four years Davis followed the fortunes of Nathan Spear, first at Monterey and later at Yerba Buena, the straggling settlement which he was to help build into the City of San Francisco. In 1842 he engaged as supercargo on the "Don Quixote" and made several trips to the Hawaiian Islands.

From 1845 onward Davis was a San Franciscan. He entered business on his own account, and in time became one of the town's prominent merchants and ship-owners.

His intimacy with native Californians has been mentioned. In 1847 he married Maria de Jesus, daughter of Don Joaquin Estudillo, a wealthy ranchero. Few men of his time had the opportunity Davis had of seeing all sides of Californian life, and none has left a record as vital and as full. He died at Hayward, California, April 19, 1909.

As boy, man, and patriarch, he saw the city he loved grow from a mere hamlet under the Mexican flag; in middle life his hand helped shape San Francisco's future; he served upon the town's ayuntamiento, or Town Council, and he was honored by its citizens who named one of its streets after him.

Many have written of the early days of California and of San Francisco, but none has caught the spirit and personality of both State and City and has passed it on to posterity as has William Heath Davis in this book which bears the title, "Seventy-five Years in California," a name chosen by him before his passing.

Much of the hitherto unpublished material now appears for the first time thanks to the courtesy of the Huntington Library and to Mr. Templeton Crocker. Gratitude is due Mr. Robert E. Cowan for his important suggestions for the betterment of this volume, notably in the accuracy of the spelling of the names of both people and ships. His meticulous care in the correction of Davis' somewhat erratic spelling is especially appreciated. The publisher wishes also to acknowledge the help he has received from Miss Dorothy Huggins of the California Historical Society, and Fred De Witt, Judge J. F. Davis, Thomas P. Burns and George Barron, of the deYoung Museum, while preparing the present volume for the press. Particular thanks are due to my friend and co-worker, Douglas S. Watson, who has been untiring in his research and in the careful editing of the Davis manuscript. Without his diligent and painstaking efforts a proper publication of the book at this time would not have been possible.

San Francisco,   JOHN HOWELL
December 15, 1928.

CALIFORNIA WAS NAMED NEW ALBION BY DRAKE IN 1579

Francis Drake is here being crowned by the "King of New Albion." The ship is doubtless the "Golden Hind," which Drake, its commander, careened and refitted somewhere on the coast of California—exact location unknown. Reproduced from the German edition of Montanus Amsterdam, 1673

TRANSLATION: The King of Albion or New England, so called because the English have become very powerful in this country of America situated in the western portion of Mexico near the Kingdoms of Anian, Tolm, Conibas, Totoneac and New Granada and California. It is separated by a great river from Canada as well as New France. It limits Norumbega to the westward; to the east great rocks surround it and the sea is upon its north. The English do much business there.

Its people are civilized, particularly the Sovereign, the Grandees, the Priests of the Law and the Magistrates. They observe justice carefully. They retain still some of the ancient idolatries. They believe nevertheless in the immortality of the soul. The sovereign and the grandees are curious and magnificent in their clothing made of beautiful skins embroidered with precious stones and fastened with golden threads. These they carry on their shoulders—their heads are ornamented with fine feathers and they deck themselves with necklaces, bracelets of pearls and precious stones.

TABLE OF CONTENTS

CHAPTER		PAGE
	HISTORICAL FOREWORD by Douglas S. Watson	xix-xxxii
I.	AUTHOR'S FIRST ARRIVAL IN CALIFORNIA	1
II.	THE MISSION OF SAN FRANCISCO DE ASIS	6
III.	WM. A. RICHARDSON'S ARRIVAL 1822	9
IV.	AUTHOR RETURNS ON "DON QUIXOTE"	16
V.	RUSSIAN AMERICAN FUR COMPANY	22
VI.	JACOB PRIMER LEESE ARRIVES IN 1833	25
VII.	ELK ON MARE ISLAND	31
VIII.	HOW THE MISSIONS WERE SUPPORTED	35
IX.	LIFE ON CALIFORNIA RANCHOS	38
X.	THE HORSE IN EARLY CALIFORNIA	43
XI.	ALVARADO'S ARREST OF AMERICANS	46
XII.	NATHAN SPEAR AND THE AUTHOR DETAINED	50
XIII.	VISIT OF DE MOFRAS TO CALIFORNIA	52
XIV.	PRIESTS AND MISSION LIFE	57
XV.	INDIAN INSURRECTIONS AND TREACHERY	63
XVI.	AUTHOR'S COURTSHIP AND MARRIAGE	71
XVII.	A SPORTSMAN'S PARADISE	76
XVIII.	CALIFORNIA AMUSEMENTS	79
XIX.	MEXICAN PUBLIC MEN AND OTHERS	84
XX.	THE HUDSON'S BAY COMPANY IN YERBA BUENA	91
XXI.	COMMODORE WILKES VISITS YERBA BUENA	95
XXII.	THE "JULIA ANN" SAILS INTO PORT	102
XXIII.	BOSTON SHIPS AND TRADERS	105
XXIV.	AMERICAN OCCUPATION OF 1842	111

TABLE OF CONTENTS

CHAPTER		PAGE
XXV.	A Lot About Thomas Ap Catesby Jones, U. S. N.	117
XXVI.	Something Concerning Don Luis Vignes	120
XXVII.	Early American Settlers in California	123
XXVIII.	Alvarado Ousts Governor Micheltorena	126
XXIX.	More About the Revolution	130
XXX.	General M. G. Vallejo's Lands and Cattle	135
XXXI.	Vallejo's Appeal for Annexation to United States	141
XXXII.	Californians and Their Ways	143
XXXIII.	William Sturgis Hinckley Builds the First Bbidge	149
XXXIV.	Ships, Hides, Customs Officials and Contraband	153
XXXV.	First Discovery of Gold in California	159
XXXVI.	Gold, Gold and More Gold	165
XXXVII.	Firewater, Bonfires and Scared Indians	169
XXXVIII.	Nathan Spear's Grist Mill; the First	174
XXXIX.	H. M. S. "Blossom" Discovers Blossom Rock	181
XL.	Don Francisco Guerrero Gives a Strawberry "Blowout"	187
XLI.	Holy Days and Holidays	195
XLII.	Yankee Turkey Shooting at Christmas	199
XLIII.	Franciscan Fathers First-Class Merchants	204
XLIV.	W. D. M. Howard, Trader, Jester and Bold Operator	210
XLV.	Samuel Brannan, the Great '46er	214
XLVI.	A Ride to Chino and a Gift to the Pope	218
XLVII.	Folsom's Foresight; and Talbot H. Green's Past	225
XLVIII.	Yoscolo, the Mission Indian Renegade	230
XLIX.	Don José de la Guerra y Noriega and His Family	236
L.	Henry Mellus; From Fo'c'sle Hand to Merchant	242
LI.	Rivalry and Goodfeeling Between Traders	246
LII.	de Pedrorena, Merchant and Stockton's Lieutenant	250
LIII.	The Great Hide and Tallow Trade	255
LIV.	Author Becomes Merchant; Buys the "Euphemia"	260
LV.	"See The American Flag Flying!"	266
LVI.	Frémont Sends for Davis	272
LVII.	Stockton the Real Conquerer; and the Conquest	278

TABLE OF CONTENTS

CHAPTER		PAGE
LVIII.	Frémont Too Busy to Talk	284
LIX.	Frémont in the Rôle of Pardoner	291
LX.	Mrs. Paty's Wine Cask Empties Mysteriously	295
LXI.	Yerba Buena's First American Alcalde: Lieutenant Bartlett U. S. N.	299
LXII.	The Gold Rush Starts; and other Incidents	305
LXIII.	Commodore Jones Extols Benicia in Vain	315
LXIV.	Davis Fails to Become Founder of Oakland	323
LXV.	Which Reads Like Part of Dana's "Two Years Before the Mast"	332
LXVI.	In Which the Author Ends His Record	338

APPENDIX

Extract from Proceedings of the San Francisco Ayuntamiento	343
Jasper O'Farrell's Signed Statement	345
Names of Residents Around the Bay of San Fancisco 1838	346
Centennial Celebration of Founding of Mission San Francisco de Asis	348
Father Gonzalez's Letter on the State of the Missions in the 1830–40 Decade	369
Padre Junípero Serra's Letter of July 3, 1769, Telling of His Arrival at San Diego	371
Statements of George Hyde and Letters in the Hyde Controversy	373
First San Francisco Directory	376
Chinese in California	379
Roster of Officers of Stevenson's Regiment	382
Stevenson's Regiment Comes to California	384
Some Particulars Regarding Stevenson's Regiment	386
Missions and Their Wealth; Hacendados and Their Property	389
Record of Ships Arriving from 1774 to 1847	397
Bibliography	411
Index	415

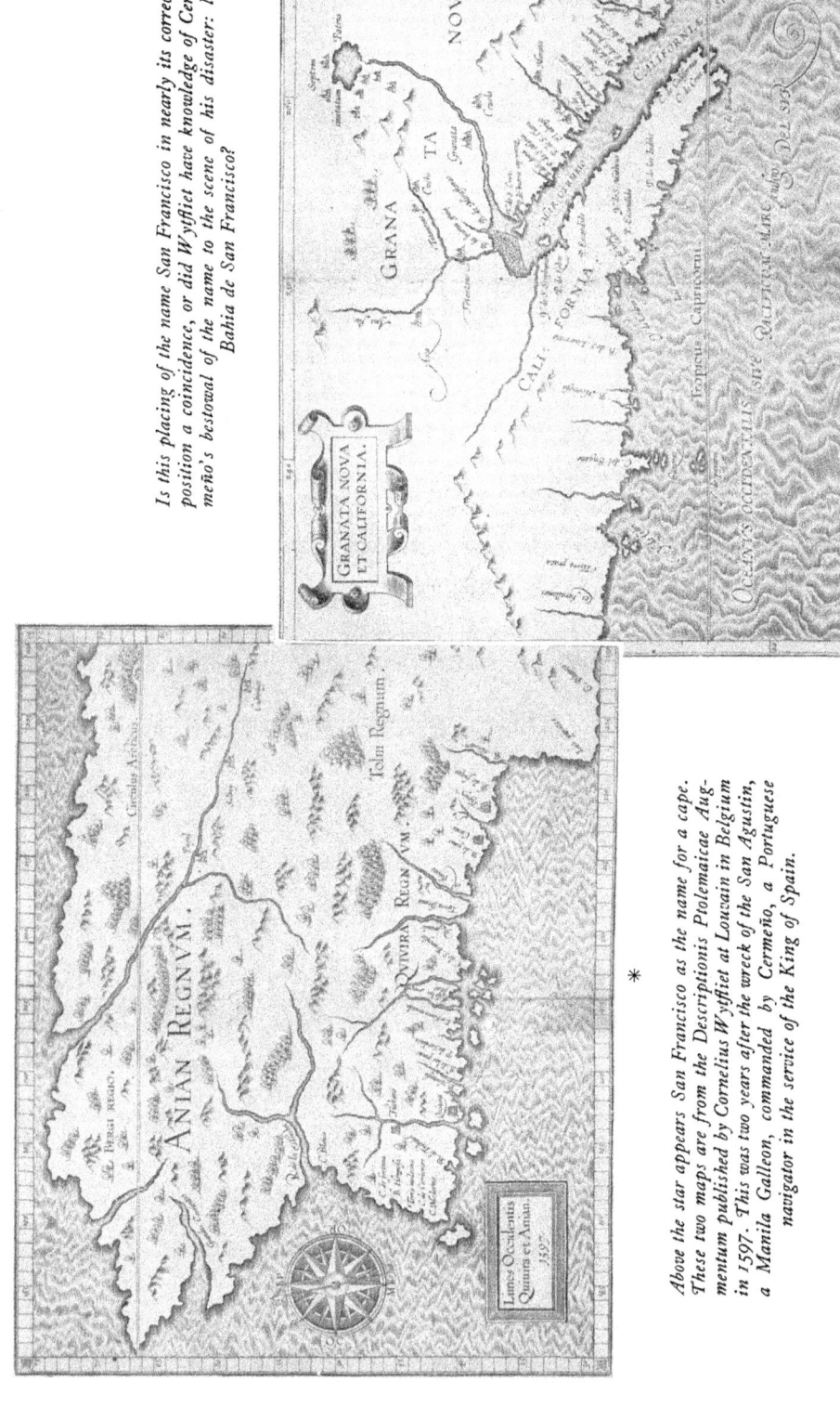

Is this placing of the name San Francisco in nearly its correct position a coincidence, or did Wytfliet have knowledge of Cermeño's bestowal of the name to the scene of his disaster: la Bahia de San Francisco?

Above the star appears San Francisco as the name for a cape. These two maps are from the Descriptionis Ptolemaicae Augmentum published by Cornelius Wytfliet at Louvain in Belgium in 1597. This was two years after the wreck of the San Agustin, a Manila Galleon, commanded by Cermeño, a Portuguese navigator in the service of the King of Spain.

MAPS FROM DESCRIPTIQNIS PTOLEMAICAE AUGMENTUM CORNELIUS WYTFLIET, LOUVAIN, 1597

LIST OF ILLUSTRATIONS

San Francisco in 1846–1847 (in color)	*Inside Front Cover*
Seal of San Francisco (in color)	” ” ”
San Francisco 1849 (in color)	*Frontispiece*
Great Seal of the State of California	vi
Portrait of William Heath Davis	vii
Crowning of Drake by the King of New Albion	xi
Map of California 1597. From Descriptionis Ptolemaicæ Augmentum	xv
California as an Island, 1666. Psalm and Marginal Note from Bishops' Bible 1568 referring to location of Land of Ophir	xix
Presidio in 1816, by Louis Choris, attached to von Kotzebue's Expedition	1
Plan del Gran Puerto de San Francisco made by Don José de Cañizares 1781	6
Jacob Primer Leese's "Dam Fine Traid" letter reproduced by courtesy of Templeton Crocker, Esq.	25
Portrait of Jacob Primer Leese	26
Celebration of Completion of Jacob Primer Leese's House, July 4, 1836	27
Elk swimming Carquinez Straits	31
The Port of San Francisco, June 1, 1849	46
A California Wedding Party 1845	71
Author's Grizzled Hairs due to Grizzly Bears	81
Extracts from the Papers of the Schooner "Julia Ann."	102
Letter from Robert Semple to William Heath Davis. Letter from Thomas O. Larkin to William Heath Davis	117
Portrait of General Mariano Guadalupe Vallejo and autograph	141
San Francisco, April, 1850, by William B. McMurtrie.	149

LIST OF ILLUSTRATIONS

	PAGE
Autograph letter of Capt. John A. Sutter introducing John Bidwell to Archibald C. Peachy; July 4, 1849. John Bidwell's autograph letter to William Heath Davis, April 13, 1895	159
Sutter's Saw Mill at Coloma where James Marshall Discovered Gold, Jan. 24, 1848	160
Alcalde Grant, signed by Jesus Noé, last Mexican Alcalde, and by Washington A. Bartlett, first American Alcalde, 1846	174
Letter of Montgomery to Leidesdorff regarding safety of Vice-Consul	174
Letter from Samuel Brannan to William Heath Davis	210
Sacramento in 1848, showing Store of S. Brannan & Co.	214
Juan Bandini's Jurupa Ranch House, Riverside, California	218
Prison Ship "Euphemia"	261
Commodore John D. Sloat's general order of July 7, 1846	266
Portrait of J. C. Frémont and autograph	272
Portrait of Commodore Robert F. Stockton	278
City of Los Angeles 1854	291
Captain Montgomery's request, "See him pleasant"	299
Report upon selection of San Francisco's first school teacher, and bill in full for San Francisco's first Public School house	305
First Public School House in San Francisco	308
City of Benicia 1854	315
U. S. Custom House owned by William Heath Davis	315
Montgomery Street, San Francisco, after the fire of May 4, 1851	317
The California Star, of April 3, 1847 (photographic reproduction)	323
Appointment of William E. Leidesdorff as Vice-Consul at Yerba Buena, Oct. 29, 1845, signed by Thomas O. Larkin. Lieutenant Joseph Warren Revere's Letter of Instructions to Mr. Kern at Sutter's Fort, July 9, 1846	338
Draft of San Francisco's First Directory in handwriting of William Heath Davis	376

Facsimile of "The Californian" of March 15th, 1848, containing advertisement of William Heath Davis and the first local mention of the discovery of gold at Sutter's Mill, January 24, 1848 . . . . *End of Index*

Sixty-eight original sketches and decorations by Douglas Rodger appearing as Chapter Headings . . . . .

Reproduction in three colors of Diego Trancoso's map of California and the Missions Fr. Junípero Serra founded. From Francisco Palóu's Life of Serra published in 1787. .*Inside rear cover*

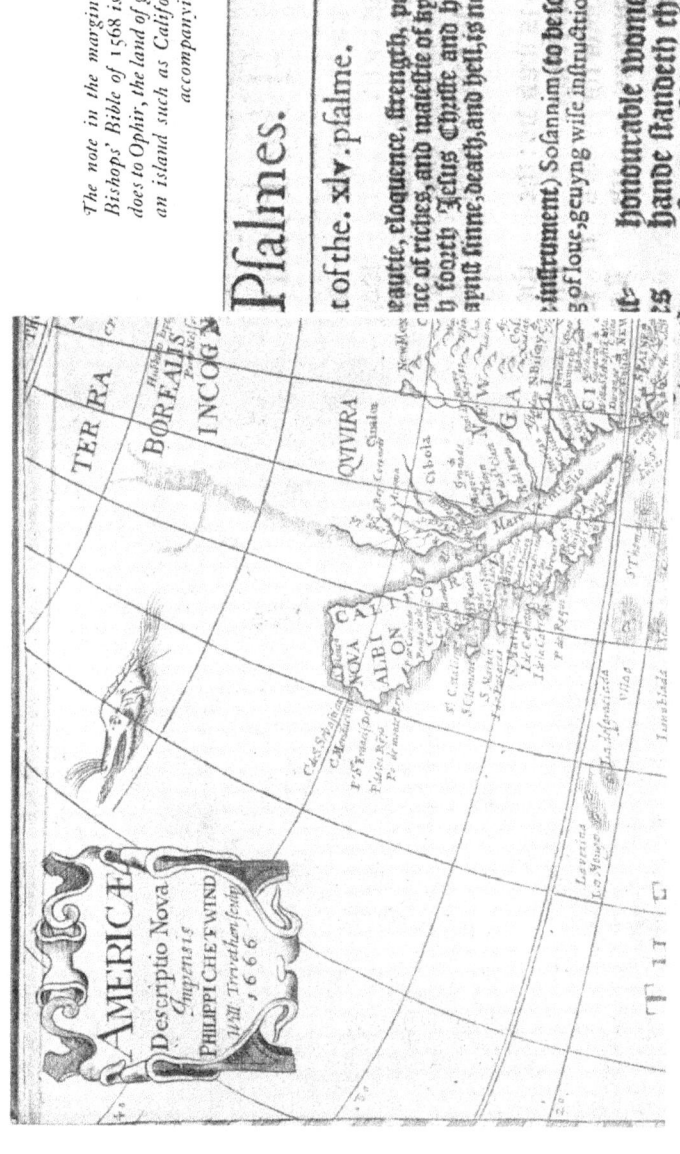

The note in the margin of the page from the so-called Bishops' Bible of 1568 is most interesting, referring as it does to Ophir, the land of gold, and the possibility of it being an island such as California is represented to be on the accompanying map dated 1666.

California here appears as an island, the northern portion bearing the name New Albion, reminiscent of the visit to our shores of Francis Drake in 1579.

CALIFORNIA: UNDER THREE FLAGS
An Historical Foreword

CALIFORNIA has been the subject of many histories; its past has furnished more curious speculation than almost any portion of the western hemisphere; and the origin of its name has excited more interest, both among laymen and historians, than even the fabled source of Solomon's gold, the land of Ophir.

The sole purpose of this sketchy outline is to serve as a background upon which the general reader may project the incidents and events of "Seventy-five Years in California" so as to render them more interesting and vivid. It makes no pretense to be other than an "adventitious aid" in helping recreate the atmosphere in which the past of the "Golden State" is enveloped.

While Cortéz, the Conqueror of Mexico, as far back as 1533 began the long series of explorations which continued, with many interruptions, for over two centuries and which have made familiar the names of Cabrillo, Drake, Cermeño and Vizcaino, it is not until the joint efforts of Gaspar de Portolá and Junípero Serra under the dual banner of Cross and Sword —the Holy Expedition of 1769, resulting in the settlement of San Diego— that it can be truly said that California's history starts.

Much has been written about the name California, and the reason for its application first to the peninsula of Baja, or Lower California, and then to both Alta, or Upper, and Lower California under the somewhat mystical designation of the Californias.

The romantic sequel to Vasco de Lobeira's equally romantic medieval novel, Amadís de Gaula, written by García Ordoñez de Montalvo and called Las Sergas de Esplandián, was found by Edward Everett Hale to contain the description of a fabulous island abounding in gold and such other delights as would attract the imaginations of the wonder-loving Spanish explorers of the Sixteenth Century, and the name of this marvelous land was California.

It is now generally conceded that this is doubtless the origin of the name and that followers of Cortéz, if not he himself, are responsible for fastening it upon the vicinity of La Paz on the eastern shore of the peninsula from which it has spread to cover the whole Pacific Coast as far north as the forty-second degree of latitude.

All now reject the supposition that California is formed from combinations of either Latin or Spanish words: calida fornax, in one instance; caliente fornella, in the other. Hot furnace, a literal translation of both suggestions, neither fits the case, nor is it as pleasing to contemplate as the scene of the hero Esplandián's romantic exploits, the land of wondrous riches, California.

Padre Serra's Expedicion Santa thrust back the curtain, and permitted the world to peek into the land we were destined to know. To follow in the footsteps of the Padres, and of Portolá, to see heart-breaking obstacles overcome, to be present at the founding of the long chain of Missions is possible in many books which lovers of California have written.

Among the many helping to shape the destiny of the new country, one name stands out from among the ruck; a light hardly less brilliant than the Padre Junípero himself; and that is Juan Bautista de Anza. All the charm of the Pastoral Period when ease and plenty ruled the land, when Indians toiled and the Dons danced, and made love to languishing-eyed señoritas, when a Californian afoot was unknown, comes from the efforts of the followers of glorious Anza and their descendents of pure Spanish blood.

How Anza in the winter of 1775-76 led his tiny army of Presidial soldiers with their wives and children through Arizona and by way of the then wilderness of the Imperial Valley from Sonora to Monterey, and in safety, is an odyssey almost as marvelous as the fabled wanderings of Ulysses. What the Church had started, the men of Anza's battalion completed. Under their protection the worthy Franciscans toiled in the Lord's vineyard, while on their part they, following the Biblical injunction, increased and multiplied. Without the influence of both of these forces, California would never have become the Lotus Land which excited the envious hopes of the more materially minded Americans.

From the roster of Anza's soldiery are drawn names still cherished as relics of our romantic past. There you will find the familiar Moraga, Grijalva, Alviso, Peralta, Garcia, Pacheco, Valencia, Sanchez, Castro, Pico, Bernal, Galindo, Berreyesa, and many others. These are the founders, the very pioneers; and it is the doings of these men and their children, mingled with those of later comers, that make up the fascinating life of the Mañana Land under the banner of Spain, and the tri-color of Mexico after the separation from the mother country.

Spain's ideal of colonization required three co-ordinate impulses: the Presidio, the Padres and their Missions, and the Pueblo. From this grouping of forces, Spanish civilization in California spread. The soldier guarded the Church, and both helped to create the town. While the avowed purpose was the Christianization of the Indians, the occupation of California was really due to jealousy of both Russia and England. The Missions were deemed but temporary footholds; a term of ten years had been set as the period of their existence. Population of the land was Spain's goal, and the fear of unwelcome intrusion was her urge.

San Diego, Santa Barbara, Monterey and San Francisco were selected for Presidios; Los Angeles, San José and Branciforte (Santa Cruz) were founded as Pueblos with the hope that by generous grants of unmeasured acres colonists would occupy the land and that Spain's sovereignty would be thereby secure.

It must be always be borne in mind that California was very difficult of access. The base for the Province at San Blas was but the half-way point in the journey from Mexico City to either San Diego or Monterey. Navigation in the Sea of Cortéz, or Gulf of California, was perilous, and the long voyage up the coast of the peninsula was only accomplished in the face of contrary winds. This isolation gave the native Californians a sense of detachment which no other Spanish colony enjoyed. It developed their spirit of independence to the extent that they never hesitated to veto the choice of governors the far away viceroy sent to rule them. This veto was absolute and was expressed on more than one occasion. The Governor was placed aboard a convenient vessel, and politely asked not to return.

With the separation of Mexico from the mother country two factions developed in California: The Mission fathers and their adherents remained loyal to Spain, while the rancheros and the military sided largely with the aspirants of independence. Later, this cleavage resulted in the secularization of the Mission establishments, from which grew the development of the great ranchos in private hands.

Again, a sectional jealousy between the official north, centered at the Departmental capital of Monterey, and the dwellers of the southland which included Santa Barbara and Los Angeles, brought about those opera bouffe martial contests in which much inferior powder was burned but no blood shed.

California might as well have been a strange island in the South Seas for all the care and thought the new Mexican republican government lavished upon it. The Californians were left to their own devices which gave the department the opportunity the natives desired; to nourish their spirit of freedom to the point where their regard for official decrees was at times negative.

With the change of flags came the dawn of what might be called the Period of Boston Ships.

Keen Yankees had made San Francisco Bay a port of supply for food and water for their whale ships. Honolulu, under its New England missionaries, was likewise often visited by these American mariners. Trade followed the pursuit of the whale, and in time the gewgaws from the Atlantic Coast—and necessities as well—became current barter for the hides and tallow of the disintegrating Mission establishments and the prospering ranchos. This commerce, forbidden by Spain, was restricted straightly under Mexican rule; but was observed largely in the breach, to the satisfaction of the natives of the department.

Supercargoes conducted the trade of the early ships visiting the Coast. These roving traders soon came ashore as resident agents, and with the growth of this profitable business, more ships and more merchants appeared in California. Boston became known, while other American cities were as if non-existent. Americans were called Boston men, and all goods from the United States went by the name of Boston goods.

A few trappers had appeared from the great beyond, braving the terrors of the solitude of the Great Basin and the Indians of the Rockies. Jedediah Smith and his party, the first white man to blaze the trail to California and Oregon, appeared at the San Gabriel Mission on the morning of November 27th, 1826, much to the astonishment of the Padres and the officials. Jedediah Smith wintered in California, and in the spring crossed the Sierra Nevadas, leaving his main party to hunt and trap on the rivers of central California, for whom he returned the following year, and made his way with two companions back to the rendezvous in the Rockies.

Jedediah Smith was the pathfinder in whose train were to come thousands and thousands of his countrymen within a score of years, whose presence on the Pacific Coast changed the destiny both of Mexico and the United States.

Some five years later we find Walker in California. He had left Captain Bonneville's party with instructions to make a rough survey of Great Salt Lake, but instead had wandered with his uncouth half-breeds and his American companions to Monterey. Walker Pass; Walker River, and Walker Lake in Nevada are reminders of this exploit. A few others risked the dangers of the overland route from the settlements at Santa Fé and found their way to Mission San Gabriel. Their stories upon their return opened the eyes of their listeners to the Wondrous Land fronting on the Southern Ocean where Boston traders were drawing wealth and yet more wealth from hides and tallow. Dana's "Two Years before the Mast" is a faithful portrait of this period. From the influence of these Boston men grew the toils which were to bind American interests so firmly that even Great Britain forebore to interfere.

As far back as 1811 Russia in the person of the Russian American Fur Company had appeared upon the scene. The cause of their coming was two-fold: necessity for a base of cereal supply for their Alaskan posts, impossible of growth in far northern latitudes; and the teeming fur-bearing mammal life of Californian waters. They preempted Bodega Bay and erected an armed post at Fort Ross. Spain's feeble grasp upon the country brought forth nothing more than a protest, and as the yearly supply ships from San Blas failed to arrive, due to the activities of the insurgents generally in Spanish America, Governor Arrillaga was glad to open trade with the intruders. The Russians remained in California until December 1841 when they sold their property to the Swiss adventurer Johann August Sutter who had arrived in San Francisco Bay in 1839, and who was destined to take a notable part in the occurrences of the years to come.

Sutter set out for California from the then frontier town of St. Louis in 1838, tramped the Oregon Trail to the Columbia River, thence he shipped to Honolulu, where he found the British brig "Clementina," and in her, by way of Sitka, Alaska, he finally made his way to his destination.

Sutter founded a principality in the wilderness where the American River (named so because of its occupation by the trappers of Jedediah Smith's company) empties into the Sacramento. Here he was lord of the marches, and here, becoming a Mexican citizen, he built his fort, armed it with Russian cannon, drilled his Indians, and surveyed his eleven square leagues of land with the complacency and with as much authority as any baron of old.

Doctor John Marsh, Harvard graduate and restless American, had slipped away from civilization to become the owner of Los Medanos rancho in Contra Costa in 1836. His home letters stirred the imaginations of others. A trickle of hardy Americans followed in his wake. John Bidwell, Talbot H. Green and Josiah Belden were members of this Bartleson party, the first overland settlers, who reached California in 1841.

At Monterey Captain J. B. R. Cooper and Thomas O. Larkin had already made their homes, while in Yerba Buena, then just taking on the dignity of a settlement, Jacob P. Leese, William S. Hinckley and William A. Leidesdorff had begun business. Nathan Spear was at this time the principal store-keeper in Monterey, while at Los Angeles Abel Stearns held a similar position. Don Luis Vignes had planted his historic vineyard at Los Alisos, and Don "Benito" Wilson on his Rancho Santa Ana del Chino was showing the lazy natives what American energy could do with the fertility of California soil. Benjamin D. Wilson (Don "Benito") had been a member of the Workman and Rowland party of settlers which had made its way overland from Santa Fé.

Here was the nucleus of American possession, and when added to the Boston men trading up and down the coast, it will be seen that Governor Alvarado had cause for his nervousness regarding subsequent arrivals.

Just north of the Salinas River, nestled in the first rises of the Gavilan Range was Natividad, the rendezvous of deserters from ships touching on the coast. Here one Isaac Graham, a Tennesseean mountaineer, an arrival of 1833 and a crack shot, had set up a distillery, and here he gathered to him spirits as reckless as himself. To obtain a true value of Graham's influence and the strength of his Natividad settlement, one must not be surprised to learn that Alvarado, soon to become governor, thanks to the rifles of fifty Natividados, solicited the former trapper's aid and obtained it.

The Presidios had almost fallen into equal decay with the secularized Missions. Political discontent was rampant. The Disputación or departmental assembly, in electing Alvarado as governor after the forced departure of ex-governor Gutierrez, even went so far as to declare California independent of Mexico; and stranger still, a proposal was offered that the name of the independent state be changed to Montezuma. This last action was immediately reconsidered and annulled along with the act of secession.

This, then, is the background of the scene when William Heath Davis arrived at Monterey to enter the employ of Nathan Spear, his uncle by marriage.

Grants of land to those Americans willing to become naturalized Mexican citizens were freely given; and daughters of many of the rich rancheros became wives of the new comers. The intercourse between native Californians and "los estranjeros," as the foreigners were called, became intimate and cordial. Each respected the other.

Back in Washington the thought of further western expansion had been born. Senator Thomas H. Benton of Missouri, the future father-in-law of Captain John C. Frémont, kept his eyes ever on the setting sun. His life was devoted to an idea: the flag of the United States must wave throughout the land from the Atlantic to the Pacific. First it was the Oregon territory that demanded his attention, but with time came the hope that Mexico might be induced to part with its California possessions, and if that were impossible, mayhap—the Texans were then fighting for their independence from Mexico—the delectable land beyond the Rockies and the Sierra Nevadas might be seized as spoils of war if it so fell out that Mexico and ourselves came into conflict.

The administration of President James K. Polk had a settled western policy as will be seen from the events which follow. And Benton deserves the title of Honorable Californian for his efforts which resulted, indirectly, it is true, in the annexation of the vast territory stretching from the Rocky Mountains to the Pacific.

What Washington wished to know was: what was this country like where Boston merchants grew rich in a few years; and so Commodore Charles Wilkes was sent with his squadron to "survey" the land. Captain John C. Frémont was detailed to approach the coast overland. Between these two, officialdom felt the true nature of the country would become known.

American war vessels hovered suspiciously along the coast, and the tide of overland immigration was gathering force. At length, the arrest of all foreigners in the department was decreed. Some fifty were seized, carried aboard ship, and dispatched to San Blas. The Mexican government disavowed this action of Governor Alvarado, returned the prisoners and compensated them for their inconvenience. Fear of the great Anglo-Saxon republic was ever uppermost in the minds of both Alvarado and his military co-adjutor, General José Castro, who were responsible for the round-up of the so-called strangers. Americans who had become Mexican citizens, or who had married into Californian families, were not disturbed.

One day in October 1842 Commodore Thomas Ap Catesby Jones sailed the U. S. ship "United States" into Monterey Bay. In Peru he had heard rumors that war had been declared between Mexico and the United States. He dropped anchor, trained his loaded guns upon the feeble fortifications of the Presidio, and, landing a force, hauled down the Mexican ensign and hoisted the Stars and Stripes.

This event was significant. The Navy was under orders to act, whenever the occasion demanded. Later advices than Jones possessed convinced him of his error, so like an officer and a gentleman the Mexican flag was replaced by him the next day, saluted, and Jones sailed away. Later he called upon Governor Micheltorena in Los Angeles and offered his official apologies.

March 8th, 1844 saw the arrival at Sutter's Fort of Captain John C. Frémont. After renewing his provision supply, he passed down the San Joaquin valley with his armed survey crew, crossed the Tehachapi, and by way of the Mojave desert, Great Salt Lake, the South Pass, reached the Missouri River in July.

His next appearance, however, stirred California to its depths. Again accompanied by Kit Carson, his inseparable guide and companion, and with a compact body of sixty armed men, Frémont arrived at Sutter's Fort on December 10th, 1845. This was the historic journey; for this time he did not avoid the Mexican settlements along the coast, but boldly came to Monterey to confer with Thomas O. Larkin who had been appointed American Consul for California the year previously.

General Castro viewed Frémont's return with trepidation, especially as orders had come from Mexican sources to stop the increasing stream of American immigration at all hazards. While it is true that Frémont had left his men encamped near San José, and had appeared without show of military display, yet when he requested permission to winter and recruit his men in the confines of the Department, it was accorded grudgingly.

Possibly Castro had prescience of what was to follow.

Frémont's movements from this time on are the history of California. But it is interesting to know that on this first visit to Monterey he was accompanied by William A. Leidesdorff, whom Larkin had appointed Vice-Consul for the United States with headquarters at Yerba Buena (San Francisco) but a few months before: October 29th, 1845.

Frémont returned to his troops then gathered at the Laguna Seco rancho, near Coyote, some fifteen miles south of San José, and instead of marching for Oregon as he had explained his plans to Alvarado and Castro, led his men across the Santa Clara valley, over the Santa Cruz mountains and into the Salinas valley where he pitched camp within twenty miles of Monterey, the capital of California.

Castro was roused. He ordered Frémont to withdraw, which he did, and next we find the Americans entrenched on Gavilan Peak, the American flag raised, and defiance offered Castro and all others in authority.

Frémont blustered. Castro mobilized his forces at San Juan. And Larkin, alarmed at the course events were taking, sent post haste to John Parrott, United States Consul at Mazatlan for help.

Without a shot being fired, but leaving his campfires burning, Frémont marched off in the dead of night, headed for the San Joaquin, and subsequently Klamath Lakes in Oregon.

Larkin's call for help bore fruit. Captain John B. Montgomery sailed the U. S. sloop-of-war "Portsmouth" into Monterey Bay in April, but the cause of the disturbance, Frémont, was then in the wilds of northern California. Montgomery stayed on for a while, and then sailed for San

Francisco Bay where he remained ready for any emergency. The emergency was soon to manifest itself.

Melodrama now enters and usurps the stage.

Archibald H. Gillespie, lieutenant of the Marine Corps, becomes a bearer of dispatches. These consisted of a duplicate message for both Larkin and Frémont, a packet of personal letters from Jessie Benton Frémont, wife of the explorer, and letters from Senator Benton to the same address.

Gillespie received his instructions in Washington from no less personage than the Secretary of State, James Buchanan, afterwards President of the United States. The route chosen to reach his destination was through Mexico, a perilous undertaking, for we were on the verge of war. Gillespie memorized his secret missive, destroyed the original, and succeeded in reaching the west coast. An American warship carried him to Monterey where he landed in April, and there he wrote from memory the dispatch for Larkin. This secret message has been the source of much research, but Professor Josiah Royce of Harvard has the honor of discovering its context and thus settling all further speculation.

Where was Frémont?

Gillespie had completed only half his mission, and he must find the Topographical Engineer wherever he might be. Disguised as an invalid seeking health, the lieutenant of Marines rode northward. At Sutter's Fort he learned that Frémont had passed onward a month before, and that the Indians of the Klamath country were restless.

With Neal, one of Frémont's men who had remained in California since the expedition of the previous year, and one other, Gillespie set out to seek his man in a wilderness filled with unfriendly savages. Frémont's trail was soon found and followed, and Neal dashed ahead to warn Frémont, who with a handful of men returned in his tracks to meet Gillespie. The meeting took place on the evening of May 9th, 1846: the day the first engagement in the Mexican war was fought at Resaca de la Palma.

Three camp fires were lighted. Frémont's faithful Delaware Indians huddled round one, for the night was sharp; Basil Lajeunesse, French-Canadian voyageur and his fellows warmed themselves at another; while Frémont listened eagerly to Gillespie's recital by the light of the third, and read the letters from his wife and Senator Benton.

Under the pines and hemlocks no thoughts of hostile Indians broke in upon Frémont's reverie. He was intent upon plans for the future and the part he was to play in the drama. He was upon the shore of his Rubicon, and he must decide. Was he clairvoyant? Did he have mystic knowledge that shots had been fired in anger on the Rio Grande thousands of miles away?

A groan disturbed the midnight quiet. Kit Carson, grasping his rifle, ran through the fitful firelight, shouting, "What was that?" In answer came a whirr of Indian arrows. The fight began, but Basil Lajeunesse had groaned for the last time, and when stillness settled again over the camp two others lay dead beside him.

The next day Frémont and Gillespie joined the main body of the party. Then followed a punitive expedition against the Klamath tribes they were destined to remember sorrowingly, for Frémont was exacting in his revenge. At length the southward march began, and camp was established at the Marysville Buttes, twin volcanic cones rising abruptly from the level plain of the Sacramento valley. Here word was given out that the head of the American survey party could be seen, and settlers and roving trappers gathered to voice their real and supposed grievances. If Frémont hesitated before, now he was all decision. He would bend circumstances to suit his plans. Castro was at San José watching the incomprehensible actions of this American Engineer, while horses to mount his summoned followers were at Sonoma. Lieutenant Arce was dispatched to get them.

The return journey began auspiciously; the Sacramento River was crossed at Knight's Landing, the horses swimming. But when the Consumnes River was neared, Ezekiel Merritt, sent by Frémont for the purpose, seized the animals, permitting Arce and his men to proceed with the parting injunction that Castro, if he wanted his mounts, must come and get them.

This was the first step in the Conquest of California.

Frémont now moved his headquarters down to Sutter's Fort. His forces were growing, for all Americans in that part of California were convinced that their leader was acting under positive governmental instructions, whereas the only communication he had received, that which Gillespie had brought to both Larkin and himself counselled an altogether different course. Buchanan had insisted upon conciliatory measures aimed to capture the whole-hearted support of the Californians, and had enjoined upon Larkin and Frémont "on all proper occasions to warn the government and the people of California of the danger of California becoming a British or French colony; to inspire them with a jealousy of European dominion; and to arouse in their bosoms that love of liberty and independence so natural to the American continent." And more, "If the people desire to unite their destiny with ours they should be received as brethren—"

Larkin was moving heaven and earth to accomplish annexation of

California by peaceful means. Already he had Castro's promise that this would come to pass by 1848, if not sooner. All the secret message conveyed was confirmation of Larkin's friendly policy, and now we behold Frémont pursuing an opposite course, and making war on his own account against the very people he was instructed to conciliate.

General Mariano G. Vallejo was the best friend the United States had in California. He was also the most influential of the department's prominent men, and yet Frémont's next move was directed against him. True, Frémont was not bold enough to appear at Sonoma in person, but he later assumed the responsibility for the actions of Ezekiel Merritt's party which arrested Vallejo, Prudon, Leese and Salvador Vallejo, the general's brother, and brought them prisoners to him at Sutter's Fort.

To follow Frémont's movements from the middle of June to the end of July, would be to give a recital of lawless acts committed against a people we hoped to win by kindness. This period includes the Bear Flag revolt, the murder of the de Haro boys and old man Berreyesa, the useless spiking of the equally useless guns at the San Francisco, the kidnapping of Robert Ridley who was acting as the Mexican collector of customs. Its consequences stirred the anger and resentment of all native Californians, and yet it was the belief of Commodore Sloat that Frémont was following government instructions that finally urged that Naval officer to raise the American flag at Monterey July 7th, 1846.

Fearing British occupation of California, Sloat had slipped away from Mazatlan, leaving the British squadron under Admiral Seymour in ignorance of his destination, and had sailed into Monterey Bay July 2nd, with the U. S. ship "Savannah."

For five days Sloat hesitated. His instructions were to seize California whenever he should hear that war had been declared between Mexico and the United States. At Mazatlan he had learned that hostilities had started along the Rio Grande, but with the fiasco of Commodore Jones in raising the flag in 1842, and having to lower it again, ever in his mind, he was excessively cautious. Sloat even went so far as to inquire if a salute to the Mexican flag would be acceptable the day the "Savannah" dropped anchor.

Sloat's belated action saved not only the Bear Flag revolters, but gave Frémont a legalized standing, without which he might properly have been regarded as a bandit and freebooter.

Frémont brought his enlarged and armed party to Monterey at Sloat's request, and it is said that the interview between the Naval commander and the instigator of hostilities, when the former learned from the latter's own lips that what had been done was without shadow of authority, was both humiliating and heated. Sloat felt he had been trapped into his seizure of California, and doubtless with the Jones matter always before him, and none too well physically at the time, he accepted the arrival of Commodore Robert F. Stockton as heaven sent, and transferring the command to him, sailed for home just twenty-two days after proclaiming California American territory.

From July 29th, 1846 the so-called Conquest of California was in energetic hands. Stockton accepted Frémont's help. The California Battalion was organized, and until the Peace of Los Angeles the following January, it played a picturesque if not an important part in the events which led to the pacification of the country.

So much has been written about Frémont as the Conqueror of California, that the leadership of other figures in the drama has been overshadowed. Kearny, coming overland from Santa Fé with his 132 men fought the only serious battle of the campaign at San Pascual. Stockton moved his forces to San Diego, and with Kearny began the march to Los Angeles. Frémont marched from Monterey southward, and at Cahuenga received the capitulation of the Californians, despite the nearby presence of his commanding officer, to whom the matter should properly have been submitted.

The end of the Frémont story, like its beginning, is irregular. Failure to obey Kearny's positive orders as the commander-in-chief appointed by the Washington authorities, resulted in his subsequent arrest and court martial. Frémont passed out of California in June 1847 with a divided reputation: the people of the north execrated him; those in the southland held him in esteem.

William Heath Davis states that Commodore Stockton was the real conqueror of California.

The outline of the conquest touching upon Frémont's actions has been given at some length, for only thus will the allusions in Davis' narrative be understandable.

Three weeks after Captain John B. Montgomery, commanding the U. S. sloop-of-war "Portsmouth" had raised the American flag over the Plaza of San Francisco on July 9th, 1846, Samuel Brannan and his Mormon followers from New York arrived in the ship "Brooklyn."

Brannan's energy and foresight had much to do with laying the foundations of commercial prosperity of San Francisco. He established the first newspaper, The California Star, in the city: this was the second in the State. Robert Semple, who took part in the Bear Flag affair, together with the Rev. Walter Colton, former chaplain of Commodore Stockton's flagship, and by him appointed Alcalde at Monterey, had begun the publication of The Californian, which Semple afterward moved to San Francisco when it was seen that the former village of Yerba Buena was certain to be center of all activities. Brannan was merchant, publisher, civic leader. His dynamic personality was always to the forefront of all movements for the betterment of general conditions. He became San Francisco's inspiration and one of its wealthiest men in the early fifties. He established a store at Sutter's Fort from which the provisions were supplied to James Marshall while he was building the saw-mill which resulted in the discovery of gold.

Brannan made his appearance in San Francisco with some of the first gold May 15th, 1848. At first the importance of the find was held in slight esteem, but soon the magnitude of the treasure grew, and the first exodus to the mines started. It is said that one time but seven able-bodied men remained in San Francisco. Desertion left officers of the Army without commands, and the word going out to the world, shiploads of gold-seekers from Honolulu, from Peru, from China, made their appearance. These first comers were soon joined by bands of Sonorans; while caravans of Americans, disregarding the unknown dangers of mountains, deserts and Indians, trekked westward to El Dorado in their covered wagons.

The military rule which had irked the liberty-loving and independent-minded immigrants came to an end with the acceptance by the people of California of the Constitution prepared by the convention at Monterey and the election of officials headed by Peter H. Burnett as Governor. From October 19th, 1849 until September 9th, of the year following, California functioned as a State without being a member of the Union, but with the arrival of the steamer Oregon at San Francisco October 19th, 1850 it was learned that Congress had voted to admit California to statehood on the previous 9th of September.

The early years of the decade beginning with 1850 brought much litigation arising out of real and fictitious Spanish and Mexican land grants; also the gradual settlement of the State's agricultural lands by American farmers. From this period on, the history of California is much a repetition of the struggles of the pioneers of other western communities, and with the completion of the transcontinental railroad in 1869, the isolation of the far west vanished, together with most of its picturesqueness.

The assimilation of Mexican California and its Americanization might be likened to the Norman Conquest of England with the Spanish speaking Californians, their customs and their laws, taking the place of the Saxons. In each instance there was a complete overthrow of a ruling people; while the intruders introduced their own language, habits of thought and ways of living, and forced the defeated to accept conditions wholly alien to them. Yet, as in Britain, somewhat of the former atmosphere and customs prevailed. Today we retain Spanish place names, we buy and sell land according to Spanish measurement, and we claim as heritage the days of the Missions and the Dons just as the British patriotically include Alfred, king of a defeated race, among the great men of England.

California has ever been a name to conjure with. Its history under three flags is filled with the mysterious. Here, after the discovery of gold, the crucial test of self-government, in a community made up almost wholly of men, brought forth orderly regard for law. Here was the meeting point of two dissimilar civilizations; the Roman ideal inherited by Spain, and the Anglo-Saxon bequeathed to America by the fathers of the Founders of the Republic. That the younger and more virile prevailed was to be expected, but in the process of reconciling their discordant elements, the picturesqueness and glamor of the romantic past have not been entirely thrown aside. The growth of American ideas amid alien surroundings, as told so intimately and with so much color by William Heath Davis, has cast upon California an air of mystery and adventure unknown to any other section of these United States.

San Francisco,   DOUGLAS S. WATSON.
December 8, 1928.

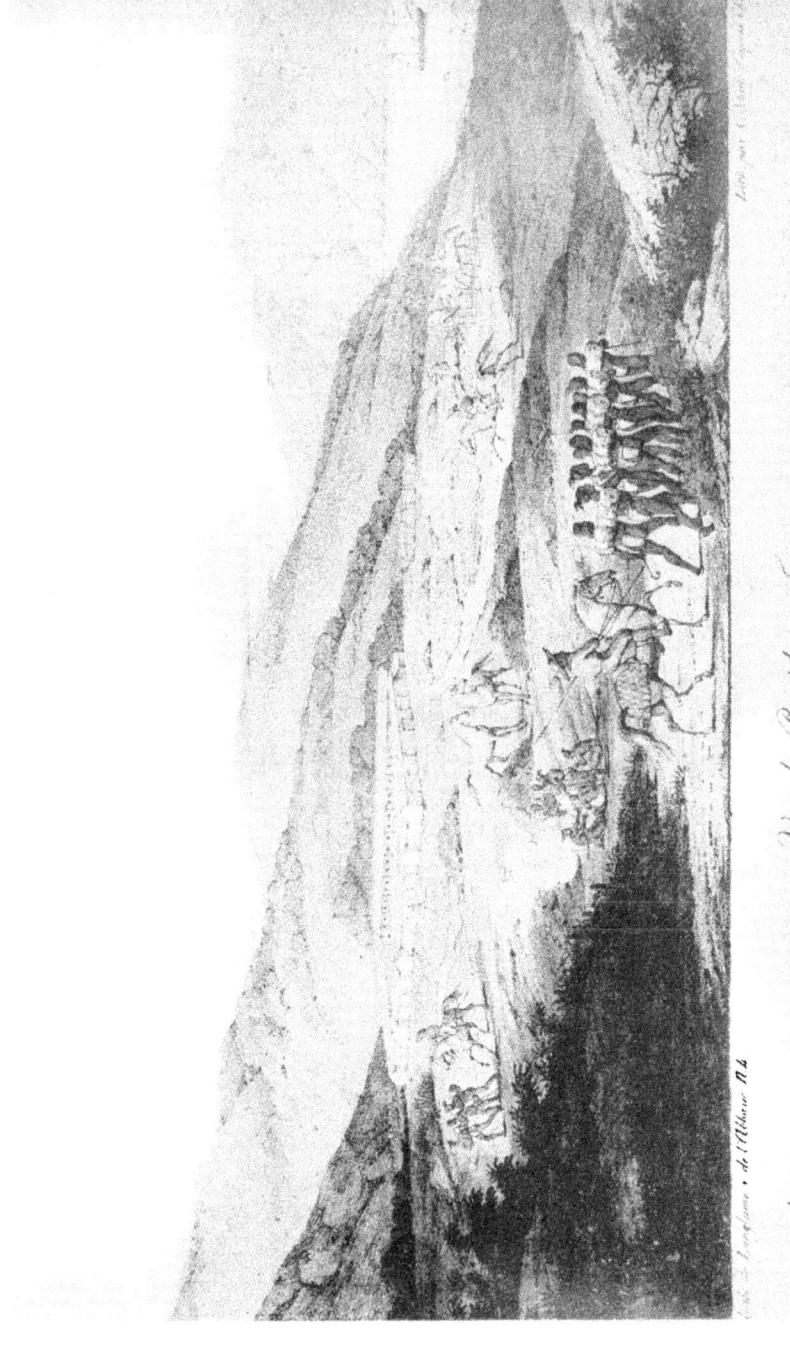

This drawing by Louis Choris, painter attached to the Kotzebue exploring expedition sent out from Russia in the ship "Rurick," shows the Presidio as it appeared in October, 1816. The quadrilateral, consisting of barracks and storerooms, has disappeared except for a portion of the southern side, now used as the Officer's Club.

CHAPTER I
Author's First Arrival in California

I FIRST came to California in 1831, seventeen years before the discovery of gold in Sutter's mill-race, and later married into a native California family of Spanish extraction. Residing in the department and the State ever since, except when absent from it on business, I have had an extended experience in the manners and customs of the people, their methods of trade, of the social and political history of the department and its successor the State, as that history was evolved through all the stirring events of that period, to the American occupation.

There is an undercurrent in social life abounding in genial interchange of amenities, which is preserved only in tradition, to be recited in family circles, and from this source I have obtained much valuable information.

All this has enabled me in these personal recollections, to rescue from oblivion events that are herein recorded, narrations of which cannot be found elsewhere. They also present an insight to the energy, enterprise, trials, misfortunes and triumphs of those men who laid the foundation of that prosperity which places California in the front rank among the most favored States of the Union.

My first visit to California was in 1831, in the bark "Louisa" of Boston, Captain George Wood, with J. C. Jones as supercargo and owner and Charles Smith as assistant supercargo. She had come from Boston with a cargo of assorted merchandise to the Sandwich Islands, where she disposed of a portion of her goods, and sailed thence to Sitka, and from there to Monterey, to Santa Barbara, to San Pedro (the port of Los Angeles), and to San Diego, trading at each of these points.

In trading at Sitka on this trip, we took furs and Russian money in payment for goods disposed of there.

At that time Sitka presented many points of interest. Besides the government fort, the different residences of the governor and his staff were fine buildings, in the shape of castles or round towers; each mounted with guns, as a protection against Indians, who were very hostile.

The office of governor was both civil and military. He and his officers were gentlemen, highly educated, refined in manners, intelligent and courteous. They received us with great hospitality.

These gentlemen were from the nobility of Russia. Their wives and daughters were exceedingly beautiful and highly accomplished; they were of medium height, delicate and symmetrical in form and figure, and exceedingly graceful in their walk and carriage. What struck me particularly was the wonderful transparency of their complexions and their rosy cheeks. At my age I was much impressed with their handsome appearance.

Most of the gentlemen and ladies spoke French and English in addition to their own language. They gave family parties and balls for our entertainment, which were conducted with great elegance and refinement.

In return we gave two or three entertainments on board the "Louisa," the vessel on each occasion being handsomely decorated with the flags of almost every nation, the Russian flag flying at the foremast. On the arrival of the governor with his staff, and the ladies of their families, he received a salute corresponding to his rank.

At San Diego we received many hides from the "Volunteer," an American bark, Captain J. O. Carter, supercargo Ebbetts; that vessel as well as the "Louisa" being owned by J. C. Jones, who was a Boston merchant engaged in trading to ports on the Pacific coast and the Islands. From San Diego we sailed for Honolulu, with a full cargo of hides and a deck load of horses. The horses were disposed of at Honolulu, and the hides taken in the vessel to Boston on her return voyage.

Among the residents of Monterey at that time were David Spence, Captain J. B. R. Cooper, Nathan Spear, James Watson, George Kinlock, William E. P. Hartnell, and these men were the most prominent of the foreigners.

The first three named were engaged in merchandising. Kinlock was a ship and house carpenter. Hartnell was an instructor in the employ of the Mexican government in the department of California, of which Monterey was the capital.

In 1833 I visited the coast again in the Boston bark "Volunteer," Captain Thomas Shaw; J. C. Jones, owner and supercargo; Sherman Peck, assistant supercargo. Jones went from Boston to the Sandwich Islands about 1820 or 1821, and became U. S. Consul, and during his consulship made voyages between Boston and the Islands and other points. During his absence his duties were performed by a deputy, Stephen Reynolds, of Boston.

We arrived at Monterey and sailed thence to San Luis Obispo, Santa Barbara, San Pedro, San Diego, and returned, touching and trading at these places. We then came to the harbor of San Francisco, and anchored in a cove known as Yerba Buena or Loma Alta Cove, Yerba Buena being San Francisco, and Loma Alta Telegraph Hill. At that time there were trading on the coast at different points the ship "Alert," of Boston, Captain Thompson; ship "California," of Boston, Captain James Arther, supercargo Alfred Robinson; the English brig "Ayacucho," Captain John Wilson, supercargo James Scott, both being owners; the American brig "Bolivar Liberator," Captain Nye; the Boston bark "Don Quixote," Captain John Meek, supercargo William S. Hinckley; and the Mexican brig "Leonidas," formerly U. S. vessel of war "Dolphin," Captain Juan Malarin, owner and supercargo Don José Antonio Aguirre.

As the "Volunteer" approached the bay of San Francisco on the trip from the south just mentioned, she was becalmed and compelled to lie to in a fog. About 11 o'clock in the forenoon the fog lifted and disappeared from the horizon, and as it did so we noticed the English brig "Ayacucho," also becalmed, lying near us, almost within hailing distance, she also having just come from the southern ports, bound for Yerba Buena.

We were then about twenty-five miles west of the entrance to the bay.

The "Ayacucho" was claimed by her owners to be the fastest vessel on the coast, and this was conceded by all the captains except Captain Shaw of the "Volunteer," who was very proud of our pretty bark, and her superior sailing qualities, and had often remarked to me that he desired an opportunity for a trial of speed between the two vessels.

The opportunity now presented itself, and he determined to avail himself of it, to the delight of all on board. The captain gave orders to prepare for the exciting race, which were obeyed with alacrity by all with smiling faces. The "Ayacucho" being a little to the west of us, took the trade wind first, it having sprung up as the fog cleared, and so had the lead.

Captain Shaw, approaching me on the quarter-deck, said, "Billy, she will not maintain that position long." The breeze freshened, both vessels put on more sail, and we began slowly and surely to gain on the brig. Captain Shaw, standing by the man at the wheel, said, "I want to pass her within hailing distance." "Aye, aye, sir," was the response. When abreast of the brig, Captain Shaw called to the steward to bring him the speaking trumpet, and on receiving it, he hailed the other vessel with "Captain Wilson how do you do?" The reply came, "I am well, thank you; Captain Shaw, you are gaining on me fast." When the stern of our vessel was about abreast of the forecastle of the brig, three cheers from the "Volunteer" rent the air, spontaneously given by the crew, and they were returned from the brig. We anchored about fifteen minutes before she did, in the present anchorage at the port of San Francisco, and our captain and all the crew were joyous and happy, as they had beaten the vessel reputed to be the fastest on the coast.

The race had been very exciting, both vessels flying their national colors, and spreading their sails to the fullest extent, the captain of each standing on the quarter-deck, watching every movement and trimming sails to catch every portion of the breeze.

In the evening, the captain and supercargo of the "Ayacucho" came on board the "Volunteer," and spent a few hours, and the race formed the subject of conversation; Wilson admitting that he was fairly beaten for the first time. A good many social glasses passed over the event, and the best feeling prevailed. This little episode was an illustration of the national feeling of pride existing between the English and Americans.

The Presidio was the military post, where all the white inhabitants lived, and was commanded by Captain M. G. Vallejo, later General Vallejo. There were probably at the barracks, including soldiers, between two and three hundred men, women and children.

The soldiers were native Californians, all vaqueros, all horsemen. Captain Vallejo was then only recently married to his beautiful bride, Doña Francisca Benicia Carrillo.* Fort Point was garrisoned, and was then known as Punta del Castillo, or Castle Point, and was also under the command of Captain Vallejo.

Among the foreigners who were here at that time were Captain William A. Richardson, a native of England, the owner of the Saucelito ranch, who was married to the daughter of the late Captain Ygnacio Martinez, who commanded the Presidio and Fort Point military posts previous to the command of Vallejo; John Read, of Ireland, who subsequently was the owner of the Read ranch adjoining the Saucelito ranch; Timothy Murphy, of Ireland, and James Black, of Scotland.

Murphy was a sea otter-hunter, making his headquarters at the Presidio and the Mission of San Rafael. Sea otter were plentiful in the bay, and at Bodega and other points along the coast. The skins were quite valuable, worth from $40 to $50, and sometimes as high as $60 apiece. They were sold to the Boston ships that traded on the coast. Read became a stock-raiser on his ranch. Richardson commanded a vessel, and traded up and down the coast, and on the coast of Peru and Chile. He made his headquarters at Yerba Buena. He got his goods at Callao and Lima, mostly English and German, which had been sent there from Europe. For them he exchanged tallow and furs which he had collected about the coast. He was sailing for a Lima house. Black was a cattle-raiser and otter-hunter, and

*Note: Benicia, California, is named for Gen'l Vallejo's wife.

became owner of ranches in Marin county. He died a few years ago, leaving to his heirs a large fortune in land and cattle.

The trade on the coast at that time was mostly a barter trade. The currency was hides and tallow, with considerable sea otter, land otter and beaver skins, the latter being obtained on the Sacramento and San Joaquin rivers.

CHAPTER II
The Mission of San Francisco de Asis

THE Mission of San Francisco de Asis, usually called the Mission Dolores, situated one league from the site of Yerba Buena, on the west side of the bay of San Francisco, contained at this time, August, 1833, about 2000 Indians, more or less civilized, well clothed. Among them were blacksmiths, shipwrights, carpenters, tailors, shoemakers and masons, all of whom had learned these trades at the Mission, under the superintendence of the Padres. They had also learned the Spanish language, as a general thing had acquired habits of industry, and had become civilized and Christianized. Many of them could read and write.

Padre Quijas was at the head of the Mission Dolores, and administrator of the establishment. He had about 10,000 head of cattle, many thousand head of horses and mares, and a vast number of sheep.

The domain of the Mission extended to what is now known as San Mateo, including the rancho of Buri-buri, formerly owned by Don José Sanchez and his family.

I visited the Mission Dolores frequently during our stay at the port here, was always kindly received by the Padre, and drank as fine red California wine as I ever have since, manufactured at the Mission from grapes brought from the Missions of Santa Clara and San José.

The Indians were captured by the military who went into the interior of the country in pursuit of them, detachments of soldiers being frequently sent out from the Presidio and other military posts in the department on these expeditions, to bring the wild Indians into the Missions to be civilized and converted to Christianity. Sometimes two or three hundred would be brought in at a time—men, women and children—from the foothill region of the Sierra Nevadas and the San Joaquin and Sacramento valleys. They were immediately turned over to the Padres at the different Missions, generally with a guard of a corporal and ten soldiers to assist the priest in keeping them until they had become somewhat tamed. They were kindly treated, and soon became domesticated and ready and eager to adopt the

CAÑIZARES' MAP OF SAN FRANCISCO BAY, 1781

From Padre Francisco Palou's Life of Junipero Serra.

L. Point Lobos	D. Lime Point	V. Mission Dolores
I. Fort Point	T. Entrance to Mission Creek (Channel Street)	S. Hunter's Point
C. Point Bonita	X. Presidio	H. San Pablo Bay

habits of civilized life. They gradually lost their desire to return to their former mode of life.

After they had become adapted to their new condition their influence on the later arrivals of Indians was very marked. These yielded much more readily to the civilizing influence exerted upon them than those first captured. They were baptized and the children christened and taught in schools and in habits of industry. Many of them were employed to look after the stock belonging to the Missions, and became expert horsemen and vaqueros.

During our stay in the bay (about three or four weeks) we sold some fifteen or twenty thousand dollars' worth of goods to Padre Quijas. We received in payment hides and tallow, sea and land otter skins, and beaver skins, and also some Spanish and Mexican doubloons, which had probably been laid away for many years.

The goods were mostly sugar, tea, coffee, clothing, and blankets for the Indians.

There were blankets manufactured at the Missions, of very coarse texture, from the wool of their sheep. They were known as Mission blankets, and used at the Missions mostly.

We also sold to the Missions of Santa Clara and San José a large amount of goods, which was sent to them in launches to what is now known as Alviso Landing, for which we received in payment hides, tallow, furs and some coin—Mexican and Spanish doubloons.

The Missions of Santa Clara and San José were richer in cattle, horses and sheep than the Mission Dolores, and each of them had a much larger number of Indians. The Mission Dolores was considered a poor Mission compared to these other two. The Mission of San Rafael was also in existence, and that was inferior to the Mission Dolores.

In 1833 there was not a single inhabitant of what is now known as the City and County of San Francisco outside of the Presidio and the Mission.

At the place where Portsmouth Square now is there was a growing crop of Irish potatoes—a patch about the size of the square—enclosed by a brush fence, the crop having been planted by Candelario Miramontes, who resided near the Presidio with his family. One of his sons loaned me a beautiful horse to ride to the Presidio and Mission Dolores whenever it suited my pleasure to do so. I had him picketed with a long rope, for pasturage, at a place which is now the block between Pacific and Jackson and Montgomery and Sansome streets.

When we left the bay of San Francisco we traded down the coast at different points. While stopping at Santa Barbara, Thomas O. Larkin, who was afterwards United States Consul at Monterey, was married on board the bark "Volunteer" by Mr. J. C. Jones, acting in his capacity as consul.

The bride was a Massachusetts lady whose name has passed from my memory. We had a wedding festival, which was attended by the élite of Santa Barbara—beautiful ladies, mothers and daughters, with their husbands and sons, all of Castillian extraction. There was music with dancing, commencing soon after the marriage, and kept up till a late hour in the evening.

Native California wine and imported sparkling champagne were freely used, and all had a very enjoyable time.

On reaching San Diego our vessel was turned over to Captain Joseph O. Carter, of the American schooner "Harriet Blanchard," both vessels being owned by J. C. Jones.

Shaw took command of the latter, and Jones and myself went in her to Honolulu, with a cargo of hides, some furs, and also thirty head of fine California horses for a deck load. Sherman remained in the "Volunteer" as supercargo. The horses were sold at Honolulu and the hides transferred to another vessel about to sail for Boston.

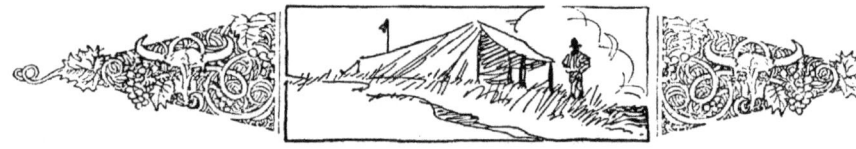

CHAPTER III
Wm. A. Richardson's Arrival 1822

ON William A. Richardson's arrival here in 1822 the Mexican flag was floating over the Province, and Governor Sola, the last Spanish ruler, who had become reconciled to the new Mexican regime, was on the point of going to Mexico as a Deputy for California to the Mexican Congress.

RICHARDSON'S PETITION TO GOVERNOR SOLA.

"William A. Richardson, a native of Great Britain, and a resident of this Province, hereby respectfully represents: that he arrived at this port of San Francisco on the second day of August last, as mate of the British Whaleship Orion, and your Worship having approved of my staying here, and it being my intention to remain permanently and become domiciled in this Province at some place with suitable climate, I most humbly pray that your Worship be pleased to grant me this privilege and favor.
(signed) William A. Richardson.
San Francisco, Presidio, Oct. 7, 1822"

THE DECREE WRITTEN ON THE MARGIN OF THE ABOVE.

"Monterey, October 12, 1822.
Being aware that the petitioner, besides being a navigator, is conversant with and engaged in the occupation of a carpenter, I hereby grant the privilege he asks for with the obligation that he shall receive and teach such young men as may be placed in his charge by my successor.
(signed) Sola."

William A. Richardson, an Englishman by birth, arrived at the Presidio of San Francisco, as chief mate of the British whaler Orion, on the second of August, 1822. He left his vessel and was permitted by the authorities to remain temporarily, but on the 7th of October, he concluded to settle permanently in California. He applied to Governor Pablo Vicente de Sola to grant him the privilege of domicile, which was acceded to on the 12th of October of the same year.

Richardson, during his stay at San Francisco, resided at the home of Lieutenant Ygnacio Martinez, then comandante of the Presidio. He noticed the difficulty of bringing the food supply for the troops at the Presidio. He at once went to work and built a launch and a boat for the purpose of transporting provisions from San José and Santa Clara Missions. This undertaking he performed in six months, with the aid of six Indians whom he taught the trade of carpentering and of shipwright; and also as boatmen in the management of the newly-built vessels. It is well known that the transportation of provisions by land was done by carts drawn by oxen. Richardson was the manager of the transporters for three years.

At the end of his charge, he married Maria Antonia, the eldest daughter of Comandante and Martina Martinez. The young couple were married at Mission Dolores by Father José Altimira; the sponsors were the comandante and one of the bride's sisters. The wedding was made the occasion of a great feast. The families of the officers and others were present at the ceremony and banquet.

Señorita Maria Antonia was considered a belle of great beauty among the handsome women of the Presidio in the thirties. There was a romance connected with this marriage.

After the Orion had dropped anchor off the Presidio, the usual old anchorage, William A. Richardson, first mate, landed a boat's crew on the beach. He found there a portion of the inhabitants of the garrison who were attracted by the arrival of a foreign vessel in the bay. Among the number were the Señoritas of the Martinez household. As Richardson leaped from the boat to the landing, Señorita Maria Antonia Martinez exclaimed, with joy in her eyes, to her lady companions, "Oh, que hombre tan hermoso el estranjero que desembarco del bote; el va hacer mi novio y yo voy hacer su esposa."—Oh, what a handsome man that foreigner just landed from the boat. He will be my bridegroom, and I will be his wife. It was love at first sight.

Richardson was equally impressed then and there with the loveliness of Doña Maria Antonia. A match was made and two hearts were entwined as one, without the formality of expressing to each other orally their love and devotion.

The union was blessed with three children: namely, Francisco, Stephen and *Mariana, who later became the wife of Manuel Torres. The Torres

*Lieutenant Wise in Chapter XII of his "Los Gringos," gives the following delightful portrait. "This anchorage (Sausalito) is a great resort for whale ships, coming from the north-west fishing grounds for water and supplies; the procurante of which was an English man, for many years a resident in the country, and possessing myriads of cattle, and a principality in land and mountains; among other valuables he was the sire of the belle of California, in the person of a young girl named Mariana. Her mother was Spanish, with the remains of great personal charms; as to the child I never saw a more patrician style of beauty and native elegance in any clime where Castillian donas bloom. She was brunette, with an oval face, magnificent dark gray eyes, with the corners of her mouth slightly curved downward, so as to give a proud and haughty expression to the face—in person she was tall, graceful

marriage was blessed with two daughters, Ruth Mariana, wife of F. E. Beck; Juana Agrapina, wife of George W. Davis, and four sons; Manuel, Alfred, Charles and Albert.

On the third day after his marriage Richardson found it necessary to go to the Mission of Solano at Sonoma, the military headquarters of the northern frontier, conveying in the vessel he had built, and which he had named Maria Antonia after his wife, a bell for the mission church.

Four or five months later he made a voyage to Sitka in the Maria Antonia to bring merchandise which was very scarce in the Department. He was back in six months with the commodities that were disposed of in San Francisco District and other parts about the Bay.

During Richardson's absence, his wife gave birth to a girl, named Mariana. With a few days difference, Mrs. Richardson's mother also gave birth to a girl, named Rafaela. On Richardson's return, the babies were held in the hands of the two mothers, who had exchanged the little ones just before the time of the first presentation to him. He was asked which was his child and at once recognized his own, which created a great deal of merriment in the two families, and among the visitors gathered for the occasion.

In 1829 Richardson started for Los Angeles to see what he could do there, and he noted that there was a great scarcity of goods. Without loss of time, he built another schooner at San Pedro in order to make a voyage to Peru, and bring back to Los Angeles and the vicinity the much desired merchandise. Before taking his departure he sent for his family. This first voyage to South America took place about 1831, and occupied nine months. He rejoined his family at the Mission of San Gabriel, where he sold some of the goods he had brought from Peru, and also sold his vessel. He bought a drove of horses, and took his family overland to Yerba Buena. He had, thus early, an idea that San Francisco, or Yerba Buena as it was then called, was destined to become a city of great importance, and in all likelihood, a part of the United States.

Richardson and his family settled in Yerba Buena in 1835. His only daughter, Mariana, was then about nine years old. There were no friction

and well shaped, and although her feet were incased in deer skin shoes, and her hands bare, they might have vied with any belles of our own. I believe the lovely Mariana was as amiable as beautiful, and I know her bright eye glancing along the delicate sights of her rifle, sent leaden missives with the deadly aim of a marksman, and that she rode like an angel, and could strike a bullock dead with one quick blow of a keen blade, but notwithstanding these domestic accomplishments and Anglo-Saxon lineage, she held the demonios Yankees in mortal abhorrence; but who could blame her, they had murdered a brace of her handsomest lovers, and this, in California, where lovers were scarce, was a crime not to be forgiven."

Note. The murder of the deHaro twins and Berryessa by Kit Carson and Frémont's Delaware Indians at San Rafael in June, 1846 is the occurrence referred to by Lieut. Wise above.

See appendix under Jasper O'Farrell's Signed Statement; page 345.

matches at the home, and their fire having become extinguished, they found themselves during two whole days without fire, and there were no neighbors at a convenient distance to get any matches from. The head of the family was then absent at Santa Clara. Fortunately, Pedro del Castillo, who was on his way from the Presidio to Mission Dolores, took a notion to go round by Loma Alta (Telegraph Hill), which was near Yerba Buena, and call upon the Richardson family. He supplied them with fire drawn with steel, flint and tinder.

Some time after Richardson had fixed his residence at Yerba Buena, he heard that a vessel was at the Presidio. He soon ascertained that it was the brig Ayacucho, commanded by his friend Captain John Wilson, who, descrying a man on the beach, sent a boat ashore, and Richardson, going on board, piloted the vessel into Yerba Buena Cove. After the vessel cast anchor, Captain Richardson and his friends, Wilson and the supercargo James Scott, came on shore and visited Richardson's tent, the domicile of the family.

This tent was the first habitation ever erected in Yerba Buena. At the time, Richardson's only neighbors were bears, coyotes and wolves. The nearest people lived either at the Presidio or at Mission Dolores. The family lived under that tent about three months, after which Richardson constructed a small wooden house, and later a large one of adobe on what is now Dupont (Grant Avenue) near the corner of Clay Street.

After Richardson came Jacob P. Leese and José Joaquin Estudillo. Lots at that time were one hundred varas square (275 x 275 feet), and were granted by the Alcalde for the sum of twenty-five dollars. Another early settler was Doña Juana Briones, who lived to be a centenarian.

During Richardson's long life in California he made friends with all who came in contact with him in social or business relations. They were firmly attached to him for his goodness. He had not a single enemy, because his heart and nature were noble. He was seized with a desire at all times to serve his fellow beings in their hours of need. He was incapable of saying no to a deserving applicant for alms. It was inconsistent with the impulses of his nature; a birth-right inherited from his pure Anglo-Saxon parents. He was a handsome man, above medium height, with an attractive face, winning manners, and a musical voice, which his daughter, Mariana, inherited.

My knowledge of the captain dates back to July 1838 when I was in the employ of Nathan Spear. Richardson was the grantee of the Saucelito rancho with thousands of cattle, horses and sheep. His family had two residences, one at Yerba Buena, an adobe dwelling, a structure of primitive architecture, which contained a parlor, commodious bedrooms and a sitting and dining room which was used at times as a ball room. The walls were thick with blinds or massive shutters closing the windows on the inside. The other residence was at Saucelito.

At the time of my acquaintance with this good man, he was Captain of the Port and Bay of San Francisco, under the immediate direction of General Vallejo, who was the comandante general. General Vallejo appreciated Richardson's experience as a sea-faring man, and as the General expressed it, Richardson was the right man in the right place. Both men respected each other, and their official and social relations were as smooth and as placid as the waters of the anchorage of Saucelito or Richardson's bay on a calm day.

I knew Mrs. Richardson personally as far back as the year 1838. She was a model of grace and dignity with a face full of expression. Doña Maria Antonia was truly entitled to be called a Spanish beauty. She was gifted with vivacity and intelligence, and a little spice of satire gave an added charm to her winning manners. She came from a family of good looking brothers and sisters.

Anterior to the year 1838 Captain Richardson had piloted vessels of war in and out of the Bay. His long practice as a mariner made him one of the best pilots for the Bay and the bar beyond the Golden Gate. Admirals and Commodores of different nationalities would communicate with him from Callao, Valparaiso and from Honolulu, that in case a vessel of their squadrons should visit San Francisco, she would fire two guns, one after the other, outside the heads. This was the signal for Richardson to go out and pilot her in. The Captain had eight trained Indians, who had become proficient boatmen. They lived on the premises at the Captain's home in Sausalito. At the report of one or two guns from outside the Bay, Captain Richardson would whistle three times which was the order for the Indian crew to repair at once to the boat which was moored close at hand. Away the surf boat would slip through the water with Richardson in the stern steering, and the aboriginal boatmen bending to their oars with a will to board the man-of-war. These Indians would do anything to serve and please the Captain. He was kind to them and they loved him.

William A. Richardson was a master mariner trading up and down the coast of California in the thirties with assorted cargoes for a Lima house, which were exchanged for hides and tallow, the currency of the country. Richardson was considered a bold navigator, but not a rash one. He was a man of judgment, and never abused it.

During the summer months the westerly winds prevail on the coast of California. It is a dead beat from San Diego to San Francisco against strong trade winds. Richardson had a perfect knowledge of the coast.

Whenever he sailed from San Diego, San Pedro, Santa Barbara, San Luis Obispo or Monterey for San Francisco, he would invariably hug the shore; in other words, he would make short tacks, from the land, and to the land, of twenty-five or thirty miles each way during daylight. But as night approached, his calculation was always correct, he would find himself two, three or four miles off the shore in order to be handy or within reach of the land breezes which generally prevail after night fall.

These winds, right off the land, from the direction of about east or east north-east, six or seven knots strong, extended only a few miles out to sea. I have observed the log at nine knots and as high as ten knot breezes an hour, with every sail set, with the sheets of the main and foresails a little free, and the braces of the yards of the upper canvas consistent with the lower canvas. At this rate of sailing slantingly along the shore line through smooth water, the vessel was approaching her destination northwardly much faster than another vessel beyond the line of the land breezes away out at sea battling against strong westerly winds to reach her port of destination from leeward or southern ports.

When Captain John C. Frémont came from Sonoma to the region now within the County of Marin in 1846, William A. Richardson was at his Saucelito rancho with his family. Frémont's visit with an armed force of about one hundred men, caused great alarm among the native Californian families residing on the north side of the Bay of San Francisco. All the women and children, numbering one hundred and more, sought refuge at Richardson's rancho, and remained there about fifteen days, camped near his residence, and he made them as comfortable as possible under the circumstances. During their stay Richardson supplied the refugees with one beef and four sheep daily, which were slaughtered for their support.

The alarm was caused by Frémont's unlawful proceedings. He also camped with his men three days at Sausalito, and forced Richardson to furnish the party with beef and mutton. Frémont personally demanded the best the place afforded, such as milk, butter, eggs, chickens and other luxuries.

Richardson went to see Frémont at San Rafael, and besought him not to permit his men to commit outrages at his home, because it was filled with helpless women and children.

Frémont took away all the broken horses, consisting of several caperonas, and left Richardson with only four saddle horses for the use of the rancho of two or three thousand head of animals. He did not pay for the animals, nor even give vouchers for them. He did the same with all the horses belonging to Timothy Murphy. Mariana, Richardson's daughter, went to see Frémont personally, and begged him to restore two of the horses which were her own riding animals.

In 1850, I owned and had the bark Hortensia lying at anchor at San Diego in ballast, ready for any adventure that might offer a profitable voyage. Richardson was our guest at the time.

When the grant was made to the original projectors of New San Diego, now the City of San Diego, there was a condition in the deed that the grantees should, within one year, build a wharf and warehouse on the site deeded by the Alcalde and Sub-Prefect. The Proprietors of the new town proposed that I should accept from them some of the realty in the new town for complying with the conditions above mentioned. This I accepted. The deed to the property was made to William A. Richardson and myself. Thus we became partners in the construction of the compulsory improvement at San Diego.

The Hortensia was well adapted as a carrier of piles and other material for the first wharf at San Diego. In June 1850, Captain Richardson sailed in the Hortensia as master, bound north for Saucelito. The morning he weighed anchor to beat down the narrow channel from the present City of San Diego to La Playa, he had only five men, one of whom was a vaquero by occupation, and not one of the five had ever been to sea as a member of a crew. He had no mate to help work the vessel up the coast against strong head winds. The Hortensia was a bark of three hundred tons measurement. I received a letter from Santa Barbara that he had made a good passage to that port, and that he would leave for Saucelito direct the following day with the same crew of five men.

This voyage in the Hortensia has always been a mystery to me; how he could navigate a vessel without mates, change watches with no one to relieve the captain, and without cook or steward provide food for those on board.

The Captain arrived at Saucelito in a remarkably quick passage, with very few hands to work the bark, to set the sails, take in reefs in the sails in stormy weather, steer the vessel day and night, and other compulsory duties necessary for the safety of the bark and all on board. Richardson was in all respects a navigator, a seaman of great self-reliance and was perfectly at home in his own vessel, provided he had plenty of corned beef on board, for he was passionately fond of that meat, even though he had scarcely help enough to work her. He hugged the shore line, the roaring surf, the rocky points usually enveloped in smothers of foam. He knew well the locations of the dangerous shoals along the coast, to these he gave plenty of sea room.

CHAPTER IV
Author Returns on "Don Quixote"

THE "Don Quixote" arrived in Santa Barbara from Boston *via* Honolulu, in May, 1838, and I was a passenger on her, this being my third trip to California. We found Governor Alvarado there, and the department in a revolutionary state. He was opposed by Don Carlos Carrillo and his brother Don José Antonio Carrillo, who were at Los Angeles.

At the above date Governor Alvarado was at his headquarters at Santa Barbara provisionally, and the brothers Carrillo were at Los Angeles. They met on the plains of Los Angeles, where a battle ensued, and four or five horses on each side were shot; but none of the soldiers lost their lives— not even one was wounded—though the conflict lasted for a day or two, as they took the precaution to keep at a safe distance from each other.

Alvarado's force was commanded by General José Castro, and the revolutionary party by José Antonio Carrillo.

Alvarado sustained his authority as governor of the department of California, and the revolutionists were considered as subdued after this bloodless conflict. Some of the leaders were taken prisoners, but shortly after released, and the remainder dispersed.

Previous to this affair our vessel was ordered by Alvarado to go from Santa Barbara to Monterey to enter, that being the only port of entry in the department.

At Monterey I stopped with Major William Warren, then keeping a store there for Nathan Spear, who had also a commercial establishment at Yerba Buena in company with Jacob P. Leese and William S. Hinckley.

During my stay there of two or three weeks, the severe earthquake of June, 1838, took place. At Monterey at that time were David Spence, Thomas O. Larkin, later U. S. consul from 1844 to 1846, John B. R. Cooper, Major William Warren, James Watson, a grocer, George Kinlock, James Stokes, merchant, Edward T. Bale, physician, a native of England, William P. Hartnell, the Mexican government instructor and interpreter. These were the prominent foreigners there. Among the Mexicans and

Californians were José Ábrego, Manuel Diaz, Don Antonio Maria Osio, Collector of the Port; Juan Malarin, Estevan Munrás, Don Pablo de la Guerra, Rafael Gonzalez, Raphael Pinto, (the last three connected with the Custom House), also, Jacinto Rodriguez, José Ameste, Don Manuel Castro, Francisco Pacheco, who were engaged in stock-raising; Mariano Soberanes, José Antonio Vallejo, also engaged in stock-raising, and a brother of General Vallejo.

At that time the following vessels were trading on the coast: The English brig "Ayacucho," the Ecuadorian brig "Delmira," Captain John Vioget, supercargo and owner Don Miguel Pedrorena; the ship "Alert," ship "California," the Mexican brig "Catalina," Captain Jo. Snook, supercargo Don Eulogio de Célis; the Mexican bark "Clarita," Captain Wolter; same supercargo as the "Catalina;" the Mexican Government schooner "California," Captain Cooper; and the Boston bark "Don Quixote," Captain John Paty.

I sailed from Monterey to Yerba Buena in the ship "Alert," well known as the vessel on which Dana served for two years, which experience gave rise to his book, "Two Years Before the Mast." She was commanded by Captain D. P. Penhallow, supercargo Thomas B. Park. The ship was owned in Boston by Bryant & Sturgis, and was on this coast trading for hides, tallow and furs.

It was at this time, while I was staying with Major William Warren that Captain Penhallow of the Alert, who was very jocular and mischievous at times at the expense of his intimate friends, played a severe trick upon "Mine host." Six or seven friends of the Major were seated at table at dinner in the evening. Among the number, Penhallow, who had brought in a live, harmless snake, wrapped up in a paper, which he quietly placed under the host's plate before he had come to the table.

Imagine the horror and indignation the noble and hospitable William Warren experienced upon turning his plate over preparatory to serving his guests. Warren was a portly man of over two hundred pounds in weight, his eyebrows and eyelids were decidedly blonde, and his complexion florid. When he saw the reptile he was startled, screamed and almost fainted, turning pale as a ghost. But it was all over in a few moments. The Major retired from the table disgusted, with a remark to Penhallow, that young Davis might serve the guests with Penhallow's snake dinner.

At first the guests suppressed their laughter, but it was impossible to conceal the mirth long, as the ludicrous features of the scene, although repulsive, were such as to cause both amazement and merriment, especially the appearance of our host who looked so scared and demoralized. Major Warren was a good, kindly man, and a favorite with supercargoes and captains, they making his store their headquarters and his table was always ready for their entertainment in the best manner. He was a great cook, an epicurean of the first order, and had kept hotels at other places with success on account of the fine table he furnished.

On arriving at Yerba Buena I went into the employ of Nathan Spear, and soon became his managing active business man.

He was a native of Boston, Mass., brother of Paul Spear, a prominent apothecary in Boston, and visited Monterey, California, as early as 1823, in the American schooner "Rover," together with Captain J. B. R. Cooper.

Mr. Nathan Spear was one of the first merchants at Monterey and Yerba Buena, and kept a stock of general merchandise, which was sold to the native California farmers and stock-raisers around the bay. The goods were carried to different points by two little schooners owned by Spear, named the "Isabel" and "Nicholas."

Mr. Spear informed me that during the earthquake of June, '38, before mentioned, a large sand-hill standing in the vicinity of what is now Frémont street, between Howard and Folsom, and between which and the bay at high tide there was a space of about twenty feet, permitting a free passage along the shore to Rincon Point (the coves of which were then much resorted to for picnics and mussel parties), was moved bodily close to the water, so as to obstruct the passage along the shore. After that no one could pass there at high tide, and we were compelled to go around back of the sand hill, and wade through the loose sand to reach that point, a much more laborious walk.

He further remarked that Loma Alta (Telegraph Hill) swayed from east to west and from west to east, as if the big mountain would tumble over. At the Mission Dolores there was no injury to church buildings or to dwellings; but at the Presidio the walls of some of the old dwellings were cracked.

The earthquake had occurred just before my arrival at Monterey. Major Warren told me that it was the severest one he had ever experienced, and it seemed to him as if the town would be destroyed during the vibration. The inhabitants were frightened out of their wits. Crockery and glassware were broken, and some of the walls of the adobe dwellings were cracked. It was a shake of no ordinary severity, and the town of Monterey was pretty well shaken up.

Early in the spring of '39, the American ship "Monsoon," of Boston, Captain George Vincent, Thomas Shaw supercargo, arrived at Yerba Buena from Monterey with an assorted cargo. My brother, Robert G. Davis, from Boston, was a clerk on board.

In the month of June the brigantine "Clementine," Captain Blinn, arrived from Honolulu, by way of Sitka. Captain John A. Sutter, with four or five Germans or Swiss, who were mechanics, and three Hawaiians and their wives were passengers. He had gone from one of the Eastern States to Honolulu, thence to Sitka, thence to California. Sutter stayed with Nathan Spear, with all his men and his outfit, and intended to go to the Sacramento valley. When he was ready to proceed, our expedition, composed of the two schooners, "Isabel" and "Nicholas," and a four-oared boat which Sutter brought with him, started with Sutter and his followers. Sutter had two pieces of artillery which he brought with him, and other arms and ammunition for defense against the Indians, if necessary. The fleet was placed under my command.

We left Yerba Buena on the 9th of August, 1839, from alongside the ship "Monsoon" (the only vessel in the bay) for the Sacramento valley, concerning which there was but little known at that time. It had no inhabitants but Indians, many of whom were Mission Indians who had left as the Missions became impoverished and located there. They returned to their former uncivilized life, making occasional visits to the different ranchos to steal horses.

The fleet was about eight days going up the river; every night we would stop at the bank, and Captain Sutter would make excursions from the river to examine the country, looking for a suitable place to establish himself. His idea was to settle, and obtain grants from the Mexican government. I think he had an understanding with that government before he went there, probably with the Mexican minister in the United States. When stopping along the bank of the river at night we could not obtain any rest on account of the immense multitude of mosquitoes which prevailed, exceeding anything we ever experienced before.

The last afternoon we anchored in front of what is now Sacramento City, and saw on the banks of the river some seven or eight hundred Indians, men, women and children. We prepared ourselves for an attack, but our fears proved groundless. They came off to our anchorage in large numbers in canoes made of tules. That afternoon we weighed anchor and went into the American river, landed, pitched tents, and made preparations to occupy the country.

Captain Sutter immediately mounted his brass cannons; all his small arms were made ready for defense against the Indians in case of necessity, and camp established.

On the way up the Sacramento river, Captain Sutter being on board my schooner, which was considered the flag-ship of the fleet, communicated to me his plans. He said, as soon as he found a suitable site he would immediately build a fort, as a means of defense against the Indians, and also against the government of the department of California, in case any hostility should be manifested in that quarter. He also mentioned his intention to form a large colony of his own countrymen to come to this coast, with a view of developing the immense Sacramento valley.

Captain Sutter was a native of Switzerland, an educated and accomplished gentlemen, and a very agreeable and entertaining companion.

Having accomplished my purpose of landing Captain Sutter at the junction of the American and Sacramento rivers with his men and his freight, the following morning we left him there, and headed the two vessels for Yerba Buena. As we moved away Captain Sutter gave us a parting salute of nine guns—the first ever fired at that place—which produced a most remarkable effect. As the heavy report of the guns and the echoes died away, the camp of the little party was surrounded by hundreds of Indians, who were excited and astonished at the unusual sound. A large number of deer, elk and other animals on the plains were startled, running to and fro, stopping to listen, their heads raised, full of curiosity and wonder, seemingly attracted and fascinated to the spot, while from the interior of the adjacent wood the howls of wolves and coyotes filled the air, and immense flocks of water fowl flew wildly about over the camp.

Standing on the deck of the "Isabel" I witnessed this remarkable sight, which filled me with astonishment and admiration, and made an indelible impression on my mind. This salute was the first echo of civilization in the primitive wilderness so soon to become populated, and developed into a great agricultural and commercial centre. We returned the salute with nine cheers from the schooners, the vessels flying the American colors. The cheers were heartily responded to by the little garrison, and thus we parted company.

The voyage down the river occupied eight days. As we approached its termination we were nearly starved. We were reduced to living on brown sugar, that being all that remained of our provisions.

The day before we reached Yerba Buena we anchored where the town of Martinez now is, the place being then known as Cañada del Hambre (Valley of Hunger), from the fact that on one occasion a company of soldiers who were out campaigning against the Indians found themselves very hungry. While at this place we were without the means of obtaining food. Our own situation coincided with that of the soldiers, and we landed with a view to kill some game or capture a steer. We adopted the latter course. Jack Rainsford, who commanded the "Isabel," killed a fine steer belonging to Don Ygnacio Martinez, our necessity compelling this step, and we were thus supplied with plenty of good beef.

On meeting Don Ygnacio Martinez subsequently and informing him of the circumstance, he said it was entirely satisfactory, and regretted that he was not there at the time to supply us with bread, butter and cheese to eat with the beef. This was certainly a fine instance of gentlemanly courtesy and generosity.

CHAPTER V
Russian American Fur Company

ON my arrival in 1838 the Russian American Fur Company had a post at Bodega and also one at Fort Ross, with headquarters at the latter place.

Pedro Kostromitinoff was the governor of the establishment, under lease from the Mexican government, which covered the privilege of hunting the sea otter and collecting forces at that point for that purpose, which lease expired a few years afterward.

Before the expiration of the lease Kostromitinoff was succeeded by Don Alexander Rotcheff, who sold the entire establishment, the improvements and everything, in 1841, to Captain John A. Sutter, of New Helvetia, which was the name of his fort on the Sacramento. The force engaged in hunting the sea otter numbered several hundred of Russians and Esquimaux, brought from Alaska with all their outfits—boats, skin canoes (made from the intestines of the whale) and their native instruments.

They were expert shooters with their Russian rifles, made for the purpose of killing otters, showing great skill in the business, which they carried on here the same as in Sitka.

Going out in their boats, the moment an otter appeared above the water a gun was raised and fired, instantly killing the animal, so expert were these hunters. Bodega was the port of outfit and delivery for the hunt.

These otters were captured in large quantities in the bay of San Francisco, and along the coast south and north of the bay; but the hunting was continued so persistently that they became scarce after a while and finally were killed out entirely. The skins varied from three and one-half to five and one-half feet in length, with a width of about three feet, and were dried at Bodega, and sent to Sitka in vessels that came, two or three yearly, for this freight, for wheat raised about the bay of San Francisco and soap made by the California farmers. The wheat and soap were for the supply of Sitka and other northern Russian posts in Alaska Territory. From Sitka these skins were sent to St. Petersburg.

Some of the men had their families with them. Don Pedro Kostromitinoff was unmarried; Don Alexander Rotcheff was a married man; and his wife was a beautiful Russian lady, of accomplishments. They lived at Fort Ross.

Sutter bought whatever the Russian Company had, the buildings and all the fixtures of the places, both at Bodega and Fort Ross, for $50,000, payable in wheat, soap and furs, in yearly installments for five years, the purchase including several thousand cattle, horses and sheep. It was all paid for in the course of time as agreed by the articles named. The wheat was raised in the Sacramento valley in and around his establishment.

At the first celebration of the fourth of July, in 1836, at Yerba Buena, the families of the prominent residents were invited to the festivity, which was managed by the Americans attached to the three or four American vessels in port, and those living on shore.

The celebration was at the residence of Jacob P. Leese, situated at a point which is now Dupont street, (Grant avenue) near Clay street.

The invitations extended to the persons living about the bay were quite generally accepted. Among the most notable of them were: Don Joaquin Estudillo, with his beautiful wife and lovely daughter Doña Concepcion; Don Ygnacio Martinez, with his handsome daughters, Doña Susana, Doña Francisca, Doña Rafaela and Doña Dolores; Captain William A. Richardson with his wife and pretty daughter, Señorita Mariana, who was one of the belles of the country; Don Victor Castro and his amiable wife, Doña Luisa, daughter of Don Ygnacio Martinez; also the sub-prefect; Don Francisco Guerrero, and his pretty wife, Doña Josefa; and Alcalde Don Francisco de Haro, with his charming daughters, Rosalia and Natividad.

Salutes were fired from the vessels at meridian of the Fourth, a grand dinner took place during the evening, and there was music as well as dancing after the banquet, kept up till the dawn of the next day.

On the fifth, picnics took place, as a continuation of the festival, generally at Point Rincon; the dance was resumed in the evening, and continued until the morning of the sixth, when the ladies had become so exhausted that the festivities ceased. This celebration was kept up year after year on the Fourth, for a long time, until the change of the government from Mexico to the United States, being attended by the native ladies of California, many of whom were noted for their beauty, and such American gentlemen as were here at the time.

Richardson was the captain of the port or bay of San Francisco for many years, an office of the department, under appointment from the Mexican governor of California; this position being equivalent to that of harbormaster under our present law. Upon vessels coming into the bay it was his duty to order them to Monterey, then the port of entry, for the purpose of entry at the custom house.

The vessels which arrived in 1839 at Monterey, entered there, and traded at coast ports, as near as I can remember, were the ship "California," Captain Arther, from Boston, William D. M. Howard, cabin boy; the vessel was consigned to Alfred Robinson and Henry Mellus, agents for Bryant & Sturgis, of Boston; the Baltimore brig "Corsair," Captain Wm. S. Hinckley, who was also owner and supercargo, from Callao; the ship "Fama," Captain Hoyer, A. B. Thompson owner and supercargo; the American schooner "Nymph," Captain Henry Paty, who was also supercargo, from Honolulu.

[TEXT OF LETTER ON OPPOSITE PAGE]

Yerba Buena
August 3th 1836

Mr Nathan Spear
    My Dear Sir:

    In the first place I must Inform you that Mr Berry passed this place for Monterey 3 days ago I mearly passed a few lines by him to let you know that I was a live. I have no news to wright you Excepting on our Buisiness here—I must let you know that I have concluded to stop in this place for Good in consequence of the great Prospect a head which is plainly four Seen—I have maid a Contract here with a couple of men to Build a house and I do think that it will be a profitable one and cost but a trifle the Present house is So open and So much Exposed that I am a fraid to leave it a lone the House which I have Contracted for is to be a fraim 60 feet Long 24 Broad 1½ Storeys high Shead in front the Length of the House 8 feet wide is to be put up here and all shingled in in the month of October for 4 hundred and 40 Dollars paid in Goods So I think that itts a Dam Good Traid if not dissapointed I have given Mr. Park and order on you for 56-4- my own private accounpt you will charge it to me I dont pay him here on accounpt of not appearing with this. I do want you by the first vessell to Send me if itts in your hands Some cand [kind] of Dark Goods for pantaloons and 1 piece of worsted vestings
    1 Gross Table Spoons
    1 Lot of flat chisells No. 2 Inch 1½-1-½-
    and I do Beliave thay you have got a Saw Such as they Saw Boards with and if in case that you have Send it to me as there is Sail for it here— I wish that you wood tell Larkins that if the Tailor has Left old Jimmys waistcot with him to Give it to you or sind it up By the first—and also tell him that Jimmy Says that he doas ow him a small trifle and he Shall Be Paid before Long.
    That timber which Mr. Milish was to of Paid Mr. Majors for find out if it is paid as I have Rec'd a Letter from Monterey from Mr. Luther Cooper informing me to have him paid as for Mr. Cooper I do not know nor maid no contract with him for it was with Mr. Majors and if in case that Majors is not Paid you will please to pay him it is 25 Dollars no more But my Respects to Mrs. Spear.

. Yours and Truly

Jacob P. Leese

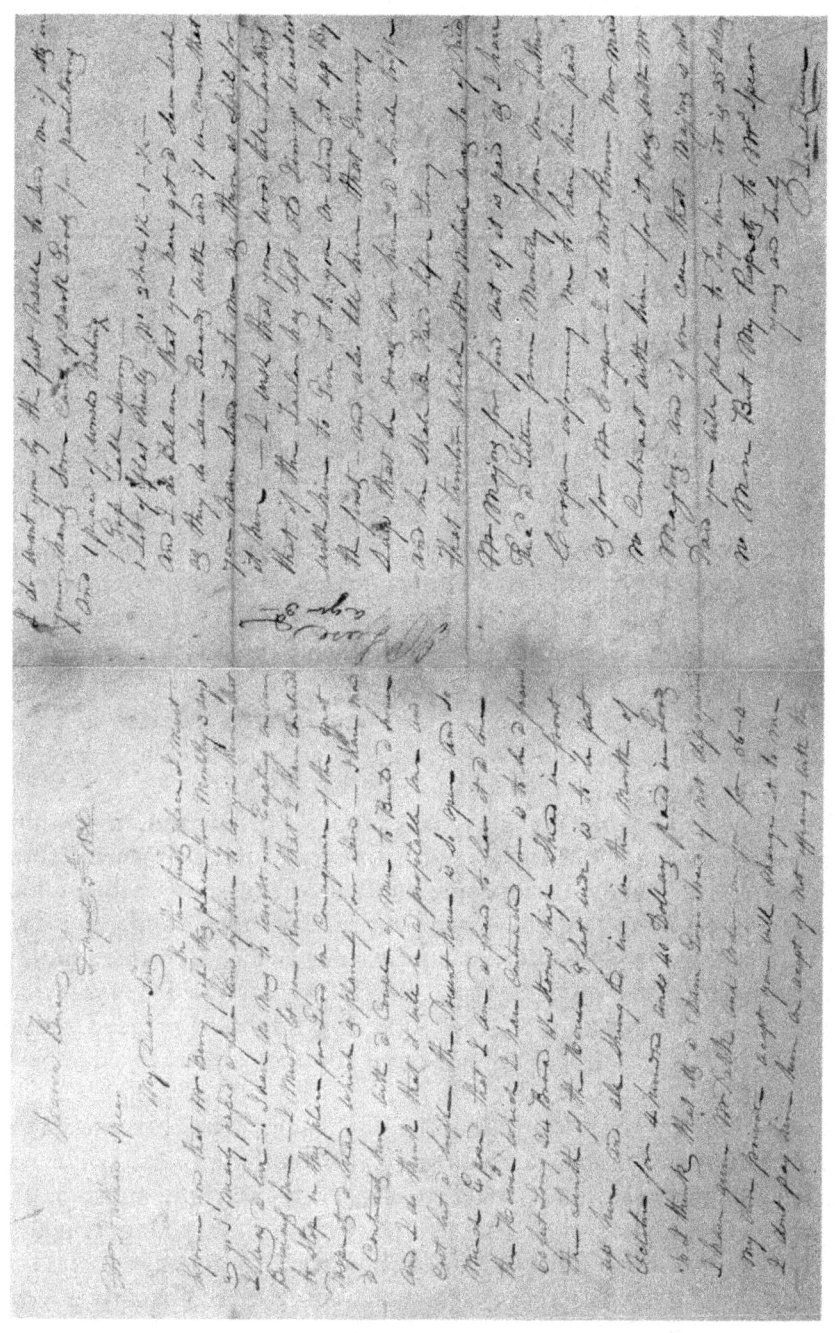

LEESE'S "DAM GOOD TRAID" LETTER TO SPEAR, UNCLE OF WILLIAM HEATH DAVIS, REGARDING THE BUILDING OF THE FIRST REAL HOUSE IN SAN FRANCISCO, THEN YERBA BUENA.

CHAPTER VI
Jacob Primer Leese Arrives in 1833

JACOB PRIMER LEESE, an old California argonaut, was born in Belmont County, Ohio, in or about 1809. He left home in 1821 and joined a company of hunters and trappers with whom he started from New Orleans bound for the Rocky Mountains. The company which had been fitted out by Caldwell, Coffee and Rogers, was known as the Independent Company. At Bent's Fort Leese became a partner of a company which had been organized there. He went to New Mexico in 1831, and was engaged in business there until 1833, when he started and traveled through the wild country to reach California.

In December 1833, while on this journey to California, and on reaching the Mesa of San Bernardino, Leese and his party found themselves short of provisions. A heavy snow storm came on, two feet of snow falling which covered everything. One day they went entirely without food, and as a last resort, Leese had to kill either his hunting dog, which he valued highly, or a mule. To kill a mule under these circumstances was a very serious matter, and so the dog was sacrificed. The dog might have been spared could the owner of the faithful animal have foreseen the early change in the weather for the better.

Only six or eight hours after killing the dog, the weather became warm, the snow melted quickly, and the bellowing of a bull was heard. He was followed and slaughtered, but proved to be a very old bull, most of the meat being so tough that even the strong teeth of the young travelers could hardly masticate it. They managed, however, to appease their hunger. A few hours later the party reached the spot where the calves were feeding and experienced no further hardships regarding food. After resting and recruiting for about three days, they pursued their journey and reached the Mission San Gabriel where they were very hospitably received by the authorities and the missionaries of the church.

The winter of 1833-4 was a very rainy one, and Leese had to sojourn in Los Angeles for about three months. He was engaged in trading with

Isaac Williams, an old mountaineer friend, who was born about fifty miles from Leese's birth place.

After remaining in the south for some time, Leese in 1836 came to Monterey, where he formed a co-partnership with Nathan Spear and William S. Hinckley to transact business at Yerba Buena. This co-partnership

JACOB PRIMER LEESE

was dissolved in 1838, when the three partners stood well in the community, but Spear had taken a dislike to Leese, due to a disagreement in the settlement of some business of the concern.

In all my intercourse with Leese, I must say that I found him genial and companionable, as well as correct in business transactions. In the early history of Yerba Buena, Leese resided on the hill with his family, and adjoining his house was the store. This structure, erected of redwood boards, one story high, with a floor extending at least one hundred feet in front with a width of about thirty feet, were it standing today would face Dupont (Grant Avenue) Street looking east, being on the south-west corner of Clay Street.

At this place for about two years Leese did a large business in supplying the ranchos bordering the Bay of San Francisco with goods. The business was done in the name of Jacob P. Leese; Spear and Hinckley appearing as silent partners of the firm. The supply of goods came from Spear's large store at Monterey and was conveyed to Yerba Buena by vessels trading on the coast.

It was at his home, adjoining the store, that the first celebration in Yerba Buena of September Sixteenth, the Mexican national holiday, occurred, and there likewise was subsequently observed with due honor

CELEBRATION OF JULY 4, 1836, AND COMPLETION OF THE FIRST HOUSE IN YERBA BUENA, BUILT BY JACOB P. LEESE

the anniversary of the independence of the United States. All the families round the Bay attended these celebrations, to each of which three days of festivities were devoted.

In the same structure Leese entertained supercargoes and captains of vessels trading on the coast, besides governors, generals, prefects and alcaldes; likewise admirals, commodores and other officers of the foreign ships of war that visited the Bay of San Francisco.

At the celebration of the American Independence in 1837, several vessels were in Yerba Buena Cove, namely: Ship Lagoda, Bradshaw, master and Thomas Shaw, supercargo, from Boston; ship California, Arther, master, supercargo William G. Gale, whose assistant was Alfred Robinson; British brig Ayacucha, John Wilson, master, Diego (James) Scott, supercargo. All these vessels were handsomely decorated for the occasion and their officers took part in the festival. Each of the American ships fired salutes at sunrise, noon and sunset. José Joaquin Estudillo and family were Leese's guests on this occasion.

About 1850 Jacob P. Leese conveyed to Thomas O. Larkin the property on Dupont (Grant Avenue) and Clay Streets in consideration of which the latter deeded his own real estate at Monterey to Leese, the same being later occupied by the Leese family. This was a barter trade. Larkin was number one, and Leese number two as to the relative value of the realty, due to the deterioration of real estate in one instance, and the rise in value in the other.

In the latter part of 1838 Leese obtained from Governor Alvarado and the departmental assembly permission to erect a building in Yerba Buena near the beach. He moved to the new quarters in the early part of the following year, continuing there until he sold the premises to the Hudson's Bay Company in 1841, when William G. Rae took possession as agent.

Leese then departed for Sonoma, where he resided and owned two fine ranchos, one bordering San Pablo Bay and the other situated at Clear Lake. Both ranchos were well stocked with cattle and fine horses, for he, as well as his brothers-in-law, Mariano G. Vallejo and Salvador Vallejo, took pains to breed properly; in other words, the stallion of each manada was not permitted to roam with its own progeny. The object of this was to avoid breeding from animals of the same blood, thus averting deterioration of the stock.

The rancho at Sonoma, called the Huichica, was only of five leagues in extent, but had very fine rich land, yielding abundance of grass for stock, which consisted of about fourteen hundred head of cattle, and three thousand horses and mares. The number of caponeras owned by Leese averaged eight or ten. It was a part of his business at that time to send horses to Oregon for sale to the Hudson's Bay Company, receiving in payment merchandise which he sold in Sonoma in exchange for hides, tallow, furs, coin, cattle and horses.

Another piece of property which Leese owned was Clark's Point, known in former times as the Punta de la Loma Alta, now Telegraph Hill. It was granted to Leese and Salvador Vallejo in 1839 by Governor Alvarado and approved by the departmental assembly. The Mexican law regulating land grants forbade the granting of land bordering on the waters of Yerba Buena Cove, but the authorities assumed the responsibility of making an exception in the case of Vallejo and Leese.

The land was two hundred by one hundred varas and was bounded by Vallejo, Front, Pacific and Davis Streets. In 1848, William S. Clark and a party of Mormons came to Yerba Buena and the former squatted on the land referred to, refusing to recognize Leese's title. Prior to this, Salvador Vallejo had transferred his interest to Leese. Clark's trespassing was during the war between the United States and Mexico, and as Leese was then a Mexican citizen, he was helpless to defend his rights.

After California became a State, Leese commenced a civil action, in 1851 or 1852, to eject the squatter from the premises, Gregory Yale, F. J. Lippitt and others representing him at Judge Norton's Court. The case was before the court a long time, during which Clark was receiving and enjoying an income from the property and with the proceeds fought Leese in the courts. After some ten years litigation, numerous persons applied to Leese to convey to them his right, title and interest in the land in controversy in severalty. He accepted their offers, this being the only way to recover something in money from his property. He was induced to give up the litigation by an apprehension that his chances in the Supreme Court of the State were very slim, as he had understood that one of the justices of that court had, away from the bench, expressed himself adversely to Leese's interests. The property became immensely valuable because it borders on the deepest water fronting the City of San Francisco. There deep sea vessels can discharge. It is now covered with very extensive warehouses where the bulk of merchandise discharged from ships is deposited on storage.

Samuel Norris was interested with Leese in mining operations shortly after the gold discovery. To convey Indian laborers and supplies, Leese had horse teams which he kept plying between Sonoma and the Feather River, then the point of interest of the mining excitement, due to the great discovery. Such teams were extremely scarce and difficult to procure for a time, until the heavy overland immigration set in.

Captain, afterwards General, Henry W. Halleck, Thomas O. Larkin and Jacob P. Leese went to the mines to see for themselves. The last named of this party drove there eleven hundred head of cattle, and sold the greater part of them to Marshall, who at that time was buying all the cattle to supply the miners with beef. The sale averaged about twenty-five dollars a head. Leese and his traveling companions were not allowed the privilege of seeing much of the gold at the time, the persons interested in the mines making it a point to keep their operations secret.

Leese made one voyage to China via Honolulu in a vessel called the Eveline. There he bought goods and brought them to San Francisco in the ship Diamond. These goods were transferred to and sold at Sonoma. The invoice cost was twenty thousand dollars, and from the sales of the merchandise Leese derived a handsome profit.

Jacob Primer Leese, a fine looking man, married at Sonoma in 1837 Señorita Rosalia Vallejo, sister of General Mariano G. Vallejo. Mrs. Leese was a tall, handsome, beautifully formed woman, full of vivacity and remarkably intelligent. She was noted for a proneness to sarcasm, which was a trait in the Vallejo family. Leese was a good marksman and he taught his wife the use of the rifle. She became quite expert with the weapon, and I have seen her make some extraordinary shots. Captain John Paty, Leese and others once had a shooting match at Rincon Point on Mission Bay, on which occasion Mrs. Leese exhibited her remarkable skill.

ELK CROSSING CARQUINEZ STRAITS

Drawn under the personal direction of William Heath Davis to illustrate his story of the vast herds of these now almost extinct animals so plentiful in California before the discovery of gold by Marshall, January 24, 1848.

CHAPTER VII
Elk on Mare Island

ON Mare Island I often saw in the years from '40 to '43, as many as two or three thousand elk, it being their habit to cross and re-cross by swimming between the island and the main land, and I remember on one occasion when on the schooner "Isabel," of sailing through a band of these elk, probably not less than a thousand, which were then crossing from Mare Island to the main land. It was a grand and exciting scene. The captain of the boat wanted to shoot at some of them, but I prevented him from doing so, because we could not stop to get the game on board and I did not like to see the elk wantonly destroyed.

These elk were killed for their hides and tallow by the rancheros in considerable numbers, at the time they slaughtered their cattle. They would go out to the haunts of the elk, and capture them by the lasso, which was used by them on all occasions, and after killing the animals, secure the hides and tallow on the spot, leaving the carcasses. The tallow of the elk was superior to that of the bullock, whiter and firmer, and made better candles.

This work was much more dangerous and exciting than the killing of cattle, and required the very best broken saddle horses and those most accustomed to the lasso, and also the best vaqueros, on account of the strength, agility, fleetness and fierceness of the elk. Great skill was also required in throwing the lasso, (the loop of which was made larger than for cattle on account of the wide-spreading horns of the elk), and in holding them after the lasso was cast.

In 1838 and 1839 the prominent ranches or cattle farms about the bay of San Francisco and in the vicinity were as follows: On the north side of the bay at the Mission of San Rafael were three or four thousand cattle and horses. At Bodega and Fort Ross, the Russian American Fur Company, which has already been described, had two or three thousand head of cattle, twelve or fifteen hundred horses and numerous sheep. At Petaluma, was the rancho of Don Mariano Guadalupe Vallejo, with about ten thousand head of cattle, four to six thousand horses and a large number of sheep.

Where the town of Santa Rosa now stands was the Rancho Santa Rosa, owned by Doña Maria Ygnacia Lopez Carrillo, with about three thousand head of cattle and twelve to fifteen hundred horses and some sheep. Adjoining the Santa Rosa on the north was the rancho of Marcus West, an Englishman, with about 1500 cattle and 500 or 600 horses.

The rancho of Don Salvador Vallejo was located in Napa Valley, and contained from 5000 or 6000 cattle and about 2000 horses; adjoining him on the east was Nicolas Higuera, with about 2000 cattle and 1000 horses; to the south of the latter Cayetano Juarez, with a few hundred cattle and horses; adjoining him on the south was the Nacional Rancho Suscol in charge of General Vallejo. This was reserved by the Mexican government for the purpose of supplying the troops of the department of California with cattle and horses. It contained 5000 head of cattle, and two or three thousand horses, in charge of a corporal and eight or ten soldiers, the latter being utilized as vaqueros for the purpose of managing this stock. It may be mentioned here as a matter of interest that all the native Californians (the term meaning those of Spanish extraction) were trained to horsemanship, and naturally became vaqueros, being very expert with the reata and skilled in the training and management of horses and cattle.

On the south side of Carquinez strait was the Rancho Pinole, owned by Don Ygnacio Martinez, with 8000 head of cattle and about 1000 horses. This rancho derived its name from the parched corn, ground up, known as pinole, and which was used everywhere and especially by the Mexican troops as food in their campaigns against the Indians; it was commonly mixed with a little *panoche* (sugar) and water, and was very palatable and nutritious. This food, together with the game killed by the soldiers, such as elk, deer, antelope—and beef, constituted their whole fare when in the field.

Adjoining this rancho, on the southeast side, was the Rancho Boca de la Cañada del Pinole, owned by Felipe Briones, with a few hundred cattle and horses; to the west of the Rancho Pinole was the San Pablo, owned by the Castro family, with four or five thousand head of cattle and one or two thousand horses.

To the south of San Pablo was the Rancho San Antonio, owned by Don Luis Peralta, who prior to his death divided the tract among his four sons, Ygnacio, Domingo, Antonio Maria and Vicente. A portion of it is now occupied by the cities of Oakland and Alameda. This rancho carried 8000 head of cattle and 2000 head of horses and mares; it extended on the south to San Leandro creek. To the east of this was the Rancho Moraga, owned by Don Joaquin Moraga, with about 800 cattle and a few hundred horses.

South of San Antonio was the Rancho San Leandro, owned by Don

José Joaquin Estudillo, with two or three thousand head of cattle, about 800 horses, and five or six thousand sheep; the present town of San Leandro is on a part of the rancho. Across San Lorenzo creek was the Rancho San Lorenzo Bajo, owned by Francisco Soto, with one to two thousand cattle, and three to four hundred horses; to the east of him was the San Lorenzo upper ranch, owned by Don Guillermo Castro, with five or six thousand cattle and two or three thousand horses.

To the east of this was the rancho owned by Don José Maria Amador and Don Dolores Pacheco residing at the Pueblo of San José, with 6000 head of cattle and one to two thousand horses. To the east of them was the rancho of Robert Livermore, an Englishman, with two or three thousand cattle and one or two thousand horses.

To the south of Francisco Soto was the Mission of San José, with 8000 head of cattle, and about 3000 horses, and eight to ten thousand sheep, and fifteen to eighteen hundred Christianized Indians, all under the charge of Don José Jesus Vallejo, the administrator of the Mission.

In the valley of San José, extending from what is called Warm Springs, as far as thirty miles to the south of the town of San José, and to the river Guadalupe on the west, there were numerous stock-raisers, having extensive ranchos, with an aggregate of not less than 100,000 head of cattle, and probably 20,000 horses, and large flocks of sheep. At the rancho of Ygnacio Alviso, where the town of Alviso is located, there were three or four thousand head of cattle and about 1500 horses.

At the Mission of Santa Clara, to the west of the river Guadalupe, there were probably 1000 to 1500 cattle and horses. This Mission, anterior to 1834, was considered one of the richest in the department, but during the revolutions and civil wars in the country the military power in the vicinity of the Mission appropriated nearly all the horses and cattle belonging to it, and it therefore became impoverished.

To the northwest of Santa Clara was the Rancho Las Pulgas, (the Fleas), owned by the heirs of Governor Argüello, with about 4000 head of cattle and 2000 horses. The towns of Belmont, Redwood City and Menlo Park are situated here.

To the northwest of the Las Pulgas was the Buri-buri rancho, with about 8000 head of cattle and 1000 horses, owned by Don José Sanchez.

Captain Henry D. Fitch, a native of New Hampshire, who came to the country in 1833 or '34, commanded vessels trading to Callao and other points on the coast, and afterwards settled at San Diego, where he married a sister of General Vallejo's wife, and engaged in merchandising. He was an honorable man, and very hospitable. Afterward, he obtained a grant of land, called Sotoyome (an Indian name) in Sonoma county, from Governor

Micheltorena. He stocked it with several thousand cattle and horses. Fitch Mountain, at Healdsburg, was named after him. He died in 1848.

At San Diego, also, was Don Juan Bandini, a native of Peru, who married one of the Estudillo family. He was a man of decided ability and of fine character. He owned several ranches in San Diego and Los Angeles counties.

Don Abel Stearns married a daughter of Bandini, Doña Arcadia, who, after Stearns' death, married Colonel Baker, after whom Bakersfield was named. She was very beautiful. Her husband was one of the wealthiest residents of the State.

At San Diego was also Don Santiago Argüello, a brother of Governor Argüello. He was a prominent man, and prefect under Governor Alvarado, in Los Angeles, and he held other offices.

To the north of the bay of San Francisco, wild Indians, from the Clear Lake country, assisted in farm work, such as making soap, *matanza* work, plowing lands for wheat, barley, beans, corn and small vegetables, onions, peas, cabbages, *calabazas, lantejas* and melons.

Civilized Indians from the Missions were scattered about the country, and many were to be found on the different ranchos. They were of peaceable disposition, were employed as vaqueros, and helped the rancheros at the planting season and at harvest time.

I have often seen the Clear Lake Indians at their *temescales,* or steaming places. A large cavity was made in the ground, six or eight feet deep, somewhat like a cellar, and tightly covered over with brush, with a little aperture for the smoke to pass out. In this cavity they made a very hot fire, and a number of them, men and women, nearly bare of clothing, went in and subjected themselves to the heating process, taking a hot air bath, keeping up a monotonous singing all the time.

They remained there from half an hour to an hour, or until entirely heated through, so that the perspiration ran off them in streams. In that condition they rushed out, plunged into a pool in the creek nearby, cooled off and washed, after which they retired to their habitations. I frequently witnessed this steaming of the Indians at the rancho of Mrs. Carrillo, at Santa Rosa, and wondered that they were not instantly killed by the sudden transition from heat to cold; but never knew any of them to be injured by the practice. These performances always took place in the night.

CHAPTER VIII
How the Missions were Supported

THE Missions exacted from the cattle owners a contribution known as *diezmo,* for the support and benefit of the clergy and for the expense of the Missions—one-tenth of the increase of the cattle. The tax was not imposed by the general government, but was solely an ecclesiastical matter decreed by the Pope of Rome or a law of the church, diligently collected by the clergy of the different Missions, and religiously contributed by the rancheros. The collection was continued as late as 1851 or 1852.

The cattle were slaughtered in the summer season; the killing commenced about the first of July and continued until the first of October, for the hides and tallow; about 200 pounds of the best part of the bullock was preserved, by drying, for future consumption, the balance of the animal being left to go to waste; it was consumed by the buzzards and wild beasts.

The tallow was tried in large pots brought by the American whale ships—such as are used to try out their blubber, and was then run into bags made of hides, each containing twenty to forty arrobas. An arroba is twenty-five pounds.

In securing the tallow, the *manteca,* or fat lying nearest the hide of the bullock, was taken off carefully, and tried out apart from the interior fat, or *sebo*. The latter constituted the tallow for shipment; about seventy-five to one hundred pounds being obtained from each creature. The former, of which forty to fifty pounds were obtained, was more carefully and nicely prepared, and was saved for domestic use; in cooking being preferred to hog's lard. Sometimes the two were mixed, the latter not being used by itself. Whenever there was more of the *manteca* than was needed for the family, the Russians were eager purchasers for shipment and for their own use. It was sold for $2 per arroba, and the *sebo* at $1.50 per arroba.

The *manteca* required much attention in trying it out. Being of a more delicate nature than the other fat and more liable to burn, it was constantly watched. When the fat of either kind was sufficiently melted and cooked it was allowed to cool partly, and while still liquid was transferred to hide bags, which were prepared to receive it by fastening at four points on the edge of four upright stakes set in the ground, the mouth of the bag being thus held open. The hides were staked out and dried, and were then ready for the market.

At the ranchos very little use was made of milch cows for milk, butter or cheese. I have frequently drank my tea or coffee, without milk, on a ranch containing from 3600 to 8000 head of cattle. But in the spring of the year, when the grass was green, the wives of the rancheros made from the milk *asaderas,* a fresh cheese, in small flat cakes, which had to be eaten the day it was made.

The horns of the animals were considered of no value by the cattle owners, and were generally secured for nothing by the trading vessels on the coast, and shipped to Boston.

The horses were never stabled. They were broken for the saddle only, and were used almost wholly for herding cattle. They were divided up into *caponeras,* or small bodies of about twenty-five each, each *caponera* having a bell mare, which was always a *yegua pinta* (calico mare), having a beautiful variety of color, whom they followed; and so accustomed were they to their leaders that the different little bands never mixed; and if by chance one got into the wrong company, he would presently go back to where he belonged.

On a rancho with 8000 head of cattle there would be, say, twelve *caponeras.* One or two of these divisions, containing the best horses, were specially for the owner of the rancho, and never used for ordinary work, but merely by the owner for his own riding purposes.

A large number of horses were needed on each rancho for herding stock, as they were used up very fast. They were numerous and cheap, and the owners placed no restraint upon the vaqueros, who rode without a particle of regard for the horses, till they soon became unfit for further use in this way. The vaqueros were continually breaking in young colts three years old and upwards, to replace those already beyond service.

There were large bands of wild horses in the Valley of the San Joaquin, which at that time was entirely unsettled. At times, a few mares, and perhaps a young stallion, would stray away from a rancho and get out of reach, until in the course of time there were collected in that valley immense herds, thousands and tens of thousands of horses, entirely wild and untamed, living and breeding by themselves, finding there plenty of good feed to sustain them.

Frequently during the summer time, young men, the sons of rancheros, would go in companies of eight or ten or twelve to the valley on their best and fleetest steeds, to capture a number of these wild horses and bring them to the ranchos. On reaching the place where a large band was collected, they prepared for the sport in this way: The saddles being removed, the horses were ridden bare-back, a piece of reata being tied loosely around the body of each horse just behind the fore legs, and the rider, having no saddle or stirrups, slipped his knees under the rope, one end of the lasso being tied to the rope also. Thus prepared, they rode toward the wild horses, who, on seeing them approach, would take alarm and rush off at great speed, the riders following. Sometimes the chase lasted for miles before they came up with the horses. On getting near enough each horseman selected his victim, pursued him, and at the right moment cast at lasso, which never failed to encircle the neck of the horse; then bringing his own horse to a stand, there was a wild struggle, the rider holding his horse firm, and the captured horse pulling and straining on the rope until he become so choked and exhausted that he was compelled to succumb.

It was very hazardous sport, and required the greatest nerve and the best horsemanship. If a rider found himself in the midst of a band of wild horses there was danger that he and his horse might be over-ridden and trampled to death. This sometimes occurred.

When fifty or sixty of the wild horses were thus captured, they were taken to the ranchos, corralled at night and herded in the daytime, until they became sufficiently subdued to be introduced among the horses of the ranch.

This was great diversion for the young men, and at the same time it added to their stock the best animals of the wild herds. It is presumed there were as many as fifteen or twenty thousand of wild horses in different bands, in the San Joaquin valley.

CHAPTER IX
Life on California Ranchos

ALTHOUGH the cattle belonging to the various ranchos were wild, yet they were under training to some extent, and were kept in subjection by constant rodeos. At stated times, say, two or three times a week at first, the cattle on a partcular ranch were driven in by the vaqueros, from all parts thereof, to a spot known as the rodeo ground, and kept there for a few hours, when they were allowed to disperse. Shortly they were collected again, once a week perhaps, and then less seldom, until after considerable training, being always driven to the same place, they came to know it. Then, whenever the herd was wanted, all that was necessary for the vaqueros to do was, say twenty-five or thirty of them, to ride out into the hills and valleys and call the cattle, shouting and screaming to them, when the animals would immediately run to the accustomed spot; presently the whole vast herd belonging to the ranch finding their way there.

At times, cattle strayed from one ranch to another and got into the wrong herd. Whenever a rodeo was to be held, the neighbors of the ranchero were given notice and attended at the time and place designated. If any of these cattle were found in the band, they were picked out, separated, and driven back to the rancho where they belonged. As the cattle were all branded, and each rancho had ear-marks, this was not difficult.

Sometimes when cattle were being herded in a rodeo, an obstinate or unruly animal, cow, steer or bull—commonly a bull—watching an opportunity, suddenly darted from the herd and ran away at full speed. The vaquero, being always on the alert and knowing his duty well, immediately dashed out after the animal. Being on a fleet horse he presently came up with the runaway, and by a dexterous movement, leaning over his horse, seized the creature by the tail, when, urging the steed to an extra effort, the horse dashed forward, giving a sudden jerk, and the tail being let go by the vaquero at the right moment, the animal was rolled over and over on the ground. When it regained its legs it was completely subdued, tamely submitted to be driven back to the herd and was not inclined to repeat the experiment.

The capture was called *coller*. It was highly enjoyed by the vaquero, and was a feat requiring no little skill, strength, nerve and horsemanship on his part. The ranchero himself when out riding with his friends, for their amusement and his own, would sometimes separate an animal from the herd, run him off to one side, gallop alongside, catch him by the tail and skillfully turn him over and over, creating a good deal of merriment. At times the sagacious animal, knowing what was coming, would draw his tail down under his body. This manœuvre did not prevent its being seized, nevertheless.

The rodeo ground was of circular shape; the vaqueros always left the cattle together in that form. When a rodeo took place, six or eight *cabestros,* or tame cattle, were brought together in a stand, or *parada,* about one hundred yards or more from the rodeo, in charge of a vaquero. When the cattle were to be selected from the rodeo, the vaqueros rode quietly in among them, in pairs, and two of them, seeing one they wanted to remove, gently approached the animal, one on each side, and, without making any disturbance, edged him along to one side of the rodeo ground opposite to where the *parada* stood. When they got just to the edge, they gave him a sudden start, by shouting *"hora"* (now), and off he went at full speed, followed by them. Seeing the *parada* a little distance off, the wild steer or cow generally made for that, or, if he or she turned to one side, was guided by the vaqueros, and, on reaching it, stopped with the tame cattle, or was compelled to if not so inclined. The cattle when taken first in this way to the *parada,* finding themselves with a strange set and few in number were uneasy; but the vaqueros continuing to bring in others, the numbers increasing rapidly, the new comers would feel more at home, and generally remained quiet. If one bolted from the *parada,* a vaquero pursued him and performed the *coller* movement, and he returned tamely and made no more trouble. As many as were required were brought to the *parada* by the vaqueros, until fifty or seventy-five were thus collected at times, as in the killing season, or a less number if selected to be returned to their owners, or for sale. Several pairs of vaqueros, or *apartadores,* were often engaged at the same time in the rodeo ground, taking out cattle to be removed and conducting them to different *paradas.*

When the owners of adjoining ranchos came to the rodeo ground to select their cattle, they brought their own *cabestros,* and their own vaqueros, who went in and picked out the cattle belonging to their special ranchos, and took them to their own *paradas.* Two or three hundred cattle belonging to a neighboring ranch would be taken from a rodeo at a time.

The work of separating the cattle, while a necessity, was really more of an amusement than a labor, and I have frequently participated in it for the sport. On such occasions many persons from the different ranchos came, as at a cattle fair in the country in our day, to exchange greetings and talk over affairs. Sometimes they would amuse themselves by joining in the work with the vaqueros, in pairs, a point being not to disturb or frighten the whole mass of cattle on the rodeo ground.

The *cabestros* had holes in their horns, with a small spike inserted, by which an unruly beast could be attached to one or two other cattle, so to be taken from one place to another, when necessary.

When the horses became disabled, or too poor for use, they were generally given away to the poorer people of the country, or to Indians who could make them useful.

The California horses were originally from Arabian stock, imported from Spain by the Padres at the time of the first establishment of the Missions. They had multiplied here extensively. At first it was very fine stock, but it became degenerated by breeding in, generation after generation, for over a hundred years. No attention was given by the rancheros to the production of good stock, either cattle or horses.

All *orejanos* (calves without ear-mark or brand) not following the cow, were considered as belonging to the rancho on which they were found.

The marking season always commenced about the first of February in the southern counties, before the hot weather came on, and ended about the middle of May, when both horses and cattle were branded, ear-marked and castrated. Rodeos were held at marking and slaughtering times, and at other periods often enough to keep the animals subdued, and accustomed to the premises of the owner.

At the killing season, cattle were driven from the rodeo ground to a particular spot on the rancho, near a brook and forest. It was usual to slaughter from fifty to one hundred at a time, generally steers three years old and upward; the cows being kept for breeding purposes. The fattest would be selected for slaughter, and about two days would be occupied in killing fifty cattle, trying out the tallow, stretching the hides and curing the small portion of meat that was preserved. The occasion was called *the matanza*.

The mode of killing cattle was thus: About fifty were driven into a corral near the *matanza* ground; a vaquero then went in on horseback and lassoed a creature by the horns, the end of the reata being already fastened to the pommel of the saddle, with as much thrown out as was necessary, only a portion being used in a small space like the corral, the remainder being held in the hand in a coil, to be let out or drawn in, as circumstances should require.

The animal was brought out of the corral, and, another vaquero coming up, the animal when it reached the spot where it was wanted was lassoed by one or both hind legs, and at that moment the horse, by a sudden movement, jerked the animal to one side or the other, and it was thrown instantly to the ground. The man who had him by the head then backed his horse, or the horse, understanding the business perfectly, backed himself, until the whole reata was straightened out; and the horse of the vaquero who had the creature by the hind legs did the same, the latter vaquero meanwhile fastening his reata more securely to the saddle, and the two lines were drawn taut. The man at the tail end, then dismounting, tied the fore legs of the animal together with an extra piece of rope, and the hind legs also, drawing all the feet together in a bunch and tying them.

During this operation the man and horse at the head stood firm, and the horse without the rider did the same, watching every movement, his ears moving back and forth; if there was any slacking of the reata from the motions of the animal, he backed a little further, without any direction from the vaquero, so intelligent and well-trained was the faithful beast. After the steer was thus tied, and powerless to rise, the reatas were taken from him entirely, and the man on foot stuck a knife in his neck. When he was dead, the two took off the skin in a short time, not over half an hour, so expert were they at the business.

At other times, not during the killing season, if a beef was required for family use, two vaqueros were detailed by the ranchero to go out and bring in a fat creature. They selected the best they could find from the cattle in the field, lassoed him and brought him in to the side or rear of the house, about 100 feet distant, and convenient to the kitchen, where the steer was lassoed by the hind legs, thrown over and killed, as above. The skin was laid back on the ground as it was taken off, and the creature was cut up on the skin. At this time nearly the whole of the meat was used, not merely the choice parts, as at the *matanza*. In cutting up the animal they first took off in a layer the *fresada* (literally, blanket), that is, the thick portion covering the ribs, which, though tough, was very sweet and palatable; and as the Californians, both men and women, old and young, were blessed with remarkably sound teeth, the toughness was no impediment to its being eaten.

I never knew an instance of a person of either sex or any age among the Californians suffering from toothache or decay of teeth, but all preserved their teeth in good condition to extreme old age; at the same time, they did not take any special care of them. I can account for the excellent preservation of the teeth only upon the ground of an extremely simple mode of living and their temperate habits.

This mode of slaughter of cattle—lying flat upon the ground—preserved a great deal more of the blood in the meat than the method in use by Americans. The meat was therefore sweeter and more nutritious than if the blood had been drained as much as possible, as is the custom with us; though the slaughtering in this way seemed somewhat repugnant to a stranger, at first. I have heard Americans express this feeling, and have experienced it myself, but we soon became accustomed to it, and were convinced that the mode of the Californians was superior to ours.

Capt. Richardson said to me that he could account for the fine appearance, the health and longevity of the Californians only from the fact that their chief article of food was beef, and the beef being dressed in the way I have described was more nutritious and sustaining than ours.

During a business visit to Los Angeles some years since, I frequently met Don Dolores Sepulveda, one of the offspring of a prominent family of that name in that section of California. Señor Sepulveda stated to me one day, speaking of the longevity of some of his countrywomen, that there were living in Los Angeles county thirty native California women with ages ranging from eighty to over one hundred years. They were well preserved mentally and physically.

In Monterey, the old capital under the Mexican regime, there are still (1889) living a number of women of Castillian extraction, who are ninety years old and upward. Señora Doña Guadalupe Briones de Miramontes lived formerly at the Presidio of San Francisco, near "Polin," the name of a spring of water celebrated for certain virtues. She is now (1889) a resident of Spanishtown, in San Mateo county, and a very old lady, being over a century in years. I have been informed that she is hale and strong, and is able to insert a thread through the small eye of a needle, preparatory to her habit of daily sewing with her hand. It was this woman who cured me of a malady and saved me from death years since. I was afflicted with the neuralgia in the head from my youth, and I had been on the point of death, but Doña Guadalupe's simple remedy relieved me of suffering probably to the end of my time.

CHAPTER X
The Horse in Early California

IN 1840 the Mission of San José ordered a slaughter of about 2000 bulls, simply for the hides, not taking any meat from them. The vaqueros rode into the fields, and lassoed and killed them on the spot, taking off the hides and little tallow and leaving the carcasses there untouched. The rule among the old rancheros here was to preserve one bull for every twenty-five cows, but in the instance above mentioned they had carelessly allowed a large number to grow up without castration. The Missions did not give so much attention to these matters as the regular ranchmen. The vaqueros of the Missions were always Indians, who were more careless in the management of the stock.

The breeding mares were divided up into *manadas,* or little bodies of twenty-five, with a stallion for each, and so accustomed were they to follow their stallion that each band kept distinct and never mixed with other *manadas*. The stallions were equally faithful to those under their charge, and never went off to other bands. It was the custom of a stallion, on the approach of a strange horse, or number of horses, to circle round his mares keeping them well together, and driving the visitors away, so jealous were they of intruders. I have never known them to mix in any way, but to keep their companies distinct. The *manadas* were formed at first by the vaqueros herding the band during the day, and at night securing them in a corral. They continued this day after day until the animals had become so accustomed to the arrangement that there was no danger of their separating. They were then left to go free, and continued together month after month and year after year. A stallion when taken away from his *manadas* and confined in a corral would squeal and neigh and manifest the greatest uneasiness and anxiety until restored to his company. Except for this training to form them into *manadas*, these mares were entirely wild and unbroken. They were never used for riding, and only occasionally for work at the harvest season. They were kept for breeding purposes, and it was not considered a proper or becoming thing for a lady or gentleman to ride a mare; it would, in fact, have been regarded as humiliating.

The tails and manes of the mares of the *manadas* were closely cut. The hair was utilized for ropes, made by the vaqueros by twisting and braiding together. Those made from the tails were used by the vaqueros for reins and halters in breaking in young colts, and those made from the manes, being of finer quality, were used by the rancheros themselves. The hair being of different colors and skillfully worked together, these hair ropes were very pretty and ornamental, as well as very strong. I once asked an old ranchero, Don Domingo Peralta, why the manes and tails of the stallions attached to the *manadas* were not cut also. He replied, *"Las yeguas los aborrecen"*—(the mares would take a dislike to them, would lose their respect and affection for them, and would not recognize them as their stallions).

When the grain was cut at harvesting, the mares were employed in threshing it. I have seen at the rancho of San Leandro four *manadas,* or 100 mares, engaged in threshing barley. While they were at work during the day the stallions were separated from them and kept in different corrals. At the end of the day, when the work was done, they were released; the mares being set free also, the stallions would go to work and separate the mares, each getting his own band together, and the mares, recognizing their own stallion, would flock round him.

The threshing was accomplished in a very primitive way: A circular piece of ground, known as *hera,* containing, say, an acre and a half, was inclosed by a fence, smooth on the inside. The ground was prepared by putting water on it, levelling and pounding it until it became firm and hard. A large quantity of grain was then thrown into this circular space, and seventy-five to one hundred mares were turned in to the place, with two or three vaqueros mounted on powerful horses, with whips in their hands, who drove the mares round and round the circle, shouting "Yeguas! Yeguas! Yeguas!" (Pronounced hay'-goo-ah.)

When the mares became dizzy from circling round in this way, they were turned and driven in the opposite direction. This was continued actively until the grain was well threshed out. The grain was winnowed in an equally primitive manner, the process requiring a day when a good breeze was blowing. The threshed grain was pushed well to one side of the inclosure by the harvesters, and a good space cleaned off. Then, with large wooden shovels, they took it up and threw it as high as possible against the wind, which blew the chaff and straw away, while the heavier grain fell down on the clean ground which had been prepared for it. In this way they got it out quite clean, also nice and whole, not broken, as it is more or less in passing through a threshing machine.

The Missions of San José and Santa Clara would use two or three hundred mares in a *hera* of four or five acres in extent. The Missions commonly raised, each, from six to eight hundred acres of wheat for their own use. The mares were also used for the threshing of beans by the same process.

CHAPTER XI
Alvarado's Arrest of Americans

THE government of the department of California imposed no tax upon the people of the country, and was mainly supported by revenue duties imposed on cargoes of foreign vessels sold in the country, which amounted to eighty to one hundred per centum of the invoice prices. This was considered very exorbitant, and offered a temptation to foreign traders to smuggle, which was largely availed of. Occasionally the government of the department would draw on the home government to assist in its financial matters.

In April, 1840, an event transpired which occasioned considerable excitement on this coast. An order was issued by Governor Alvarado, through the prefect Don José Ramon Estrada, for the arrest of all the resident Americans in the department, with some exceptions. General Manuel Castro, who is still living at Monterey, recently (1889) informed me that this movement originated with Governor Alvarado and General José Castro; that they had been informed that the Americans were preparing to rise against the government of the department, take possession of it, assassinate them, and assume control of the department affairs in behalf of the United States; that Alvarado and Castro becoming alarmed for their personal safety, as well as that of the department, in order to prevent this outbreak, issued the order above mentioned. Don Manuel, in giving me this information, said, with a smile, he did not think the Americans had any such design. He thought Alvarado and General José Castro were unduly alarmed. This is Don Manuel Castro's version of the matter. My own opinion is that Governor Alvarado had been secretly instructed by the home government to be constantly on the alert for any movements or designs of the Americans for getting possession of the country, and becoming alarmed himself, ordered the arrest.

Governor Alvarado issued his orders through the prefect to the different sub-prefects and alcaldes of the department to arrest all Americans within their several districts. This was accomplished, the arrests being

THE PORT OF SAN FRANCISCO, JUNE 1, 1849

From the original drawing of Geo. H. Baker, made at date expressly for the "New York Tribune" and published in that paper's issue Aug. 28, 1849. About two hundred vessels were then detained here, their crews leaving for the mines on arrival in port. Only a portion of these can be shown. The view is from Rincon Hill, looking N. W., showing San Francisco Bay, Mt. Tamalpais, Angel Island and the hills of Marin in the distance. In the mean distance lies the embryo city flanked by Telegraph and Russian hills. Population estimated at 2000, all adults, with few women. Many living in tents.

made by the military, under the instructions of the civil officers. About seventy persons were thus arrested, nearly all Americans; a few of other nationalities were also taken, under the mistaken impression that they were Americans. While these arrests were being made General Vallejo, with his staff and about seventy soldiers, came from Sonoma to Yerba Buena and placed the town under martial orders for a few days, when he left with his forces for Monterey. [Yerba Buena contained at that time about twenty-five inhabitants, men, women and children all told.] The captives were sent to Monterey, some by water and some by land, under military guard, as soon as possible after the arrest. They were put into the government house under a military guard, and were kept there until all were collected, being well treated. They were then transported to San Blas in the Mexican bark "Jóven Guipuzcoana," Captain Joseph Snook, an Englishman who had sworn allegiance to the Mexican government. They were accompanied by General José Castro, who was in charge of them. The owner of the vessel was Don José Antonio Aguirre, a native of Spain, an old merchant of this coast, living at Santa Barbara.* Prominent among the prisoners was a pioneer to the coast from Tennessee, by the name of Isaac Graham, who lived at Santa Cruz. He was an old hunter and trapper, and at the time of his arrest was engaged in stock-raising and getting out lumber, having a water-mill there, and owned the Rancho Zayanta.

The news of the arrest was communicated to Washington as speedily as possible by Thomas O. Larkin, afterwards United States consul at Monterey, and orders were sent out through the United States Minister at Mexico, to Commodore Claxton, in command of the Pacific squadron, to look into the matter, and he dispatched the United States sloop of war "St Louis," Captain Forrest, to Monterey. She arrived there shortly after the departure of the "Jóven Guipuzcoana" with the prisoners. In fact the two vessels passed each other shortly before the "St. Louis" arrived, the captain, of course, not being aware that the other vessel contained the prisoners. She remained there a short time and went southward, not visiting the bay of San Francisco at that time. She again visited the upper coast in the summer of 1841, coming direct to the bay of San Francisco, and proceeding thence to Monterey.

This movement was one of the manifestations of the old feeling of jealousy which existed on the part of the Mexican government towards the government of the United States. There had for some time existed a suspicion on the part of the Mexican officials of California against the

---

*Graham was a Tennessean. Prior to his arrest he lived at Natividad in the Salinas Valley. —"Beginnings of San Francisco"—Eldredge. P. 232.

Americans in the department, which was, doubtless, natural enough, as they desired to retain their positions with all the honors and benefits pertaining thereto. A fear prevailed that the Americans in the department of California, although few in number, might band together and conspire against the legitimate government, overpower and take possession of it. Consequently, in order to be on the safe side and avert this danger, they thought it best to arrest these Americans and get them out of the department.

This feeling of distrust or partial hostility on the part of the officials was well understood among the Americans in the department, who, however, I am convinced, had no design whatever against the government, at least no such idea was ever discussed or suggested to my knowledge, although for a long time it had been the common talk among the Americans when among themselves or in company with the rancheros that at some future time the United States would hold possession of California, and that our government would never permit any other nation to be the possessors of this territory.

But the idea of the few Americans then in California upsetting the government of that department existed only in the minds of the officials, strengthened, doubtless, by advices from the home government of Mexico to be constantly on the alert and avert anything of the kind, if threatened. While the officials were thus jealous and inimical, on the other hand, the rancheros, the owners of the large estates and the immense herds of cattle and horses, of whom I have spoken, were exceedingly friendly to the Americans and the United States government. They often expressed to me and to other Americans in the department the hope that at some time the Stars and Stripes would float over California, and she become a part of the United States. In their intercourse with the American traders and others who had visited the coast they could not fail to perceive the American superiority in intelligence, education and business ability. They naturally felt a respect for the government of the country to which such men belonged, and a desire that they might also share in these advantages for themselves and their children; that their children might be better educated, their agricultural methods improved, their lands better cultivated and enhanced in value, their horses and cattle made more valuable by improving the stock, and other desirable things secured, all of which they were sufficiently intelligent to appreciate and desire for themselves, and so, without reserve, they frankly expressed their liking for the Americans and their wish to be united with them.

These Californians frequently expressed to me their dislike of the constant revolutions to which the Mexican people were addicted, and said they would feel better protected under the American government and more secure in life and property, than under the Mexican government. In these revolutions their sons were often wrested from them and forced into the army, in the service of the party then dominant and nearest at hand. They were taken from fourteen years old and upwards, much to the dread and distress of the parents, though it may be mentioned that the risks of the service were not very great, since it was a rare thing for anybody to be killed in these revolutions.

The women of California, without exception, were wholly loyal to their own government, and hated the idea of any change; although they respected the Americans, treated them with great cordiality and politeness, and entertained them hospitably at their homes, they would not countenance the suggestion that the United States or any other foreign power should assume control of the country.

CHAPTER XII
Nathan Spear and the Author Detained

NATHAN SPEAR was arrested with the other Americans, and taken to Monterey by a guard of soldiers, but was soon released by the governor, who had been a clerk for Spear in former years at Monterey and had a high esteem for him. The governor, therefore, made an exception in his behalf. At that time I was in the employ of Spear, the principal manager of his commercial house at Yerba Buena. I was also arrested and taken to the headquarters of the subprefect, Don Francisco Guerrero, at the Mission Dolores, and was there a prisoner for twenty-four hours. During my incarceration I was very kindly treated by the sub-prefect and his amiable wife, Doña Josefa, daughter of Don Francisco de Haro, who was alcalde at that time. In the evening I was entertained by this lady with a beautiful little dancing party at her house, at which were present six or eight lovely young ladies and about as many young California gentlemen.

We had a delightful time. On that occasion, Doña Josefa, who had been married only a year, and who was a graceful woman, with full, brilliant black eyes, wore her hair unconfined, flowing at full length, rich and luxuriant, reaching nearly to her feet; as she moved in the figures of the dance she presented a fascinating picture of youth and beauty that I could not but admire. The dancing continued till a late hour, and the affair was so very enjoyable that I hardly realized that I was a prisoner of State. The sub-prefect assumed the responsibility of releasing me in the morning, and remarked at the time that he would receive an order to that effect from the seat of government, procured by Spear. This subsequently proved to be correct, and I had no further trouble.

There were a few exceptions to this general arrest of Americans, among them Don Abel Stearns at Los Angeles, he being a very early pioneer to this country, a prominent and wealthy merchant at that time, and always very highly respected by the officials. He had been in the country so long that he was rather considered as belonging to it, though he was a Bostonian originally. Another was Don Juan B. Cooper at Monterey, who had also been long in the country, having arrived here in 1823 in the American schooner "Thaddeus." He had been a shipmaster, and at the time of the arrest was engaged in the business of stock-raising. He was married to a sister of General Vallejo, was intimate with the officials and respected by them.

There were also a few other old residents, who had married into California families, who were excepted; among them William G. Dana, Francis Branch, Daniel Hill, Lewis T. Burton and Isaac Sparks, all of Santa Barbara. None of the agents, supercargoes or captains of vessels on the coast at the time of this arrest were molested; only those who resided here continuously.

When the news of this arrest was communicated to the State Department at Washington by Thomas O. Larkin, later the United States consul at Monterey, instructions were sent to the United States Minister at the City of Mexico, and through his intercession with the Mexican government these prisoners were released in a month or two after their arrival at San Blas, whence they had been transported to Tepic. While they were at the latter place orders came from the Mexican government for the release of the prisoners, and for the imprisonment of General Castro. The Mexican government disclaimed having authorized the arrest of these people, and its prompt action in ordering their release, and causing Castro to be imprisoned, was probably for the purpose of giving greater effect to this disclaimer and making everything appear as favorable as possible to the American government. At the same time I have no doubt the Mexican government was really at the bottom of the whole movement, directly or indirectly, but after the event had transpired, thought best, for prudential reasons, to discountenance it, not desiring to provoke any difficulty with the United States. Further to strengthen the position of the Mexican government in this phase of the matter, it promised the United States Minister that these people should be indemnified for the trouble and inconvenience to which they had been subjected by this movement.

CHAPTER XIII
Visit of de Mofras to California

THE population of the department of California about 1838-39 was probably from ten to twelve thousand, exclusive of Christianized Indians, who numbered about twenty thousand.

In 1840, de Mofras, a Frenchman, visited the coast in a French frigate (name forgotten), and landed at Yerba Buena. He was a French official, a kind of traveling ambassador to observe the different countries of the world. I think he came here from the coast of Peru and Chile. There were but few houses here at the time, and the most prominent was the residence and commercial establishment of Nathan Spear on the spot which is now the north-west corner of Clay and Montgomery streets. He was invited by Spear to become his guest. He was there several months, making that his headquarters, traveling about the bay and to different points in the interior. As I was in Spear's employ I saw a good deal of de Mofras, became quite well acquainted with him, and was much pleased with him, as were all those with whom he came in contact. He was an educated gentleman, master of several languages besides his own, among them English, Spanish, and German. He was a close observer of everything, and, like most Frenchmen, excited in his conversation and manner. In my business trips about the bay in the schooner "Isabel," he frequently accompanied me. On one occasion, in coming up to the town in the schooner from Read's ranch, on the opposite side of the bay, the captain of the vessel went a little too near the flat off North Beach, and the schooner grounded. We were compelled to lie there for an hour or two, waiting for the tide to float us off. Monsieur de Mofras soon became impatient and excited, and finally he got so restless and uneasy that he could no longer restrain himself. In spite of my persuasions and remonstrances he leaped overboard, with his clothes on, waded and swam ashore, and proceeded dripping wet to the house. On his arrival there, Spear was astonished to see him in that plight, and at first thought the schooner had been wrecked. I used to joke with him afterwards about his jumping overboard, and he confessed to me that he would not do it again; that in a deep place between the shoal and the beach, it was with great difficulty he kept from drowning, as his long boots had filled with water and the weight of his clothes bore him down.

It was understood that de Mofras was on a tour of general observation for the French government. During his visit here he was in correspondence with the officials at home, but it is not known that his visit had any political bearing or significance, and if he had any instructions in this direction from the government he did not disclose them. During his stay on the coast he visited General Sutter in Sacramento valley stopping there a month or two; also General Vallejo at the military headquarters at Sonoma, sojourning there one or two weeks. He also visited Monterey, the seat of the government, where he was courteously and hospitably received by Governor Alvarado and the other officials. Next, he visited Don Alexander Rotcheff at the Russian American Fur Company's headquarters at Fort Ross, and he went also to other prominent points. He was very cordially received and entertained by Rotcheff and his wife, both of whom spoke the French language perfectly, and de Mofras therefore felt quite at home in their company.

Don Alexander when visiting Yerba Buena spoke of de Mofras and praised him. The visit to Sutter pleased him greatly. He spoke of Sutter in the highest terms, and thought his establishment and operations in the Sacramento valley would people and develop that immense country sooner than it could otherwise have been done, as he believed Sutter would induce a large immigration to that point by the numerous letters he had written home to his own country and to the United States. De Mofras was very favorably impressed with California, and he frequently spoke of its future importance, thinking it would some day be a great country, and he freely expressed his opinion that it would belong to the United States. Considering its natural resources and advantages he thought that under the United States government it would become a rich and important section. His admiration and astonishment at the bay of San Francisco were frequently expressed, and I have seen him many times stand in front of Mr. Spear's store, at the corner of Montgomery and Clay streets, which was then quite near the water, and go into raptures on looking at the bay, stretching out his arms with enthusiasm and exclaiming with delight, Frenchman-like, at the broad and beautiful expanse of water before us, predicting that it would be a great field for commerce; and saying again and again, he had never seen anything like it and the more he traveled over it the more he was impressed with its grandeur and importance.

Spear had a very high opinion of de Mofras, and I will mention a little incident which occurred one day when de Mofras was stopping at Spear's house. We were at dinner, and the servant in passing a plate to de Mofras accidently touched his glass with it, which gave out a sharp ring, and instantly de Mofras placed one of his fingers on the glass to stop the sound. Spear mentioned it afterward as an illustration of the good breeding of the Frenchman.

A curious tradition was current in regard to the bay of San Francisco, which greatly interested de Mofras, as well as myself and others who heard it. Captain Richardson, who has been mentioned before in this narrative, had in his employ at that time an Indian by the name of Monica. He was about eighty years of age, but still active and vigorous, and was employed by Captain Richardson as boatman on the bay, in launches which were used to run between the shipping and different points to convey goods back and forth. This old Indian told Captain Richardson that the story had been handed down from his remote ancestors, that a long way back there was no Golden Gate; that between Fort Point and right across to the north it was all closed by a mountain range, and there was no access to the ocean there, but the natural outlet of the bay was through the Santa Clara valley, across the Salinas plains, to the bay of Monterey; that in a tremendous convulsion of nature the mountain barrier between the bay and the ocean was thrown down and a passage made where the Golden Gate now is. That became the entrance to the bay. In the course of time the Santa Clara valley and the other land between the lower end of the bay of San Francisco and the bay of Monterey became drained and elevated.

In this connection, I may mention that I have seen sea-shells which were brought up from a depth of 108 feet in boring an artesian well at San Leandro, and I learn that shells were found in Alameda at a depth of about 100 feet.

Captain Richardson frequently alluded to this tradition in the presence of Nathan Spear, Monsieur de Mofras and myself. De Mofras being a scientific man, he became so impressed with this statement that he rode out to Fort Point two or three times to examine personally the features of that part of the bay, and from his observations there and of the country between here and the bay of Monterey he expressed his opinion that the theory or tradition was probably correct. In frequent conversations at the dinner table he became quite enthusiastic in dilating upon the geological appearance and indications of the country, especially in reference to this story related by the old Indian Monica in regard to the Golden Gate.

Near the Presidio, about three-quarters of a mile southeast from the barracks in the grounds of the Miramontes family, was a very remarkable spring called "Polin"—an Indian name. The spring was celebrated from a very remote period for its virtues, which were handed down from the Indians for several generations, and afterward through the Californians. It is claimed that it possessed the remarkable power of producing fecundity in women who were childless, and who partook of its waters. Many authentic instances could be quoted in support of this assumption. In proof it may be mentioned that the Miramontes family, living on the spot, had twenty children, and other families living in that neighborhood were blessed with a large progeny. Many who came to the place from a distance, by the advice of friends, to test the wonderful qualities of the water, were alike rewarded for their faith by a happy increase in their families. The first wife of William D. M. Howard, a well known early San Franciscan, for several years without children, went hither by the advice of Mrs. Miramontes, and at the proper time was blessed with a lovely little daughter. Other instances might be given in proof of its efficacy in this direction.

The winter of 1839-40 was a severe one in California, an immense quantity of rain falling. It poured down for forty days and nights, with but little cessation. Old Domingo Peralta, who had come across the bay to Yerba Buena with his family, in a boat, to obtain supplies, was caught here and obliged to remain several weeks, stopping at Spear's house with his large family of ten or twelve persons until he could re-cross the bay to get home.

After Captain Sutter had established himself in the Sacramento valley, he sent a boat to Yerba Buena about once in two weeks for the purpose of obtaining supplies for his station, Spear being his agent. During the prolonged storms of this year the whole country was flooded, and communication was consequently interrupted, and we didn't hear from Captain Sutter for more than a month. At last a boat made its appearance, bringing a letter from him, in which he described the country as one vast expanse of water. Among the stories he mentioned was one of seeing the deer, elk and other animals crowded together in large numbers on every little prominence which appeared above the waters, to protect themselves from being carried away by the flood. The boat, in endeavoring to return, was unable to stem the current, which was so strong and rapid as to keep her on the passage several weeks before she reached Sutter's place again. The boat's captain was a Swiss, and the boatmen Indians, formerly of the Missions, who had returned to their wild Indian life.

Some years before my first arrival here in 1831, there was an exceedingly dry season. The priest at the head of the Mission of Santa Clara ordered the destruction of several thousand head of horses and mares belonging to the Mission, which was accomplished by drowning them in the Guadalupe river, in order to preserve the feed for the cattle, as there was not enough for all, and the cattle were regarded as of more value than the horses.

CHAPTER XIV
Priests and Mission Life

THE priests of California belonged to the Order of Franciscans. Their ordinary dress was a loose woolen garment, made whole and put on over the head, reaching nearly to the ground, of a plain drab or brownish hue, which was the color of the Order. The dress was made with wide sleeves, a hood falling back on the shoulders, which could be drawn over the head when it was desired by the wearer, if the weather was cold or unpleasant; and at the waist was a girdle and tassels of the same material tied around the dress or habit, the tassels hanging down in front. Sometimes they were left untied. One requirement of the Order was that every priest should have shaven on the crown of the head a circular spot about three or four inches in diameter. This I noticed among all of them. As the hair commenced growing it was again shaved, and this spot was always kept bare.

The priests at the various Missions were usually men of very pure character, particularly the Spanish priests. The first priests who established the Missions were directly from Spain. They were superior men in point of talent, education, morals and executive ability, as the success of the Missions under their establishment and administration showed. They seemed to be entirely disinterested, their aim and ambition being to develop the country, and civilize and Christianize the Indians, for which purpose the Missions were established. They worked zealously and untiringly in this behalf, and to them must be given the credit for what advancement in civilization, intelligence, industry, good habits and good morals pertained to the country at that day, when they laid the foundation of the present advanced civilization and development of the country.

After the independence of Mexico, and its separation from Spain, the Missions of California passed under the control of Mexican priests, who were also men of culture and attainments, generally of excellent character, but as a class they were inferior to their predecessors. They were always hospitable to strangers, all visitors were kindly received and entertained with the best they could offer, and the table was well supplied. The wine which they made at the Missions was of a superior quality and equal to any that I have drunk elsewhere.

In trading through the country and traveling from point to point it was customary for travelers to stop at the Missions as frequently and as long as they desired. This was expected as a matter of course by the priests, and had the traveler neglected to avail himself of the privilege it would have been regarded as an offense by the good Fathers. On approaching the Mission the traveler would be met at the door or at the wide veranda by the Padre, who would greet him warmly, embrace him and invite him in, and he was furnished with the best the Mission afforded at the table, given one of the best rooms to sleep in, attended by servants, and everything possible was done to make him at home and comfortable during his stay. On leaving he was furnished with a fresh horse, and a good vaquero was appointed to attend him to the next Mission, where he was received and entertained with the same hospitality, and so on as far as the journey extended.

The last of the Mexican priests was Father Gonzalez, who presided in '38 at the Mission of San José and who died some years ago at the Mission of Santa Barbara at a very advanced age. He was a noble man, a true Christian, very much respected and beloved by all his people, and by all who knew him. Whenever I went there he always welcomed me in the most cordial manner, and the moment I saw him I felt drawn toward him as by a lodestone. He would take me in and say, *"Sienta usted hijito"* (sit down, my little son), and seating himself close by my side, he entertained me in such delightful manner by his conversation, which flowed easily and naturally in a continuous stream, that one hardly realized that he was only an humble priest. His people greatly honored and loved him, and he was known among them as "The Saint on Earth." There were some exceptions among the priests as to general rectitude and excellence of character, as there are everywhere; but as a class they were a fine body of men of superior character, and accomplished a vast deal of good. The priests were much respected by the people, who looked to them for advice and guidance.

The supercargoes of the vessels that were trading on the coast, of course had occasion to visit all the settlements in the interior or along the coast to conduct their business with the people, and to travel back and forth up and down the country. In visiting down the coast they usually went on the vessels, which had a fair wind most of the time going south; but on coming up there was commonly a head wind, which made the voyage tedious, and the supercargoes then took to land and came up on horseback, accompanied by a vaquero, stopping along from one Mission to another or at some rancho, where they were always welcome, and where they were supplied with fresh horses whenever they required them, free of charge, by the Fathers or the rancheros. These horses were furnished as a matter of course with entire freedom and hospitality by the farmers and the Padres. When the traveler reached another stopping place he was provided with a fresh horse, and such a thing as continuing the journey on the horse he rode the day before was not to be thought of, so polite and courteous were these generous Californians.

The traveler had no further care or thought in regard to the horse he had been using, but left him where he happened to be, and the Padre or ranchero would undertake to send him back, or if this was not convenient it was no matter, as the owner would never ask any questions concerning his safety or return. It would have been considered impoliteness for the guest to express any concern about the horse or what was to become of him. Sometimes the traveler was furnished by the rancheros with part of a *caponera*, ten or twelve horses with a bell mare, and a vaquero, in order that he might continue his journey to the end without looking for other horses. He would travel along from day to day, changing his horse each day and sometimes oftener, and also that of his vaquero, and on reaching his journey's end the vaquero would return with the horses.

In later years, say after 1844, some of the smaller rancheros gave more attention to horses than cattle, making it a specialty to have always on hand several fine *caponeras* for the accommodation of travelers, who in these latter years were accustomed to hire the number of horses they required for their journey, with a bell mare, and a vaquero to accompany them, or at times the owner of the horses himself went with them. Santa Barbara, and to some extent Los Angeles, were points especially where horses were furnished in this way.

Some of the supercargoes of the vessels owned their horses, to the number of twelve to fifteen, and employed a vaquero continuously. When the supercargoes were at sea the vaqueros looked after these horses, and took them from point to point to meet the vessel when she would come into a certain port. When the supercargo landed he would find his horses there, and journey with them from place to place as his business required. The vaquero, while waiting for the vessel, would stay with some family, probably one of his relatives, of whom he most likely had many in various parts of California, and the horses would feed in the vicinity. Many supercargoes preferred this method, as they could always thus have the horses and vaqueros to which they were accustomed.

As the supercargo came to a Mission or rancho near a port, he would stop a few days waiting for the vessel to come along, and its approach was sometimes announced by a vaquero, and sometimes by a gun from the vessel. The supercargo would then go down and take with him the customers to whom he was to bill the goods from the vessel. The rancheros would attend him with their loads of hides and tallow to pay their indebtedness incurred on a former trip, or to make new purchases by exchanging them for goods. They would convey their hides and tallow in large wagons of very primitive fashion. The body of the vehicle was set on the axles, having no spring, but with four wheels (the smaller wagons with two) sawed out of a tree four feet in diameter, and about a foot thick, a solid block or section, with a hole in the middle for the axle. Sticks were set up perpendicularly along the sides and covered with hides stretched across them, thus inclosing the body of the wagon. In this way they brought back the goods they bought.

The wagons were drawn by oxen, with a nearly straight yoke fitting the top of the neck just back of the horns, and fastened with a piece of soft hide, and attached thereto and to the wagon. Families sometimes took long journeys in these wagons fitted up with more style, the sides being lined with calico or sheeting, or even light silk, with mattresses on the floor of the wagon. With cooking and eating arrangements they went along comfortably, camping by a spring, and sleeping in the wagon, traveling days at a time.

The people lived in adobe houses, and the houses had tile roofs; they were comfortable and roomy, warm in the winter and cool in the summer. Their furniture was generally plain, mostly imported from Boston in the ships that came to the coast to trade. Generally the houses had floors, but without carpets in the earlier days. Some of the humble people had no floors to their houses, but the ground became perfectly hard and firm as if cemented.

The women were exceedingly clean and neat in their houses and persons and in all their domestic arrangements. One of their peculiarities was the excellence and neatness of their beds and bedding, which were often elegant in appearance, highly and tastefully ornamented, the coverlids and pillow cases being sometimes of satin and trimmed with beautiful and costly lace. The women were plainly and becomingly attired, but were not such devotees of fashion as at the present day, and did not indulge in jewelry to excess.

Their tables were frugally furnished, the food clean and inviting, consisting mainly of good beef broiled on an iron rod, or steaks with onions, also mutton, chicken, eggs, each family keeping a good stock of fowls. The bread was *tortillas;* sometimes it was made with yeast. Beans were a staple dish with them, admirably cooked, corn, also potatoes; and red peppers were their favorite seasoning. A delicious dish was made of chicken and green corn, partly cooked and put together, then wrapped in the green leaves of the corn, tied with the same and boiled called *tamales*. Their meat stews were excellent when not too highly seasoned with red pepper.

The people were sober, sometimes using California wine, but not to excess. They were not given to strong drink, and it was a rare occurrence to see an intoxicated Californian. The men were good husbands generally, the women good wives, both faithful to their domestic relations. The California women, married or unmarried, of all classes, were the most virtuous I have ever seen. There were exceptions, but they were exceedingly rare.

The single men were not so much so, associating to some extent with Indian women, although the married men were generally excellent husbands and kind fathers.

During my long and intimate acquaintance with Californians, I have found the women as a class much brighter, quicker in their perceptions, and generally smarter than the men. Their husbands oftentimes looked to them for advice and direction in their general business affairs. The people had but limited opportunities for education. As a rule they were not much educated; but they had abundant instinct and native talent, and the women were full of natural dignity and self-possession; they talked well and intelligently, and appeared to much better advantage than might have been supposed from their meagre educational facilities.

The families of the wealthier classes had more or less education; their contact with the foreign population was an advantage to them in this respect. There were no established schools outside the Missions, and what little education the young people obtained, they picked up in the family, learning to read and write among themselves. They seemed to have a talent and taste for music. Many of the women played the guitar skillfully, and the young men the violin. In almost every family there were one or more musicians, and everywhere music was a familiar sound. Of course, they had no scientific and technical musical instruction.

The houses of the rancheros were usually built upon entirely open ground, devoid of trees, generally elevated, overlooking a wide stretch of the country round, in order that they might look out to a distance on all sides, and see what was going on, and notice if any intruders were about the rancho for the purpose of stealing cattle or horses, in which way they were occasionally annoyed by the Indians, or perhaps by some vicious countrymen; and the house was placed where there was a spring or running water. These houses stood out bare and plain, with no adornment of trees, shrubbery or flowers, and there were no structures, except the kitchens, attached to the main buildings. Even in the towns it was a rare thing to see flowers or shrubbery about the houses of the Californians.

I have often inquired of the rancheros, on seeing a beautiful and shaded spot, why they did not select it for their residence, and they would always answer it was too near the forest—they having in view always security against the Indians.

CHAPTER XV
Indian Insurrections and Treachery

OCCASIONALLY the Indians who had been at the Missions, and had become well informed in regard to the surrounding neighborhood and the different ranches in the vicinity, would desert the Missions, retreat to their old haunts and join the uncivilized Indians. At times they would come back with some of the wild Indians to the farms, for the purpose of raiding upon them, and capturing the domesticated horses. They would come quietly in the night, and carry off one or two *caponeras* of horses, sometimes as many as five or six, and drive them back to the Indian country for their own use.

In the morning a ranchero would discover that he was without horses for the use of the ranch. He would then borrow some horses from his neighbor, and ten or twelve men would collect together and go in pursuit of the raiders. They were nearly always successful in overtaking the thieves and recovering their horses, though oftentimes not without a fierce fight with the Indians, who were armed with bows and arrows, and the Californians with horse carbines. At these combats the Indians frequently lost some of their number, and often as many as eight or ten were killed. The Californians were sometimes wounded and occasionally killed. Once in a while, but very seldom, the Indians were successful in eluding pursuit, and got safely away with the horses, beyond recovery.

In the early part of '39, nearly all the saddle horses belonging to Captain Ygnacio Martinez, at the rancho Pinole, were thus carried off by the Indians, and his son Don José Martinez, (whose niece I afterward married), with eight or ten of his neighbors, went in pursuit of them, and though they succeeded in recovering the animals, they lost one of their number, Felipe Briones, who was killed by an arrow. The fight on that occasion was exceedingly severe, and the Indians became so incensed, and their numbers increased so much, that the little party deemed it too hazardous to continue the fight, and retreated, taking with them the recovered horses, but were compelled to leave the body of Briones on the field. Two days afterward the party went back and recovered it, but found it terribly mutilated. Some eight or ten of the Indians were killed by the Californians in that fight.

Juan Prado Mesa was the comandante of the San Francisco Presidio, and frequently left his post to go in campaigns against the Indians with part of his command. He was always considered a successful Indian fighter. He was a brave and good man. On one occasion he was wounded with an arrow, which ultimately carried him to his grave. He was blessed with a large family. I became very well acquainted with him, and he frequently furnished me with fine saddle horses and a vaquero to make my business circuit around the bay. He was under the immediate command of General Vallejo, with whom he was intimate, and sometimes he confided to me secret movements of the government.

The Californians were early risers. The ranchero would frequently receive a cup of coffee or chocolate in bed, from the hands of a servant, and on getting up immediately order one of the vaqueros to bring him a certain horse which he indicated, every horse in a *caponera* having a name, which was generally bestowed on account of some peculiarity of the animal. He then mounted and rode off about the rancho, attended by a vaquero, coming back to breakfast between eight and nine o'clock.

This breakfast was a solid meal, consisting of *carne asada* (meat broiled on a spit), beefsteak with rich gravy or with onions, eggs, beans, *tortillas,* sometimes bread and coffee, the latter often made of peas. After breakfast the ranchero would call for his horse again, usually selecting a different one, not because the first was fatigued, but as a matter of fancy or pride, and ride off again around the farm or to visit the neighbors. He was gone till twelve or one o'clock, when he returned for dinner, which was similar to breakfast, after which he again departed, returning about dusk in the evening for supper, this being mainly a repetition of the two former meals.

Although there was so little variety in their food from one day to another, everything was cooked so well and so neatly and made so inviting, the matron of the house giving her personal attention to everything, that the meals were always relished.

When the rancheros thus rode about, during the leisure season, which was between the marking time and the *matanza* or killing time, and from the end of the *matanza* to the spring time again, the more wealthy of them were generally dressed in a good deal of style, with short breeches extending to the knee, ornamented with gold or silver lace at the bottom, with *botas* (leggings) below, made of fine soft deer skin, well tanned and finished, richly colored, and stamped with beautiful devices (these articles having been imported from Mexico, where they were manufactured), and tied at the knee with a silk cord, two or three times wound around the leg, with heavy gold or silver tassels hanging below the knee. They wore long vests, with filagree buttons of gold or silver, while those of more ordinary means had them of brass. They wore no long coats, but a kind of jacket of good length, most generally of dark blue cloth, also adorned with filagree buttons. Over that was the long *serape* or *poncho,* made in Mexico and imported from there, costing from $20 to $100, according to the quality of the cloth and the richness of the ornamentation.

The *serape* and the *poncho* were made in the same way as to size and cut of the garments, but the former was of a coarser texture than the latter, and of a variety of colors and patterns, while the *poncho* was of dark blue or black cloth, of finer quality, generally broadcloth. The *serape* was always plain, while the *poncho* was heavily trimmed with gold or silver fringe around the edges, and a little below the collars around the shoulders.

They wore hats imported from Mexico and Peru, generally stiff; the finer quality of softer material—*vicūna,* a kind of beaver skin obtained in those countries. Their saddles were silver-mounted, embroidered with silver or gold, the bridle heavily mounted with silver, and the reins made of the most select hair of the horse's mane, and at a distance of every foot or so there was a link of silver connecting the different parts together. The tree of the saddle was similar to that now in use by the Spaniards, and covered with the *mochila,* which was of leather. It extended beyond the saddle to the shoulder of the horse in front and back to the flank, and downwards on either side, half way between the rider's knee and foot. This was plainly made, sometimes stamped with ornamental figures on the side and sometimes without stamping. Over this was the *coraza,* a leather covering of finer texture, a little larger and extending beyond the *mochila* all around, so as to cover it completely. It was elaborately stamped with handsome ornamental devices.

Behind the saddle, and attached thereto, was the *anqueta,* of leather, of half-moon shape, covering the top of the hindquarters of the horse, but not reaching to the tail; which was also elaborately stamped with figures and lined with sheep skin, the wool side next to the horse. This was an ornament, and also a convenience in case the rider chose to take a person behind him on the horse. Frequently some gallant young man would take a lady on the horse with him, putting her in the saddle in front and himself riding on the *anqueta* behind.

The stirrups were cut out of a solid block of wood, about two and a half inches in thickness. They were very large and heavy. The strap was passed through a little hole near the top. The *tapadera* was made of two circular pieces of very stout leather, about twelve to fifteen inches in diameter, the outer one a little smaller than the inner one, fastened together with strips of deer skin called *gamuza,* the saddle strap passing through two holes near the top to attach it to the stirrup; so that when the foot was placed in the stirrup the *tapadera* was in front, concealed it, and protected the foot of the rider from the brush and brambles in going through the woods.

This was the saddle for everyday use of the rancheros and vaqueros, that of the former being somewhat nicer and better finished. The reins for everyday use were made of deer or calfskin or other soft leather, cut in thin strips and nicely braided and twisted together, and at the end of the reins was attached an extra piece of the same with a ring, which was used as a whip. Their spurs were inlaid with gold and silver, and the straps of the spurs worked with silver and gold thread.

When thus mounted and fully equipped, these men presented a magnificent appearance, especially on the feast days of the Saints, which were celebrated at the Missions. Then they were arrayed in their finest and most costly habiliments, and their horses in their gayest and most expensive trappings. They were usually large, well developed men, and presented an imposing aspect. The outfit of a ranchero and his horse, thus equipped, I have known to cost several thousand dollars.

The gentleman who carried a lady in this way, before him on a horse, was considered as occupying a post of honor, and it was customary when a bride was to be married in church, which was usual in those days, for a relative to take her before him in this fashion on his horse to the church where the ceremony was to be performed. This service, which involved the greatest responsibility and trust on the part of the gentleman, was discharged by him in the most gallant and polite manner possible.

On the occasion of my marriage, in 1847, the bride was taken in this way to the church by her uncle, Don José Martinez. On these occasions the horse was adorned in the most sumptuous manner, the *anqueta* and *coraza* being beautifully worked with ornamental devices in gold and silver thread. The bride rode on her own saddle, sometimes by herself, which was made like the gentleman's but a little smaller, and without stirrups, in place of which a piece of silk—red, blue or green—perhaps a yard wide and two or three yards long, joined at the two ends, was gracefully hung over the saddle, puffed like a bunch of flowers at the fastening, and hung down at one side of the horse in a loop, in which the lady lightly rested her foot.

The ladies were domestic and exceedingly industrious, although the wealthier class had plenty of Indian servants. They were skillful with their needles, making the garments for their families, which were generally numerous. The women were proficient in sewing. They also did a good deal of nicer needlework of fancy kinds—embroidery, etc.—in which they excelled, all for family use. Their domestic occupations took up most of their time.

Both men and women preserved their hair in all its fullness and color, and it was rare to see a gray-headed person. A man fifty years of age, even, had not a single gray hair in his head or beard, and I don't remember ever seeing, either among the vaqueros or the rancheros, or among the women, a single bald headed person. I frequently asked them what was the cause of this remarkably good preservation of their hair, and they would shrug their shoulders, and say they supposed it was on account of their quiet way of living and freedom from worry and anxiety.

The native Californians were about the happiest and most contented people I ever saw, as also were the early foreigners who settled among them and intermarried with them, adopted their habits and customs, and became, as it were, a part of themselves.

Among the Californians there was more or less caste, and the wealthier families were somewhat aristocratic and did not associate freely with the humbler classes; in towns the wealthy families were decidedly proud and select, the wives and daughters especially. These people were naturally, whether rich or poor, of a proud nature, and though always exceedingly polite, courteous and friendly, they were possessed of a native dignity, an inborn aristocracy, which was apparent in their bearing, walk, and general demeanor. They were descended from the best families of Spain, and never seemed to forget their origin, even if their outward surroundings did not correspond to their inward feeling. Of course among the weathier classes this pride was more manifest than among the poorer.

In my long intercourse with these people, extending over many years, I never knew an instance of incivility of any kind. They were always ready to reply to a question, and answered in the politest manner, even the humblest of them; and in passing along the road, the poorest vaquero would salute you politely. If you wanted any little favor of him, like delivering a message to another rancho, or anything of that sort, he was ready to oblige, and did it with an air of courtesy and grace and freedom of manner that were very pleasing. They showed everywhere and always this spirit of accommodation, both men and women. The latter, though reserved and dignified, always answered politely and sweetly, and generally bestowed upon you a smile, which, coming from a handsome face, was charming in the extreme. This kindness of manner was no affectation, but genuine goodness, and commanded one's admiration and respect.

I was astonished at the endurance of the California women in holding out, night after night, in dancing, of which they never seemed to weary, but kept on with an appearance of freshness and elasticity that was as charming as surprising. Their actions, movements and bearing were as full of life and animation after several nights of dancing as at the beginning, while the men, on the other hand, became wearied, showing that their powers of endurance were not equal to those of the ladies. I have frequently heard the latter ridiculing the gentlemen for not holding out unfatigued to the end of a festival of this kind.

The rancheros and their household generally retired early, about eight o'clock, unless a *valecito casaro* (little home-party) was on hand, when this lasted till twelve or one. They were fond of these gatherings, and almost every family having some musician of its own, music and dancing were indulged in, and a very pleasant time enjoyed. I have attended many of them and always was agreeably entertained. These parties were usually impromptu, without formality, and were often held for the entertainment of a guest who might be stopping at the house. The balls or larger parties were of more importance, and usually occurred in the towns. On the occasion of the marriage of a son or daughter of a ranchero they took place on the rancho, the marriage being celebrated amid great festivities, lasting several days.

Fandango was a term for a dance or entertainment among the lower classes, where neighbors and others were invited in, and engaged themselves without any great degree of formality. The entertainments of the wealthy and aristocratic class were more exclusive in character; invitations were more carefully given, more formality observed, and of course, more elegance and refinement prevailed. An entertainment of this character was known as a *baile*.

In November, 1838, I was a guest at the wedding party given at the marriage of Don José Martinez to the daughter of Don Ygnacio Peralta, which lasted about a week, dancing being kept up all the night with a company of at least one hundred men and women from the adjoining ranchos, about three hours after daylight being given to sleep, after which picnics in the woods were held during the forenoon, and the afternoon was devoted to bull fighting. This programme was continued for a week, when I myself had become so exhausted for want of regular sleep that I was glad to escape. The bride and bridegroom were not given any seclusion until the third night.

On this occasion Doña Rafaela Martinez, wife of Dr. Tennent, and sister of the bridegroom, a young woman full of life and vivacity, very attractive and graceful in manner, seized upon me and led me on to the floor with the waltzers. I was ignorant of waltzing up to that moment. She began moving around the room with me in the waltz, and in some unaccountable manner, perhaps owing to her magnetism, I soon found myself going through the figure with ease. After that I had no difficulty in keeping my place with the other waltzers, and was reckoned as one of them. I waltzed with my fascinating partner a good portion of the night.

During this festivity, Don José Martinez, who was a wonderful horseman, performed some feats which astonished me. For instance, while riding at the greatest speed, he leaned over his saddle to one side, as he swept along, and picked up from the ground a small coin, which had been put there to try his skill, and then went on without slackening his speed.

Some years after that I was visiting him, and while we were out taking a ride over his rancho, we came to an exceedingly steep hill, almost perpendicular; at the top was a bull quietly feeding. He looked up and said, "Do you see that bull?" "Yes," said I. "Now," said he, "we will have some fun. I am going up there to drive him down and lasso him on the way." It seemed impossible owing to the steepness of the declivity. Nevertheless, he did it, rode up to the top, started the bull down at full speed, and actually lassoed the animal on the way, threw him down, and the bull at once commenced rolling down the steep side of the hill, over and over, until he reached the bottom, José following on his horse and slackening up the riata as he went along. He was a graceful rider.

After many years of happiness with his excellent wife, during which they were blessed with six or eight children, Don José Martinez became a widower. A few years after this he married an English lady, a sister of Dr. Samuel J. Tennent, who was then living at Pinole ranch, and who married a sister of Don José Martinez. Dr. Tennent lived on a portion of the ranch inherited by his wife. The marriage of Don José to a lady outside of his own countrywomen was rather an unusual occurrence among the Californians. The marriage proved a happy one, and half a dozen children resulted therefrom. This lady is now living in San Francisco (1889).

Don José Martinez had the largest kind of a heart, and if anyone called at his house who was in need of a horse, he was never refused, and the people of the surrounding country were constantly in receipt of favors at his hands. If one wanted a bullock, and had not the means to pay for it, he would send out a vaquero to lasso one and bring it in and tie it to a *cabestro* (a steer broken for that purpose), so that the man could take it home, and told him he might pay for it when convenient, or if not convenient, it was no matter. So with a horse which he might furnish, it didn't matter whether the animal was returned or not. This generosity was continual and seemed to have no limit. At his death, which occurred in 1864, his funeral was attended by a vast concourse of people from all the surrounding country, who came in wagons, buggies and carriages to the number of several hundred vehicles, such was the high appreciation in which he was held by the community. I never saw such respect paid to the memory of any other person. If true generosity and genuine philanthropy entitle a man to a place in the kingdom of Heaven, I am sure that Don José Martinez is received there as one of the chief guests.

A CALIFORNIA WEDDING PARTY IN 1845

This is another of the quaint illustrations William Heath Davis had made for "Seventy-five Years in California," the publication of which was prevented by the loss of his manuscript in the San Francisco catastrophe of April 18, 1906.

CHAPTER XVI
Author's Courtship and Marriage

SOON after I reached maturity, thoughts of domestic and settle-down life overtook me. I concluded I could manage my growing business more advantageously by being introduced in the Court of Hymen to a daughter of the soil of California of Spanish extraction.

In the fall of 1842 the historic bark Don Quixote was at anchor at Santa Barbara; also another historic bark, the Jóven Guipuzcoana, a Mexican vessel. Both were traders on the coast and were bound for the windward or northern ports. I was then the supercargo of the Don Quixote and was accustomed to visit all places of business in the towns, also the residences of the haciendados for orders for goods.

I remember one sunny afternoon being in the store of Don José Antonio Aguirre to sell him an invoice of goods to replenish his stock. A young lady whose face impressed me appeared there and made a small purchase. She and her father, Don Joaquin Estudillo were guests of Mrs. Aguirre, a niece of the latter and first cousin of the former. Father and daughter were waiting for the departure of the Jóven Guipuzcoana to take passage on her for their home at San Leandro on the east side of the Bay of San Francisco. It was on this trip the Señorita was made prisoner of war by Commodore Jones, when the Mexican bark was captured which I have mentioned elsewhere. My relations with the rancheros as a merchant made me acquainted with Senor Estudillo and his family. He had known my father when he (Estudillo) was a Custom House officer sailing up and down the coast as a guard on various vessels at different times. My interest in the family increased as I called at the mansion during my journeys around the Bay for my pro rata of the trade, and it was appreciated by the good people.

About the latter part of 1843, I found myself seriously in love with the young señorita I had previously seen at Santa Barbara. The program was soon made up in my mind, how I should proceed in this delicate dilemma. I approached the mother of the fair one, and bluntly told her that I desired her daughter Maria for my life companion; remarking in a half-serious, half-playful manner that I knew it took two to make a bargain. The good señora smiled approvingly, as I thought, but without uttering a single word in reply to my suggestion. I continued to speak of my attachment which could only be completed by uniting the hands of those who had already exchanged the love of their hearts.

On an occasion like this, very often a favorite aunt of the lady sought in marriage would be appealed to for intercession in behalf of the suitor, and this stratagem was resorted to in my case. But I had strong opposition in the family in the person of an elder sister. Whenever I called at the house she expressed friendship, but it was assumed and fictitious. It was very apparent that she was envious of her younger sister marrying before herself. La Señorita Maria had numerous admirers who were also soliciting her hand, some of wealthy and influential families, and naturally she was proud of the adulations bestowed upon her and hesitated to make her choice.

I was located at Yerba Buena as agent for Paty, McKinley & Co. In the summer of 1845 I wrote a letter to Don Joaquin Estudillo, begging him to communicate my wish to his daughter, and adding, that if my proffer were agreeable, if he would write, I would come to San Leandro to visit the family. In the course of time a reply came in the negative, which was due to the work and influence of the elder sister with the parents and without the knowledge of Señorita Maria, as it subsequently proved.

The Don Quixote arrived in August of the same year. In the rush and multiplicity of business, the closing of the Yerba Buena house, preparatory to our departure for the leeward coast and Honolulu, my matrimonial affair disappeared from my mind, only to return after we had left the Bay. In March 1846, I arrived at Monterey in my own vessel with a cargo of goods for the California market. There I met Henry Mellus, who was awaiting one of his vessels from Southern California. One starlight evening after dinner at the hospitable mansion of Thomas O. Larkin, our American Consul on the coast, Mr. Mellus suggested that we stroll toward the beach and listen to the surf.

During our quiet walk he remarked to me: "Don Guillermo, I have something to impart to you that concerns you deeply, regarding one of the daughters of Don Joaquin Estudillo of San Leandro. I have heard the true story about your love affair, and my authority is undoubted, and when it was related to me it seemed incredible, but it was true, nevertheless. La Señorita Maria never knew you had written her father, and she was in ignorance of the letter he sent you declining your proffer of marriage. I really pity the poor girl," he said, "for what she has suffered during your absence from the coast. I am sure when she learns of your return, she will be more than delighted to see you at her home."

My vessel arrived at Yerba Buena in April, and my business kept me so incessantly employed during our short stay that I was unable to visit the eastern shore of the bay to call on Don Joaquin and his family.

The brig sailed to Sausalito to water before proceeding to the southern ports for trade. It was now the 20th. of May, after the usual showers of that month, and the hills and mountains towering above us as we lay at our anchorage were in the height of their loveliness and splendor, and the scenery was enchanting in the extreme.

I learned to my delight that Miss Maria Estudillo was at the home of her favorite aunt, Mrs. Richardson, ostensibly on a visit to her but in reality to meet the one she esteemed. I called on the ladies and was cordially received with an embrace by Señora Richardson, and a warm greeting from the señoritas. I observed that the young lady from San Leandro was impressed with my presence which demonstrated clearly in my mind a rooted affection for the one seated by her side, and it was mutual.

The custom of embracing by the señoras or heads of families had existed since the foundation of the Department. It was only practiced or extended to friends and acquaintances of long standing, by married ladies who had become mothers, as a mark of extreme courtesy. I have never known of an instance of a young woman or daughters of matrons extending this to others than near relatives, because it would be considered highly improper by the parents and others.

This mode of salutation was an act demonstrating clearly to the visitor that the reception was genuine and the impulse of a noble nature. It was performed in the most modest and delicate manner: the lady would simply extend her arms around the gentleman, and in return, he would do the same; she looking to the right smilingly, he to the left. Our free and easy American style of kissing was not practiced.

I invited Captain Richardson, Señora Richardson, Miss Richardson and Miss Estudillo to dine on board my vessel as my guests. In addition to these, Nathan Spear, ex-Alcalde Wm. S. Hinckley, Captain Russom, R. M. Sherman, the clerk, and Mr. Lee, the first mate, were members of the party. The menu comprised chicken soup; chicken salad, boiled turkey and ham; roast muscovy ducks; sweet potatoes; other vegetables and fruits; custards, cakes and confections. Having arrived from Honolulu so recently, we were well supplied with poultry and other products of the Islands. California wine was not in general use at that time as a beverage, but we had claret, white wine, champagne, and sherry. The dinner passed off pleasantly.

The day when we were heaving anchor Captain Russom handed me a spy glass and directed my attention to two young ladies who were seated on a natural carpet of flowers covering the brow of a commanding hill which overlooked the vessel then unfolding her canvas to the breeze. One of these ladies was picking the wild flowers within her reach, while the other held her handkerchief to her face. Captain Russom was thoughtful, and showed his gallantry to the fair ones by dipping the flag, flying at the mizzen gaff, several times. And, of course, the author waved his handkerchief. In this act of farewell he was joined by Sherman, and we both waved until we were hidden from view as the brig approached the Golden Gate.

Later our engagement was made formal in the presence of the family, and I received an embrace from each of its members, including the elder sister.

There was a law of the Roman Catholic Church that no Protestant could marry a Catholic woman without the former becoming a convert. So, if a young man wished to obtain the hand of a California lady in marriage he was compelled to turn Catholic. I remember well when the two brothers Henry and Francis Mellus, who married sisters, were converted to the Roman faith before their marriages. They, however, proved to be sincere in their change from Protestantism, and were known to be devout. The author became a Roman Catholic several years before his wedding.

The rule of the church was rigid regarding marriage in those days, but now, by dispensation from the Pope, it is permitted for Catholics and non-Catholics to marry in countries of mixed population.

During my wooing of over two years, I do not remember having spoken a hundred words to the young lady when we were alone, but I was permitted to converse with her in the presence of her parents, especially her mother. This was an unwritten law or custom of Spanish families from time immemorial. Their sense of propriety demanded that during courtship the young people should talk and see each other only in the presence of relatives of the prospective wife. When this rule was invaded the young lady would expect or was prepared for a reprimand from her mother or father, who demanded that there should be no repetition of the indiscretion, hence it was a rare occurrence.

About a week before the wedding, Don Joaquin sent about twenty milch cows from his rancho around the bay to San Francisco to be used in the preparation of the marriage feast, for milk was scarce in town. He alson sent a caponera of his fine horses for use during the festival. The animals were allowed to roam the hills and valleys of San Francisco which was then a mere cow pasture with a population of less than one thousand inhabitants, including both Mission Dolores and the Presidio. This livestock was under the constant care of vaqueros to prevent them retracing their steps over the same route by which they had come from San Leandro. Such was the instinct and attachment of these animals for the place of their nativity that if turned loose and not restrained in any way, they would have arrived at the rancho in a short time. This has been known to occur.

The first Alcalde under American occupation, Lieutenant Washington A. Bartlett, changed the dating of official documents from Yerba Buena to San Francisco in 1847. General Kearny, the Military Governor, approved of this for it was but a restatement of the name which existed under Mexican rule as a district comprising Yerba Buena, Mission Dolores and the Presidio, and had never been changed.

Miss Maria Estudillo and I were married at the Mission of San Francisco de Asis, sometimes called Mission Dolores, in November 1847. The bride was carried by her uncle, Don José Martinez, to the church on a spirited jet black horse from Pinole, taken from his own caponera of blacks. It was in keeping with the ancient custom on such occasions for a relative thus to convey the bride, if she was not mounted by herself; as carriages and buggies were not in use at so early a period. The animal was superbly caparisoned with gold and silver mounted saddle and bridle, and Don José was dressed in the costly festal habiliments of olden times.

At the ball in the evening Don José was a prominent actor. He danced the Jarabe, an ancient dance of the country, which is performed by a gentleman and lady facing each other. At a certain stage of the amusement both would stop, when one would deliver several verses in rhyme, at the end of which the dancing was resumed, the lady approaching in a circle, round and round her partner and back to her place, bowing gracefully to her companion, her dainty feet in full view. This was repeated by the Don in a similar manner; and both would then dance with the rapidity of lightning in a circle of small diameter, going round and round artistically and with grace, accompanying their movements with appropriate gesticulations. Sometimes two ladies and gentlemen would dance the Jarabe and then it was even more amusing and attractive. This elicited applause from the audience.

The order of dances embraced quadrilles, waltzes, contra-dances and la Jota. The festivities were kept up continuously as the company was eager to commemorate the occasion with a genuine marriage festival such as was enjoyed by their forefathers. At intervals during the night a cold luncheon of poultry, ham, cakes, coffee, champagne and other wines was served.

CHAPTER XVII
Sportsman's Paradise

IN mid-winter all animals on haciendas become thin and poor in flesh. This was the dull season of the year among the merchants and but little business was transacted. But the fleet of small vessels owned in Yerba Buena was kept busy going to the different estuaries of the bay to collect hides that had accumulated during the winter months from cattle slaughtered for use of the haciendas.

One morning in March 1840 at the breakfast table, Nathan Spear remarked that this being the quiet part of the year around the bay that the crews of the "Isabel" and "Nicholas" were not at work sufficiently long at a time to keep them from getting rusty. "I think," he decided, "that it would be well to send the "Isabel" over to Yerba Buena Island with a crew of four men to cut and load her with wood for cooking purposes."

The eastern part of the island at that time was almost covered with scrub oak trees, the wood of which was very hard and made a strong fire. I replied that I would accompany the wood cutters and consider it my vacation, and would take my gun and fishing tackle along so I could supply the camp with fish and game. "I will go to the Mission Dolores after our breakfast to obtain permission from the sub-Prefect or Alcalde to cut wood on Yerba Buena Island," I said, and Spear agreed.

Spear had a good stable of rough redwood boards on the premises next to the store which contained several very fine horses, and I saddled the old man's favorite buckskin. He was long in body and well put together, with a head and ears as if carved by a sculptor, with a neck which looked as if his dam had been sired by a deer. I was young, but eighteen years old, full of fun and frolic, a good fast rider, and away we went through the sandhills to Mission Dolores. The spirited and speedy horse seemed inspired with my errand to interview the dignitaries of the District of San Francisco.

Preparations for visiting the island were soon made, and as an absence of eight or ten days was contemplated, a goodly supply of eatables had to be provided. Nathan Spear being an epicure of no ordinary taste, was liberal and supplied us with the best his store afforded.

We camped on a piece of level ground or mesa just above the beach and west of the cove. We had two tents, the men occupying one, the author the other. The little schooner was moored east of the camp but in full view. I arranged my time methodically: to read a little, to fish a little and to shoot a little at the wild game that flew over our white tents in great numbers. My first morning as a resident of the solitary isle was devoted to fishing, selecting a spot north-west of the camp near a spring of soft water which bubbled over the rocks. My success as an angler was beyond expectation and a surprise to me. In less than no time I had a pail full of several varieties of fish which made the sport quite exhilarating. For dinner we had fish fresh from the water cooked with California bacon cured by that historic personage Nathan Spear. One of the men who proved to be a good cocinero prepared our first midday meal on Yerba Buena Island, and all relished it greatly. I soon became ambitious as an angler and rose at the peep of day, but I had my doubt if the fish would take the bait at such an early hour, but to my joy they did so with eagerness. I soon returned with a fine mess of live and fluttering fish for breakfast. This time I had fished from what is now known as "Torpedo Point." Probably I was the first fisherman who ever threw a line and hook into the clear waters of San Francisco Bay from Yerba Buena, or, as it is popularly known, Goat Island. I caught so many fish from day to day that the men dried them, and in all probability this curing gave San Francisco its first shipment of dried fish.

I also devoted much time to shooting ducks. They were plentiful and fat, and of many varieties: mallard, canvasback, widgeon and teal. My favorite spot for shooting was the top of the hill overlooking the village of Yerba Buena. The ducks would appear in flocks, darkening the air, and so great was their number that it required no skill to kill them on the wing. As they fell to the ground they often burst open, being so fat and heavy. After I had discharged the two barrels I would be surrounded with dead and wounded birds, and the flock would wheel about to share the fate of the first victims. I hastened to re-load so as to take them on the wing again, and the stupid birds would fall to the ground as thick as hailstones. I am sure I was the first hunter on the Island.

I killed so many of this savory game that we preserved them like the fish to swell the first export from the Island. I became so interested and excited over my success as angler and hunter that the reading matter in my tent went undisturbed.

On my return to town I presented Nathan Spear with several dozens of ducks and plenty of fish for the table. He was more than delighted at the sight of "so many good things to eat," as he expressed it, and remarked that I looked sleek from the good living I had enjoyed while on the Island.

CHAPTER XVIII
Californian Amusements

BESIDES indulgence in music and dancing, the men found their recreation, as they did their occupation, chiefly on horseback.

Horse racing was one of their favorite amusements, which they occasionally enjoyed; especially on the Saints' feast days, which were general holidays. The vaqueros were then relieved from duty, wore their best clothes, and were allowed to mount the best horses and to have their sport. These races were usually from two to four hundred yards and participated in by only two horses at a time. Bets were made in cattle and horses, and large numbers of animals were lost and won on these occasions; at times one hundred up to several hundred head of cattle were bet on the result of a single short race. They generally put up their *vaquillas,* (heifers). They had no money to wager, but plenty of cattle. Sometimes horses were also bet, but not often.

There was on one occasion a famous race at Los Angeles of nine miles, between the horses of two wealthy rancheros, and an immense amount of property changed hands on the result of the race, cattle and horses, mostly the former. This race attracted quite a large crowd of people, and was considered a great affair for that day. Don José Ramon Carrillo, of the Santa Rosa ranch, was extremely fond of horses, a very expert and accomplished horseman himself, and a brave and good fellow. On his rancho he had a number of fine *caponeras,* I think as many as ten or twelve, all of the best horses. In 1844 I bought a fine horse of him for which I paid $50, which at that day was a large price; he was a splendid animal, a dark yellow, darker than buckskin. I bought another, equally as good, a dapple gray, for $20, all he asked for him. Either of them to-day would be worth $200. Don José was passionately fond of bear-hunting, and talked of this sport and of his love of horses with the greatest enthusiasm, and never seemed to be at ease unless he was on a horse.

On several occasions when I was visiting him in the summer season, when the bears were plenty, he was always engaged in hunting them, and tried to persuade me to join him in the sport, urging me to become a bear-hunter, saying he would teach me to lasso bears and make me as good as himself in that line. But my experience with bears (as related a few pages further on) had satisfied me, and I always declined absolutely to become a participant.

In 1844 Don José Ramon ran a race with the first horse he had sold me, at the Mission Dolores, against a horse owned by Francisco Sanchez, named Palomino, and was just barely beaten, the distance being 300 yards. Thereupon, William Rae, of the Hudson's Bay Company's post, put up a mouse-colored horse named Grullo for a race of 600 yards against mine, and the bets were doubled, and Don José Ramon, with my horse, won by a long distance. He was much pleased with his success, and Rae was much chagrined with the failure of his horse. At this occurence, James Alexander Forbes, then and for several years previous British vice-consul, was the judge of the race.

The bull-fighting was usually held on one of the Saints' days. The bull was turned into an enclosure, and the horsemen would come in, mounted on their best animals, and fight the bull for the entertainment of the spectators, killing him finally. Sometimes a bear and bull fight would take place, another amusement they had at the killing season at the *matanza* spot.

When cattle were slaughtered, bears came to the place at night to feast on the meat that was left after the hides and tallow were taken. The bears coming, the rancheros, with vaqueros, would go there for the purpose of lassoing them. This was one of their greatest sports; highly exciting and dangerous, but the bear always got the worst of it. One would lasso a bear by the neck, and another lasso the same beast by the hindfoot, and then pulling in different directions the poor bear was soon strained and strangled to death. Sometimes half a dozen or more would be taken in a single night in this way.

At one time I was encamped at the embarcadero of Temescal, a place between where the Oakland long wharf and Berkeley are now, in order to receive hides and tallow from the cattle that were slaughtered not far away, which articles I was collecting for my employer, Nathan Spear. I was there for several days with one man, the boats meantime taking down loads of the hides and tallow to Yerba Buena and returning empty. One night I sent my man up to Don Vicente Peralta's house, on an errand, and remained in my tent alone all night, to my great peril, as I soon discovered.

The *matanza* ground was about a mile from my tent, and Peralta and his vaqueros came down in the night to lasso the bears for sport. Some of them got away from their enemies and made for my tent, probably being attracted to it as a strange object looming up white in the darkness; with the curiosity which such animals are known to possess, they proceeded to investigate it. I sat in the tent and heard these animals circling round and round outside for several hours, going off at times and returning. I was in constant fear that they might push their noses under the canvas, work themselves into the tent and devour me, and had they not been full from feasting on the *matanza* meat I should probably have fallen a victim to their hunger.

AUTHOR'S GRIZZLED HAIRS DUE TO GRIZZLY BEARS

As I sat there quietly and listened to their deep breathing and movements outside, I was filled with fear and anxiety, and it may easily be imagined how much I was relieved when finally the beasts went off for good and left me alone. I attribute my prematurely gray hairs to the alarm I felt on that occasion.

On giving Don Vicente Peralta a narrative of my narrow escape from being devoured by the bears which he and his vaqueros had stampeded to my tent, he laughed heartily, but became serious when he realized the gravity of my situation, and remarked that there were not enough men at the place that night to lasso all the bears, and three of them had escaped, as he supposed to the mountains. He said they were not hungry, having made a hearty supper from the slaughtered cattle, but he thought it was best to be on the safe side; that they were not to be trusted at any time, and a youth of my fine appearance might be tempting to them.

After this occurrence whenever I had occasion to stop over night there, he would send a vaquero with a horse, and kind messages from himself and wife to be their guest for the night, which invitations I gladly accepted. He asked me once or twice to accompany him on his bear-hunting expeditions, but I always declined, preferring the company of his handsome wife for the evening to the possible danger of being devoured by the *osos,* taking warning from my past critical experience.

Don Vicente was about six feet tall, finely proportioned, straight as an arrow, weighing about 225 pounds, hospitable, kind, and full of native dignity. His surroundings were in keeping with his appearance, manners and tastes.

I have ridden in company with him going to the Feast of San José, when he was attired in a costly suit trimmed with gold and silver lace, sitting with ease and grace on his horse, which was equally well equipped, followed by two mounted and well-dressed *mozos* twenty feet in the rear, and his wife about two or three hundred yards distant with her splendidly mounted cavalcade, the whole forming a picture worthy of admiration.

On one occasion in 1840 I stopped at his house during one of my trading expeditions, remaining over night. In the morning, when about ready to depart, he said to me, *"No se abure."* (Don't be in a hurry.) "Let's take a ride out this beautiful April morning. You see how handsome the hills are; it is the pleasantest part of the year. Just now the cattle and horses are beginning to change their coats, and everything is fresh and new. Let's take a ride and enjoy the day."

Don Vicente being one of our best customers, with whom I was anxious to keep on good terms, I accepted the invitation, being also pleased to enjoy the day as he proposed. He mounted me on a splendid horse and taking another himself, we went along enjoying the freshness and beauty of everything about us exceedingly. Presently Don Vicente said, "We will now have a little fun and I want you to assist me. You see among those cattle there a three-year-old cow. I select her because she is the fleetest. Your horse is well trained and will follow the movements of the game. You must take care that he does not unsaddle you by his quick movements. Now let us go for her!"

We let the horses out and they immediately rushed away, and in a few moments we lapped the cow, one on either side. He leaned over and caught the creature by the tail, and instantly she was turned over and over toward me, and my horse, at the right moment, leaped to one side to allow room for the animal's movements. It was very exciting, and I shall never forget the exhilaration of the chase and the leap made by the horse to get out of her way when the creature was thrown.

The native Californians were not naturally gamblers. I have seen some of the lower classes gamble for small sums with cards, but have never known the wealthy rancheros, or the higher class in towns, to indulge in gambling, except on special occasions, like feast days of the Saints or at a horse-race.

The merchants sold to the rancheros and other Californians whatever goods they wanted, to any reasonable amount, and gave them credit from one killing season to another. I have never known of a single instance in which a note or other written obligation was required of them. At the time of purchasing they were furnished with bills of the goods, which were charged in the account books, and in all my intercourse and experience in trade with them, extending over many years, I never knew a case of dishonesty on their part. They always kept their business engagements, paid their bills promptly at the proper time in hides and tallow, which were the currency of the country, and sometimes, though seldom, in money. They regarded their verbal promise as binding and sacred, relied upon their honor, and were always faithful. This may be said of all their relations with others; they were faithful in their promises and engagements of every kind. They were too proud to condescend to do anything mean or disgraceful. This honesty and integrity were eminently characteristic of these early Californians. As much cannot be said of some of their descendants, who have become demoralized, and are not like their ancestors in this regard.

CHAPTER XIX
Mexican Public Men and Others

AT the head of the government of the department of California was, of course, the governor, who resided at Monterey, then the seat of government. The next officer in rank was the prefect, whose position was somewhat similar in rank to that of lieutenant-governor at the present day, only he was much more of an executive officer. He resided at Monterey also. Through him all orders emanating from the governor were issued to officers of lower rank—the sub-prefects—who presided over districts of considerable extent; for instance, that in the vicinity of Yerba Buena comprised San Francisco and Contra Costa, the latter being the name of all the country on the east side of the bay.

The alcaldes presided over the towns, and were supervised by the sub-prefects. There was also a secretary of state at Monterey, who was the immediate counselor of the governor, generally a man of education and of more than ordinary ability. The commander-in-chief of the forces of the department also usually resided at Monterey, although in the case of General Vallejo there was an exception, he residing at Sonoma by permission of the supreme government of Mexico.

The governor's cabinet consisted of the prefect, the secretary of state and the commander-in-chief. The government was both civil and military in character. The office of the prefect was of great importance. The whole civil administration of affairs went through his hands. His orders were issued to the various sub-prefects of the department, and they in turn issued them to the alcaldes. In matters of doubt concerning the titles to pueblo lands and other questions which the alcaldes were called to pass upon, the sub-prefects were often consulted, and questions of importance referred from the alcaldes to the prefect, through the sub-perfects, and by him laid before the governor and cabinet for final decisions.

There was also the junta departmental, comprising seven members, which assembled at the seat of government once a year. The members were elected from different sections of the department, and remained in session each year from one to three months, according to the business to be disposed of. The oldest of their number was made chairman or president of this assembly, and held his office during its existence. The governor of the department could also preside over the assembly.

This body was largely occupied in passing upon titles to lands which had been conveyed by the governor to different persons, these grants being certified by the secretary of state. The grants were generally bestowed as a reward for services rendered the country in a military capacity, though there were some exceptions where grants were given to other persons at the option of the governor. He had full power to issue these grants, subject to approval or disapproval by the assembly. If they were approved, the title was considered perfect; if not approved, the title was considered inchoate, subject to further consideration and action by the junta.

In case of death of the governor, or other vacancy of his office the president of the junta departmental became governor *pro tem.* until a new appointment was made by the supreme authority in Mexico. I recollect of only one instance where the president of the assembly became governor *pro tem.*, and that was on the occasion of the revolution against Governor Micheltorena, when he was displaced, and Don Pio Pico who was then president of the junta departmental, was made provisional governor.

In 1834 or '35 an ayuntamiento, or town council, was formed for San Francisco, consisting of one alcalde, two regidores and a sindico, which body resided first at the Presidio; afterwards at the Mission.

There were no regularly established courts in the department at that time. The alcalde exercised the office of judge, jury, lawyers and all, inasmuch as no lawyers were employed; in fact there were none in the department. The plaintiff and defendant simply appeared before the alcalde, and stated their case on either side, produced their witnesses, if they had any, and the alcalde decided the case speedily; generally on the spot, without delay.

I believe that more substantial justice was done in this way than in the courts of the present day, with all their elaborate machinery and prolonged course of proceedings.

The alcalde decided all cases of minor importance, and the penalty for lesser crimes was fine or imprisonment. Cases of more magnitude, like those of murder and other high crimes, were brought before the governor and cabinet at Monterey, and their decision in the matter was final. The governor had full power to condemn or discharge a prisoner, or to pardon him after sentence. The fate of the prisoner rested entirely in his hands. There was no hanging in those days, but when a prisoner was convicted of a capital offense and condemned to death he was shot by the military. Criminals, such as burglars, horse thieves, cattle thieves, perpetrators of assaults, were arrested by the sindico, and turned over to the military commander of the post, if within convenient distance, otherwise to an alcalde's posse, and imprisoned in the calaboose, and guarded by citizens specially appointed by the alcalde for the occasion until the time for examination or trial.

These alcaldes as a class were men of good, strong common sense, and many of them had a fair education. As a rule they were honest in their administration of justice and sought to give every man his dues. I had occasion to appear before them frequently in my business transactions, with reference to hides that were not branded according to law, and other matters. I always found them ready upon a proper representation of the case to do what was just to all concerned.

The alcalde was an important personage in the town. His insignia of office consisted of a cane of light colored wood, handsomely finished, and ornamented at the top with silver or gold. Below the knob were holes in the cane, through which was drawn black silk cord, attached to tassels of the same material, hanging below. The alcaldes carried this staff on all occasions, and especially when about to perform any official act, such as ordering an arrest. Great respect and deference were paid to the cane and its bearer by the people at large. He was treated with great courtesy and politeness and looked up to as a person of undisputed authority. The administration of the governor and his cabinet, and of the various sub-prefects, was just and satisfactory to the people, and I have never known any instance to the contrary.

Juan B. Alvarado, who was governor of California when I came to this coast, was a native Californian. His mother was a sister of General Vallejo. He was educated at Monterey by an English instructor, W. E. P. Hartnell. When quite a young man, he was clerk to Nathan Spear, then a merchant at Monterey. I have frequently heard Spear speak in terms of the warmest admiration of his honesty and great ability. Spear himself was well read and intelligent, and I have heard him say that he took such an interest in young Alvarado, as he called him, that he was in the habit of imparting to him when in his employ a good deal of information about other countries and governments. Alvarado, who had a thirst for knowledge, was an eager listener, and received it gratefully; for a considerable portion of his acquirements he was indebted to Spear. In his early life he was more or less connected with the governing officials at Monterey, and then showed his talent in that direction.

It was in 1836 or '37, I think that Alvarado wrote a letter to President Bustamente, then at the head of the Republic of Mexico, about some governmental matters connected with the department of California, in which his ability was recognized by the president; for, shortly after this, he appointed Alvarado governor of the department, which position he held until he was superseded by Micheltorena in the latter part of '42. In his administration of affairs he showed talent, and was friendly to all foreigners. Spear and other well-informed Americans often spoke highly of Alvarado's military tact. Although not educated with a view to military life at all, he seemed to have a natural aptitude for military tactics and remarkable ability for planning military movements.

José Castro, the second in command in the army, was an educated military man. Living at the headquarters of the government, he frequently consulted Alvarado on important military matters, and relied largely upon his opinions and advice. General Castro was a man of fair military ability, of excellent character, very popular, and much liked by his countrymen.

General Vallejo was a more reserved man than Alvarado. He was a native of California and lived continuously in Sonoma, with his family, attending to his immense herds of cattle and horses, and did not participate in active movements in the field. He occasionally visited Monterey, where his mother and nephew, the governor, resided. He was hospitable, and received the merchant traders on the coast at his fine mansion at Sonoma and entertained them handsomely. He was courteous to the higher class of foreigners, but had no taste for the companionship of the rougher class, miners, trappers and other adventurers whom he denominated "white Indians."

In the month of December, 1839, Jacob P. Leese, who was a brother-in-law of General Vallejo, Thomas Shaw, supercargo of the ship "Monsoon," of Boston, and myself, crossed the bay to Sonoma Landing in the schooner "Isabel," and appeared at General Vallejo's house in the evening. We were very cordially received, handsomely entertained at dinner, and invited to pass the night, which we did. On retiring we were shown to our several apartments; I found an elegant bed with beautifully trimmed and embroidered sheets and coverlid and pillows; but on getting in to it I discovered there were no blankets, an oversight of the servant, and as the whole house had retired I could not arouse anybody to secure them, but lay there shivering and shaking through the night, wishing there were a little less elegance and a little more comfort.

I saw General Vallejo in Sonoma many times. His selection of horses for his own use was one of the finest in the country, comprising a large number of beautiful animals, well trained. I have seen him taking his morning and evening ride on horseback (there were no carriages in Sonoma at that time) and sitting on his fine horse in the most natural and graceful manner. He was considered skillful in the use of the lasso, and also expert in the *colliar,* or catching the bull by the tail and overturning him when going at full speed, as before described. This was a favorite amusement amongst the rancheros, and any one of them, though he might be the possessor of many thousands of cattle and horses, who was not fully up to the mark in the skillful and daring manœuvers of using the lasso and in *colliar* and other feats of that kind, was looked upon as lacking in those accomplishments which were befitting a genuine Californian.

General Vallejo received a school education under the instruction of W. E. P. Hartnell at Monterey. Being naturally fond of study, and appreciating the advantages of education of a higher order, and having great ambition for learning, he has continued his studious habits during his whole life, gathering books here and there whenever opportunity offered, sometimes from vessels coming to the coast, and if there were any special books he wanted he would send to Mexico, to Spain, to France, to England, to the United States, or to any part of the world to procure them. Having accumulated large wealth in his younger days he has always gratified his tastes in that direction. In visiting him in the earlier days I would find him in his library surrounded by his books, in which he took the greatest delight and pride. He illustrates in the best manner the oft quoted phrase, "a gentleman and a scholar."

Don Pablo de la Guerra was a native Californian, and a pupil and brother-in-law of Hartnell, the latter having married one of the de la Guerra sisters. He was a man fond of reading, an accomplished scholar, speaking his own language in the best manner, and also the English fluently and correctly. He was in the government service, and in 1845 became Collector of the Port. His father was Don José de la Guerra, a native of Spain, who always resided at Santa Barbara, and who married one of the Carrillo family there. The four brothers of the lady—Don Carlos, Anastacio, Domingo and José Antonio Carrillo—were each of them at least six feet in height, weighing over 200 pounds, and finely proportioned. Don Carlos was the leader in the revolution against Governor Alvarado to displace him in 1838.

Don José Antonio resided at Los Angeles, and was considered a leading man of talent in that part of the country, being surpassed only by Alvarado in intellect. During this revolution he was a most efficient worker in the movement to place his brother Don Carlos in the position of governor.

Don Pablo de la Guerra was a member of the first Constitutional

Convention in '49, and assisted greatly in the formation of the constitution. He was several times elected to the Senate, (State) representing Santa Barbara and San Luis Obispo. He often presided over the Senate in the absence of the regular officer, and was frequently asked to become a candidate for governor of the State, but declined.

Mr. Alfred Robinson, sometimes known as Don Alfredo Robinson, who still lives (1889) in San Francisco, married a sister of Don Pablo de la Guerra and of Doña Augusta Jimeno. I never saw the lady, but she must have been fine looking, coming, as she did, from a handsome family. This wedding is described in Dana's "Two Years Before the Mast."

Don Manuel Jimeno, who was secretary of state under Alvarado, was a native of Mexico, and emigrated to California when very young. He married one of Don Pablo de la Guerra's sisters, Doña Augusta. He was considered a man of learning and a statesman. I think he held also the position of secretary of state under Micheltorena. He was familiar with the laws of Mexico which were in force in the department of California, and filled the office with credit to himself and the department. His wife was an accomplished lady, very entertaining in her conversation, overflowing with wit and vivacity. I have frequently heard her, after the change of the government to that of the United States, express her utter disapprobation in the most sarcastic language; but she was so intelligent and her manner so captivating, that the listener was overcome with admiration of her brightness and the pungency and appropriateness of her speech.

In a patriotic outburst, Señora Doña Augusta Jimeno exclaimed one day that she would delight to have the ears of the officers of the United States squadron for a necklace, such was her hatred of the new rulers of her country. But, with all this, it was well known in Monterey that whenever an officer of the army or navy was taken sick Mrs. Jimeno was the first to visit the patient and bestow on him the known kindness so characteristic of the native California ladies, with encouraging words, and delicacies suitable to his condition. This would show that she disliked them as conquerors of her country, but respected them as individuals. Some years after Mrs. Jimeno became a widow, she married Dr. Ord of the United States army.

Mariano Pacheco, the brother of the governor, was with me for two years as clerk in Yerba Buena, in 1843 and '44.

Doña Ramona, the mother of Governor Pacheco, when I first knew her in 1838, at Santa Barbara, was a handsome woman, queenly in her walk and bearing, and among her countrywomen, who were noted for their beauty, she was one of the most attractive. Her first husband, Don Francisco Pacheco, was an accomplished musician, playing the violin with great skill and taste.

After the death of her first husband Mrs. Pacheco married Captain John Wilson, an old Scotchman, and lived at Santa Barbara. She was kind to all the merchants who visited that port. In 1842 and '43 I was at Santa Barbara as supercargo of the "Don Quixote," and often dined with her. Frequently when the hour arrived, and I was not there, she would send a servant round the town to find me, with the message, *"Doña Ramona esta esperando a usted para la comida."* (Doña Ramona is waiting dinner for you.) I would sometimes tell her not to wait for me, that my business might prevent me coming, and I could not be prompt at her fine dinner, but she would always send for me. Her kindness to me is among my pleasantest recollections.

CHAPTER XX
The Hudson's Bay Company in Yerba Buena

THE Hudson's Bay Company was a commercial corporation existing under charter granted by Charles II. in 1670. During the first half of the XIX century it had posts and stores for trade with Indians and trappers at Astoria, Fort Vancouver and other points on the Columbia. The head agent, residing at Vancouver, was given the title of "governor." In 1821 McLoughlin was appointed governor for the company of all the country in the Oregon Territory west of the Rocky Mountains.

In the spring of 1841 Governor McLoughlin (who was a large man) and suite came from the Hudson's Bay Company's post, on the Columbia river, in the bark "Cowlitz," to Yerba Buena, for the purpose of establishing a post of the company at this point. The governor was also called Dr. McLoughlin. He was talkative and companionable. The four or five gentlemen who accompanied him were also large men, of refinement, and appeared to be men of prominence. They purchased a portion of a block of land, with a house, from Jacob P. Leese, bounded by Montgomery street on the west,* Sacramento on the south, Clay on the north, on the east coming near to the water mark of the bay. They purchased four fifty varas, being two-thirds of the whole block. The house was a large wooden two-story building, occupied by Leese and his family. The price paid for the property was $4800, half in coin and half in goods. The "Cowlitz" remained about two weeks at Yerba Buena, and then the governor and his party left in her for Monterey, and proceeded thence to their post on the Columbia river. The building was not given up by Leese until the arrival of William G. Rae, son-in-law of Dr. McLoughlin, from the Columbia river post, with a large stock of goods in the "Cowlitz." He opened the new post in September, 1841, and took possession of the property. The goods were sent from England to the Hudson's Bay Com-

---

*This is an error. Leese sold the Hudson's Bay Company the Easterly two thirds of the block bounded by Kearny, Sacramento, Clay and Montgomery Streets. If the word "East" be substituted for "West" Davis' description may stand.

pany's station on the Columbia and then transshipped here, the vessel going to Monterey to make entry at the Custom House. Rae made use of the building for a store; he kept a large miscellaneous assortment of English goods, and the company traded in the same way that other merchants did on the coast, sending out their little launches and schooners to collect hides and tallow about the bay, and to deliver goods, and they did a good business until the death of Rae in January, 1845. They had no large vessels trading up and down the coast.

Rae was a Scotchman, tall and handsome, and much of a gentleman. I became intimately acquainted with him, and have played "whist" at his house many times until daylight. He was fond of this game, a skillful player, and always selected me for his partner, as he considered me a good player also. We sometimes bet a *real* (equivalent to twelve and a half cents) each on the result of the game—never more than this sum—which was bet in order to make the game more interesting.

One evening there were three sets of gentlemen playing "whist" in Mr. Rae's rooms, he and I being partners as usual. During one of the games I saw by a significant look from him that he had a poor hand, and that he rather conceded the game to our opponents; to which I assented. As the game proceeded, I had only two hearts in my hand, the ace and the king; I deliberately threw away the king, which seemed to astonish him, as I saw by a kind of dry smile on his countenance. This trick was my partner's already, but as I could not follow suit I played the king of hearts, and thus enabled my partner to use his cards to advantage, and when hearts were played afterward my low trumps secured other tricks, and the game was decided in our favor. This greatly delighted Rae, who expressed his unbounded satisfaction, and so emphatically that all the playing in the room stopped, and his enthusiasm created general hilarity. He said to the other gentleman that this movement of mine in the game was one of the best conceived that he ever witnessed, and complimented me highly for my skill. If he had just made $10,000 by some lucky stroke of business he could not have been more delighted.

The games of "whist" and "twenty-one" were favorite amusements of the people in those days, and generally indulged in, there being no public amusements of any kind. Rae had with him his wife, the daughter of Governor McLoughlin, and two or three interesting children.

The other third of the block containing the Hudson's Bay store was owned by John J. Vioget, a Swiss, who lived there, and had a kind of public house, with a billiard-room and bar, which at that time was the only place of resort for the entertainment of captains, supercargoes, merchants and clerks of the town. He had also occasional visitors from the ranchos whenever they came to town to make their purchases and transact business. Among these visitors was Don José Joaquin Estudillo, of the San Leandro Rancho, also a large man, but not so tall as Rae.

One day Rae, Estudillo and a number of others happened to be at Vioget's house, which was a sort of exchange or meeting place for comparing notes on business matters, talking over affairs in general. At the same time a little amusement was perhaps indulged in. Some were chatting, some smoking, some playing billiards, and presently Rae challenged Estudillo to a contest at wrestling, to prove who was the best man. The challenge was accepted, and they stood up facing each other; on the word being given they came together and Rae was immediately thrown, to his great amazement. At the second trial he was thrown again, and this was repeated a third, fourth and fifth time, until Rae frankly acknowledged that his opponent was the better wrestler, and he himself was fairly beaten. He invited us to join him in a glass of wine.

Rae was much respected. He was liberal to those less favored by circumstances than himself, frequently giving little presents to persons who came to his store of things most needed by them. His table was always finely supplied with the best of everything, and he had a generous sideboard and entertained a great deal of company. He and Spear were the chief entertainers. There being no hotels at that time, the hospitalities of the town devolved mostly upon these two gentlemen. The captains, supercargoes and other strangers were always welcome at Rae's house, and it was a pleasure to him to entertain them. He had the true California nature and feeling in this respect.

Rae had a clerk named Robert Ridley, who was a regular English cockney, a good-looking fellow. He married the daughter of Juana Briones, the first settler at North Beach. He was singular and comical, and was considered the funny man of the town. Everybody knew him, and he was popular and liked by all. He knew everyone's business, was the newscarrier and gossip of the place, and was at home in every house. He imagined he was a lady's man, and at times stirred up a little excitement among the feminines. He was a great teller of extravagant stories—a regular Munchausen—and withal was considered the life and fun of the place.

I met him one fine spring morning between seven and eight o'clock. "Bill," said he, "how many *London Docks* do you suppose I have taken already before breakfast this morning?" "About a dozen," I answered; "your usual allowance." "I can discount that," said he; "I have taken twenty-three!"—and he was apparently sober at the time.

Rae told me the same day that two large decanters filled with dark

English brandy on the sideboard in his dining-room had been emptied, and he accused Bob of having drank the contents, which the latter acknowledged having done, astonishing as it may seem. Like most Englishmen, he was not easily affected by this habit, and it was for a long time a question whether King Brandy should rule or Bob; but finally his strong English constitution yielded to the superior authority of the former, and poor Bob died more than twenty years ago at the Mission Dolores (1889).

The business of the Hudson's Bay Company's post was quite successful up to January, 1845, when it was discovered that Rae was unfaithful to his wife, having succumbed to the fascinations of a California lady. Upon this becoming public, Rae, who was a sensitive man, was so overcome with mortification and disgrace that he shot himself. After his death the British vice-consul, James Alexander Forbes, took possession of the post, and was instructed by the managers of the general post on the Columbia river to close out the business of the company at Yerba Buena as soon as practicable. This was done in the course of a few months, and the land and house sold to Mellus & Howard for $5000. They afterward opened a commercial establishment there, using the building as a store, and in the winter of 1849-50 this building was converted into the United States Hotel, which became a popular resort.

CHAPTER XXI
Commodore Wilkes Visits Yerba Buena

IN 1841 the squadron in command of Commodore Wilkes visited the Columbia river on an exploring expedition, the fleet consisting of the United States sloop of war "Vincennes," which was the flag ship, the sloop of war "Peacock," commanded by Captain Hudson, and the brig "Porpoise." In going into the Columbia, across the bar, the "Peacock" was lost, and became a total wreck, but the officers and crew were rescued and taken on the two other vessels. Sailing thence, after the completion of their work on the Columbia, the "Vincennes" and "Porpoise" arrived in the bay of San Francisco in July and anchored off Saucelito. Soon after, the numerous boats of the vessels were prepared for the survey of the Sacramento river. Commodore Wilkes headed the party, and they were engaged for about two months in exploring that river and some of its branches. During the survey they frequently visited Captain Sutter, and I have often heard the officers speak of his hospitality to them at his establishment on the Sacramento. They also made some surveys of San Francisco bay, remaining here until October.

Commodore Wilkes was not a man to impress a stranger favorably at first sight, being rather severe and forbidding in aspect, not genial and companionable, and not popular with his officers, though they gave him credit for being very thorough in his discipline and duties, and there is no doubt he was a great explorer and a thoroughly scientific man. He was an indefatigable worker and accomplished a great deal, but, unlike other distinguished commanders who visited the coast, he was not given to sociability and had no entertainments on board his vessel; although several were given by his officers, who were a genial set, fond of enjoyments. I partook of their hospitality on several occasions, and had a very pleasant time.

Wilkes was visited by General Vallejo and his brother Captain Salvador Vallejo, on board the "Vincennes," and the general was received with a salute and all the naval courtesies due to the commander-in-chief of the forces of the department of California. He was also visited by Governor Alexander Rotcheff, of the Russian American Fur Company at Fort Ross, and I afterward heard Rotcheff say, when speaking of his visit to Wilkes, that he took great interest in this exploring expedition. In his visits to Spear, which he made frequently, he told us with enthusiasm of his listening for hours to Wilkes and his officers in their accounts of their visits to the South Sea Islands and other parts of the globe, and their descriptions of the habits, manners, character and mode of life of the natives. Some of the officers of the squadron visited Rotcheff at Fort Ross, and were handsomely entertained by him during their brief stay. It was sixty or seventy miles from Saucelito to Fort Ross, and to enable the officers to get there conveniently, Rotcheff sent down a number of his finest horses, with a vaquero, to take them up, having adopted the Spanish fashion of herding horses in *caponeras,* and being well furnished with fine stock. He returned the officers in the same way, after their visit. Some of these navy officers also visited General Vallejo at Sonoma, and were entertained by him very agreeably.

The supplies for the ward-rooms of the two vessels while in port, were obtained from Spear, and as I was his active business man, I became well acquainted with the officers. I found them fine fellows, full of life, and ready for any enjoyment that came along. They would sometimes send over a boat for supplies in the morning, and address me a line, saying they would be over in the evening, a dozen of them or so. Meanwhile I would dispatch a boy out to my friend Guerrero, the sub-prefect, at the Mission Dolores, asking him to send me a dozen horses and saddles, which he would kindly do. If there were not saddles enough, I made them up in town. When the party arrived in town about dusk, the horses would be ready, and mounting them, we rode out to Guerrero's house. The young men and women in the neighborhood were invited in, and we would have a little dance, the party generally lasting till morning. The young fellows from the ship enjoyed it highly after their long life at sea.

Commodore Wilkes seldom came ashore at Yerba Buena, being a very busy man, and when not engaged in surveying outside, was industriously occupied on the vessel in working out the results of his explorations and surveys, and recording them.

Spear appreciated Wilkes' labors, and the commodore took quite a liking to him and invited him to dine on board the vessel several times, and they had several interviews. Spear had great respect and admiration for the commodore, which was reciprocated by him, whenever he found a man who could understand and appreciate his work, which was everything to him, he became more affable and companionable than with others.

Wilkes more particularly esteemed Spear from the fact that he was an American, and one of the first American settlers on the coast, having come here in 1823; and also from the fact that he had done a great deal through his correspondence with friends in the east to inform the United States government of the great resources and future importance of California, describing minutely its climate, soil, productions and commercial advantages. His principal correspondent was his brother, Paul Spear, a wealthy druggist of Boston, who communicated through friends in Washington this information to the authorities. Spear also predicted to me and others that at some future time mineral discoveries of importance would be made here.

These efforts of Spear to make the advantages of California known to the government, and his views and opinions in regard thereto, greatly interested Wilkes, and he commended him warmly for what he had done in that direction. Spear was the first merchant who established himself on shore in California, first at Monterey, afterward with a branch at Yerba Buena, to which place he went later himself.

Governor Alvarado, who felt very grateful to Spear for the aid he had given him in his younger days, and with whom he always maintained a cordial friendship, often suggested to Spear that he should become a Mexican citizen, and urged this upon him repeatedly, in order that he might bestow upon him a grant of eleven leagues of land, which was the extent allowed by law, and which grant could only be made to a citizen of Mexico, and he assured him that he would be most happy to do this if Spear would only comply with his suggestion; but Spear persistently refused to renounce his allegiance to his own country, which he honored and loved too much to wish to change his nationality, even for so tempting an offer, although many Americans and other foreigners had done so for the purpose of obtaining grants of land from the Mexican government. During their friendly intercourse the governor would sometimes say to Spear, "Don Nathan, it is only a question of time when this country will belong to your government. I regret this, but such is undoubtedly the ruling of Providence;" or something to that effect.

Spear told me that in his conversations with Wilkes in visiting him on the vessel, the commodore expressed himself repeatedly as more than delighted with the bay of San Francisco and the Sacramento river, and said there was no question as to the future greatness and importance which would ensue when the bay and the other commercial advantages of this territory were availed of. He said that California would surely belong to our government at some time in the future. It was understood, and was, in fact, stated by Wilkes to Spear, that the chief object of his visit to California was to obtain and report accurate information in regard to the bay of San Francisco to the government at Washington, with a view of future acquisition. Wilkes, on being informed that de Mofras had been the guest of Spear while stopping at Yerba Buena, was greatly interested, and inquired carefully and particularly about de Mofras' visit to California, asking Spear for all the details of his movements here and his conversations. He was particularly anxious to know if de Mofras ever divulged that the French government had any designs or intentions in regard to the bay of San Francisco.

In my visit to the officers of the vessels the conversation in the wardroom would frequently turn upon the bay of San Francisco, and they often declared their admiration, and said that in all their visits to other parts of the world they had seen nothing to equal it. The more they became conversant with it in their surveys the more they were impressed with its importance, and they would sometimes exclaim, "This is ours!" referring to the future, when the United States government should hold possession of this part of the country.

During my early residence here British men-of-war came to the coast and to the bay of San Francisco about once a year or so, remaining two or three weeks at a time, touching also at Monterey, and sometimes going north to visit the British possessions. They generally landed at *Saucelito, at which point they replenished their supplies to some extent. Captain Richardson, the owner of *Saucelito Rancho, an Englishman, was a social man and very obliging, and he made it pleasant for them to go there. He supplied them with wood from his ranch, also beef, and allowed them to procure water from the springs on his place. It was the impression among the foreign residents here, especially the Americans, that these visits of British government vessels had some significance; that they called here under instructions from the British government, to observe in a quiet way, the bay, the surrounding country, its facilities, the people, the probable resources of California, and to note whatever was going on, with some view to the future possibly of England's obtaining possession. American men-of-war came here more frequently, in the same way, and stopped several weeks at a time. In fact, there was nearly always a United States government vessel either at Yerba Buena or Monterey, or somewhere in the neighborhood, often more than one, up to the time when the country came into our possession.

It was the impression then, and doubtless the fact, that the American war vessels were sent for the purpose of keeping an eye on the vessels of other nations, particularly the British, as bearing upon the future of

*Americanized into Sausalito. The Spanish Saucelito means: little willow.

California; and in my intercourse with the commanders and officers of the United States government vessels, they expressed to me their suspicion or fear that the English had designs upon the country, and the hope that they would not be permitted to anticipate any movements our own government might contemplate, and get ahead of us in securing an advantage in California.

In Spear's interviews with Wilkes when he visited him on board the "Vincennes," the commodore freely conversed with him about the future of the Pacific coast, and stated that the British government was the only power which the United States had cause to feel any concern about in reference to California, and said further, that the United States squadron in the Pacific was specially instructed to keep an eye on the movements of the British vessels of war in this ocean, with a view of intercepting any movement that they might make looking toward securing possession of California. The commodore at this time showed that he had no special liking for the English, as was subsequently evinced in his memorable capture of Mason and Slidell from a British vessel during our civil war. In one of his conversations with Spear he said, with that frankness and freedom from reserve which characterized his speech with those in whom he felt confidence, "These Britishers shall never get possession of California. Our government is constantly on the alert to prevent any such design. We are their equal, and a little more, as has been proved in the past." This greatly delighted Spear, who was a thorough American, and longed to have the country come under the American flag. Wilkes also informed Spear that Thomas O. Larkin afterwards our consul at Monterey was specially instructed by the government authorities at Washington, through the secretary of state, to constantly advise the government of all the movements of the English on this coast.

During the visit of Wilkes' squadron to the Fiji Islands, prior to coming to California, a chief of high rank had been taken captive in one of the fights which frequently occurred between the different tribes. The chief was held by his captors for ransom. Wilkes being desirous of securing a Fijian to take home with him, paid the ransom in presents of such articles as he had on board his vessel to the captors, who thereupon released their prisoner, and Wilkes took him on board his vessel and brought him to California. He was a thorough savage and cannibal. In my visits to the "Vincennes" I frequently saw him. He was confined in a room of good size, in the forepart of the vessel, constantly guarded by a marine. He was a man of large and powerful frame, with rather a square countenance, and a cunning look in his eyes, but not ferocious in his appearance and manner. He was very dark in his complexion, something between a negro and a Malay, and had a heavy head of hair, looking like an immense bunch of oakum—probably two feet in diameter from side to side, and a foot high from the top of his head, giving him a very singular appearance. He seemed to regard this hair as sacredly as the Chinese do their pigtails, and when the officers of the vessel suggested that some of it be clipped off, for the benefit of his health, he begged most piteously, with tears in his eyes, that they would not touch it, saying he would rather die, or submit to any torture or disgrace, than be deprived of it. When first taken he was of great size, weighing probably 250 pounds, but while imprisoned on the vessel he had become reduced to about 200. I once went into his place of confinement, and saluted him, and shook hands with him. He returned the salute with a kind of nod, showing some appreciation of the attention paid him. He was carefully and kindly provided for; everything was done that could be for his health and comfort, as the commodore was desirous of getting him to Washington; but his confinement wore upon him; he was impatient and uneasy, and I subsequently learned that he died on the voyage eastward after the vessel left here.

Captain Richardson repeated to Commodore Wilkes the tradition of the old Indian Monica with regard to Golden Gate at one time having been closed, and subsequently rent apart by some great convulsion of nature, making an outlet for the waters of the bay through to the ocean, and Wilkes became greatly interested in the matter. With some of his scientific corps, together with Captain Richardson, he went out to the Golden Gate in one of his boats to carefully observe the two points on either side; having become familiar with the bay in their surveys, which extended as far up as Alviso and the surrounding country, they could form an intelligent opinion in the matter. They said they thought it probable that the story of the old Indian was correct, and that the bay once found an outlet through the San José valley into Monterey bay. The botanist of the party, with whom I was quite intimate, particularly expressed his belief in the correctness of this theory or tradition. The commodore was so interested in the matter that he had the old Indian Monica brought on board his vessel by Captain Richardson, and questioned him closely all about it himself. Monica was treated with great courtesy on this occasion and was shown all over the vessel. The Fiji captive was also exhibited to him, and he regarded him with much interest and curiosity, especially as Captain Richardson explained to him that in his own country he was a great fighter; that after a battle between the different tribes the bodies of the slain were taken by the victors and devoured as a grand feast.

Commodore Wilkes had with him a full scientific corps, all the various departments covered by the expedition being represented, in the ablest manner. Probably there never was sent out by the government a more thoroughly skilled and learned set of men. The regular officers of the vessels also were very well fitted for their work, highly capable, and were of great aid to the commodore in his labors. The first surgeon of the fleet, Dr. Holmes, I discovered in conversation was a distant relative of mine. When I told him of my grandfather and other relatives in Massachusetts I was treated with great attention. Doctor Oliver Wendell Holmes, the author, is of the same family, and was named after my grandfather, Oliver.

Captain Richardson who had come here in 1822, was much liked by Wilkes, though an Englishman, inasmuch as he was a thorough sailor and pilot, and well acquainted with the bay of San Francisco, and he was also an agreeable and obliging gentleman. He gave Wilkes a good deal of information about different parts of the bay, indicated points for examination and survey, and his suggestions were of aid to Wilkes and were found by him of much value. When the commodore was about to leave the bay of San Francisco for Monterey, he requested Richardson to pilot the vessel out to sea. Richardson advised him not to leave on the day appointed, as there had been a strong south-east wind blowing, the bar was very rough, breaking almost across, and he thought it too hazardous. The commodore being of a very determined nature—headstrong, as Richardson expressed it—was not easily changed from his purpose when he had once made up his mind to anything. He said he would go nevertheless, and asked Richardson to be on board at a certain hour. The vessels accordingly started, but on nearing the bar it was decided to come to anchor just inside, which they did. During their stay there, the swell of the sea swept over the "Vincennes," and broke loose and set in motion some spars on the upper deck, which killed two of the marines on board.

CHAPTER XXII
The "Julia Ann" Sails Into Port

FROM 1835 to 1839 Captain Eliab Grimes, of Boston, was a wealthy merchant at Honolulu, engaged in general trade. He imported his goods from Boston, and sent out once a year from the Islands for the purpose of hunting the sea-otters on the coast of California, the American brig "Conroy," owned by him, and commanded by Captain James Bancroft, an Englishman by birth, but a citizen of the United States by naturalization. Bancroft lived at Honolulu. On these voyages the vessel first proceeded to the coast of Alaska, where she took on board from sixty to seventy of the native Indians as hunters, with their light-skin canoes, and then brought them down to the coast of California, the favorite hunting ground being off shore between Santa Barbara and San Diego. They generally arrived there early in the spring, and continued the work during the summer and until late in the autumn, when the season expired. They were always very successful in securing a large number of skins, and when the hunting was over, the vessel returned to Alaska to leave the hunters and their canoes, and proceeded thence to Honolulu. As these skins were very valuable, Captain Grimes and Captain Bancroft, the latter having an interest in the vessel and the voyage, became wealthy. Hunting sea-otters on the coast of California without permission of the authorities was contrary to the laws of Mexico. Captain Bancroft had no such permission and was therefore violating the law. But as the government had no revenue cutters to enforce it, the offenders pursued their profitable occupation without interference.

In 1837 the government of the department of California bought of Captain John Paty a schooner of about a hundred tons, named the "California," but she was not fitted for revenue-cutter service, having only one or two small guns, and she was used chiefly to carry dispatches between Monterey and Mazatlan and San Blas, in communication between the department of California and the supreme government at Mexico.

Captain Bancroft married at Honolulu in 1836, and on the last voy-

These extracts from the log and papers of the schooner Julia Ann *are in the handwriting of William A. Leidesdorff, who reached Yerba Buena in 1841. The barter account gives a perfect picture of trade methods in vogue in California before the discovery of gold at Sutter's Mill.*

Leidesdorff's signature appears on this account with a member of his crew.

Leidesdorff's rise to affluence is told interestingly by Davis in his narrative.

age he ever made, in 1839, he was accompanied by his wife. In the summer of that year, the brig was lying at anchor at the Island of Santa Cruz, off Santa Barbara; one day the Indians returning in their canoes from the hunt, towards evening, collected around the vessel, and Captain Bancroft spoke to them from the deck in their own language, and inquired about their success for the day. Their report did not satisfy him, as they had not obtained the usual number of otters, and he began to talk severely to them, reprimanding them for their ill success, thinking he could say what he pleased to them. Upon this, they rushed on board the vessel in large numbers, pointing at him their loaded rifles with which they killed the otter, in the use of which they were expert, and commenced firing. He fell upon the deck. Meanwhile, his wife, who was in the cabin, and who always had more or less dread of these Indians, hearing the tumult above, hastened up; seeing her husband lying bleeding on the quarter-deck, and the Indians around him, she flew to the spot and fell upon him, covering his body completely with her own to protect him from his assailants. The assault continued, and she was severely wounded. Captain Bancroft died on the spot. The natives were quieted after a time, when the mate took command of the vessel, and returned them to Alaska. He then sailed for the Islands with Mrs. Bancroft and the body of her husband, which was preserved, for burial at Honolulu. She survived but a few weeks after reaching her home, though attended by the best medical skill. Her life might have been saved had she consented to submit to a surgical operation which was proposed, but she declined to have it performed. After the tragic death of her husband she had no desire to live.

In the spring of 1839 there arrived in the bay of San Francisco from British Columbia a British vessel of war, Captain Belcher, which anchored east of Yerba Buena. She was on an exploring expedition in the Pacific Ocean. Soon after the vessel dropped anchor Captain Belcher came ashore, accompanied by some of his officers, and called at Spear's store and also at Jacob P. Leese's residence. Captain Belcher stated to Mr. Spear that he would remain in the bay a few weeks and make some surveys of our miniature inland sea and the Sacramento river. The work of the ship while in the bay was never made known to anyone here, at the time, to my knowledge. She remained at Yerba Buena but twenty-four hours, and then departed for Saucelito, where she was anchored during the work of her boats around the bay and on the Sacramento river. Captain Richardson, owner of the Saucelito rancho, said but little or nothing in regard to Captain Belcher's visit and his surveys of the bay and rivers.

At this early period, and several years before Wilke's exploring expedition, it would seem that England had her attention directed to the value and importance of the bay of San Francisco from its geographical position as the commercial center of the Pacific Ocean trade in the future.

The schooner "Julia Ann," Captain William A. Leidesdorff, who is well known in the history of San Francisco, left New York about January, 1841, for the coast of California through the Straits of Magellan. J. C. Jones, former United States consul at Honolulu, who owned the schooner, left New York sometime afterward in a sailing vessel to meet the "Julia Ann" at Panama. He proceeded to the Isthmus on the Atlantic side, crossed to Panama, and expected to find the vessel there on his arrival, but was compelled to wait sixty days before she appeared.

During her passage through the Straits she encountered many delays and perils, having almost constant head-winds, and being in great dread of the Indians, who were cannibals and who swarmed about the vessel in their canoes, a little distance off, apparently waiting an opportunity to pounce upon the schooner and capture all on board. A constant watch was therefore kept up to prevent such a calamity. They finally got through the Straits, and were greatly relieved to find themselves beyond the reach of the savages. They arrived at Panama just as Jones was about chartering another vessel to take him up the coast, thinking his own must be lost. Robert G. Davis, a brother of mine, was a passenger on board the schooner; also John Weed, of a very wealthy family of New York; who took the voyage for the benefit of his health. My brother had a stock of merchandise aboard for sale on the coast. She arrived at Monterey in June, 1841. This was Leidesdorff's first visit here.

In January, 1842, I left Nathan Spear and took passage on the ship "Alert," Captain Phelps, to Monterey, and there found the bark "Don Quixote," Captain John Paty, and I made arrangements with him to become supercargo of that vessel, and at once assumed that position. We came to Yerba Buena, remained here a few weeks trading around the bay, and I made very successful sales and collections for Paty. On leaving here we proceeded to Monterey. About the last of February we sailed from there for Honolulu with a cargo of hides and otter and beaver skins, which we disposed of on reaching there, and purchased a full cargo of goods for the market of California.

These goods had been brought principally from Boston and New York, and some from England, France and Germany. There was only five per cent. duty on foreign goods imported into the Islands in those days, and Honolulu was a depot where the ships brought their goods from different parts of the world, and from there they were sent out to supply the whole western coast of America; points in California, the Columbia river, the British and Russian possessions north, and also to Mexican ports.

CHAPTER XXIII
Boston Ships and Traders

THE "Don Quixote" left Honolulu on the 31st of May and returned to this coast, entered at Monterey, and traded along the coast for the remainder of the year; and she left Santa Barbara, returning to Honolulu, in February, 1843; sailing thence, she arrived at Yerba Buena on the 20th of May.

On this voyage also we brought to port a full cargo of merchandise. Immediately the sub-prefect came on board and ordered us to Monterey for entry. I knew the sub-prefect well, and told him the tide would not admit of our leaving till the next day. He then placed a guard upon the vessel to remain with us until we left the port, not a regular custom house officer, but a citizen selected by him for this special duty. We had a purpose in coming to Yerba Buena first. The duties on goods imported into California were very high at that time, and this was a great temptation to merchants trading on the coast to avoid them as far as possible. The invoice cost of our cargo at Honolulu was $20,000 and the duties would have amounted to nearly or quite as much, averaging about 100 per cent. While the merchants and captains trading on the coast desired to keep on friendly terms with the Mexican government, and had no thought or intention of opposing it in any way, at the same time they did not entertain so much affection for it as to induce them to contribute to its revenues any more than they could well avoid, and so whenever they saw an opportunity to outwit the custom house authorities they availed themselves of it.

Soon after the guard was placed on board, one of us who knew him very well, approached him and told him we were going to lock him up in a state room. "What?" said he in surprise; "What's the matter?" We laughed, and told him not to be alarmed, and he soon understood, apparently what we were aiming at. He was told that he could have his supper and could take his smoke, and then go into the state-room, where he would find a nice bed, a bottle of Madeira, a bottle of aguardiente, cigars, and everything to make him comfortable, and that the door would be locked and the key taken away, and he was to go to sleep and take it easy, and in the morning he would be let out and given $20 in gold. "Don't say any more," he replied; "that's enough."

Accordingly, after finishing his supper and his cigar, he went into the state-room, as desired, the door was locked and the key laid aside, and nothing further was heard from him till the next morning. We put on all the boats and men, and during the night worked industriously and landed about half our cargo, all the more valuable goods—silks, etc., on which the duty was the highest, and a large quantity of sugar. The tide favored us, and we put the goods on the bench near Spear's store, and the men rolled them in. We ceased our labors about four o'clock in the morning, well satisfied with our night's work.

There was another vessel in the harbor, the ship "Admittance," of Boston, Captain Paterson, Henry Mellus supercargo, afterward of the firm of Mellus & Howard. We muffled our oars in order not to attract the attention of the officers and crew of that vessel, but our movements were observed by them, as they informed us sometime afterward. We had, however, no fear of them, for we knew they would not report us as they might sometime themselves be engaged in similar business, and they were interested in keeping quiet. The penalties for smuggling were very severe under the Mexican law—death in some cases. We left on the following day for Monterey, to enter the remainder of the cargo, first recompensing our guard, as promised, and putting him ashore, and on reaching the port of entry we duly entered the goods on board and paid the duties, to the satisfaction of the custom house, having saved a handsome sum by our night's operations, concerning which no suspicion was ever created in the minds of the sub-prefect or custom house officers.

I propose to say something in regard to the evasion of the revenue laws of Mexico by the merchants of California in early days, in order that the matter may be fully understood and regarded in its true light; to show that those who were transgressors of the law in this respect were not considered as law-breakers in any odious sense, but were in entire good standing in the community, and were, to a certain extent, benefiting the people and doing a service to the country.

In entering goods at the custom house, the revenue officers did not require any oath from the merchants as to the correctness of the invoices presented by them; in fact, no oath of any kind was required of them; and the practice was to prepare fictitious invoices, and pay $10,000 instead of $40,000 on a cargo of the value of the last named sum. The duties on goods imported from foreign countries were very high, averaging about 100 per cent., as previously stated; so that a cargo of miscellaneous goods costing in Boston $50,000 would be subject to duties of about the same amount on entering at the custom house, making $100,000, to which must be added, as a legitimate part of the cost of the goods, various expenses, such as the cost of the voyage from Boston to this coast and back, including the stay of the vessel here and her sailing up and down the coast (about three years being consumed in the whole voyage from Boston out and return), the wear and tear of the vessel, the wages of the crew, the pay of the officers, the commission of the supercargo, the supplies of the ship in provisions, the cost of purchasing and collecting hides and tallow and preparing the hides for the return voyage, the long credit given to the rancheros and other purchasers of goods, besides the numberless other expenses, little and great, all immediately or remotely connected with the expedition; and also the interest on the capital invested; all together making the cost of the business very heavy.

These expenses were to be reimbursed from the profits arising from the exchange here, for hides, of the cargo from Boston and the sale of the hides there. In order to make this profitable the merchants found it necessary to evade the payment of duties to the Mexican government so far as practicable, and these duties were evaded to a very considerable extent, probably one-half.

Had the shipper been compelled, under a more stringent administration of the law, to pay the full amount of duties, he could not have made a fair profit out of the business. Moreover, he would have been compelled to charge so high a price for his goods that it would have been a severe tax upon the rancheros who required them.

It will be seen, therefore, that not only was the temptation to smuggle very great, under the facilities presented by a loose administration of the revenue laws, but there were excellent reasons why the payment of duties should be evaded. They operated to such an extent that the merchant did not feel under that moral restraint, especially in the absence of the oath, which under other circumstances he might have experienced. If he defrauded the government, he was helping the people.

It would not have been good policy to crowd or cripple the farmers by making them pay exorbitant prices for their goods. This would have reacted upon the merchants and been injurious to the department. To give a higher price for his goods, on account of the larger duties paid by the merchant, the farmer would have been compelled to slaughter a larger number of cattle to secure the requisite quantity of hides and tallow to pay for them, thereby subtracting so much more from his wealth and the wealth of the department. The merchants, therefore, not only benefited themselves by this evasion of the duties, but, to a greater or less extent, protected the farmer at the same time. Although I never knew an instance of the bribery of an official by a merchant, yet the officers of the revenue must have had in their own minds an idea that the customs laws were evaded.

The relations of the officials and the merchants were very pleasant. They associated together in the most friendly manner. The merchants always made it agreeable for the officials whenever they came aboard the vessels, treating them courteously and hospitably. The high rate of duties was sometimes alluded to, when the officers would smilingly say that they themselves considered the duties as very high. They would add that they presumed the government of Mexico knew what it was about when it fixed the rates. I have heard them admit that if the duties had been lower the government would probably have secured more revenue. Although I don't mean to intimate that they connived with the merchants knowingly to defraud the government, yet they certainly were not very sharpsighted or severe in the discharge of their vocation. However, had they been ever so vigilant and desirous of rigidly enforcing the laws, they were really powerless to do so efficiently, for they had no detectives, no revenue cutters—none of those numerous aids and facilities for detecting the offender against the laws which prevail in these latter days.

It was then considered as no disgrace for a merchant to evade the revenue laws to such an extent as he thought proper to take the risk; some doing so more than others; although it was never talked about among the merchants themselves, or made public in any way. There was a kind of tacit understanding that this was the general custom, and it was all right and proper to get as many goods in free of duty as possible, and it was encouraged by the rancheros themselves, as many were not solicitous of assisting the remote general government at Mexico by payment of exorbitant taxes in duties upon the necessaries of life required by them. Had the merchant been compelled to make oath, it would have been respected. The merchants, who were all foreigners, were an honorable and high-minded set of men, and would not have perjured themselves to evade the duties.

A large amount of goods could easily be concealed in the lining of a vessel, or a false lining be built, at no great expense around the sides of the ship, behind which they could be stowed away. There were numerous other hiding places which could be availed of. The captain, with the aid of the mates and the ship's carpenter, could make whatever arrangements or alterations were necessary to conceal successfully a large amount of goods. When the vessel reached the port of entry, the customs officers would go through the formality of making an examination of the ship; but they did it in quite a superficial way. They were so exceedingly well-mannered that they did not wish to appear impolite, and so they did not make any critical and offensive scrutiny of the arrangements and contents of the vessel.

Portions of the cargoes of vessels trading from South America and the Sandwich Islands were sometimes deposited upon the Islands off Santa Barbara, when the vessels approached the coast, before coming to the port of entry. I know of one instance in which about two-thirds of the cargo of a vessel from Honolulu was landed upon the Island of San Nicolas, about seventy miles south-east of Santa Barbara, after which the vessel entered at the custom house, paid the duties on the remainder of the cargo, and then returned to the Island and took in the portion she had left there. She then went on her way, trading about the coast as usual. Invoices also were arranged to suit the plans of the merchants. Goods were sometimes landed at night at Yerba Buena and other points outside of the port of entry, and at the port of entry itself, by eluding the officers, before entry was made. The rancheros, in a general way, would hint to the merchants that they ought to smuggle all the goods they could; they knowing they would get what they purchased cheaper than if all the duties were paid.

At Monterey we found the Baltimore bark "George Henry," Captain Stephen Smith, which had arrived a few days before from Callao, and had on board a steam saw-mill, the first ever brought to this coast. It was set in operation in the woods near Bodega for sawing lumber. Smith had visited California in 1841 and purchased of Captain Sutter all his title and interest in Bodega, and also bought, for work of the mill, the rancho Blucher, near Bodega, covered with timber, mostly redwood.

In a few weeks we came to Yerba Buena, (our vessel, after having made entry and paid duties at the custom house, being free to go anywhere on coast trade) and took on board in the daytime and openly what we had secretly landed on the night of the 20th of May, transporting small lots at a time. This created no suspicion, as Spear, having a large stock of goods on hand at his store, might be supposed to be shipping a quantity of them down the coast. We left again, and traded along the coast as far as San Diego. There a new firm was formed, that of Paty, McKinley & Co., for general trading purposes, consisting of Captain John Paty, of the "Don Quixote," James McKinley and Henry D. Fitch. The vessel went in as a part of the stock of the concern, being still under the command of Captain Paty. We then returned to Yerba Buena, after having touched at intermediate ports, and taking on at San Pedro some cargo belonging to McKinley & Fitch, which came into general stock. On reaching Yerba Buena, we landed about half the cargo of the vessel at Richardson's old adobe building, which stood where Dupont street is now, between Clay and Washington, and was then owned by McKinley, he having bought it of Richardson a few years previous. I then quit the vessel, Mr. McKinley taking my place as supercargo, while I remained at Yerba Buena with the goods, as commercial agent of the firm. I did a large business for them until September, 1845, the vessel meanwhile trading along the coast, visiting the bay of San Francisco three or four times during this period to supply me with stock from the stores on board.

CHAPTER XXIV
American Occupation of 1842

ONE of the most interesting events in the history of California was the first taking of Monterey by Commodore Jones, in 1842. The following account has been kindly offered for my use by Mr. S. S. Culverwell, who was a participant in that affair, and who now (1889) resides in San Francisco.

CULVERWELL'S STORY OF THE CAPTURE

About August, 1842, the American squadron, under Commodore A. Jones, was lying at Callao, Peru. I was on board the frigate "United States." The sloop of war "Cyane," Captain Stringham, was near by. Commodore Jones was on the "United States," also Captain Armstrong, First Lieutenant Lardner and Surgeon Maxwell, who recently died in San Francisco. There was also a British squadron in the harbor of Callao, of which I think the "Vanguard" was the admiral's ship. It was understood among the ship's company that we were to sail soon, as everything was in readiness for departure at short notice, but to what point we were destined nobody knew. It seemed to be the opinion, and was generally understood, that our sailing depended upon the movements of the British fleet, which was very closely watched by our vessels. One evening there was a ball given on the admiral's ship, at which the officers of our vessels were present, and on that occasion they learned that the English were to sail the next morning, but their destination was a secret. By this our own movements were guided; for early the next morning we were under way, bound for Monterey, California. During the whole passage, the ship's company was exercised in practicing the guns and apparently preparing for something extraordinary. It leaked out in a few days that the commodore's instructions were to keep watch of the British fleet, and, if anything should occur which looked suspicious, he was to get ahead, and take possession of Monterey.

When we reached the bay of Monterey, the "Cyane" and the "United States" came to anchor opposite the fort, and the same afternoon the commodore sent a message ashore to the alcalde or governor to surrender the place. The answer was returned that he was not in town. The ships' crews were at quarters on board all night. I was a boy of sixteen at that time—a powder boy, stationed in what was called the "slaughter house," just abreast of the main mast. I remember the remarks made by the old salts on the night we were lying there at our moorings, looking up at lights in the fort and seeing men with lanterns running around here and there. The sailors surmised that any moment the guns of the fort might open fire upon us, and if they had done so, the general impression was that they would have given us a pretty lively shaking up. The gunners on board our vessel said the first time their guns were let loose we would catch the whole of them just where we stood in the "slaughter house," and that one gun in the fort would do us more damage than our whole broadside of twenty-six guns could do them. The crews of both our vessels were at the guns all night to be ready for action, and our officers were watching intently the movements at the castle or fort. If any demonstration had been made, both ships would have opened fire immediately. The night passed off quietly however.

The next morning at nine o'clock, the officers, marines and sailors were landed, and marching up to the fort, took possession of it, hoisted the American flag, and, to my recollection, retained possession about twenty-four hours. But there seemed to have been a mistake as to the intention of the English, for the fleet did not make its appearance at Monterey.

We gave the place up, and returned to Callao; there learned that Commodore Jones had been ordered home, and that Commodore Dallas was on his way out to relieve him. (This was only hearsay.) Our cruise of three years not being more than half finished, Commodore Jones wished to complete it and go home on his ship, and so kept out of the way of Dallas. We left Callao and sailed for the Sandwich Islands. After our visit there, we went to all the groups of islands in the Pacific Ocean. When the time of the cruise was up, we went to Valparaiso. Meanwhile, after we left Callao, Commodore Dallas, on board the United States frigate "Congress," followed us around from one place to another, but not overtaking us; for he would arrive at a place just after we had left; and so, by dodging the "Congress" in this way, Commodore Jones completed his cruise and took the "old wagon," as the frigate "United States" was called, around to the Atlantic side, home.

I understand that an official investigation of the commodore's action at Monterey took place, which resulted in exonerating Commodore Jones from blame for his action in the matter, and that he was presented with a gold-hilted sword for the vigilance which he had displayed in this affair.

Mr. Culverwell's contribution is made use of, it being an accurate statement, by an eye-witness, of the events detailed.

While I was at Santa Barbara with the "Don Quixote" about the latter part of September, 1842, the "Jóven Guipuzcoana," Captain Snook, was there also. He departed a few days before we did and proceeded up the coast to Monterey, trading along as usual. His vessel left the port of Monterey sometime in October. As she was beating out of that bay they saw two war vessels approaching from the south, and according to the usual custom raised the Mexican flag, she being a Mexican bark; and the two vessels approaching raised the English flag. When they got pretty near, a shot was fired from one of them across the bow of the "Jóven Guipuzcoana" for that vessel to stop, which demand she complied with. Shortly after, she was hailed with an order to throw her foreyards back, which she did, and waited quietly not knowing what was the matter, until a boat put off from one of the other vessels and came alongside. The boat contained a lieutenant, midshipman, the ordinary boat's crew, and eight or ten men besides. When they came aboard his vessel Captain Snook observed that the officers wore the uniform of the United States navy, which puzzled him a good deal; the vessels bore the English flag. They asked him to surrender the vessel to them, which he immediately did. They remained on board, and the three vessels came to anchor in the bay of Monterey, just under the bluff where the fort or castle stood, and then the English flag was hauled down on the two vessels of war and the American flag raised instead. These vessels were the United States frigate "United States" and the sloop-of-war "Cyane."

When the "Jóven Guipuzcoana" left Santa Barbara, Don José Joaquin Estudillo was on board, with his daughter, whom he had left with her aunt when quite young at San Diego, where she had since lived. He had not seen her for ten years, and was now taking her to their home at San Leandro. When the vessel was captured as above described, in going out of Monterey, this young lady and also Mrs. Snook, the captain's wife, became prisoners of war. I learned from the former, who afterward became my wife, the facts in regard to what transpired on the vessel. The two ladies being in their state-rooms unaware of what had transpired, Captain Snook went to his wife's room and told her that they were prisoners; whereupon that lady hastened to Miss Estudillo's room and informed her, in tears, that they had been captured. The officer in command told Captain Snook that his presence was required on board the frigate "United States," and that his orders from the commodore were that no one should go ashore; that all on board were prisoners of war, ladies included. Captain Snook then had an interview with the commodore, and coming aboard his own vessel, he found his wife very much agitated and frightened. She presently prevailed upon the captain to return and request permission of the commodore for herself and Miss Estudillo to be put ashore. The request was granted, and the next morning early the two ladies were landed. During the night Captain Snook had the oars of the boats muffled, and quietly landed nearly the whole cargo of the vessel, in order to save it for the owner, unknown, of course, to the American vessels of war. Early in the morning an officer from the "United States" came on board and took an inventory of what remained of the cargo, which was very little.

Soon after the vessels had anchored at Monterey, Commodore Jones sent an officer on shore to demand the surrender of the town. The authorities at Monterey had noticed the two vessels coming in under the English flag, which was presently replaced by the American, and also the return of the "Jóven Guipuzcoana" with them, and their suspicions were aroused. They supposed that war had been declared between the United States and Mexico, and thought the vessels had probably come to take the town. Upon this, Governor Alvarado left Monterey for his rancho Alisal, twenty-six miles distant, accompanied by a body-guard of forty cavalrymen, not wishing to incur the humiliation of surrendering the town himself. In leaving, he instructed the comandante, Captain Mariano Silva, that if the surrender of the town was demanded to comply with the request, inasmuch as they had not force enough to resist successfully. When the officer who went on shore to demand the surrender found that the governor was not there, he was met by the comandante, to whom he delivered the message, and who complied. It was stipulated between them, as it was late in the day, the formal surrender should take place the next morning at nine o'clock. The following morning the officers, marines and sailors were landed in large force and proceeded, a portion to the fort, and a portion to government headquarters. As they marched up from the landing, through the town, they made quite a display, with the American flag flying and the band playing the national air. The native Californians resident in the town were horror-stricken, especially the officials and the women, the latter going about the streets or looking from their windows with their hair hanging loosely about them and tears streaming from their eyes, bewailing the loss of their country, the humiliation of their flag, and fearing that their lives and property might also be sacrificed. T. O. Larkin, later United States consul, with David Spence and other prominent foreigners, sought to pacify them assuring them that if the country was lost to them forever, they should be protected.

Commodore Jones' force marched through the streets, and a manifesto was read at intervals declaring that as war existed between the United States and Mexico, he, as commander of all the American forces on the Pacific and representing the government of the United States in that quarter, had been ordered to take possession of the department of California; and in doing so, his purpose was not to injure the peaceable inhabitants of the department; that he would give them every assurance that they should be protected in their lives and property; and moreover, the laws of Mexico, under which they had lived, should continue in force; and those officials who might wish to continue in their positions and administer the laws honestly and justly, were at liberty to do so. On reaching the government headquarters the formal surrender took place, and the United States flag was raised.

Thomas Oliver Larkin and other prominent Americans at Monterey had received from Mexico newspapers and letters giving much later intelligence than Commodore Jones had received at Callao before his departure from that port, which showed that up to the time of their issue no war existed between the two countries.

After the town had been taken possession of, Commodore Jones examined these letters and papers giving the latest intelligence, and, on doing so, became convinced that war had not been declared, and saw that his action in the premises had been, to say the least, premature. Accordingly, he determined to surrender the place to the authorities of the department and leave them in possession, as before. He therefore sent an officer to the comandante, Don Mariano Silva, to say he was satisfied from the facts he had collected from Thomas O. Larkin and other American residents at Monterey that he ought to surrender the place to the Mexican authorities, and would formally do so on the following day at a certain hour. The next morning the troops were drawn up in front of the government headquarters and at the fort. At a signal, the American flag was hauled down and the Mexican flag raised at both points. A salute was then fired from the two vessels in honor of the Mexican flag, and this was responded to by a salute from the fort. All the courtesies due from one nation to another were shown; and the town of Monterey was fully restored to the possession and power of its former possessors, twenty-four hours after it was taken from them. The commodore and officers, some twelve or fifteen, in full uniform, then called on the government officers, to pay their respects; and the war was at an end. In return, the officials called on the commodore and his officers on the flag-ship, and were warmly welcomed, entertained, and honored with a salute befitting their rank. The Mexican bark was also released and permitted to go on her business unmolested.

About four or five days after these exciting events I reached Monterey on the "Don Quixote." Shortly after, Captain Paty and myself called on Commodore Jones on board his vessel, and were immediately made to feel at ease in his company. He impressed us as a man of decided ability, and withal social and genial. We listened with great interest and admiration to his account of his movements at Monterey and his reasons therefor, which he gave us in full. He said he had been instructed by the government to keep a close watch upon the movements of the British squadron in the Pacific, and on learning at Callao that their vessels were about to leave, though he did not know for what destination, thinking the objective point might be Monterey, he started a little in advance. He reached that place without seeing them. Believing that the war which seemed imminent between the United States and Mexico had already commenced, he took possession of the place, being determined to anticipate the British in case they had any design of doing the same thing.

As he proceeded in his narrative, he warmed up with enthusiasm, and declared what he had done was in perfect good faith. Although he had no positive instructions to take Monterey, what he had done was in accordance with the general instructions of the government not to be outdone by the British. Straightening himself up, as he went on in his narrative, he said: "Although I was doubtless hasty in my action, it was better to be a little too soon than an hour too late. The delay might have been fatal. I felt the immense responsibility resting upon me. Had I arrived here and found the British flag floating over Monterey, it would have been no easy thing to displace it. In fact, to attempt to do so would have been equivalent to a declaration of war between the United States and Great Britain, and had I allowed the British to get the advantage of me in securing Monterey, I would have been disgraced forever." He said that when he came to anchor before Monterey he had springs placed upon the cable, so as to move the vessel round in case of necessity, but he was very happy that there had been no occasion to fire upon the town; although, he added, that if any demonstration of hostility or show of resistance had been made, he would have met it promptly, first notifying the proper authorities to have the women and children removed, as he did not want to shed a drop of their blood, and then, if necessary, he would have opened upon the fort and battered it to pieces.

The commodore went on to say that he was very favorably impressed with California; that this was his first visit, but he was familiar with it from reading and other information he had gathered about it; that he liked the climate and the appearance of the country, and that it was destined to be of great importance, and that it must belong to the United States. He dwelt at length upon the importance of our government getting possession of it, and not letting the British do so in advance of us. He said there was no other nation to fear in this connection, and that he and all his predecessors here had been charged to be always on the watch for the British fleet in these waters, and that doubtless his successors would be likewise instructed.

The commodore in his conversation with us expressed a considerable degree of pride at having been the first to raise the American flag on the soil of California, and seemed to regard this movement, although so briefly terminated, as having given us the first right in the future, and to have established a priority of claim on the part of the United States to the possession of the country when it should pass from the control of Mexico.

[TEXT OF LETTERS ON OPPOSITE PAGE]

Yerba Buena Oct. 9th 1846

Dear Sir:

You are hereby authorized to purchase for me a tract of land at least one mile square beginning at low water mark on the south side of the strates of Carquinas six hundred feet West of the mouth of a small creek which emties near the narrowest part of the strates thence Eastward with the strates, South, West and Northward for quantity the said land at present belonging to Don Ygnacio Martinez.

You are authorized to make the above purchase on the best terms you can obtain but not to exceed five hundred dollars and draw on me for the money at this place.

By so doing you will oblige
Your most ob't serv't.
R. Semple

Mr. Wm. H. Davis,
Yerba Buena.

Monterey March 11 1847

Mr. William H. Davis
Dear Sir

during your stay here I endeavoured to speak with you on the importance of keeping to yourself the information you gave me respecting another Persons having a deed for the land we spoke of but I always forgot it when you was in the house. I now write to you on the subject.

I understand that some Brickmakers are about working on my land. I wish Mr Sherman to have them enter into contract with him paying me as near five per cent as he can obtain for the clay firewood and other privileges. This is of importance to me. Write me soon.

I am in haste
yrs
Thomas O. Larkin

Send me
black stock

CONTEMPORARY LETTERS FROM R. SEMPLE AND THOMAS O. LARKIN TO DAVIS

These hitherto unpublished documents reveal the prominent position William Heath Davis held among the leading American actors in the California drama of 1846–47. It will be noted that only the beginning and the end of the Larkin letter is reproduced.

CHAPTER XXV
A Lot About Thomas Ap Catesby Jones, U. S. N.

WE remained in the harbor of Monterey with the "Don Quixote" about a week, and made frequent visits to the flag-ship, and had many pleasant interviews with the commodore and his officers. It was years since I had heard any good music, and we enjoyed hearing the fine band play at sunset on the quarter-deck of the frigate. Captain Paty and myself sent a little present of fine California wine to the commodore and Captain Armstrong, which we had procured from the vineyard of Don Luis Vignes at Los Angeles. It was highly appreciated by the recipients.

While we were at Monterey, an elegant entertainment was given by Thomas Oliver Larkin and other American residents, at the government house, to the commodore and the officers of the vessels. Captain Paty and myself were among the guests. The music, dancing and feasting lasted till a late hour. The commodore had sent messages to Governor Alvarado at his rancho to come in and see him; that he was a gentleman whose acquaintance he was desirous of making; that he would be most happy to entertain him aboard his vessel. Alvarado replied courteously, declining the invitation, saying that while he was still governor of California, he might, by such a visit, in some way compromise himself, or the commodore in his subsequent intercourse with Micheltorena, the newly appointed governor, who was at Los Angeles on his way to the seat of government; and said that he referred all matters concerning the recent taking of Monterey to him.

Commodore Jones was much respected by his officers and also very popular with them. During my visits to the vessel, I got the impression from what I heard that Commodore Jones was especially selected for service in the Pacific Ocean to watch and counteract any movements that might be made toward the acquirement of California by any government, other than our own; not only because of his superiority as a naval commander, but on account of his intelligence, sagacity, diplomatic talent and courage; these qualities rendering him peculiarly fitted for an undertaking requiring delicacy and tact in its management.

Had Alvarado known of the coming of Jones beforehand, he would have made preparations to defend Monterey and sink some or all of the fleet, by firing from the castle; as was done on a former occasion, in 1818, when two insurgent vessels, manned by Spaniards from South America, without any government authority came into the harbor of Monterey with the intention of capturing the town; and one of them, the "Negra," was sunk by guns fired from the fort. As she was going down, those on board made signs and shouted to those on shore to have mercy on them, and stop firing. Captain Gomez, commanding the artillery, ordered the firing to cease. The men from the sinking vessel, and those from the other one also, then all came ashore in their boats; and instead of being grateful for the kindness shown them in sparing their lives, they marched up with their arms, overpowered the governor and his forces and took possession of the town. The governor, Don Pablo Vicente de Sola, with the other officers of the government and the garrison and the families living in that vicinity, had to take flight into the country. The enemy burned the town and the garrison buildings, and then went away.

We departed from Monterey in the "Don Quixote," leaving the two United States vessels, and proceeded to Yerba Buena. During the stay of the "Don Quixote," lasting several weeks, Commodore Jones arrived in the sloop-of-war "Cyane," which was made flag-ship before leaving Monterey, the frigate "United States" having been sent to Honolulu for naval stores, that place being the depot for provisions, etc., of the Pacific squadron. She made the trip from Monterey to Honolulu and back in twenty-nine days, the quickest ever known at that time, and I don't think it has been beaten since by any sailing vessel. This included four days stopping at Honolulu to take in stores. Captain Eliab Grimes was on board of her on her voyage out from Monterey as the guest of Captain Armstrong. She made the run to Honolulu in ten days. Captain Grimes said she might have performed it in eight days, but it was always their habit to shorten sail at evening and proceed under less canvas during the night. He tried to persuade them to keep on full sail during the night, as well as the day, but Captain Armstrong could not be induced to alter the custom; so the voyage was longer than it otherwise need have been.

The "Cyane" lay at Saucelito during her stay here, and the commodore visited Yerba Buena. I was very busy arranging for my business and saw but little of him at that time. Spear saw him frequently, and both he and Richardson spoke in high terms of the commodore as a well-informed man.

In January, 1843, Don José Joaquin Estudillo, accompanied by his wife and his daughters, Doña Concepcion and Doña Maria Jesus (the latter of whom a few months before had been captured at Monterey by Commodore Jones, as already described), visited Captain Richardson's family at Saucelito, Mrs. Richardson and Mrs. Estudillo being sisters. During this visit Captain Richardson and his wife and daughter and the Estudillo family were invited by Commodore Jones to a little party on board the "Cyane." As they passed over the gangway of the vessel the commodore and his officers stood there to receive them, and showed the greatest warmth and courtesy toward them. Captain Richardson introduced Don José as the father of the young lady who a few months before had been captured by the commodore at Monterey. "What!" exclaimed the commodore; "is this the father of the fair captive who, under the rules of war, I was compelled to make prisoner for a time?" and at the same moment took Estudillo warmly by his hand, threw his arms around him and embraced him heartily, as was the fashion of the Californians. After all the introductions were made and affable greetings extended, the commodore showed the highest gallantry by remarking that the only thing he regretted was having to surrender Monterey after having taken it. They had a delightful entertainment, dancing until late in the evening, the ladies above mentioned being present.

On this occasion the commodore showed great attention and politeness to Don José, and was exceedingly affable to the ladies, doing everything in his power to make their visit agreeable, and setting before them a very handsome dinner. During the dinner the commodore carved with difficulty, one of his hands being distorted from a wound received during an engagement between the vessel on which he was a midshipman and a vessel of the enemy, during the war of 1812 with England. He excused himself for his want of skill in carving, explaining the cause of the difficulty. A number of the officers on board the "Cyane" spoke the Spanish language fluently, which added to the interest of the festivity.

During the stay of the vessel in the bay the commodore's habit was to go on shore in the morning and hunt for small game, sport he greatly enjoyed. He would frequently lunch with Captain Richardson on shore, and there he met the Estudillo family. The "Cyane" left here and went down to Monterey about the time the "United States" was expected back. On the arrival there of the latter vessel she was made the flag-ship again, and both ships left for San Pedro.

CHAPTER XXVI
Something Concerning Don Luis Vignes

COMMODORE JONES called on Micheltorena at Los Angeles, with his suite of officers, in full uniform, and the commodore and the new governor had a long conference in regard to the taking of Monterey, lasting several days. The explanations of the former were politely received by the latter and a cordial understanding arrived at between the two.

During his stay there a banquet was given to Commodore Jones and his officers by Micheltorena, winding up with a grand ball. Mr. Henry Mellus was present, and has informed me it was a brilliant affair. All the wealth and beauty of Los Angeles and surrounding country were present. The commodore and his officers expressed themselves as highly delighted. They also spoke flatteringly of Los Angeles and its neighborhood, calling it the Eden of the earth. They were charmed with the vineyards and orchards, with the orange groves, seeing the golden fruit hanging on the trees in the month of January. The most extensive cultivator at that time (1843) was Louis Vignes, who invited them to his place and entertained them. They were delighted with his California wines, of different vintages, some as much as eight or ten years old, of fine quality. They were interested in going through his cellars, where the wines of different years were stored in large quantities in pipes. Vignes presented the commodore and the officers with several barrels of this choice wine, which were gratefully accepted. He remarked that he desired them to preserve some of it to take to Washington to give to the President of the United States, that he might know what excellent wine was produced in California.

Don Luis, as the Californians called him, was a Frenchman, who came to Monterey in the bark "Louisa" with me in 1831 from Boston, touching at Honolulu and Sitka. From Monterey he went to San Pedro, shortly afterward established himself at Los Angeles, and before long had the largest vineyard in California. At that early day he imported cuttings of different varieties of grapes, in small quantities, which were put up with great care and sent from France to Boston; thence they came out in the vessels trading on this coast, to be experimented with in wine producing. He took great pride in the business. I regard him as the pioneer not only in wine making, but in the orange cultivation, he being the first man to raise oranges in Los Angeles and the first to establish a vineyard of any pretension. In 1833 I called to see him at his house and found him well established. My old friend was overjoyed to see me and received me most hospitably; I remained two or three days with him. I was a boy at that time, and he said to me most warmly, "William, I only regret that I am not of your age. With my knowledge of vine and orange cultivation and of the soil and climate of California, I forsee that these two are to have a great future; this is just the place to grow them to perfection." He was then about fifty years old, full of zeal and enterprise. He was one of the most valuable men who ever came to California, and the father of the wine industry here. He had an intelligent appreciation of the extent and importance of this interest in the future.

In 1842, nine years afterward, I again called to see him. He asked me if I remembered what he had said to me when I was last there, about the California wine, its importance and value, and remarked that he would now prove to me that his predictions were correct, and would show me what he could do for California. He then took me and a friend who was with me into his cellar and showed us the different vintages stored there, and brought out several bottles of his old wine, which were tested and commended. He said he had written home to France representing the advantages of California for wine making, telling them that he believed the day would come when California would rival "la belle France" in wine producing of all varieties, not only in quantity, but in quality, not even excepting champagne; and that he had also induced several of his relations and a number of his more intelligent countrymen to come to California to settle near Los Angeles, and engage in the business. He also manufactured aguardiente in considerable quantities, as did other wine producers. This liquor was considered by the old settlers as a superior article when three or four years old. Beyond that, it still further improved in quality, being of a finer flavor, entirely pure, and was regarded as a wholesome drink. It was made from the old Mission grapes. When first produced it was clear and colorless, like gin or alcohol, but gradually assumed a slight tint with age, and when six, eight or ten years old, became of fine amber color, and was then a rich, oily liquor, very palatable.

The merchants bought the aguardiente and also the wines, in considerable lots, directly from the vineyards, and sold it to their customers at Monterey, Yerba Buena, and other points along the coast. At that time I was familiar with wines of different kinds, and was regarded as an expert in determining their quality and value, and I considered the aguardiente as vastly superior to the brandy made in those days. Some of it is probably still kept at Los Angeles.

Don Luis was truly one of the most enlightened pioneers of the coast. In May, 1852, I saw him again for the last time, visiting him at his home, accompanied by John H. Saunders, who recently died at San Rafael. Vignes was then quite old, but his intellect was unimpaired. The Don was full of history of wine matters, and kept up a constant stream of conversation, proud of his success, and overflowing with brilliant anticipations of the future of this interest in which he was so wrapped up, as bearing upon the prosperity of the state and its commercial importance. His vineyard was entered by an immense gate, just outside of which there was a splendid sycamore tree of great age. From this circumstance Vignes was known as Don Luis del Aliso, *aliso* being the Spanish word for sycamore. He greatly admired the huge tree and was proud of it and of being called by that name, by which he was more familiarly known. His choice old wine could be drunk with impunity. It had an agreeable, exhilarating and strengthening effect, but no unpleasant after-consequences. He was known by everybody in the vicinity of Los Angeles, and appreciated. He was generous to the poor; in their distress he helped them in bread, money and wine. When they came to him he advised ths mothers of young children to give them a little wine as an internal antiseptic, so that they might grow up strong, as in his own country; or on the same principle, perhaps, that doctors prescribe whisky and milk, as a cure for diphtheria.

I am sure that all of the residents of California who were living here at the time of Don Luis will endorse what I have said in regard to him and his influence upon the prosperity of the country. It is to be hoped that historians will do justice to his character, his labors and foresight.

CHAPTER XXVII
Early American Settlers in California

SOME of the foreigners at Santa Barbara dated their residence at that place back to 1830 and 1831. Among them were William G. Dana, a nephew of my father; Daniel Hill, Francis Branch and A. B. Thompson, who were all natives of Massachusetts. They were engaged in merchandising and stock-raising. Isaac Sparks and George Nidever were natives of Kentucky, and otter-hunters by profession. Lewis T. Burton was also an otter-hunter, who left an only son a considerable fortune in land. Michael Burke was a native of Ireland, and Robert Elwell was a native of Boston. The latter was a comical character, with a peculiar sharp countenance, a prominent nose, and a queer look. He had considerable native wit, and made fun for others. He himself was made fun of by the captains, supercargoes and merchants who came to the place; and was altogether of use as a clown. He married a daughter of Don Juan Sanchez, a prominent ranchero.

After 1833, Dr. Nicholas A. Den, a native of Ireland, came to Santa Barbara and practiced his profession there. He married a daughter of Daniel Hill, who had married into the Ortega family. Dr. Den was as homely a man as I ever saw. His wife, still living, (1887) preserves her beauty. Her hair was remarkable in its color of *melchocha,* or pulled candy made from molasses. It was very luxuriant, falling profusely over her shoulders nearly to her feet. Dr. Den was an intelligent, educated and accomplished gentleman, and much liked. He has a brother, a physician, now (1889) living at Los Angeles, and commonly known in Southern California as Don Ricardo, a man of learning, and universally respected.

At Santa Barbara also was Captain Thomas W. Robbins, formerly a shipmaster, a Boston man, married to a daughter of Don Carlos Carrillo. When I was there in 1842 he kept a store of general merchandise, and which was a kind of headquarters for the captains and supercargoes of vessels lying in port. He was generous and liked by everybody. At his table, as well as at Mrs. Wilson's, the captains and supercargoes of vessels were always welcome.

Captain Paty and myself were dining with him in 1842, and he told us of an old Indian cook who had been with him many years, and had been carefully instructed, as indeed, his good dinners testified. He said that although the man was faithful and quiet, and attended well to his duties, he was obliged about every six months to give him a tremendous whipping; only because at those times the Indian came and begged his master to give him a good thrashing, saying it was necessary, to make him a good cook for the next six months. Robbins felt forced to comply, much against his will, for he was a kind-hearted man and treated his servants well; but the Indian assured him it must be done, otherwise he would become lazy and negligent.

Captain Robbins had before mentioned this several times, and on this occasion, in order to fortify his statement, while we were busy with our dinner and talking and laughing with the wife of our host and their beautiful children, he whispered to a servant in the dining-room to call the old Indian. Presently, in he came, a stalwart man, weighing probably 200 pounds, strong and well preserved, with rather a pleasing cast of countenance, and polite in his manners, the result of his good training in the family. Captain Robbins addressed him in Spanish, saying, "I have said to my guests that I have had to whip you soundly, against my will, about once in six months, because you desired it and persisted in having it done, to make you a good cook for the next half year. Is it so?" The old Indian looked sharply at Captain Paty and myself and answered, *"Es verdad, señores."* ("It is true, sir.") A roar of laughter followed from all present, as the cook retreated to the kitchen, laughing heartily himself.

In my father-in-law's family at San Leandro there was an Indian by the name of Juan José, now (1887) seventy years of age, well preserved and strong, who was taken when a child, reared and always retained by them. He was usually obedient and tractable, but occasionally would become lazy and insolent, when it was found necessary to give him a good whipping; which was done (not by his own request, however); whereupon he became civil and obedient and attended faithfully to his duties. The effect of this management has always been apparent; goodness, as it were, being whipped into him.

I knew Don Teodoro Arrellanes in Santa Barbara. He was a thorough ranchero. He was then perhaps fifty-five years of age, six feet in height, very straight, weighing 220 pounds; was genial and polite; had a numerous family, and owned extensive tracts of land, comprising many leagues; among them the Rancho Guadalupe, near Santa Maria, with as many as

20,000 cattle and thousands of horses. Among the rancheros he was looked upon as a kind of chief in that portion of country, by reason of his good judgment and knowledge of matters pertaining to ranchos. On one occasion I said to him: "Don Teodoro, how is it you have accumulated so much wealth—such an immense number of cattle and horses?" He smilingly answered: "The labor is to get the first 2000, and after that they increase very fast, under ordinary care and management. They require a great deal of care and thought, to make the best rodeo cattle and to prevent them from running entirely wild, and to make the horses useful for their purpose." Sometimes cattle escaped from the ranchos to the mountains, forgot their former training, and become entirely wild; when vaqueros would go out into the mountains, lasso them, and bring them, tied to the *cabestros,* to be slaughtered or tamed.

John J. Warner, a native of Connecticut, came to California in 1831. He owned the Rancho Agua Caliente in San Diego county, containing eleven leagues. He resided there and also at Los Angeles; was somewhat a literary man, and he spoke Spanish fluently. He has represented Los Angeles and San Diego counties in the State Legislature. The Californians valued his friendship, and also his good counsel whenever they were in need of advice.

The intermarriage of the foreigners in early times with the Californians produced a fine race of children, who partook of the characteristics of both parents. The stock, as usual, was improved by the mingling of the different nationalities.

CHAPTER XXVIII
Alvarado Ousts Governor Micheltorena

THE revolution against Micheltorena by Alvarado and Castro, in 1844, was not on account of bad government or misrule by Micheltorena, or from a dislike of him by the responsible men of the country. The wealthy ranch-owners and others were not in favor of revolution. They desired peace, naturally, as they had everything to lose by conflict and nothing to gain. It originated as much from the restless nature of Alvarado and his ambition to rule, as anything else. Having when young been connected with public affairs, and afterward governor of the department, he could not rest quietly and see the government administered by anybody else.

General Castro, who had been displaced when Micheltorena came into power, was ambitious, and naturally joined with Alvarado; and the two, having been intimately connected for a long time, stirred up the people to revolution. There was also a good deal of feeling by many against the troops who came into the country with Micheltorena, especially by the residents of Monterey, where the troops were quartered; they alleging that the soldiers stole their chickens and committed other small depredations. They might have done something worse, though there is no evidence of it.

Alvarado and Castro collected several hundred men about the bay of San Francisco and got them together on the Salinas plains, mounted, and armed with all kinds of weapons such as they could pick up, most of their arms being of no great efficiency. They had also a few old cannons. At this place they were met by Micheltorena and his force from Monterey, and a skirmish ensued. The insurgents retreated to the Laguna San Antonio, followed by Micheltorena. They remained there several days, during which some firing and maneuvering took place; but nobody was killed.

From that point, Alvarado and Castro with their troops retreated, and commenced a march south for the purpose of visiting the different ranchos, creating sympathy for their cause and obtaining recruits, horses and provisions.

Alvarado had great power of speech and argument. He was eloquent in behalf of his movement, and though the people generally disliked it, he induced some of the rancheros to join him. Many of the younger men were taken against their will as recruits for his army. He also secured a large number of horses, some of which were given to him voluntarily, and others were taken by force.

I was at that time in Los Angeles. It was known by the people there that a revolution prevailed at the north. But the soldiers at the barracks and the rancheros were loyal to the government. Alvarado knowing this, prevented any information going ahead of him to notify the military of his coming. He reached the neighborhood of Los Angeles and went into the town quietly before daylight, and surprised the soldiers at quarters. Some resistance was made, two of the defenders being killed. The garrison was overpowered and obliged to yield the post, and a guard was placed over the captives. Alvarado took possession of the plaza, where the barracks were located, and also of the government offices, including those of the alcalde and prefect. The officers who resisted were made prisoners. He then set his wits to work to bring the people under his influence, and immediately had a conference with Don Pio Pico, a very wealthy ranchero in that place, a man of large influence, brother of Don Andres Pico, also wealthy, popular and influential; the two owning sixty or seventy leagues of land in what are now Los Angeles and San Diego counties. This interview was followed by several others. Alvarado used his great powers of persuasion with Don Pio to induce him to join his cause and pursuade the people of the surrounding neighborhood to come into the movement, and contribute hundreds of their fine horses to the army. Among other inducements by him, he promised Pio Pico the governorship of the department, if Micheltorena should be deposed. Being at that time president of the junta departmental, he was assured the place was lawfully his; and he was finally so influenced that he promised to aid Alvarado to the extent of his power. Don Andres Pico was also prevailed upon to join the movement. Through the activity and great influence of the Pico brothers, several hundred new recruits were collected, and added to Alvarado's army. Hundeds and hundreds of the finest of saddle horses were contributed also. I saw *caponera* after *caponera*, day after day, brought to the military headquarters, at the town plaza, from the neighboring ranchos. Alvarado and Castro were busy in receiving recruits, distributing them and the horses to the different commands, and reorganizing the forces for the battle which was expected to take place. The work continued actively for several weeks. At that time military affairs took precedence of everything else in Los Angeles.

Ever since the conflict between Carrillo and Alvarado in 1838, and even prior to that time, there had existed a jealousy between the two sections of the country north and south, the northern portion of the people, say from San Luis Obispo north, being the Alvarado party; and the southern portion, from Santa Barbara south, the Carrillo and Pico party. The leaders in the north were Alvarado and General José Castro, but the master spirit was Alvarado. In the south the leaders were Don José Antonio Carrillo and his brother Don Carlos, and the brothers Pico.

In this outbreak, General Vallejo was considered non-committal, not taking active part, preferring to attend to his own affairs. Alvarado, thus engaged, feared the influence of José Antonio Carrillo. After he had won over the Pico brothers, he approached him in the same way he had approached them, but found in him, as he had anticipated, more confirmed and strenuous opposition to his plans. Carrillo was superior to the Pico brothers in intellect, but Alvarado was superior to them all. He finally prevailed upon Don José Antonio to give him some assistance. José Antonio's ambition originally, in the revolution of 1838, was to make his brother Don Carlos governor; to prove to Alvarado and to his countrymen, as I frequently heard him say, that he himself was the brains of the department.

After the skirmish near Salinas, Micheltorena was joined by Captain Sutter, with fifty or sixty riflemen, from the Sacramento valley, among them Dr. John Marsh, one of the first comers, P. B. Reading, and other early settlers, who probably had no particular preference one side or the other in the revolution. Their aim and desire was to secure large grants of land, in addition to what they already possessed, and which they would have undoubtedly obtained as a reward for military services in defending the country had Micheltorena remained in power. Sutter kept also in the Sacramento valley 300 Indian riflemen, whom he had trained as soldiers, for his own defense.

Micheltorena followed Alvarado southward; but as the main portion of his troops was infantry, and his cannons had to be transported, his progress was necessarily slow. When Alvarado and his force left Los Angeles to meet Micheltorena, several of the American residents and other foreigners who had joined his army accompanied him; among them Alexander Bell, a leading merchant. He requested me to take charge of his store during his absence, and in case he should meet the fate of a soldier I should turn everything over to his widow. In leaving, he gave me the key of his safe, and said it contained considerable money. In those days there were no banks. Every merchant was his own banker. Bell was considered as always having a good supply of money on hand, and I felt a little nervous the first night; as there were a good many doubtful characters about Los Angeles, I feared that some of them might break in, and take possession of the funds. I was not disturbed however. Perhaps Alvarado had taken all this class along with him as part of his army.

In January, 1845, the two armies came together in the valley of San Fernando, one of the most beautiful portions of Los Angeles county. Alvarado had seven or eight hundred men, well mounted but poorly armed. About nine o'clock one clear morning, a day or two after the departure of the troops, the first cannonading was heard in Los Angeles, and we knew that the battle had commenced. Directly to the north was a high hill. As soon as the firing was heard, all the people remaining in the town— men, women and children, ran to the top of this hill. As the wind was blowing from the north, the firing was distinctly heard, five leagues away on the battlefield, throughout the day. All the business places in town were closed.

The scene upon the hill was a remarkable one. Women and children with crosses in their hands, kneeling and praying to the Saints for the safety and protection of their fathers, brothers, sons, husbands, lovers, cousins—that they might not be killed in the battle; indifferent to their personal appearance, tears streaming from their eyes, and their hair blown about by the wind, which had increased to quite a breeze. Don Abel Stearns, myself and others tried to calm and pacify them, assuring them that there was probably no danger; somewhat against our convictions, it is true, judging from what we heard of the firing and from our knowledge of Micheltorena's disciplined force, his battery, and the riflemen he had with him. During the day the scene on the hill continued. The night that followed was a gloomy one, caused by the lamentations of the women and children.

It afterward proved that our assurances to the women were correct; for not a single person was killed in this remarkable battle, only a few horses being shot. The next day the strife ended; Micheltorena capitulated, and agreed to leave the country with his troops, arms and followers.

CHAPTER XXIX
More About the Revolution

ON THE day following the grand battle in San Fernando valley many of the prominent men from both armies arrived at Los Angeles, among them Captain Sutter, Dr. Marsh, Bidwell, Bell and others. Sutter and some of his friends came first to the headquarters of Don Abel Stearns, who received them kindly. They were so thickly covered with dust that one could hardly recognize them. I was glad to meet my old friend Captain Sutter, whom I had not seen for several years. That night he was the guest of Charles W. Flügge, a conspicuous German merchant of Los Angeles, who had lived at fort New Helvetia, and been connected with Sutter in business. I spent the evening there very pleasantly, talking over old times with Captain Sutter, and sipping some fine California wine of Don Luis del Aliso's vintage till a late hour in the night.

James McKinley was present at the battle as a spectator, not taking an active part. Towards the close of the day he volunteered to Alvarado and Castro to act as mediator between them and Micheltorena and endeavor to bring about an agreement of the two armies. He was encouraged to do so; and upon his representations the conflict was terminated.

During the settlement of the terms, before the capitulation, the insurgent Californians urged upon Micheltorena, as one of the conditions, that General Vallejo should be deposed as commander-in-chief, and General Castro appointed in his place. This was agreed to; and from that time General Castro occupied that position.

The capitulation of Micheltorena was not compulsory, inasmuch as his force of skilled and disciplined soldiers, and their arms, equipments of every kind, and supply of ammunition, were altogether superior to those of Alvarado; but it was the result wholly of Micheltorena's good feeling toward the people of California, and which led him to refrain from injuring them, as he might easily have done, and to a serious extent. From my knowledge of him and my personal acquaintance with him, I regarded him as a humane man. The forbearance he showed on this occasion in the face of great provocation, proves this to have been the case. He was not only a military man, but a statesman, and took a broad and comprehensive view of the whole matter. Captain Sutter, during the evening, in giving me an account of the day's battle, said that Micheltorena had ordered his command not to injure the Californians in the force opposed to him, but to fire over their heads, as he had no desire to kill them. This order was given to the other captains also. Sutter's men being sharpshooters and skillful in the use of their rifles, might have done terrible execution, had they not been directed to the contrary. Moreover, the Americans who accompanied Sutter had lived for many years among the Californians; some had intermarried with them; had become identified with them, and the natural sympathies of these men were, of course, not against them.

Had Micheltorena conquered the Californians in this conflict, and killed a number, it might have added to his military reputation, but it would have made him very unpopular with the people and embittered them against him, especially the families of those killed, and their friends. Thereafter his position as governor would not have been a pleasant or an easy one, for he would have been subjected to constant harassment from people opposed to him; who would have considered that they had been greatly injured at his hands, and would finally have driven him away.

A few days after the battle, Micheltorena moved his forces to Palo Verde, about four miles from San Pedro, where our vessel, the "Don Quixote," then lay. Don Pio Pico became provisional governor of the department, after the capitulation, by virtue of his holding the position of president of the junta departmental, and immediately entered into negotiations with Captain Paty and myself to charter the "Don Quixote" to convey Micheltorena and his forces to Monterey, and thence to San Blas, taking in the remainder of the troops at Monterey. After several day's conference we came to an agreement. Pico chartered the vessel for that purpose for $11,000. While these negotiations were pending, Captain Paty and myself called upon Micheltorena a number of times with reference to the transportation of the troops, the room required for their accommodation, and other details. In about two weeks after the agreement was made the vessel was ready to receive the troops, and they embarked upon her.

We had a pleasant trip of seven and a half days to Monterey. Micheltorena talked freely about the late battle. He said he was a friend of the Californians; that he had been sent here to protect and not to destroy them; that he thought they were a brave people, but they were ill prepared for a battle-field; their cannons were of little account, their small arms still worse, and they could not procure others from any source, the government having possession of them all; that they had done their best to defeat him, but that was an impossibility. He said his forces were drilled soldiers and well armed; his officers educated military men; that he had eight or ten fine brass guns, four to eight-pounders, properly mounted, an inexhaustible supply of ammunition; and that he could have made sad havoc among the opposing force; but he gave orders to the artillerymen and soldiers to shoot over the heads of the insurgents and avoid killing or wounding any; that he had been sent by the supreme government of Mexico, as soldier, and governor of the department, and had endeavored to do his duty.

Micheltorena stood nearly six feet in height, was straight, of handsome appearance, with a military air and bearing. He spoke the French language correctly and fluently, and his own language so finely that it was a pleasure to listen to him. He was a good diplomatist, as well as a good general, and was liked by the solid men of the department. He tried to serve the people well and to please them. Probably no trouble would have arisen had there been no Alvarado in the department, always restless, and ambitious to rule again, and always interfering with the rightful governor, and exciting other ex-officials to create an agitation, so they might be restored to their former positions, under a new administration.

Alvarado and his party tried to arouse the sympathies of the rancheros, with whom Micheltorena was popular, and who loved order and peace, by alleging grievances suffered by the people under Micheltorena rule, little by little instilling dissatisfaction into the people's mind, as pretexts for revolt against the government. The grievances were mainly imaginary, for, as before remarked, the only tangible thing that could be complained of was the stealing of some chickens by soldiers, which certainly was rather a slender basis for rebellion. Of course Alvarado must offer some reasonable excuse. Although his own ambition was doubtless the motive and propelling force in the movement, it would not have been politic for him to admit this; nor would he have met with aid and encouragement on this ground. He therefore made use of some trivial complaints against the Mexican soldiers, enlarging upon and exaggerating alleged offences, until the Mexicans were made to appear in the eyes of the people as a terrible set of scoundrels, whose presence was highly dangerous to the country, and whom it was necessary, for the protection of the lives and property of the people, to get rid of.

This is my opinion of the matter, though I am aware that it differs from that of a few others. It is based upon my own observation and that of many others and my knowledge of Alvarado and his supporters.

During the voyage to Monterey I observed the soldiers closely. Some of them were rather hard-looking, but the main body of them was quite the contrary, and whenever I passed near any of them they politely raised their hats, and saluted me with *"Buenos dias."* Their conduct during the voyage was creditable to themselves and to the commanding general and his officers. It was a common remark among those belonging to our vessel, how well the troops behaved. Confined as they were for several days, had they been the villains represented, it would have come out in some way during the voyage. General Micheltorena and Captain Paty were brother Masons, and they played chess every night until two or three o'clock in the morning. The former drank wine at meals, was an inveterate cigarito smoker, fond of talking, a graceful, entertaining conversationalist. He went to bed late, and took chocolate in bed in the morning.

Captain Sutter spoke of Micheltorena as a soldier and gentleman of high character, and had great respect for him. He referred to his conduct and treatment of the Californians, and thought they were fortunate to be opposed by so kind-hearted and humane a commander as Micheltorena.

At Monterey the "Don Quixote" received the portion of the army, one-quarter of his entire force of 600, which was stationed there during the campaign, and the families of the officers, as well as Mrs. General Micheltorena. She was a lady of refinement, and was much beloved by the California ladies.

The vessel sailed for San Blas, after stopping a week at Monterey. Captain Paty spoke in praise of the conduct of all on board, and particularly of his respect and liking for Mrs. Micheltorena. The governor said to Paty that he regretted that the captain was not amongst the many grantees to whom he had given land during his administration; and would have been glad to have known that the captain was provided for in this way. Expressing a partiality for California, he said it was only a question of time when the department would become great and wealthy. He doubted the ability of his own government to keep California as a part of the domain of Mexico, on account of its geographical position; its great distance from the capital; the difficulty and expense of transporting troops so far, and maintaining them for its defense, together with the fact that the government had no navy; that the department in its defenseless condition was a constant source of trouble and anxiety to Mexico, and he thought it was inevitably destined to pass out of her control.

Captain Sutter and a number of men under his command in the battle with Alvarado were granted large tracts of land in the Sacramento valley by Micheltorena; among them Bidwell, Job Dye, Thomes, Toomes, Reading, Knight and Dr. John Marsh (the latter receiving a grant from Alvarado). After Micheltorena went away, Alvarado was made collector of the port under Governor Pico, and Don Manuel Castro was made prefect.

Alvarado had shown his ambitious spirit in 1836, and desire to rule, by creating, for imaginary grievances, a revolution against Governor Chico, who had been sent here by the supreme government of Mexico to take charge of department affairs and had administered the office of governor for a year or two. He succeeded in his designs, and sent Chico out of the country. As usual on such occasions, no blood was shed. Alvarado so directed the movements of his generals and maneuvered with so much tact that he succeeded in his efforts, without sacrificing any lives. Strange to say, upon this success of Alvarado in revolutionizing the government, instead of an army being sent from Mexico by that government to capture him and take him there as a rebel against his country, he received from President Bustamente an appointment as governor of California, upon his representing the matter in a letter of marked ability to that dignitary.

When Micheltorena first arrived in the department in 1842, with his troops from Mexico, he landed at San Diego, where he was welcomed by the people from all the surrounding country. He had a reception lasting several days. As he was about leaving, he was waited upon by a deputation of citizens of Los Angeles who brought him an invitation from the prefect, Don Santiago Argüello, brother of ex-Governor Argüello, to attend the celebration of the anniversary of the Independence of Mexico at this place on the sixteenth of September. He accepted the invitation and subsequently participated in the exercises of the day. On leaving San Diego to proceed north, he was accompanied by a private party, going in the same direction, consisting of Don José Joaquin Estudillo, and his daughter; who after became my wife; and his brother and family. The journey occupied several days. The troops seemed well disciplined and orderly, and were apparently well bred men, quiet, polite and respectful in behavior. On reaching the Mission of San Juan Capistrano, the general halted with his forces for a rest of a day or two, during which he gave a grand outdoor entertainment, or picnic, in a beautiful valley back of the Mission, to which all the people of the neighborhood were invited. He prevailed upon the Estudillo party to stop and participate in the festivities. Among other diversions for the entertainment of the guests, the troops were drawn up in military order and went through their evolutions, the band played, and dancing was enjoyed. From there they continued on to Los Angeles, where the general was received with all the honors becoming his position and rank. The town was alive with enthusiasm. The day of the anniversary was a gala day. Horse racing and bull-fighting were a part of the performance. The Californians were dressed in their most costly habiliments, and their horses were superbly equipped.

CHAPTER XXX
General M. G. Vallejo's Lands and Cattle

GENERAL Mariano Guadalupe Vallejo had as many as 25,000 head of cattle on his two ranchos. One of these ranchos was called the Petaluma, and the other the Temblec, between Sonoma and Petaluma. At one time he owned another rancho at Santa Rosa which afterward became the property of Doña Maria Ygnacia Lopez de Carrillo. He had besides about 2,000 head of horses and about 24,000 head of sheep.

The General maintained very friendly relations with the Indians, toward whom he always acted in a most humane manner. His right-hand ally, in all his intercourse with the neighboring tribes, was the high chief, Francisco Solano, who stood over six feet and who possessed a very good intellect. This chief had received some education from the Mission padres and appreciated the advantages of civilization. He was companionable and pleasant in his manner and deportment, and was much respected by every one who knew him. At his death he was buried on a small island in Petaluma Creek. The burial took place with all the honors under the direction of another chief named Camilo.

I knew this chief, who was a fine, intelligent and shrewd man. He often came over to San Francisco to purchase goods from Nathan Spear, whose agent I then was. He owned 600 cattle, numerous horses and sheep, and was quite a noted breeder. He was punctual in meeting his obligations, and owing to this and to his affability and intelligence, was highly esteemed by us all. He could read and write, and keep accounts, having been educated by the old missionaries. Camilo was the grantee of a rancho of about two leagues of land, known as "Olompali," bordering on the Bay of San Francisco between the ranchos Petaluma and Novato. He was likewise a wheat raiser, and sold his crops to the Russians.

As a proof of General Vallejo's clearheadedness I will state that he always treated both Solano and Camilo with high consideration, because it was through these men that he conquered and controlled the numerous tribes of Indians without shedding blood. It was also by their assistance that he had command of all the laborers he needed for the vast improvements he introduced in Sonoma and Petaluma.

The General was a large grower of wheat at his hacienda, Petaluma. He employed several hundred men to plow, sow and harrow the vast fields he had under cultivation. These laborers were trained in the art of plowing and sowing at the Missions with the Padres as instructors. The General also employed uncivilized Indians, known as "gentiles," as assistant plowmen and harvesters. Plowing the soil was done wholly by oxen, a pair to a plow. Thus the primitive cultivator penetrated the earth but a few inches. The soil being virgin and rich in quality, however, produced fabulous crops.

The measurement of the production of a wheat field was by the quantity of seed sown. The California "fanega" weighed one hundred and thirty-three pounds. It has been known that crops of wheat raised on the lands of the Mission of San José returned one hundred fanegas for every fanega sown. Thus was the yield estimated. Acres were not known in early California among the "labradores" who tilled the ground. Their smallest land measurement was the square league.

The General was very fond of superintending the work as it progressed. Among the crops he planted were wheat, barley, oats, beans, peas, garvanzo and lanteja. He raised great quanities of these articles of food on his haciendas. I have watched his management as a farmer with interest, particularly at harvest time, and he always appeared to take pride in the title of "labrador." Vallejo found a market for his wheat with the Russians who came regularly every year with two, and sometimes four, vessels to transport to Alaska their purchases from Vallejo; Salvador, his brother; Nicolas Higuera; Cayetano Juarez; the Missions of San José and Santa Clara and others, for the support of their settlements throughout that vast territory.

The General's home consumption of wheat was considerable; it was made into flour for the maintenance of his soldiers at Sonoma, and to feed the workers at his several haciendas. At his principal rancho, Petaluma, he had to house and feed six hundred vaqueros and laborers. The grand old structure of two stories in height with piazzas, and court yard in the rear stood upon a commanding eminence. It was a rule generally among the haciendados to select an elevated site for the home of the family.

At the Petaluma mansion the General entertained captains, supercargoes and other visitors of distinction and did it sumptuously.

Nathan Spear had a grist mill which, as related elsewhere in these pages, was imported from Baltimore via Callao, and put up in San Francisco on the north side of Clay Street, on the middle fifty vara lot between Montgomery and Kearny Streets. This mill was run by a six mule power, of which there were four changes, and turned out from twenty-five to fifty barrels of good flour a day. Besides milling for himself, he ground for the wheat growers bordering on the bay. I have known Vallejo to have had five or six hundred fanegas of wheat at the mill at one time to be ground into flour. He divided the result; in other words, he gave one-half for milling, free of cost of the sacks and transportation of the grain from Petaluma and the freight of the flour back to Petaluma or Sonoma.

Spear owned several vessels which he used in his business. These carried grain and flour to and from the different embarcaderos around the bay. Salvador Vallejo and other tillers of the soil were patronizers of the Spear grist mill which was founded at the village of Yerba Buena in the winter of 1839-40. Nathan Spear was not only an enterprising merchant originally from Boston, but a true American, who loved his country far above the temptation of a grant of eleven square leagues of the best land in the Department of California, which he could have had by denouncing his mother country to become a naturalized citizen of Mexico.

Spear's mill was in full operation from the day it began grinding until 1845. This mill was considered of great benefit to California because it supplied a great part of the flour used in the Department for half a decade. Nathan Spear after many years of labor as a merchant became a sick man from heart trouble, and in 1845 moved from San Francisco to Doctor Edward T. Bale's hacienda, a grant of several leagues of land, upon a part of which the town of St. Helena is now located. Spear was an American and Bale was a Britisher. There was a mutual love between these early argonauts which lasted to the end of their existence. Bale was considered a scientific and talented man in his profession as physician and surgeon by the early men of California. I have heard Spear speak of him most highly, praising his skill.

General Vallejo had several grist mills at Petaluma of the most primitive pattern. These were run by one horse with an Indian boy by the side of the animal wielding a cow-hide whip to keep him going for the grist. Throughout the Department these one horse power grist mills were attached to each household, giving a daily supply of flour for the hacienda's kitchen. Elsewhere in this volume I have given an account of the primitive grist mills used in California.

General Vallejo would never tolerate injustice or brutality toward the natives. Notwithstanding his friendship for Solano, he once had the chief arrested for an alleged complicity in the sale of Indian children, and cleared him only when satisfied that the charge was unfounded.

The Nacional rancho at Soscol had about 14,000 head of cattle, and a large number of horses. These cattle used to stray to a long distance along the margin of Suisun Bay. This rancho was under the control of General Vallejo from the time he founded the military headquarters at Sonoma. He was virtually the owner of all the cattle on the north side of San Francisco Bay, which were originally reputed to be Mission or government property, but eventually he became the acknowledged proprietor of all these animals.

Including Petaluma, Temblec and another rancho, the total of cattle on all these estates reached the enormous number of fifty thousand head. This made the General the largest cattle owner in early California. Don Guadalupe, as he was generally called by his countrymen and the merchants, castrated, earmarked and branded about the first of March each year some ten thousand calves, or one-fifth of his great herds. An increase of one to every five head on the hacienda was the basis of the yearly estimate among the hacendados. This mode of counting had been tested and proven as you would the balance sheets of a commercial house. To verify the rule, they counted the cattle as they went out of the corral, before the number became too great on a hacienda.

Hacendado Vallejo during the matanza season slaughtered eight thousand steers of three years of age or over, for their hides, tallow and manteca. It was a rule among the hacendados to slaughter as a yearly income about four-fifths of the yearly increase of the herds. The "novillos" or steers averaged to each animal about six arrobas (twenty-five pounds to the arroba) of tallow and manteca; four arrobas of the former to each steer at one and one-half dollars the arroba, and two arrobas of the latter at two dollars the arroba—a total of eighty thousand dollars. Add to this sixteen thousand dollars for the hides and some notion of the General's income from only one product of his haciendas is obtained.

Petaluma was the matanza ground for the "novillos" from the other ranchos, with the exception of Soscol. The matanza steers were killed at that rancho separately from the rest. During the killing season at the home rancho, I have observed the numerous try-pots bubbling with the melted tallow and manteca, the latter being the delicate fat that lies between the hide and the ribs of the animal. Of course, the improvements and management of this extensive estate were patterned after the early Missions. Under General Vallejo's rule everything was neat, and everything was in its right place. Among these early raisers of stock enough of the "novillos" were carried over from one season to another for their own consumption.

The Californians were fond of frolicking and having good times out of doors in the open country of their domains. Such entertainments were called "Meriendas." These commenced in the spring of the year after the work of branding and ear-marking the calves was over, a task that signalized the hacienda's new accession of wealth, and continued to the months of Indian Summer, which were considered the best of the year. The atmosphere then is tempered, it is soft and balmy, and you feel that you are all the time rubbing against silk of the highest finish in texture. Such is my observation of the climate of California during my many years here. I have been repeatedly asked if the climate of the State has changed since the year 1831. Of course, my replies were always in the negative. There is no difference between the climate of old California and new California.

The meats relished most on these playful excursions in the open air were from terneras or yearling heifers. The tender and nutritious morsels were broiled over a bed of coals, prepared from a branch of some ancient live oak, by means of an iron spit which an expert "asador," a servant of the household, watched over. This functionary also prepared other choice tidbits such as *"tripas de leche"* and *"mollejas"* or sweetbreads. At these meriendas I have participated with the other guests from neighboring ranchos in the good things prepared under the direct supervision of La Señora de la Casa. While the guests were seated on the ground relishing the good food spread before them on snow white linen, the ladies found time to gather and arrange miniature bouquets of the flowers within their reach. These nosegays were called by the gentlemen, souvenirs de la merienda.

Elsewhere I have spoken of the arrest of the foreigners in California. While these arrests were being made, General Vallejo, with his staff and about seventy soldiers, all mounted on fine horses and well equipped with carbines, sabres and pistols, arrived in San Francisco from Sonoma on their way to Monterey. The General was attired in undress uniform, mounted on a spirited dapple gray, and was attended by Col. Victor Prudon; Major José de los Santos Berreyesa and Lieut. Lázaro Piña, who composed his staff. This body of troops was transported from Sausalito by Capt. William A. Richardson in several of his undecked barges which had been built and owned by the Missions bordering the bay long years before.

They were landed at Thompson's Cove between Clark and Buckalew Points. It was no small undertaking on the part of Richardson to ferry the horses across the Bay, because at Saucelito there was no convenience, no wharf at that time for embarking animals on board a launch. The same difficulty existed at Yerba Buena. General Vallejo with his staff, followed by the cavalry two abreast, rode along what is now Montgomery Street to the residence of his brother-in-law, Jacob P. Leese, between Clay and Sacramento Streets. The military made a fine appearance with their large handsome horses. Sonoma had the reputation of raising the best and largest animals in the Department.

General Vallejo placed the settlement of Yerba Buena, Mission Dolores and the Presidio under martial law. Yerba Buena contained at that time about fifty inhabitants, all told; men, women and children. Mission Dolores and the Presidio housed several hundred. During his sojourn of several days, the General was visited at his headquarters, the home of Jacob P. Leese, by the dignitaries, the inhabitants, the captains and supercargoes of the vessels in port in order to pay their respects to the Commanding General of the Department. On his departure the civil authorities resumed their duties as usual. Alvarado evidently was worried and unsettled in his mind regarding the course to pursue relative to the expulsion of the Americans. He needed the presence of his uncle to consult and counsel with at this critical period of his rule as Governor of California, for Mariano G. Vallejo was always considered a most conservative man in the management of public affairs while he held office in the government.

GENERAL MARIANO GUADALUPE VALLEJO
A staunch supporter of American ideas.

CHAPTER XXXI
Vallejo's Appeal For Annexation to United States

AT A meeting held at the home in Monterey of United States Consul Thomas O. Larkin toward the end of March 1846 of the civil and military officers of the Department of California to treat on the future of California, some of the persons present expressed their feelings in favor of independence of Mexico pure and simple; others favored a French protectorate; still others preferred English protection.

Several, among them Rafael Gonzales, Victor Prudon and Mariano G. Vallejo, favored annexation to the United States. Lieut. Col. Prudon made a warm speech in favor of the last proposition. Vallejo could not coincide in opinion with those who favored a European protectorate as he felt convinced that California could not maintain her independence if left entirely to her own resources.

Referring to the proposed plan of asking for the protection of England or France, he said that public men in Europe could not take the vivid interest in California's future that she needs. He thought it would be neither honorable nor worthy of the Californians to go to far off Europe for a master. There was no bond of sympathy between her and those nations separated from her by two broad oceans. Superadded to that was the fact that Californians were republicans, and they would undergo the utmost suffering, even death, rather than assent to become the subjects of a monarch. Ill treated as the Californians had been by the so-called republican rulers of Mexico, they had never thought of giving up their birth rights as republican citizens; they had even cherished republican equality. He for one, would certainly oppose every attempt to present to the world the sad spectacle of a free American people begging for vassalage; asking for a European crowned head to become their master. He was not afraid of Mexico, who possessed neither navy or army, nor resources to support any sufficient force to land and hold California in subjection. He then argued in favor of accepting annexation to the United States. He contradicted those who said that by annexation to the United

States California would lose her political status. Vallejo explained the constitution of the United States and how under it California would have representation in Congress as well as any other State of the Republic. He counselled that no ill-feeling should be shown toward the immigrants who had come overland; they had come to farm ranches, and to establish industries; and California with them will prosper beyond her wildest dreams. He concluded by saying that California ought to detach herself from Mexico, and ask for admission "to form a part of the great confederation known as the United States of North (sic) America."

Prudon having noticed that several of the persons present approved Vallejo's proposal, asked Comandante Castro to put it to a vote. General Castro did not assent, and the discussion continued. The meeting finally adjourned to reconvene at a later hour.

Vallejo thought that the partisans of monarchy had it all cut and dried, and prevailed on the friends of the United States to leave Monterey. They did so, and when the hour of voting came, there was no quorum, and no definite result could be arrived at.

CHAPTER XXXII
Californians and Their Ways

THE Californians seldom intermarried with the Indians; but they mixed with them to a certain extent; and in visiting the Missions, one would sometimes see fine looking children belonging to the Indian women, the offspring of their association with California men. In some cases, these children of Indian women were deserted by their parents; or their mothers were of so worthless a character that the children would have suffered in their hands and been neglected. They were then adopted into California families, christened with the name of the family, reared in a proper way by them, kindly treated, employed as nurses and domestics, and not regarded as common servants. In those days there were no foundling and orphan asylums, and the priests of the Missions felt it incumbent upon them to exercise an oversight of unfortunate children. Sometimes they called the attention of the matrons of the families to them, and thus secured their adoption. Children were also taken into families without any suggestion from the priest whatever. The Indian women of California were far better stock than those of Mexico, which accounts in a measure for their finer children. The climate may also have had an effect in the better development of Indian offspring in California, than in Mexico.

The French ship "Leon," of about 700 tons, Captain Bonnet, arrived at Saucelito in 1844, and thence took a cargo of young cattle to the Society and Marquesas Islands (which were under dominion of France) for breeding purposes—to stock the islands. There were two or three hundred head, most of them supplied by Captain Richardson. They were sold at six dollars apiece, which at that time was considered a good price, the regular price for heifers being three dollars. The same vessel returned the following year for another cargo of stock cattle, which was supplied by Captain Richardson, as before.

In November, 1844, James McKinley and myself left San Diego and went overland to Santa Anita, a rancho situated a few miles north of the Mission San Gabriel, in a pretty valley about eight or nine miles easterly from Los Angeles. Hugo Reid, a Scotchman, lived at Santa Anita. He was a skillful accountant, and we brought along with us, on a pack animal, a large pile of account books belonging to the business of Paty, McKinley & Fitch, who were about dissolving their partnership. We remained at Reid's house most of the months of November and December, adjusting and settling the books, with his aid. Reid had been disappointed in love in his own country; his intended bride having thrown him over, so to speak; and he left the country in disgust, vowing he should marry some one of the same name as she who had slighted him, even though an Indian woman. He came to California and fell in with a woman of pure Indian blood, named Victoria, the name of his former love, and married her.

Upon our visit at Reid's house, we found that they were living very happily together. They had one daughter, a beautiful girl of about eighteen, born some years before their marriage, of another English father. We were surprised and delighted with the excellence and neatness of the housekeeping of the Indian wife, which could not have been excelled. The beds which were furnished us to sleep in were exquisitely neat, with coverlids of satin, the sheets and pillow cases trimmed with lace and highly ornamented, as with the Californians. It was one of the striking peculiarities of Californians, that the chief expense of the household of the poorer families was lavished upon the bed; and though the other furniture may have been meagre and other useful articles, such as knives and forks, scanty in supply, the bed was always excellent, and handsomely decorated; sumptuously often, with those of more means. I never knew an exception in any household. This was an evidence of good taste and refinement and that they were peers of other civilized people.

In the fall of 1841 a French vessel laden with a valuable cargo, consisting of silks, brandy and other costly goods, commanded and owned by Limantour (afterwards well known in California in connection with land matters), arrived on this coast, intending to come to Yerba Buena. In seeking to come into the bay of San Francisco, an inlet near Point Reyes was mistaken for the entrance to the harbor, and she went ashore. The motive for coming to Yerba Buena first, with an after design of entering the goods at the custom house in Monterey and proceeding thence to Mazatlan, arose from the fact that under the Mexican laws she could land goods at Mazatlan by showing papers representing that she had paid duties at Monterey; and by entering the goods there rather than at Mazatlan money could be saved on the duties, as the custom house officers were supposed to be less vigilant and less strict at the former place than at the latter. After the vessel went ashore, Limantour and his crew landed in boats near the Point, were furnished with horses by a ranchero in the neighborhood, and came over to Saucelito.

Captain Richardson brought Limantour across the bay to Yerba Buena, and communicated the first news of the loss of the vessel. The "Don Quixote," Captain Paty, being in port, after several days of negotiation between Paty and Limantour, the latter chartered the vessel for two or three thousand dollars to go up to the wreck and save what she could. The "Don Quixote" was a good sailer, easily handled, and Captain Paty took her quickly to the wreck and in two or three weeks was back in Yerba Buena with nearly the whole cargo, most of it in fine condition. The weather had been good and the sea smooth, the southerly winds not having commenced, which favored the saving of the goods. After the "Don Quixote" returned she was ordered to Monterey to enter and pay duties, and she went accordingly. Limantour having lost his vessel, abandoned his trip to Mazatlan. His goods were disposed of to different vessels in port; some to residents.

Limantour established himself for a time at Yerba Buena, where he sold much of the merchandise, and then proceeded in a small schooner of forty or fifty tons down the coast and disposed of the remainder. Silk was largely used by the California ladies, the wealthier class dressing in that material. The rich men of the department were generous to their wives and daughters, never refusing them what they required in dry goods and other materials. Limantour's silks therefore found ready purchasers. The vessel subsequently became a total wreck and went to pieces where she struck.

In the winter of 1844-45 a little incident occurred which produced some local excitement. Captain Libbey, of the bark "Tasso," had made several voyages to the coast and had become enamored of a young California lady, who was also beloved by Chico Haro. Libbey was a good-natured man, but rather gross in his appearance. His attentions were not reciprocated by the lady. The two rivals met one day in Vioget's saloon, which was kept at that time by Juan Padillo, who succeeded Hinckley as alcalde. They had imbibed rather freely of California aguardiente, which when newly made, is very stimulating. Ramon Haro, brother of Chico, the brothers Francisco and Ysidro Sanchez, uncles of the two Haros, were present, and they all had drunk more or less. A drunken row ensued, high words were used, and during the melee Captain Libbey was stabbed by Chico Haro. His brother Ramon was supposed to be an accomplice in the matter. The Sanchez brothers were also more or less connected with it. This occurrence is mentioned, because breaches of the peace were rare; disturbances of any kind being very unusual.

I have before stated that the Californians, as a class, were a sober people, and drank little; but the Sanchez family was an exception; and though not habitual drunkards, they imbibed freely, one only of them, Don José de la Cruz Sanchez, being temperate. After the stabbing, Alcalde Hinckley did his duty promptly by arresting the two Haro brothers and Ysidro Sanchez. They were immediately tried, and Ysidro was released. The two Haros were found guilty and sentenced to the calaboose of the Pueblo San José for six months each. The whole matter occupied but a brief time, Hinckley showing great alacrity in the administration of the law. Libbey was not dangerously stabbed, and presently recovered.

I have already spoken of the fine appearance and development of many of the Californians; and in this connection shall mention General Vallejo's three brothers, all well proportioned men, of large stature; one now living (1888) is over eighty years of age. The Bernals, of San José; the Berreyesas, of whom Don José Santos was particularly noble-looking and intelligent; the half-brothers of Governor Alvarado, at Monterey; the Estrades, the Soberanes family, the Munrás family, also of Monterey, were fine-looking men; also the Santa Cruz Castros, three or four brothers; Don Pablo de la Guerra's brothers, at Santa Barbara, they were his equals in good looks.

Don Antonio Maria Lugo, of Los Angeles, was genial and witty, about eighty years of age, yet active and elastic, sitting on his horse as straight as an arrow, with his reata on the saddle, and as skillful in its use as any of his vaqueros. He was an eccentric old gentleman. He had a wife aged twenty or twenty-two—his third or fourth. In 1846 I visited him. After cordially welcoming me, he introduced me to his wife, and in the same breath, and as I shook hands with her, said, in a joking way, with a cunning smile, *"No se enamore de mi joven esposa."* He had numbers of children, grandchildren and great-grandchildren. Los Angeles was largely populated from his family. Referring to this circumstance, he said to me, quietly, *"Don Guillermo, yo he cumplido mi deber a mi pais."*

At Los Angeles, also, were Don Tomás Yorba and his brothers, splendid looking, proud and dignified in address and manners, the cream of the country. The wife of Don Tomás was Doña Vicenta, a graceful woman. The Sepulvedas, of Los Angeles, also were fine physical specimens of the people. At San Diego, the Argüellos, sons of the prefect, were finely formed men, well proportioned. Mrs. General Castro, of Monterey, Doña Modeste, was beautiful, queenly in her appearance and bearing. The wife of David Spence, sister of Prefect Estrada, was of medium size, with fine figure and beautiful, transparent complexion. The two sisters of General Vallejo, one the widow of Captain Cooper, the other the wife of Jacob P. Leese, were also striking in beauty. The latter, Doña Rosalia, was considered in former days a very attractive woman, fascinating and vivacious. Mrs. Leese learned from her husband the use of the rifle, shooting with the greatest accuracy. Jacob P. Leese was among the sharpshooters in early Indian campaigns. On the Fourth of July celebration in 1839 I saw a specimen of her skill with the rifle, which was wonderful, shooting at birds on the wing at a great distance, and killing them.

When James McKinley and myself were on our way from San Diego to Santa Anita, in November, 1844, to visit Hugo Reid, we stopped a day and night at the Mission of San Luis Rey, where we met Father José Maria Zalvidea, one of the last of the old priests from Spain still remaining in California. He was strong and healthy, although about eighty years of age. There was also a Mexican priest in charge of the Mission.

Father Zalvidea spent most of his time in walking back and forth in the spacious piazza of the Mission, with his prayer-book open in his hand, saying his prayers, hour after hour. I stood there for some time observing him, and every time he reached the end of the piazza he would give me a little side glance and nod of recognition, and say *"Vamos si, señor"* a number of times in succession. Whenever he met me or anyone else through the day or evening he would make the same greeting, and never anything else. If anyone spoke to him he would listen attentively until the speaker had finished, apparently hearing and understanding everything that was said, but he made no reply other than the words I have quoted. During such interviews he would never look a person square in the face, but always gazed a little one side, round the corner, as it were. One might have supposed he was demented from this singular conduct. I inquired if this was so of Mr. McKinley, who had known him for ten years or more, and he replied that he was always the same; that his mind was perfectly clear and unimpaired; that he was so absorbed in his devotions that he did not care to hold any intercourse with the world or converse on worldly topics, but gave his whole life and attention to religion.

Father Zalvidea was much beloved by the people, who looked upon him as a saint on earth, on account of the purity and excellence of his character. Among his eccentricities was his custom, at meals, of mixing different kinds of food thoroughly together on one plate,—meat, fish, vegetables, pie, pudding, sweet and sour—a little of everything. After they were thoroughly mingled, he would eat the preparation, instead of taking the different dishes separately, or in such combinations as were usual. This was accounted for by others as being a continual act of penance on his part. In other words, he did not care to enjoy his meals, and so made them distasteful; partaking of food merely to maintain existence. Whenever any ladies called on him, as they frequently did, to make some little present as a mark of their esteem, he never looked at them, but turned his face away, and extending his hand to one side received the gift, saying, *"Vamos si señora; muchas gracias."* He never offered his hand in salutation to a lady. At times, in taking his walks for exercise in the vicinity of the Mission, the priest was seen to touch his head lightly on either side with a finger, throw his hands out with a quick, spasmodic motion, and snap his fingers; as if casting out devils. On such occasions he was heard to exclaim, *"Vete, satanas!"*—some improper thought, as he conceived, probably having entered his mind.

Resuming my business in Yerba Buena in April, 1845, I visited old customers around the bay, and was very successful in making collections prior to and during the killing season of that year; and I accumulated many hides, bags of tallow and furs, and had sold out the entire stock of goods by the time the "Don Quixote" arrived again in August, after having safely landed Micheltorena and his troops at San Blas.

AN EXTREMELY RARE AND EARLY PRINT

CHAPTER XXXIII
William Sturgis Hinckley Builds the First Bridge

WILLIAM STURGIS HINCKLEY joined Nathan Spear in the latter part of 1838, in business at Yerba Buena. Hinckley was a native of Hingham, Massachusetts, nephew of William Sturgis, of Boston. He was an educated man, of pleasant address. He had been some years engaged in business in the Sandwich Islands, whence he came to this coast and traded awhile in vessels, until he established himself at Yerba Buena. He was popular with both the foreign and the native population. When I arrived at Santa Barbara, in May, 1838, Hinckley was there, and visited Alvarado's headquarters frequently, the two being intimate friends. Hinckley highly estimated Alvarado's talent and had a warm esteem for him, which feeling was reciprocated by the governor, who was in the habit of communicating his plans to Hinckley confidentially. Alvarado was much appreciated by intelligent foreigners, who recognized his general superiority, he being an excellent looking man, and possessing great geniality and tact.

At this time Carrillo was in active opposition to the governor, seeking to oust him from his position. Hinckley greatly assisted Alvarado with advice and suggestions regarding his preparations to repress Carrillo. One evening they were engaged in private conversation in the governor's rooms, discussing their plans. Alvarado had a one-eyed secretary, who was a fellow capable and accomplished enough, with talent for writing official dispatches and papers, and a useful man, but withal prying and inquisitive. Gas was not in use in those days, and sperm and adamantine candles were rare. Bullock and elk tallow candles were commonly used for lights, with old-fashioned snuffers, having a little square box attached to receive the wick when snuffed off. The secretary, on this occasion, every few minutes dodged into the room where Alvarado and Hinckley were engaged in conversation, ostensibly for the purpose of snuffing the candles, showing thereby his politeness and attention, but really to catch the drift of the conversation and find out what was going on. He was so assiduous in the performance of his self-imposed duty, that the two gentlemen presently discovered his intention. Not liking to be so frequently interrupted, Hinckley, who was fond of a practical joke, emptied the snuffers of the bits of burnt wick, and poured in a little gunpowder (it being war time gunpowder was handy), and the two gentlemen then retired to a remote corner of the room. Soon after, the faithful secretary came again and applied the snuffers, when an explosion followed that startled and nearly capsized him. He immediately broke out of the room, and the two gentlemen indulged in a burst of laughter. From the adjoining apartments, the governor's aids and General Castro hurried in, alarmed at first by the explosion, but relieved by hearing the laughter that followed. On being informed, they joined in and added to the general merriment. The secretary finally made his appearance and shared in the fun, admitting that he had been victimized.

In 1839 Hinckley went to Callao and brought the brig "Corsair," of which he was part owner and supercargo, to Yerba Buena, loaded with assorted merchandise. In 1840 he became a permanent resident here. In 1842 he married Doña Susana, daughter of Don Ygnacio Martinez, his first wife having died in 1840 in Massachusetts. In 1844 he was elected first-alcalde of the district of San Francisco, headquarters at Yerba Buena. Being well fitted for the office of alcalde, he discharged the duties of the position in a manner very creditable to himself and to the satisfaction of the Californians and foreign residents.

On the block now bounded by Washington, Jackson, Montgomery and Kearny streets was a salt-water lagoon, or little lake, connected with the bay by a small creek. When the tide came in the lake was filled. At all stages of the tide there was considerable water remaining in it. To reach Clark's point, to the north of the creek, the settled portion of the town being to the south of it, the people would have to get across the best way they could, by wading, or jumping across in some places. One of Captain Hinckley's acts as alcalde was to cause the construction of a little bridge across the creek, thereby adding much to the convenience of the people who had occasion to go to the other side. This was regarded as a great public improvement, and people came from far and near to look at and admire it, especially the native Californians, who arrived from the Mission and elsewhere, with their wives and children, to contemplate the remarkable structure.

During his administration as alcalde there were two or three little disturbances among the lower orders at Vioget's saloon and elsewhere, this saloon then being rented to Juan Padillo, a Mexican. Alcalde Hinckley, on being informed, would immediately go to the spot, and raising his *baston,* command them in tones of authority to desist from disturbance. Everything at once became quiet, and the disorder ceased; showing the respect with which they regarded the American alcalde and his insignia of office.

Hinckley prevailed upon the prefect at Monterey to order a survey of Yerba Buena. The survey was made, and a plan of the town drawn and mapped, being the first survey of the kind of any importance. He took great interest in having the streets properly located and the plan executed in the best manner. No names at that time were given to any of the streets.

When Governor Micheltorena was opposed by Alvarado and Castro, he was at first favored by Hinckley as the legal governor of the department. Respecting his own oath of office, he naturally felt it his duty to stand by the regularly constituted authorities. However, when Alvarado had succeeded in turning the current of popular feeling against Micheltorena, and had roused the people to revolution, Hinckley could not resist the movement, and joined the Alvarado party, becoming an active participant in its operations.

During the Bear Flag excitement Hinckley stood firmly by the Mexican Government, and was outspoken in its favor.

After the expiration of his term of office, he retained his friendship for the Californians and Mexicans. Before his death, which occurred in June, 1846, talk of war between Mexico and the United States was prevalent. The sloop-of-war "Portsmouth," Captain Montgomery, was then lying at Yerba Buena, and though Hinckley was an American, his feeling in favor of the Mexican rule was so strong that he used to have some warm discussions on the subject with Captain Montgomery and other officers of the vessel.

Francisco Guerrero I regarded as one of the most important men in the district. He was a Mexican by birth. Shortly after I made his acquaintance, in the year 1838, I found him to be an intellectual man. About 1839 he was made alcalde, or *juez de paz,* and a few years after, was appointed sub-prefect. In these offices he performed his duties most strictly, but not discourteously. On the occasion of the detention of Spear and myself at the time of the general arrest of the foreigners, he came in person to Spear's house and mentioned in the politest manner that he had an order from headquarters to arrest us, which he very much regretted, saying that Spear and myself need not feel any alarm; that everybody knew us, and that he would go with Spear part of the way, as if they were traveling together, and that no indignity should be put upon him as a prisoner; making the exercise of authority as light and as little disagreeable as possible. And so in the other arrests, he was so polite that those who were detained could not be otherwise than pleased with him. He knew them all and showed no domineering spirit, but treated them as friends rather than otherwise, and at the same time he did his duty strictly.

Guerrero encouraged the immigration of foreigners to California and their settlement, and defended them in their rights after they got here. He saw that the country must necessarily pass from the control of Mexico. In his administration of office he gave great satisfaction, showing no partiality to his countrymen over foreigners, treating all with equal justice. Albeit a thorough Mexican, and loving his country, he had, as he often expressed it, no dislike to Americans. He admired them as a progressive people, and saw that they would ultimately control. On one occasion, in conversation with him, I suggested that he had better look out for a rainy day, and secure some land for himself; that Governor Alvarado, in consideration of his official services, would give him a grant, and that the land about the bay of San Francisco would some day be valuable. He replied that he had already taken steps to secure a grant at Half Moon bay, five or six leagues in extent; that he had received a permit from the government to occupy it, and in due time would get his title. He was very social in his nature and fond of little dances, which were frequently had at his house, joining in the festivity with great enthusiasm.

Guerrero was one of the few real founders of San Francisco. A street at the Mission was named after him. In 1851 he was murdered, in broad daylight, at the corner of Mission and Twelfth streets, by a Frenchman, who came up behind him, mounted on horseback, and struck him on the back of the head with a slungshot. It is supposed that parties interested in the Santillan land claim were the instigators of the murder. They wished to get Guerrero out of the way, as he would have been a damaging witness against their claim; being afraid of his influence and ability and independence of character; knowing he would not hesitate to expose the fraudulent nature of the claim. His widow is still living, and maintains her fine and dignified appearance and the graceful walk of her earlier years (1890).

CHAPTER XXXIV
Ships, Hides, Custom Officials and Contraband

THERE is not in existence, to my knowledge, any maritime or commercial report of arrivals, or statement of the volume of business, in the port of San Francisco (Yerba Buena) for the two decades preceding the latter part of the year 1846, at which time the United States government established a custom house here, the first collector being appointed by Commodore Stockton, commander of the naval squadron.

It has been my purpose in these pages to furnish as complete a list as possible of the arrivals of vessels* in the years from 1831 to 1846, both at Yerba Buena and at Monterey, the capital, where the only custom house in the department was located.

The Boston ships which came here in early days with goods to sell, and took back hides, remained about two years, going up and down the coast several times. The round trip from San Diego, touching at San Pedro, Santa Barbara, San Luis Obispo, San Simeon, Monterey, Santa Cruz and Yerba Buena, occupied three or four months; so that during the two years they made seven or eight trips of this kind, selling their goods collecting hides and tallow at different points, and on reaching San Diego deposited their collection of hides and tallow in warehouses, each of the vessels having a house for that purpose.

At that port the hides were prepared for shipment by soaking them for twenty-four or forty-eight hours in large vats of brine, to preserve them against the attacks of moths and other insects. They were then spread out on the smooth sandy beach to dry, and afterward hung on ropes and beaten by the sailors with a sort of flail, a contrivance made of a wooden stick three and a half feet long, to which was fastened a strip of hide and a short piece of wood of heavier kind than the other, to swing freely. Armed with these beating-sticks, two sailors passed along each side the row of hides and beat them thoroughly, removing all the dust and sand.

After two years, a full cargo having been gathered, and stored at San

*See appendix: List of Ship Arrivals.

Diego, the ship was loaded, carrying to Boston 38,000 to 45,000 hides. In loading the vessel, a rude press, made of boards and worked with ropes and pullies, was used to press the hides firmly together in the hold. I saw this done in 1831 at San Diego, when the cargo of the bark "Volunteer" was transferred to the bark "Louisa." The vessels trading between California and Peru took no hides to Callao. If they collected any they exchanged them with the hide ships for tallow, no tallow going to Boston. Tallow vessels also had houses at San Diego for the deposit of bags of that article. The tallow was used in Peru for making soap and candles and for consumption in the silver mines of the country.

Prior to 1843, whalers from the Atlantic coast would occasionally touch at a California port, either San Diego, San Pedro, Santa Barbara, San Luis Obispo, Monterey, or the bay of San Francisco, for supplies of beef and vegetables, and for water. In 1843, '44, '45, a considerable number of whalers came to San Francisco bay, and anchored off Saucelito; as that was a convenient place to obtain water, Captain Richardson invited them to come and take what they wanted from his springs, which were reached from the beach. The shipping was generally supplied with water from those springs. There was also a spring of good water at about where the northeast corner of Clay and Montgomery streets is now, from which whalers and merchantmen sometimes got a supply. As many as thirty or forty whalers were in the bay at one time during each of these years. They were not required to enter at the custom house. They generally had on board a few thousand dollars' worth of goods for trading, and were allowed by the custom house authorities to exchange goods for supplies for their own use, at any point where they touched along the coast, to the extent of $400, but were not allowed to sell goods for cash.

After 1842 there was an officer of the customs stationed at Yerba Buena to keep a general oversight of the shipping. The whalers, however, became so numerous in the bay that he found it impossible to attend to them all, not having guards sufficient to place one on each.

The farmers were much benefited by these vessels, inasmuch as they obtained from them goods at a cheap rate, in exchange for supplies. In consequence of there being so little supervision over them the whalers traded with the farmers and others for supplies, freely, not adhering to the $400 rule, but doing pretty much as they pleased.

In making my usual trading expeditions, the rancheros whom I met would ask me if I thought as many of the whalers would come another year as were there then. I told them I thought even more would come, as they had been encouraged by finding good supplies of vegetables, and would probably come again and advise other ships to come. They asked my advice as to what they should plant for sale to the ships another year. I told them to plant Irish potatoes, cabbages, pumpkins and onions, as those were the vegetables the vessels mainly depended upon.

Among those who were most active and energetic in furnishing supplies of this kind, and interested in planting for the purpose, were Don Vicente Peralta, the Castros of San Pablo, Don Antonio Maria Peralta, Don Ygnacio Peralta, and Don José Joaquin Estudillo, all on the east side of the bay. The Californians, although mainly engaged in cattle raising, were fond of agriculture, and would have engaged in it extensively had there been any market for their products. When an opportunity presented itself, as in the case of supplying the whaleships, they availed themselves of it, and commenced planting.

The vessels usually remained from four to six weeks getting in their supplies, which took some time, as they had to send out their boats to the different ranchos about the bay, there being no produce merchants in those days. They were delayed also in painting and repairing, and waiting, perhaps, for the proper time to arrive when whales would be in season at the whaling ground. Most of the crews were given their liberty on shore, and a sailor would occasionally desert, and settle among the rancheros; if a good man, industrious, and willing to work, especially if he had some mechanical skill at carpentry or other useful industry, he was encouraged by the rancheros to stay, and was treated with kindness; but if indolent and worthless fellows deserted, while kindly treated, they were not encouraged to remain, but were presented with horses, and perhaps some clothes, and persuaded to ride away to some other rancho.

As the time for the whaling fleet to visit the port approached, the farmers who had raised a supply of vegetables looked forward to their coming, hoping to dispose of their produce, and obtain goods in exchange at a low rate.

In 1843 or '44 a young Irishman named O'Farrell deserted from an American whaleship lying at Saucelito, having been employed as a cooper on board, and went to the Mission of San Rafael, then under the charge of Timothy Murphy, as administrator. From there he went to Bodega, bought a large tract of land, and engaged in cattle raising. He subsequently assisted as civil engineer in the survey of a portion of the city of San Francisco, as laid down on the present official map. Afterward he was elected to the State Legislature from Sonoma county; for one term held the important position of State Harbor Commissioner; and Jasper O'Farrell's* name is prominent in the history of the state.

While acting as the agent of Paty, McKinley & Co., at Yerba Buena,

---

* See appendix; Jasper O'Farrell's Signed Statement page 345.

in 1843, '44 and '45, I occupied a large adobe building on the spot which is now the west side of Grant avenue, near Clay. Requiring only a portion of it for my store and residence, three large rooms remained unoccupied. When the custom's agent Benito Diaz, (who was not very scrupulous) came to reside at Yerba Buena, I invited him to occupy these rooms with his family, free of charge; and he did so. He had under his command four boatmen, and a four-oared boat with which he went all around the bay to visit vessels. I was on friendly terms with him, and at times after he had come home for the day, I would request and obtain the use of his boat and crew for the evening, he asking me no questions. Thus provided, I visited the whaleships, and purchased goods from them at a very low figure, white and brown cottons, calicos, handkerchiefs, and other cheap stuffs, paying cash. My arrangements with Paty, McKinley & Co., were such that while I was conducting their business, I was allowed to trade on my own account, if such would not interfere with their trade. My goods were bought and sold for cash, while theirs were sold only for hides and tallow. Although money was scarce, I was enabled to sell articles so low that the rancheros managed to raise the funds to pay for them.

In securing commodities from the whaleships I had them landed by the captains in large water casks, each end of the cask being filled with Boston pilot bread to the depth of eighteen or twenty inches. The casks were landed on the beach, and were supposed to be empty, but if any official felt curious enough to make an examination, and open the cask, the pilot bread would be seen. It was common to purchase bread supplies from the vessels for use on shore; there were no bakeries, and the pilot bread was much liked. It would therefore appear all right to the inquiring officers. Nathan Spear, William G. Rae, William A. Leidesdorff and others doing business at Yerba Buena got goods from the whalers by the same method, and considerable trade was carried on in this covert manner. During these two or three years, I made outside of my regular salary from my employers two or three thousand dollars.

The revenue regulations were so little respected and so loosely enforced, that this traffic with whalers was safe. In 1845, the whaleship "Magnolia," Captain Simmons, was at Yerba Buena. He was afterward of the firm of Simmons, Hutchinson & Co., at San Francisco; in 1849 one of the heaviest houses on the coast, doing a large business.

Captain Jim Smith, of the whaleship "Hibernia," from New Bedford, was here in 1844. He afterward established a line of packets between San Francisco and Honolulu. Captain Smith was a Democrat, and Captain Eliab Grimes, before mentioned in this narrative, was a Whig, and in 1844 they met in Nathan Spear's parlor, which was a resort of prominent merchants and strangers in the town, and often engaged in very warm political discussions, both being men of intelligence, aptness of expression, and erudition in the history and doctrines of their political parties. Each ably defended his party and its men and measures, the discussions lasting usually several hours and attracting an interested audience of fifteen or twenty persons—captains, supercargoes and merchants, to whom anything of the kind was a great treat, in the dearth of other amusements.

Captain Smith had the advantage of Captain Grimes in keeping his temper and being always cool and collected, while Grimes would get very much heated and would swear furiously at his adversary. In that remote part of the country forty-five years ago (.1889), in that little Mexican town of about seventy or eighty inhabitants, the influence of the fierce contest between Democrats and Whigs which was being waged all over the Union was felt and had an effect.

Captain Eliab Grimes, during the war with England in 1812, was a young lieutenant of an American privateer, an hermaphrodite brig, which did great service in our cause, and captured many prizes, burning the vessels and landing the officers and crews at some convenient point, after securing what money and other valuables were on board. So successful was the privateer that each officer acquired a little fortune. Giving an account of his experiences on board, he said that one morning they saw a vessel far off flying the English flag, supposed to be a merchantman, but on approaching, she proved to be a British man-of-war, and a fast sailer, which bore down upon them; a stiff breeze blowing at the time. The privateer began to run away as fast as her sails would carry her, but the gale increasing, the war vessel made better headway, and their capture seemed imminent. Fortunately, the wind lightened, giving the American vessel an advantage, as she could sail faster than her pursuer in a light wind, and toward night she increased the distance between them and escaped.

William G. Rae, who was present when the captain related the adventure, remarked, with a touch of national pride, he being an Englishman: "Captain Grimes, if the wind hadn't moderated, you would have had to surrender the brig." "No!" retorted Grimes, flashing up; "I'll be d—d if we would; we would have scuttled the old brig and sunk her before we would have surrendered." It is true; their decision and resolution would have proved unconquerable.

Rae and Grimes were on very friendly terms. They were given much to discussion, and for hours together opposed each other in wordy controversy about national matters, the American Revolution, the last war with Great Britain, ably defending to the utmost each his own country. Rae, having a liking for the Americans, was not offended with Grimes' ebullitions, but took them all in good part, carrying on the discussion mainly as an intellectual pastime and for the entertainment of the listeners, who enjoyed the debates.

Captain Grimes was an intimate friend of my father. They made several voyages together, one as passenger in the other's vessel, and my only brother was named after Captain Grimes. The captain was a noble-hearted man, very much esteemed and loved both at Honolulu and Yerba Buena. In 1841 or 1842 he obtained from Alvarado a grant of eleven leagues of land near Sacramento city, which afterward came into the possession of Sam Norris, and was known as the Norris ranch.

When Captain Grimes died, in 1848, he had 16,000 or 18,000 head of rodeo cattle on his ranch, obtained in these few years by his good management, system and skill. He was attentive to details, such as having the right proportion of bulls to cows. I merely allude to this by way of comparing the American and Californian styles of management. His funeral was attended by the people of all the surrounding country, who came to pay the last tribute of respect and affection to his memory.

[TEXT OF LETTERS ON OPPOSITE PAGE]

Chico, Cal. April 13, 1895

Hon W. H. Davis,
    San Francisco, Cal.

Dear Sir,—By the S. F. Call of recent date I notice a reference to yourself and the book you are proposing to publish.

May I ask of you a question? Namely, The exact date of the death of Juan Bautista Alvarado? He was Governor in 1841 when I arrived in California—and till superseded by Micheltorena in 1844. The reason I ask you the date is because I have seen it incorrectly printed, unless in error myself. Californians, of whom we may ask information of men and events in early days, are becoming remarkably few. You are the only literary one of *ante bellum* and *ante aurum* times (so far as I know).

Just a line in reply will greatly oblige me. Pardon the intrusion and believe me,

Yours very truly
    John Bidwell

---

7 o'clock July 4th 1849

Archd C. Peachy, Esq.
    Dear Sir:

Yesterday I has had the pleasure of sending a letter to you by Olimpio, I hope you now in possession of it. I tooke the liberty to introduce to you my friend Mr. Bidwell, he can give you every information about the Country as he knows her through and through; he told me that he know a good place for a town near the Butes, perhaps it would be good if you Lieutt Meynard & myself lay out one there.

Excuse my haste and believe me my dear Sir! very respectfully
    your
        Obedient Servant & friend
            J. A. Sutter

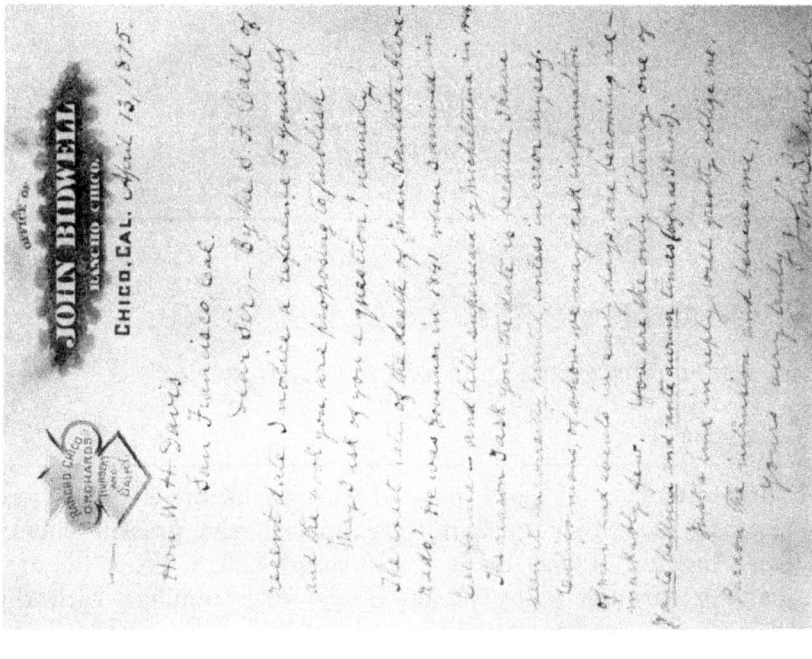

JOHN BIDWELL TO DAVIS

*Bidwell reached California as a member of the Bartleson Party—
the first overland caravan of settlers—in 1841*

JOHN A. SUTTER'S LETTER INTRODUCING BIDWELL

*Davis transported Sutter and his goods to the site of his "New Helvetia"
settlement, now Sacramento, in 1839*

CHAPTER XXXV
First Discovery of Gold In California

THE first discovery of gold in California to be made public was in 1840 in the valley of San Fernando, in the present county of Los Angeles. It was made by some Mexicans, from Sonora, who were passing through going north. They were familiar with the gold placers in their own country, had their attention attracted to the locality, and made the discovery. A good deal of gold from this source found its way to Los Angeles into the hands of the storekeepers. Henry Mellus, in trading along the coast, used to visit Los Angeles, his vessel lying meanwhile at San Pedro. In his business with the merchants there he collected about $5,000 in gold dust, which was of fine quality, in scales as from placer diggings. Other merchants also collected some. Mellus remitted $5,000 in gold dust to Boston by the ship "Alert," and also made other similar remittances. I saw at Yerba Buena, and handled, some of the dust which Mellus had obtained. That year and the next, probably eighty to one hundred thousand dollars worth of gold dust was taken from these diggings. The finding of gold continued there for several years, up to the time of what is known as the big gold discovery in the Sacramento valley, but the results were small.

The coin generally used by the merchants was Spanish and Mexican doubloons (gold); also American gold coin. Silver money of Mexican, Peruvian and United States coin was likewise in circulation. I never saw in California any of the paper money in use in the East.

In the early days, while California was still under Spanish rule, the proportion of men who had immigrated to the new country was largely in excess of the women. To equalize the difference, and furnish wives for the single men, more particularly for the soldiers, a representation was made by the governor of the department to the Spanish authorities of the facts, whereupon the home government made arrangements for the conveyance to California of a considerable number of women of Spanish extraction, from Mexico. Some came by water, by vessels chartered by the Government expressly for this purpose, and others came by land, under official auspices.

The motive was to prevent, so far as possible, the mixing of the Spanish race in California with the native Indians of the country. The Spaniards were naturally proud of their own blood, and wanted to keep it uncontaminated. Hence this movement on the part of the government. The want of women was thus supplied in a measure, but as late as 1838, and along up to 1846, the men exceeded the women in number, and some mixture with the Indians occurred.

SUTTER'S SAW MILL AT COLOMA BUILT BY JAMES MARSHALL, AND IN THE RACE OF WHICH HE DISCOVERED GOLD ON THE MORNING OF JANUARY 24, 1848. REPRODUCED FROM A DRAWING MADE AT THE TIME.

It was customary for the young men of the Californians to marry early. In this they were encouraged by their parents, partly because they desired to have the sparsely settled country populated as rapidly as possible, and partly also that the young men might thereby escape being drafted into the army. Under the Mexican law the commanding general of the army had power to levy upon the people for as many men as he might want to recruit his military force. From time to time, he designated such young men of different families as he chose to be taken for the purpose. It was nothing less than most arbitrary conscription. There was no redress. The rancheros were compelled to give up their sons when called upon, however wealthy, as money would not be accepted in lieu of the services of the young men.

The unmarried were only taken, the commanding general being so considerate as to leave the married men to care for their families. The motive for early marriage, therefore, was strong; in frequent instances boys of sixteen and seventeen taking wives unto themselves. The designs of the commander were often thus frustrated, and draft evaded by young men who were on the alert to escape military service.

A squad of ten soldiers, commanded by a sergeant, was sent out in 1838 by General Vallejo, from Sonoma, for the purpose of picking up recruits at the ranchos. A young man living in the vicinity of the general's headquarters getting information of this movement, and of the direction in which the squad was going, rode off post-haste to Suscol and across the National Ranch. As fast as one horse tired he lassoed another. Continuing on his course he reached the Straits of Carquinez, where he abandoned horse and saddle, and was quickly ferried across in a *tule bolsa* by the Indians. Taking his chances of lassoeing on foot one of Don Ygnacio Martinez' fine horses, rather a difficult feat, he rapidly pursued his journey until he reached San Pablo. There he gave information of the coming of the recruiting squad to his friend Castro, then a boy fifteen or sixteen years old, who immediately mounted a fleet horse and rode to the rancho of his neighbor, Martinez, and informed his son of about the same age, that the conscripting officer was coming. The two then rode off rapidly southward, changing their horses when necessary, and stopping at the ranch houses along for food and a little rest, until they reached the old Mission of San Juan Bautista, which was located in a wide valley of remarkable beauty, half way between Castroville and Gilroy. At the Mission they were within a district under command of General José Castro, who was a relative of one of the boys, and could feel at ease. They remained there until they thought it safe to return home. The following year both of these young men were married, Castro to the sister of his friend Martinez, and the latter to a daughter of Don José Joaquin Moraga, at the time owner of the valuable Moraga grant of six leagues.

The Californian parents had dread of their sons being drafted into the army, and the young men themselves had no liking for it. Some of the more wealthy rancheros had pre-arranged and reliable communications with their relations or friends living in Sonoma, who gave them information whenever a squad of soldiers was about to be sent out to gather up recruits, and of the direction the squad would take. At such times young men would be sent off for a month or two from the rancho, either hunting game, or to the great San Joaquin valley to lasso some of the numerous wild horses there.

The farmers were peace-loving men, and disliked to have their children forced into the army. They would protest, in the presence of their friends, against General Vallejo's or Castro's taking their boys for soldiers, asking what they wanted of them when the country was at peace, not at war or likely to be, saying that the general had a hundred or two soldiers already, which was a force amply sufficient to send out to capture or chastise wild Indians, and that any further increase must be only for the purpose of gratifying personal ambition and love of power and display; that if the Americans came to take the country, if they ever should, the few hundred soldiers he might have under him would not prevent the carrying out of their designs.

After Captain Sutter had settled at the fort New Helvetia, he was in the habit, at times, of sending fresh salmon to Yerba Buena.

The fish were fresh-salted or smoked. Nathan Spear, who was an epicure, and lover of good things, appreciated these fish very highly. The idea suggested itself to his mind that something profitable might be done in salmon fishing on the Sacramento river. Not wishing to trespass upon Captain Sutter's ground, although, of course, Sutter had no exclusive right to the fish in the river, Spear wrote to him on the subject, and received encouragement to go up and engage in fishing there for salmon. He made several trips in 1840 and '41 in the schooner "Isabel," camping on the bank of the Sacramento in a comfortable tent, and superintended the catching of the fish by the crew of his schooner and by Indians experienced in fishing, furnished by Captain Sutter. He took large quantities of salmon, filling the hold of the "Isabel" with fish packed in bulk; transported them to Yerba Buena, and disposed of them at satisfactory prices, packed in barrels and kegs of different sizes, to visiting vessels and to residents, making a good profit.

To Nathan Spear, therefore, is due the credit of having inaugurated the salmon fishery on this coast as a business, and of developing, to a considerable extent, an enterprise which has since grown to large proportions. On the last trip to the river in salmon catching Mrs. Spear accompanied her husband.

While John Parrott was United States commercial agent (consul) at Mazatlan in 1844 or '45, and also engaged in trade, an English brig named the "Star of the West" arrived there from England, with a cargo consigned to Parrott, the invoice cost of which was $120,000. The duties on this cargo would have amounted to that sum; probably more. Parrott wished to save paying a large proportion of them, and thinking he could do better by entering the vessel at Monterey, than at Mazatlan, he hoisted sail, and started for the former place. Just before reaching Monterey, the vessel went ashore at Punta de los Lobos, Carmel bay, and became a total wreck. All persons on board were saved; also a large part of the cargo, one-half or two-thirds. The goods were originally intended to be taken from Mazatlan into the interior of Mexico, upon mules, this being the only mode of transportation, and had been packed in England with reference to that, in not very bulky square packages, admirably put up, solid and compact, and encased with water-proof wrapping. So securely were they covered, that although many of them were taken from the water in the hold of the vessel, and others picked up while floating about the bay, yet the contents were not in the least injured, and were in as good a condition as if they had been landed from a vessel at the wharf. When the wreck became known at Monterey, the people of that place flocked by hundreds to the spot, and commenced saving as much of the cargo as possible. There being nothing to prevent, each became a wrecker on his own account, and saved what he could for his own benefit.

Captain J. R. B. Cooper was successful in securing a large amount of these goods. He took down from Monterey a number of the old-fashioned, solid-wheel wagons, drawn by oxen, the creaking and screeching of the vehicles, for want of grease on the axles, being heard for miles. With the aid of sailors whom he brought to the wreck he secured a large share of the spoils, many wagon loads; took them to Monterey, and made a small fortune out of the proceeds. Cooper was an old sea captain, and understood the business. Others saved smaller quantities. The custom house permitted them to be taken as "damaged goods," without payment of duty, although, no damage was apparent on opening the packages. The landing of the goods was attended with great risk and danger, three of the native Californians losing their lives at this time—José Antonio Rodriguez, Francisco Gonzalez and Francisco Mesa. None of the wrecked goods was recovered by Mr. Parrott. His protests and demands were ignored. It was a scramble, and he could not procure men or teams.

In 1840 or '41 there arrived at Yerba Buena from Mazatlan two Americans, one named Hiram Teal, a merchant; the other Rufus Titcomb, his clerk. Teal brought on a vessel about twenty thousand dollars' worth of Mexican goods; such as silk and cotton rebozos, serapes, ponchos, mangos, costly and ordinary; silver mounted and gilt spurs, saddles, ornamented and ordinary, *armas de pelo*, or riding robes for protecting the legs and body up to the waist; silver headstalls for horses, hair bridle reins, and other fancy and ornamental goods; an assortment of Mexican products. Teal opened a store and sold these goods to the hacendados principally. Many were also sold to Captain Sutter, who paid for them in land-otter and beaver skins. Teal was here about two years disposing of his merchandise, and he made probably $30,000 out of the venture; and had also bought some of Limantour's goods, which he sold with his own.

I have heard him speak highly of the people of New Mexico with whom he had lived, in respect to their honesty and fair dealing; that during the whole mercantile course there, of several years, during which he dealt largely with them, giving them credit for their purchases when required, he never lost a dollar in all his transactions. They were kind and hospitable; their kindness was genuine, and not affected. He said the happiest part of his life was spent among them. He obtained his goods for his store at Santa Fé, mostly from St. Louis, overland, commencing there with three or four thousand dollars. The twenty thousand dollars' worth of goods he brought from Mazatlan to Yerba Buena showed how successful he had been in New Mexico. At Yerba Buena he was much respected by Spear, Rae, and other prominent merchants, and liked by the people in general. He was fond of chess, and also made frequently one of a party at whist, playing chess in the daytime with Rae, and whist in the evening. After selling his goods here, Teal returned to New Mexico. Both he and Titcomb were originally from New England.

CHAPTER XXXVI
Gold, Gold, and More Gold.

THE existence of gold in the Sacramento valley and vicinity was known to the Padres long prior to what is commonly known as the gold discovery of 1848. Many of the Indians connected with the Missions were from that part of the country, and after becoming civilized, they were permitted to go to and fro between the Missions and their old homes, leave of absence being granted for the purpose. Sometimes on returning to the Mission after a visit of this kind, an Indian would bring little pieces of shining metal to the priest, approach him with an air of mystery indicating he had something to communicate, and display what he had found. The priest was to the Indian the embodiment of all wisdom and knowledge, and naturally the one to whom he would disclose anything of importance. Probably he had a suspicion that these shining bits were gold, having some indefinite idea of the value of that metal. He would be asked where he had obtained it, and would name the spot, a certain slough or river bottom, where he had picked it up, or say that in digging for some root he had unearthed it. Upon getting all the information the Indian could give, the priest, with a solemn air, would caution the Indian not to impart to anyone else knowledge of the discovery, assuring him if he further divulged such information the wrath of God would be visited upon him. Having the most entire confidence in the priest and in everything he said, the Indian never uttered a word in regard to finding the gold, and kept the matter secret in his own breast.

In my business trips about the bay of San Francisco and neighborhood I visited the Missions, and became intimately acquainted with Father Muro, of the Mission of San José, and Father Mercado, of the Mission of Santa Clara. Both these priests always welcomed me. Father Mercado, whenever I was in the neighborhood transacting my business with the people, would send a messenger for me to come and dine with him. His table was bountifully supplied; and during Lent, when meat was forbidden, he had everything else that was allowable, fish of different kinds, eggs cooked in various styles, and little delicacies of one kind and another, furnishing a meal of which a prince might have partaken with the greatest satisfaction.

The priests naturally had confidence in the merchants who supplied them with goods and whose position gave them influence, and it was through them that they had communication with the world outside.

Father Muro, while I was visiting him along in 1843 or 1844, at the time I was agent of Paty, McKinley & Co., at Yerba Buena, mentioned to me his knowledge of the existence of gold in the Sacramento valley as a great secret, requiring me to promise not to divulge it. I have never mentioned it to this day to anyone. Afterward, in conversation with Father Mercado, the same subject was gradually and cautiously broached, and he confided to me his knowledge of the existence of gold in the same locality. Both of the priests stated that their information was obtained from Indians. Father Mercado was a brilliant conversationalist, and talked with greatest fluency, in a steady stream of discourse hour after hour; and I greatly enjoyed hearing him. After he had imparted the news of gold in the Sacramento valley, I would interrupt the discourse, and, for the sake of argument, suggest that it would be better to make the matter known to induce Americans and others to come here, urging that with their enterprise and skill, they would rapidly open and develop the country, build towns, and engage in numberless undertakings which would tend to the enrichment and prosperity of the country, increase the value of lands, enhance the price of cattle, and benefit the people. He would answer that the immigration would be dangerous; that they would pour in by thousands and overrun the country; Protestants would swarm here, and the Catholic religion would be endangered; the work of the Missions would be interfered with, and as the Californians had no means of defense, no navy nor army, the Americans would soon obtain supreme control; that they would undoubtedly at some time come in force, and all this would happen; but if no inducements were offered, the change might not take place in his time.

I never heard from any one, except the two priests, of gold in Northern California prior to its discovery in 1848 at Sutter's mill. In the year 1851, I, with others, made an expedition into lower California from San Diego in search of gold. There information had been given by Indians to priests under similar circumstances.

About the year 1837 there was an Indian outbreak in what is now San Diego county. A family by the name of Ybarra, consisting of the father, the mother, two young daughters, and a son about twelve years of age, lived at the rancho of San Ysidro. They had in their employ an old Indian woman, who had been christianized at the Mission, a very faithful and good woman, a *comadre* to her mistress, the godmother of one of the Indian woman's children. This relation was frequently assumed by the California ladies, it being a mandate of the Catholic Church everywhere, that any child that is christened shall be attended by a godfather and godmother, and the Californians performed this religious duty toward the children of the poorer classes, including the Indians. The serving woman got information of an attack upon the rancho which had been planned by Indians in the mountains, and a week before the occurrences here mentioned she warned the family of the approach. She urged and begged that they at once remove to the Presidio of San Diego for protection. Her mistress was anxious to follow the advice, but Ybarra himself discarded it. He did not believe that the Indians contemplated a movement.

The Californians were a brave people, especially in opposition to the Indians, whether they went out in pursuit of them to recover stolen horses, or otherwise. They were always prepared to resist an attack by them in their own homes, and did not fear them, but considered that three or four, or eight or ten of their number were sufficient to vanquish ten times that many Indians.

Ybarra had with him two vaqueros on the ranch, and did not think it necessary to pay heed to the statement of the woman, who, the night before the attack, repeated with emphasis, her advice for the family to leave, saying the next day the Indians would surely be there and carry out their plans. The next morning at nine o'clock, while Ybarra and his vaqueros were at the corral, about 150 yards from the house, engaged in lassoing horses, with the intention of starting for San Diego, the Indians stealthily approached, to the number of seventy-five or one hundred. The three men in the corral, seeing them very near, immediately ran toward the house to secure arms. This design, however, was thwarted by a little Indian boy employed in the family, who, seeing them coming as they neared the house, shut and barred the door and prevented them from entering. He must have had knowledge of the designs of the Indians, and been in complicity with them, as by this act of the little villain, the three unarmed men were left outside at the mercy of the miscreant savages, and were speedily killed. The Indians then broke into the house, and made a movement immediately to kill Doña Juana, the mistress, but the old Indian woman defended her at the peril of her own life; interceded with the Indians and supplicated them to spare her mistress. This they did. The two daughters were also captured by the Indians and made prisoners. All the houses of the rancho were burned. The mother was ordered by the savages to leave the house, and go on foot to San Diego. She set forth entirely disrobed. On approaching San Diego Mission she was clothed by a friendly woman, who came out and met her. In proceeding through a wheat field on the rancho she met her little son, who had gone out in the morning and had not encountered the savages. He now learned from his mother of the murder of his father and the two vaqueros, and the capture of his sisters. He was sent ahead to give information of the attack to the first Californian he might meet.

News of what had happened was immediately communicated to the Rancho Tia Juana, owned and occupied by Don Santiago Argüello, a beautiful piece of land having a fine stream of living water running through it. At that time several California families were encamped there, spending a portion of the summer; the Bandinis, Alvarados and others. There were also several young ladies and girls, one of them Miss Estudillo.

At the Rancho Tia Juana the intelligence created much consternation, and the camps of the several families were immediately broken up. They proceeded to San Diego, accompanied by the Argüello family, who took with them as many of their horses as they conveniently could. The Indians shortly after reached the place, burned the houses, and secured the stock which the owner had left behind in the fields.

CHAPTER XXXVII
Firewater, Bonfires and Scared Indians

THE third night the Indians intended to fall upon the Rancho Jesus Maria, occupied by Don José Lopez with his wife and two daughters. News of the Indian outbreak reaching San Diego, it was resolved to send out a force for his protection and to rescue, if possible, the two girls captured at San Ysidro.

Don José Lopez had a large vineyard and manufactured wine, of which he occasionally imbibed more than was consistent with a well-regulated head. On the evening when the Indians were to attack him he was filled with wine, which led him to some extraordinary demonstrations. He went out and built a number of large bonfires in the vicinity of his house, and then commenced shouting vociferously, making a great noise for his own entertainment only. As the Indians approached the place they sent out a spy in advance to reconnoitre and ascertain if everything was favorable for attack. The spy seeing the fires burning, and hearing this loud and continued shouting, concluded that the Californians were there in force, and so reported to the main body of Indians, who deemed it prudent to retire.

This is the only instance I remember where any particular benefit resulted from the freaks of an intoxicated man, who probably could not have done anything better to drive away the Indians had he been aware of their presence and designs.

The next day the force arrived, and Lopez and family were escorted to San Diego, the main body of the troops going in pursuit of the Indians.

Ybarra, at the time he was murdered, had in San Diego two sons, who joined the company in pursuit, as they were anxious to learn everything possible regarding the fate of their sisters. They were soon informed by a captured spy that two of the chiefs had made them their wives. The company followed into the mountains, until they reached a rugged and broken country wholly inaccessible to horses, and were obliged to stop, the narrow defiles affording innumerable hiding places for Indians and giving them an advantage over the approaching enemy. Had the Californians attempted to advance on foot they would have met with certain death, for the Indians swarmed in force, knew the region intimately, and would have picked the troops off one by one. The two brothers Ybarra, however, urged on by the desire to rescue their sisters, advanced further into the mountains than the rest of the company, actually saw the girls in the midst of the savages, and got within a short distance of them, but were so badly wounded by the arrows showered upon them that they were compelled to return. After that, up to the time Miss Estudillo left San Diego, in 1842, nothing further was heard of the two girls.

Opposite the house where she was living with her aunt was the residence of Ybarra's two sons and their families. Doña Juana, the mother, lived with them in San Diego up to the time of her death, which occurred about a year after her husband was murdered; this terrible occurrence and the loss of her daughters also, proving too great a blow for her. During this time she never ceased to lament their sad fate. It was heart-rending to listen to her expressions of grief, weeping and wailing for the loss of her husband and children, like Rachel refusing to be comforted. Her distress often made the people weep who heard her lamentations.

Prior to the incidents above related, the same tribe of Indians had made several attacks upon the Presidio of San Diego for purpose of plunder, and the capture of women, but were frustrated; and also pursued and severely chastised. The savages in that part of the country had the reputation of being braver and better fighters than those in the north. The San Diego Indians ate the meat of horses as well as of cattle.

In 1838 there were living at the Presidio of San Diego the following families: The Estudillos, the Argüellos, the Bandinis, the Alvarados, Governor Pico's family, the Marrons, the Machados, the Ybarras, the Serranos, the Carrillos, the Lopez family, the Fitch family and a number of others.

One of the daughters of the Alvarado family married Captain Snook. After her marriage two of her younger sisters resided with her a portion of the time. One of them had acquired considerable knowledge of Indian language. Several of these families had Indian men for cooks. One evening after supper, the young lady just mentioned, Doña Guadalupe Alvarado, overheard the cooks in earnest conversation in the Indian language. As soon as the words were caught by her ear she was startled and surprised, and drawing nearer heard all that was said. She discovered that the Indian cooks from the different families had gathered in the kitchen of the house and were discussing a plan of attack upon the town by members of their tribe. It appeared that arrangements had been completed for the capture of the town the following night, and that the cooks in the several families were to lend their aid.

In the council of the cooks, it came out that each on the following night was to communicate with a spy from the main body of Indians, and take stations for this purpose on top of the hill overlooking the town, where the old Presidio and first garrison quarters of the Spaniards in California formerly stood. They were to inform the spies of the condition of each family, whether or not it was sufficiently off guard at the time to warrant an attack. There happened to be present in the house Don Pio Pico and Don Andres Pico, who were making a friendly call on the family. They were a good deal startled at the statement made by the young lady, and represented that they would give the conspiracy immediate attention. The people of San Diego at that period had their houses well supplied with arms and were always on the watch for Indian movements. Accordingly, during the night they organized a company of citizens and arranged that at daylight each house should be visited, and the cook secured. This was successfully accomplished. As each of the conspirators came out of the house in the early morning he was lassoed, and all were taken a little distance from town, where it was proposed to shoot them. They expressed a desire to be allowed to die as Christians, to confess to the priest and to receive the sacrament. This request was granted; the priest heard the confession of each and administered the rites of the church. A trench of suitable depth was then dug, and the Indians made to kneel close beside it. Then on being shot, each fell into the ditch, where he was buried. Eight or ten Indians were executed at this time.

While these proceedings were taking place a messenger was sent to one of the Boston hide-ships lying in the port requesting that a cannon might be loaned to the town, to assist in its defense. The cannon was sent over, with a suitable supply of ammunition. At night a party of citizens visited the spot where the Indian spy was to appear, and succeeded in capturing him. He steadily refused to confess, though assured that he would soon die, as his friends had done before him. One of his ears was cut off, and he was given to understand that the other one would follow, and that he would be mutilated little by little until he made the statement required of him; whereupon, his resolution gave way, and he made a confession indicating where the Indians were encamped, and telling all that he knew.

This mode of extorting a confession, although repulsive to those who participated in it, was the only way of securing the desired information. After the spy had divulged all he knew, he was shot without ceremony, he being an unconverted Indian and not desiring the services of the priest.

The next day the citizens were out in force, found and surprised the Indians and engaged them in battle; numbers of them were killed, but none of the Californians.

The last time Miss Estudillo saw any of these savages was in 1840 while visiting at the house of Don Juan Bandini, who owned and occupied the Rancho Jurupa, in what is now Riverside county. Her aunt, Doña Dolores Estudillo, was Bandini's first wife, and at her death, left several children. He afterward married a daughter of the Prefect, Don Santiago Argüello, who, at the time now mentioned, was mistress of the household. The house was situated at an elevation, and the view from it commanded a wide range of country. One day they all noticed from the house a body of Indians in the distance, who were collecting horses they had stolen from the Mission San Gabriel and the Rancho Santa Ana in that neighborhood. As Bandini had but few men with him at the time, and the Indians were in large numbers, he did not deem it prudent to attack, and attempt the rescue of the animals. He therefore permitted them to move off to their retreats without any pursuit.

In 1838, at Yerba Buena, I made the acquaintance of James Berry, an Irishman of intelligence and education, who had come here from Mexico or South America. He had traveled all over the world. Spear was attracted to him, and Berry stayed at his house while in Yerba Buena. He spent a good deal of his time at the Mission of San Rafael with Timothy Murphy, one of his countrymen, and Father Quijas. He was a Spanish scholar and spoke Spanish perfectly. In 1839 Governor Alvarado gave him a grant of eleven leagues of land at Punta Reyes, and he stocked the rancho with horses and cattle.

The ship "Alciope" of Boston, Captain Clap, arrived at Yerba Buena in the summer of 1840 with an assorted cargo, from Honolulu. She had been chartered by A. B. Thompson, who disposed of her goods here, and then loaded her with hides and tallow. She went down the coast exchanging the tallow for hides, with the tallow vessels bound for Callao, and proceeded to the Islands; from there to Boston.

At the Fourth of July celebration while at Yerba Buena on this trip, being the only vessel in the bay at the time, she was handsomely decorated with flags of different nations. Salutes were fired by the vessel at sunrise, noon and sunset. A grand picnic was held at the Rincon, which was attended by all Americans and other foreigners of the town, by the elite of the Californians from town and country, and by the officers of the vessel. The foreigners, English, Irish, Germans and French, joined in the festivities with all the enthusiasm of the Americans, and the Californians likewise, prominent among whom was Don Francisco Guerrero, who did all in his power to make the occasion enjoyable to those participating. In the evening there was a ball at Captain Richardson's house on the hill, Clay street and Grant avenue, which was attended by those who had joined in the picnic. Late in the evening a splendid dinner was served, and dancing continued till daylight. The whole celebration passed off in the pleasantest manner and was greatly enjoyed by all. To enable the prominent families around the bay to attend, boats and schooners were sent to different points a day or two previous to the Fourth to bring them in, and they were returned in the same way after the event.

CHAPTER XXXVIII
Nathan Spear's Grist Mill; the First

ABOUT September, 1838, there arrived at Yerba Buena the hermaphrodite brig "Fearnaught," Captain Robert H. Dare, from Realejo, Central America, with a cargo mostly of *panoche* (hard sugar) put up in boxes in solid form, each box containing a cake of about three arrobas in weight, and resembling packages of maple sugar. The vessel also brought a little coffee. She remained in the harbor a long time. The *panoche* sold readily to the California people, who had a liking for sweet things, and were very fond of it, the children eating it in lumps like candy, the grown people doing the same. Captain Dare was an Englishman, a regular John Bull, a very good sort of man, punctual and correct in all his business engagements. There also came in the vessel an American by the name of John Perry, who had lived at Realejo for many years as a merchant. He visited California on this trip for his health. He was a peculiar man, although very intelligent, possessed of wide information, and a Spanish scholar, speaking and writing the language fluently. He retained the friendship and confidence of his business associates to the time of his death. After the vessel had disposed of her goods she returned to Realejo. Perry remained here for about a year and a half, stopping with Spear, and assisting in the business, taking charge of the store while I was cruising about the bay. Spear, of course, had a general oversight of affairs, but did not confine himself closely to the store at Yerba Buena, as he had a store at Monterey also, to which place he went frequently. He also made little trips into the country round about on matters of business. Besides this, having a smattering of medical knowledge, and a good supply of medicines, he was called upon to attend the sick in various directions, which he did willingly, making no charge for his services.

Perry was married to one of the ladies of Realejo, and appeared to be very devoted to his wife and children. Having an intimate knowledge of the character, habits and manners of the people of Central America, he

[TEXT OF LETTER ON OPPOSITE PAGE]

U S Ship Portsmouth
Yerba Buena July 6th 1846

Sir

I have received your note and in reply, would recommend your coming on board the Portsmouth for this night, as to say the least the propriety of sending an armed force on shore except in case of sudden & extreme immergency, as appeared to be the case on the night of the fourth, may well be questioned. Still, if the Alcaldy, the only remaining officer of the town will join with you in a statement of the necessity of an armed force to protect your person & property I will not hesitate to comply with your request.

Resply Your Obt Ser

Jno. B. Montgomery
Commander

To
William A. Leidesdorff Esqr
Vice Consul of the U. States
Yerba Buena

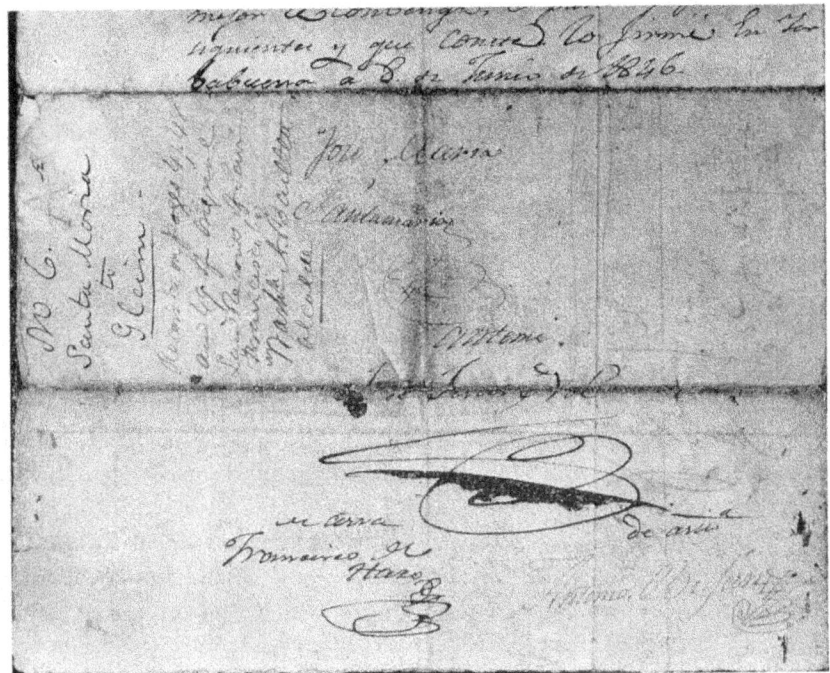

BARTLETT CARRIES ON FOR NOÉ

This Alcalde Grant bears the signatures of José de Jesus Noé, last Mexican Alcalde, and Washington A. Bartlett, first American Alcalde at San Francisco.

This letter is the outcome of the rather boisterous Fourth of July celebration of 1846, five days before the American flag was raised over the future San Francisco.

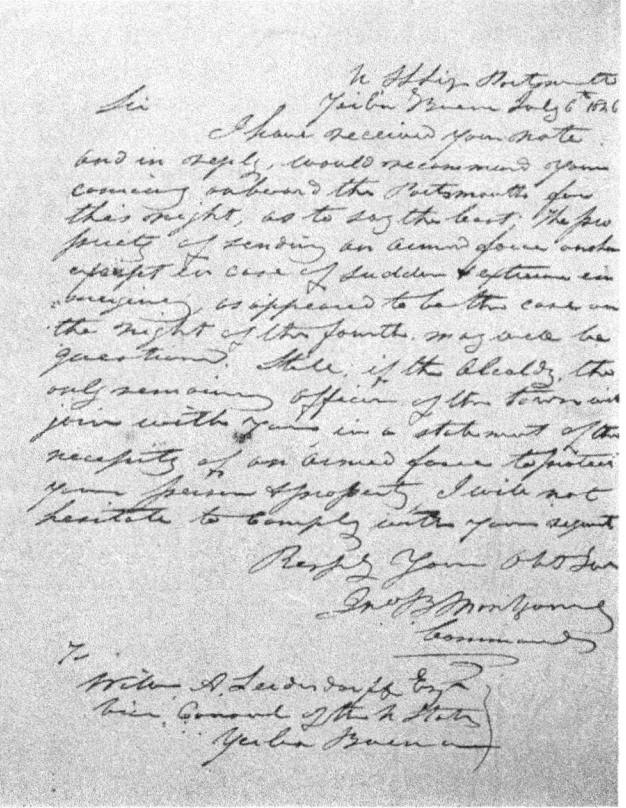

MONTGOMERY ALLAYS LEIDESDORFF'S FEARS.

"KENT HALL" APPEARS ON THE BEACH

entertained us with descriptions of the country, its inhabitants and their history.

In 1838, and prior to that time, the Mexican law applicable to the department of California forbade anybody in any seaport building nearer the water than 200 varas, so that facilities for smuggling might not exist, as if the houses were close to shore. Under this agreement Jacob P. Leese and Captain Wm. A. Richardson were living on what is now Grant avenue, and conducting business there. This was considerably beyond the 200 vara limit, and as they could not be down near the water, which they would have preferred for their business, they went higher up than was necessary under the law, this elevation giving them, however, a good view of the surrounding country and bay.

About the beginning of 1838, the Boston bark, "Kent," Captain Steel, was lying in the bay of San Francisco, and Spear bought of him a good-sized ship's house, and placed it near the beach, at what is now the northwest corner of Clay and Montgomery streets. As a special friend, Alvarado, the governor, gave him permission to occupy it there, he then being the only person who was permitted to be near the margin of Loma Alta cove. Very soon afterward he built a store adjoining "Kent Hall," by which name the ship's house was known, though only 12x18 feet in dimensions. About that time Spear and Leese dissolved their partnership, and the business on the hill was discontinued, Leese still having his residence there. Spear opened business at the new place near the water. He had no title to the lot, simply a permission from the governor to occupy it. Perry, finding that the climate of California agreed with him and that his health had improved, determined to make Yerba Buena his home in the future. He was inclined to become a Mexican citizen.

Spear encouraged him in this inclination, as being of great advantage, for thereby he might, under the law, become a grantee of such lands as the governor should be disposed to bestow upon him. He also thought Perry might assist him in acquiring a title to the lot occupied by his store. Perry went by land to Monterey, with strong letters of introduction from Spear to Alvarado, in the spring of '39. The governor made him a citizen of Mexico, and granted to him, in his own name, the fifty vara lot occupied by Spear. Upon his return, Perry deeded the property to him, although under the law, strictly applied, Spear could not hold the land under such transfer. In a short time Leese obtained a similar permit from the governor to build near the water, and did so. After that, Vioget and John Fuller did the same. They were followed by others as the town increased and foreigners came in. Spear continued to occupy the place until the change of government in 1846. Perry returned to Realejo in the spring of 1840, his health not firmly established, and died there within a year.

In 1839, early in the year, the brig "Daniel O'Connell," an English vessel, arrived at Yerba Buena from Payta, Peru, with a cargo of Peruvian and other foreign goods, having on board a considerable quantity of *pisco* or *italia,* a fine delicate liquor manufactured at a place called Pisco. He had also a considerable lot of vicuña hats, and a good many *ponchos,* similar to those brought from Mexico. Spear assisted the captain and supercargo in disposing of the goods. She left here for Peru in the Spring of 1840 with a cargo of tallow.

In 1839 the brig "Corsair," Captain William S. Hinckley, arrived from Monterey. Hinckley was afterward alcalde. While at Monterey he said something about evading the custom house laws, and was heard to talk imprudently in Spear's store. I cautioned him in a friendly way. A few days after, Don Pablo de la Guerra, a custom house officer, and other officials, arrived from Monterey; Hinckley was arrested, and kept under arrest for about a week at Spear's store while an examination was made by the officers. An inspection was made of the vessel, the sailing master and other officers were cross-questioned; but nothing could be proved against him, and he was discharged.

Hinckley being a man with good powers of speech and persuasion, brought these personal forces to bear in his defense against the charge of smuggling. Besides this, he showed the officials all the attentions possible during the examination. This is the only instance, with the exception of A. B. Thompson, supercargo of the "Loriot," that I remember, of an arrest in those days on a charge of evading the revenue laws.

On this trip the "Corsair" landed at Yerba Buena, consigned to Spear & Hinckley, the machinery for a grist mill, from Callao, manufactured at Baltimore. Shortly after, the machinery was put up in a heavy-frame wooden building, two stories high, on the north side of Clay street, in the middle of a fifty vara lot between Kearny and Montgomery streets. This was the first grist mill in California. It was operated by six mules, Spear having some eighteen or twenty for this work. A man by the name of Daniel Sill was the miller. The mill made a considerable quantity of fine flour, from wheat raised by the rancheros round the bay, each of them having a patch, and some of them fields of good size.

The mill probably turned out twenty to twenty-five barrels of flour a day, which was put up in fifty and one-hundred-pound sacks and sold to farmers and to the vessels. A flour mill run by water was established about the same time at San José by William Gulnac, an American, who married a Lower California lady. He first emigrated to Honolulu, with his family, and from there came to Monterey in the bark "Volunteer," in 1833. He went thence to San José. Those two were the only flouring mills in the department for a long while. Prior to their establishment the ranchero made his flour by crushing the wheat by means of an apparatus composed of two circular stones a yard in diameter, set up out of doors near the kitchen of his house, a shaft being affixed to the upper stone and turned by mule power. The grain thus ground fell upon a platform about eight or ten feet in diameter, under the lower stone; a hopper was affixed to the upper stone, into which the wheat was poured. After a quantity had gone through this process it was ground over again two or three times in the same manner; the flour was then sifted out in hand sieves, and was ready for use. The poorer people who did not have a mill of this kind were provided with a *metate,* a flat stone, about 12x18 inches, with a little rim on the two long sides, and supported on three legs five or six inches high of unequal length, the flat surface inclining at an angle of about thirty-five degrees. The operator, resting on his knees, crushed and abraded the grain by moving a hand-stone forcibly downwards over the flat surface until the grain was well cracked. At the foot of the incline it fell into a dish placed beneath. The process was repeated several times and until the grain was sufficiently pulverized for use. If corn was crushed for *tortillas,* or tamales, the whole of the grain was made use of. The *metate* was also used for grinding chili pepper, when dry—for seasoning; also for meat, instead of chopping.

Sill, the miller, was an old mountaineer who had come across the plains in 1831 or '32, and lived about the bay of San Francisco, either at a Mission or with a ranchero. He was industrious and useful, possessed of a deal of common sense, but of no education; quiet and well behaved; a splendid hunter and marksman, having brought from his eastern home his old rifle, of a very primitive pattern, but unerring in execution in his hands. If he ever drew it upon a coon, a bear or a lark, the result was that the game had to come down. While employed as miller he was fond of going out Sunday mornings for a little hunt. I was often invited to accompany him. We would start about nine o'clock and go over to a place called Rincon, a flat between Rincon Hill and Mission Bay, and a resort for deer, the place being covered with a thick growth of scrub oak and willows, which afforded them good shelter. Presently, perhaps four or five deer would appear in sight, and Sill, drawing his old rifle to his shoulder, always got one. "Now, William," he would say, "go for the yellow horse." This was one of Spear's animals, and was known as the deer horse. I would go and saddle him, and ride over to the hunting ground. By that time, Sill usually had another deer. Slinging the two carcasses across the animal, we would return in triumph to town.

The native Californians were not fond of hunting, and so the deer were little disturbed, save by the few hunters who came into the country from other parts. Sill spent a portion of his time in the Sacramento valley, trapping beaver and land-otter, for their skins, which were very valuable. He also killed elk, for their hides and tallow. There was a blacksmith's shop connected with the mill, and Sill, who had a natural aptitude for all trades, was the blacksmith as well as the miller, the first one in San Francisco. Afterward, old Frank Westgate was employed as blacksmith. He understood that work; but was a hard drinker. Sill remained as miller for Spear until about 1842 or '43, when his disposition to rove, impelled him to take his departure. He went to the upper Sacramento valley, and lived a while with Peter Lassen, a Dane, who had settled there under a grant. At times he stopped with some of the other settlers; with Sutter for a while at New Helvetia. As he always made himself useful, he was welcomed wherever he went.

About March, 1841, the Ecuadorian brig "Jóven Carolina," from Guayaquil, arrived, commanded by an Ecuadorian who was always known as Captain Miguelon, (which signifies large Michael.) The captain was of a broad and liberal nature, kind and humane in his treatment of the men on board his vessel; the friend of everybody; overflowing with good humor, though at the same time an excellent business man. Being one of the jolliest and best-natured of gentlemen, he took great delight in the society of ladies. They often visited him on board the brig. The vessel brought a cargo mostly of cocoa, with a quantity of coffee, from Central America, and some Peruvian commodities. She remained at Yerba Buena until November, disposing of the goods, all of them being sold in the bay, a portion to vessels trading on the coast. The Californians were fond of cocoa and chocolate; the manufacture of the latter from the cocoa was done by women, who prepared a choice article with the hand-mill or *metate*.

The vessel went back to Guayaquil, and thence to Peru, with tallow. Shortly before she sailed, Captain Miguelon, who owned the vessel, urged me to go to Guayaquil with him, saying that on arrival there, I should be supercargo; we would then return to California and dispose of the goods. The offer was an excellent one, but I declined it, thinking I could do better by remaining where I was.

One day in January, 1842, after I had joined Captain Paty, as supercargo, I started with Edward L. Stetson, the young clerk of the vessel, accompanied by a vaquero, from Don Domingo Peralta's rancho, near the present site of Berkeley, for the pueblo of San José. Stetson had just come from Charlestown, Massachusetts.

It had been raining hard, and the creeks were swollen, running over their banks, the country flooded all round; the winter having been a severe one. On reaching Alameda creek at the crossing near Vallejo's Mill, we found it was overflowing, and the current very swift. In that condition it was dangerous to cross. I had often crossed under similar circumstances, and I consulted with the vaquero as to the expediency of proceeding; he replied, "Just as you please." Stetson said it looked very risky. I told him to keep perfectly cool and steady, as the horse would have all he could do to take him over, and he must not do anything to excite the animal or throw him off his balance. The vaquero went first, Stetson next and I followed. About half way across, the vaquero's horse, a large white colt, unbroken, lost his footing, and he and the rider rolled over and over in the stream, but after a hard tussle brought up on the opposite side, the vaquero having stuck to the horse all the time. When this happened Stetson began to weaken, got unsteady, nervous, and, turning round, looked very white, remarking that it was the worst scrape he ever got into. I told him not to look around, which might embarrass the horse, but to look ahead, to hold on and keep cool. However, he began to shake, and presently down the horse went, and the two began to roll over and over. He lost his hold upon the saddle and floundered about in the stream, his long limbs projecting here and there, as the current swept him away. Notwithstanding the peril he was in, I could not resist laughing at his ridiculous appearance. The horse got across, and Stetson brought up on a little island. Getting across the stream dry on my horse, I called out to him to rest awhile, and then swim ashore the best he could. Being a swimmer, he finally plunged in, and with hard work in the swift water reached shore, minus his hat and a fifty dollar serape. We gave the vaquero a dollar, and he returned in an hour with the serape, having been fortunate enough to recover it.

We resumed our horses, and on reaching the Mission of San José were cordially welcomed by Father Muro. Stetson and the vaquero were furnished with clothing while their own was drying, the difficulty being to find garments which would accommodate Stetson's long limbs, and at the best the bottom of his pantaloons came half way up to the knee. Considerable merriment was had at his expense. We remained two nights, waiting for the Coyote creek to fall somewhat, as we had to cross that stream. The Coyote was not dangerous to cross, and we reached the old town of San José without mishap.

There were no bridges in those days. In April, 1839, a bridal party, numbering twenty or thirty persons, went from Pinole to the Mission of San José. In crossing San Leandro, San Lorenzo and Alameda creeks they had difficulty, because of the high water. In returning the next day they found the streams still higher, and the difficulty increased. On coming to the San Leandro creek they found the water so high that it was unsafe to cross, and the entire party was detained there several days.

The first steamer appeared on the bay of San Francisco in 1847. She was built by the Russians at Sitka, and brought on one of their vessels to Bodega, where the machinery was put into her. She was a side-wheel boat, and was owned by William A. Leidesdorff, who had bought her of the Russians. On the trial trip in the bay she passed round Goat Island, when all the native and foreign residents gazed with curiosity and astonishment. The excitement was great, and the day one of general rejoicing. The machinery, shortly proving a failure, was removed, and she became a sailing vessel about the bay.

When Captain John Paty landed General Micheltorena and the troops at San Blas he found there a man by the name of William M. Smith, whom he brought to Yerba Buena on the return voyage. He was afterward known as "Jim Crow" Smith, on account of his ability to mimic southern negroes. Coming originally from Georgia, he had been a circus rider in Mexico, and was considerable of a pistol-shooter, with a good deal of bravado about him. When in liquor, if crossed, he was a dangerous man. He could assume the air and manner of a gentleman, but through all the superficial polish the circus rider was discernible more or less. He had considerable native ability, though not much education, and spoke the Spanish language well. After an employment by William A. Leidesdorff to collect hides and tallow, he became a partner of Frank Ward in the fall of 1847, the firm being Ward & Smith, dealers in general merchandise. In the capacity of first auctioneer in Yerba Buena, he built himself up and made money, as any man could do in those days who was industrious. He prospered, and secured the respect and confidence of the people. In 1848 he married the widow of William S. Hinckley, and in 1849 or '50 moved to Martinez, and built a residence about a mile from the town. Up to the latter part of '53 he behaved very well. Being an accurate shot with a pistol he could knock the head off a bird or break the neck of a bottle at any reasonable distance. One day after he had been drinking with José Antonio Sanchez and some others, he requested Sanchez to stand off about twenty paces and put a bottle on his head, and let him break it with a pistol shot. The latter complied, and Smith shattered the bottle, though intoxicated at the time. The performance was repeated several times. Fond of using his pistol, he finally committed suicide at his home in Martinez in 1854.

CHAPTER XXXIX
H. M. S. "Blossom" Discovers Blossom Rock

DON MARTINEZ became comandante of the Presidio of San Francisco in 1819, succeeding Don Luis Argüello, who was appointed provisional governor, and with his family lived at the Presidio. In later years I had a conversation with one of his daughters, Doña Encarnacion Altamirano, who, at the time above mentioned, was twelve years old. She remembers that there was a little *baluarte,* or fortification, of triangular shape, located near the intersection of Van Ness avenue and the bay shore, at what is now known as Black Point. The fort, she said, was mounted with a cannon pointing to the bay. There were no barracks at the place, no buildings of any kind. There was no guard, only this single gun mounted on the *baluarte.* I asked the object of the arrangement, and she replied it was intended for defense, to be availed of in the event vessels of an enemy succeeded in getting past Fort Point and coming up the bay. The little fort was in charge of the comandante, and the artillery was kept in good condition. It remained there for several years, and up to the time the family removed from the Presidio to the Pinole Rancho. The gun was occasionally fired at the celebration of some festival, the powder for this purpose being brought from the Presidio. Shot for the gun was kept near it at the fortification, ready for use in case of necessity.

In 1826 the ship "Blossom," a British man-of-war, Captain Beechey, visited the bay of San Francisco, and remained several weeks. The captain made the first discovery of the sunken obstruction to navigation known as Blossom Rock, which he named after his ship, and laid it down on his chart. I have known of a number of vessels getting on this rock. In 1830 the East India ship "Seringapatam" came into the bay for supplies. She was loaded with East India goods—silks and other articles adapted to the Mexican trade, being bound to ports in Mexico. She remained a week or two. In leaving, she struck on the rock, and hung there until a change of tide; when she floated off and proceeded on her voyage. Being built of teak wood in the strongest manner, the ship received no injury. She was commanded by English officers, who were attired in the East India Company uniform. The crew was composed entirely of Malays. It will be remembered that Blossom Rock was blown up and removed under the direction of engineer A. von Schmidt.

One of the characteristics of Californians in early days was the great respect which the children showed their parents. I have observed instances of this deference; among which, the son coming into the presence of his parents, in their own house, removed his hat with politeness, and always remained standing, perhaps in conversation with them, until he was asked to be seated.

The Californians were not given to drinking, though fond of tobacco smoking, the habit being universal amongst the men. Sometimes the ladies of Southern California indulged in smoking in order to be sociable; and some of the women of Northern California were addicted to the same habit—a few among the lower classes. The Mexican ladies, however, were fond of smoking; the rich as well as the poor. This was the custom in their own country, and those who came to California brought it with them. The cigaritos which they smoked were small, made of delicate paper, and the tobacco very fine.

The Mexican as well as the California ladies were noted for their small feet and hands, which is a characteristic of the Spanish race. The Mexican ladies when smoking were in the habit of holding the cigarito between the thumb and finger; the rich using a gold or silver holder, to prevent staining the fingers with the tobacco, and the poorer classes a holder made of *gamuza,* or fine deer skin—with two little pockets, into which they slipped the thumb and finger. Holding up the cigarito, as they placed it in the mouth or removed it, they displayed their pretty little hands to advantage, the fingers extended with an air of coquetry, all very graceful and becoming, and quite captivating to the observer.

But, however, habituated to the indulgence, no boy or man, though the latter might be sixty years of age, ever smoked in the presence of his parents. I remember this regulation was conformed to while Don Ygnacio Peralta was one time visiting his father Don Luis, at the latter's house in the Pueblo of San José; the son, then over sixty years, standing until the old gentleman requested him to be seated. During a long interview, in which they talked continually, the son, though ill at ease, refrained from smoking; the father meanwhile enjoying himself happily in that way; but such a breath of decorum and filial respect as for the other to smoke at the same time was not to be thought of. If a young man was smoking in the street, and met an old man coming along, so great was the feeling of respect and deference for the latter, that the former would cease smoking and throw his cigar away, and politely raise his hat in salutation, whether they were acquainted or total strangers. The vaqueros and other servants of the house showed the same politeness to their masters, always removing their hats when they came into their presence, and never smoking before them.

Notions of propriety and morality were so strict among the people that young people engaged to be married were permitted little association by themselves.

They were scarcely allowed to see each other or to converse together, except in the presence of their parents. This was my own experience in an engagement of over two years. The courtship was usually arranged by the mother of the young lady, or sometimes a favorite aunt was sought and first consulted by the young gentleman who desired the daughter or niece in marriage. If the suitor was considered a worthy person by the father, the young lady was communicated with, after which a request in writing came from the young man to the father. If the application was deemed satisfactory he sent a written reply. Time, however, was taken for consideration, and no haste displayed. It would be an excellent thing if, in this respect, the old Spanish custom, having so much of simplicity and purity, prevailed to-day. Although the young ladies were not so highly educated as at the present time, yet on going into a family one could see at a glance that artlessness, affection and modesty were the characteristics of the feminine portion thereof, and these merits in my estimation transcend all others.

In November, 1838, having been invited to a wedding, together with Captain Hinckley I crossed the bay in the schooner "Isabel," and arrived just before sunset of a clear November afternoon, at the embarcadero on San Antonio creek, (East Oakland.) Reaching the landing, we were met by a younger brother of the bridegroom, mounted on a splendid black horse, both horse and rider being attired in the richest manner and presenting a very attractive sight. At the same time there appeared upon the brow of the hill, perhaps twenty yards away, a full *caponera* of *palominos,* or cream-colored horses, for the wedding cavalcade. They raised their heads, pausing a moment, startled it seemed at sight of the vessel, and as the bright sun struck full upon them, their colored bodies, of light golden hue, and dazzling manes, shone resplendent. The picture has ever since remained in my mind. They were attended by vaqueros, who cast their lassos and secured two of them for Captain Hinckley and myself, we having brought our saddles with us, a necessity in those days, though you were a guest. The bridegroom had two *caponeras* for the use of the bridal party;

one of *canelos,* or red roan horses, and the other of twenty-five black horses. Horses of mixed color were better animals than those of a single color.

On returning from the wedding, which took place at the Mission of San José, as the bridal party approached the mansion at Pinole, a salute of welcome was fired by the father of the bridegroom from a brass cannon, which he, as a military man, kept mounted in the little plaza in front of his dwelling for the protection of the family.

The spring was the dullest season of the year, as the cattle then became quite poor, and not many were killed. Cattle were killed for the use of the rancheros in winter. They were in good condition until spring. The merchants made collections of hides and tallow which accumulated from the slaughter for farm use. In the spring of 1840, business being quiet, I took the schooner "Isabel" over to Yerba Buena Island, now Goat Island, with four men, and camped there for a week; the men cutting the scrub oak on the Island, and filling up the schooner. Permission had been asked of the alcalde to go over and cut wood, which he had granted. I took my fishing tackle and books along. While the men were cutting wood, I fished from the shore, and passed a week very pleasantly as I have related elsewhere.

In 1842 or '43 Spear and Fuller having obtained possession of five or six goats from Captain Nye, of the ship "Fama," placed them upon Yerba Buena Island, by permission of the alcalde. They found subsistence there, multiplied rapidly, and in 1848 and '49 amounted in number to several hundred. From this circumstance the place derived its name of Goat Island.

Spear would occasionally send over to the Island to get a kid or two for his table, the meat being very palatable, and would invite the neighbors to partake.

In the fall of '48 and the early part of '49, after the rush of adventurers to California in the gold excitement, some of them amused themselves by going over to Goat Island and shooting the goats. Meat was scarce, goat meat was considered acceptable, and commanded a good price. Spear and Fuller caused notices to be published in the newspapers forbidding the killing of the goats by trespassers; but those who thought it fine sport to shoot the goats scampering over the island, wholly wild and untamed, gave no heed to the notices.

After this commenced, Spear said to me one day, "Give me my price for my half interest in the goats on the Island." I replied that I did not need them. He said that he did not want to be bothered, and I had better take them, whereupon, to oblige the old gentlemen, I gave him a previously stipulated sum for the goats. It proved a poor investment, for nearly all the goats were killed by the reckless shooters, and not a cent of value did I ever get out of the speculation.

Old Jack Fuller, by which name he was familiarly known, was an Englishman, and an excellent cook. He had been employed by Spear in that capacity. He was also a butcher, and on special occasions, such as festivals, acted as caterer, and could get up an excellent dinner or feast when required. He was well liked by everybody, and met with great success in this line of business. He came originally with Spear to the coast in the schooner "Thaddeus," from Boston, in 1823. He owned property on Kearny street, cornering on Sacramento and California streets, which became valuable about the time of his death. Old Jack was always' good natured, and never dangerous, but would occasionally imbibe too much and run off the track. While in this condition he was given to the most astounding stories, of an innocent kind, however, and that never harmed anybody.

In the fall of 1843 I erected on the beach, between Clay and California streets, about midway between Montgomery and Sansome, a large hide shed, roughly built of boards, securely inclosed and convenient, so at high tide the vessels that brought hides to the place could come right to the door of the house and deliver them. In the summer of '44 I had about 4,000 hides collected there, awaiting shipment. On the afternoon of the 18th of August there came a heavy rain, which lasted continuously for eighteen hours, quite as severe as rains in December or January, very remarkable for a summer in California. As the house was not built for protection against the rains, but only for summer use, my hides got thoroughly wet through, as did those of other persons who had houses near and at other points on the bay. I was obliged to take them all out and dry them on the beach.

When Captain Grimes was settled at Sacramento on his ranch he still made his headquarters at Yerba Buena with Spear, and when here occupied Kent Hall.

The captain, though temperate, and never getting the worse for liquor, was fond of a glass now and then, as most old captains are, and always kept a liquor case well supplied with the choicest brands of liquors. This was known to his friends, and it was always considered a treat to join the old gentleman in a glass. Kent Hall and the liquor case became quite a byword among his associates. Various expedients were used to get the captain into good humor preliminary to taking advantage of the hospitality, and many purely original yarns were given out as sober fact for his entertainment and edification. Looking sternly over his spectacles at the narrator he would refuse to lend a willing ear, or would apply to their talk some emphatic and disparaging epithet. He had traveled extensively over the world, was intelligent and well read, sensible, a man of liberal ideas, and not easily humbugged. It was therefore necessary for those who had designs upon his liquor case to sharpen up their wits and present very plausible, comical stories to interest the old captain sufficiently to persuade him to the point. William D. M. Howard and William G. Rae were the chief leaders in these movements. They would always succeed in bringing the old gentlemen round by telling something a little more ridiculous or astonishing than had been before related; and when the liquor case was opened—to their satisfaction and delight, those who were near at hand were also invited.

CHAPTER XL
Don Francisco Guerrero Gives a Strawberry "Blow out"

LITTLE festivals and recreations among neighbors, without much formality, were usual with the California families, there being scarcely any amusements. On the hills toward the ocean, between the Presidio and Fort Point, and south as far as Lake Lobos, there were large patches of wild strawberries, which grew very plentifully and ripened in the spring. At that time families would resort to the place for the purpose of gathering and partaking of the fruit, camping out for several days at a time; many coming from the surrounding country north and south of the bay, and as far as Sonoma and Santa Clara. This innocent and healthful recreation was a great enjoyment.

I joined a party gathering strawberries, in 1844, the camp consisting of the families of Wm. G. Rae, Captain Richardson, Nathan Spear, Captain Prado Mesa, Don Francisco Guerrero, Bob Ridley and some others. Other camps were scattered about in the neighborhood. The little village of Yerba Buena was nearly depopulated for the time. We were absent about a week.

Before the camp broke up that year, Don Francisco Guerrero gave a grand *merienda* or picnic, in a little valley north of our camp, looking toward the ocean. He provided, among other things, several bullocks and calves, which were prepared as *carne asada*—meat roasted on spits over a bed of coals—this being much superior to other modes of cooking the meat. Guerrero invited to this festival all the people who were camped on the strawberry grounds, numbering several hundred men, women and children; and they enjoyed themselves heartily. Rae, Spear and myself insisted on furnishing the wine for the occasion, although Guerrero had intended doing it himself. While camping, we were visited by W. D. M. Howard and Henry Mellus, supercargos and agents of vessels, and by other supercargoes and captains of vessels in port at the time. Their visit added greatly to the variety and enjoyment of the occasion. Most prominent among those furnishing fun and amusement for the camp was Howard.

One evening he retired into a tent, and, unknown to the ladies, blackened his face with burnt cork, put on a crushed hat and some old clothes, and in this guise appeared among the company as a Southern negro; acting out the character to perfection. At first, the ladies were frightened, and it was some time before his identity was disclosed. On another evening he appeared as a down-east Yankee, dressed in the peculiar garments suited to that character, and created a great deal of diversion by the representation.

On the way home, after the breaking up of the camp, our special company halted at the Mission Dolores. Here Guerrero gave a *baile* in the hall of the Mission, in which all participated and had a grand time, winding up our strawberry festival. Evenings at the camp were spent in singing, telling stories and playing twenty-one and whist.

These gatherings commenced with the first settlement of the country by the Spaniards, the Indians making known the place the strawberries grew. After the custom of camping had been inaugurated, it was regularly kept up year after year, and continued until the change of government and the country became thickly settled.

Captain John Paty first visited this coast in the schooner "Clarion" from Boston, in 1836. This schooner was afterward the "California." She was sold to Governor Alvarado for the use of the government. Captain Paty, who had been a sailor all his life, was probably as good a navigator as ever lived. He had visited nearly all parts of the world, and was very popular in California, much liked by everybody; also highly regarded by the officers of the local government. The government employed him several times, with his vessel. He took Micheltorena and his troops from California to San Blas. Subsequently Señor Castillero, in April 1846, went in Paty's vessel to San Blas, as commissioner, sent by Governor Pico to treat with the home government on some business. Paty was fond of letter writing, and in his communications with friends at the East he spoke well of the climate, soil, advantages and capabilities of California, and dwelt upon the benefit which would result if the American government should obtain possession, and what a misfortune it would be if it should fall into the hands of any other power. After the change of government he and some others started a line of packets between San Francisco and Honolulu. They afterward combined with J. C. Merrill & Co. in the business. His line was the first started between these places. Captain Paty commanded one of the vessels, and his vessel was so popular as a carrier, that he took a great many persons between these ports. They would wait to go with him, he being a favorite. On his arrival in San Francisco, on the completion of his hundredth voyage between this port and the Islands, about 1865 or '66, the event was celebrated by his many good friends in San Francisco by a banquet given in his honor. On his return to Honolulu, a similar celebration took place, in which his family, then at Honolulu, joined.

Rae, Spear and Grimes were especial friends of Paty; he being, as has been said, one of the circle of whist players at Rae's rooms. The captain's wife and two children accompanied him on some of the trips of the vessel to San Francisco in 1842 and '43.

Theodore Cordua, a Prussian, came to the coast in the "Don Quixote," from Honolulu, as a passenger in 1842, his first visit here. He was an old acquaintance of Captain Sutter in his native country. When Sutter settled in the Sacramento valley, he corresponded with Cordua and urged him to come here. After his arrival he visited Sutter. Through the latter's influence he was granted eleven leagues of land by the Mexican government, first having become naturalized. The grant was made to him by Micheltorena. The tract in the Sacramento valley known as the Cordua ranch is a part of his grant. He was a large, portly man, and a general favorite with everybody. He spoke excellent English. Whenever he came to Yerba Buena he was much sought after by the people, on account of his companionable qualities, being a great whist player, and very fond of the game.

There was another German, Charles W. Flügge, who came in 1843, and went to Sutter's place. He was intelligent, and a thorough business man, but exceedingly high-tempered; was an intimate friend of Cordua, both being from the same country. Flugge opened a store at New Helvetia in company with Sutter. He knew nothing of Spanish on his arrival, but by diligent study, and intercourse with the Indians about the fort, (many of whom were old Mission Indians, and had learned Spanish) he became proficient in that language, and wrote and spoke it fluently. In 1844 he went to Los Angeles and established himself in business with James McKinley. At that time I bought of him for $40 the fifty vara lot at the northwest corner of California and Montgomery streets, where Wells, Fargo & Co.'s office was situated for many years.*

The Californians of the present day are a good deal degenerated, as compared with their fathers—the old stock, as I found them when I first came to the country, and for several years succeeding, up to the time of the change of government in 1846. I distinctly remember how they impressed me, when I first saw them, as a boy in 1831 and 1833—a race of men of large stature and of fine, handsome appearance. There are several causes for the deterioration in these people which is now so apparent, the chief of which is the unjust treatment they received from the American government, in the matter of their landed property. Before the change of gov-

*The site of Davis' four story brick building mentioned elsewhere; and now occupied by the "Financial Center Building."

ernment, they were in full and happy possession of their ranchos, under the titles emanating from the Spanish and Mexican governments; and considered themselves entirely secure in their properties.

They were then a wealthy people, probably more so than the people of any other Spanish country, according to the number of the population; that is, their average wealth was greater than that of the people of Spain, or any of the countries peopled from Spain originally. For a time after California passed into the hands of the United States, their wealth increased, owing to the demand for horses and cattle (of which their wealth consisted) for the supply of the troops that were sent here, and of the United States squadron and vessels, and ships of other nations that began to arrive.

After the discovery of gold, when the people came in large numbers, this good fortune continued for a time, until the Californians had troubles in regard to their land titles, arising first from the inroads of squatters, who trespassed upon their ranchos, took possession of considerable portions of the land, drove off cattle, interfered with the grazing, annoyed and despoiled the ranchos, and invaded the rights of the possessors.

The first settlers had to fight with the Indians for possession of the land, and some of them lost their lives in the conflicts. The treaty of Guadalupe Hidalgo recognized the rights of the Californians to their lands under the Mexican titles; but by subsequent legislation of Congress they were required to prove their titles before the United States Land Commission and the Courts. This was an unnecessary hardship imposed upon them, and involved them in ligitation and expense, which was a new and perplexing experience, even if no unfair advantage had been taken of them. They did not understand our language, and in order to be properly represented before the commission and the courts, they were obliged to employ American counsel. Many of these lawyers were quite unscrupulous, and took advantage of the Californians, who were honest and simple-hearted. Where they could not pay ready money for the legal services which were charged at a high rate, the lawyers required promissory notes of them. When the notes became due, and remained unpaid, the holders attached their land and obtained possession of it. The depredations of the squatters continued and of others also, who by one means or another had obtained possession; or the owners were so much involved in efforts to defend themselves that they became dispirited, crushed, poor and miserable. The sons of noble families grew up in want and poverty; became dissipated and demoralized. Thus the old stock rapidly deteriorated and went into decay. The subject of the land troubles of the Californians will be further alluded to.

A few old California families have retained a considerable portion of their property. They have maintained their dignity and pride. They are the same as in the earlier days, unchanged, kind, hospitable and honorable. I may mention as among these exceptions, Don Francisco Galindo, the owner of the Galindo Hotel in Oakland. His father died some years ago, nearly one hundred years of age. (1890)

Recently (1888) in San Diego, I met the widow of Captain John Paty. She was on a visit to one of her married daughters who resided there, the wife of Lieutenant Benson, of the United States army. Another daughter married a lieutenant in the United States navy, and lived at Vallejo. I remarked to the mother that she was represented in the American government. I found her a well preserved lady of over sixty, plump and fine looking. She had recently arrived from Honolulu, near which she then resided. The lady had a beautiful home in Nuuanu valley, at the foot of which is Honolulu.

Mrs. Paty came to the Islands the first time in 1834, in the brig "Avon," of about one hundred and eighty tons, commanded by her husband. In 1836, Mrs. Paty returned to Boston with her husband. On this trip the bark was loaded with sperm-oil, from the wreck of an American whaleship. The outer harbor of Honolulu is nothing more than an open roadstead, exposed to southerly winds. The whaler driven from her mooring there on to a reef, was unable to get off, and finally went to pieces, the cargo of oil being saved. While the "Don Quixote" was moored at long wharf in Boston, on this trip, the bark "Cervantes" was at the same pier, the two vessels almost touching each other. This was thought to be a singular coincidence, meeting of barks having such memorable names,—one the actor and the other the writer, so renowned throughout the civilized world. The two captains were proud of their vessels, and both became great friends during their stay in Boston. Mrs. Paty made her home at Honolulu after 1837, and while her husband was engaged in trading between the Islands, Valparaiso and Callao, and the coast of California. In 1842 she accompanied him from Honolulu, and arrived at Monterey about June. She went in the vessel south and back again to Monterey, arriving there in October, 1842, just after Commodore Jones had taken and given it up, as before described. She was from Charlestown, Massachusetts; a woman of fine character, good education, of great intelligence and with excellent conversational powers. I think she was the third American lady who came to this coast; Mrs. T. O. Larkin and Mrs. Nathan Spear preceding her. She was a pioneer of whom the country might well be proud. These ladies being then the only American women on the coast were treated with the greatest courtesy and distinction by the officers of the United States squadron.

On arriving at Monterey, she was invited to the flag-ship, and entertained in the pleasantest manner. The invitation was several times repeated, the presence of the ladies being considered a great compliment to those aboard the vessel. It certainly was a most agreeable surprise and gratification to the officers to find in this remote part of the world some of their country-women, so refined and intelligent.

I was present on one of the occasions aboard the flag-ship, when Mrs. Paty remarked in a facetious manner, "What a pity, Commodore Jones, that you gave up this beautiful department, after having taken possession." He replied that he would gladly have kept it, but he was compelled to relinquish it; that he took it in order not to be behind time, in case the British contemplated a similar movement, supposing at the time that war existed between the United States and Mexico; but he had found this was an error; having no good reason for holding on, he gave it up. When I told Mrs. Paty, at my last interview, that I should give a sketch of her husband in an account of California and its people, she expressed her gratification, and said she hoped I would do him full justice, for he was deserving of everything I could say in his favor. She added, "You must call him Commodore Paty, and not simply Captain Paty."

In February, 1846, the king of the Sandwich Islands conferred on Captain Paty the title of Commodore, officially, and he became to some extent the representative of the Sandwich Islands to protect their interests on this coast. He wore on special occasions the Hawaiian uniform. The merchants of San Francisco recognized and confirmed his title of Commodore. Among themselves they bestowed on him the title of Commodore of all the fleet trading between the Islands and this port.

He was a kind-hearted man. I never knew him to refuse a favor to any one, though often he complied, when appealed to, much against his own interests. As his agent and business man, I was mindful of his customers— as to their reliability, and while always ready to trust native Californians for whatever goods they wanted, knowing they would be sure to pay for them, I found it was not best to trust such foreign residents as were of doubtful financial responsibility. Men of this character would come to me and ask for credit, which I was compelled to refuse. They would then sometimes go to Paty himself, stating their case; and he, full of the milk of human kindness, could not find it in his heart to refuse them. He would call me aside and say he thought we should accommodate them. I would remonstrate, and declare that we might as well charge the items to profit and loss account at once; that it was about the same as giving the goods away; that I knew it was for his interest not to, but if he gave me a peremptory order to deliver them, I would do so. "Well," he would say, "I hate to refuse; I think you had better." The articles were delivered accordingly, and that was the last we knew of the transaction, except as it remained on the books.

On some of these occasions Mrs. Paty was present, and, being of a firmer disposition than her husband in business matters, would intimate to the captain that it was foolish to interfere in behalf of the impecunious customers.

The doubtful purchasers were not those who had settled and built up homes, but mostly runaway sailors, some of whom used to go to the redwoods about the bay and to the redwoods of Santa Cruz and Monterey to cut lumber for building purposes, there being no saw-mills in the department. They were rather uncertain and roving. Few of them settled down and became permanent residents. They generally spent money as fast as it was earned. The hunters and trappers who came across the mountains and remained in California were of a different type; and though lacking in the graces of civilization, were honorable, and true to their word, sober, and industrious in the line of their occupation (most of them continuing as hunters and trappers), and we could trust them confidently, knowing if they wanted goods they would pay.

At the time of Commodore Wilkes' stay in the harbor of San Francisco, Captain Paty was here with his vessel. Having traveled extensively all over the world, and being an old sailor and splendid navigator, Wilkes enjoyed his society. Many of the places where Wilkes had been and others to which he intended to go, Paty had visited. He often went aboard the flag-ship to spend a few hours, when the two navigators would interchange ideas. Wilkes obtained information from him in regard to the Pacific ocean and its islands, and the places at which he intended to touch. Paty was pleased with Wilkes because of his scientific acquirements, the old commodore making the interviews instructive, as he always did to the few for whom he felt respect and in whom he had confidence.

Mrs. Paty recalled to my mind, at San Diego, an incident which took place at the grand entertainment given by the citizens of Monterey, upon the restoration of the town to the Mexican authorities, after the capture by Commodore Jones. Captain Armstrong, of the flag-ship, was a heavy man, and Captain Paty was small and wiry. Both were fond of dancing, and there was an animated contest between them to see who could waltz the longest, to the amusement of the company. They continued on the floor a long time, the California ladies seeming never to tire of dancing. Paty secured a victory over his big rival, who succumbed to fatigue.

Another incident was also brought to mind. When Micheltorena and his troops were conveyed to San Blas, calling at Monterey, she quit the vessel before it left San Pedro, and it was my pleasure to convey Mrs. Paty to Los Angeles, where she was to remain at William Wolfskill's house, awaiting the captain's return from Mexico. It was a beautiful, balmy morning in March, when the season in that part of the country is much more advanced than further north. We traveled in the old-fashioned primitive carriage or wagon, with solid wheels, drawn by oxen. The gañan, or driver, a Californian, was mounted on a horse, and rode by the side of the oxen, armed with a slender stick with a sharp pointed spike attached to the end, for the purpose of urging the creatures along. Being a light-hearted young man he beguiled the monotony of the journey by singing sentimental songs in the Spanish language, in a melodious voice, which were also quite entertaining to us. The vehicle was comfortably furnished, and we were well provided with eatables—chickens, hams, etc., the journey occupying the whole day. I took precaution to instruct the driver to supply himself with some grease for the axles, to prevent the sharp squeaking and screeching which otherwise would have been heard for several miles. When I last saw Mrs. Paty, the novelty of her experience at that time was referred to,—a refined Boston lady traveling in such rude fashion through a wild country. We had a good laugh over the reminiscences.

Wolfskill, of Los Angeles, above mentioned, had a vineyard which was then in good bearing, and second only in importance to that of Vignes.

During her stay at Los Angeles Mrs. Paty visited an Indian woman living in the neighborhood, 130 years of age, and found her well preserved and in possession of her faculties, but her face was extremely wrinkled, and resembled a piece of dried and crinkled parchment. She presented the appearance of a living mummy. She recalled the arrival of the first missionaries to the coast, being then a full-grown woman. Mrs. Paty had also found at Santa Barbara, previously, an Indian woman 116 years of age.

Mrs. Paty was as fully intelligent as her talented husband. She wrote many letters to her friends East, gentlemen as well as ladies, describing the country here, and setting forth its beauties, thus doing a great deal to make it known to the rich and influential citizens of Boston and elsewhere. She did as much in this respect, and did as well, as any man could have done. Prior to my wife's marriage, she and Mrs. Paty were friends, and in 1849 Mrs. Paty lived with us while her husband was away on one of his voyages. Recently they met at San Diego, and were delighted to see each other and talk over old times. Since Captain Paty's death great respect and polite attention by the captains of steamers and vessels on this coast, who held the commodore in high honor, had been accorded his widow, who was much gratified at this kindly regard for his memory. She had a son at Honolulu, John Henry Paty, a partner in the banking house of Bishop & Company.

CHAPTER XLI
Holy Days and Holidays

MRS. BENNETT arrived in Yerba Buena, from Missouri, about 1842, with her husband and a large family of children. I mention her first, as she was unmistakably the head of the family,—a large, powerful woman, uncultivated, but well-meaning and very industrious. Her word was law, and her husband stood in becoming awe of her. Their children were respectably brought up, the family being supported by sewing, washing, ironing; raising chickens, turkeys and ducks. I trusted her for goods frequently, not knowing, or caring much, whether they were ever paid for; but they always were. She was an honest, good woman, and while not regarded as an equal by the better cultivated and more aristocratic ladies, she was always pleasantly received in their houses; as foreign ladies were scarce and class distinctions not rigidly observed.

The carnival festival which is celebrated with merriment and revelry in Catholic countries during the week preceding Lent, was observed by the Californians. They had various little entertainments; among them, dancing parties; a supper served late in the evening being one of the agreeable features of these gatherings. The Californians made the most of all their festivals, and, according to their usual habits, observed this one fully, giving themselves up to amusement during its continuance.

One of the amusements the Californians brought with them from Spain and Mexico, was the custom during the carnival season each year, of breaking upon the heads of the opposite sex, egg-shells filled with fine scraps of pretty-colored silver or gold paper, or with cologne water, or some harmless and agreeable substance. It was in the nature of a game or trick played upon one another, the idea being to catch the victim unawares, and gently smash the egg and distribute its contents over the head. A gentleman, for instance, would call upon a lady, and be pleasantly received and entertained. When his attention was attractively occupied, the fair hostess would deftly tap his head with the egg, which, breaking, would cover his head with the bright scraps of paper, or with the cologne; and a good laugh would ensue at the success of the stratagem. The gentleman, in turn, in calling upon the ladies, would go provided with these pleasant missiles, and would seize opportunities to break them on the heads of the fair entertainers. This custom was observed all through the department. It has long been practiced in Spanish countries. Much maneuvering and various ingenious devices were resorted to by the ladies to catch the gentlemen off guard, in order to accomplish the delicate feat. The gentlemen, at the same time, exercised all their tact and skill to get a similar advantage. When successful, and the lady or gentleman's head received the contents of the egg, whatever company was present joined in the outburst of merriment. Only one egg at a time was broken, more than one being considered improper, though it was allowable to repeat the process with another shortly after, if the opportunity could be secured.

At this festival in 1841, I remember calling upon Señorita Doña Encarnacion Briones, living at North Beach, who afterward became Mrs. Robert Ridley, a sprightly and pretty girl. I was provided with eight or ten of these festival eggs, hoping to break some of them upon the head of my entertainer, but notwithstanding my skillful designing and planning, I entirely failed to dispose of one of them, while she, on the contrary, by her wit and cunning, got the advantage of me, and broke several upon my head, throwing me off guard by her fascinations and feminine artifices. On my taking leave, feeling somewhat chagrined at my want of success, she playfully remarked, in the most graceful manner, "*Usted vino a trasquilar, pero fué trasquilado.*" (You came to shear, but you have been shorn.)

Mrs. Paty, Mrs. Larkin, Mrs. Spear, Mrs. Rae and the other ladies took delight in this amusement. Wm. D. M. Howard, who was ready for any fun, enjoyed the diversion greatly, and had great satisfaction in performing the feat of egg-breaking. The ladies, at the same time, regarded it as quite a victory when they secured the advantage of him. Henry and Francis Mellus were considered as ladies' men and were very fond of this sport.

The captains, supercargoes and merchants here at the time regarded carnival week as a kind of visiting season, similar to our New Year's day. The ladies at this time were prepared for calls from the gentleman. The festival was anticipated with pleasure. At the parties which took place egg-breaking was practiced; the contra-dances, waltzes and quadrilles were chiefly danced. There was a very ancient dance known as the *jota,* which was more particularly for the older people. As the dancing went on, all kinds of devices and schemes were contrived to break the eggs, but without interfering with the figures. The ladies at these times wore their hair unconfined, and flowing gracefully over the shoulders, so that when the eggs were broken the cologne should dry quickly, or, if the eggs contained bits of gold and silver paper, the bright spangles showered upon the hair should present a pretty appearance, as it waved about them while they swept through the dance. At this time the floor became quite thickly strewn with egg-shells, besides being well sprinkled with cologne water.

The season was observed with somewhat more display and pretension at Monterey and Los Angeles than elsewhere, the former being the capital, and the latter the largest town in the department. Picnic parties were attended at Point Pinos, near Monterey, the people taking with them baskets of choice eatables and enjoying the day. The ladies and gentlemen at these out-door parties would watch for opportunities to break carnival eggs.

At the festival in 1843, the sport of egg-breaking with a party of ladies and gentlemen, in the courtyard, went beyond its legitimate bounds; those engaged finally commenced throwing water at each other, Mrs. Bennett being the leader of the feminines in the innovation. The practice of this amusement in the street, however, was entirely confined to those of the humbler position; and it happened but rarely.

The three holy days of Lent, *Jueves Santo, Viernes Santo, Sabado de Gloria* (Holy Thursday, Good Friday and Holy Saturday) were rigidly observed by the Californians, the ladies dressing in black, when attending church during these days. It was the practice of the Spanish vessels in the harbor to have their yards drawn nearly perpendicular alongside the masts, a custom always observed in Spanish countries. The vessels of other nationalities here at the time also fell in with the observance, out of deference to the religious views of the Californians and respect for their church. If a vessel neglected to comply, a request was made of the captain to do so by the alcalde or prefect.

I have heard sub-Prefect Guerrero request Captain Nye, of the brig "Bolivar Liberator," to respect the holy days by drawing up the yards of the vessel.

The ship "Alert" arrived at the beginning of 1840, from Boston, in command of Captain William D. Phelps, the vessel and cargo consigned to Alfred Robinson and Henry Mellus. Captain Phelps was a Boston man, an extensive traveler, and became popular on the coast. My brother Robert and myself were once invited to spend an evening on board the "Alert," when Captain Phelps entertained us with an account of his travels over the world. He said that while his vessel lay in the Mediterranean Sea, he conceived a great desire to visit Jerusalem—which he found means to gratify, so impressed was he with that city and its relation to the events narrated in the Scriptures. When in the sacred city, his religious emotions overcame him and he knelt and prayed several times. On his return to Boston, he was impelled to join a church, and had retained his connection with it continuously since. At the same time, he was not bigoted, but entered heartily in all little festivities. He believed his visit to Jerusalem was the most valuable part of his experience, and his observations there to be worth more than all he had seen in the rest of the world.

Captain Phelps was an excellent shot with the rifle, very fond of hunting deer, elk, rabbits, ducks, geese, quail and other birds; and kept his vessel in game while in port. Being an epicure, he always selected the choicest game to supply his table and that of his friends—Rae, Spear and others. Phelps approaching the store on landing of mornings from the vessel, would meet Spear on the outside, leaning against the gate near the water, looking for the captain. The latter would call out, "Good morning, Don Natan," (foreigners having adopted the California style of addressing each other by their first names) and Spear would respond in the same cordial way. Captain Phelps had a curious peculiarity of hesitating and stammering as he commenced to talk, his right cheek quivering rapidly until he got along farther in his speech and warmed up a little, when his language came fluently and the pulsation of the face ceased. He was a good observer, and a man of excellent judgment, and also entitled to much credit, with others heretofore mentioned, for making California known on the Atlantic side, by letters, recording his observations and experiences. They were well written, and calculated to make a good impression in regard to the department of California. He frequently read to us portions of the letters, and we recognized their truthfulness and his happy mode of communicating impressions of the country. He also visited Wilkes, and was handsomely entertained, and, like Paty, became a favorite of the commodore.

In speaking of those who did so much by their correspondence in the early days, to make California known, I want to give credit to the ladies and gentlemen, especially Mrs. Paty among the former, from Massachusetts. The vessels which came to trade in the earliest days were almost exclusively from Boston. It was from their officers that the best information regarding the new country was communicated to the National authorities, who were thus made alive to the necessity of keeping an eye on the distant territory, as having a bearing upon the growth and security of the Republic. It doubtless led to the frequent visits, and afterward almost constant presence, of United States vessels of war with unquestionably a purpose in view.

CHAPTER XLII
Yankee Turkey Shooting at Christmas

THE New Englanders and other foreigners were fond of keeping up the custom of turkey-shooting on Christmas eve. A shooting match of the kind occurred on Christmas, 1841, at which were present William G. Rae, Captain Phelps, William S. Hinckley, Vioget, Nathan Spear, Henry Mellus, my brother Robert, myself and others; all taking part in the sport. Captain Phelps had left his rifle in the corner of Spear's store on the night of shooting the turkeys. The second day, the 26th, he came ashore about breakfast time. The captain took up the rifle, confident that it was not loaded, but had been discharged when last in use. Placing a cap on the nipple, he told my brother to hold the muzzle against his (Phelps') ear and pull the trigger, so that he might feel if any air came from the gun and thereby ascertain if it was clean. My brother obeyed. The cap exploded, but the gun was not fired. He put on another cap, and told my brother to hold his hand out straight. The captain then placed the muzzle in the center of the palm, pulled the trigger and fired. This time a ball came out, passing through Robert's hand, through the wall separating the store from the dining-room, and through the opposite wall, lodging in an adobe beyond. On taking a line between the two bullet holes in the dining-room it was ascertained that, if Mrs. Spear had occupied her seat at the breakfast table the bullet would have passed directly through her chest.

The chief Christmas amusements of the Californians were horse-racing and cock-fighting. The finest Christmas dinners I ever partook of were at their tables.

Among the early vessels which came to the coast was the ship "Eagle," of Boston, owned and commanded by my father, William Heath Davis. The middle name was given to him by his uncle, General Heath, one of Washington's fighting generals of revolutionary times. The vessel was brought by him to the Sandwich Islands about 1814, thence sailed over to the Russian settlements in Alaska, thence to California about 1816. Two other trips were made by my father to California, during one of which my mother accompanied him, shortly after their marriage. He also traded in this vessel between the Sandwich Islands and China; taking from the Islands cargoes of sandal wood, which was plentiful and cheap there, but valuable in China, and used by the Chinese in religious ceremonies in their Joss houses and temples, and for other special purposes. It commanded a high price. Silks, teas, lacquered wares and other goods were brought from China, of which he sold a portion in the Islands, and then went across to the Russian possessions on the northwest coast of America, thence to California, to dispose of the remainder.

On trips to California he went into some of the less prominent ports. At the time he was accompanied by his wife the vessel called in at Refugio, a rancho about fifteen or twenty miles west of Santa Barbara. Many of the wealthier Californians came to this place and purchased from the vessel choice articles of merchandise, as also did the Padres. The captain did not take hides and tallow in payment, but the rancheros and the priests brought with them bags of Spanish doubloons, and paid for their purchases in coin, or in sea otter skins, which were then plentiful.

The Padres were the chief customers of the vessels, and spent freely from their well-filled coin bags or from their ample stores of otter skins which they had accumulated. They did what they could to stimulate and increase the hunting of the sea otters, inducing the Californians and others who were skilled in the work to go out and shoot them; frequently fitting out the boats and furnishing and paying the hunters themselves or buying the skins from men not in their employ. The otters were taken largely in the bay of San Francisco and all along the coast. The Padres considered themselves the rightful owners, and were jealous of the Russians, who at that time were making immense fortunes out of the business; and so did all they could to get a portion of it into their own hands. They collected the skins for the enrichment of the Missions, being desirous of making their Missions wealthy, and conducting them in an extensive and liberal manner,—with thousands of Indians around to civilize and Christianize. They also had immense herds of cattle and horses to look after. Seeing this opportunity to add to their wealth, they eagerly availed themselves of it. The goods which they bought from the vessel were not for their personal use and enjoyment, but most of them were resold to the rancheros at a profit, and so helped to swell the funds of the Missions over which they presided. The good Fathers had no strong boxes in those days to keep their coin and other valuables in; they concealed their treasure under the tile flooring of their rooms. The Padres also received from members of the church, money, simply for safe keeping,—a practice of the Catholic people which is continued to this day, showing implicit confidence in their spiritual advisers. The first iron safe in this part of the country was brought here in 1846.

While trading at this trip, my mother was much interested in observing the Padres, clad in their peculiar dress, and also the rancheros, with their fine costumes and equipments. The vessel, at Refugio, was visited by Don Ygnacio Martinez, then comandante of the Presidio of Santa Barbara. Learning that a strange vessel was anchored twenty miles to the west, he, in his official capacity, dressed in full military costume, accompanied by an officer and two soldiers, went off to the vessel, where he was received in the most friendly and gracious manner, and entertained with sumptuous dinners. He afterward said he was overwhelmed by the kindness and entertainment he met with on board the vessel, and that he could only accept half what was proffered with such grace and generosity. My mother, in describing the occurrences to me recounted the admirable appearance of the comandante, and that she never saw so many piles of gold (Spanish doubloons) as were collected on board the vessel,—the result of sales of goods to the rancheros and Padres. Speaking of these events to me and asked how much my father realized from his cargo, she said, many thousands in gold, and a large number of sea otter skins, which were taken to China, where they brought from $80 to $100 each.

Captain Martinez saw me the first time, in Yerba Buena, at Spear's store, in 1838, and, without introduction, came forward and embraced me cordially, saying, "I am sure you are the son of Don Guillermo Davis, whom I knew, and whose vessel I had visited"; and expatiated upon the kind treatment he had received on board. He had recognized me by my likeness to my father.

Captain John Meek commanded and owned a part of the "Don Quixote" when on this coast in 1832, that vessel being then engaged in trading between here and the Sandwich Islands. Meek was among the early pioneers, having arrived in the ship "Eagle," as first officer, with my father, about 1816. He made two voyages subsequently in the same position on the same vessel. He was from Marblehead, Massachusetts. He has stated to me that my father's voyages in the "Eagle" were very successful; and that on each voyage he realized about $25,000 profit, in Spanish doubloons and sea otter skins, from sales in California, aside from profits in the Russian settlements. He said that my father's vessel was among the first that came from Boston to trade here (perhaps the very first), which gave him a great advantage, as he had no rivalry or competition; and besides he spoke Spanish fluently. Probably his success, when it became known in Boston, on his return from China with a cargo of China goods, stimulated others to engage in the trade, and brought other vessels here.

Captain Meek discoursed to me upon the fine appearance of the California men, and the beauty of the women. He remembered Don Ygnacio Martinez and his visit to the "Eagle" when stopping at Refugio, as before described. In one of his first voyages here in the "Don Quixote," he received a present from Martinez, who was then comandante of the Presidio at San Francisco, of three heifers and a young bull, in recognition of the kindness of my father and Captain Meek to him during his visits to the "Eagle." On his return to the Islands, Captain Meek carried these animals with him.

In 1871 I visited Honolulu and called on the captain, and the history of these cattle was recounted, he having then between four and five thousand head on his "Big Tree Rancho," about thirty miles from Honolulu. He had been supplying that city and the foreign men-of-war, and other vessels, for many years with beef cattle—all from the increase of the little band presented to him by Martinez. In later years the stock had been improved by the introduction of blooded bulls from England and the United States. At the time of receiving the cattle from Martinez, the captain presented to his daughter, then Mrs. Estudillo, a China camphor-wood trunk, covered with black leather, with the captain's initials (J. M.) upon it, which were also the initials of the recipient's maiden name—Juana Martinez.

During this visit I saw a California horse, from Santa Barbara, thirty-three years old, which had been in color a dark iron-gray, but was then nearly milk white, from his great age. He was perfectly sound, and Captain Meek drove him nearly every day round the city. He was about sixteen hands high. With the exception of a slight rheumatism in his hind legs, the horse had remained well during the many years of the captain's ownership.

About 1833 Don Antonio José Cot, a Spanish merchant of the department, chartered and loaded the "Don Quixote" with tallow, for Callao, Peru. She there took aboard an assorted cargo, and proceeded thence to Honolulu, where she landed a portion of it, and came to this coast with the remainder. On this trip from Callao to the Islands she averaged 200 miles a day for nearly the whole distance, the quickest passage known at that time. I doubt whether any sailing vessel has beaten it since. She was a very fast sailer, noted for speedy voyages. Once she went from Boston to Smyrna, on the Mediterranean Sea, and back to Boston, at a speed averaging nine knots an hour both ways. In the spring of 1846 she made the run from Honolulu to Monterey in ten days.

When Mrs. Estudillo's father returned from his visit to the "Eagle" at the Refugio, bringing with him the fine presents he had received, and the purchases he had made—silks, satins, crape shawls, fancy silk handkerchiefs, satin shoes, sewing silk of all colors, and other elegant finery of various kinds, with beautiful articles of lacquered ware, she and the family were quite overcome with astonishment and delight, for they had never seen anything so rich and beautiful.

Refugio was the rancho of the Ortega family. The "Eagle" arriving there the first time, my father was very watchful and cautious, as it was a strange coast, and he didn't know how he would be received. On his visits to the Russian Settlements, at the north, he had obtained such information as he could in regard to California, the Missions, etc. His purpose in coming here was to secure as many sea otter skins as possible, and to enter into communication with the Padres. He therefore went as near to Santa Barbara and the other Missions in that part of the country as he thought prudent, and anchored off the rancho of Ortega. Noticing that some of the people had come down to the beach to investigate, he questioned if it would be safe to go ashore, not knowing but he and his crew might be made prisoners. The strangers appearing harmless and quiet, he and his second officer ventured off from the ship in a boat, and introducing himself in Spanish, he was courteously received.

Asked what the vessel was doing there, my father replied that he would like some beef for the ship's use. He engaged in conversation with the Californians in their own language, and invited Señor Ortega on board the ship. The invitation was accepted, and he was entertained on board. On leaving the vessel he was presented with a number of choice and elegant articles from the cargo, which not only pleased him, but had an excellent effect upon the Californians in leading them to favorably regard their visitors. Information of the vessel's arrival was communicated to Santa Barbara, which resulted in the comandante's coming up, as before described.

The presents he received, increased the good opinion of the inhabitants for the new comers, and no difficulty whatever was encountered after such happy beginning of the acquaintance.

In the three voyages of the "Eagle" to this coast, stopping at Refugio each time, my father collected, in payment for goods sold, beside the money received, about 1500 sea otter skins, allowing in barter $30 for each.

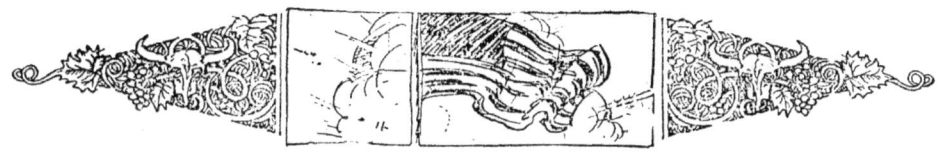

CHAPTER XLIII
Franciscan Fathers First Class Merchants

THE Padres had stores at the Missions, to supply the wants of the Indians, as well as the Californians in the employ of the Missions. Their stock was necessarily large. They also supplied the rancheros with goods, taking in payment hides, tallow, fur and cattle. They also traded with the fur hunters, and gave in exchange for skins, goods and also gold and silver coin. The Fathers were first-class merchants. When they made purchases from vessels trading on the coast, they exhibited good judgment in their selections and were close buyers. The "Volunteer," in 1833, sold to the Missions bordering on the bay considerable quantities of goods, for cash. I remember that our supercargo, Sherman Peck, spoke of the missionaries as shrewd purchasers, and strictly reliable men. It was a pleasure to deal with them. The Padres, bought goods cheaper than the rancheros; their purchases being always larger, a reduction was made in prices, as a matter of policy, and to encourage good relations already existing.

One Mission would assist another with hides and tallow, or with fur, skins, or money, in payment for goods which it had purchased. The priest sometimes gave an order on another Mission, in favor of the supercargo, to furnish what was required. While my father was trading at the Refugio, the vessel had to wait several days, for payment for a portion of the goods sold to the Mission of Santa Barbara. Having paid over such gold and otter skins as it had on hand, this Mission sent out to the Mission of San Buenaventura at the east, and Santa Ynez on the west, for a further supply of skins, and coin, to pay for the balance of the goods. These numerous Missions were in reality one institution, with a common interest. The advancement of one was the general good and welfare of all. The goods purchased by one Mission were sometimes sent to others, partly for use, and in part for sale, as the range of distribution was thus widened. When one Mission had furnished another with money, or fur skins, or hides, or tallow, to assist it in paying for a large purchase, although there was no obligation to return the same, yet the Fathers were proud men, and it was their custom to return what they had borrowed, when they were able to do so from their new accumulations. While their interests were one, there was at the same time a friendly ambition on the part of each to conduct his Mission successfully, and not be outdone by any other Mission.

The Padres were the original pioneers of California, beyond all others. They have left behind them, as mementos of their zeal and industry in the work in which they were engaged, the Missions they built and conducted, besides other evidences, less tangible, of their influence for the welfare of the people of California and the whole world.

It is a curious fact that nearly all the men prominent in otter and beaver hunting in the early days of California were from the southern, or slave states, of the Union. Isaac J. Sparks, of Santa Barbara, who died some years ago, was from Kentucky; also George Nidever, who lived at Santa Barbara. Lewis T. Burton, of Santa Barbara, who died in May, 1870, was a native of Tennessee, and arrived in Santa Barbara in 1833, or before, and followed the occupation of otter hunting until it was no longer profitable. Samuel J. Hensley, of San Francisco and San José, who at one time was president of the California Steam Navigation Company, and who died some years since, was from a southern state. Daniel Sill was a native of Kentucky, as was also Isaac Graham.*

P. B. Reading, who was the Whig candidate for governor of California against John Bigler in 1851, was a native of Canada, of English parentage, but, I believe, lived in a southern state in early life.

The four last named followed the profession of trapping beavers and land-otters on the Sacramento and San Joaquin rivers and tributaries. These men were experts in the pursuit of fur-producing animals, and were the earliest trappers of Anglo-Saxon extraction. They made a good deal of money; beavers and otters being numerous at that time.

Among the early otter hunters in California was George Yount, who came from Missouri, probably about 1831 or '32, and settled in Napa valley. Tim Black came from Scotland about the same time, and lived at San Rafael. Timothy Murphy also resided at San Rafael. Francis Branch, who arrived in Santa Barbara in 1833, and afterward removed to San Luis Obispo, where he owned a large ranch, was a native of one of the New England states.

The priests had instructed some of the Mission Indians before the arrival of the early foreigners, in the work of trapping otters. The Mis-

*See note page 47.

sions in the neighborhood of the bay of San Francisco secured large quantities of furs from the Indian trappers.

During my business intercourse with the Father in charge of the Mission San José I received from him in the year 1844 several thousand dollars' worth of beaver and land-otter skins which had been collected by his Indians on the Sacramento and San Joaquin rivers. On my visiting the Mission Dolores in 1833 with Mr. Peck, supercargo, and Captain Shaw, of the bark "Volunteer," we went into the "otter-room," so-called, a large apartment in the upper story or attic of the building. From the rafters and additional light timbers which had been placed across the room were hung the otter skins which the Mission had collected and had on hand at that time; there being probably eighty to one hundred ready for sale, or exchange in trade. We got them all.

Otter skins were preserved on board vessels taking them to China, in empty rum casks, which were dry and clean, but still retained the odor of rum. The furs were packed, with heads put in the casks, and they were thus secure against moths and other insects, and not exposed to dampness. All the vessels adopted this mode, which proved to be an excellent one.

The exportation of sea otter skins and river furs was very large. Besides those exported by the Russians, the Boston ships took a great many home with them, as did also vessels to other ports.

As the hunting increased, the animals diminished and the exportations became less; but late as 1840 and along to 1844 Henry Mellus made shipments of sea otter, land-otter and beaver skins amounting to $15,000 or $20,000 each. Land-otters and beavers were then not so scarce as sea otters.

Among the Californians it was a custom to call all persons, of either sex, by a Christian name, the younger people especially being so addressed. The older persons, if men, had the prefix of "Don" or "Señor Don" given to their Christian names, and were rarely known by their surnames. The ladies were addressed with the prefix of "Doña" or "Señorita Doña" to Christian names, if unmarried, and "Señora Doña," if married.

Shortly after arriving at Monterey in the bark "Louise," in 1831, I was playing about the deck one day with Louis Vignes, he having come from Honolulu in the same vessel. The main hatch being uncovered for the discharge of the cargo, in running round the opening, I slipped, lost my balance and fell into the hold. Taken up insensible, I remained so for some hours, having broken my arm. Our consul at Honolulu, Mr. J. C. Jones, was a stepfather of mine. He came over on the same trip, and was on shore. Word having been sent to him, he brought aboard Dr. Douglas, who set my arm carefully, and treated me very kindly. This doctor was a Scotchman, of learning and extensive scientific acquirements; a naturalist, who also gave attention to botany, and was a collector of rare and curious specimens from the animal and vegetable kingdoms. He had traveled all about the world; had come recently from South America, and was making the tour of California. He was a grand, good man.

At Monterey the doctor was the guest of David Spence, his countryman. Having visited the various Missions, and made the acquaintance of the Padres, for whom he had great respect and attachment, he spoke of their learning and of the great good being done by them in this wild and unsettled territory, and commended their missionary work—with the limited means at command—not only in Christianizing and educating the Indians in schools and churches, but in teaching various useful trades.

Dr. Douglas, being brave and fearless, usually traveled on foot through the country, and refused the services of guides or vaqueros whom the good Fathers or rancheros would urge him to take with him. Two or three years after the accident, the doctor visited the Sandwich Islands for the purpose of pursuing his researches, and traveled over the island of Hawaii unattended, engaged in procuring specimens. Here he became widely known and much esteemed. At that time large numbers of wild cattle ranged in the mountains of the island, portions of different bands that had strayed away. The younger cattle, from long neglect, had become uncontrollable, and roamed without restraint of any kind, no one claiming ownership in them. They were hunted by foreigners and natives, and trapped in pits five or six feet deep, dug along the mountain sides, and covered lightly with branches of trees and brush. The cattle, in ranging, fell into these holes, and being unable to extricate themselves, hunters could easily dispatch them. If the meat was fit for food, a portion of it would be saved; but the main object of the slaughter was the securing of hides and tallow.

Pursuing his favorite occupation for some time on the island, Dr. Douglas disappearing suddenly, began to be inquired about by many. The British consul projected a search, assisted by the king, the American consul and other foreigners resident at Honolulu. Rewards were offered; and the governor of the Island sent out to look for the doctor. After diligent search his body was discovered in one of the cattle pits, having evidently been there several days. A live bull was found in the hole with him. His faithful dog who had accompanied him in all his travels was found watching at the edge of the pit. It is supposed that the doctor approached too near the edge to look at the animal imprisoned there, and, slipping in accidentally, was killed by the bull.

I have before spoken in terms of commendation concerning the chastity existing with California women. So great was the horror of the older Californians to any exception in this respect that the guilty parties, when discovered were dealt with severely. The man who offended was imprisoned for two or three years, and put to hard work as a prisoner. The woman was disgraced by cutting off her hair close to the head. In San Diego, a man named Lavaleta had seduced a young girl. He was imprisoned; but the comandante of the Presidio had compassion upon the woman and prevented her hair being cut. Taken into his family, she was kindly treated. She afterward married a respectable man, and lived the life of a good woman.

I remember another case in San Diego where the parents of the young woman were very severe. Her hair was cut off close to her head, and she was placed in jail, and also put to work to sweep the streets of the town with the other prisoners.

The Indians of California used artfully constructed traps for bears. They dug a large hole, about five or six feet deep, directly under the branch of a tree, covered it with brush and a light coating of earth, and made all smooth on top. From the branch would be suspended a quarter of beef. Bruin would scent the meat, and, approaching without suspicion, would fall headlong into the pit. Shooting with bow and arrows, the Indian, having come out of his place of concealment, would presently kill the bear. After he had acquired the use of firearms there was no delay in thus dispatching the animal. In 1840, and subsequent years, numbers of bears were trapped in the vicinity of San Leandro, about a mile and a half from the present town. The young men of a family, accompanied by an Indian servant, would go out and secure a bear, having great enjoyment in the sport.

Doña Luisa Avila de Gafia, a California lady, born in the city of Los Angeles, a relative of two noted families there of great wealth, and married to a citizen of Mexico,—was attractive for her remarkably fine personal appearance and superior conversational powers. On Christmas, 1880, she was visiting in San Diego, and I was interested in her account of her life in the city of Mexico, where she had lived for a number of years. Although fifty-six years of age she had not a gray hair in her head, as was proven by loosening her hair and having the ladies present at the dinner party make an examination of the luxuriant tresses. Her teeth were very fine. The lady related, that when Juarez was elected president of the Mexican Republic, Miramon, with his forces, opposed him, and designed effecting his capture, so as to prevent him taking the office. Doña Luisa, having large estates in Los Angeles county, plenty of resources and ready money (as had also her husband), proposed to Juarez to furnish him with means, horses, escort, funds—everything needed, for him and his family to make a safe retreat to the mountains, where he could remain until such time as his friends should organize a sufficient force to defeat Miramon and his schemes, after which he could safely take the position of president of the Republic. Juarez accepted her proposal, and she actually carried the plans into effect, with entire success. Juarez followed the advice to fly to the mountains, receiving from time to time intelligence of what was going on in the city. When it was prudent to return he did so, and took his seat as president, the designs of Miramon having been frustrated by the diplomacy, skill, generosity and energy of this magnanimous lady. Subsequently, during the administration of Juarez, her friendly services in his behalf were duly recognized, and appreciation accorded from Mrs. Juarez also. De Gafia, the husband, distinguished himself in the engagement of the Californians against Commodore Stockton at San Gabriel, in the winter of 1846-47, having then a command in the native forces. In that fight he behaved bravely. Subsequently he acted as United States consul at Tepic.

CHAPTER XLIV
W. D. M. Howard, Trader, Jester and Bold Operator

WILLIAM D. M. HOWARD belonged to a respectable family of the city of Boston. In his youth, getting himself and his companions into mischief of one kind or another, his mother hoped to subdue and cure him of his wayward tendency by sending him to sea before the mast, in the ship "California," Captain Arthur, bound for this coast.

The good captain had compassion on the lad and after they had got to sea took him as cabin boy, in which capacity he arrived at Monterey in the early part of 1839. The vessel proceeded thence to San Pedro; and Howard became clerk for Abel Stearns, who was then a merchant at Los Angeles, the first of the foreign merchants, and doing a large business. Alfred Robinson or Henry Mellus, and perhaps Captain Arthur, used influence in getting Howard into this position. The young man had become docile by his sea experience; and applied himself diligently to his new labors, having a bright and active mind, and showing indications that he would make a successful merchant. In 1840, he went home, *via* Mexico, to see his relatives, and returned here in 1842 with Captain Arthur, of the vessel he first came in. The ship touched at Honolulu on her way to California. Aboard, as a passenger, was a young lady, Miss Mary Warren, the daughter of Major William Warren, of Boston. During the voyage young Howard became enamored of the young lady, who was pretty and fascinating. They were married at the house of Captain Grimes, while the vessel remained at Honolulu, and the bride and groom came to Monterey in the ship, after a stay of a few weeks at the Islands.

Reaching Monterey about this time in the "Don Quixote," I met my friend Howard and was introduced to his wife. During the visit, Howard surprised me by announcing a discovery he had made that we were second cousins; that his mother was a niece of my father; and that the name of my family was his second given name. He made me a present of a work called "Day and Night," in two volumes. The "California" pro-

[TEXT OF LETTER ON OPPOSITE PAGE]

Escondido Oct. 5th, 1888

Friend Davis

Excuse delay. Mr Devoll had moved, I got your address of him when down last week.

I am here for life—the finest place in the State, which is saying Mucho; The finest Climate, Soil, Water and scenery now going—Am going to put out an Orange Orchard in the Spring (Sweet ones) 20 acres plowed virgin soil and waiting for the rains.

I will send you a map and Book of the place for your friends. You need not look for any change here for the better under one year, then look out and stand from under, then the R.R. will be under way from here to N.Y. direct, the water works finished, and the R.R.'s in full blast and things generally on the uphill grade. Land now is down to a reasonable price, and people are lookin westward again; houses to rent everywhere, big and little. I went to the El Cahone Valley last week, and was much pleased, but I think this is the finest Climate, not quite so warm; today I bought 50 acres more here, you know my old propensity; but I will try and not load up this time. It is a general falt of mankind but all will have to come down finally, water will find its level and man too, he should have no more than his capacity to handle.

Tell Sherman this is the Climate for him and all his rich friends, rich men first and poor men follow, here and Mexico too. And now we must have a solid North for a "Solid South," a Country that will not protect itself is a Rebel, and may emigrate the same as Chinese, let the "Solid South" take Cuba and run their machine and not experiment on the work of our fathers or us either. Let the Mormons go to Mexico, they will very soon get Polygamy wiped out of them.

My regards to all old Pioneers,

yours truly

Saml Brannan

LETTER FROM SAMUEL BRANNAN TO THE AUTHOR

ceeded down the coast, trading, and the "Don Quixote" came to Yerba.

Before this second trip of the "California," she had been sold by Bryant & Sturgis to William G. Read, a capitalist of Boston, by whom she was loaded, and sent out, with three supercargoes: Captain Arthur, Captain Clapp, who commanded the "Alciope" when she was here in 1840, and William D. M. Howard. They did not get along very harmoniously. Captain Arther, though an excellent navigator and ship master, was not much of a business man, neither was Captain Clap; but Howard, with a natural aptitude for business, had profited by his experience with Stearns in 1839 and '40, in developing business capacity, and was the chief supercargo. The others were jealous of his superior ability. The cargo having been disposed of, the vessel returned to Boston with hides, but Howard and his wife remained at Los Angeles. Read had written to Howard meantime that he would dispatch to him the "Vandalia," of four or five hundred tons. The ship arrived here in the latter part of 1843. Howard, being sole supercargo, traded up and down the coast (sometimes taking his wife with him), and sold the cargo at a good profit for the owners. In 1846 he sent the vessel back to Boston with hides, otter and beaver skins, and other furs.

The vessel while in the harbor of San Francisco, entertained many of the ladies at impromptu receptions. Howard often joined them in Philopena—sharing with them double almonds, the one calling out Philopena first, on their next meeting, being entitled to a present. It cost him a good many pairs of gloves, and other articles, to discharge these obligations.

In 1845 he formed a copartnership, under the style of Mellus & Howard, with Henry Mellus, who for several years had been employed by Boston merchants as agent and supercargo. The business of the Hudson's Bay Company in Yerba Buena having been terminated by the death of Rae, the premises occupied by that company were purchased by the new firm. Late in 1848 they built a new store on the southwest corner of Clay and Montgomery streets; abandoned the Hudson's Bay building and took Talbot H. Green, a new partner into the business. Then the style of the firm was changed to Mellus, Howard & Co.

Howard was a bold operator, liking to do things on a grand scale—sometimes rather reckless in his purchases, but generally successful. Henry Mellus was the best merchant in town, he having been thoroughly educated in business. My store in 1846 and 1847 was on the northwest corner of Clay and Montgomery streets. Howard was accustomed to late suppers, and often after I had retired for the night at Kent Hall he would rap at my door and call out that I must come over and have supper with him, persisting until I complied.

Going across to the store, we feasted on turkey, chicken and champagne, or whatever his larder afforded; talking, laughing and enjoying ourselves for two or three hours, sometimes with other company.

The American flag was hoisted in 1846, and the town was placed under martial law. Watson, captain of the marines of the American man-of-war "Portsmouth" (Commander Montgomery), was in charge, with a corps from the vessel. The flag was raised on what is now Portsmouth Square. A guard was stationed at the Mexican custom house, an adobe building on the square. The Californians made no resistance to the raising of the flag at various points in the department; but some weeks afterward they decided to oppose the complete surrender of the country. At Los Angeles, Santa Barbara and San José, attacks were made upon the little guards of soldiers there stationed, and they were driven away. News reaching Yerba Buena, the remainder of the marine corps on board the "Portsmouth" was sent on shore, making a force of twenty-five. The opposition of the Californians led to the preparations by Commodore Stockton and the battle of San Gabriel, which will be spoken of hereafter.

Howard, myself and a few other merchants were furnished by Watson with the countersign, which was changed every night. We were out on a visit one evening, and were crossing Portsmouth Square, on the way home, about eleven o'clock, when we were hailed by the guard on duty: "Halt! who goes there?" "Friends;" we answered. "Advance and give the countersign!" commanded the sentry. We advanced, but both Howard and myself had forgotten it. We explained our position. The guard said he was obliged to take us to the guard-house, which he accordingly did, armed with his musket, one of us on each side of him. Fortunately, Captain Watson was still up, and, on seeing us approach under arrest, burst out laughing. He dismissed the guard, and entertained us very hospitably for two or three hours. Howard was a capital mimic. He often personated the peculiarities of others in a good-natured way; was a fine actor, and very successful in playing practical jokes on his friends. If Grimes flew into a rage over the practice of some of these artifices, the former used his mirth and persuasive abilities with success, in calming down the old captain.

Robert Ridley, in 1845, built a one-story cottage, with a piazza round it, on the southwest corner of California and Montgomery streets, back about twenty varas (fifty-five feet) from each of the streets. He sold this place to William A. Leidesdorff, who lived there from 1846 to the time of his death in May, '48. In the summer of 1847 Commodore Biddle arrived from China in the line-of-battle ship "Columbus," and was the guest of Leidesdorff. While he was there, Don José Joaquin Estudillo with his wife and two daughters, and myself called to pay our respects. As we approached the house from the Montgomery street side and passed the pretty flower garden which Leidesdorff had at the time, we were met by him and the commodore. The latter seeming to be in a playful mood, presented each of the ladies with a miniature bouquet of two or three flowers plucked from the garden. To me he presented a single dry straw picked from the ground.

Upon the death of Leidesdorff, Howard was appointed administrator of the estate, with two bondsmen, each in $50,000, of whom I was one. Howard then took possession of the cottage as a residence, and occupied it up to the beginning of '49. While there, he received a good deal of company,—merchants, captains, supercargoes, army and navy officers and other strangers. Mrs. Howard came up from Los Angeles, where she had been spending considerable time, a daughter being born to her there, and joined her husband at the Leidesdorff cottage in 1848. She left San Francisco in January, 1849, by the American ship "Rhone" for Honolulu, hoping to secure in the Islands the restoration of her failing health, but she died in three or four months after her arrival, while staying with the family of William Hooper, the United States consul.

In the autumn of 1849 Howard was married again, the bride being Miss Poett, daughter of Dr. Poett, who, with his wife, had resided many years in Santiago, Chili, where the young lady was born. They came to California in '49. Before the marriage he had purchased a house and lot on the northeast corner of Stockton and Washington streets. It was there he was married and afterward lived, until 1851, when he moved to Mission street, between Third and Fourth, and built one of four cottages—of similar design and appearance, the others having been constructed, one by George Mellus, one by Talbot H. Green and one by Sam. Brannan. Howard had by his second wife one child, (1899) still living. His first child died at Los Angeles.

Mellus, Howard & Co., in 1848 and '49, after the discovery of gold, did an extensive and profitable business. They had a branch store at Sutter's Fort, with Sam. Brannan as partner and manager (he having no interest in the San Francisco house), and sold goods and supplies of all kinds to the miners. The business at Brannan's branch store required continuous supplies from the San Francisco house, and he would sometimes come to the city and nearly empty my store and the stores of others, buying everything we had.

CHAPTER XLV
Samuel Brannan, the Great 46'er

E. MICKLE AND COMPANY were a mercantile house established in San Francisco since 1848. They came here from Valparaiso. A master of a ship consigned to this firm, during his stay in port, obtained several grants of 50 vara lots from the Alcalde. Two of these lots were located on what is the easterly line of Montgomery Street between Sacramento and California Streets. Previous to his departure, the ship captain gave to the head clerk for E. Mickle and Company a letter of instructions regarding the lots. Shortly afterward, the agent put up a large notice on a board placed on a knoll near the center of the property, stating that it was for lease.

Samuel Brannan leased the land and after occupying it for about a year the firm of Osborn and Brannan built a store on a portion of the property. The store was situated on the first 50 vara lot from Sacramento Street, and about twenty feet back from the east line of Montgomery Street. Brannan's firm was then doing a large business as merchants. Brannan subsequently purchased from the owner's agent both lots for $9000, in gold dust, and a deed of conveyance was duly executed to him by the agent. The purchaser then improved a portion of the property with fine buildings. [Note: these were destroyed in the fire of April 18th, 1906.]

Ten years later Brannan sold twenty-five feet on Montgomery Street, where the old bank of Donohoe, Kelly & Co. afterward did business. The purchasers did a large drygoods business there for several years. When they finally closed up, they wished to divide their property but could not agree upon the valuation of land they had bought from Brannan. In view of this, they concluded to offer it for sale at public auction so that each of the partners could bid for it what he thought proper. It was so offered and purchased by one of the partners. Investigation of the title was made by O. C. Pratt and Alexander Campbell, senior, forming the legal firm of Pratt and Campbell, who discovered that Brannan's title

SACRAMENTO CITY IN 1848

This curious print was prepared under the direction of William Heath Davis before his death in 1909. The store of S. Brannan & Co., in which W. D. M. Howard and Henry Mellus were partners with Samuel Brannan, is said to have furnished the provisions used by Marshall while building the sawmill at Coloma where gold was discovered by him January 24, 1848.

was merely one of possession, as the clerk of E. Mickle and Company from whom he had purchased had had no legal authority or power of attorney to sell. This great difficulty was gotten over by Brannan's attorney obtaining a deed from the original owner, then residing in Wisconsin, by payment of a further sum of money. Brannan paid his attorney a large fee, said to be $50,000, for his services in this transaction in addition to the expenses of himself and his assistant. But it was worth fully that amount, for it saved Brannan a much larger sum.

The incident above related shows the loose manner in which real estate transactions were handled in the early days in this city. Litigation arising from land titles was common.

Brannan's confiding disposition and carelessness in business is shown in the following: A person named Charles E. Norton, who had resided many years in Mexico, was on a visit to San Francisco. Through Norton Dr. Hitchcock, Ferdinand Vassault and others purchased the Baraten mines in Cosala. Norton made his headquarters in Vassault's office, where he had a number of beautiful specimens of gold ore. Some of his acquaintances from Mexico would come to see him there, and they told Vassault that they had several valuable mines in their country which they desired to sell. On one occasion Brannan came in, made the acquaintance of the Mexicans, and had a long talk with them about the mines they claimed to represent. Brannan invited them to visit him at his office several days later when he would talk further with them. After several interviews with the Mexicans, Brannan told Vassault that he had made up his mind to buy two, and possibly three, of the mines they claimed to own; adding that if he did make the purchase, he would like Vassault to take an interest in them with him. It was agreed that they should meet the Mexicans at Brannan's office, but when Vassault arrived, Brannan informed him that he had already agreed upon the price to be paid for the mines, namely $200,000; of which $10,000 was to paid down to bind the bargain. Brannan was to make an investigation within a given time, and if everything was as represented the balance of the purchase money would then be paid.

On the table of his private office there were several samples of beautiful ore represented as having come from the mines bargained for. Vassault examined them carefully; and calling Brannan aside, told him that the Mexicans were dishonest and warned him not to pay them any money. He informed Brannan that while examining the specimens of ore lying on the table, his suspicions had been aroused.

Vassault then picked up one of the specimens and showing it to the spokesman for the Mexicans asked if the rock in his hand had actually come out of one of their mines. The man answered in the affirmative. Vassault did the same with all specimens, and received the same reply. Calling Brannan out of the room, Vassault requested him to let the matter rest until the next day, but Brannan declined, saying he had the documents for the purchase prepared and the check drawn, and that he wished to close the business that afternoon. Vassault then asked Brannan to excuse himself from the Mexicans for a half hour, which was done, and the strangers retired. Vassault then told Brannan that the specimens were his, that they had been given to him by his friend Charles E. Norton, and that they had been stolen from his office three days before.

When the Mexicans returned to Brannan's office at the end of the half hour, they were ordered to leave it, and thus ended the attempted swindle. Vassault saved Brannan from a loss of at least ten thousand dollars.

During the French intervention in Mexico, at the time Maximilian was being supported by them, Brannan assisted President Juarez and his supporters, furnishing them with arms, ammunition and supplies. For this he was afterwards paid forty thousand dollars in money by the Mexican government, and also given a large tract of land in Sonora. This land was of no benefit to Brannan, however, for it was situated in the Yaqui region where the Indians were hostile to the government, so that Brannan was unable to take possession of his grant.

Samuel Brannan, when himself, was liked by every one who knew him. He was kind hearted, confiding and generous to a fault; and always ready to open his purse for the relief of the needy. He had a sort of bluntness toward poor people who called upon him for assistance, and would ask questions regarding their necessity, but invariably ended the interview with a generous gift and the remark: "Come again if there is further need of my assistance."

There is hardly a man who has done more for the city of San Francisco or the State of California than Samuel Brannan. He laid out the city of Sacramento, and was the first to project a railroad from that city to a distance of about 28 miles. He had the rails and ties at Sacramento and was about to commence work when Messrs. Stanford, Huntington, Hopkins and Crocker prevailed upon him to sell them the materials for their own project: the Central Pacific Railway.

Brannan likewise laid out the town of Calistoga, and developed the springs there, making known their medicinal qualities. He was the publisher of the first newspaper in San Francisco, the California Star which he started in 1847. This paper was later united with the Californian, first published in Monterey, and brought to San Francisco in May 1847.

The two were afterward issued united, becoming the Alta California.

Without fear of contradiction I may say that Samuel Brannan was one of the most public spirited men in San Francisco; and that his hand and heart in the early days were in every enterprise for the promotion of education and the general prosperity of the state of his adoption.

CHAPTER XLVI
A Ride to Chino and Gift to the Pope

DON VICTOR CASTRO, in addition to raising cattle and vegetables, was a boatman. He owned a schooner launch and a whaleboat, the latter he had obtained from one of the whale ships in exchange for vegetables. This whale boat of Castro's was the only ferry that connected Yerba Buena and Sausalito, socially and commercially, with the opposite or eastern shore of the bay, known in early days as Contra Costa.

Of course, the hide shippers ran boats on the bay, but only for the delivery of merchandise or in search of cargoes of hides and tallow. The merchants of Yerba Buena also had their boats for the same purpose.

Cerritos, a part of the San Pablo rancho, was a sort of terminus for travelers coming to or going from the eastern shore until as late as 1850-51 when the steam ferry began making trips from San Francisco up the San Antonio creek or estuary.

Don Victor was kind and obliging to his callers. He entertained them as guests at his home while his boatmen were making ready for the row across the bay. Obadiah Livermore who died here a few years ago was one of his boatmen in the winter of 1849-50. When Castro was unable to go himself, Livermore took his place and landed the passengers on San Francisco side. This very whaleboat of Victor Castro's has carried matrons and their daughters to and from the early festivals held in San Francisco commemorative of the natal day of Mexico and that of her sister republic. I have partaken of the hospitality of Don Victor and his lovely wife, Doña Luisa Martinez, often. Like all early Californians of Spanish extraction they were generous to a fault. I have tried to reciprocate the kindness of Señor and Señora Castro, and whenever they came to San Francisco they were entertained at our home by Mrs. Davis, who was a niece of Doña Luisa.

I was the guest of Abel Stearns at Los Angeles, when one very warm morning before six o'clock, I was awakened by a knocking on my bed-

Photograph by W. K. Love, Riverside, California.

RANCH HOUSE OF LOUIS RUBIDOUX, OWNER OF THE JURUPA RANCHO FROM 1849 TO 1869.
NOW RIVERSIDE, CALIFORNIA

This adobe house was originally built by Don Juan Bandini and Abel Stearns in 1839 as their home and occupied by them as such until 1843. The Jurupa Grant was made to Don Juan Bandini, September 28, 1838, by Governor Juan B. Alvarado. Later, ownership of portions of the grant passed to Don Benito Wilson and Don Julian (Isaac) Williams. Rubidoux purchased the entire rancho in 1848–1849.

THE GREAT HACIENDA—EL CHINO

room door, which opened on a wide piazza and court yard, by a young good looking vaquero of Spanish extraction. As I opened the door he said, "El caballo esta ensillado; es un animal muy bueno para el camino,"—the horse is saddled, and he is a very fine animal for the road. I made my toilet quickly and was mounted shortly on a beautiful bay horse, sixteen hands high, lengthy in appearance, with head, ears, nostrils and neck worthy of being carved by a sculptor. I was soon out of the Pueblo and on the highway to El Chino rancho. As the sun rose over the mountains to the east its rays were hot and the horse sweated freely. Moving along at a steady gallop, I was greeted by the haciendados, then in the midst of the matanza and all customers of mine, with shouts of, "Cuanto tiempo va a demorar el buque en San Pedro?"—How long will the vessel remain in San Pedro? I would reply, "Two weeks"—Dos semanas. "We will dispatch the wagons with hides and tallow for you the coming week," they told me good naturedly.

On this trip I collected or set in motion the wagons all along the route to San Pedro. Some of the rancheros would recognize me at a distance, and riding up to meet me would say, "Your pay is ready and the hides and tallow will be sent in a few days more." There were fat steers in the corrals, visible from my position in the road. These were marked for slaughter, and vaqueros were separating out others. Everybody was busy: trying out fat, curing hides, cutting up meat for drying. As I rode along I could see no evidence of change. It was too soon to look for the new order of things, for the government under American officials was less than a year in existence. After a canter of an hour or so I would walk my horse to give him a breathing spell, but the spirited animal was eager to reach the end of the journey, and was restless to go from a walk to a lope.

I was riding through the rich valley of Los Angeles, in the month of August 1847. The plains were covered with its moving wealth, some of which was being converted into currency, hides and tallow, to pay for the necessities imported. As I passed along I would ask a ranchero about the condition of the cattle. His answer would be, "The steers are fat and they will yield one with another six arrobas of fat at least. The year has been very grassy and good for slaughtering cattle."

I arrived at the great hacienda—El Chino—an hour before midday, after a ride of forty miles, with the thermometer at one hundred in the shade. The noble animal was as strong and as gay as at the commencement of the journey. A sumptuous dinner was relished after my ride. At table were more than twenty persons, among whom was the family of the proprietor.

I took a great interest in the big establishment, receiving from the American haciendado every attention possible. His treatment of me was a reminder of the cordial receptions of the old Spanish haciendados. Don Julian—Isaac Williams was known among Californians by that name—offered me a fresh horse for my return, but my animal was fresh enough to take me back in lively style.

I found the enterprising man in the midst of his *matanza,* with more than a thousand steers slaughtered, the work to be continued until two thousand or more were killed. I observed with great interest the try-pots bubbling with the melted tallow and *manteca,* the latter, the delicate fat that lies between the hide and meat of the animal. He was preparing this to add to the exports of the hacienda.

Isaac Williams informed me that he would start the wagons within two days with several thousand dollars of hides and tallow for my vessel at San Pedro. I reached Los Angeles before sunset after a very hot ride with the grand horse perfectly unfatigued. This shows that the California horses were originally from fine stock, and their endurance was really astonishing.

Isaac Williams was one of the first Americans to come to the Department of California, and was known by the name of Don Julian, from the similarity in sound of Williams to Julian in the ears of the Californians of that time. He gave as one reason of his coming here that he wanted to see the setting sun in the furthest West. He became the owner of several leagues of land and thousands of animals.

In June, 1846, Don Julian came on board my vessel at San Pedro, and I sold him a large quantity of goods, the payment for which was to be made in the following 1847 *matanza.* The hacienda Santa Ana del Chino, containing eight leagues of land, was situated about thirty miles from where Pomona is now located. Don Julian's home was built in the heart of a fertile valley, in which were thirty thousand horned cattle, sheep and horses. It seemed to me like a young Mission with American ideas added to the ancient notions of improvements.

His income, say, from two thousand five hundred steers killed, would be from the tallow and *manteca,* at six arrobas to each animal, fifteen thousand arrobas or twenty-five thousand dollars; add to this five thousand dollars for the hides, the amount would be thirty thousand dollars. This is an illustration of the incomes of the haciendados, proportionate to the number of cattle they slaughtered at the *matanza* season; exclusive of the sales of cattle, horses, wool and sheep.

The homes of the haciendados were generally large dwellings, one-story in height, built of adobes, with very thick walls as a protection against the attacks of the Indians. The floors in the dwellings of the more wealthy class were planked, and the rooms were partitioned off in sizes to suit the requirements of the families, and furnished with plain, neat furniture, generally imported from Boston. The homes of the poor, usually had no flooring except the adobe soil, which had been stamped and pounded until it was as smooth and hard as slate, and resembled it in color. These rooms were warm in winter and cool in summer. The buildings were erected on the general plan of the Missions, with broad piazzas; a courtyard was entered through a wide passage way, protected by massive wooden doors.

Many of the hacendados lived in the towns in the winter months; but in the spring of the year their households moved to their country homes, where they generally remained until the autumn or close of the *matanza* season.

During these times of dwelling at the haciendas, visits were received from the merchants, supercargoes and the residents of the towns. They were entertained in the most hospitable manner, with picnics in the day time to some picturesque spot on the rancho and in the evening a family *baile* was invariably heralded by the melody of the violin and harp. I have often been a guest at such gatherings, which were the sweetest part of my life, and thought these native Californians of Spanish extraction, were as a rule, as sincere people as ever lived under the canopy of heaven.

I look back almost two generations ago to those merry days with pride and joy, at the kindness which I received and the manliness and simplicity of the welcome of the fathers of families, and the womanly deportment of their wives and daughters, and their innocent amusements.

When I arrived at the Stearn's I went at once to my room, and without undressing, threw myself on the bed. It was not long before I was sound asleep. The servant came to my door and knocked and knocked to tell me supper was ready. He reported to Doña Arcadia that it was impossible to waken me. She herself came to the door and repeated the knocks, but the journey of eighty miles with the intense heat had overpowered my whole system. It would have taken a cannon blast near my bed to have gotten me up. At the breakfast table the next morning I made an apology to Señora Stearns, the good lady of the home, saying that it was not in my power to have complied with her rule for supper, assuring her also that I knew I had lost a fine meal.

One spring forenoon in the early Fifties I made a visit to San Francisco. I was living at San Leandro in Alameda County at the time. On the corner of Montgomery and Sacramento Streets I accidentally met Captain John A. Sutter. Our greeting was most cordial and spontaneous, for we had not seen each other since January 1845 in Los Angeles just after the capitulation of San Fernando between Castro and Micheltorena, which resulted from Micheltorena's voluntary offer and determination to leave the Department of California for San Blas, Mexico, with his army, as mentioned elsewhere.

The old captain said, "Let us go to some quiet place. There is a room in the rear of Barry and Patten's resort where we will be away from the noise of the street."

Sutter was faultlessly attired and looked young and fresh. He ordered a nice luncheon with a bottle of Heidseick, and as we ate and sipped the sparkling beverage we indulged in many reminiscences of our trip to the American River away back in 1839.

The subject of his conversation was his treatment by the early merchants of Yerba Buena and Nathan Spear, who had stood by him, especially the latter in the beginning of the settlement in the Sacramento Valley, when the existence of New Helvetia, his colony, was in the balance. After the severe winter of 1839-40, the success of Sutter's undertaking was assured. He had familiarized himself with the unknown wealth of the rivers in beaver and the valleys in elk, deer, bear and other fur-bearing animals. The tallow derived from the elk was an article of commerce and in good demand at two dollars the arroba. Beaver and land otter were plentiful in the streams and tule flats. There was a large Indian village of about one thousand on the present site of Sacramento. These Indians were converted Mission aborigines, and they were expert hunters. Sutter soon learned of the richness of his possessions, and at once set to work to utilize the skill of these hunters. The Indians proved a source of great revenue to the Captain. They were paid by him so much a skin for their catch. In this and other ways, Sutter emerged into prosperity and influence which was recognized by the merchants afloat and ashore, and the wealthy haciendados of the Department.

Sutter appreciated Spear's faith in his integrity, and his ability as a leader, and sent him a large shipment of furs in payment for supplies which Spear had booked against the Captain in his critical days, financially.

We talked and sipped, and sipped and smoked and the subject turned to the discovery of gold. The Indians from a very early period had learned something of its value. This knowledge they had obtained from Padres at the Missions. It was from the rich finds by Indians and deposited by them at the Missions that gold to the value of six or seven thousand dollars was obtained, which placed in a fine silk purse made especially for the purpose, was sent to Rome as a present to the Pope many years before the finding of the placer diggings in San Fernando

Valley. Bishop Garcia Diego, the first bishop of the Roman Catholic Church in California, was the donor.

The Captain continued the story of his experiences of a score of years in the great Sacramento Valley, and said that they were the happiest years of his life, because he had been in a position to do good to the immigrants and others in need, with plenty to give and no compensation to ask.

The Buri-buri rancho derived its name from an Indian tribe that inhabited the land between San Mateo and the puertezuelo of San Francisco. They also claimed the western shore of the Pacific Ocean as their fishing grounds. In 1838 the Buri-buri hacienda contained more than eight thousand cattle and numerous horses and sheep. It was the property of Don José Sanchez. His name appears elsewhere as a leader of military expeditions against the Indians.

Redwood City inherited its name from the forests of redwood trees growing among the hills to its rear. In former years under both Mexican and American rule there was a large trade from the embarcadero of Las Pulgas in redwood lumber. At first the timber was gotten out with primitive hand saws, but later saws driven by water and steam power denuded the sierra of its wealth and grandeur. These forests were first penetrated by the Mission Padres, Lieutenant Moraga and a few soldiers. They saw a forest of timber suitable for the erection of the Mission San Francisco de Asis. Timbers, planking and boards were cut and prepared with primitive rip and crosscut saws by the hands of the priests themselves, aided by Indians. As fast as this lumber was ready it was hauled to the embarcadero of Las Pulgas (Redwood City) and San Francisquito (Mayfield) and transported to the embarcadero or Mission Creek in schooners and launches built by the Padres.

Palo Alto, the home of the late Senator Stanford and the location of the great university bearing his name, takes its appellation from an ancient monarch of the forest standing near the bank of San Francisquito creek. The base of this mammoth tree was a favorite luncheon spot with early day wayfarers, and merchants engaged in trade for hides and tallow. I have partaken of my noon repast a great many times under the shade of its branches. The lunch generally consisted of well prepared chickens, tamales, lambs tongues and hard boiled eggs, with tortillas and fine white bread, and invariably a bottle of old Mission wine.

In the mountain forests and on the prairie country in back of and on either side of San Francisquito creek there were hundreds and hundreds of black, cinnamon and grizzly bears which roamed the country, living on acorns from the live oaks studding the flat lands. In the season of matanza, they feasted on the rejected meats of the slaughter of the steers belonging to Santa Clara Mission the owner of the ground. At this season vaqueros and their masters amused themselves in the exciting night pastime of lassoing and strangling the brutes to death. Bears have been known to angle with their paws for live and dead fish in the waters of the Pacific Ocean on the western shore of San Mateo County.

Don José Joaquin Estudillo, father of Mrs. Davis, once told me that during one night he and ten soldiers from the San Francisco Presidio, where he was stationed as an officer anterior to 1835, lassoed and killed forty bears in the woods at San Francisquito, one of the numerous ranchos of Mission Santa Clara. They had a relay of horses trained to this work, and the soldiers having been originally vaqueros were quite at home in the sport.

It was matanza time and the bears were attracted by the smell of meat. Señor Estudillo said it was very exciting, and they were so interested in dispatching bears that they forgot the lateness of the hour. The animals were lassoed by the throat and the hind legs with a horseman on each end, the two pulling in opposite directions until the poor brute succumbed. The fun was kept up till daylight. When they were through they were completely exhausted, and then it was they discovered how much work they had done.

Prior to Henry Mellus' downward voyage in the ship "Barnstable" in 1846 from San Francisco to San Pedro, the Californians had revolted. In order to save him from being arrested by the Californians, Don Manuel Requena, then Alcalde of the Pueblo of Los Angeles, contrived a very novel way of preventing Mellus from being taken prisoner.

He sent a confidential Indian to San Pedro, ostensibly to fish, but with a letter bound round his foot with a cloth. The Indian, pretending to be lame, walked and limped with the aid of a stick, and passed through the lines of the unsuspecting Californians. The letter was delivered safely. It cautioned Mellus not to land at San Pedro by any means for he would be caught by the Californians guarding the springs of water then used by men-of-war when in port and by American vessels. This was the only fresh water at San Pedro, a few miles from the rancho Palos Verdes, belonging to Don Juan Sepúlveda.

CHAPTER XLVII
Folsom's Foresight; and Talbot H. Green's Past

THE Leidesdorff estate, when Howard took charge of it, was in debt about $60,000. In its management and settlement he showed his business ability. It embraced a great deal of property. Everything was arranged by Howard in the most satisfactory manner. C. V. Gillespie was his managing assistant in this business. J. L. Folsom, quartermaster, United States army, in San Francisco, noticing the rapid rise in real estate, consequent upon the discovery of gold and the rush of people to California, and knowing that the Leidesdorff property would rapidly become valuable, slipped away from the city and proceeded to the island of St. Croix, one of the West Indies, where Leidesdorff was born, and where his mother Ann Maria Spark, and her family, were living. His father was a Dane, who had emigrated to St. Croix.

Folsom bought of the heirs the entire estate in California, paying therefor the sum of $75,000 cash, and afterwards $15,000 or $20,000 more. On returning, after having secured the deed, the property was turned over to him, it being then worth several hundred thousand dollars.

I was elected to the ayuntamiento of San Francisco in 1848 and also in 1849.* My friend Howard having conceived the idea that I would like to be a member, insisted upon my taking the nomination, which I accordingly did. While a member of the council, I had the honor of suggesting the name of a street in San Francisco after its first citizen, William D. M. Howard; which suggestion was adopted.

He organized, in the year 1849, the first military company in San Francisco, under the name of California Guard, composed of one hundred members, of whom I was one. He made a good commanding officer, and drilled the company efficiently; taking much pleasure and pride in this work, having acquired in the East in his younger days considerable military skill. Without ambition for political office or civil position of any kind—although, with his talents and popularity, he might easily have

*See appendix: Extract of Proceedings; page 343.

attained any position in the department—his aspirations were of a military character, and his tastes were in that direction. At the same time he was a persistent and honest worker for his friends. If he thought that a certain man should fill a certain position in civil affairs, he would set the forces in motion to that end; electioneer for him, and by his efforts carry him through successfully.

Having a fine ear for music, and great appreciation of it, Howard had also a taste for theatricals, and was a good amateur actor. He happened to be at Santa Barbara with the "Vandalia" in 1845, while the ship "Admittance" was there. John C. Jones was going as passenger to Boston, and had secured a cabin for his accommodation. Jones was considered a good actor of Shakespearean characters, and while the vessels were at Santa Barbara he and Howard got up a performance (in which both personated characters) for a large company assembled. It was very successful, affording a good deal of entertainment to themselves and the audience; being the first introduction of Shakespeare to this wild country.

Just after my marriage, in November, 1847, Howard serenaded us on two occasions with a band of music, at our house in Yerba Buena. When the band had played a number of airs on the piazza, we got up and dressed, opened the doors, and invited Howard and the musicians in. Mr. and Mrs. Estudillo being also with us, we had quite a party. Champagne was freely opened, and a few pleasant hours were enjoyed.

Mellus having had an attack of apoplexy in 1850, which impaired his health, soon after sold out his share in the business to Howard and Green, receiving therefor $150,000 here, and also one-half of $40,000 which he and Howard had on deposit in Boston. After his withdrawal he retired to private life in that city. His brother Frank afterward went into the concern, but shortly withdrew.

Sometime in 1850 Talbot H. Green was recognized by H. P. Hepburn, a lawyer from Philadelphia, who had known him at the East, as Paul Geddes. Hepburn was walking in Montgomery street with a number of gentlemen, among them Ferdinand Vassault, and looking across the street, exclaimed, "Why, there's Paul Geddes!" "That's Talbot H. Green," said one. "No," responded Hepburn; "it is Paul Geddes; I know him as well as I do myself." The circumstances under which he had suddenly left the East soon became known throughout the city, and the discovery created quite a sensation, as Green at the time was a candidate for the office of Mayor of San Francisco. Howard had put him forward for that position.

Green stoutly denied that he was Paul Geddes and contradicted all the accusations, affirming that he was Talbot H. Green, and always had been. To prove the truth of his statement, he offered to go East and obtain evidence to satisfy anybody interested of that fact. Vassault was called on by Howard and asked if it was correct, as reported, that Hepburn had made the disclosure about Green, in Vassault's presence. The latter confirmed the report, and the former appeared much surprised and excited.

Green soon left for the East and did not return for a number of years. Howard continued the business by himself.

The great fire of 1851, which destroyed the business portion of San Francisco, and, in fact, almost the whole city, leaving a little rim on the outside like the tire of a wheel—the wheel itself being gone—burned out Howard, who at the time had a large stock of goods, and also his buildings in different parts of the town. He became so crippled in consequence that he was on the verge of bankruptcy.

The town was rebuilt, however, and in 1853 real estate had increased so much in value that he had not only recovered his losses by the fire, but had become a rich man. He visited Boston in that year. The fact of the resuscitation of San Francisco and the great increase in the value of property there were of course well known at the East. When Howard reached Boston he was looked upon as a millionaire. This excited the jealousy of Mellus, who, although wealthy himself, was not satisfied; and he instituted a suit against Howard, employing the famous Rufus Choate as his counsel; his complaint being that he was not in his right mind at the time of his settlement with Howard in 1850, and that he had not received the full value of his share of the partnership property at that time. The suit was, however, abandoned, as Howard could prove unquestionably that Mellus was sufficiently sane to know what he was about, and had sold his interest with full knowledge of its value. Besides, at the time of settlement, the friends of Mellus, his brothers and others, were consulted; they were aware that in the transaction there was no deception on the part of the purchaser.

After his return from Boston, in 1854, he was so enraged at Mellus' unfriendly action in commencing suit, that he caused the name of the street which had been called after him to be changed to "Natoma," which name it still bears.

Howard was the leader and one of the most active organizers in the establishment of the California Pioneer Society in 1850, and due credit should be given him for these efforts. He was the first president of the society, and remained as such till 1853. At the Pioneer Hall was a portrait of him, but I regret it was not a very correct likeness; a better one was owned by Don Alfredo Robinson.

I never knew Howard to decline granting a favor or refuse to contribute to a charitable enterprise. In any scheme of the kind he was always one of the first to act, not from ostentation or a desire for display, but from real philanthropy and generosity. Among other things, I remember his subscribing $300 to build the first Catholic church, on Vallejo street, in the fall of 1848, for which I made some collections at the request of Judge (afterward Governor) Burnett, and I was a treasurer of the fund.

In 1850 or 1851 Mellus & Howard purchased, in Boston, a first-class fire engine, one of such machines as were in use in those days, worked by hand, selected by Mellus while he was East on a visit, the firm paying for it, and the freight also, from their private funds. On its arrival in 1851 they presented it to the city of San Francisco, this being among the first, if not the very first, of the engines which the city possessed. It was named the "Howard."

A fire company was organized, of which Howard was made foreman. Charles R. Bond was secretary, Ferdinand Vassault, William Burling, A. S. Dungan, G. B. Post, R. S. Watson, Charles Warner, R. L. Ogden, Thomas J. Haynes and other well-known gentlemen—all merchants, the first citizens of San Francisco—were original members; also Beverly C. Sanders, banker, and collector of the port; Sam. Brannan and George H. Howard, capitalists. In fact all the members of this company were men of wealth and high standing, none others being admitted. At the organization of the company and the election of officers there was a jolly time. One of the participants one time remarked to me that the champagne was unlimited. There were about forty members, and they had their headquarters in an iron building, imported from England, situated on the west side of Montgomery street, a little south of California, where the engine was kept. On occasions of fires, Howard, as foreman, and the other members of the company, appeared in their firemen's caps and uniforms, and worked the engine—aided by volunteers from the outside, when necessary.

The subject of this sketch may be regarded as one of the founders of San Francisco. His enterprise, energy and wealth helped build it up and stimulated its prosperity. He had its interests always at heart; and where he could be of service in anything tending to its growth and advancement, he was foremost.

In personal appearance, he can be described as an ideal nobleman, six feet in height, erect, of commanding figure, with sandy beard (generally clean shaven), full, ruddy cheeks, laughing eyes, and soft and musical voice.

During his visit to Boston in 1853, Howard contracted a severe cold which settled on his lungs. After his return here in 1854, he commenced to pine away. He gradually grew worse, until he became hardly more than a skeleton of his former self, having lost perhaps half his weight. He was then living at the Oriental Hotel, Bush and Battery streets, with his family.

Larkin went up to the hotel one day to see him. He looked about the parlor, passing a man sitting there and was continuing his search, when the man in the chair called out, "For God's sake, Larkin, why don't you speak to me?"—and, to his astonishment, he perceived that it was Howard, so changed that he hardly knew him. His death was much lamented, laudatory obituary notices appearing in the *Alta* and *Herald*. The columns of the latter were dressed in mourning, as a token of respect.

Howard left a fine estate, which was divided between his widow and son. His widow afterward married his brother George; and after the latter's death, she married her present husband, Mr. Bowie.

CHAPTER XLVIII
Yoscolo, the Mission Indian Renegade

AFTER the change of flag, the laws of Mexico (civil and criminal) were continued as the predominating laws of the department, but the U. S. military commander of the territory was at the head. If a doubt arose concerning any alleged illegal exercise of authority by an alcalde (who was an elective officer) or by prefects (who were appointed by the governor), the dispute could be referred to the military governor, and his decision thereon might be final; he had power, for cause, to remove the alcalde from office; but I know of no instance of the arbitrary exercise of this power.

Pio Pico was the last of the governors under the Mexican regime, holding from January, 1845, to the time of hoisting the American flag at Monterey July 7th, 1846.

Commodore J. D. Sloat, of the U. S. navy, was the first military commander under our flag. He was succeeded by Commodore R. F. Stockton in July, 1846. Colonel Frémont was the military governor during a part of 1847. The latter was succeeded by General Kearny, and he, by Colonel Mason. The last of the military governors was General Riley, during whose administration the first constitution of the state was formed at Monterey in 1849. It was ratified at the general election November 13, 1849; the population at that time being about 120,000, of whom 80,000 (estimated) were American, 20,000 foreigners, and 20,000 native Californians.

Peter H. Burnett was elected governor at that election, under the constitution. On the 20th of December, 1849 (before the admission of the state into the Union, September, 1850), he entered upon the discharge of his duties at the capital, the pueblo of San José. Before the expiration of his term of office he resigned the governorship, and John McDougal, the lieutenant-governor, served out the remainder of the term, a little less than a year.

Governor McDougal was jolly and open-hearted, but his habits were against him, and occasionally he would imbibe too much.

The next election took place in the fall of 1851, John Bigler being elected governor of the state for the term of two years from January 1, 1852. His majority was 441 votes over P. B. Reading, the Whig candidate; the whole vote being about 50,000.

In 1849, Central wharf was built in San Francisco, so named from Central wharf of Boston. It was located where Commercial street is now, commencing a little to the west of Sansome street, and running 400 feet into the bay. Howard was one of the most active movers in this enterprise, and owned a large amount of the stock. The wharf proved to be useful, and was a valuable piece of property, bringing in a large income. At the public sale of tide lands by Alcalde Hyde, in October, 1847, Mellus and Howard bought the block bounded by Clay, Sacramento, Sansome and Battery streets, and they gave the company a slip of land about thirty-five feet wide for the building of the wharf. Its construction and use enhanced the value of the remainder of the block, and increased the wealth of the firm.

Afterward, in 1849, the alcalde, with the approval of the ayuntamiento, granted to the Central Wharf Company a block of tide land east of this block, and the wharf was extended to Front street the same width as the portion before built. In 1850 Colonel J. D. Stevenson and Dr. W. C. Parker secured the title to the block in front of that just mentioned, bounded by Front, Clay, Davis and Sacramento streets, and they granted to the Central Wharf Company, for a consideration, a strip the width of the wharf for a further extension, which was made as far as where Davis street now is. After that the city gave the company the right of way as far as Drumm street, and the wharf was built to that point.

The first section of wharf extending to Battery street, cost $110,000, and from Battery to Drumm $200,000. On the organization of the wharf company, C. V. Gillespie was elected president, and I was chosen treasurer. At the first meeting after the organization I reported having collected $23,000 from the stockholders. The stock was paid for as soon as subscribed. At the second meeting I reported that the subscriptions had all been paid in, amounting to $200,000. I then relinquished my position as treasurer, having more business on hand of my own than I could find time to attend to. I had accepted the position at first solely to oblige Howard.

From the time of the building of the first portion, the wharf beame an important feature of the city; and in the winter of 1849-50 it presented a scene of bustle and activity, day after day, such as, I presume, hardly has been equalled elsewhere in the world at any time.

An immense fleet of vessels from all parts of the globe, numbering eight or nine hundred, were anchored in the bay, east of the city, between Clark's Point (now about Broadway street) and the Rincon (now about

Harrison street), presenting a very striking picture—like an immense forest stripped of its foliage.

Central Wharf was the thoroughfare for communication with the vessels, and was crowded from morning till night with drays and wagons coming and going. Sailors, miners, and others of all nationalities, speaking a great variety of tongues, moved busily about; steamers were arriving and departing, schooners were taking in merchandise for the mines, boats were crowding in here and there—the whole resembling a great beehive, where at first glance everything appeared to be noise, confusion and disorder.

The city of San Francisco of 1905 with its extensive commerce and four hundred thousand people, presents no such grand spectacle of enterprise and activity as was centered at that pier, in its infancy.

The wharf at that time was a prominent feature of the view from the hill residences west. On leaving my home at Stockton and Jackson streets for the store on a fine morning, looking down, the sight was panoramic in the extreme—the living mass of human beings moving to and fro seeming in the distance not unlike an army in battle on the edge of a forest, represented by the wilderness of masts of vessels majestically riding at their moorings, gathered from all parts of the known world. The scene was one of the most memorable within my recollection.

Visiting the Missions of Carmel, Santa Barbara and San Diego in 1831, I was impressed with the neatness and order about them, and the respectable appearance of the Indians. The men dressed in white shirts and blue drill or cotton pants; many of them with shoes, which were manufactured at the Missions, from bullock hides, deer and elk skins, dressed and tanned there. The government of the Indians was systematic and well designed. A few of the Indians, in whom the Padres had confidence, were selected to act as alcaldes or *capitanes,* each over a certain number, for whose good conduct he was held in some degree responsible. If any offense against the regulations of the Mission was committed, the case was reported to the Padre, who determined what punishment should be inflicted on the culprit. The good impression was confirmed by a visit to the Mission Dolores in 1833, where were gathered from 2000 to 2500 Indians, the order and discipline among them being so apparent and perfect as to excite the admiration of the beholder. It seemed like a military camp.

Captain Shaw, of the "Volunteer," was a severe disciplinarian, and his vessel was as neat in every respect as a man-of-war; he also remarked upon the neatness and good order of the people, and everything connected with the Mission, saying the system could not be surpassed on a war vessel. There were no ragged children or vulgar-looking women. In visiting other Missions during that year, I noticed a similar condition; good order and cleanliness prevailed. I made the same observations at the Mission of San José in 1838, where two or three thousand Indians were collected—all having an appearance of neatness, and all being under good discipline. At that time the Mission of Santa Clara was falling into decay, owing to the loss of some of its lands, and it was made a centre for military operations.

At the Mission of San José in 1839, I saw an Indian whipped on the bare back, for some offense he had committed, this being one of their punishments. The Mission was not then under the charge of Father Gonzales, but of Don José Jesus Vallejo. In a year or two the control was again given to the Padre, and Don José withdrew. This was the richest Mission in the Department at that time.

Among the Indians who were educated at the Missions, two became prominent—Stanislaus at the Mission of San José, after whom Stanislaus River and County were named; and Yoscolo, at the Mission of Santa Clara. They were educated by the Fathers. Both showed ability and promise in their youth. Yoscolo when twenty-one years of age, was made the chief of the whole body of Indians at the Mission, responsible of course to the Padres for the management of them. In this position he displayed tact in the control of the Indians.

At one time some of them committed trespasses which displeased the Padres and they proposed punishing Yoscolo, who refused to submit to it. At this stage he was joined by 500 of the Indians over whom he had command, and they all assumed a hostile attitude.

The Indians were armed with bows and arrows, having been allowed to retain these weapons, as it was considered there was no danger in their doing so, and they were needed in killing game.

The outbreak occurred in the night. The five hundred, led by Yoscolo, broke open the Mission stores and helped themselves to blankets and whatever articles they could easily carry away.

A small guard was usually placed at each Mission by the governor, consisting of ten or fifteen soldiers, from the troops of the nearest Presidio, under the charge of a corporal or sergeant. At the Mission of Santa Clara there was a guard of this kind, under the command of Juan Prado Mesa. But against so large a force it would have been powerless.

After breaking into the stores and helping themselves, they entered the convent attached to the Mission, and seized about two hundred young Indian girls whom they took away with them.

It is probable that the sole object of the émeute was to secure possession of the girls, and that Yoscolo had planned for some time to effect this purpose; that the offense for which he had incurred the displeasure of the Fathers and rendered himself amenable to punishment was committed as a pretext for the outbreak; that his five hundred followers had all been fully instructed beforehand as to the performance; and that the weapons had also been secured, and everything pre-arranged. Yoscolo was a young man of talent and bravery, as afterward was shown, and capable of conducting an intrigue of this kind. Besides the plunder from the stores, and the two hundred girls, about two thousand head of horses belonging to the Mission of Santa Clara and also some owned by the citizens of the pueblo of San José, were taken by the Indians. As they went on south they gathered in the stock of others. They made good their retreat, and reached the Mariposa mountains without opposition.

An instance is not known of Indians doing harm to any of the Padres, so great was the respect in which the Fathers were held.

Stanislaus had sometime previous left the Mission of San José and taken command of numerous tribes at Mariposa, numbering about 4,000. He, also, was well educated, brave and talented, but preferred the freedom of wild life and the exercise of authority over the tribes, to the tame civilization of the Missions.

Yoscolo sought Stanislaus, cultivated his friendship, and the two joined forces, the former becoming the leader. These events occured in May, 1831.

The government took steps immediately to pursue and chastise the offenders. General Vallejo collected a force from the different presidios, and called also for volunteers. In two or three weeks he had organized a body of 200 men, armed and equipped, for the pursuit.

The Indians were encamped on the Stanislaus river to the number of several thousand,—men, women and children, for fishing and general enjoyment.

The Californians reached the camp and prepared to attack it. As soon as the presence of the troops was known, the enemy formed an ingenious plan to evade them. A large number of bundles of grass were set afloat down the stream, and as the current took them past General Vallejo's camp, in the indistinct light of the moon the soldiers mistook them for Indians, and supposed that their wily foes were getting away in a body; whereupon, the entire force set out in pursuit of the supposed aborigines, who, after being followed some distance down the stream, were discovered actually to be men of straw. Meanwhile, the real Indians had taken up their march to the interior and where they were safe from all pursuit, as no white man would follow them into those well-nigh inaccessible retreats.

Some time after, Yoscolo, with about 200 picked men, made an attack in the night upon the Mission of Santa Clara, for the purpose of plunder. Breaking into the stores, they helped themselves to whatever they chose to carry off, making good their escape. They took up their position at a pass in the Santa Cruz mountains, known as "La Cuesta de los Gatos," which name was given from the circumstance that wild cats in great numbers were about there in former times. Here Yoscolo relied upon his ability to hold out against any attack of the Californians.

This new outrage on the part of these Indians aroused the military spirit of the Californians anew. Juan Prado Mesa gathered one hundred men in a few days, with whom he marched against the enemy, taking with him also a piece of artillery.

Mesa was a great Indian fighter. He knew his enemies, and did not underestimate their cunning and ability; yet, at the same time, he had no fear of them. Yoscolo, seeing him approach, came out from his retreat, and with his force went part way down the mountain to meet him. A desperate encounter ensued, in which both sides showed great intrepidity. The Indian leader marshaled his forces in the form of a square, in true military style, and ordered his men to lie down and discharge the arrows from a recumbent position, in which there would be less risk of being hit by the bullets of their opponents, who were armed with old-fashioned muskets, carbines and flint-lock pistols. The battle raged all day, the savages showing great stubbornness in continuing it. Only when their arrows had all been discharged did they finally yield to the Californians. Their leader, when taken, was found to be wounded. He and the more prominent of the band under him were immediately beheaded. The remainder were turned over to the Mission of Santa Clara to be civilized and Christianized anew. About one hundred Indians were killed and wounded in this battle. Of the Californians only eight or ten were killed, but a large number were wounded. Among the killed were two brothers Cibrian, of a well-known family of the pueblo of San José.

Yoscolo's head was affixed by the hair to the top of a pole planted in front of the church at Santa Clara, and remained there for several days as a warning to other Indians.

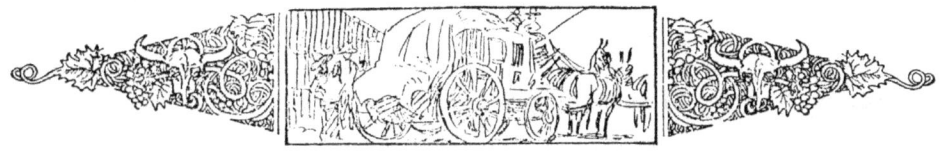

CHAPTER XLIX
Don José de la Guerra y Noriega and His Family

STANISLAUS, with a force of about eighty Indians, came down from the mountains in May, 1840, to the rancho of Guillermo Castro, at San Lorenzo, and to the rancho of the Peraltas, at San Antonio (East Oakland), and captured several hundred head of horses. A day or two after, Castro, with seventeen men, went in pursuit. A fight took place on the banks of the San Joaquin river. Stanislaus formed his men in military order; and directed them to lie down, and not to discharge the arrows at random, but to make sure of a white man each time. The battle lasted about three hours, during which two of the bravest of the fighters, the Romero brothers, were wounded. One of them could not help expressing admiration for the bravery of Stanislaus, as he noticed his conduct during the fight, and he informed Castro, who was in command, that it would be impossible to win, as the Indians were in superior force and were well supplied with arrows. The Californians then withdrew, with their recovered horses. The loss of the enemy could not be definitely ascertained, but it was considerable in killed and wounded.

In the summer of 1841 the Indians of the Clear Lake region committed some depredations, and troops, to the number of fifty or sixty, were sent out under command of Captain Salvador Vallejo to vanquish them. Reaching the Indians, he found them in their *temescales,* and as they emerged from the steaming huts, one or two at a time, they were barbarously shot or cut down, until about 150 men, women and children had been slaughtered. When the news of the massacre reached Yerba Buena, the people were horrified. I remember that Spear spoke of it as nothing but butchery, for which there was no justification; and the officers of Wilkes' expedition regarded it in the same light.

No doubt the Indians deserved some chastisement for the offenses, or at least their leaders did, but no such punishment as was inflicted.

Solano, after whom Solano county was called, was a noted chief. He exercised great influence over the tribes, and had the confidence and respect of General Vallejo, who conferred with him, and communicated to him his wishes and views. He assisted the general in keeping the Indians in subjection.

In 1843, sixty or seventy Indians, commanded by the brother of Yoscolo came to the rancho San Pablo, stole several hundred horses and then retreated. One of the owners of the rancho, with his brother and four other Californians, and two domesticated Indians, went in pursuit. The thieves were found in the neighborhood of Mount Diablo. The little party approached, and succeeded in capturing two of the Indians, whom they put to instant death.

The main body of the Indians coming up, a fight took place, lasting two or three hours, during which the horse of the leader of the party was killed under him. He made a barricade of the body of the animal and fought behind it, and in the fight he shot the leader of the savages dead with his pistol,—the same chief who had killed Briones in 1839. After the fall of their leader the others became dismayed, and retreated, leaving three or four dead upon the field and abandoning the stolen horses.

The Indians sometimes fought with poisoned arrows. In fighting expeditions the Californians were usually accompanied by an Indian doctor, who was provided with an herb which he used as an antidote to the poison. Indians, themselves, also made use of it. When a man was wounded by an arrow the Indian doctor applied his mouth to the wound and sucked out the blood and the poison with it. He then chewed some of the herb and injected it into the wound.

Some time prior to 1860 a man named O'Connor obtained possession of a portion of the Rancho San Pablo by purchase, transfer or otherwise. The ranchero permitted him to remain, respecting his claim, and did not distrust him so long as he remained upon his own premises, but would not allow the slightest encroachment upon land the owner occupied as a homestead.

Squatters would take possession of lands belonging to the Californians. A certain ranchero, by his coolness and bravery, succeeded in driving them from his premises and in keeping them off, sometimes facing guns and pistols. He never had to fire upon a man, though fully armed on these occasions and on the alert to use his weapons, if necessary. The owner of the rancho, one day in 1860, riding over his land, mounted on a fine horse, with a reata on his saddle, noticed that some laborers employed by O'Connor had come over the border and were at work upon his land. He peremptorily ordered them off, and threatened to thrash them with the reata if they did not instantly obey. O'Connor coming up to interfere, commenced an angry dispute, drew a pistol, and was in the act of firing at the ranchero when the latter quickly flung out the lasso and caught O'Connor round the neck. The rider putting spurs to his horse, the unfortunate man was dragged along at a furious rate. Luckily, the ranchero's son happened to be near at hand, also mounted on a swift steed. He rushed forward in pursuit, and dexterously cut the reata between horse and victim, thus saving the latter's life. A witness, giving an account of the occurrence, said, he never saw anything more admirable than the whole performance, in coolness, quickness and courage.

The reata was a slender woven cord about eighty feet in length, and made of very strong leather or strips of hide untanned. In the hands of a Californian it was not only a very useful implement, as well as means of amusement at times, but was also a powerful weapon, as has been shown by the instance just mentioned. It was carefully handled, as much so as a firearm but accidents sometimes happened from its use.

A ranchero of my acquaintance was once in the act of securing the reata to the pommel of the saddle, just after a steer had been lassoed, when his hand got under the lasso, between it and the saddle, and the strain which came at that instant almost severed the fingers of his hand from the remainder. In two or three weeks thereafter lock-jaw set in, from which he died. There are numbers of instances where a Californian has lost a thumb or forefinger of the right hand by having it caught and cut off in the same manner by the reata, while in the act of securing it to the saddle.

To the Californian the lasso was an indispensable part of his equipment on all occasions when he started away from home. In expeditions against the Indians and in military campaigns, every man took his reata along with him, not only for use for ordinary purposes, but as a weapon of offense and defense in cases of necessity. If, on starting out, he had been compelled to choose between pistol and reata which to take with him, he would have chosen the latter as being the more useful of the two.

I remember where the use of the reata in an extraordinary way saved a man's life. Between San Luis Obispo and Guadalupe, the regular road in some parts was quite sandy. Traveling over it was heavy work. Another and at times better road ran nearer the ocean, part of the way along the beach when the tide served. Don Luis Estudillo happened to be going from Guadalupe to San Luis Obispo one day in the spring of 1875, and reached the Arroyo Grande at the moment a wagon and four horses, driven by a young man, were struggling in the water, after an attempt to ford, when the tide was high, at the point where the beach road crossed that estuary. Seeing the stranger in this plight, being borne out by the current into the ocean and hearing his cries for help, Don Luis prepared to assist in a rescue. He knew it would not be prudent to plunge his horse into the swift tide, so he rode in only a short distance, and casting the reata the full length, with all his force, it just reached far enough. The loop passed over the young man's head and went round his neck. Calling loudly to him to catch hold with his hands, so that he would not be strangled, Don Luis then gently drew him ashore, and saved his life. The horses and wagon were carried out to sea and lost.

About the year 1801 José de la Guerra y Noriega, a captain in the Spanish army, came from Mexico and located at Santa Barbara, as comandante of that presidio. He was born about 1775 at Novales Santander, in Spain. When Mexico severed allegiance to Spain he resigned his commission in the army and was elected as *diputado* to represent the department at the capital city. During his residence in California he acquired immense wealth in lands, cattle, horses, sheep and money. He owned the Las Positas rancho, of twelve leagues, and the Simi rancho, of fourteen leagues, about half way between Santa Barbara and Los Angeles, the two ranchos being nearly adjoining. Each rancho had from 5000 to 6000 head of cattle and about 2000 horses. He also owned the Callegua rancho, of five leagues, with 2000 head of cattle and a large number of horses; also El Conejo rancho, of three leagues, with 1000 head of cattle and many horses, and the San Julian rancho, of eleven leagues, with 10,000 head of cattle and a large number of horses. His possessions covered a vast area, and were equal to a small kingdom. In all these ranchos the horses aggregated 5000 to 8000. His sons were José Antonio, Francisco, Pablo, Joaquin Miguel, and Antonio Maria. His daughters were Teresa, wife of Hartnell; Augusta, wife of Jimeno; Anita, wife of Don Alfredo Robinson, and Maria Antonia, wife of Lataillade, and after his death, of Gaspar.

I became well acquainted with the old gentleman in 1842. He still retained his title of captain, by which he was always called. I sold him large quantities of goods at different times. He was a close buyer, generally paying cash (Mexican and Spanish doubloons). What money the vessels collected was used for the purchase of hides. Being introduced by Henry Mellus to the captain in 1842, he received me with a good deal of dignity and coolness, and rather pompously; but on learning that I was the son of Don Guillermo Davis, who had visited the coast many years before, he welcomed me cordially; paying my father many compliments; saying that he knew him well, and had bought from him largely. I was afterward quite a favorite of his, and came to know him well. While supercargo of the "Don Quixote" in 1842 and '43 I made four or five sales to him, ranging from $2000 to $4000 each.

On these occasions Noriega took me to the attic of his house, where he kept his treasure, the room being used exclusively for that purpose.

There was no stairway, the attic being reached by a ladder, which was removed when not in use. In this room were two old-fashioned Spanish chairs, and ranged round about were twelve or fifteen *coras*—strong, compactly-woven baskets, of different sizes, made by Indians, the largest holding, perhaps, half a bushel—all of which contained gold, some nearly full. The money amounted to a considerable sum in the aggregate. I was astonished to see so much coin in the possession of one person in a country where the wealth consisted mainly of horses and cattle. The old gentleman said that the attic was the safest place in which to keep it. I asked him how he managed to collect so much gold, and he replied that it was the accumulations of all the years he had been on the coast. The Spanish soldiers, when they were paid off, spent their money freely, and he had supplied them with what they wanted, having carried on a store of his own.

Many articles were also required to supply his ranchos, and he paid his vaqueros in goods, as they had not much use for money; and on these he made more or less profit. He also sold his hides and tallow, besides otter and other fur skins, for cash; and had thus collected his great treasure. He had no occasion to spend money except for purchases from the vessels. Being a good merchant and shrewd manager, he knew how to take care of money. Noriega had also at Santa Barbara a vineyard, from which he made wine and aguardiente.

In 1846 I owned one-third of the brig "Euphemia," the other two-thirds being owned by Captain Grimes and his nephew Hiram Grimes. I was supercargo, and being at Santa Barbara with the vessel, Captain Noriega asked to see the invoice of my goods, and seemed very anxious to purchase. That day and the next, I sold him about ten thousand dollars' worth, for which he paid coin. After visiting San Diego on this trip, and returning in January, 1847, I sold him goods to the amount of three or four thousand dollars more, which he paid for in cash and in hides.

Some of the old gentleman's boys were a little wild. Knowing that their father had plenty of money and the place where it was deposited, they devised a plan to secure some of it for their own use. The ladder was kept in the old captain's bedroom, beyond their reach. So they climbed to the roof from the outside, and took off two or three of the tiles, beneath which were standing these baskets of gold. Reaching down into the baskets with an improvised pitchfork, they drew out as many coins as they thought it advisable to take. How often this operation was repeated and how much of the old gentleman's treasure thus disappeared is not known, but the trick was soon discovered and reported, and this mode of abstraction was brought to an end. As the captain did not know how much money he had in the baskets, of course he could not tell how much he had lost.

LENDING TO LESS FORTUNATE LANDOWNERS

When I first knew him, he was nearly seventy and retained his fine personal appearance. He was the sire of many handsome sons and daughters.

Being the wealthiest man in that part of California, and having so much money, he was applied to by the rancheros for loans when they were in need of funds. The loans were made on promises to repay in beef cattle at the killing season, or in heifers, or in hides and tallow after cattle had been killed; the lender taking the borrower's word as security, as was the custom.

In the spring of the year, the number of heifers agreed upon would be delivered to him to add to his own stock, heifers being more easily domesticated in a new place than older cattle; or at the *matanza* season the beef cattle or the hides and tallow would be delivered, and the debt thus cancelled.

When cattle, old or young, were transferred from one rancho to another, as was frequently the case in the dealings of the rancheros with each other, it was generally done in the spring of the year, the new feed being then plentiful, and they were easier *aquerenciado,* or domesticated, in their new pasture than at any other season. A band of cattle taken to another rancho, would be placed under the charge of vaqueros, and watched and herded at first very carefully. Becoming accustomed to the new place, and less restless and uneasy, they were allowed more liberty of range, and at night were coralled. After some weeks, they were habituated to their new surroundings, and turned in with the other cattle, becoming a part of the general band belonging to the rancho.

CHAPTER L
Henry Mellus: From Fo'c'sle Hand to Merchant

THE ship "Courier" arrived at Monterey, from Boston, on the 3d of July, 1826, Captain Cunningham master and supercargo, and traded on the coast, collecting hides and tallow. Thomas Shaw, who came out from Boston in the vessel as a carpenter, after her arrival was made clerk and assistant supercargo. He was supercargo of the "Lagoda," when she was here in 1835, and also of the "Monsoon" which arrived here in 1839. George Vincent was second mate of the "Courier," and commanded the "Monsoon" in 1839. He also commanded the ship "Sterling," which left Boston, in October, 1843, and arrived here early in 1844. She was consigned to Thomas B. Park. Henry Richardson came out on this trip from Boston, as clerk of the vessel, and died here of typhoid fever. He was a young man of great promise, and his death was much lamented by those who knew him. Captain Vincent also commanded the brig "Sabine," which left Boston in the early part of 1848, arriving here in the midst of the gold excitement. Holbrook was owner and supercargo.

The ship "Monsoon" was lying in the harbor, in 1839, and Sutter left from along-side for the Sacramento valley, with the schooners "Isabel" and "Nicolas" and his own four-oared boats, as previously described. Just prior to our leaving, the whole company was invited on board the ship for a little farewell entertainment. We were handsomely treated; toasts were given, and a pleasant time enjoyed. As the visitors left the vessel to embark on their expedition, they were followed by friendly expressions and best wishes of Captain Vincent, his officers and crew. After 1848 the captain continued to reside in San Francisco, and made one or two trips to Mexico to purchase goods. In 1850 I had my office in the brick building at the northwest corner of Sacramento and Montgomery streets, on the second floor, where Captain Vincent also had an office and kept his valuables. The second story was reached by a flight of stairs from an alley that connected with Montgomery street. While the great fire of May, 1851, was raging, the captain rushed up to the office to secure his property, and in returning was caught by the fire at the foot of the stairs in the alley, and there perished, his body being nearly consumed to ashes.

In 1837 Thomas B. Park came out in the ship "Alert" from Boston, in the capacity of assistant supercargo. On Robinson's return to Boston in the same year, in the ship "California," Park took his place as agent, and remained here ten or twelve years, and up to his death. He was an educated merchant and gentleman. Though not liking the rough travel of a new country, and the rambling kind of trade peculiar to California, where a good deal of push and energy were required, but preferring much to be in his own office attending to his correspondence, with bookkeeper and clerks at hand, whom he could direct in the business, still he was willing to adapt himself to the circumstances, and did travel about to secure his trade; sought out his customers and followed them up, sold his goods, and filled his vessels with hides. But he consumed more time than others, not moving actively, nor pushing the business very vigorously.

There was a great deal of competition in the early days in the selling of goods from vessels, particularly at Yerba Buena, which was a distributing point. Whenever there were two or more vessels here at a time, the supercargoes were very active in getting round in their boats, up the creeks, or with their horses and vaqueros, to various points about the bay, in order to be first at the different ranchos and Missions, to sell goods, and collect hides and tallow. The rancheros preferred to buy from the vessel rather than from the local stores, for the reason that they then got supplies at first hand, and, as they thought, to better advantage.

Henry Mellus came to the coast in the brig "Pilgrim," before the mast, in 1834, Frank Thompson, captain. The vessel was consigned to Alfred Robinson. When the brig arrived, the ship "Alert," Captain E. F. Faucon, was here, Alfred Robinson, agent and supercargo. He transferred Mellus from the vessel, and employed him as clerk. Most of the Boston ships in those days had on board three or four boys, of good families, who were sent here to get a little experience, and learn something of nautical life. Mellus was one of them. The "Pilgrim," a smaller vessel than the others belonging to the same owners, was sent as a tender to assist them at rancho landings, such as at the Refugio and other points distant from the regular ports, and to deliver goods and receive hides and tallow.

Robinson was thorough and systematic in all mercantile matters—a man of good commercial schooling. He had a great dislike for the "Alert's" captain, Faucon, and also for John H. Everett, the clerk of the vessel, who certainly were very disagreeable.

In order to get them away from the coast as quickly as possible, Robinson loaded the "Pilgrim" rapidly, transferred Faucon and Everett, and dispatched them, with the brig, home.

In 1837 Mellus returned to Boston, with Robinson, in the ship "California," the agency being left in charge of Park. Returning in 1839, as assistant supercargo of the "California," Mellus for a time co-operated with Park in the agency, and showed great aptness for business, becoming a successful merchant in San Francisco. He was not so demonstrative and unreserved as Howard, but said very little, and that little to the point. Though unostentatious, he was always pleasant and agreeable, and magnetic in manner. An excellent manager, he planned everything carefully beforehand, and all the details of his business were executed without jar or confusion. Everything moved smoothly, just as designed, and came to a successful issue. He kept his plans to himself. When he sent off his boats from the vessel's side, no one unconnected with the vessel knew their destinations, and no advantage could be taken by competitors. In 1846 he married Anita Johnson, the daughter of an Englishman who had married a Mexican lady from Sonora. Anita was born in Los Angeles. She was pretty and attractive. A number of children followed the marriage After relinquishing the agency for Bryant & Sturgis in 1848, Mellus went to Boston with his family on a visit. He returned to this coast in the winter of 1849-50, at which time he had an attack of apoplexy. He partially recovered, but never was the Henry Mellus of former days. H. F. Teschemacher and he were close friends, and he was also on the same friendly terms with Alfred Robinson.

Mellus' family lived at Los Angeles after his marriage. On one occasion a grand party took place there, at which were present Mr. and Mrs. Mellus, Teschemacher, and other company, among whom was a young officer of the United States army named Bonnycastle. During the dancing, Mrs. Mellus and Bonnycastle happened to be in the same set, and at this time the army officer was grossly guilty of the impropriety of pressing the lady's hand ardently. She immediately left the room, feeling much aggrieved, and informed her husband of what had occurred. The result was a challenge from Mellus to Bonnycastle, which was accepted. The latter having the choice of weapons, selected rifles, at forty paces.

On the morning appointed for the meeting Mellus was reclining on a lounge in his house, very uneasy, and much excited at the prospect before him. Being of a very sensitive nature, the contemplated duel was quite contrary to his inclinations and tastes. He looked forward to it with forebodings which he could not control. A friend much attached to him came into the room, and seeing his nervous condition, proposed a compromise, urging that since he was a respectable man of family, with a good many duties, whereas his adversary was a single man, the risks would be much less with the latter. He proposed to take Mellus' place as a principal in the duel, and insisted upon it so strongly that Mellus finally yielded, and allowed him to do so.

The parties met, and fired, Bonnycastle being wounded in the hand. A ring on one of his fingers was hit by the bullet and carried away, and the finger shattered. Thus the duel terminated.

Up to the time of the attack of apoplexy, Mellus was known as a man of remarkably strong mind, with head always clear; but afterward it was evident that his intellect was somewhat impaired, although his conversation was rational and intelligent. I remember meeting him at San Diego in 1850, whither he had gone for his health. He frequently came to the house where my wife and I were staying; and he seemed solicitous about his diet, saying that he dared not imbibe wines of any kind, having to be very careful of himself.

The action on the part of Mellus, in relation to Howard, created a feeling against him in San Francisco and on the coast among those who had known them here in the former days, and he became quite unpopular; but I did not join in the outcry against him. My regard for him remained undiminished.

After he had retired from Mellus, Howard & Co., his brother Frank went into the concern as partner, and the style of the firm became Howard, Mellus & Co. Frank shortly after withdrew; the firm name was changed to Howard & Green, and so continued to the time the partnership was dissolved by the exposure of Green and his departure from the city.

CHAPTER LI
Rivalry and Goodfeeling Between Traders

REFERRING again to the competition among the early merchants, I recollect some instances of pretty sharp practice in the collection of hides and tallow. Merchants trusted the rancheros largely for the goods they sold them, and the indebtedness was paid after cattle were killed. The ranchero being more or less in debt at all times, would promise a merchant to supply him with a certain quantity of hides and tallow at a stipulated time; but shortly before the specified date the ranchero would be called upon by another merchant to whom he was likewise indebted for goods, and who was also anxious to secure hides and tallow, on account of what was owing to him, and also to make up a cargo for shipment. By persistent efforts and persuasion he would so work upon the ranchero—who was good-natured and obliging, and desirous of accommodating all his friends, as far as he was able—as to secure for himself a a large part of the hides and tallow which had been promised to the first one, and carry them off triumphantly, somewhat to the chagrin and discomfiture of the merchant who had the first contract, who, coming shortly afterward, would find that his competitor had got ahead of him. The ranchero would then make the best of it, explaining that he could not resist the importunities of the other, and had been obliged to let the hides and tallow go to the first arrival. To make good his original promise, he would let the second comer have the hides and tallow remaining, and would collect everything about the place that could be made available, even frequently ordering more cattle to be slaughtered, the hides taken off, and some tallow melted out forthwith.

When this happened, hides were often taken in a green state, and staked out and dried by the merchants at Yerba Buena. I have frequently had them spread, by stakes, at the vacant space by the water side, between Washington and California streets, which was then a meadow, covered with short green grass. I have also seen them hung up thickly on ropes stretched over the decks of vessels, the same way the clothes of the crew of a man-of-war are hung in the rigging to dry. The tallow in a very soft state was sometimes taken on the vessel—before it had cooled and hardened, after having been put into the bags.

It was impossible for the rancheros to pay all the merchants at once, as it required time to kill a large number of cattle and prepare the hides and tallow. The merchant who reached the rancho first, generally had the best bargain, though in the course of time the others usually got their share.

In 1841 a ranchero had promised to deliver to me a quantity of hides and tallow on a certain day. I went at the time specified, to the ranch landing with the schooner "Isabel," expecting a full load, but I found that Henry Mellus had preceded me the day before, with one of his schooners, and had secured nearly the entire stock. Upon my appearing, the ranchero and his sons expressed a good deal of concern and many regrets. They went to work and collected all the dry hides they could find on the place, had a lot of bulls slaughtered immediately, and the hides taken off, and some of the *matanza* tallow tried out, so that before I left I made up nearly a schooner load. This cutting under and getting the first grab, was common, and well understood among the merchants, but it never caused any ill-feeling, as it was considered perfectly fair. They joked and laughed about it among themselves, and it was not thought that any injury was done or unfair advantage taken. The quickest, most enterprising and industrious, it was conceded, should be the winners. The last man might be the first on some other occasion. There was never any disagreement or hard feeling, or quarrel of any kind, or even a coolness where two merchants would not speak to each other. At all times they were on the most friendly footing; entire good feeling prevailed. Of various nationalities—American, French, English, Scotch, German and Spanish, as a class they were intelligent, high-minded and honorable.

Mr. Frank Mellus, a younger brother of Henry, came from Boston in 1840, in the "Alert," and was employed as clerk and educated by Henry in business. On his arrival, he was green-looking and bashful, and he always retained boyish appearance and bearing. He failed to command that respect and deference which was felt towards his brother. He was a good fellow however, though impulsive and easily excited, and proved to be quite smart and efficient. The Californians gave him the nickname of *Fulminante* (percussion cap), by reason of his excitability. He married Adelaide Johnson, a sister of Henry's wife, a very handsome and vivacious young lady. George Mellus another brother came to the coast in 1849.

In 1850 a beautiful bark, of several hundred tons, owned by Henry Mellus, Don Alfredo Robinson and others, arrived from Boston with a cargo designed especially for Los Angeles. She anchored at San Pedro and discharged the goods. The vessel was named after the Christian name of a California lady, then the wife of a very wealthy gentleman living in one of the southern counties. Several years since, this lady, while at the Palace Hotel, was called upon by an acquaintance of hers, a Spanish-American gentleman, who, in the course of conversation, asked if she would sing; she replied, facetiously and with the utmost good nature, *"No puedo cantar, pero puedo encantar"* (Cannot sing, but I can enchant.)

Spear and Henry Mellus were very good friends. Each called the other *compadre,* though this relation did not actually exist between them. I have heard Spear speak in the highest terms of Mellus, and compliment him for good business judgment.

The following is a list of the vessels which were sent out to Henry Mellus by Bryant & Sturgis, while acting as their agent: ship "California," Captain Arthur; ship "Alert," Captain Phelps; ship "Barnstable," (first voyage) Captain Hatch; ship "Barnstable," (second voyage) Captain Hall; ship "Admittance," Captain Peterson; bark "Tasso," Captain Libbey; and bark "Olga," Captain Bull.

Don José Antonio Aguirre was one of the most prominent early merchants of California. At the time of the separation of Mexico from the Spanish government, he was in business in the city of Mexico, and largely interested in trade with Manila and Canton, which was carried on extensively between those places and Mexico. The importation of cargoes of Manila and China goods, was a branch of the business he conducted. He remained loyal to Spain after the separation, and in consequence was expelled from Mexico, as was the case with many other loyal Spaniards. Coming to California he made his mercantile headquarters at Santa Barbara and San Diego. He owned the brig "Leonidas," and afterward the "Jóven Guipuzcoana." Fine-looking and of commanding appearance, though of rather a severe bearing toward strangers, his manners were affable and genial to those who knew him well. He was a genuine merchant, thoroughly educated. His first wife was a daughter of Prefect Estudillo, of San Diego. In 1842 Aguirre had the finest residence in Santa Barbara. His wife dying there, he afterward married her sister. He was a great church man, and a favorite of the missionaries. He had visited the United States; was well-read, and was appreciative of our institutions and government.

In conversing with me he gave expression to his views with regard to us; he thought that at the rate we were progressing in time we would be the greatest nation on earth. One thing about which he spoke seemed to have produced in him amazement: that in the courts, which he sometimes visited from interest or curiosity, during the trial of a case, he would hear the arguments on either side, in which the opposing counsel appeared to be the greatest enemies, ready to tear each other to pieces, and yet, after the trial was closed, they would calm down and be the best of friends; and the same peculiarity was noticeable in our elections, when the prejudices and passions of men were excited on opposite sides; when resentments were aroused, hot words were exchanged, and all kinds of abusive things were said; yet, after the election, the combatants came together on the best of terms. He thought this a fine trait in the American character, and spoke of it with admiration.

Aguirre was my guest from the early part of 1848 up to the end of 1849. Spear was there at the same time, and Aguirre and he became cronies. Often they had dissensions, but only upon political and national affairs.

The proposition that the United States might acquire Cuba by conquest or purchase had been broached, and Spear argued in favor of it, which would anger Aguirre, and he would denounce the project in severe terms, declaring in emphatic language that Spain would fight to the last drop of blood before she would surrender the island.

This worthy gentleman had a large estate. The San Jacinto Nuevo Rancho, of eleven leagues, and several other smaller ranchos in San Diego county, and two or three leagues in Los Angeles county, were among his possessions, besides many cattle and horses. Four children and his wife survived him. The widow afterward married another Spaniard named Ferrer, who squandered all the property which the first husband had left to her.

CHAPTER LII
de Pedrorena, Merchant and Stockton's Lieutenant

IN 1838 Don Miguel de Pedrorena, a resident of Peru, arrived here, being at the time part owner and supercargo of the "Delmira." The vessel was under the Peruvian flag, and John Vioget was her captain.

The "Delmira" was loaded with tallow, and left the coast in 1839, Don Miguel remaining here. In 1840 the brig "Juan José," Captain Duncan, was sent to him from Peru, he being part owner and supercargo. The other owners, whom he represented, were in Lima—a wealthy house. Most of their goods were imported from Europe to Peru, and they sought to increase their business by these ventures to California. The "Juan José" loaded with tallow, and returned to Peru. Afterward she made another voyage hither for the same sort of cargo.

Don Miguel was a native of Spain, and belonged to one of the first families of Madrid. After receiving an education in his own country he was sent to London, where he was educated in English, becoming a complete scholar. Most of the Castillian race of the upper class are proud and aristocratic; but Don Miguel, though of high birth, was exceedingly affable, polite, gracious in manner and bearing, and, in every respect, a true gentleman. He married a daughter of Prefect Estudillo, and resided in San Diego until the time of his death in 1850, leaving one son, Miguel, and two daughters, Elena and Ysabel. He was a member of the convention at Monterey in 1849, for the formation of the state constitution. He owned the Cajon Rancho and San Jacinto Nuevo Rancho, each containing eleven leagues, with some cattle and horses. Notwithstanding these large holdings of land he was in rather straightened circumstances in his latter years, and so much in need of money that when I visited San Diego in the early part of 1850 he offered to sell me thirty-two (32) quarter-blocks of land (102 lots) in San Diego at a low figure. He had acquired the property in the winter of 1849-50, at the alcalde's sale. I did not care for the land, but being flush, and having a large income from my business, I took the land, paying him thirteen or fourteen hundred dollars for it.

In Madrid he had several brothers and other relatives, one of his brothers being a Minister at that time in the Cabinet of the reigning monarch. During the last two or three years of his life, these relatives becoming aware of his unfortunate circumstances, wrote to him repeatedly, urging him to come home to Spain, and bring his family with him. They sent him means, and assured him that he would be welcomed. Though poor, his proud disposition led him to decline all these offers. Popular with everybody in the department, the recollections of him by those who knew him are exceedingly pleasant. Spear was much attracted toward him on account of his fine scholarship and great store of information. He did all he could to make the acquaintance mutually agreeable.

When Commodore Stockton was making his preparations for the recapture of Los Angeles, in the latter part of 1846, at San Diego, at which point the fleet then lay, Don Miguel Pedrorena offered his services as cavalryman, which were accepted. He also rendered aid to Stockton before he started on the expedition, by procuring him supplies of horses. Being an active man, familiar with the country and people, he did this very readily. Don Santiaguito E. Argüello also volunteered his services to Stockton, and assisted Pedrorena. Both of these men were appointed captains in Stockton's force, and both had cavalry commands. Major Samuel J. Hensley, who joined Stockton at Yerba Buena in the fall of 1846, and went with him to San Diego in the "Congress," also joined Pedrorena and Argüello in scouring the country for horses, and getting as many of the Californians as they could to join the expedition. Hensley also had a command under Stockton. Not only before the force started, but during their progress from San Diego to the river of San Gabriel, these three men rendered invaluable service to the commodore by inducing other Californians to join and augment the force. I think there were about one hundred Californians on Stockton's side, when the conflict took place. Hensley, who had been in the country a good while, was an accomplished horseman, entirely at home in the saddle. He and Pedrorena and Argüello were brave men, cool, collected, self-possessed, determined, and consequently were of value. In the battle they all displayd great judgment and bravery.

Don Santiaguito was an Indian fighter, and had been always foremost in proceeding promptly against the Indians whenever they committed depredations on the people, as they often did. He organized many of the hasty expeditions which were gotten up on the spur of the moment to pursue and chastise them on such occasions, and was very successful in overtaking and punishing them as they deserved. Often he was in a good deal of danger in the engagements, and I have known him at times to be in very critical circumstances, but never in the least flurried or excited—always calm and collected, fully aware of what he was about, bringing himself finally out all right. This man was a nephew of Don Luis Argüello, the first native California governor of the department.

In 1834 Alfred Robinson and William G. Gale, who were associated in the agency for Bryant & Sturgis, were at Santa Barbara, awaiting the arrival of the ship "California" at that port. One day seeing a vessel approach the town, between the islands, they went toward the beach and made her out to be their vessel. On their way they met Thomas Shaw, supercargo of the "Lagoda," coming up to the town, when Robinson called out exultingly to him, "Look out, Shaw! There's the 'California' coming; you'll have some competition now."

The Missions were rich at the time, and the two agents, in order to make large sales of goods, concocted an ingenious plan, which they carried into effect, as follows: After the captain had been ordered to take the ship to Monterey, they started up the coast on horses, with their invoices of goods. Pretending to be rivals, Gale would go first, on coming to a Mission, and present his invoice to the Padres, and after they had made large selections from the list, Robinson, who was much liked by the Fathers and friendly with all of them, smilingly presented his invoice, and made extensive sales also. Repeating this at other Missions, by the time Monterey was reached they had sold an enormous quantity of merchandise. Each had prepared a list of the cargo.

Gale was known on the coast by the name of Don Guillermo el Cuatro Ojos (Four Eyes), from the fact that he wore glasses; this name having been bestowed by the Californians, who were given to nicknaming a person with anything peculiar in his appearance or manner. By such name he was known to everybody during his stay here. The custom prevailed more particularly in the southern portion of the department, where two ladies, cousins of my wife, were nicknamed, one *"Nutria"* (Sea Otter) and the other *"Pichona"* (Dove), and so addressed to this day (1892).

The Padres not only taught the Indians to build vessels and boats, but instructed them also in their management, and made sailors of them. They were sometimes employed as such by myself and other merchants at Yerba Buena, upon boats that were attached to the vessels, or that were owned on shore, in the delivery of goods and collecting hides and tallow. The Padres also instructed the Indians how to shoot and capture otters in the best manner. Hence, their accumulation of so large a number of fur skins, when the sea otters were plentiful about the bay and along the coast.

I remember that in 1833, hides and tallow were brought to the vessel in schooners and launches manned and commanded by Indians, from the Mission Dolores and the Missions of San José, Santa Clara and San Rafael, the vessels and boats having been built at the Missions by the Indians, under instructions from the Padres, after designs and models prepared by them of a very ancient pattern. They reminded me of illustrations of old Spanish vessels.

Richardson owned one of these vessels, built at the Mission of San Rafael, called the "Tava," and the old Indian Monico was one of the crew, who were all Indians. Old Domingo Peralta had another of these peculiar boats, built at one of the Missions. Nathan Spear had control of a boat of this kind in 1839, belonging to the Mission of San José. It will be seen that the Padres, in addition to their missionary work and the teaching of various trades to the Indians, were also shipwrights and skilled workmen in the building of vessels and boats.

About 1833 the brig "Loriot," Captain Nye, arrived from Honolulu with a cargo of merchandise, A. B. Thompson, supercargo. Shortly after, orders were sent from Monterey to have the vessel and cargo seized, upon the presumption that full duties had not been paid. Don José Sanchez was directed to board the vessel and arrest Thompson. He accordingly proceeded to do so, accompanied by a squad of soldiers. Reaching the deck of the vessel and approaching to make the arrest, Sanchez drew a pistol and aimed it at Thompson, who instantly struck it from the officer's hand, and at the same moment knocked him down and jumped upon him. The soldiers came to Sanchez' aid and gave him protection. Thompson was taken ashore and imprisoned at the Presidio, where he remained for some considerable time. After his arrest the whole cargo was removed to shore, together with the stores of the vessel, and the sails were unbent and taken away. Finally an order was received from headquarters to release the cargo and other property of the vessel and to liberate Thompson, which was carried into effect. During the detention the cargo and stores deteriorated in condition, particularly the latter, which were also much diminished in quantity.

The trip of the "Loriot" to Honolulu from Boston, prior to her coming here, was one of the longest on record—occupying two hundred days. On this voyage, Henry, a younger brother of Captain Paty, came out, also Eli Southworth, both from Plymouth, Mass. Henry was part owner of the "Don Quixote," and in the year 1840, while the vessel was on a voyage from Valparaiso to Honolulu, many of the crew were sick from small-pox contracted in Chili, and several died on the passage, which so affected the mind of Henry that though not taking the disease, he became demented. Looking into a mirror in his state-room, he took a razor and cut his throat. He was buried at sea. Southworth was interested in the "Don Quixote." From 1843 to 1845 he was with me in Yerba Buena as my clerk. After 1849 he went to the redwoods, and engaged men in getting out lumber for a number of years, but did not make a success of the venture, financially. In 1853 he came to live at my house at San Leandro, and remained there until he died, in 1857.

As an exception to the uniformity of friendship and good feeling which prevailed on the coast in early days between the foreigners and Californians, and, in fact, between all classes in all their relations, I wish to mention that Everett, who has been spoken of as coming here in the "Alert," was a disagreeable man. He arrived again in the bark "Tasso," as supercargo, with Captain Hastings, in 1840. Mean, selfish, and repulsive in his appearance and manners, his unhappy disposition was shown by his continually quarreling with Captain Hastings, who was a gentleman. However, notwithstanding his unpopularity and the general disfavor with which he was regarded, he succeeded in filling his vessel, for the reason that the people were in want of the goods which he had brought, and therefore they took them in exchange for hides and tallow. Everett, contrary to the usual custom of the merchants, never made presents to the people, or showed them any friendly courtesies. They themselves were always generous to strangers, making them welcome to whatever they had. They would have disdained an offer of compensation for such kindness. But the merchants, having been so well treated by them, and having shared, more or less, in their hospitality, naturally reciprocated the good feeling, and showed their appreciation and friendship by making presents from time to time, thereby cultivating a kindly spirit.

CHAPTER LIII
The Great Hide and Tallow Trade

GOVERNOR PACHECO, a boy in 1842, was sent to Honolulu to be educated. After remaining about two years, under the tuition of Mr. and Mrs. Johnston, he returned. The ship "Sterling" then being in port, he went on board, and for a year or more traveled about in company with Thomas B. Park, supercargo, from whom he received a good deal of instruction in mercantile matters; it being a fine opportunity for the young man, who was bright and teachable. In 1861 he went to Europe, on a tour of travel and observation. At that time, and prior, his stepfather, Captain Wilson, and his mother and the family owned several extensive ranchos in San Luis Obispo county, adjoining one another, which the captain had bought from different owners, and which contained fourteen thousand to sixteen thousand head of cattle, and many horses; being a large number of cattle for a single owner at that date. After the death of Captain Wilson, the family met with the misfortune of losing the cattle and horses by starvation in the dry season of 1864, nearly all of their stock perishing for lack of feed. At this time vaqueros were busily employed taking off the hides. They were obliged to work very speedily (so many cattle were dead, and others dying day by day), to save the skins in marketable condition. The hiring of men was expensive, and left but little profit on the hides. The great loss was the beginning and cause of financial troubles, and they lost nearly the whole of their land.

A statement of the export of hides and tallow from the department of California, from 1826 to 1848, has been prepared by me, gathered partly from actual knowledge of the cargoes taken by particular vessels, and partly estimated from the size of the vessels which loaded previous to my residence here; these vessels always taking full cargoes on their return to the Atlantic coast, viz:

	No. of Hides
Ship "Brookline," departure 1831	40,000
Ship "Courier," Capt. Cunningham, departure 1828	40,000

	No. of Hides
Bark "Louisa," Capt. Wood, departure 1831	25,000
Bark "Volunteer," Capt Carter, departure 1832	20,000
Ship "California," departure 1833	40,000
Brig "Newcastle," departure 1833	10,000
Brig "Plant," tender to "California" 1833	10,000
Schooner "Harriet Blanchard," departure 1833	8,000
Bark "Volunteer," Capt. Carter, departure 1834	20,000
Brig "Roxana," tender to "California" 1834	10,000
Brig "Pilgrim," Captain Faucon, departure 1834	10,000
Ship "Alert," Capt. Frank Thompson, departure 1834	40,000
Ship "Lagoda," Capt. Bradshaw, departure 1836	40,000
Bark "Kent," Capt. Steel, departure winter 1836-37	30,000
Brig "Bolivar Liberator," Capt. Nye, three or four trips, departures 1836 to 1843	60,000
Ship "California," Capt. Arther, departure 1837	40,000
Ship "Rasselas," Capt. Carter, Honolulu, departure 1837	35,000
Ship "Alert," Capt. Penhallow, departure winter 1838-39	40,000
Bark "Don Quixote," Captain Paty, four or five trips to Honolulu, departures 1838 to 1845	60,000
Ship "Alciope," Capt. Clap, departure 1840	30,000
Ship, "California," Capt. Arther, departure winter 1840-41	40,000
Ship "Monsoon," Capt. Vincent, departure winter 1840-41	40,000
Bark "Tasso," Capt. Hastings, departure winter 1841-42	35,000
Ship "Alert," Capt. Phelps, departure winter 1842-43	40,000
Ship "Barnstable," Capt. Hatch, departure 1843-44	40,000
Ship "California," Capt. Arther, departure 1843-44	40,000
Ship "Fama," Capt. Hoyer, departure 1843-44	20,000
Ship "Admittance," Capt. Peterson, departure 1845	40,000
Ship "Sterling," Capt. Vincent, departure 1845	30,000
Ship "Vandalia," Capt. Everett, departure 1846	40,000
Ship "Barnstable," Capt. Hall, departure winter 1846-47	40,000
Bark "Tasso," Capt. Libbey, departure 1847	35,000
Bark "Olga," Capt. Bull, departure winter 1847-48	25,000
Total	1,068,000

Probably an underestimate. The actual number of hides exported approximated one million and a quarter.

With regard to the amount of tallow exported during the above period—I have already mentioned that the killing season was when the cattle were the fattest, each bullock producing on an average three to four arrobas (twenty-five pounds) of tallow, besides the *manteca* reserved for home use. In the winter season, when cattle were killed for home consumption and for the use of the vessels, the tallow would average perhaps not over one arroba to the bullock. Taking the whole year through, I place the product of tallow, for export, at two arrobas for each animal killed, which, for the one million and a quarter, would give 62,500,000 pounds of tallow.

The Californians cut up a great many hides for the use of the ranchos. Strips of the skins were used for reatas and in building corrals, also for covering wagons and for many other purposes. Many of the rancheros tanned their own leather, for *corazas, mochilas, anguilas* and *tapaderas.* Some of the sons of the rancheros were shoemakers, and made shoes for home use. The soles of the shoes were made from the leather, and tanned deer skin was used for the uppers. The hides were also used to cover the trees of the saddles and for other purposes. Large quantities of tallow were used by the rancheros for candles and for soap. Large amounts of the latter were made by the rancheros of the valleys of San José, Gilroy and Pajaro and sold to the Russians for export to Alaska.

A vessel in the bay, about once a week ordered a bullock for ship's use from one of the ranchos nearest by, which would be brought in alive by a vaquero, aided by a *cabestro,* to the meadow between Washington and California streets at the water side. A little below Spear's store there was a scaffolding, with fall and tackle, for hoisting the cattle by the horns after being killed, erected by some ship's crew for the use of the vessel and left there. Each of the vessels in the bay had a signal deposited at the store, and when a bullock was brought in for a vessel, or if, for any other purpose it was desirable to give notice, the signal was displayed. If the tide was up to the beach, then a boat would be sent ashore, or if a bullock was expected, perhaps it would be sighted, with the aid of a glass, from the vessel, and the crew coming ashore, prepared with knives, the animal was dispatched, cut up, and the meat taken aboard, together with the hide, which was stretched above the deck, or against the main rigging, to dry. Sometimes the cattle were killed in the primitive method, and cut up without hoisting, thus leaving more of the blood in the beef. They were so killed and the meat prepared at Thompson's Cove, which was a little bay south of Clark's Point, and between that and Buckalew or Watchman's Point, where Thompson had a hide house. Cattle were likewise slaughtered at Monterey, San Luis Obispo, Santa Barbara, San Pedro and San Diego, and at other ports or landings, on the beach, for the use of vessels. The cattle were slaughtered upon the ground, and cut up as they lay, no hoisting apparatus being used.

Captain Steel came here in command of the bark "Kent," in 1835, from Boston. He was good-natured and jocular, a vegetarian, and during his stay never touched meat. The Fourth of July being celebrated in Yerba Buena in 1836, by a public dinner, Captain Steel was present, and also John Vioget, two men who were like Damon and Pythias—of the same disposition and temperament, and always around about the same time. At this banquet, Steele christened Vioget as Blucher (after the officer who saved Wellington from defeat at Waterloo). By that title he was afterward known on the coast; called by it even more than by his real name.

Vioget was one of the principals in an incident of somewhat ridiculous nature. In 1841 a Russian by the name of Don Andres Hoeppner, was employed for a considerable time by General Vallejo as teacher of music for his daughters, at Sonoma, and frequently visited Yerba Buena. Being an excellent musician—playing with taste and skill the piano, violin and guitar—he was popular and well liked, such men being much appreciated by the people, who had little in the way of good music or amusements. Being sociable and companionable he frequented Vioget's saloon, and became a particular friend of the proprietor.

The latter was known on the coast as a great eater, and prided himself on that reputation. Hoeppner and several others being in the saloon one day enjoying themselves, the question of gormandising was brought before the company, and he challenged Vioget to a contest to determine who was the biggest eater in the department. Hoeppner not being known or suspected in connection with gastronomic feats, the challenge was instantly accepted, and a day was fixed for the contest. Invitations were sent out to the merchants to attend. I was invited, as were also Spear and others.

When the trial commenced pancakes were brought on, plate after plate, and speedily devoured. Hoeppner was one plate ahead. The next course was beefsteaks, all of which disappeared as rapidly as had the other, Hoeppner led a little on the steaks. Next was *gisado,* a meat stew in the Spanish style—a delicious dish, several plates of which were consumed. Next came *asado,* or beef broiled on the spit, many plates. Hoeppner a little ahead. After this, beans, Spanish style, large quantities of which were disposed of; succeeded by *tamales,* corn prepared as before described, each of the contestants eating at least a dozen. An immense pudding then appeared, followed by pies of various kinds, which were largely consumed. All the food had been prepared in the nicest manner, and made inviting, by skilled cooks—old Jack Fuller and assistant. The wind up was black coffee, but during the meal no drink was taken. Vioget gave out on the pies. Hoeppner, still eating, was declared the winner. All were astonished at the quantity of viands that went down the throats of those two men. After concluding their repast they got up and moved round, smoked, drank a little wine, played billiards, and appeared to suffer no inconvenience from the meal each had consumed.

Vioget was of large frame; Hoeppner taller, nearly six feet in height, slender, but well proportioned. I have no doubt each of the gormands ate food enough to satisfy a dozen hungry men. Both contestants were good musicians, Vioget playing the violin as finely as Hoeppner. The former was also an excellent civil engineer, and had been employed by Captain Sutter in surveying his lands. Don Andres Hoeppner's wife was a Russian lady, a pretty little woman, and, like women in general at Yerba Buena, was much appreciated.

Vioget was afterward captain of the brig "Euphemia," in 1848. Referring to his defeat in the eating match, he said that if he had been as young as Hoeppner the latter would not have had any show at all. He was some fifteen or twenty years older.

CHAPTER LIV
Author Becomes Merchant: Buys the "Euphemia"

I WENT over to Honolulu in 1845 as supercargo of the "Don Quixote," with Captain Paty, and while there a partnership was proposed between him, his brother William and myself, under which the ownership of the vessel was to be transferred, one-half to me and one-fourth to each of the brothers; but we could not agree upon her valuation. William Paty thought the vessel was worth $8000, which I thought was too high. Captain Meek agreed with me, saying that, considering her age, $5000 or $6000 would be a good price for the bark. The negotiations, therefore, fell through, and my relations with Captain Paty ceased, under the circumstances much to my regret.

Afterward, several merchants and firms at Honolulu, among them Stephen Reynolds, who had been the United States vice-consul, E. & H. Grimes, and Starkey, Janion & Co. (a heavy English house), made propositions to furnish me with a vessel to trade on the California coast, the business to be partly mine. The offer of E. & H. Grimes was accepted. We purchased the "Euphemia," an English brig which had been employed by Henry Skinner & Co. in the Chinese trade. Then came a difficulty with regard to the papers and flag of the vessel, inasmuch as the Grimes and myself were Americans. We had selected an Englishman by the name of Thomas Russom for captain, a very good man, who was then at Honolulu; and to sail under the English flag we should have been obliged to have the papers made out in the captain's name; but we did not think it advisable to entrust so much to one man not directly interested with us, however responsible and trustworthy he might be. In order to avoid the difficulty, Hiram Grimes, who had a good deal of influence with the premier, Mr. Wiley (an old Scotchman, who had lived in South America many years), succeeded in getting the vessel registered in his name, under the Hawaiian flag.

We then purchased the cargo of the vessel, which occupied a month, selecting with care and judgment such articles as were suited to the California trade, picking here and there the best we could obtain. At the same time the Patys also purchased a cargo for the "Don Quixote." The "Euphemia," with her cargo, cost between $50,000 and $60,000, my share being $17,000 or $18,000. Having saved my salary for several

PRISON SHIP "EUPHEMIA" FORMERLY OWNED BY
WILLIAM HEATH DAVIS

years, and accumulated money by speculations with the whalers, etc. I was able to pay about half this amount into the concern, leaving the other payable in six months, for which I gave my note to E. & H. Grimes (the first note I ever gave). In contracting with them it was stipulated that the business on this coast should be done in the name of William H. Davis only, their names not appearing.

My mother was living in Honolulu and was wealthy, owning a large number of cattle, which were good property, as they were always in demand by the ships of war, whalers and other vessels visiting the Islands. She offered me money to assist in carrying on the business, but I declined it, preferring to act within my own resources; and I really did not need it.

These vessels both left Honolulu February 26, 1846. A strong southeasterly gale sprang up, which was in their favor, and in less than two weeks' time the bark anchored at Monterey. Our brig had occasion to touch at a lower coast port before calling at Monterey, and did not reach that place until the last day of March. The "Don Quixote" was then ready to leave for San Blas, she having been chartered to take Castillero as commissioner to represent California in the City of Mexico.

Soon after we anchored, I went on board that vessel and was warmly greeted by Captain Paty and Eli Southworth, they having feared that some misfortune had happened, on account of the long delay of the brig. I then went ashore and called on General Castro, comandante-general of the department.

During this visit I ventured upon a little diplomacy, in order to place myself on a good footing with the officials, as this was my first venture of any magnitude on my own behalf. I noticed that the window and door-frames and woodwork about the headquarters were unpainted, and mentioned to the general that I had on board my vessel some paints and oils, and with his approval I would send a few kegs ashore for his use. He said those materials were scarce and he should receive them with a great deal of pleasure.

On this occasion I was accompanied by United States Consul Larkin. While we were there I was introduced to Mrs. General Castro, and we chatted for some time very pleasantly. I saw by the general's expression, when she went into the next room for a few minutes, that he was proud of her. Larkin found an opportunity to communicate, enthusiastically, "Isn't she beautiful?" and I responded, with equal enthusiasm, "Indeed, she is."

On returning to my vessel I sent and borrowed two cannons from the bark, got them aboard, and fired a salute in honor of the Mexican flag, which was promptly returned by the comandante from the fort. Thus, my introduction to the port of Monterey as a merchant in my own behalf was happily accomplished, and everything made smooth for future trade.

Then I called on the collector, Don Pablo de la Guerra. He was living with his sister, Mrs. Jimeno. He said at once that the other vessel had been there two or three weeks, and that my brig had only just got in; as both had sailed the same day, he wanted to know how that was. I said to him, "Look at the brig. She is more like a box than anything else. She is no sailer." He responded that I was correct; that she was indeed like a box, and it was not surprising that she had made a long voyage. I sent to Don Pablo from my cargo a basket of champagne, and to Mrs. Jimeno some sweet potatoes and cocoanuts, which were regarded as luxuries at Monterey.

It was customary when a vessel came into port to enter, to give the management of the custom house business to a shore merchant, who acted as broker. He made the entry, assuming the responsibility of the transaction—paving the way, if any difficulties arose. Larkin, Hartnell, Spear and Spence sometimes acted in a similar capacity. The merchant received a proper commission for the service. On this occasion I employed Larkin to make the entry.

The law required the collector and his officers to go on board any vessel arriving with dutiable goods and make a thorough examination. Captains or supercargoes would invite merchants from on shore and other friends to accompany the officials. Quite a party assembled, the event being made one of entertainment. A handsome collation was provided of meats, fowls, jams, jellies, pies, cakes, fruits, champagne and other wines of which all would partake, and an enjoyable time be had. We spread a table, and received and entertained the guests as handsomely as any one could. Among those present were: Henry Mellus, Captain Eliab Grimes, Don José Ábrego, Larkin, de la Guerra, the collector, and two or three of his officers, one of whom was Don Rafael Pinto, an attaché of the customs service (*aduana*) for a great many years.

The custom house inspector was a curious old Mexican who had lost his teeth, and his sentences were mumbled in a queer way; but he was polite and gentlemanly withal, and while going through the formality of looking about the vessel to examine her, I accompanied him. The main hatch was off, and I said that if he wished to go down into the hold, I would have a ladder brought for his accommodation, and that he should be assisted down. He replied that he was not very particular. I remarked that there were a good many scorpions among the cargo. These creatures had got in at the Islands, and in the warm latitude they had bred very fast. When I mentioned scorpions, he stepped back, really frightened, and making up a ludicrous face, declared vehemently that he had no desire to go into the hold—thoroughly alarmed at the idea. The duties on the cargo amounted to ten thousand dollars.

The merchants, when they entered goods, used to pay about half the duties in cash, and give their notes for the remainder, payable in sixty or ninety days, the custom house allowing them this accommodation. Not having sufficient money to pay these duties—although Captain Grimes and other merchants offered to procure it for me, which offer I declined—a plan was adopted to realize more speedily upon the cargo than could have been done on the vessel and selling there, as was common. Obtaining the use for a short time of a large room in the custom house, with ample space for my purpose, the crew brought the cargo ashore, and the ship's carpenter put up a table eighty feet long, in the room so secured, on which I sampled the goods for sale. William F. Swasey, who had recently come to the coast, was looking for employment, and I engaged him to assist me.

The plan was an admirable success. Men, women and children gathered in crowds, finding it much more convenient than to go aboard the vessel, where the goods couldn't have been seen to advantage. They were also attracted by the novelty of the arrangements. They bought in quantities to suit. Within a week I had taken some five thousand dollars in cash, on sales amounting to fifteen thousand dollars; so that I was able to pay half of the cash duties demanded, and had some money left. My notes went into the custom house for the remainder.

The collector and his officers were always in debt to the merchants for goods. The notes they gave were sometimes turned in for duties, the customs officers arranging the matter with the government. The collector of course reported to the government all duties collected, this being its only source of revenue; and if in need of money for government use, the governor would direct the collector to negotiate to the best advantage with merchants what paper he had, at a discount. Or frequently the government owed merchants for supplies used by the troops, such as muskets, ammunition, shoes and other clothing, and would require money for the troops, who were regularly paid; and used the notes in settlement with the merchants, and to obtain money to pay the troops. The merchants were glad to take notes (which had been given for duties), either in liquidation of their claims, or for cash loaned, as they would be paid at maturity, in hides and tallow, by the parties who signed them. Mellus was at Monterey before I arrived, and he waited until I came, and secured in part liquidation of his firm's claim against the government most of the notes I gave the collector.

On my arrival, Captain Eliab Grimes was at Consul Larkin's house. He greeted me gruffly, and said, "Well, Hiram has been playing the devil down there, buying a vessel and cargo for $50,000 or $60,000, and sending her up here!" The captain, being the main man of the concern, naturally felt some doubt about his nephew and myself (who were young men) succeeding in this speculation. I told him I had paid about $9,000 in cash on my interest, and was owing about as much more, to be paid in six months. "Well, do you expect to pay it?" he asked, rather savagely. "I hope to do so," was my reply. Producing the well known liquor case, which he carried with him wherever he went, we had a glass or two together, and he asked for all the details of the venture in partnership with his nephew and himself.

I narrated the transactions in full, at which he seemed to feel reassured. He had been greatly concerned about our buying the vessel and cargo. He was also pleased afterward, when I informed him of my success in the sale of the goods at the custom house, of which he had expressed doubt when I first mentioned the plan to him—having thought it would fail; and Mellus was of the same opinion. The goods not disposed of were taken on board again, and we sailed for Santa Cruz. I made many sales there, taking my pay in lumber and hides and tallow, to be delivered at a future time. I then sent the vessel to Yerba Buena, and came up by land, making sales at San José, Santa Clara and other places, by invoice, to the rancheros and merchants—doing well. Reaching Yerba Buena about the 25th of April, I found that Spear had vacated his store and moved to Napa, on account of ill health. Hinckley was in town. Bob Ridley was keeping the Vioget house, with his family, and I lodged with him.

The next morning I met Howard, who was here with the "Vandalia," and for a day or so was a guest on board his vessel, until my own arrived, while I sold to rancheros round the bay until I had no goods remaining. Josiah Belden assisted me in this work as one of my clerks. The vessel then went over to Saucelito to get in a supply of water. While she was there, Spear, who had come down from Napa, Hinckley and myself, went over to spend a night on board. We had a good supper, and a jolly time—talking over old matters, smoking, singing and drinking champagne nearly the whole night. Captain Russom was an admirable singer, and he entertained us with songs, and the whole company also sang.

This was the 20th of May, 1846, a heavy southeast gale blowing, and during the evening the captain went on deck to order the second anchor dropped, for the greater security of the vessel. It rained hard all night.

The next day I visited Captain Richardson. The day after, Captain and Mrs. Richardson, Miss Richardson and Miss Estudillo came on board the brig by my invitation. Our steward and cook prepared a choice dinner, which the guests enjoyed. I invited the ladies to the salesroom and made them some presents. I remember having given Mrs. Richardson some white silk handkerchiefs and fancy goods, from the cargo. Meeting her a few years ago she said she still had the handkerchiefs. (1890).

CHAPTER LV
"See The American Flag Flying!"

SHORTLY after, the "Euphemia" left Saucelito, bound south, and we took on board at a southern coast port an additional cargo of merchandise. About the last day of May we arrived at San Pedro, and sold there twenty-five thousand dollars' worth of goods. Thence we sailed to Santa Barbara, where additional sales were made, to the extent of eight or ten thousand dollars; thence to Monterey, arriving in July, 1846. On rounding Point Pinos we were surprised to see the United States vessels of war at anchor, and the Stars and Stripes floating from the staff over the town.

On the voyage up, Captain Russom, myself and the two mates, Lee and Colbath, and also the clerk, R. M. Sherman, who were New England men, had many little discussions about the probability of Monterey being taken by the English. Owing to the rumors of war between the United States and Mexico, we were expecting it. The captain being an Englishman, we Americans teased him, and boasted that our country would certainly be the foremost. He descanted upon the pluck and enterprise of his countrymen, and declared that they would certainly plant their flag in Monterey before the Americans had a chance. As we rounded the Point and saw our flag floating serenely over the town, we called out exultantly, "There it is, Captain Russom! See the American flag flying!" He was discomfited, but made the best of it, frankly saying that his countrymen were beaten. The "Euphemia" was the first vessel to enter Monterey after the American acquisition.

Going ashore, on ascending the steps of the wharf, I was met by U. S. Consul Larkin, who introduced me to Commodore Sloat, standing by his side. The commodore extended his hand, and said: "I am glad to make your acquaintance, my dear sir, and to welcome you to *American soil!*"

In the course of his conversation he said, "Thank God! we have got ahead of Seymour." He said that he had determined to take the country at all hazards, and he had done it. The commodore was an agile, nervous

[TEXT OF GENERAL ORDER ON OPPOSITE PAGE]

GENERAL ORDER

Flag Ship Savannah
7 July 1846

We are now about to land on the territory of Mexico with whom the U.States is at war. To strike their flag and hoist our own in place of it, is our duty. It is not only our duty to take California, but to preserve it afterwards as part of the U.States, at all hazards, and to accomplish this it is of the first importance to cultivate the good opinions of the inhabitants, and reconcile them to the change. We know how to take care of those who oppose us, but it is the peaceful and unoffending inhabitants whom we must reconcile. I scarcely consider it necessary for me to caution American Seamen and Marines against the detestable crime of plundering and maltreating unoffending inhabitants.

That no one may misunderstand his duty the following Regulations must be strictly adhered to, as no violation can hope to escape the severest punishment.

1st. On landing no man is to leave the shore until the Commanding officer gives the order to march.

2nd. No gun is to be fired, or other act of hostility committed without express orders from the officer commanding the party.

3rd. The officers and Boat keepers will keep their respective Boats as close to the Shore as they will safely float taking care they do not lay aground and *remain* in them prepared to defend themselves against attack, and attentively watch for signals from the ships as well as from the party on shore.

4th. No man is to quit the ranks, or to enter any house for any pretence whatever, without express orders from an officer. Let every man avoid insult or offence to any unoffending inhabitant, and especially avoid that eternal disgrace which would be attached to our names and our country's name, by indignity offered to a Single female, even let her standing be however low it may.

5th. Plunder of every kind is strictly forbidden, not only does the plundering of the smallest article from a prize forfeit all claim to prize money, but the offender must expect to be severely punished.

6th. Finally, let me entreat you, one and all, not to tarnish our hope of bright success by any act that we shall be ashamed to acknowledge before God and our Country.

John D. Sloat
Commander-in-Chief
of the U. S. Naval forces
in the Pacific Ocean

COMMODORE JOHN D. SLOAT'S GENERAL ORDER OF JULY 7, 1846

The fine American spirit of this document displays Sloat's character better than a chapter long portrait.

little man, and was extremely well satisfied wth the exploit, his face being illumined with a perpetual smile of satisfaction.

My vessel happened to have a variety of stores of which the vessels of the squadron were in need, and these wants I supplied, visiting the purser of the flagship frequently in the transactions.

There I made the acquaintance of Post-Captain Mervine, and saw him every day, the week I remained there; sometimes visiting him in his cabin, by his invitation. He was portly, well proportioned, quick and energetic in his manner, and impressed me as a man of resolution and decision of character. He gave me a little account of matters prior to the fleet's arrival. He said the "Savannah" and "Cyane" were at Mazatlan, oscillating between that port and San Blas, waiting for the news of the declaration of war, and the English ship "Collingwood," Admiral Seymour, was there at the same time. Captain Mervine said they were watching Seymour and he was watching them. If the "Savannah" ran from Mazatlan to San Blas, the "Collingwood" followed her; or, if the "Collingwood" ran from one place to another, the "Savannah" was after her. Commodore Sloat, while on shore, having received, unofficially, private information that war had been declared between the United States and Mexico, slipped away one night with his vessels and sailed for Monterey, making all speed possible, not knowing but they should find the "Collingwood" there before them. Arriving first, however, on July 2nd, Commodore Sloat hesitated as to what he should do.

On the night of the 6th of July, a council of war was called, at which were present the Commodore, Captain Mervine, Captain Dupont of the "Cyane," and other officers of the squadron, to discuss the matter, and to settle upon a line of action.

Captain Mervine declared to me that Sloat still seemed irresolute. At the council, the captain said: "You hesitate, Commodore Sloat, but delay is dangerous; the 'Collingwood' is right at our heels. You know when we approached this port we thought we might find her here before us and the English flag raised on shore, in which case we should have had to fight. It is more than your commission is worth to hesitate in this matter. Although you have no direct official information of the declaration of war between the two countries, the unofficial news is to the effect that war had been declared. If we don't hoist the American flag, the English will take possession of this capital; so there is no time to be lost. It is our duty to ourselves and to the country to run up the flag at once."

Captain Mervine remarked further, that he talked so emphatically at the council of war that his suggestions prevailed. The next morning the United States flag floated over the town.

Mervine was outspoken and frank, unquestionably a better qualified officer than Sloat. He was impatient at the commodore's slowness and vacillation. It was owing to the captain's decision and right comprehension of the situation, in my opinion, that the flag was raised.

Eight days thereafter, the "Collingwood" came into the bay. My vessel then lay at Santa Cruz, and we heard the salutes. James Alexander Forbes, British vice-consul at the time, was in Monterey shortly after the "Collingwood" arrived. He learned from the officers of the ship, as he informed me, that, as they rounded the Point, and the United States men-of-war were discovered, and the American flag came in sight, floating over the town, the British admiral stamped his foot in rage, and flung his hat upon the deck. His chagrin at the advantage which the Americans had gained over him in this matter caused these demonstrations.

The American flag was flying in Yerba Buena when I reached there overland from Santa Cruz. The United States ship "Portsmouth," Captain Montgomery, was in port. I made the acquaintance of the captain, and breakfasted with him one morning, by his invitation, aboard the ship. He said, among other discussions regarding the situation, that he felt some anxiety about the relations of our government with England, in connection with the Oregon Question, or the boundary line dispute between the United States and British Columbia; he thought that any time we might learn that war had been declared between the two countries; that the vessel was ready for action, although he was short of his full fighting complement, as his marines were ashore, on guard, under Captain Watson, yet he believed he could do good execution with his vessel should an enemy be encountered.

While we were talking, it was reported to the captain that a strange vessel was in sight, coming up the bay; whereupon he ran out on deck to sight her, and gave orders to have the men immediately beat to quarters. This was done—a pretty sight which interested me very much. Every man stood at his post ready for action. It might have been an English war vessel approaching, and the captain though it best to be prepared for hostilities. Soon discovered it to be a merchant vessel, we returned to the cabin. Washington A. Bartlett, third-lieutenant on the "Portsmouth," afterward alcalde at Yerba Buena, told me this was an usual occurrence on board— beating the men to quarters and getting ready as a vessel came in sight.

When my brig arrived, I took possession of Spear's vacant premises, and transferred the remainder of the cargo, opening a store for the sale of the goods. The vessel was then sent to Santa Cruz, to load with lumber for Honolulu. Leaving the store in charge of employees, I went by land to meet the vessel about the time the loading of cargo was completed, and there found that the captain, and Sherman, the clerk, were somewhat worried at my delay of a day or two, fearing I might have been murdered by Indians in crossing the Santa Cruz mountains. The brig being just ready, we took her over to Monterey, where I prepared her papers and accounts.

At this time I found Commodore Stockton had arrived there in the "Congress," had relieved Commodore Sloat, and taken command of the forces on the Pacific Coast, Post-Captain Mervine had taken out some of the guns of the frigate "Savannah" and mounted them on the fort overlooking the bay. His men were drilling there, and were practicing in firing at water targets—throwing bombs, to see at what distance they would explode—all with reference to the possibility of war with England. He invited me to the fort once or twice to witness the practice, which was very interesting.

The "Euphemia" was dispatched to Honolulu, with the cargo of lumber and some furs. Remittances were also sent by her in what were known as "Purser's Bills," which I took in exchange for supplies furnished the United States vessels, these bills being drawn by the pursers on the department in Washington, and countersigned by the commander. It was a convenient method of remittance, the bills being at a premium. I also sent $1,800 in gold. Returned to Yerba Buena shortly after, when the United States flag-ship "Congress" came into the bay, with the commodore on board.

When Commodore Stockton first arrived at Monterey with the "Congress," he sent for Captain Richardson to come from Saucelito to pilot the vessel. In August the "Congress" left Monterey for San Pedro. From there Stockton went to Los Angeles to confirm and more fully establish the possession of the country by the United States, to make himself known to the people, to begin friendly relations with them, as their commander-in-chief, to make the acquaintance of the wealthy rancheros and to endeavor to impress upon them that he was their friend.

The "Congress" soon returned to Monterey, and came from there to Yerba Buena, Captain Richardson, pilot; who, while on the vessel, gave the commodore valuable information about the country and the people. These two men became great friends.

Upon the arrival of the "Congress," several of the citizens of Yerba Buena called on Commodore Stockton aboard the vessel to pay their respects, among whom I remember were Spear, Captain Grimes, Howard and Leidesdorff—perhaps seven or eight in all, including myself. We were handsomely received by the commodore and were favorably struck with his appearance, which was that of a gentleman and thorough commander. He was fine-looking, of dark complexion; frank and off-hand in manners and conversation; active and energetic. There was nothing weak or effeminate about him. He at once impressed us as a strong man and of decided ability.

We remained about half an hour, the commodore making us feel at home, inquiring individually of the pioneers about their first coming to the country, their experience here, etc., so that we were soon well acquainted with him.

A few days afterward, upon the first landing of the commodore, a celebration was held, which was a grand success. Extensive preparations had been made. Notice having been sent into the surrounding country, the people came to town in great numbers.

Colonel Wm. H. Russell made a speech, welcoming the commodore, as he landed from his barge, which came close to shore (the tide being high) at about where Clay street is now, between Montgomery and Sansome. Russell spoke in bombastic, spread-eagle style, saying, "I meet and welcome you on the shore"—giving much emphasis to the consonants.

A procession was formed, which marched from the corner of Sacramento and Montgomery streets to Washington street, up Washington to Kearny, to Clay, to Dupont, along Dupont to Washington, thence down the hill to Montgomery again. These streets, with the exception of Kearny, had been named by Bartlett. Some blocks were enclosed by fences— the three bounded by Montgomery and Kearny streets, east and west, and by Jackson and Sacramento, north and south—these blocks being identical with those between these streets to-day; also a portion of the block between Sacramento and California streets, the southeast corner of that block being separately enclosed (a 50-vara lot by itself), parties owning in that block having built cross-fences. On reaching Montgomery street, those who had formed the procession gathered about a platform which had been erected near where Clay now intersects Montgomery street. The commodore was invited to make a speech, which he did in the most enthusiastic manner, and quite at length, and referred facetiously to Russell's eloquent speech of welcome to California.

At that time the news had been received of the revolt of some of the Californians, and the re-capture by them of points which the Americans had taken possession of; and Stockton, in his address, referred to this, saying he was there to protect and defend the country, to fight her battles, if need be, and to establish and maintain her interests.

Guerrero, the Sanchez Brothers, Vasquez, and all the rancheros in the immediate vicinity, had each sent in a number of horses for the procession —the choicest from their *caponeras,* the largest and most handsome, numbering one hundred or more. After the speaking was over, an escort of horsemen rode with the commodore to the Presidio, which he desired to visit; thence across to the Mission Dolores, getting back to Yerba Buena near sunset, when we dispersed.

We rode very rapidly, Stockton himself being a fine horseman. On our return the horses were covered with foam.

The procession was the first that ever took place in California in a civil celebration. It attracted large numbers of women and children from all the neighborhood. It was a demonstration of welcome, not only by Americans proper, but by those of all nationalities who had made this new country their home; and (with some exceptions) by the Californians also, who, although their government was now to be superseded by that of strangers, nevertheless accepted the situation gracefully. On this occasion most of the Californians joined in the celebration, entering into it with spirit, and contributing to its success. For that early day, it was an imposing display and very creditable to the people.

The ovation was unexpected by Commodore Stockton, and much appreciated, since it showed the good feeling of the masses of the people toward the American government and for him as its representative, and that the Californians regarded him as a friend rather than an enemy.

When the news was received, shortly after the "Congress" arrived, that the Californians at Los Angeles, Santa Barbara and other points in the south had revolted, and replaced the Mexican flag, Stockton dispatched orders to Monterey for Captain Mervine to proceed with the "Savannah" to San Pedro, to protect American interests at Los Angeles. Mervine, on reaching San Pedro, landed his marines and most of his crew, with some artillery. Taking command, he moved towards Los Angeles. He had some animals with which to transport his guns. To prepare for anticipated conflicts with the Californians, it was the custom for the commanders and officers of the government vessels, while lying at the different ports, to drill the crews for army service. The officers themselves possessed more or less military knowledge, but they familiarized themselves still further with that branch of the service. In the various expeditions inland, a portion of the naval force on the coast was utilized as infantry men, and, occasionally, as cavalry men, according to circumstances. As Mervine proceeded, the Californians began to surround the little army and disturb it with threatened attacks. When the rancho of Manuel Dominguez was reached, about half way between the port and Los Angeles, a battle ensued, lasting several hours, in which Mervine displayed great daring in leading his men forward, but without avail; it resulted in the defeat of the Americans, who retreated to San Pedro, and boarded their vessel. Several of the sailors and marines were killed in the engagement.

CHAPTER LVI
Frémont Sends For Davis

THE news of Mervine's defeat reaching Commodore Stockton, he sent orders to the captain to remain at San Pedro. In the meantime he actively organized a force to proceed south. The intelligence of this rebuff caused him to forward operations vigorously, his aim being to secure a sufficient force to make thorough work in overcoming the refractory Californians and establishing the American supremacy.

Small arms of all kinds were very scarce in the country, and Stockton was desirous of collecting all he could for his proposed expedition. One morning a midshipman from the "Congress" presented the commodore's compliments, and said the Commodore desired me to purchase for him a quantity of small arms, pistols, rifles, etc. I sent out several of my clerks to the little shops, bar-rooms, and all the places in Yerba Buena where it seemed probable any arms could be found, and collected a considerable number, many of which were obtained from the Mormons, who had recently arrived. The arms were turned over to Commodore Stockton, who paid for them, and also thanked me for the service.

About the latter part of October, 1846, the commodore sailed with the "Congress" for San Diego. The "Portsmouth," Captain Montgomery, was ordered to proceed there also, and left some time subsequent. These vessels, on reaching that point, were joined by the "Savannah," Captain Mervine, the "Cyane," Captain Dupont, and the sloop of war "Dale." The sloop of war "Warren," Captain Hull, remained at Yerba Buena.

Captain Montgomery was highly regarded by the people, and became a great favorite with all classes, both American and foreign, and also with the Californians. He was about fifty years of age, with a pleasant, intelligent face; a man of considerable ability, officer-like in appearance, and in demeanor polite to all; kind and conciliatory in his intercourse with the people, winning their esteem and affection. He was much liked by his officers, who spoke of him as one of the best commanders in the service. During the six or seven months that he remained at Yerba Buena, he never had

From a daguerreotype by Brady.

The value of Frémont's actions in California in 1846 are still matters of controversy.

the slightest trouble with any one. Captain Hull, who succeeded him in command of the district, on the contrary, was frequently in hot water; getting into various difficulties; inclined to be over-particular and fussy. Although a good officer, attending strictly to his duties, he showed an impatient disposition, noticing trifling affairs and matters; whereas Montgomery would not have taken notice of them. A man of small mind, Hull was unpopular with the people, but at the same time had his friends, among them Captain Grimes.

Two sons of Captain Montgomery came out in the "Portsmouth" with him, aged respectively twenty-one and seventeen years. Toward the latter part of November, 1846, these two young men were sent by their father, in one of the "Portsmouth's" boats, accompanied by a crew of eight sailors and a boatswain, with a considerable amount of money to pay the troops—to Sutter's Fort, on the Sacramento. They were never heard of after their departure, and no trace of them or of the boat was ever found, nor any clue as to their fate. It is presumed that the boat capsized off Angel Island, in crossing the bay, and it and the occupants were swept out to sea. The winter commenced early that year; heavy southeast winds and rains prevailed, and it was stormy when the boat left. A thorough search was made and the whole country notified of the loss, but with no result. The sad disaster was a great blow to Captain Montgomery, and weighed very heavily upon him.

When Captain Montgomery and the people of Yerba Buena became aware that the boat had failed to reach Sacramento, they at once concluded that some disaster must have happened. The first impression on the captain's mind and that of others, was that the two young men might have been murdered by the sailors in the boat for the sake of the money; who had then seized it and swamped the boat, and gone into the interior. That idea prevailed for some time, but after wide information had been given of the disappearance, and every effort made to get some intelligence, as none of the sailors were ever seen by any one on shore, and they could not have stayed in the country nor have gone out of it without the fact being known, this belief gave way to the more plausible supposition that the boat was swamped and carried out to sea.

About the middle of November my brig arrived at Yerba Buena from Honolulu with a splendid cargo, consisting largely of liquors, and a good assortment of miscellaneous goods well adapted to the market. It was one of the first cargoes, perhaps the very first, that paid duties in San Francisco, under the American government.

When the vessel left for Honolulu in August, I ordered her to come back to Yerba Buena, being convinced, as the country had passed into our possession, this would be a port of entry by the time she got back; foreseeing that San Francisco was to be the commercial mart, and that Monterey would cease to be the headquarters for shipping.

The liquor was mostly New England rum, exported from Boston to the Islands. Having plenty of cash on hand, I at once paid the duties on the goods, which were thirty per cent on all articles of the invoice cost, amounting to $5000 or $6000. The law required the duties to be paid as soon as goods were entered.

Captain William A. Richardson, of Saucelito, was appointed the first Collector of the Port by Commodore Stockton, in recognition of his services as pilot while on the "Congress."

In addition to other useful information given to the commodore by Richardson, after the revolt of the Californians had become known, he also explained to Stockton that the disturbance did not commence with the wealthier and better class of rancheros, but with officials and ex-officials who were desirous of remaining in power, and that they had stirred up the floating or irresponsible class, who had little or nothing to lose, in opposition to the new government.

My New England rum cost in Honolulu $1.00 per gallon; the duty of thirty cents made it $1.30. Liquors at that time had become very scarce, and on the arrival of the vessel a great demand began for it. I sold it speedily at from $3.00 to $4.00 per gallon; could hardly land it fast enough to supply the want. Going a short distance from my store, I would be hailed by one person or another, "Got any more of that New England rum? I want a cask of it."

Before returning to my store, I would have seven or eight orders in my head to put down in the order-book. The whole invoice was disposed of at a splendid profit, most of it having been delivered from the vessel.

From the first trip of the "Euphemia," business had been very prosperous. The last success in my transactions bought me up in wealth, influence and commercial importance, to a level with Mellus & Howard, whose establishment to that time had been considered the leading one.

Soon after the brig's arrival, I commenced preparing her for a trip south, to be near the seat of war. Landing some of the goods she recently brought from Honolulu, I put on board goods from the store, arranging the cargo especially to supply the wants of the army and navy, and not with reference to selling to rancheros. I had tea, coffee, sugar, clothing, boots and shoes, assorted liquors, foreign wines of the best quality, ale and porter, flour and other articles, which I knew would be in demand by the squadron and the military forces. We left the beginning of December, and proceeded to Monterey, having on board Mrs. Thomas O. Larkin, with some of her children.

Larkin, sometime before, had been captured by the Californians at Salinas, while journeying from Monterey to Yerba Buena. Having dealt with them largely, and always having treated them kindly, he naturally thought that the Californians would not molest him, but that he would be allowed to pass through the lines. He was mistaken. They thought it important to seize the former United States official. He was well treated, although there was one Californian, Joaquin de la Torre, who was inclined to be ugly, and showed a disposition to harm Larkin. Whereupon, Don Manuel Castro put an immediate stop to any such proceedings. Castro ordered a guard of ten men placed over Larkin for his protection. This man de la Torre was considered, among his countrymen, as a person of low instinct.

Mrs. Larkin was much troubled about her husband's imprisonment, and despondent on the trip to Monterey, which occupied a day and a night. I did my best to cheer her, saying, that her husband, having been acquainted with the Californians for so many years, was entirely safe. Nevertheless, she continued dispirited, and evidently felt anxious.

About this time, Bartlett, then alcalde, went into the country for some cattle, and while attending to the business, he also was arrested and made prisoner by the Californians. Another occurrence took place. C. E. Pickett had uttered some remark offensive to Captain Hull, and on its coming to his ears, he had Pickett arrested, and ordered him to remain on my premises as a prisoner of war; saying to him, that if he went away from my store he would have him imprisoned on board the "Warren" in close quarters. Pickett was very indignant, but thought it prudent to comply.

At Monterey I delivered ten casks of the rum, and also sold largely of other goods, nearly all the sales being for cash.

We proceeded thence to Santa Barbara, where I sold to Noriega, as before stated, and also sold to others.

On our way there from Monterey, on Christmas Day, 1846, we were off San Luis Obispo in a tremendous gale of wind from the southeast, with a boisterous sea. My excellent cook and steward, who still remained with me, had prepared a choice dinner, but the sea prevented our sitting at table, and we were compelled to partake of the turkey and other viands in the bunks.

Money circulated freely at the points where the United States vessels of war visited, as disbursements were made at all these places, and the contents of the pursers' strong boxes became much diminished; those who had anything to sell reaping the advantage.

The fitting out of the battalion by Commodore Stockton, before he left for the south, required a large expenditure on the part of the naval officers. The pursers could replenish their exchequers, however, by the issue of their bills drawn upon the government at Washington, there being plenty of money in the hands of the merchants.

While I was at Captain Noriega's house in Santa Barbara, negotiating with him, there came to the house Major Snyder, Major Reading, and King, the commissary, all of whom I knew. They said, Colonel Frémont desired to see me at his camp, about a mile from town. I told them I would call on the colonel as soon as I had finished my business with Captain Noriega. They replied that the colonel wished me to go without delay. Whereupon, I complied (it being war time) somewhat against my will. I surmised the colonel wished to obtain supplies, and while I wanted to assist the government, and to do everything I could toward making the men under Frémont comfortable, at the same time I did not care to become his creditor.

My companions to the camp gave an account of the condition of the men composing the battalion, saying, that their necessities were very great, and that they were in next to a starving condition, being without flour, sugar, tea or coffee; beef supplies being all they could procure; and that many of them were without shoes or hats. On reaching headquarters, I noticed that many of the men were ragged and dilapidated.

This battalion had been collected by Stockton before he left Yerba Buena. He caused it to be widely known that a battalion would be formed, and called for volunteers, and sent officers into the country in every direction to obtain recruits; and about four hundred were collected at Yerba Buena, consisting mainly of Americans, with a few English, Irish, Scotch, German, and of other nationalities. Some of them were rather rough, but many among them were intelligent men—Bryant, afterward alcalde of San Francisco, also William H. Russell, a big man from Kentucky, who came to Yerba Buena in 1846 across the plains. He was good-natured, but self-esteem was a great weakness in his composition. Sometimes this vanity was carried to a ridiculous extent in the telling of yarns. His friends laughed at his assumption of superiority, and made jokes at his expense. Often when they were ridiculing him with fictitious praises of his attainments, and assumed a deference to his authority, he thought they were in earnest and that they were rendering tribute to his importance. He therefore never took offense at anything they said. I knew him very well; he was generally liked, and had no enemies.

The following anecdote in regard to him was frequently told: In coming to California overland, while camping at night, the owls were sometimes heard in the distance, calling out in their peculiar, deep tones, sounding not unlike the human voice. One evening after the colonel's party had camped, he was perambulating outside, and, hearing the owls, fancied they were addressing him, with, "Who comes there?" He promptly responded in sonorous tones, "Colonel William H. Russell, of Kentucky—a bosom friend of Henry Clay." This little performance was afterward a source of bantering among his friends.

Frémont was placed in command of the battalion by Stockton, and he marched with it southward. The start was made in the winter. The weather being very severe, many hardships were suffered by the troops on the march, and when they arrived at Santa Barbara a considerable number of them were in weak condition. The arms I had collected for Stockton were put into the hands of these men, a good many of whom I knew—probably one hundred to one hundred and fifty out of the four hundred. Some of them told me that while crossing the Santa Ynez mountains in the night, Frémont showed considerable nerve in leading his men, the road being very steep and a tremendous storm raging.

On reaching Frémont's tent I found him walking to and fro in front of it. After salutations, he said he had sent to see what I could do towards furnishing supplies for his troops, who were greatly in need, beef being about the only food in camp. I told him I would be happy to supply the battalion with flour, tea, coffee, sugar and clothing. He said that I could see the quartermaster and commissary and arrange with them about the quantities, etc.; that there was no money in the camp at that time, but that I would surely be paid; that they would doubtless capture Los Angeles within six weeks, and I could depend on getting my money then, and he pledged his word he would pay for the supplies within that time.

Major Snyder was quartermaster and King was the commissary. After consulting with them as to what they wanted, and they had given me acknowledgments of indebtedness amounting to about $6000, the goods from the vessel were landed next day. Concluding my business at Santa Barbara, I proceeded to San Diego.

CHAPTER LVII
Stockton, the Real Conqueror and the Conquest

THERE was an understanding between Stockton and Frémont, as part of the former's plan, that Frémont should approach Los Angeles, halt at a point not far from there at a specified time, send word to Stockton at San Diego of that fact, when Stockton would advance from the south, and thus inclose the Californians between the two forces.

Stockton waited at San Diego for that intelligence from Frémont, which, however, did not arrive. Having become impatient at the long and mysterious delay, Stockton decided to move on Los Angeles without tarrying further for Frémont.

While waiting, Stockton had not been idle. On the arrival of the fleet at San Diego, he landed his sailors from the different vessels, and moved up to the presidio, or old town of San Diego. By invitation of Bandini, he took possession of a portion of his residence and made it the military headquarters. His sailors were encamped at that place, and the whole presidio was turned into a military camp. The commodore had also the band from the "Congress" quartered at the mansion.

The commodore was accustomed to have the band play during the dinner hour, and to invite the Bandini family and ladies of San Diego to dine with him and to listen to the excellent music, which invitations they were pleased to avail themselves of, and afterwards spoke of these occasions with enthusiasm. The ladies also praised the commodore and his officers, and evidently appreciated the courtesy and attention.

Don Bandini had in his dwelling a very large hall, where he gave dancing parties during the commodore's stay in San Diego, in which he and his officers and the best families of the town participated, the band of the squadron furnishing the music. Bandini himself was a musician, and was noted as a dancer. He understood fully how to manage an entertainment of the kind, with his charming wife. These gatherings were highly enjoyed by all who were present.

COMMODORE ROBERT F. STOCKTON
William Heath Davis assigns the title of Conqueror of California to Stockton.

He owned the Guadalupe rancho in Lower California, comprising eleven leagues of land, with 4,000 or 5,000 head of cattle, 2,000 horses, and numerous sheep. In Riverside county he owned the Jurupa rancho, with 4,000 or 5,000 head of cattle and 2,000 or 3,000 horses. He had another rancho a few leagues below the boundary line between the United States and Mexico, called Tecate. He was a well-educated man, representing the department of California in the city of Mexico for some time.

Stockton's sailors were drilled in military tactics at the presidio of San Diego, and practiced in various army evolutions as soldiers—infantry, artillerymen and cavalry—in preparation for the coming campaign. The commodore wanted to do his work thoroughly, and make sure of conquering.

The Californians had risen quite generally through that part of the country. Stockton's preparations were extensive, and his organization complete and effective. The necessity was urgent of at once bringing the whole department into subjection to the new order of affairs. Meanwhile Santiaguito Argüello, Don Miguel de Pedrorena and Hensley were actively recruiting, and gathering horses, for Stockton's command.

While these preparations were going forward, news was received of General Kearny's arrival at or near Warner's rancho, in San Diego county, from New Mexico, to take the position of commander-in-chief of the United States forces in California. The information was brought by Captain Snook, who has been mentioned in connection with Commodore Jones' taking possession of Monterey, in 1842. He had given up sea voyaging and bought a rancho in San Diego county in the vicinity of San Pasqual. On getting this intelligence, Lieutenant Beale was sent out by the commodore to meet Kearny and guide him to San Diego.

On reaching San Pasqual, at which place Kearny had then arrived, Beale found that the general had from 120 to 130 men with him, all suffering severely from cold and lack of food. The winter was an unusually severe one, snow and frost prevailing, which was very seldom known in that latitude, and the men had experienced many hardships on the way from New Mexico to this point. They had no horses, only mules. Lieutenant Beale informed General Kearny that he had been sent by the commodore as a guide, and that it would be advisable to avoid meeting Don Andres Pico and his force of cavalry, consisting of about 90 men, who were then in the vicinity of San Diego, having been dispatched from the main body of Californians near Los Angeles for the purpose of watching Stockton's movements and preparations, and communicating information of the same to headquarters. Commodore Stockton, knowing of Pico's presence in the neighborhood, and that he had a well-mounted force, in fine condition, thought it best for Kearny's troops not to meet them, probably surmising that the latter were not in very good fighting condition, after their long march during the cold weather; or, probably, he had been informed of this by Captain Snook. Upon Lieutenant Beale's communicating Commodore Stockton's views to Kearny, the latter promptly responded, "No, sir; I will go and fight them," and declined to act upon the suggestion of the commodore.

Beale had observed the starved appearance of the men and their bad circumstances generally. He intimated to Kearny that as they were worn out with their recent march and had not found time to recruit, they were hardly in a fit condition to meet the Californians, who were numerous, as well as brave, and not to be despised as enemies. He also represented that the mules would be no match for the horses in a battle, even if in the best condition. Kearny declined to be influenced by the argument, being determined to have a fight. He was saved the necessity of moving to meet the Californians, however, for the latter having learned of Kearny's force at San Pasqual, shortly appeared there, and, led by Don Andres Pico, made an attack upon the 6th of December.

When the Californians observed the appearance of Kearny's men, and how they were mounted, they remarked to each other, "*Aqui vamos hacer matanza.*" ("Here we are going to have a slaughter.") They were mounted on fresh horses, and were armed with sharp-pointed lances and with pistols, in the use of which weapons they were very expert. A furious charge was made upon Kearny's force, whereupon all the mules ran away as fast as their legs would convey them, pursued by the Californians, who used their lances with great effect, killing about twenty-five of Kearny's men and wounding a large number (including General Kearny) of the remainder (nearly all of them in the back), who were all in the predicament of being unable to control the half-starved mules which they rode at the time of the stampede. The general, however, managed to rally his men and the mules, and, taking a position, held it against the attacking forces, who were not able to dislodge him. The Californians withdrawing from the immediate scene of action, Kearny buried his dead, while expecting that at any moment the enemy would renew the fight.

In this conflict Beale was slightly wounded in the head. At his suggestion Kearny moved his force to the top of Escondido mountain, which lay in the direction of San Diego, marching in solid form, so as to be able the better to resist any attack that might be made, the mountain offering advantages for defence which could not be procured below. While there encamped they were surrounded and besieged by Pico and his troops who made another attack, but without success.

In the battle just described, Don Andres Pico, who was brave and honorable, displayed so much courage and coolness as to excite the admiration of the Americans. He never did an act beneath the dignity of an officer or contrary to the rules of war, and was humane and generous. If he saw one of the enemy wounded, he instantly called upon his men to spare the life of the wounded soldier. Kind and hospitable, Pico was held in great esteem by the Americans who knew him.

While Kearny was thus besieged, Lieutenant Beale volunteered to make his way through the enemy's lines and communicate to Stockton the intelligence of the general's position and circumstances. It was an act of great daring; but by traveling in the night only, and part of the time crawling on his hands and knees, to avoid discovery, he finally reached San Diego, nearly dead from exhaustion, his hands and limbs badly scored.

When he came into San Diego he was little more than a skeleton; his friends hardly knew him. He gave an account of what had transpired and of the condition of Kearny's force. As soon as his mind was relieved of the message he became utterly prostrated from the sufferings he had undergone, and shortly after was delirious. It was some time before he recovered. Stockton and the other officers of the squadron showed him every attention.

A force of two hundred men, with some light artillery, was immediately sent to rescue Kearny's troops and escort them to San Diego, also conveyances for the wounded, with full supplies of provisions. The Californians moved back as this force approached, not venturing further demonstrations. The troops, with the wounded, were brought to San Diego.

Stockton continued his preparations on an extensive scale for the conflict. He delayed a further movement in order to allow the recovery of the wounded men. Kearny demanded of Stockton the position of commander-in-chief of the territory, by virtue of an appointment to that place by the President. The navy officer declined to yield the command, claiming that the men whom he had organized and drilled for the conflict belonged to the United States ships which he commanded; that he had spent his time and labor in making preparations; had transformed his sailors into soldiers; had exercised and trained them in military tactics; that he had gathered horses and men, had organized a force of cavalry, and had made all his arrangements to conquer the Californians and show them that the country was now a part of the United States. He claimed the honor of accomplishing this, and declined to be superseded by another.

There was more or less controversy about their respective ranks, which was not definitely settled.

Meanwhile, Stockton continued his preparations. Kearny having made his demand and Stockton having refused to comply, the former could do nothing but quietly submit. When the expedition was ready to start, he volunteered to join with such of his dragoons as were able to do service, about eighty in all, which offer was accepted by Stockton, Kearny simply commanding his own men under the commodore's orders. When they moved forward, about the first of January, 1847, Stockton had between seven hundred and eight hundred men, including Kearny's force.

During the march, and afterward, the natives in Stockton's army were mounted as cavalrymen, and were assigned to picket duty, a very responsible service—which showed the confidence the commodore placed in them. They were specially adapted for this duty, being genuine horsemen, and knowing the country thoroughly. They were, moreover, faithful and trustworthy.

Arriving at the river San Gabriel, the Californians were found in force on the opposite side, in an advantageous position. The river was swollen from previous heavy rains. On the eighth, the two armies commenced an artillery fight, in which Stockton exhibited great skill, coolness and bravery. During the engagement one of the artillerymen was killed by a shot from the enemy, while firing his gun. Stockton, who was near by, immediately took charge of the gun, and so accurate was his aim that he did marked execution in the enemy's ranks. In the navy the commodore was known as a practical artillerist, and afterward was the inventor of a powerful piece of ordnance. Under cover of the artillery fire, his force crossed the river, the movement being accomplished with considerable difficulty, and was followed by the artillery.

The fighting continued on that day and the next, the Californians making several charges upon the United States troops. The commodore had formed his army into a hollow square, which the enemy attacked on every side simultaneously; but they were unable to penetrate it, and were repulsed each time. The Californians were all mounted, there being no infantry in their army. They relied upon their horsemanship and their lances to break Stockton's lines; but he knew their mode of attack and was prepared for it. The line of troops in front kneeled down and received the charge of the cavalry at the point of the bayonet, those in the rear thus being enabled to fire over the heads of those in the front rank.

Twenty-five or thirty of the Californians were killed, and a great many wounded; while Stockton's loss did not exceed ten killed, with a few wounded.

Doubtless the actual number of the Californians killed will never be known, they having concealed their loss, not being willing to make a statement in regard thereto. Many more of the Californians would have been killed and wounded during their charges upon Stockton's force, but for skillful maneuvers in horsemanship which they employed in making their attacks.

Forcing their horses forward, in approaching Stockton's line, every horseman in their ranks threw himself over to one side, bending far down, so that no part of his body, except one leg, appeared above the saddle. When the columns met, and the horseman was required to use the lance or do other effective service, he remained but a few seconds in the saddle; and in the retreat he threw himslf over along the side of the horse, and rode rapidly in that position, guiding the steed skillfully at the same time. By these tactics, the cavalry of the enemy avoided presenting themselves as conspicuous marks for the riflemen.

Stockton had three or four hundred head of beef cattle which he had brought from San Diego, or had gathered along the route, for the use of his army. In forming the square to receive the attacks of the Californians, the cattle were placed within the lines, and also his baggage-wagons and supplies.

The enemy made desperate attempts to break through at the point where the cattle were stationed, but without success.

It might seem difficult to keep a large body of rodeo cattle within the military square during the progress of a battle. But the animals were placed in charge of the mounted Californians of Stockton's force. They were rancheros and were thoroughly familiar with the handling of stock; they made it their duty to see that the cattle were kept intact on this occasion. The creatures gradually became accustomed to the movements of the army and were held in place even during the discharge of cannon and small arms. Stockton's infantry and artillery repulsed the attacks, and he managed the animals so well that no part of his square was broken on any side. The Californians finding that our army was too powerful for them finally withdrew from the field.

CHAPTER LVIII

Frémont Too Busy to Talk

THE Californians retreated toward the San Fernando Mission, near which point they were confronted by Frémont's battalion, which had advanced that far on the way south; and they capitulated to him. This was the whole of Frémont's participation in the conflict.

Meanwhile Stockton marched his army into Los Angeles, to the tune of "The Star Spangled Banner." Frémont also soon arrived.

The Californians finding themselves beaten, and seeing the number and determination of their opponents and their superiority in arms, in military organization and in generalship, quietly yielded, dispersed, and went about their business, refusing to contend further against the United States.

The city of Los Angeles, after our army entered and took possession, was orderly and not at all disturbed; the citizens moved to and fro, in the usual way, as if her angelic sanctity was not in the least ruffled.

Stockton appointed Frémont governor of California. He, perhaps, was influenced to this course by Kearny's previous abrupt demand for the position of commander-in-chief. Frémont took the office, and Stockton returned to San Diego, with his army, including Kearny's force. He embarked his men on the vessels and took command of the squadron again.

I arrived at San Diego about the time of the battle, with the "Euphemia," in company with the bark "Tasso." The two vessels left Santa Barbara at the same time, a heavy gale having then abated. A light easterly wind prevailed, which required us to beat down all the way. We sailed so near to each other that we carried on a conversation from one vessel to the other. The "Tasso" lowered a boat, and Captain Libbey and supercargo Teschemacher came aboard our vessel, staying for an hour or two and partaking of refreshments. On reaching San Diego we waited for war news.

Meanwhile, I sold to the different vessels of the squadron $3,000 to $4,000 worth of provisions, its own stores having been largely used for the supply of the troops; received purser's bills in payment; also sold to Bandini and to my old friend Captain Fitch, who were merchants there.

The dragoons of Kearny's force who were wounded in the battle of San Pasqual, about twenty or thirty in number, when brought into San Diego had been distributed among the different families. Dr. R. F. Maxwell, then surgeon of the "Cyane," was in attendance on the men. He took me and Teschemacher with him to visit them. They all had the utmost horror of Californians. The attack upon them had been sudden and vigorous, and they had been pursued by the Californians, relentlessly, and grievously wounded, the lances having been wielded with such skill and precision that many of the dragoons were killed.

This was an entirely new experience to the American soldiers. As there had been no opportunity offered to face their enemy in a fair fight, a terrible impression had been made upon their minds of the warlike character of the native Californians.

One young man in particular, of about twenty, with an intelligent face, suddenly became delirious while we were visiting him, and called out in terror, thinking the Californians were upon him. The San Diego ladies were very kind to these men, visiting and nursing them, preparing little delicacies for them and doing all in their power to make them comfortable.

After the troops had returned to San Diego from the battle of San Gabriel, Kearny made inquiries for a young Californian of the opposing force who had distinguished himself in the battle of San Pasqual by his courage and valor. He had singled out General Kearny individually and sprung at him as chief of the enemy. When he had succeeded in wounding the general, and the latter had fallen, the young Californian desisted from the attack and spared his life. After some inquiry, Kearny succeeded in finding out who he was. Upon his solicitation the young man called on the general, who greeted him warmly, and praised him for his bravery and soldierly behavior.

As soon as we received news of Stockton's victory over the Californians, Teschemacher and myself started by land for Los Angeles, ordering our vessels to proceed to San Pedro. The first night out we slept at the rancho of Santa Margarita, in charge of Don José Antonio Pico. He was called Teniente (Lieutenant) Pico, from his long service in the army. I had known him in 1841, '42, '43, in Sonoma, in General Vallejo's army. This rancho was owned by Governor Pico and Don Andres Pico, and was one of the most beautiful places in the country. Here I saw the first sugarcane growing in California, around a mound near the house, in the center of which, at the top, was a natural spring of water. Some of the stalks were nearly as large as my arm.

Arriving in the evening, we were received with great hospitality by Don Antonio and his family; had an excellent supper; and talked and smoked, and sipped California wine to a late hour, enjoying ourselves heartily.

The next morning I was up early, and, on going out, saw the sugar-cane. I expressed my surprise to Don Antonio, who was already out on the porch, (with a black silk handkerchief tied over his head, the four ends meeting at the back of his neck.) On receiving permission to cut some of the sugar-cane, I feasted on its sweetness before breakfast.

We got an early start, Don Antonio insisting that he should send back to San Diego the horses and vaqueros we had engaged there to take us to Los Angeles; furnishing us with true California hospitality six of his own horses and a vaquero to continue the journey, three of the horses to go ahead loose, to be used when those we started with had become tired. Not wishing to slight his generosity, we accepted them, and proceeded.

We stopped next at the rancho of Santa Ana, owned by the beautiful and fascinating widow of Don Tomás Yorba, who had extensive land possessions, and great numbers of cattle and horses. She managed her rancho with much ability. The lady was one of my best customers. In June, 1846, I sold her from $2,000 to $3,000 worth of goods, she having come to the vessel at San Pedro to buy them. Here we passed the night. She also insisted upon furnishing us with fresh horses to Los Angeles, having herself before we appeared in the morning dispatched ours and the vaquero back to Teniente Pico.

Returning the vaqueros and horses was frequently done when guests remained over night. She provided us with two horses and another vaquero. It had been raining for some days, and the Santa Ana river was high.

While we were making our preparations to start, Doña Vicenta, her fine hair streaming over her shoulders, a picture of womanly grace and beauty, gave orders to her *mayor–domo* to group four or five *manadas,* which was done. Having the horses together, the vaqueros drove them into the river, across to the other shore, and then immediately back to the same place. As they returned, Doña Vicenta said: "The river is now prepared for you to cross." The object of the movement of the large number of horses had been to trample down and harden the soft sediment or river quicksand at the bottom, so that we could cross on our horses with greater ease and safety, without risk to horse or man. When we were all prepared to start, the band of horses was driven over the river again at the same place, and we followed immediately in their wake.

This proceeding, which I have frequently seen in other places, for the same purpose, showed the extreme kindness of the lady to her guests. While here, we drank some good California wine, five or six years' old, manufactured by Tomás Yorba, Doña Vicenta's deceased husband. They had a large vineyard, and made wine for their use, and also for sale to others, and I purchased of her several hundred dollars' worth of wine and aguardiente, to be transported to my vessel at San Pedro, and resold. There was no higgling about the price, she simply named it when she said I could have the articles.

The common custom in dealings between the merchants and the Californians, was for the purchaser not to take occasion to ask the price; the seller quietly naming it at once. There was a perfect understanding between the parties, and confidence was felt on both sides that no advantage would be taken; the price stated was at once accepted as the correct one. Mrs. Yorba was the aunt of Mrs. Gafia, wife of the American consul at Tepic, Mexico, before mentioned. She lived afterwards at Anaheim, where her married daughters also resided.

After crossing the Santa Ana, the next important stream was the San Gabriel, which we reached toward the end of the day, having made rather slow progress in the muddy roads. We found the river very swift, and, halting at the brink, looked inquiringly towards each other. Addressing the vaquero by name, I said: *"Que se parece á usted? El rio está bravo"* (What do you think? The river is mad.) He replied, it was dangerous but we could manage to cross. I asked Teschemacher what he thought, and he said he supposed we should have to try. We went in, at the suggestion of the vaquero all three abreast, so that he could keep us in sight. About a third of the way across, the vaquero's horse suddenly turned over, and went under the swift water. He came up again, the vaquero still clinging fast to him. The animal gave a snort, shook the water from his ears and went forward to shore. Teschemacher's horse made a side motion, as if to turn over, but the rider leaned to the other side, and the animal, regaining his balance, swam across. My horse had no trouble, but took me steadily and safely over. The horses had to swim most of the way. We got to Los Angeles about seven or eight o'clock P. M. We were going to Don Abel Stearns' house; as we approached, Charles W. Flügge met us and took us to his apartments, where he prepared some hot punch, which warmed us, after which Doña Arcadia Stearns provided us with an excellent supper. Dry garments and shoes were given us, and several hours were spent there talking, enjoying ourselves, and drinking California wine until we felt in a very happy frame of mind, though none of us were intoxicated. Mrs. Stearns provided each of us a room, and we slept very comfortably in her excellent beds.

The captains, supercargoes and merchants in the early days of California were nearly all good drinkers. They partook freely of California wine and aguardiente, which, from its excellence and purity, seemed to have no deleterious effect. I never knew of an instance of a drunkard among them.

While we were proceeding from San Diego to Los Angeles, Stockton and his force passed in the opposite direction, by another road, going to San Diego. On the second day after reaching Los Angeles I called on Colonel Frémont who was then Governor of California. The first person I saw at headquarters was Colonel William H. Russell. He had been made Secretary of State by Frémont, and he gave me a little account of the movements of the battalion, the capitulation, etc. I told him I had called to see Colonel Frémont on business, and that I should like to make a settlement of my claim against him; that my vessel was at San Pedro, and I probably should not be at Los Angeles more than a week. He answered, in his flourishing style, that the colonel was extremely busy; that he had a great many callers and very important matters to attend to; and asked if it would make any difference if he did not present the matter to the colonel until the morrow. I told him that a day's delay would make no difference.

Russell worshiped Frémont as a great hero, carrying his admiration to a ridiculous extent, thinking Frémont appreciated him. I called the next day at headquarters, and was again put off by Russell, who told me that Colonel Frémont was engaged in writing dispatches to Washington, and could not by any means be disturbed. Seizing me by both hands, and shaking them warmly, he said, with a good deal of fervor, that he should consider it a personal favor if I would call the next day, when he would secure the attention of the governor to my business; upon which the interview ended.

I called every day during the week, and was each time unable to see Frémont, although Colonel Russell informed him I had called, the plea being that his great press of business would not admit of it. I became convinced that he was trifling and purposely avoided an interview. On the seventh day I sent to him by Colonel Russell the quartermaster's and commissary's receipts for the goods I had delivered, and requested their approval by Frémont. I was told to call in the afternoon, at which time I at last succeeded in getting the papers, containing Frémont's endorsement as Governor of California.

Meanwhile, during this week, I was busy in making sales at Los Angeles and collecting wine and aguardiente, of which I purchased considerable quantities, taking much of it in pay for goods previously delivered; also collecting hides, tallow and money. I made large sales. The country having been at war, the supplies of the people had become exhausted.

I did not regret having furnished the supplies for the soldiers, knowing how much they were in need of them, nor the assistance I had rendered the government in so doing; thus indirectly aiding in conquering the country. Nor did I regret that I was not to receive my pay when I found it was not forthcoming, although it had been absolutely promised by Frémont; but I considered in view of Col. Frémont's relation to me as a creditor and of the great accommodation I had rendered to him at Santa Barbara, when his force was in distress, and of his promise to settle on reaching Los Angeles, that I was entitled to courteous treatment. If he was not prepared to redeem his promise, he could at least have said so in a fair, square, and manly way.

In January, 1848, my partnership with E. and H. Grimes was dissolved, and in settlement I turned these two papers over to them. Several years afterward I knew that the claim was still unpaid, though I think it eventually was settled.

Commodore Stockton became U. S. Senator from New Jersey in 1851 and interested himself personally to see that the indebtedness which he had contracted, as agent of the government, for supplies on this coast received attention at Washington.

I may mention one instance: Don Santiaguito Argüello, furnished large quantities of army supplies to Stockton from his extensive rancho eleven or twelve miles from San Diego—several hundred head of cattle and horses, and for which he had a claim against the government amounting to $14,000. The claim was sent to Washington by Major Lee, commissary-general for the Pacific coast. Stockton's attention being called to it, he exerted himself effectually in its settlement, and in a few months Argüello received his money.

I regard Stockton as the real conqueror of California and as a man of very large mind, great judgment, and extraordinary foresight evinced in his whole career. His visit to Los Angeles shortly after coming to the coast and his friendly overtures to the Californians at that place, and afterward at Yerba Buena, showed his wisdom and discernment. When the news of the revolt of the Californians was received, he showed his good judgment in the preparations he made, first here in the north, and afterward in San Diego, looking months ahead for the conflict, and arranging to meet it systematically and thoroughly. Instead of hastily going forward with a small and unorganized and imperfectly drilled army, he took pains to instruct his officers and men for their new work; and at the same time, no doubt, improved and qualified himself in army tactics. The gathering of recruits, horses and supplies from the country and equipping, drilling and organizing his troops for the campaign, required laborious effort.

*In striking contrast to this mode of proceeding was Kearny's hasty and ill-judged action in fighting Pico's force, with half-starved and fatigued men mounted on mules, which was precipitated by Kearny, against the combined judgment of Stockton and Beale.

We have another example of Stockton's foresight and good sense, in sending out a man to warn Kearny of there being in the vicinity a more powerful enemy (Pico), and to proceed to San Diego without meeting that foe. Had any less capable man than Stockton been commander-in-chief at that period on the Pacific coast, the insurrection of the Californians would have been a serious affair. The conflict might have been prolonged with further effusion of blood.

*For a complete statement of an eye witness of the engagement at San Pasqual to which Davis here refers see "Notes of a military reconnoissance" William Helmesley Emory [30th Congress, 1st session, Ex. doc. No. 41] Washington 1848.

CITY OF LOS ANGELES, 1854

The chapel facing the Plaza—"Nuestra Señora la Regina de los Angeles"—is in use today as a parish church. The low hills in the background are Boyle Heights, while the higher ground beyond is the Puentes, which rise to the northward of Whittier.

CHAPTER LIX
Frémont in the Rôle of Pardoner

WHEN Frémont's battalion was passing down to Los Angeles from the north, near San Luis Obispo, Jesus "Totoi" Pico was arrested as a spy and charged with the design of conveying to the Californians information of Frémont's approach. Brought before Frémont and tried by court-martial, he was found guilty and condemned to be shot. The arrest took place near the man's own home at San Luis Obispo, and it was deemed improbable that he had designed acting as charged, especially in view of the fact that the Californians were well-posted as to Frémont's movements during the whole progress of the march. If the prisoner had been found any considerable distance from his home, between Yerba Buena and Los Angeles, the case would have looked more suspicious against him. He declared his innocence. As the time for the execution approached, Pico's wife and family were much alarmed. Mrs. Pico, accompanied by her children, appeared before Frémont to intercede for her husband. She knelt before him and pleaded eloquently for her husband. The commander relented, and gave Pico a pardon. They afterward became friends, and the latter went with Frémont on his march south.

In my visits to the camp at Santa Barbara, I saw "Totoi" Pico two or three times and conversed with him. He spoke of Frémont's great kindness to him, after he had been pardoned, and of the attentions that had been shown him.

In conversation with many of the prominent Californians, at various times, after their defeat in the battle of San Gabriel, they expressed themselves freely against the Mexicans, saying that they considered the Mexican government had appeared badly in the war between that country and the United States; that the fact that General Scott had been allowed to march from Vera Cruz to the City of Mexico, with hardly a show of resistance by the Mexicans, seemed to indicate there was a concerted plan between Santa Ana and the United States government to permit the success of the latter's army in Mexico. They seemed to think also that

Mexico was very delinquent in its duty to California, in not sending an army to resist the capture of the territory by the United States; and remarked that the Mexican government had sold them like so many sheep. They said their own effort against the United States forces was in part to show that they were not Mexicans and cowards, but had some patriotism and love for their country. Although they could not successfully hope to resist so powerful a nation as the United States, yet they had proved their devotion to California in not quietly submitting to be conquered, without a sign of resistance.

On leaving San Pedro, I sailed for Santa Barbara, with Louis McLane and Josiah Belden on board as passengers; also José Ramon Estudillo, who had been impressed into the service by the Californians in Contra Costa (San Leandro) and taken south by them. He was in the fight of San Gabriel. McLane was a passed midshipman in the navy aboard one of the United States vessels, and held a position on shore as captain, (with other officers) for the protection of the flag, and had accompanied Frémont's battalion. McLane was permitted to return and take his old position at Monterey. He came on my vessel for this purpose. We touched at Santa Barbara, and were four days beating up from there to Point Concepcion, against a strong head-wind. Seeing that we had before us a tedious voyage, the captain, at my request, anchored under the lee of the Point, and Belden, McLane and myself left our vessel and went ashore, determined to come up to Monterey by land. At the Cojo rancho, Don Anastasio Carrillo's *mayor-domo* brought us a *caponera,* and we took three good horses and a vaquero and proceeded inland to the Rancho Nipomo, owned by William G. Dana. When we arrived, we found there H. F. Teschemacher and Dr. Nicholas A. Den, the former having left his vessel at Santa Barbara to come up by land. The next morning I ordered the vaquero back to the Rancho Cojo, with Carrillo's horses and a note to the owner explaining the liberty I had taken in borrowing them.

Belden, McLane and myself each bought two horses from Dana to continue our journey. Den and Teschemacher had brought their horses from Santa Barbara, with a vaquero, and a tent on a pack animal. We joined in one party, all sleeping in the tent, camping out and cooking our own food. We spent several days on the journey. The weather was delightful, cool and clear, the country fresh and beautiful, with grass and wild flowers growing luxuriantly all the way from the Cojo to Monterey; and we enjoyed ourselves exceedingly.

On reaching Monterey, the "Tasso" and the "Euphemia" were already there, they having got a favorable slant of wind after leaving Point Concepcion. I continued my trip by land to Yerba Buena, ordering my vessel to proceed there, and, on arriving, found that my friend and employee, R. M. Sherman, had done a good business during my absence. When the "Euphemia" came into the bay (March, 1847,) I had on board over $20,000 in coin (Mexican dollars and doubloons) and purser's bills, the result of sales during the trip south and back, besides what was trusted out.

I also had aboard a large quantity of California wine and aguardiente, which were just as good as gold, and better, because there was a sure sale for both at a profit. Some of the original cargo also remained.

I was greeted by Captain Grimes, who reported that my mother was very ill at Honolulu. I therefore made preparations to go hence. On giving Captain Grimes an account of my business trip down south and the result, he was greatly pleased. His face broke out in a smile all over, and he said: "William, you have done wonders."

On the 31st of March, sailed for Honolulu, on the "Euphemia" with Pickett aboard, he having requested me to take him down to visit the Islands. I had about $30,000, including what Sherman had collected during my absence south, a portion of which was in Mexican dollars, twenty bags of $1,000 each. We left in a south-east storm, but after a day or two it abated, and with gentle trade winds the ocean was as smooth as glass. A whitehall boat could have made the passage. On arriving at Honolulu after a voyage of twenty days, I was met by the pilot in the outer harbor, Stephen Reynolds, a Boston merchant at Honolulu, who had been previously United States vice-consul there. He had lived at Honolulu many years, and had become wealthy, importing goods from Boston; and yet he acted as pilot. The pilotage was very lucrative. He immediately gave the sailors their orders, and we were shortly anchored in the harbor. I was met on the wharf by Alexander G. Abell. He was then United States consul at Honolulu, and was of the firm of Abell, McClure & Cheevers, engaged in the trade between the Islands and California. The two latter had taken a large cargo in the brig "Francisca" to the Pacific Coast, leaving Mr. Abell to manage the business at Honolulu. He asked if I had any remittance for him, and when informed I had not, he seemed disappointed; he could not imagine what his partners were doing in California, not to have disposed of the goods, or a part of them, and remitted the proceeds. I knew that they had mismanaged the business and were too fond of drinking, and enjoying themselves, to make a success of it.

Mr. Reynolds, who was a special friend of my mother, accompanied me to her house, and on the way asked me what amount I had brought for Grimes; on my replying, about $30,000, he stared in amazement and could hardly believe it. He said he was overjoyed, for the house had got into trouble financially; this amount would save them from a great disaster; and it did, when I turned the money over to the concern.

The presence of so large a fleet of vessels on the coast, as well as the increasing immigration to California, had stimulated business, and money was plentiful at Honolulu. The Sandwich Islands, then being our nearest neighbors, were greatly benefited.

I found my mother very ill. Her death occurred four days after my arrival.

I reached Honolulu on Sunday. While I was at my mother's house, with Reynolds, I was sent for by Hiram Grimes from his residence, the stores and other business places being all closed on that day.

Honolulu seemed very much like a thriving New England town, both in the business and residence portions. A person could easily imagine himself in one of the suburbs of Boston, in passing through its streets.

I spent most of my time with my mother until her death. After the funeral, I commenced loading my vessel for the return voyage.

CHAPTER LX
Mrs. Paty's Wine Cask Empties Mysteriously

SHORTLY after the Missions were first instituted in California, the rancheros, in a small way, commenced to establish their ranchos, getting grants from the government beyond the Mission lands, and obtaining a few cattle from the Fathers. Many of them were ignorant, uncultivated, and quite unused to the luxuries of life. A man of this kind one day visited the Mission of San Luis Obispo, and was kindly received by the good Father.

During the visit a servant was directed to bring in some refreshments. A lunch was served, and, among other things, a steaming pot of tea. A cup was set before the ranchero, and he was invited to help himself. Never having drank any tea, he was puzzled how to proceed, but presently lifting off the lid of the teapot, he dipped the spoon in, and, taking out some of the leaves, placed them in his cup, added sugar, and began to eat the new dish; whereupon the good Father kindly and politely explained that the tea was to be drank, and not to be eaten.

In 1842, the "Don Quixote" arrived at Honolulu, and found there the beautiful clipper-built ship "Congress," from New York. The vessel was engaged in the China trade, plying regularly between New York and China. On that trip she had brought supplies for the missionaries, of whom there were a good many at the Sandwich Islands and at other islands in the Pacific ocean.

The Missions in New York and Boston, in those days, sent out large quantities of supplies, including books and papers, from their headquarters, to Honolulu, that being a distributing point. I have known vessels to come there with goods for the missionaries exclusively. The "Congress," after discharging, waited at Honolulu some time before sailing for China, partly by reason of the typhoons which prevailed in the China seas at that season of the year, and which her captain wished to avoid; and partly to receive expected advices from the owners in New York, by the way of Mexico.

The speediest mode of communication between the United States and the Pacific islands was by vessel from New York, or other Atlantic ports, to Vera Cruz; thence across, by mule conveyance to Mazatlan or San Blas; letters being addressed to the care of the United States Consuls at those seaports.

Vessels were constantly going and coming between the Mexican coast and Honolulu, being owned in the latter place and employed in the China trade. They brought cargoes of goods to the Islands; disposed of a portion of them there, and went thence to San Blas or Mazatlan with the remainder. The cargoes were purchased with special reference to the Mexican trade of the interior, whither they were sent from the coast. The consuls forwarded by these vessels such letters and dispatches as they had received from the Atlantic side, and frequent communication was thus had. In 1834 or 1835 the brig "Griffin," Captain William C. Little, originally a Boston vessel, was engaged in trade between China, Honolulu and the coast of Mexico. She was on a voyage from Honolulu to Mazatlan, with a partial cargo of China goods, but did not reach Mexico. She was never heard of more. All the hides shipped from California to the Islands were re-shipped to Boston.

The captain of the ship "Congress," having heard of the feats of the "Don Quixote" as a fast sailer, was anxious to have a trial of speed, as he prided himself upon the sailing qualities of his own vessel. Therefore, when he was ready for sea, he waited a few days for the bark to discharge and take return cargo of miscellaneous goods for California.

The two vessels came out of the harbor of Honolulu together. Great interest was manifested in this race. When we left the town the houses and every little elevation were covered with people, who had gathered to witness the contest. The "Don Quixote" being well known, and having a history as a fast vessel, was the favorite.

Our bark passed out first, and after we had got fairly clear of the harbor, we lay to, to allow the pilot to go ashore. He and his crew exchanged parting salutations with us, standing up in the boat, taking off their hats and cheering. Just then the "Congress" came up with us. We loosened and spread out our studding sails, and the "Congress" did the same, until both vessels had all their canvas to the breeze, sailing gaily away. Looking back we saw the crowds on shore, waving us farewell, until they were lost to view in the distance.

The two vessels kept pretty near for some time, but the "Don Quixote" gained, little by little, upon her rival, until, when twenty or thirty miles out to sea, she was fairly ahead. As night came on, the vessels parted, each on its own course.

Captain Paty kept everything about the bark in the neatest condition. It may be said in general that the captains who came to the California coast in those days were gentlemanly, intelligent and well-read. Each took pride and delight in his own vessel, thinking her the finest that sailed the ocean, and was always ready, when opportunity offered, for a trial of speed. The "Euphemia" was an exception; we never boasted of her sailing qualities.

In 1842 the "Alert" and the "Don Quixote" happened to be in Monterey, and were ready to leave at the same time. When this was noticed, much interest was manifested in the circumstance. They had to make many tacks to get out of the bay, and Captain Phelps of the "Alert," did his best to crowd the bark, but the former was really no match for the latter, which easily took the lead. During this trial, Captain Paty ordered the chain cable moved from the bow to midships, and the sailors shifted it with great alacrity, entering into the spirit of the occasion as sailors always do when their own vessel is put to a test. I have witnessed several ocean races; the great enthusiasm of the crews at such times was noticeable, the sailors being proud of their vessel, which was their home. They were as much attached to it as landsmen to their domiciles and surroundings.

In the summer of 1844, the "Admittance" and "Don Quixote" were both trading on the coast, and were at Santa Barbara together. They were ready to leave on the same day, both bound to Monterey. The captains and supercargoes of the vessels, and their friends, arranged that there should be a trial of speed between them. The "Admittance" was a good sailer and a beautiful ship. Captain Peterson, her master, being a first-class navigator, the vessels were evenly matched. They were obliged to beat all the way up against the prevailing head-winds. The "Don Quixote" anchored at Monterey twenty-four hours in advance of the other. Captain Paty as a bold navigator, with good judgment had no superior. He took chances which a more cautious captain would not have dared to take. His plan was to sleep in the daytime, allowing his mates to sail the vessel when everything was clear, and at night to take charge himself.

As he understood the coast thoroughly, he kept inshore as much as possible after sunset, to get the advantage of the land breeze, which prevailed nearly all night, but extended only a few miles from shore. He took short tacks to get the breeze, while Captain Peterson kept much further out to sea, and lost the advantage. Before the vessels left Santa Barbara, there were numerous bets made by the officers and their friends on shore, as to the result of the trial, mostly of wines, cigars and small articles, no money being wagered.

All the early vessels that came out from Boston to trade on the coast had on board small quantities of choice wine casked, belonging to their owners, usually sherry and madeira, put under the special charge of the captain, simply to make the voyage to California and back, and not to be touched on the way, it being sent for the improvement it received on the voyage through continuous agitation.

In 1842, Mrs. Paty was presented by Don Luis Vignes with a cask of California wine, while the captain's bark was at San Pedro, and she had it put on board for the benefit of the sea travel, until such time as the vessel should reach Honolulu, when the intention was to have it bottled.

Captain Paty and his officers were accustomed to a little wine at dinner; and after tasting the Vignes wine, they found it so agreeable that they could not resist drinking of it while on the voyage. The good lady, who was aboard, never suspected it was her wine that was disappearing day by day, she herself being a participant in the abstraction. Captain Paty and I presented Commodore Jones, at Monterey, with some of this identical wine, as being superior to anything else that could be procured for the purpose. The vessel reaching Honolulu, Mrs. Paty inquired for the cask and was much chagrined to find that the contents had wholly disappeared.

[TEXT OF LETTER ON OPPOSITE PAGE]

U.S. Ship Portsmouth
Yerba Buena July 8th 1846

Sir,

At ½ past seven oclock tomorrow morning I propose landing a considerable body of men under arms and to march them from the boats to the flagstaff in Yerba Buena, upon which, at 8 oclock I shall hoist the Flag of the U.States under a salute of twenty one guns from the Portsmouth, after which the Proclamation of the Commander in Chief Commodore Sloat, will be read in both languages for the information of all classes.

I will thank you therefore to have it translated and ready for that purpose at the appointed hour—and be pleased to present my compliments to the Alcaldy—and say if agreeable to him I shall be gratified to see him pleasant on the occasion, that I may, under the authority of the Proclamation, confirm him in his official position, until the pleasure of the Commander in Chief shall be known.

Very Respectfully
etc, etc.

Jno B Montgomery
Commander

To
    William A. Leidesdorff Esq
    Vice Consul of the U.States
    Yerba Buena

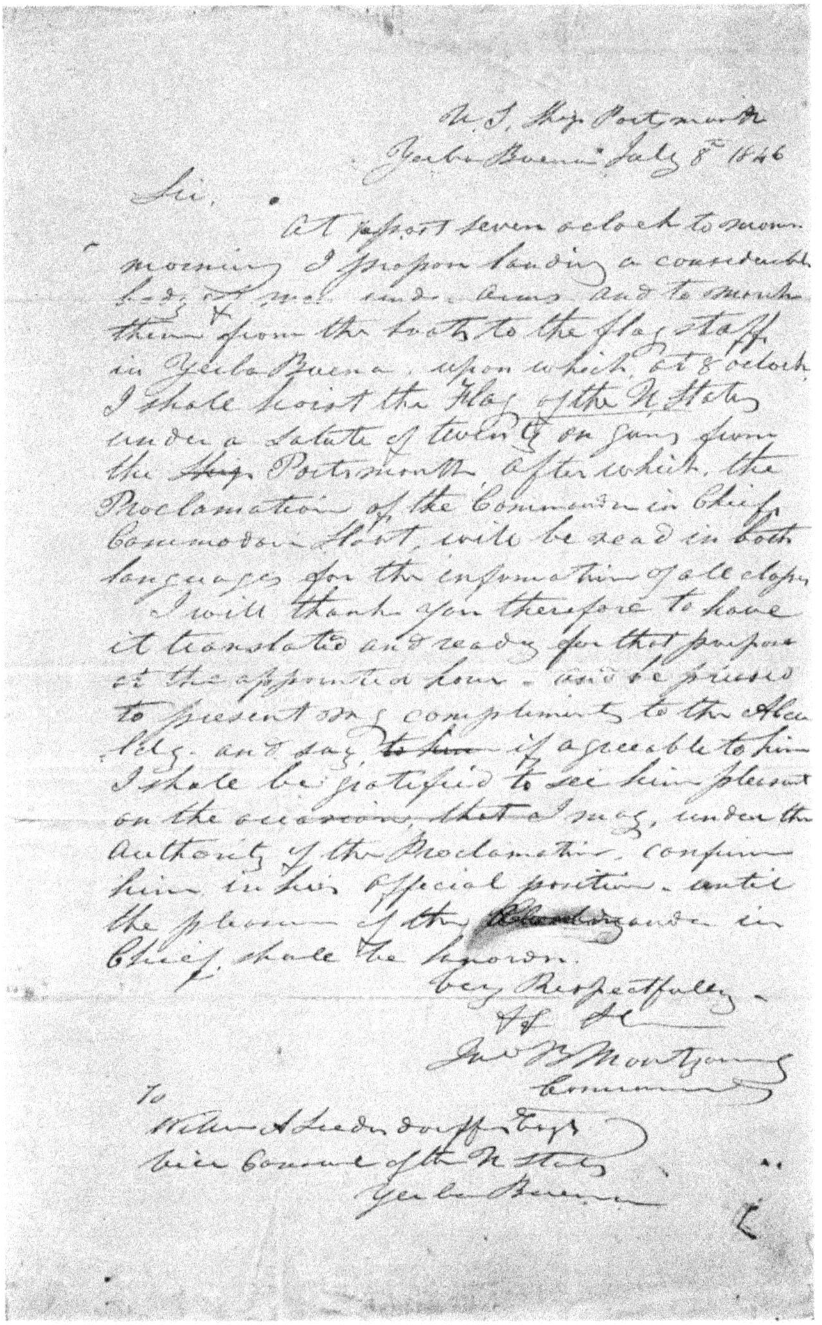

U. S. Ship Portsmouth
Yerba Buena July 8th 1846

Sir,

At passed seven oclock to morrow morning I propose landing a considerable body of men under arms and to march them from the boat to the flag staff in Yerba Buena, upon which at 8 oclock I shall hoist the Flag of the U. States under a Salute of twenty one guns from the Ship Portsmouth, after which, the Proclamation of the Commander in Chief, Commodore Sloat, will be read in both languages for the information of all classes.

I will thank you therefore to have it translated and ready for that purpose at the appointed hour — and be pleased to present my compliments to the Alcalde, and say to him if agreeable to him I shall be gratified to see him pleasant on the occasion, that I may, under the authority of the Proclamation, confirm him in his official position — until the pleasure of the Commander in Chief shall be known.

Very Respectfully
&c &c
Jno B Montgomery
Commander

To
William A Leidesdorff Esqr
Vice Consul of the U. States
Yerba Buena

CAPTAIN MONTGOMERY'S "SEE HIM PLEASANT" REQUEST
Written the day before American occupation of Yerba Buena, this letter, with its humorous slip of the pen, has extraordinary interest for San Franciscans.

CHAPTER LXI
Yerba Buena's First American Alcalde Lieut. Bartlett, U. S. N.

SOON after the United States flag was hoisted on shore at the port of San Francisco, July, 9th, 1846, Captain Montgomery selected Lieutenant Bartlett, of the "Portsmouth" to act as first-alcalde of Yerba Buena. He was capable, speaking the Spanish language, which was a great advantage. George Hyde was appointed at the same time as second-alcalde, he having arrived here as secretary to Commodore Stockton, in the frigate "Congress." He had joined that vessel for the purpose of coming to California. Mr. Hyde was a Pennsylvanian, of wealthy family and of the highest respectability. Commodore Biddle was from the same State, and their families were intimate. When the commodore visited Yerba Buena in 1847, he remembered Hyde at once, and they were on very friendly terms. George Hyde retained the office of second-alcalde only two days, and then resigned.

When Bartlett was made prisoner by the Californians, Hyde was appointed in his place by Captain Hull, in December, 1846; and held that position until Bartlett's release and return, when the latter again resumed the alcaldeship.

There was an election for alcalde in October, 1846, in which Bartlett, who still held the office, was a candidate, with Bob Ridley the opposing aspirant. The latter was badly beaten by Bartlett who was elected by a handsome majority. The popular voice of the people was then expressed for the first time, under the American system, since the change of flag in the department.

Prior to 1841, Jacob P. Leese obtained a grant of two leagues of land, from the government of California, known as Cañada Guadalupe, y Visitacion, y Rodeo Viejo, bounded as follows: On the east by the bay of San Francisco, on the south the San Bruno Mountains or Buri-buri rancho, on the west by the rancho of San Miguel, owned by Don José Jesus Noé, and on the north by the rancho of Doña Carmel Cibrian. In 1841 Robert Ridley was granted by Governor Alvarado, four or six leagues of land on the north side of the bay of San Francisco in Sonoma district (now Sonoma county.) In 1841, Leese deeded to Ridley his two league grant. In return, Ridley conveyed to Leese his four or six leagues of land, in consideration of the other conveyance to him. It was a barter trade between the parties and the only transaction of the character—exchanging land grants—that ever occurred to my knowledge in California, under the Mexican regime. Duboce avenue in San Francisco was at one time called Ridley street after Robert Ridley.

In 1847, when George Hyde was alcalde of San Francisco much jealousy existed and there were many bickerings between rival land owners, which caused an idle charge, that was subsequently proved entirely unfounded, to be made against Mr. Hyde, of having, in his official capacity, tampered with the map and survey of the city. The alcalde demanded an investigation, and by order of Colonel Mason, then acting as military governor of the department, the town council was directed to take evidence and report on the subject.

The commission met on the 1st or 2d of November, 1847, and organized by appointing R. A. Parker, chairman. On motion of E. P. Jones, Mr. Harrison, a clerk in the custom-house and commissary's office, was appointed to take down the evidence. The first and only witness called was one Grayson, also a clerk in the commissary department. He was sworn, and testified that he knew who had made the defacement on the map, and that it was the alcalde, Mr. Hyde. On cross-examination, he stated that he did not see the alcalde do it, but presumed that he must have done it, because the map belonged to the alcalde's office. This was all the testimony taken on the charge. The clerk was directed to make and keep a fair copy, or report, of the proceedings.

On the following evening the commission met again, when the committee preferring the charge admitted that it had no further evidence. Mr. Hyde then demanded that the evidence, as taken, be read over before closing the proceedings. The clerk objected to this as unnecessary. He was required to do so, however, when it was discovered that he omitted the entire cross-examination. When asked his reason for the omission, he alleged that he did not think it was of any consequence. Significantly requested to *step down and out,* he did so promptly. Alcalde Hyde proposed to introduce testimony from the records of the court the object of which would develop itself, as the evidence was read, and which would probably aid in showing who did tamper with the map and surveys.

The hearing occupied three evenings, when it became apparent who the interested parties were and what the motive was for making a change in the lots and survey—that it was work which originated in Mr. Alcalde

Bryant's office to accommodate certain individuals and for whose benefit it was done; and that Mr. Hyde had nothing whatever to do with the business. The exposure resulted in a row among the parties concerned, which was ended by the commission's adjourning until the next evening.

The committee making the charge failed to again appear. It could not be prevailed on to meet and it did not meet the commission until the 4th day of December, a month afterwards. At that date it met to accommodate Mr. Sam. Brannan, who was the author of a second and different charge, to wit: that the alcalde had granted a lot to other persons, which had been promised by his predecessor, Bryant, to Mr. Brannan's mother-in-law. Alcalde Hyde denied any knowledge of such promise. He asserted that this was the first he had heard of it, and, if true, the act of conferring the grant by him was unintentional. Mr. Hyde's clerk, who had also been clerk under Mr. Bryant, testified that he had recorded the grant referred to and had brought to Alcalde Hyde for his signature both the grant and record, which were signed. He had not informed Mr. Hyde of the fact of Alcalde Bryant's promise, because he had forgotten it. He could not say whether Alcalde Hyde knew of it or not. Mr. Brannan was satisfied; and declared that Alcalde Hyde had been entirely vindicated.

The last proceedings occupied but one evening, and the commission adjourned. The committee that had preferred the first charges never appeared again, notwithstanding frequent calls and solicitations of Mr. Hyde and of the board of commissioners.

Affairs ran along from December 4th to the first day of March, 1848, when a horse race occurred. Under the excitement of the occasion, some of the citizens, deeply interested by heavy betting on the result, fell into personal altercation which terminated in two of them, Leidesdorff and McDougal, being bound over by Alcalde Hyde to keep the peace. Therefrom grew subsequent proceedings, embracing the application to Governor Mason for the removal of Mr. Hyde from office. It was a secretly concocted affair, not heard of until the reply of the Governor reached San Francisco, a couple of weeks later. Leidesdorff swore vengeance against Hyde, and took that method of effecting it. He and E. P. Jones, an unscrupulous person, secretly addressed a letter to Governor Mason, wording it in a deceptive manner, which influenced Mr. W. D. M. Howard and Mr. Robert A. Parker to sign it. The latter were under the impression that it merely asked for the removal of Alcalde Hyde, on account of the alleged arbitrary act of placing Mr. Leidesdorff under arrest. Mr. Hyde, considering himself injured by these secret assaults, sent in his resignation, to take effect April 1st, and at the same time apprised the governor of the facts relative to the horse race altercation and the meeting of the town council, adding that it had held no session as a board of commissioners since December 4, 1847.

The governor asked the four gentlemen who had signed the communication for a report of the evidence before the commissioners as to the charges, taken in accordance with his previous directions. Messrs. Howard and Parker, finding themselves seriously entrapped, declined to associate further with Jones and Leidesdorff. The two last named gentlemen, concluding it would be better for them also to withdraw from their compromising position, asked the governor to consider their letter as private correspondence, instead of relating to official matters. Thus, so far as the council was concerned, the entire affair had an insignificant ending. C. L. Ross, a member of the self-appointed citizens' committee represented a ring composed of several persons who coached the entire proceedings under the charges. As matters developed, it was soon known that malice was at the bottom of the whole business.

Mr. Hyde, at the time he sought to influence the governor to postpone the sale of the beach and water lots, also pointed out to him the necessity of reconstructing of the ayuntamiento, or Town Council, to which the district of San Francisco was entitled. In view of the sale leaving a large balance of funds on hand, ample security ought to be provided for its safety; and the employment of these moneys for various improvements ought not to be left to the disposal of the alcalde alone. A safe and commodious jail was a necessity urgently demanded, also the erection of a school house. Various other suggestions were offered by Mr. Hyde. He secured the appointment of T. M. Leavenworth as second-alcalde, and obtained a promise that a Court of First Instance should be provided for the district as soon as practicable.

Bartlett continued in office until the arrival of Commodore Biddle, in June, 1847, when he was ordered on board his vessel for duty as Lieutenant. Mr. Hyde was then appointed alcalde by General Kearny and held the office until April 3rd, 1848.

When General Kearny became military governor here in 1847, he approved the change of name from Yerba Buena to San Francisco as already in use by Alcalde Bartlett.

Don José Ramon Carrillo, before mentioned as a distinguished bear hunter, notwithstanding his fondness for the exciting sport, was himself as gentle as a lamb. There always appeared on his face whether in conversation or not, a peculiar smile, which indicated his good nature. On one occasion he was out in the woods, with his companions, in Sonoma county, where he lived, and they saw a bear a little distance off. He proposed to the others to go on foot and fight the animal alone, to which they assented.

He had a large sharp knife, and taking the *mochila* from his saddle he held it in his left hand as a shield, and thus accoutered approached the bear, which immediately showed fight. The combat began. Carrillo, as the bear charged upon him and attempted to seize him, held up his shield to repel the assault, and with his knife in the other hand made skillful thrusts at the animal, with telling effect. Before long the creature lay dead before him.

On another occasion he was riding alone through the woods, when, seeing a bear a little distance away, he went after him on his horse, prepared to throw his reata and lasso him. That part of the country was overgrown with *chamiza,* so that the ground was a good deal hidden. The chase had hardly commenced when the bear plunged suddenly into a ditch, perhaps five or six feet deep. Before Carrillo could check his horse, the animal and himself plunged headlong into it also. He immediately distangled himself from his horse, and, while doing so, the bear showed signs of retreating. Under circumstances of the kind, a bear is apt to lose all his courage and is not inclined to fight, and in this instance the suddenness of the shock seemed to have knocked all the savageness out of him.

Don José Ramon instantly took in the situation; and saw that in such close quarters with the animal, with no room to move about to use his reata or otherwise defend himself, his situation would be a dangerous one should the courage of the bear revive; and that his safety was in allowing him to get away. The bear commenced to climb up the steep sides of the pit, where it was very difficult to get any kind of a hold, and Carrillo, with wonderful presence of mind, placed his strong arms under the brute's hind-quarters and, exerting all his strength, gave him a good lift. The bear having the good sense to rightly appreciate this friendly assistance, struggled forward, got out, and scampered away, leaving the horse and his master to climb out as best they could.

In 1850, Don José Ramon Carrillo married the widow of Don Tomás Yorba; and in 1851, as I was about leaving San Diego, I sold to him my furniture there, which he added to the establishment at Santa Ana where he lived with his wife. In 1861, as he was riding towards his home one night some one waylaid him on the road and shot him dead. He was found there as he fell. The perpetrator of the crime was never discovered.

In 1836 or '37, Don José Martinez started from the mansion at Pinole to go out for a little sport at bear hunting, with several companions. This rancho is situated in a deep valley, with high hills on either side. When they had got some little distance from the house they fancied they heard a bear not far away, and Don José rode off ahead of the others, up the side of the hill, and suddenly came close upon a bear, himself unprepared for an attack. The bear made a dash at him, and with his claw raked him down the leg, ripping his trousers, tearing off the shoe and stocking and just giving the foot a scratch. As the horse pressed forward, the Don held on to his saddle with all his might, to save himself from being torn to pieces. The strength of the bear's stroke having been spent upon the clothing, which gave way, the rider passed on and escaped. His companions soon coming up, the creature was speedily lassoed and killed.

Doña Encarnacion, the widow of one of the Peraltas, the present wife of Don Manuel Ayala, resided at Temescal, where she had a beautiful home, one of the handsomest in the country. In 1840, while she was Mrs. Peralta, she lived a quarter of a mile from her later residence in a northeasterly direction. About where her home was she had a large vegetable garden, or *milpa,* and cultivated watermelons. One day in the month of August, she walked down from her house at midday to look at her garden and see how her melons and vegetables were getting on. As she was about to return to the house, just as she had left the garden, she saw a short distance off five or six horsemen, among them her husband, gathered about an immense bear which they had just lassoed. It was the *matanza* season, and the animal had been attracted to the spot by the smell of the meat. He had come down from the mountains to feast upon the carcasses of the slaughtered cattle, but, contrary to the usual custom, had boldly approached in the broad light of day instead of at night. He was a monster, the largest that had ever been seen there, strong and savage, having broken one of the reatas. It required the strength of all the men to manage and hold him. Doña Encarnacion was a good deal startled at the sight of the struggling beast. Her husband made a motion to her to go back to the *milpa,* which she did, staying until the bear was fully secured and subdued. This was in the open country, with no concealment of woods or shrubbery.

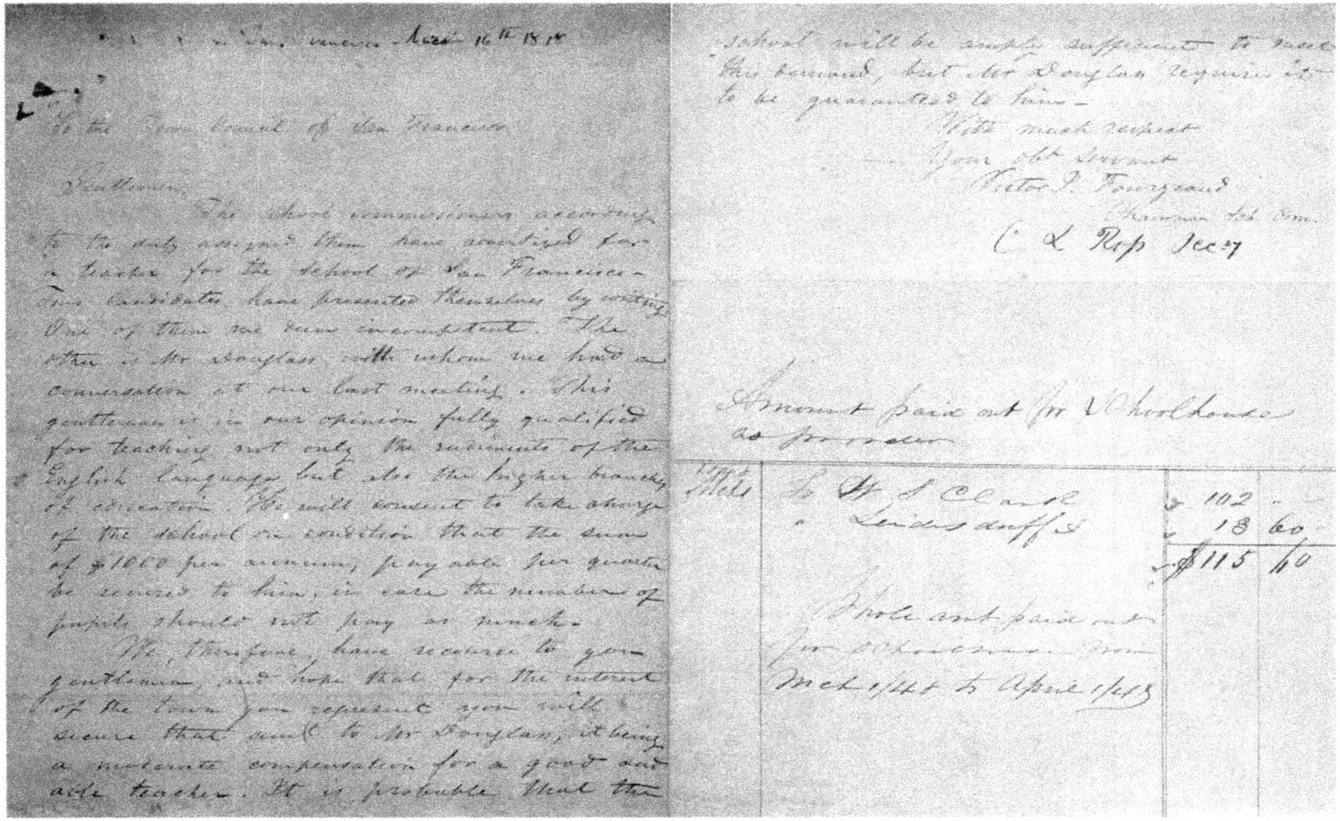

[illegible] Mar 16th 1848

To the Town Council of San Francisco

Gentlemen,

The school commissioners according to the duty assigned them have advertised for a teacher for the school of San Francisco. Two candidates have presented themselves by writing. One of them we deem incompetent. The other is Mr Douglas with whom we had a conversation at our last meeting. This gentleman is in our opinion fully qualified for teaching not only the rudiments of the English language but also the higher branches of education. He will consent to take charge of the school on condition that the sum of $1000 per annum, payable per quarter be secured to him, in case the number of pupils should not pay as much.

We, therefore, have recourse to you gentlemen, and hope that for the interest of the town you represent you will secure that sum to Mr Douglas, it being a moderate compensation for a good and able teacher. It is probable that the school will be amply sufficient to meet this demand, but Mr Douglas requires it to be guaranteed to him.

With much respect
Your obt Servant
Victor J. Fourgeaud
Chairman Sch. Com.

C L Rep Dec 7

Amount paid out for Schoolhouse as per order

1848 Mch	To W. S. Clark	102	..
	" [illegible]	18	60
		$115	60
	Whole amt paid out for Schoolhouse from Mch 1/48 to April 1/48		

REPORT UPON THE SELECTION OF MR. THOMAS DOUGLAS, GRADUATE OF YALE COLLEGE, AS SAN FRANCISCO'S FIRST PUBLIC SCHOOL TEACHER; TOGETHER WITH BILL IN FULL FOR SAN FRANCISCO'S FIRST PUBLIC SCHOOL HOUSE

CHAPTER LXII
The Gold Rush Starts; and Other Incidents

AFTER my return to the coast, with the brig "Euphemia," in March, 1846, an idea came into my mind, that in the course of business events, I would prepare a voyage for Callao, Peru, with the "Euphemia" or some other vessel, carrying a cargo of tallow for that market. In this I was inspired by the big gains of vessels that were fitted out from Callao with assorted merchandise for the coast of California. In return for goods the vessels brought here, they went back to Peru with tallow as a remittance, which was sold at one hundred per cent profit over the cost of the same here. In the fall of 1847 I commenced getting ready for the new field of operations. At Saucelito I deposited the tallow collected from debtors to myself around the bay, and from vessels trading on the coast, in exchange for hides. In December following, the brig sailed for San Diego, to touch at intermediate ports for collections of more tallow. I had contracted with Don Eulogio de Célis for a lot of tallow he had stored at San Diego, to make up a full cargo. Before the brig reached Monterey, she encountered a southeast gale of wind, and sprung a leak. In the course of a week, a courier arrived from Monterey with a letter from R. M. Sherman, who was supercargo, informing me that they had arrived there, and that the vessel was in a leaky condition. The bark "Natalia," of Valparaiso, was leaving for Monterey at the time the bad news reached me, and I took passage on her. The brig returned to San Francisco; the voyage to Callao having been abandoned for lack of a vessel to convey the cargo. Had she been favored with her usual luck, the venture would have been carried out, with a prospect of a profitable result for her owners. The proceeds of the tallow would have been invested in general merchandise, as Callao was then a depository for goods from Europe and the United States. But, the adage, "Man proposes, God disposes," proved true in this instance, and the vessel was sent to Honolulu for repairs, with her cargo of tallow, Mr. Sherman as supercargo. The tallow was sold there at a loss.

While the "Euphemia" was being overhauled and put in order, Sherman was busy buying a return cargo, and his selections proved suitable for the mines, which were discovered during his absence. The "Euphemia" arrived at San Francisco just in the nick of time, in June, 1848, a few days after the first appearance here of the gold from Sacramento.

On the evening of Mr. Sherman's arrival, Mr. W. D. M. Howard invited eight of his intimate friends (among the number the writer) to partake of a fine dinner, in honor of and to welcome Sherman's return. It was in the early hours of morning that this group of young argonauts retired to their homes, after an hilarious and enjoyable feast.

In the fall of 1849, the "Euphemia" was chartered by W. D. M. Howard, Hiram Grimes, Joseph P. Thompson, Eulogio de Célis and myself, for a voyage to Mazatlan for Mexican goods, with a capital of $45,000 in gold dust. Célis furnished $15,000, and went as supercargo; Howard and myself, $10,000 each, and the other two of the company $5,000 apiece. At my suggestion, Howard and I called on board the flag-ship "Ohio," and asked Commodore Jones to give the "Euphemia" an American flag, instead of the Hawaiian, which he readily did. The occasion of the interchange of flags was celebrated with sparkling wine on board the brig, by a large company of friends, including Commodore Jones. The voyage to Mexico proved to be a success to those interested in the enterprise.

Sometime in 1850 I sold the "Euphemia" to the city of San Francisco, to be used as a prison brig, and she was moored alongside Long Wharf for a time.

Thus ended the career of one of the luckiest vessels to her owners that I have known in my long business experience. She was homely and a slow sailer, but carried more than double her tonnage in freight. On her first voyage to California she cleared $30,000 the day I obtained the receipt for the duties and Custom House permission to trade up and down the coast. Her numerous voyages to Honolulu and San Francisco were very prosperous financially, and during my ownership only one accident occurred to the "Euphemia."

The "Jóven Guipuzcoana" was owned by Mr. Aguirre, as I have before stated. In the beginning of December, 1848, Major Reading, of the firm of Hensley, Reading & Co., of Sacramento, was in my store one morning. The subject of conversation between the Major and myself on that occasion was the high price of flour that ruled in the market. Reading suggested getting up a voyage to Oregon for a cargo of flour. I replied, "Yes, I have a vessel in port already manned, belonging to Aguirre." The Major wanted to know how soon she could sail. I said, "Right away, as she is already prepared for sea." Reading asked how much money would be required for the speculation. I replied, "$15,000, in this manner: Hensley, Reading & Co. should pay in $5,000—Aguirre and myself $10,000." I then asked Reading, who would go supercargo, and suggested one of his partners, Jacob R. Snyder.

In two days from that time, the bark was on her way to Portland, with a spanking breeze at her stern from the southeast. She arrived at the Columbia river and went to Portland in remarkably quick time. Three or four days after her arrival, Mr. Snyder succeeded in buying a full cargo of flour for the vessel, at reasonable prices. While she was getting ready to start on the return voyage the Columbia river froze over, and the vessel remained from December, 1848, to April, 1849, walled in by ice. During the time the bark was detained, many vessels arrived from Chili with flour. The consequence was, when our flour reached here it had no price in the market. It was sent in the vessel to Sacramento, and jobbed out at fair prices, so that we lost no money, but made some profit.

P. B. Reading was the Whig candidate for Governor of California, in the election of 1851, against John Bigler, the Democratic candidate for the same office. Being a Whig, I voted for the former, who was defeated by Bigler.

The American flag was raised at Yerba Buena, by Captain Montgomery, of the "Portsmouth," as before stated, July 9th, 1846.

The ship "Brooklyn," Captain Richardson, arrived from New York about the last of the same month. The vessel brought passengers to the number of two hundred and thirty, and I was the first aboard after she dropped anchor, to welcome the new comers to our embryo American town. It was on this occasion I met Sam. Brannan for the first time, who was a passenger. The "Brooklyn" came with an organized military company, at the head of which was Brannan as its leader. They arrived a little too late for their object—to hoist our national standard; as the good work had already been accomplished by our squadron.

Many of the new comers pitched their tents on a lot of mine, on Washington street near Montgomery. These additions to our small village, proved to be desirable, as they were an industrious, hard-working and thrifty class of people, intelligent and sober. Among them were carpenters and house builders. After their arrival, the echoes of mechanics' hammers vibrated through the sand hills of Yerba Buena. From every direction in the village, the signs of progress under the change and that of the American system, became apparent.

Soon after Brannan's arrival, he commenced business in a spirit of push and energy; and at once manifested an interest in California's prosperity which he has assisted materially to develop and in promoting her varied resources. He was always found at the front, with open purse, in any enterprise to forward the interest of the State of his adoption. If there is a man who is deserving of recognition from the State of California and the city of San Francisco, it is Sam Brannan. He assisted to lay the corner-stone of the city's commercial greatness.

FIRST PUBLIC SCHOOL HOUSE IN SAN FRANCISCO, SITUATED ON PORTSMOUTH SQUARE, AND FIRST USED APRIL 3, 1848

After the discovery of gold, at Sutter's mill-race in January 1848, and the news had spread over the Pacific Ocean, vessels began to come in with merchandise, from Honolulu, Mazatlan, San Blas, Valparaiso, Callao, Chinese and other Pacific ports.

By the time the first steamer arrived from Panama with eastern passengers, there were already anchored in the bay of San Franicsco, quite a fleet of vessels of nearly all nations, which had come to receive their share of the newly discovered treasure, in exchange for goods, which were in much demand to supply the wants of those who had gone in great numbers to the mines from all portions of the department, and of the passengers by vessels. In the month of June, 1848, two miners came to my store with fine scale gold dust. I had seen similar gold from the San Fernando mines in Los Angeles county. But withal I was in doubt as to the genuineness of the bright metal before me. The miners and myself called on James C.

Ward, a neighboring merchant. He proved to be incompetent to determine whether it was gold or not. We four men went to Buckalew, a jeweler and watchmaker. Mr. Buckalew applied the *aqua fortis,* and at once pronounced the metal pure gold. I bought the dust, over one hundred dollars' worth, at sixteen dollars per ounce, from the two miners, and paid them half in coin and half in goods.

*This gold was the first to arrive in San Francisco to be used in trade and I was the first purchaser of the product of the mines. All merchants transacted an immense business, and there was no trouble in selling goods, if we had them to sell. The receipts of gold from the mines was so great, and the means of weighing it so limited, that we had trouble from the scarcity of scales. Buckalew being the only maker of scales was kept at work from morning till night manufacturing to fill orders.

Gold and silver coin became very scarce in the market. The duties on goods from foreign ports, had to be paid in coin, and the merchants were unable to comply with the custom laws. An arrangement was made with the Collector of the Port, to receive gold dust on deposit from them, at ten dollars per ounce, for duties, redeemable at the end of sixty days with coin. Most of the gold pledged for duties was sold at auction by the government, at the expiration of the time, for about ten dollars per ounce, and less in some instances. This action of the government was a great hardship to the merchants, as they incurred a loss of six dollars for each ounce thus sold, and particularly when it was known at the Treasury Department in Washington, that the true value of the gold was from eighteen to twenty dollars per ounce, assayed and made into coin at the Mint in Philadelphia.

David Carter, of Boston, in the summer of 1848, formed a copartnership with me, for carrying on commercial business, between California and the Eastern States. Mr. Carter left here in the fall of 1848, by way of Central America. He carried with him about thirty thousand dollars in gold dust, to be coined at the United States Mint above named, and it was the first gold coined at that time from California. I had a small interest in this gold shipment.

One bright morning in February, 1849, the California, the first steamer from New York arrived here from Panama with the first gold-seekers from the Atlantic States. As she rounded Telegraph Hill, the vessel careened to the shore side, from the rush of passengers to get a look at the town. The United States Pacific naval squadron was anchored between Telegraph and Rincon Hills. Commodore Jones' flag-ship was the "Ohio." The other vessels were the "Portsmouth," "St. Mary," "Cyane," "Dale" and "Warren."

*Samuel Brannan brought the first samples of gold to San Francisco, May 15, 1848.

The sight of the steamer, with her immense load of humanity, inspired the Commodore to order a general salute from the vessels of the fleet simultaneously. After the first broadsides from them they were enveloped in a cloud of smoke, until the end of the greeting of twenty-one guns from each ship. The handling of the guns was so admirable that the firing appeared as if from one only. The echoes of the cannonading vibrated among the hills and valleys of the surrounding country of the bay, as heralding the future greatness of California.

Commodore Jones, who first planted the American flag in California, in 1842, was the first to fire the memorable salute in the bay of San Francisco welcoming the immigrants who came subsequent to the discovery of gold. The Commodore was proud of being the first of our naval officers to welcome the new immigration that subsequently laid the foundation of California, destined to assume the front rank among the States of the Union. The scene is fresh in my mind; the view of the spectacle being grand, inspiring and awakening the deepest enthusiasm. In this steamer came the agent, Alfred Robinson, of the Pacific Mail Steamship Company, which had just been organized in New York; and the "California" was the first vessel built by that Company and sent out to the Pacific coast as the forerunner of a commercial fleet propelled by steam.

Don Alfredo Robinson came to California in the ship "Brookline," of Boston, in 1829, as assistant supercargo. He arrived at Monterey and in the same year came to San Francisco. He has now attained the ripe age of over four score years and is mentally and physically hale and strong, with the exception that he has become almost totally blind. Of the very earliest settlers of California Mr. Robinson stands first on the list of the few remaining argonauts. Jacob P. Leese comes second, J. J. Warner, number three, (if he is still living) and the writer, number four. It will not take many more years before the names here mentioned will disappear, as things of the past (1889).

Immediately below my home, north of Jackson and west of Stockton streets, there existed a hollow or little valley, with low, rolling hills on each side. In it in the summer of 1849, quite a village of tents was temporarily inhabited by people from all parts of the world, preparatory to departing for the mines. One night in the early hours of morning my slumber was disturbed by screams of women and children from the hamlet of canvas. While I was reflecting, in a half awake and half asleep condition, as if emerging from a dream or nightmare, I heard a sharp knock at the door of my dwelling. In opening it, there stood before me several women, trembling with fright. They had escaped from their temporary homes; the poor creatures came to my house for protection, which I gave them. One of the number, who proved to be a cultivated Chilean lady, Doña Rosa Gaskell, asked my wife to permit them to remain for the rest of the night. Mrs. Gaskell was terribly alarmed for her life. Her husband had gone to the mines. During the melee at the scene of disturbance, the tents and their fixtures were destroyed, and many persons were injured bodily by the hands of a band of ruffians who styled themselves the "Hounds."

The town became alarmed and excited over this affair, and energetic measures were at once adopted to prevent a repetition of the outrage by these desperadoes. Mr. Samuel Brannan took the lead in the matter. Under his directions we organized patrols, and the town was divided into districts, each district guarded by a body of men under arms. I was appointed the head of seven, to guard north of Washington and east of Montgomery streets, running to the bay from these thoroughfares. For several weeks I shouldered one of Uncle Sam's shining muskets with bayonet, parading all night near the habitations of the roughest elements of the town.

While we were protecting the place Mr. Brannan was active and did good work. The breakers-of-the peace were arrested as fast as they were found and identified. They were placed on board the sloop-of-war "Warren," in irons, preparatory to their trial by a Court of the Territory.

Mr. and Mrs. C. V. Gillespie arrived here in the American brig "Eagle," from Canton, in the beginning of February, 1848. With this vessel another American lady was added to the number of the very few that were already here, who with the male population were all very glad to welcome this estimable lady to the new American town.

Hall McAllister brought letters of introduction to Mr. Gillespie from the East, at the time when the "Hound" excitement was at its highest pitch. Horace Hawes was the prosecuting attorney against the evil-doers and disturbers of the tranquility of the town. C. V. Gillespie, who was a member of the committee of safety, suggested to Mr. Hawes the name of Mr. McAllister as a young man of talent and learned in the profession of the law, to be associated with him in the prosecution of the "Hounds." This was the cause of his participating in those events. He prosecuted the prisoners for the Territory with marked ability. That trial established his legal talent, which developed up to the time of his demise, and stamped him the foremost barrister of the city of San Francisco and of the State of his adoption. I may safely remark here, that he probably had no superior in the Union in the law, considering that Mr. McAllister was master of all branches of practice in his profession. The "Hounds" were convicted after a stubborn and able defence by their attorney, Myron Norton. R. M. Sherman and Wm. H. Tillinghast were appointed a committee, to board the "Warren," to interview some of the prisoners.

Some years after this occurrence, a young lady, a cousin of Sherman, met an older lady accidentally in New York. The subject of their conversation turned on California. The former mentioned that she had a cousin in California named Richard M. Sherman. The latter replied that she was familiar with a part of the early history of the Golden State. She had a son, by the name of Higgins, who was one of the gang of "Hounds," that were tried and convicted for the crime above named. It was a singular coincidence, that Sherman who was active in the exciting event and had waited on Higgins in his official capacity, as a committeeman, was a relative of the young woman. Higgins, the "Hound," was the son of the older lady.

The pressure was great for the first twelve months or more after the discovery of gold, to transport passengers and goods more speedily to the mines. The only transporters of passengers and goods were sailing schooners and launches. Early in 1849, Mr. John Parrott suggested to me the project of building a steam vessel, for commerce on these inland waters. Captain William A. Richardson, John Parrott and myself were to form a copartnership, with a cash capital of $45,000, as a beginning for our enterprise. Mr. Parrott was to leave for New York immediately, and to contract with a builder for a steamboat of about 200 tons capacity, to ply between San Francisco and Sacramento, with passengers and freight. He departed on the U. S. flagship "Ohio," by way of Mazatlan, for New York, in February, 1849; and on arriving there, he found that Jim Blair was then constructing a stern-wheel boat for the bay of San Francisco and rivers adjacent thereto. In a letter from Mr. Parrott to Richardson and myself, he discouraged our scheme, for the reason that the steamer already under construction for Blair would supply the demand of the increasing trade with the interior, and he thought that our undertaking would prove financially disastrous.

This news was anything but pleasant to the captain and myself, as the traffic with the mines had multiplied to such an extent that every man living here was astonished to witness the millions of wealth that were pouring into the town of tents.

I wrote to Mr. Parrott that there was business enough for our steamboat if she was built; yea, and eight or ten more with her, to meet the commercial demands of the bay and its tributaries. In his answer to my letter, he thought that my judgment was erroneous, and that he was right. The project was abandoned, through him, to the injury of himself and his associates. The business would have produced for us hundreds of thousands, if not a million or more of dollars. I am sustained in this assertion by events that transpired subsequently in this line of business.

Richardson and myself got our money back from New York, after waiting a long while. Blair's boat was called "Sutter," after the pioneer of Sacramento Valley, and she did a large and profitable business for her owner.

Mr. Lafayette Maynard was the owner of a part of block of real estate, bounded by Sacramento, Sansome and California streets, which bore his name. He had been a lieutenant in the United States navy, and was familiar with the art of surveying harbors and rivers. He took Wilkes' survey of the Sacramento river, and examined it critically for an object. He went to capitalists in New York, explained and demonstrated to them that it was practicable and feasible for a deep sea steamer of 600 or 800 tons measurement to navigate the river to Sacramento city. The steamer "Senator" was purchased by a syndicate, for the purpose suggested by Maynard, and he was included in the company. At the time of the transaction, she was a packet out of New York, running on the Sound. She departed immediately for San Francisco through the Straits of Magellan, and arrived here early in September, 1849. Samuel Brannan, W. D. M. Howard, (and, I think,) Bezar Simmons, and myself, made up the party of four who boarded her soon after she dropped anchor. Mr. Brannan, who was the originator of the project, was selected by us as our spokesman. He soon made known the object of our visit, and offered the captain or agent of the steamer the large sum of $250,000, in gold dust, at sixteen dollars per ounce, for her sale to us. This offer was rejected with smiles, by those representing the steamer. Mr. Brannan again asked them what would they take for the vessel. The answer came that she was not for sale. So ended our trip to the most historic vessel of the days of forty-nine.

It was often remarked that the "Senator" had carried enough gold from Sacramento to San Francisco to sink her two or three times over with the weight of the precious metal. Add to this the passage and freight money, the former two ounces for the trip, and the latter from forty dollars to eighty dollars per ton, and the amount received was enormous. It would probably take two or three similar steamers to convey the freighted gold, and the gold and silver coin she had earned for her owners during the height of our gold production.

The "Old Senator," by which name she was familiarly known, is now moored in the waters of Australia, as a coal vessel. Had she possessed intelligence, she might have been too proud of her nationality, and for her deeds of the past in the accumulation of wealth to the country of her birth, to become a naturalized subject of a British colony, by the change of flags.

Had Mr. Parrott exercised his known foresight and great business ability, our steamboat would have been one of the early conveyances on the waters of the bay of San Francisco, in competing for our pro rata of the enormous business, that was done principally by a few vessels moved by steam, of a commerce that excited the business men of the known world.

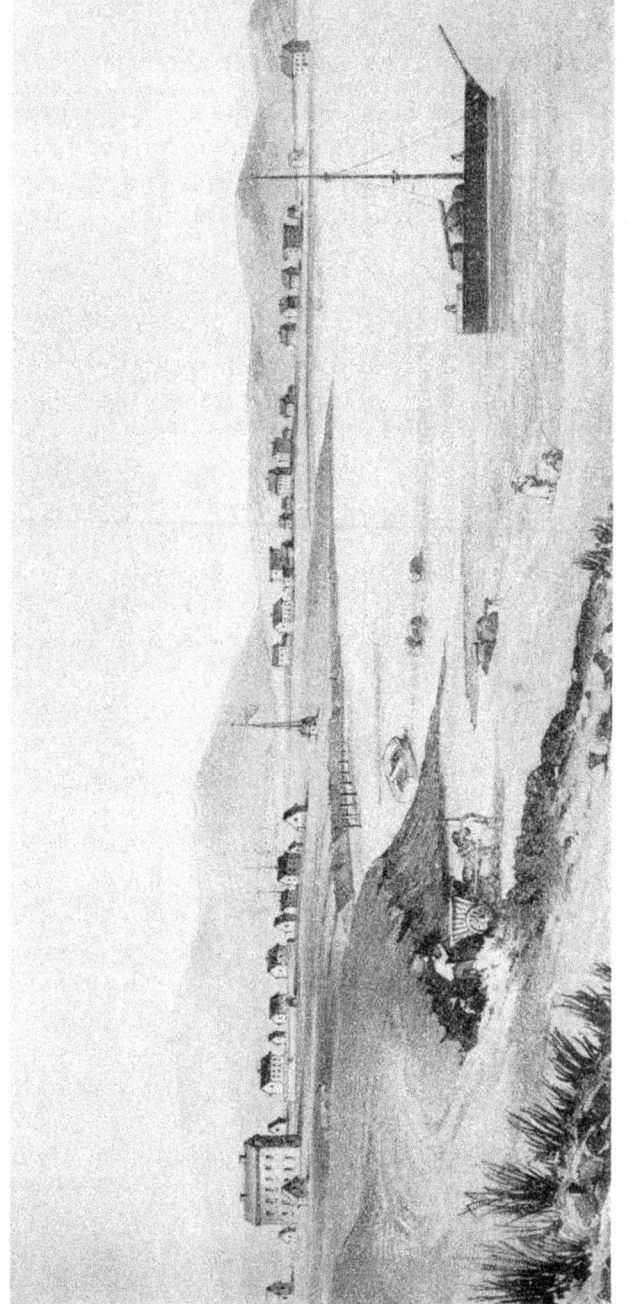

CITY OF BENICIA, 1854

Under the name "Francisca," Robert Semple and General Mariano G. Vallejo with Thomas O. Larkin projected here the city which they and many of the higher officers of both the Army and Navy felt would supplant the growing settlement of Yerba Buena. General Vallejo's wife was named Francisca Benicia; hence the choice of Benicia instead of Francisca when Alcalde Washington A. Bartlett in 1847 decreed that Yerba Buena should be known in the future by the ancient name of San Francisco.

CHAPTER LXIII
Commodore Jones Extols Benicia in Vain

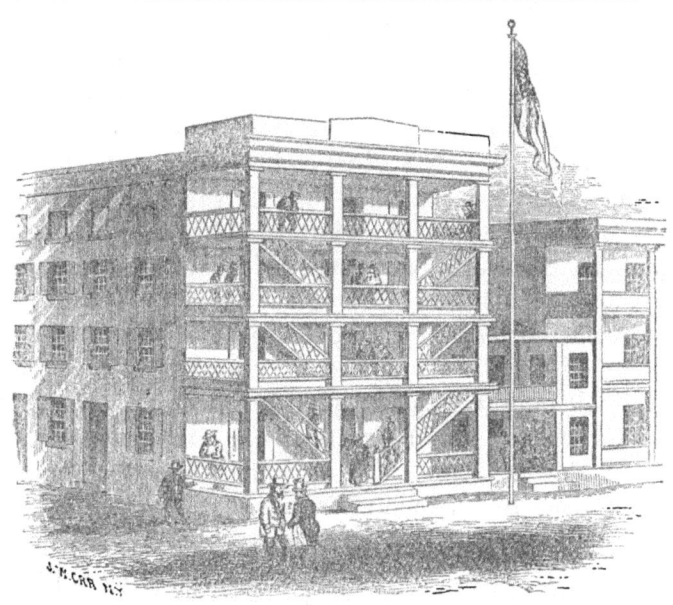

UNITED STATES CUSTOM HOUSE, NORTHWEST CORNER CALIFORNIA
AND MONTGOMERY STREETS, OWNED BY WILLIAM HEATH DAVIS,
DESTROYED IN FIRE OF MAY 4, 1851

THE first brick building of more than one story erected in San Francisco was commenced in September, 1849, by the writer, at the northwest corner of Montgomery and California streets; forty feet on the first and eighty feet on the latter street, four stories high, with a cellar. The bricks and cement, and other materials, were brought from Boston. The winter of 1849-'50 was so rainy that the work on the structure was stopped early in November, and re-commenced in April, 1850.

The rains were heavy, and teaming difficult on Montgomery between California and Jackson streets, and California, Sacramento, Clay, Washington and Jackson streets. The miniature city of that day was a lake of mud. To enable the pedestrians to move about, boxes of Virginia tobacco and kegs of New England nails were placed along the streets, about a foot or two apart, for sidewalks. On these goods the people traveled, by leaping from a box to a keg, and from a keg of nails to a box of tobacco, and thus the inhabitants managed to reach their places of business and their homes. The influx of tobacco and nails was so great that the articles had no market value, but they were of use for the purposes above described.

One lovely morning in April, 1850, Commodore Jones approached me where my building was being put up, and said he had a business proposition for my consideration. The naval commander of the Pacific squadron immediately gave me the details of it; which was for me to stop building, and to undo what had been done; and he would transport all the materials of my structure to Benicia in one of his ships of war, free of charge for freight.

He and other Benicians were to deed me a very eligible piece of real estate in the city of the Carquinez free of cost, conditioned that I should erect a large brick building on the site. The Commodore went into the particulars of the commercial advantages of Benicia over San Francisco, in extended and able remarks, such as a man of talent and of vast information would surely make. After listening to the historical naval officer's praises of the interior deep sea harbor, with all due respect to his high rank, I said: "I beg to differ with you. In my judgment San Francisco is destined to be the harbor and business emporium on the Bay of San Francisco, from her geographical position and accessibility for vessels from the ocean." I thanked the Commodore for having spent more than an hour in attempting to convince me from his standpoint of the superior advantages possessed by Benicia for being the future big city of California, but was compelled to differ with him nevertheless. At this time and previously, there had been a vigorous move on the part of a few men, to locate San Francisco at Benicia for all time, as the great city on the waters of San Francisco Bay. Among the schemers were Robert Semple, General Vallejo, Thomas O. Larkin, Henry D. Cook, William M. Steuart, and the heads of the United States army and navy on the coast. I was talked to by some of the parties above named, before Commodore Jones interviewed me who made propositions of magnitude in my interest, from their view of the subject. They wanted me to give up the city that I had assisted to build from its infancy, and to establish my large business at Benicia; which was something that I could not accede to.

That building after it was finished, I leased to the United States Government in June, 1850, for a Custom House. The rental was to be three thousand dollars per month, or thirty-six thousand dollars per year for three years to run. In the great fire of May, 1851, the Custom House

LOOKING SOUTH ALONG MONTGOMERY FROM TELEGRAPH HILL
AFTER FIRE OF MAY 4, 1851

succumbed to the devouring element; also other buildings and merchandise I owned, both of which produced me an income of over ten thousand dollars monthly, before the fire. The Collector retained possession of the premises for over a month, guarding the treasure which was saved in the vault, which proved to be thoroughly fireproof. The structure was filled with bonded goods from cellar to top. The lease terminated with the destruction of the building, and ended one of my monthly incomes. But I demanded of the Collector pay for the detention of the premises after the fire, the sum of $6,000. He referred me to the Treasury Department at Washington for my compensation. In the course of many months, I received three thousand dollars through Colonel J. D. Stevenson, who was my attorney in the matter.

Thomas Butler King was the Collector of the Port at that time. The removal of the treasure from the ruins of my building, to the new custom-house, Palmer, Cook & Co's. old banking house, northwest corner of Kearny and Washington streets, constituted a procession of about fifty armed men, which was headed by the Collector with pistol in hand. This action on the part of King, was ridiculed and censured by the citizens as doubting the honesty of the inhabitants of the young city. The numerous law-abiding citizens that lined Montgomery street to view the transfer of the treasure, would have protected the Government funds from any attack that might have been made, without the aid of the accompanying guard.

One evening in December, 1848, Señor Aguirre and myself were seated by a blazing fire, in the sitting room of my home in San Francisco. The wind was blowing from the southeast, the windows of the dwelling rattled with the storm, and the piazza was drenched by the spattering of the silvery drops that fell from the dark clouds overhead. I said to Don José Antonio, that the "Jóven Guipuzcoana" sailed but a week or two since for Oregon, for a cargo of flour, and I had another business proposition in my mind, to make for his consideration:—"You and I both have money lying idle. Let us arrange a voyage to China, for a cargo of Chinese goods, for this market." He replied that he had confidence in my business ability, and any suggestion coming from me he would gladly assist to carry out. I said, "Let us charter the ship Rhone for the object and I will prevail on her owners to join us."

Mr. Aguirre was an old merchant that traded between Mexico and China, mentioned previously, and was familiar with the cost of goods in China; also with the prices of the articles when sold here. I asked him what capital we would require for the expedition. He said, not less than $100,000, to make it profitable and that $120,000 would be still better. I replied, "All right; we will put in $40,000, and I think Finley, Johnson & Co. will invest $40,000; and I am sure Cross, Hobson & Co., will make up the balance." He suggested that I had better move in the matter soon. The following day I arranged with the two firms above named, and by noon the Rhone was chartered. The beginning of January, 1849, the American ship Rhone departed for Canton *via* Honolulu. She took with her $120,000 in gold dust at sixteen dollars per ounce, less $4,000 which Cross, Hobson & Co. were unable to provide to make up the full amount of their portion.

Mr. Finley who was also an old China trader between Baltimore and China, went as supercargo, to attend to the business of the Rhone. The ship returned to San Francisco in the summer of 1849 with a cargo of goods.

Mr. Finley had a written instruction, on the eve of his departure, to invest the funds under his charge wholly for China goods and no other. About half of the cargo proved to be European and American goods, and the market of San Francisco was glutted with such articles. The entire cargo of the vessel was sold peremptorily at auction by Brannan & Osborn. During the sale W. D. M. Howard and I were standing side by side and offering bids to the auctioneer. Mr. Howard said to me, "Why, if the invoice of the Rhone had all been Chinese goods, the Rhone's cargo would have yielded you a very large profit, over the capital you invested." The owners of the cargo made a profit of more than one hundred per cent. on the Chinese goods, but lost on the other goods, in consequence of Finley's acting contrary to his instructions. Had Mr. Finley followed the old adage, "Obey orders or break owners," the rule would have been reversed in this instance to: "Obey orders and enrich owners."

Let me remark right here, that it was the unanimous wish of the charterers of the Rhone, that I should go as supercargo instead of Finley, and the latter urged me over and over to accept the appointment, and relieve him of the responsibility of the undertaking. Had I gone one thing is certain, I would have obeyed my instructions to the letter. In the end however we lost no money, but made a profit.

In the summer of 1849, and after the arrival of the ship Rhone from Canton, my friend Aguirre conceived the idea for a business voyage to the Southern ports of California. He had in my safe between $100,000 and $200,000 in doubloons and gold dust, and he was eager to do something with it.

The bark Rochelle, of Boston, was in port, and Aguirre wanted me to charter her for our joint account, and I did so. Captain John Paty was in town without a ship, and he was engaged for master of the vessel. In a short time she was filled with goods, on freight for different points on the coast, and with merchandise on our own account. She sailed for Monterey, and after she had passed Point Pinos in the night, the wind shifted to the southeast. In order to reach the anchorage of Monterey, she had to make tacks, and beat against the wind. In standing in towards the shore on which were the picnic grounds of olden times, south of Point Pinos, she struck on a rocky point, in the darkness and sprung a leak. Captain Paty, however, managed to get her off and came to anchor. In a few days after the accident, a courier arrived from Monterey, with letters from Aguirre and Paty, informing me of the mishap. At that time I was the owner of a Baltimore-built bark of about three hundred tons burden, named Hortensia, which was lying here in the stream, preparatory to a departure later in the year for Valparaiso in ballast for a cargo of flour, on my own account for this market. This unexpected news changed the programme of the Hortensia's intended voyage to Chile. In twenty-four hours after the receipt of my mail from Monterey, the Hortensia was on her way to the scene of the disaster, with her owner as passenger. The cargo of the disabled vessel was transferred to the Hortensia and she performed the delivery of the goods at ports south of Monterey as far as San Diego. The Rochelle venture after all the serious and costly accident proved profitable finally.

This was the first misfortune that had occurred to Captain Paty during his long career on the coast as mariner and shipmaster. He looked very much depressed, when he reached the deck of the Hortensia, after we had dropped anchor. The misfortune of the Rochelle was a good thing for the Hortensia, as it proved afterward. The influx of flour from Chile during the winter of 1849-50 was so great that its price came down, and the shippers of the article suffered heavy losses.

In 1850 and part of 1851, Mrs. Davis lived at San Diego in her own house. During a visit to her in the latter year, I was invited by a nephew of one of the early governors of California, to join him and his brothers, in a gold-hunting expedition to Lower California. Our company consisted of the three Argüellos, myself, two servants, and two pack mules, for our baggage and provisions. During our journey through the sparsely populated country, to the Mission of Santo Tomás, we camped every night near a spring or stream of running water. Don Ramon Argüello, who acted as our guide, would pitch our tents, after the ground had been cleared of brushes and scrub oak, in a circle of about 300 feet circumference, the boundary of which was encircled with a rim of fire. This was done to protect us from nightly attacks of rattlesnakes while we slept. The territory was infested with these repulsive and dangerous reptiles. Every day during our march, Don Ramon would kill, on an average, a dozen of these snakes. He would eat a portion of their bodies, after it was broiled over a hot fire, and often remarked to me, that it was more nutritious than the meat of a fat chicken. He tried to prevail on his brothers, to share with him in his "tidbits," as he called them.

We stopped as we moved along at the rancheros' old adobes, and received their hospitalities—a repetition of the treatment of strangers in Upper California in the days gone by. We drank very good native wine, from the vineyards of the pioneers of the department. We were several days in reaching Santo Tomás, where we camped in the ancient olive orchard of the Mission, under the shade of its trees. The trees were lofty, their planting having been the work of the early missionaries, more than a century before my visit there.

Here Don Manuel Castro who was the military commander of this part of the country, joined our party, with five soldiers and a corporal, as an escort, to our journey of discovery. General Castro also provided us with an Indian, who was to interpret for us, with an old chief, for whom we were in search, to obtain information of the hidden bonanza.

The expedition arrived at Trinidad, a valley in a mountain of over four thousand feet above the level of the sea, twenty to thirty miles back from the Pacific Ocean. Here we dispatched the interpreter with another Indian for Chief Zapaje. In three days time our couriers returned with the chief and other aborigines. Our camp fed them well, before our big talk took place over the object of our visit, with Zapaje. General Castro was a talented man and a man of persuasive power of language. He commenced first to convince the chief, that if he would make known the coveted spot and uncover it to us, he would present him with a *manada* of mares, ten saddle horses, and twenty-five head of cows for himself and his tribe. The old man was unmoved with this generous proposition from Castro. The latter asked him through the interpreter, what was his objection to lead us where the placer existed after this offer of so much property. He replied that more than seventy years ago, he was instructed by the Fathers of Santo Tomás never to divulge to any one, outside of the Church, the covered wealth of Lower California; if he did he would incur the wrath of God, and would die instantly. These early teachings of the Fathers were indelible in the minds of these Christianized Mission Indians, who were deeply impressed with the Church notions, of keeping the world ignorant of the whereabouts of this buried ore.

Don Santiaguito Argüello next argued with the chief, to tell him where the gold existed, and offered him one hundred head of cows, one *manada* of mares, and five tame horses, if he would reveal the secret. The chief turned a deaf ear to this proffer, and told the interpreter to tell Señor Argüello, whom he had known when a youth, that he would die soon after telling it.

I was the third to have the final argument with the stubborn Indian. I commenced telling him that I was a merchant of San Francisco, the owner of bales of Turkey red handkerchiefs, calico, brown sheeting, colored blankets, tobacco, and other articles suitable to the Indian tastes of California; if he would show us where the mine was located, I would give him two bales of handkerchiefs, two of calico, two of cotton, fifty pairs of blankets, tobacco and other articles of value; conditioned that he bring us some of the gold first; after that we would meet him at this place with our presents, and follow him with the animals and goods to the location of the placer, where the whole property would be delivered to him. His answer to my liberal proposition was the same as already mentioned.

Here our hopes vanished for discovering the rumored deposits of gold, known to exist in primitive days of missionary regime. It was well known to the early inhabitants of that part of the peninsula, that gold existed; and the priests handled plenty of it, through the Indians of the Missions. But the secret of the deposits was kept by the priests, as a matter of policy and from political and religious convictions; and by the Indians because of their superstitions.

On our way back to San Diego, we were intercepted at the ruins of the Mission of San Vicente by Don Emigdio Vega. He was a member of a prominent family of that name, in Los Angeles County, who were large cattle owners. Señor Vega offered to sell me seven hundred head of tame milch cows, many of them with suckling calves, and fifty head *cabestros*, for seven thousand dollars. I said to him I had no time to spare to go and see his cattle. He referred me to one of the Argüellos who was present. The latter said that he had seen the stock, and that they were large fine cattle. I accepted Vega's offer and bought the animals.

In May, 1852, I visited San Diego, and received from Argüello the cattle I had bought of Vega the year before.

On my way north with the band of cattle, I stopped at Los Angeles about two weeks, during which time I bought of Don Eulogio de Célis, seven hundred large steers for thirteen dollars each. With this purchase it made the drove a large one. The band arrived at San Leandro in August, where they were re-branded and re-earmarked with my iron and earmark. The stock was removed to "San Joaquin" in the fall of 1852, and José Antonio Estudillo, a brother of Mrs. Davis took charge of them. The consideration for his care over my cattle, being one-half of the increase from the cows.

The item telling of the departure of the "Euphemia" with specie consigned to E. & H. Grimes, Oahu, is the subject of an interesting episode detailed in the text. The names of Sutter, Brannan, E. P. Jones, Major P. B. Reading, all appearing in this early issue of San Francisco's first newspaper, are frequently met with in Davis' narrative.

CHAPTER LXIV
Davis Fails to Become Founder of Oakland

PREVIOUS to my departure for Southern California, I had a corral built, large enough to contain my cattle, on my mother-in-law's portion of the Pinole rancho, which I had named "San Joaquin," after the husband of the proprietress of the land she had inherited from her father and mother, Don Ygnacio and Doña Martina Martinez. Mrs. Estudillo added to her interest by purchases from several of her sisters, who were also heirs of the Pinole. In titling the new rancho, I simply added San to the Joaquin, then it became the name of a Saint. The Californians were in the habit generally of naming their ranchos after Saints; probably from religious convictions that the Ruler on High in all things would aid and guide them in their daily pursuits. But it did not save them from the avaricious enemies of the Spanish and Mexican grants.

Señora Doña Juana Estudillo was the possessor of over seven thousand acres of valuable land, a part of the original "Pinole." She had the tract enclosed and improved with good fences and buildings. Under ordinary management it could have been made to produce from rents of the land enough income to have supported Mrs. Estudillo and her children. But the rancho was subsequently sold for thirty-eight thousand dollars.

Probably the present owner and the original purchaser from Mrs. Estudillo of the "San Joaquin" would not sell it for half a million dollars. The Central and Southern Pacific Railroad have acquired rights of way through the estate (1884).

In the end, my cattle speculation proved a success, for many steers were sold in the fall and winter of 1853 and 1854, for fifty, sixty and as high as seventy dollars for each animal. There were many of them stolen from the rancho, for lack of watchfulness on the part of the man who had the supervision of the animals. Schooners and launches came to the beach along the northern boundary of the rancho in the night, and the very vaqueros under pay from Estudillo to guard the cattle against thieves, were the men (villains) delivering to the boats, not only my cattle, but also those that were owned by the Estudillos themselves. My loss in this way amounted to more than ten thousand dollars.

In 1853, the cattle at San Leandro were pretty well hemmed in by the squatters, and deprived of their pasturage, on their native soil. So it was compulsory on the part of the owners, to remove them to "San Joaquin," for grazing, to keep them from dying for want of grass and water.

My cattle and the herd from San Leandro made a rodeo of over four thousand cattle, a very respectable number compared with the round-up of the early days of the department.

Don José Ramon Estudillo, another brother of Mrs. Davis, was fond of the sport of lassoing elk. He told me once that on this identical spot of "San Joaquin," he had seen many of these beasts of the forest grazing with the stock of the Pinole rancho.

After new San Diego was laid out, lumber was wanted for building purposes, by the projectors of the newly made plot, and by others; also by the quarter-master of the post, for government improvements.

About the latter end of the summer of 1850, the brig "Cybele" of three hundred and fifty tons burden, arrived from Portland, Maine, loaded with a cargo of lumber and bricks. Mr. Bond of the firm of Hussey, Bond & Hale, offered me soon after the "Cybele" dropped anchor, the brig with her load of three hundred thousand feet of pine lumber, eight or ten houses already framed, and forty thousand bricks, for ten thousand dollars, and I bought the vessel and cargo just as she came from the East. The following day she sailed for San Diego, with the same captain that brought her to San Francisco.

The purchase proved profitable. About eighty thousand feet of the same lumber were re-shipped to San Francisco from San Diego in the winter of 1851-52, and I realized from it seventy dollars per thousand feet, free of freight. At the time of the arrival of the "Cybele," building materials were a glut in the market of San Francisco. The vessel was similar to the "Euphemia," as a great carrier, for her tonnage.

It was evident after the change of flag that the growth of San Francisco would be rapid, even without subsequent discovery of gold and the influx of immigration caused by it. The resources of the department were endless, as an agricultural and horticultural country; also, for grazing purposes. The latter had been demonstrated by the early settlers under the Mexican rule. This prospective wealth of California was sufficient to build and support one large city on the coast San Francisco, being geographically well situated for the commerce of the world, with her rich country bordering on the bay, and rich valleys accessible by water.

In my travels around the bay on business, I had observed a picturesque spot for a town on the estuary of San Antonio, due east from San Francisco. The site was known in early times as Encinal de Temescal, on Vicente Peralta's portion of the division of the Rancho San Antonio, segregated by Don Luis Peralta, his father. This site is the present city of Oakland.

My relation with Don Vicente was good, socially and commercially. In the fall of 1846, he was in my store making purchases. I told him I had a proposition to make for his consideration, and I desired him to dine with me that evening. After dinner I broached the matter, by saying to him: "You are the owner of the Encinal de Temescal, and there is a spot on that part of your rancho that pleases me for a town." He wanted to know the exact location of the place, and I pointed it out to him on a rough map I had prepared for the purpose. I offered him five thousand dollars cash for two-thirds of the Encinal, to build a church of his faith, also to construct a wharf and run a ferry-boat from San Francisco to the intended town, all of which to be at my cost and expense. Whenever sales of lots were made, we would both sign the deeds, and each take his pro rata of the money. Don Vicente, in reply to my talk, said that he would take the matter under advisement and let me know.

He inquired the extent of the land I sought to purchase. I described it to him on my sketch, which made Fifteenth street from the bay to Lake Merritt the northern boundary, and thence from Lake Merritt, following the meandering of the shore boundary of the present city of Oakland to the intersection of Fifteenth street with the shore line of the bay of San Francisco. When we met again, Don Vicente was not prepared to give me an answer.

While my mind was full of my project, I interviewed and explained to W. D. M. Howard, Sam. Brannan, Henry Mellus, Alcalde Hyde, James C. Ward, Wm. A. Leidesdorff, Robert Ridley, Frank Ward, Hiram Grimes, Wm. M. Smith, Robert A. Parker, Francisco Guerrero, Josiah Belden, Bezar Simmons, C. L. Ross, R. M. Sherman, and many others of the leading citizens of San Francisco, my programme for a "Brooklyn" for San Francisco—an outlet for the coming city. Each of these gentlemen was willing and anxious to buy a block or more of land for a retreat so near the metropolis, whenever I completed my arrangements with Peralta, and mapped the town.

During my numerous conversations with him at various times on the subject before me, I told him that if he declined to accept my generous offer, he would suffer essentially, from a business standpoint; that his land would be squatted on, and his cattle slaughtered without his knowledge at night by evil-doers, and the meat shipped to San Francisco and sold.

(Beef was selling here at retail from three-quarters of a dollar to one dollar per pound. I paid the latter price to supply my table with meat in the winter of 1849-'50.) That if he sold me the land I would have the tract inclosed at once with a good fence; I would start the town with the best and wealthiest people of San Francisco, which would be a body-guard against the appropriation of his property without his knowledge and consent. "Well," he said, "I must get the consent of my father for my action in the matter." This was simply done to put me off, as he hated to part with any land, although convinced that it would be for his benefit to put some of his possessions into money. It was the old notion of the big rancheros of the department to have leagues of land, with thousands of animals.

I went to see his father at the city of San José, accompanied by James Alex. Forbes (British vice-Consul for California, who was married to a sister of Mrs. Vicente Peralta,) who knew the old man well. Old Peralta said that the land I desired to buy from his son Vicente absolutely belonged to the latter. I preserved in my project year after year, to induce Don Vicente to yield to my liberal proffer, as I considered I was doing him a kindness. But it was of no avail, and the stubborn man stood alone in his singular notion, against the judgment and advice of his good wife, of the British vice-Consul (his brother-in-law), of the Catholic priest, and other friends of Don Vicente, all of whom advised him to accept my proposition by all means.

In the meantime, boatmen from San Francisco were bringing meat from the cattle belonging to Vicente Peralta to the city. These cattle were killed with rifles in the night, under the shadow of the Encinal, by parties who had already squatted on his lands. At one time Peralta and a vaquero came suddenly on a party of men, in the night, who were quartering a beef, preparatory to shipment to San Francisco. The squatters immediately pointed their guns at Peralta and his vaquero, who departed, in order to save their lives. This slaughtering of his animals began as early as 1848, before the discovery of gold. In the fore-part of 1850 I made my last call on Don Vicente on this business, to renew once more my offer. At this time the Encinal de Temescal was well covered with squatters. But I received the same reply as before. Probably the loss to Peralta in cattle would exceed one hundred thousand dollars. I have heard it estimated by others much above my figures.

He sold the site that I wanted to buy from him in the fall of 1850, to Colonel Jack Hays, Major John C. Caperton, Col. Irving, Alexander Cost, John Freaner and others, for eleven thousand dollars, after spending more than the amount he received, in fruitless lawsuits, for the possession of his lands from the squatters. Everything that I had predicted to Peralta, several years before the date above named, proved to be a reality, and he lost a large fortune by his stupidity, in refusing to have me associated with him in the ownership of some of his land. I had selected the best men in San Francisco, as founders of the new town I had conceived to build. Probably we would have prevented Carpentier, Adams, Moon and others, from becoming citizens of the town, adverse to our title.

Several years after the above event, one bright spring morning, I met Don Vicente accidentally on Broadway in Oakland. He was glad to see me, and invited me to a costly French breakfast. During our enjoyable meal, he referred to our old social and business relations, and at last he broke out with an expression in his own language: *"Yo fui muy tonto, de no aver aceptado su proposicion, tocante al Encinal de Temescal."* (I was very foolish not to have accepted your proposition, in regard to the Encinal de Temescal.) In reply I said to him: *"Es inutil de llorar por leche derramada."* (It is useless to cry over milk already spilt.)

The following narrative concerning an historical Rancho in Alameda County, is a fair illustration of certain events throughout the State generally, after the change of government, in respect to the difficulties and annoyances endured by the early settlers, and legal owners of the land and rightful possessors, in retaining their homes from the grasp of unscrupulous squatters and adventurers.

In 1834 and 1835, Don José Joaquin Estudillo was living at the Presidio of San Francisco, and was elected first-alcalde of the district at the time. In the latter part of 1835 or the beginning of 1836, he removed to Rancho Pinole, and in the same year he located with his family at San Leandro.

José Joaquin Estudillo settled on the Rancho San Leandro in 1836. He first obtained a written permit from the governor of the department to occupy the land. After he had located there with his family, he petitioned Governor Alvarado for a title. While the Governor had the matter under consideration, Guillermo Castro, who owned the adjoining rancho San Lorenzo of six leagues to the east of San Leandro, was intriguing with Alvarado to obtain a grant of the same land. Governor Alvarado had married a first cousin of Castro. Although the former was on intimate terms with Estudillo, the governor was rather inclined to favor his cousin.

Estudillo and Castro were both summoned by the governor to appear before him, to determine the petitions of the two applicants. Estudillo triumphed over Castro in the controversy. The former received his title papers in 1842 for one league of land, more or less, within and according to the following boundaries: on the west the Bay of San Francisco, on the north the arroyo (creek) San Leandro, on the east the first ridge of mountains or hills, and on the south the arroyo San Lorenzo. The consideration of the grant was the military services rendered by the grantee to his country. At the time that Don Joaquin settled on this land, he commenced with three hundred vaquillas (heifers) to breed from. On his death in 1852, he left to his heirs about three thousand head of cattle, the increase of the original number after those he used and sold. Señor Estudillo had a peculiar idea of breeding white cattle; it was that it would enable him to see his stock at a great distance. In his large herd you could observe them more distinctly from their whiteness over the other cattle of the rancho.

I well remember the occasion of the visit of Doña Martina, the mother of Mrs. Estudillo to San Leandro in 1850. Mrs. Martinez viewed the rancho of San Leandro from the cupola of her daughter's residence. She admired Don Joaquin's idea of breeding white cattle, because she saw they could be distinguished when far away. This lady was the owner of the Pinole rancho with thousands of animals.

In 1851 men commenced settling on the San Leandro rancho, against the wishes of its legal owner. The squatters had started a story that Estudillo had changed his title papers from one league to two leagues of land. Estudillo's grant called for one league, more or less, in accordance with the diseño (plat) and all the land contained therein belonged to the grantee. It was so decided by the government of the United States, and a patent was issued to Estudillo for seven thousand and ten acres of land. Don José Joaquin was an educated, intelligent and upright man, and he had nothing to gain from a pecuniary standpoint in making the alterations as alleged by the squatters, as the ownership of the tract was already in him. Besides, all title papers before delivery to the grantee were recorded in the government archives at Monterey. The scheme of the enemies of the title was inconsistent with the facts. Squatting first made its appearance along the banks of the San Lorenzo creek, at a place subsequently known as "Squatterville." It soon spread over the entire rancho. From the incipiency of the epidemic, the sons and sons-in-law of Señor Estudillo opposed the evil-doers in seizing the land. At times when we encountered these men in their different holdings, there was a tendency or appearance towards a bloody affray. But among them, there were conservative counsellors and prudent squatters, who invariably prevailed on the rougher class to avoid bloodshed.

Only in one instance was this good advice disregarded. A young, intelligent man from Vermont, by the name of Albert W. Scott, was severely wounded by a pistol shot through the body, by one of the leaders of the squatters named Caleb Wray. Young Scott was helping John C. Pelton, who had been employed by the family to erect fences on the rancho, to prevent further invasion of the land, if possible, by the wrong doers. Scott recovered after many months of good nursing by the mother of the Estudillos. Since his narrow escape from death in protecting the rightful owners of the San Leandro, Mr. Scott has become a prominent merchant in San Francisco, and he has met with good success in business. He has been elected once or twice on the Board of Education in this city; also, he was elected several times as Supervisor of his district in the city.

Once in the spring of 1852, during my temporary absence to the Southern country, the cattle of the rancho that were raised along the San Lorenzo creek and vicinity, suffered greatly for want of water. The squatters had fenced in the entrance to the creek, and prevented the stock from getting to the only place where they could be enabled to drink. John B. Ward happened to know Captain Chisholm, one of the squatters on the creek, and he prevailed upon him, to allow the poor animals to take their daily beverage of pure fresh water, and keep them from dying from thirst.

Some of these men were very malicious, and they often shot and wounded horses and cattle that were raised on the rancho and they always did so under the cover of darkness.

While the controversy with the squatters was progressing in these exciting times of 1851, 1852, 1853 and 1854, Mr. Ward and myself were asked by the lawyers of the rancho to bring them the title papers. Mr. Ward undertook to do so, and carried the papers in his breast coat pocket. On leaving the embarcadero of San Leandro in a small launch, in the night, on his way to San Francisco he assisted the crew of the craft in poling and rowing through the meandering of the creek. While thus engaged, the papers fell out of his pocket into the water, and in the darkness of the night were lost. This created another furore by the enemies of the title. During all these turbulent times the members of the family were in constant fear of their personal safety.

The family instituted several ejectment suits against the squatters. In each trial the jury disagreed, but the majority of them in each case were against the wrong holders of the land. Thereupon John B. Ward, the lawyers and myself, formed a plan, which afterward proved successful in bringing the squatters to terms. An interest in the land was deeded to one Clement Boyreau, an alien. This enabled us to reach the jurisdiction of the United States Circuit Court. The squatters were sued by Boyreau in that Court. The trial lasted several weeks, and Judge Hoffman, who had been sitting with Judge McAllister during the trial, rendered a decision favorable to the plaintiff. This just verdict of the Federal Court overthrew the squatters. They then took leases from the family, pending the decision of the United States Supreme Court, on the appeal regarding the title proper.

After the compromise in 1856 with the squatters, those that occupied the lands at Squatterville, bought at thirty dollars per acre one thousand acres; terms, one-third cash, the remaining unpaid amount in one and two years in equal payments, at ten per cent interest per annum.

In 1854 or 1855 the voters of Alameda county were dissatisfied with the location of the county seat at Alvarado, because it was not central, being within a short distance of the northern boundary of Santa Clara county. There was an election ordered for a choice of the county seat by popular vote. There were several candidates in the field, among them San Leandro, which succeeded over the other competitors. The county seat was removed from Alvarado, and the family mansion was surrendered to the county for a temporary court-house.

This structure was subsequently destroyed by fire in the night. There were many conjectures by the people of the county as to the origin of the fire. Probably it was the work of a vicious man, in order that the county seat might be removed back to Alvarado. After the fire the county seat still remained at San Leandro.

The people of Alvarado eventually succeeded in getting back the records, through some technicality of the law.

But again it was put back to San Leandro, where it remained for years. Subsequently there was a law enacted for its removal to Oakland.

While Mr. Ward and myself were canvassing the county for San Leandro, a plan was submitted by us to Mrs. Estudillo and her children to lay out a town for the coming county seat, if we were successful. San Leandro succeeded in the election, and a deed was executed to the county by the family, of a site for the county buildings. Two hundred acres of land were also reserved and a town was mapped, which is the present town of San Leandro. A fine hotel was built by the family, and named after the founder of San Leandro, "Estudillo."

In 1856 and 1857 which were the last years of my management of the San Leandro, with Ward, the income of the rancho was more than forty thousand dollars yearly for rents of land. This enabled Mr. Ward and myself to discharge most of the liabilities that were incurred in our expensive litigations to recover the productive lands of the rancho. It thereafter produced a large revenue to the family from the very men who originally were adverse to our title. When I ceased to be one of the business managers, I left the estate with more money due from the sales of land, than the rancho was owing for our costly lawsuits. The San Leandro rancho was considered by many good judges of land, the best and richest soil under the canopy of Heaven. The income of it was enough for two, yea, three Estudillo families.

CHAPTER LXV
Which Reads Like Part of Dana's "Two Years Before the Mast"

THERE were several ports in the department, where the hides were transported to the vessels from the shore through the surf, namely: Santa Barbara, San Luis Obispo, Santa Cruz and Monterey (the latter before the wharf was built by the government.) The ship's long boat was moored just outside the rollers, with two sailors on board to receive the cargo from the surf boats. The latter were hauled upon the beach out of the reach of the waves, and loaded, say, with ten hides each. The men would watch for the first, second and third rollers to comb and foam, and before the fourth made its appearance, the boats were pushed into the water energetically, with a man or two on board each to scull to the launch and unload the hides. This was repeated until the latter was loaded and towed to the ship. Between the third and fourth rollers, there is a lull of a minute at the most in the movements of these dangerous billows of the sea. The steersman of a surf boat, in approaching the shore, watched his opportunity for the fourth roller always, and guided her straight for the landing, and went in flying with the breaker, with the stern elevated to an angle with the bow of about thirty degrees, at a velocity of about 12 to 15 miles an hour, and during this exciting speed for a small boat, the oarsmen peaked the ends of their oars to the bottom of the boat whereby their outer ends were elevated beyond the reach of the roaring sea. All this work in landing and embarking for the vessels had to be done quickly, to avoid being swamped by non-compliance with the movements of the swell of the ocean, and for the salvation of life and property in those early days when wharves had not been built. But the crew and others of the ships, became experts with years of experience in voyages up and down the coast of California.

There were other sea ports on the coast from which the rancheros shipped hides and tallow, namely: El Cojo (Point Concepcion,) La Gaviota, and Refugio before mentioned. The Mission of San Juan Capistrano, about sixty miles south of Los Angeles, in the days of her glory in wealth, exported hides and tallow, from the beach known by that name and not far distant from the Mission. These large estates transported their productions in the same way as I have above described. Occasionally the surf landings were rougher than at other times, from the action of the winds. When the beach was very rough after a heavy wind along the coast, tallow in bags was put in the water and towed to the vessels, and dried thoroughly on deck before being placed in the hold.

A native California lady named Señora Doña Josefa Estrada Ábrego, half-sister of Governor Alvarado, resided at Monterey in 1842 (still living there—1889) at the time Commodore Jones raised the American flag over that city. She was one of the most beautiful and intelligent of her sex. Like all her people, she felt deep chagrin that the fortunes of war should bring about a change which would compel her to submit to the new order of things.

Commodore Jones as a gentleman, aside from his official rank, was an acceptable visitor in the families of the native Californians, where he was treated with courtesy, which he reciprocated in kind, as one who fully appreciated the situation, and would not permit himself to be outdone in gallantry.

One day he called at the Ábrego mansion, and alluded to the fine appearance of the assembled children—especially extolling the manly bearing of the boys. Acknowledging the compliments with a smile and graceful obeisance, la Señora said, good naturedly, but with ill-concealed warmth: "I am only sorry, Commodore, my sons were not old enough to offer resistance when you captured our city." To which Commodore Jones replied: "The sentiment does you honor, madame. As lovers of their country, it would certainly have been their duty to do so. "Señora Ábrego, it may be remarked, is at this writing (October, 1888,) 74 years of age and in a remarkable state of mental and physical preservation.

The writer was interviewed by a reporter of the San Diego *Sun*, in December, 1887, to whom he imparted the following information:

"In the year 1831, our three vessels were at La Playa, preparatory to one of them loading for Boston. It was at this time that Mr. Jones removed to the Presidio above Old Town, taking with him a cook from one of the vessels, two stewards and two servants. He rented a home at the Presidio, which was then located at the present ruins, on the eminence just above the palm trees in Old Town. The military headquarters and the soldiers of this department were located there. In fact, all the inhabitants of this section were living at the Presidio. It was quite a lively town. At our house, which was a building of six or eight rooms, we entertained many beautiful Spanish women at dinners, and also at dancing parties. We were there about two or three months, and during that time one of the vessels in the bay was loading for Boston.

"The location of the Presidio was chosen from a military point of view, to protect the citizens of this miniature city, from the ferocious and savage Indians of those days. In the town the inhabitants, soldiers and citizens numbered between 400 and 500. Quite a large place. There was a great deal of gaiety and refinement here. The people were the élite of this portion of the department of California. In the garrison were some Mexican and not a few native Spanish soldiers. What is now called Old Town, was at that date laid out, but was not built for some time thereafter. Whenever a ship came to anchor at La Playa, saddle horses were at once dispatched from the Presidio to bring up the supercargo and captain. The voyage of these vessels from Boston, usually occupied from one hundred and fifty to one hundred and seventy-five days. Monterey being the seat of the government of California, and the port of entry of the department, all vessels were compelled to enter that port first. After paying the necessary duties, they were allowed to trade at any of the towns along the coast, as far south as Lower California.

"I returned to the coast in the Boston bark "Don Quixote," Captain John Paty, in 1838, having been absent about two years. Afterwards I became supercargo of the same vessel. During my two year's absence, the town (or Presidio) on the hill gradually changed its location to where Old Town now exists. The population was about the same, with possibly a natural increase. The rancheros of the vicinity usually kept their families at the Presidio as a protection against the Indians.

"From 1838 to the present time I have been a resident of California.

"Of the new town of San Diego, now the city of San Diego, I can say that I was its founder. In 1850, the American and Mexican commissions, appointed to establish the boundary line, were at Old Town. Andrew B. Gray, the chief engineer and surveyor for the United States, who was with the commission, introduced himself to me one day at Old Town. In February, 1850, he explained to me the advantages of the locality known as "Punta de los Muertos" (Point of the dead), from the circumstance that in the year 1787 a Spanish squadron anchored within a stone's throw of the present site of the city of San Diego. During the stay of the fleet, surveying the bay of San Diego for the first time, several sailors and marines died and were interred on a sand spit, adjacent to where my wharf stood, and was named as above. The piles of my structure are still imbedded in the sands, as if there had been premeditation to mark them as the tomb-marks of those deceased early explorers of the Pacific ocean and of the inlet of San Diego, during the days of Spain's greatness. I have seen "Punta de los Muertos" on Pantoja's chart of his explorations of the waters of the Pacific.

"Messrs. José Antonio Aguirre, Miguel Pedrorena, Andrew B. Gray, T. D. Johns and myself were the projectors and original proprietors of what is now known as the city of San Diego. All my co-proprietors have since died, and I remain alone of the party, and am a witness of the marvellous events and changes that have since transpired in this vicinity during more than a generation.

"The first building in new San Diego was put up by myself as a private residence. The building still stands, being known as the San Diego hotel. I also put up a number of other houses. The cottage built by Andrew B. Gray is still standing, and is called "The Hermitage." George F. Hooper also built a cottage, which is still standing near my house in new San Diego. Under the conditions of our deed, we were to build a substantial wharf and warehouse. The other proprietors of the town deeded to me their interest in Block 20, where the wharf was to be built. The wharf was completed in six months after getting our title in March, 1850, at a cost of $60,000. The piles of the old wharf are still to be seen on the old wharf site in Block 20. At that time I predicted that San Diego would become a great commercial seaport from its fine geographical position and from the fact that it was the only good harbor south of San Francisco. Had it not been for our civil war, railroads would have reached here years before Stanford's road was built, for our wharf was ready for business."

In the winter of 1861-62 unusually heavy rains fell in San Diego County, being thirty inches, the average fall for that section of the State being nine inches.

There were collected together six hundred or seven hundred soldiers of the United States Army, at the military depot in San Diego, from Arizona to go East, and from the East and San Francisco to go to Arizona, to guard the territory against the Confederates. During those unparalled storms, the country around the depot became miry and the travel for heavy teaming impossible. The fuel at the soldiers' quarters gave out, and there was no way to replenish the supply for the troops, to keep them alive with warm food. My wharf and warehouse were still in existence near the depot, and earning me several hundred dollars per month for wharfage and storage. The commanding officer of the post decided to use my property for fire-wood, as a military necessity. Being war time, it was demolished for that purpose, and I lost my income.

A few years after the occurrence, I went to work and collected evidence, in connection with the destruction of the wharf and warehouse. I appealed to Congress with the facts I had obtained for compensation for my loss. The Senate passed a bill unanimously, appropriating sixty thousand dollars as my pay; but it was defeated in the House. At last, Congress enacted a law creating General Saxton (Quartermaster-General of the Pacific Coast) as a Commissioner, to take testimony in California. Several sessions were held in San Francisco; also three or four at San Diego, where the property was located. The testimony before the Commissioner was overwhelming in my behalf. After these proceedings the claim was before the House, Congress after Congress, asking that body to appropriate a just and equitable amount, under the Commissioner's investigation and report, for my reimbursement. In 1884-85 I was voted $6,000 in full payment for the sixty thousand dollars, which the Senate had allowed. While I was in Washington attending to the matter, a member of Congress remarked to me one day:—"The Government has the power to take your property, and you get your pay the best way you can, if you ever get it." This was said by the gentleman in a general way.

The depot block which I have mentioned above was donated to the government, by the original proprietors of New San Diego, at my suggestion, together with another block of land adjacent to the depot, and a wharf privilege for all time. The real estate has become very valuable, as well as the water property, since the rapid growth of the city next to Mexico, on the water front of California.

Speaking of the old historic building, at the military headquarters, which has been the receptacle for government stores since the year 1850: The lamented General Nathaniel Lyon of our civil war times, was quartermaster during the construction of the building. On its completion Captain Lyon said to me one evening: "I am going to give a *bayle* at the building, with the aid of my brother officers. Will you assist me to get up the amusements?" I replied, "Certainly, I will help you with pleasure." Captain Santiaguito Argüello was selected to invite the fair sex, from the old town, from the ranchos, and from the city of the angels. The assemblage of women constituted the élite of San Diego and Los Angeles, which places were noted in early times for their handsome women. The party dispersed in the early hours of morning, guided by the dim light of a constellation to their homes. Thus terminated an enjoyable reunion more than a generation since.

Some three or four years since, I met General Vallejo, in the courtyard of the Palace Hotel, conversing with a few intelligent-looking American tourists. I remarked to him on his youthful appearance, for a man of his ripe age. He said he was the living patriarch of his countrymen, many of whom have passed away at great ages. "Yes, General," I said, "I well remember seeing you at the Presidio of San Francisco in 1833. You were then the comandante of that military post—a young soldier in the Mexican army." The General addressing the strangers, told of his sports of early days. He said right where we all stood, he lassoed a large bear with his reata. He was noted for his horsemanship among the rancheros of the department. The listeners from the East looked at the General with a good deal of curiosity. They were astonished that the man who stood before them, was an actor in the exciting scenes of the primitive days of the Golden State at Yerba Buena which was then only inhabited by the wild beasts of the forest. Now look back two generations, and see at the site of the incident above named, the magnificent Palace Hotel and its beautiful surroundings.

CHAPTER LXVI
In Which the Author Ends His Record

I HAVE mentioned previously that I was on my way from Santa Cruz when the national standard was hoisted over San Francisco on the 9th of July, 1846. I arrived only a day or two after the occurrence. My name appears on the list of the inhabitants of Yerba Buena on the day the American flag waved over the little village for the first time, this place having been my residence for many years.

Several years anterior to 1838 there was a Chinaman on board the brig "Bolivar," Captain Nye, as a servant in the cabin, and he remained on the coast during the stay of the vessel. Probably this man of the Celestial Empire was the first that visited California until the commencement of 1848.

The American brig "Eagle" arrived here from Canton, China, on the 2d of February, 1848, with two Chinamen and a Chinawoman, who were looked upon as curiosities by some of the inhabitants of the growing town of San Francisco, who had never seen people of that nationality before. During the winter of 1848 and 1849 it was observable that Chinamen were multiplying by immigration rapidly. The Mongolians soon availed themselves, in the new field, of their pro rata of the large business that was being done here during the gold excitement. At that particular time there was no expression of alarm from the people of San Francisco that the Chinese would overrun the city of the bay and the State of California.

In the multiplicity of matters upon which I have written, I have unintentionally omitted to narrate the manner in which the merchants generally kept their gold. Among the receptacles for the gold dust were tin pans, tin pots and also a vessel used as a piece of furniture for the sleeping apartments. The bright metal was placed in those after being weighed, and a tag attached on which was marked the number of ounces.

As I am closing my work, it is but proper to make a few remarks in reference to the Vigilantes of 1856. The subject has been written upon so often, that I deem it would be a repetition to write of the exciting scenes

[TEXT OF LETTERS ON OPPOSITE PAGE]

          Consulate of the United States
          Sn Francisco October 29th 1845

Sir

 Believing it of sufficient importance to the American commercial interests, to have an Agent for the Government of the United States, I wish to appoint you as my Vice Consul for this port.

 You will please inform me if you are willing to accept this appointment and enter upon its duties immediately

      I am Sir
       with respect
       Yr. Obt. Svt.

         Thomas O. Larkin

William A. Leidesdorff Esq
 Sn Francisco.

         Sonoma July 9th 1846

My dear sir,

 I forward to you a flag, the standard of the United States, to be hoisted at the fort at New Helvetia.

 I also forward to you by the same bearer the proclamation of Commodore John D. Sloat dated at Monterey July 7th 1846, on which day, he landed and with the forces of the U. S. took formal possession of that part of California announcing his intention of doing the same by the rest of it.

 In conformity with his instructions Capt. Montgomery has this day hoisted the national flag under a salute at Yerba Buena and I have done the same at this place, and am ordered to announce the same to you by express, on the receipt of which it is * * * * *

Larkin's letter appointing William A. Leidesdorff Vice-Consul of the United States of America at Yerba Buena, later known by its original designation of San Francisco.

Lieutenant Joseph Warren Revere was dispatched by Captain Montgomery to take possession of Sonoma. This letter of Revere's is addressed to Mr. Kern, of Fremont's survey party, then in charge at Sutter's Fort.

TWO EARLY DOCUMENTS

then enacted to save life and property, from the ruffians who infested and controlled the city of San Francisco, in carrying out their evil designs a generation ago. The men who composed the Vigilance Committee were determined to demonstrate to the whole country that San Francisco was and is as now an American town, and that her citizens were to perpetuate that title at that critical period of her history for all time to come. They did their work well; and restored order and obedience to the law of the land.

The citizens who came forward to the rescue, deserve the everlasting gratitude of the people of the Pacific coast.

In calling to mind incidents in which my old associates were connected, the act of doing so has revived many personal circumstances which though not needed in the book were pleasing; also many scenes of enjoyment with those who have departed from life and will be seen no more. Such events have awakened at times, mournful sensations, for

"There is many a lass I've loved is dead,
And many a lad grown old;
And when that lesson strikes my head,
My weary heart grows cold."

Other remembrances have brought back happy associations with friends, and seasons past; between the gladness of some and the sadness of others, there arise sentiments, which, in the language of Ossian, "Like the swaying of the wind in the pine tops, are pleasing and mournful to the soul."

APPENDIX

EXTRACT FROM PROCEEDINGS OF THE SAN FRANCISCO AYUNTAMIENTO OR CITY COUNCIL

NOTE: This was first meeting to be held after San Francisco's first serious fire; that of December 24, 1849. Ed.

FORTY-FIRST MEETING

At a meeting of the Town Council held January 2, 1850, there were present: Messrs. *Steuart, *Brannan, *Ellis, *Green, †Price, *Davis and *Turk. Hon. John W. *Geary, presiding.

The minutes of the previous meeting having been read and approved,

Communication from B. Nollner, concerning a grant of a 50 vara lot, laid on the table.

Communication from the Prefect referred to a committee previously appointed for a similar communication. Col. Steuart, chairman.

Communication from W. C. Rogers returned.

Communication from J. Gilbert laid on table.

Communication from S. C. Simmons laid on table.

Petition of A. Melhado laid on table.

Petition of S. W. Hastings, Earl and McIntosh for relief from loss sustained from fire. Referred to judiciary committee.

Petition of Z. Snyder and J. D. Atkinson to assist J. B. Brown. Laid on table.

Petition of W. S. *Clark laid on table, and the Alcalde authorized to strike the lot referred to from the catalogue, if he deem it proper.

The following report of Wm. Heath Davis, Chairman of Committee on Expenditures, read and accepted: to wit, that the following bills be paid.

Wm. M. *Eddy, and others, surveying	$3,487.80
Tucker, Pierson & Co., coffins	550.
Joel Allen, coffins	800.
Geo. Smith & Co., burying the dead	570.
Charles Marshall, boarding bill	79.
Robert Beck, furnishing Station House	89.50
Brooks & Friel, furnishing Station House	76.50
E. Laffan, rent	150.
Robert Beck, holding inquest	22.
John Riker, posting bills	20.
Shepherd & Devor, candles	47.50

C. W. Cornell & Co., coffins	$ 300.
Tucker, Pierson & Co., coffins	156.
E Laffan, rent	460.
Chas. S. Hallock, coffins	780.
Wm. W. Whaites, candles	93.
Eastman & Barr, rope, at fire Dec. 24	10.
Chas. E. Hitchcock, Street Inspector	185.
Chas. E. Hitchcock, Street Inspector	300.
Samuel J. Clark, Jr., Coroner's fees	60.
C. C. Parker, Lumber	74.
Total	$8,310.30

Report of Col. Steuart, Chairman of Committee on Health and Police, read and laid on the table for future consideration.

Report of S. Brannan, Chairman of Committee to whom was referred petition of P. Dexter Tiffany, offering lot for sale for public use of the Town,—read and accepted.

Report of Frank Turk,* Esq., Chairman of Committee to consider petition of H. *McAllister, asking confirmation to title of 50 vara lot, No. 432, read and accepted.

On motion of Col. Steuart, the rules were suspended to take into consideration the report of the Committee on Health and Police. After adopting five sections of said report, it was again laid on the table.

On motion of Mr. Brannan, Resolved that a Committee of two be appointed by the chair to draft a petition to the Governor for the suspension of the Prefect and Justice Colton, for malfeasance in office.

Messrs. Turk and Price were appointed.

On motion of Col. Steuart, Resolved, that the Secretary be authorized to procure an iron chest suitable for the safe keeping of the books and papers containing the proceedings of this council.

On motion, adjourned.   H. L. Dodge, Secretary.

*Each of the names starred in the above is today the name of a San Francisco street.
†Present day Eighth Street in San Francisco was known as late as 1854 as Price Street.

JASPER O'FARRELL'S SIGNED STATEMENT

SIGNED STATEMENT OF JASPER O'FARRELL REGARDING THE MURDER OF JOSÉ R. BERREYESA AND THE DE HARO TWINS, PUBLISHED IN THE LOS ANGELES STAR, SEPTEMBER 27, 1856.

"I was at San Rafael in June 1846 when the then Captain Frémont arrived at that Mission with his troops. The second day after his arrival there was a boat landed three men at the mouth of the estero on Point San Pedro. As soon as they were descried by Frémont there were three men (of whom Kit Carson was one) detailed to meet them. They mounted their horses and after advancing about one hundred yards halted and Carson returned to where Frémont was standing on the corridor of the Mission, in company with Gillespie, myself, and others, and said: "Captain, shall I take these men prisoners?" In response Frémont waved his hand and said: "I have got no room for prisoners." They then advanced to within fifty yards of the three unfortunate and unarmed Californians, alighted from their horses, and deliberately shot them. One of them was an old and respected Californian, Don José R. Berreyesa, whose son was the Alcalde of Sonoma. The two others were twin brothers and sons of Don Francisco de Haro, a citizen of the Pueblo of Yerba Buena. I saw Carson some two years ago and spoke to him of this act and he assured me that then and since he regretted to be compelled to shoot those men, but Frémont was bloodthirsty enough to order otherwise, and he further remarked that it was not the only brutal act he was compelled to commit while under his command.

"I should not have taken the trouble of making this public but that the veracity of a pamphlet published by C. E. Pickett, Esq., in which he mentions the circumstance has been questioned—a history which I am compelled to say is, alas, too true—and from having seen a circular addressed to the native Californians by Frémont, or some of his friends, calling on them to rally to his support, I therefore give the above act publicity, so as to exhibit some of that warrior's tender mercies and chivalrous exploits, and must say that I feel degraded in soiling paper with the name of a man whom, for that act, I must always look upon with contempt and consider as a murderer and a coward."

(signed) JASPER O'FARRELL.

The copy of the Los Angeles Star from which the above is taken is in the collection of the Historical Society of Southern California.

NAMES OF RESIDENTS AROUND THE BAY OF SAN FRANCISCO
1838

In 1838 the following were the prominent families around the bay of San Francisco: At the Mission Dolores were Francisco de Haro, then alcalde who was married to the daughter of Don José Sanchez; Francisco Guerrero, who was afterward alcalde and sub-prefect; Tiburcio Vasquez, Doña Carmen Cibrian, Candelario Valencia, married to the daughter of Don José Sanchez; Jesus Valencia, married to another daughter of Sanchez; Don Jesus Noe. The residence of Don José Sanchez was at Buri Buri, which place he owned. It contained 8000 head of cattle and a great many horses and mares. His sons, who lived there also, were José La Cruz, Francisco, Manuel, Chino and Ysidro. Captain Juan Prado Mesa, who resided with his family at the Presidio, was in command of the military post there.

At the Rancho Pinole, near Martinez, resided Teniente Ygnacio Martinez, with his family. At the Rancho San Pablo, Don Joaquin Castro, with his mother, Doña Gabriella Berreyesa de Castro, and his brothers, Antonio, Gabriel, Victor and Jesus Maria. At Temescal were Don Domingo Peralta and Vicente Peralta. At San Antonio, Ygnacio Peralta and his family, and Antonio Maria Peralta and his family. At the Rancho San Leandro resided Don José Joaquin Estudillo and family. At the Rancho San Lorenzo, Guillermo Castro and family. At the Mission of San José, José Jesus Vallejo, brother of General Vallejo, who was then administrator of that Mission, which retained some of its former wealth. At Milpitas resided Don José Crisóstomo Galindo and family; James Alexander Forbes, who was married to a daughter of the latter, and was then acting as British vice-consul, a native of Scotland. He was a thorough Spanish scholar. There were also José Maria Alviso (chico) and family. At Agua Caliente was Don Fulgencio Higuera and family. At the Pueblo San José, Don Antonio Suñol, a native of Spain, a merchant; the Bernal families; Don Antonio Maria Pico and family; Don Luis Peralta, the father of those before mentioned, with his daughters, he being then nearly a hundred years old. He was a native of Sonora, and had emigrated to this part of the country when a boy. At Santa Clara were Doña Soledad Ortega Argüello, widow of Don Luis Argüello, one of the early governors of the department of California, who owned the Rancho Las Pulgas (which means the Fleas) in San Mateo county, long possessed by his heirs; also Don Ygnacio Alviso, with his amiable wife, to whom I am indebted for numerous kindnesses.

At these different places there were many others, mostly foreigners, engaged in commercial pursuits.

At Sonoma were General M. G. Vallejo and family, he being commander-in-chief of the forces of the department. His military headquarters were at that place. He owned the Rancho Petaluma, with thousands of cattle and horses. The Rancho Suscol was a national ranch under his control, heavily stocked with cattle and horses. At Sonoma, also, was Salvador Vallejo, brother of the general, who owned a large ranch in Napa Valley, with thousands of cattle and horses. Nicolas Higuera lived at Napa, and was engaged raising stock; so were Cayetano Juarez and Don Joaquin Piña and family. At Santa Rosa resided Doña Maria Ygnacia Lopez de Carrillo, with her beautiful daughters, Juana and Felicidad. Mrs. Carrillo was the grandmother of ex-governor Romualdo Pacheco and mother-in-law of General Vallejo. At San Rafael were Timothy Murphy, Ygnacio Pacheco and family, and Domingo Sais. At Read's Ranch was John Read, who married the daughter of Don José Sanchez, with his family. At Saucelito were Captain William A. Richardson and family.

CENTENNIAL CELEBRATION OF FOUNDING OF MISSION SAN FRANCISCO DE ASIS

The Centennial Celebration on Sunday, October 8, 1876, of the founding of the Presidio of San Francisco and the Mission Dolores, may be truly described as a memorable event in the annals of the commercial metropolis of California.

I am indebted to Mr. P. J. Thomas, the compiler and publisher of a valuable work upon the founding of the Mission of San Francisco de Asis, and historical reminiscences of other Missions of California, and which includes an account of the procession and the religious and civic exercises held at the celebration of the foundation of the above Mission in its hundredth year—for the privilege of incorporating in this volume two very interesting addresses delivered on that occasion.

At the Mechanics' Pavilion at least eleven thousand persons were assembled. Among other prominent citizens, the Governor of the State; His Grace, the Most Reverend Archbishop Alemany; the Mayor of City and County of San Francisco; Hon. John W. Dwinelle and General M. G. Vallejo, orators of the day; the Collector of the Port of San Francisco; Consuls from foreign countries; Col. Peter Donahue and Gustave Touchard, were present.

The Spanish, Mexican and South American elements were largely represented in the immense throng, which was graced by the presence of many members of the clergy of the Province.

At the Old Mission grounds on the corner of Sixteenth and Dolores streets, the celebration was inaugurated with the solemnity befitting so important an anniversary. The exercises commenced with a Grand Pontifical Mass at 10 A. M. Beneath a tasteful gothic arch, adorned with ferns, ivy, clematis, and wreaths of flowers and tropical plants, the temporary altar was erected. The choir excellently rendered Beethoven's Mass in C, as well as the Offertory *Ave Maria,* by Loretz.

At the conclusion of the Gospel, His Grace the Most Rev. Archbishop advanced from the altar to the front of the platform occupied by the choir, and stated that instead of the sermon promised by the Right Rev. Bishop Grace, of St. Paul, Minnesota, which would not be delivered, owing to the unexpected illness of that revered prelate, he would himself address those present. The Archbishop then delivered the following discourse:

THE ARCHBISHOP'S ADDRESS

Dearly Beloved: This is a day of joy and exultation, both to the citizens of San Francisco, and, in a certain sense, to those of the whole State of California, especially to the children of Christian light, for to-day we celebrate the Centennial of the Foundation of this Mission, and of this vast metropolis of the Pacific Coast.

If our illustrious nation has justly been celebrating with rejoicing the Centennial of its existence, and the other nations of the world have been admiring the gigantic steps with which our Republic has advanced in a hundred years towards every kind of progress, with equal right and joy we are solemnizing to-day the hundredth anniversary of the existence of San Francisco as a civil and religious community, because we are especially interested in the establishment and prosperous duration of its double edifice, the foundations of which were laid in this place by our forefathers a hundred years ago.

A Centennial may be likened to a prominent, elevated spot, on which the traveler loves to rest, not only to cast a glance at the distance gained, but also to view the balance of his journey, and pursue it with fresh vigor. Thus, our Centennial affords us the pleasure of admiring the noble deeds of our ancestors, and the opportunity of encouraging ourselves to follow the course of a true civilization, and of our real and permanent interests. Others may perhaps speak of the Presidio of San Francisco developing itself in these last years into a great capital; they may assign to it in the near future a prominent place among the cities distinguished not less for their wealth and magnificent edifices, than for their artistic and literary talent. I will endeavor to limit my few words to religious recollections, inspired not only by the present festival and hallowed spot, but also by particular persons that have come to take part in the celebration; for we have in our midst the children of St. Ignatius, St. Francis and St. Dominic, the first Christian pioneers of both Californias, and we now occupy the same place occupied a century ago by other ministers and other people, guided by the same end, and undertaking the same work which we now have on hand—the true happiness of man through the code of the Gospel.

The spiritual soldiers of Loyola had already amazed the kings of Castile and Aragon, when, few in number and with no other resources than their breviary and their apostolic charity, they conquered what the invincible Cortéz and the Spanish armadas had not been able to subdue. By their charity and patience they had gained the hearts of the wild tribes of Lower California, and with arduous and apostolic labors they had established sixteen Missions in that peninsula. Sad human vicissitudes had already determined that the sons of St. Francis, and, soon after, those of St. Dominic, should succeed to the charge of these Missions; when a magnanimous heart, a great priest, a zealous apostle, desirous of the good of souls and of enriching them with the real treasures of Christian faith the Very Rev. Father Junípero Serra, President of the Franciscan Missionaries, willingly offered to come with his fellow-laborers to found establishments of religion and Christian beneficence in this, our California. This country had never before been inhabited by civilized man; no one could vouch for his safety in it; no one had known of its fertility and immense mineral treasures. But it was known to them that in it there were souls created by the Almighty, redeemed by His divine Son, who, buried in the darkness of paganism, had never seen the rays of the Christian light; and this was enough to induce them to undertake the great sacrifice of exiling themselves to these unexplored shores, ignorant whether it would cost them their lives; but certain that it would subject them to numberless privations and arduous labors.

It is easy for us now to come and live in this land, already well known for the benignity of its climate, the fertility of its soil, its precious treasures, its magnificent edifices inhabitated by persons of cultivated manners; but who can sufficiently appreciate the greatness of the sacrifice of those Franciscan Missionaries, who, guided by the spirit of Padre Junípero, or rather by that of apostolic charity, came first to live in this unknown country, among a barbarous people, who might, perhaps, repay their heroic sacrifices with ingratitude or even a fatal arrow! Yet they knew that the Son of God had not promised his Apostles any other reward in this world than that of being allowed to drink of the chalice of His passion for the benefit of man. Animated with such apostolic sentiments, those religious men came to our California, and having established the Mission of San Diego in 1769, and that of Monterey in 1770, they turned their attention to the foundation of the Mission of San Francisco.

And here I may mention the curious fact that the beautiful bay of San Francisco was singularly discovered by land, under the auspicious exploits of the missionaries; for it had ever remained veiled to all European eyes, notwithstanding the various vessels which had periodically passed in front of the Golden Gate. Some had inclined to the opinion that Sir Francis Drake had entered our port toward the close of the sixteenth century; but it is generally held as correct, what Humboldt and DeMofras assert, that the port visited by Drake was that of Bodega, or the one bearing his name around La Punta de los Reyes.

The first Europeans that ever saw our magnificent bay were those who composed the missionary expedition which came overland from San Diego, about the middle of July, 1769, to examine the already known port of Monterey; during which it happened that after the exploring party had passed the place now known as La Soledad, instead of turning west to their left, in the direction of Monterey, they continued their journey northwest, until they found themselves in full view of the bay of San Francisco.

But the Mission of San Francisco was not founded until the 8th day of October, 1776. Three weeks before—namely, the 17th of the preceding September—the Presidio of this place had been founded with the usual formalities; and, according to the wishes and instructions of the Viceroy of Mexico, the Missionary Fathers, accompanied by the civil authorities of the Presidio, performed the memorable work of the foundation of the Mission with all possible solemnity and formality; the account of which is given us by the faithful historian and eye-witness of the ceremony, Rev. Father Palóu, in the following words:

"Being left alone with the three young men, the work of cutting timber was commenced in order to begin the construction of the chapel and houses in which to live. On the arrival of the vessel we had sufficient timber, and with the help of some sailors furnished by Captain Quiros, in a short time a house was built thirty feet long and fifteen wide, all of plastered wood, with its roof of tule, and, adjoining it, of the same materials, a church was built fifty-two feet long, with a room for the sacristy behind the altar; and it was adorned in the best way possible with various kinds of drapery, and with the banners and pennants of the vessel. On the 8th of said month, the Lieutenant having arrived the evening before, the foundation took place, at which assisted the gentlemen of the vessel, with all the crew (except those necessary to guard the vessel), as well as the commander of the Presidio, with all the soldiers and people, re-

THE ARCHBISHOP'S ADDRESS

taining in the fort only the most necessary. I sang the Mass, with ministers, which, being ended, a procession was formed, in which was borne an image of our Seraphic Father, St. Francis, the patron of the Port, of the Presidio and of the Mission. The solemnity was celebrated with repeated salutes of fire-arms, and the swivel-guns which had been brought over from the vessel for the purpose, as also by the firing of rockets."

Thus, a hundred years ago, on this spot, with solemn Mass and festive procession, with holy blessings and the *Te Deum*, the standard of the Cross was elevated, the law of the Gospel was proclaimed, the work of conversion and civilization of the gentiles was solemnly inaugurated.

I should now beg leave to examine the means adopted by our forefathers to accomplish the noble object which they proposed to themselves, or rather the general system and special laws enacted and executed by our Christian ancestors, for the Christian civilization—the temporal and eternal welfare of the Indians. In order to have an affair of such magnitude duly attended to, the Spanish crown had constantly attached to its court a royal Council, composed of men distinguished for their wisdom, prudence and rectitude. This Council was especially devoted to the welfare of the Indians; and to that end it was guided by a special provision in the last will and testament of Queen Isabella "the Catholic, which deserves to be written in letters of gold. In that order she declares that, in taking possession of the islands and lands of the ocean, her principal intention was "to endeavor to induce and bring the inhabitants thereof and to convert them to our Holy Catholic faith, and to send to said islands and continent prelates and *religious* clergymen, and other persons learned and fearing God, in order to instruct the inhabitants thereof in the Catholic faith, and to teach them good morals, and to pay all the attention to that. I beseech my lord, the king, most affectionately, and I charge and command the princess, my daughter, and the prince, her husband, that they perform and fulfill that, and that this be their principal aim, and bestow much care to it; and that they never consent to tolerate that the Indians and inhabitants of those islands and continent, discovered or to be discovered, receive any injury in their persons or property, but that they enjoin that they may be well and justly treated, and that they remedy any wrong which they may have received."

It is not possible that Blackstone, the celebrated English jurist, in laying down the laws of equity which should guide princes in their conquests of American countries and peoples, may have studied them in the testament of Isabella; yet, no doubt, he was guided by the principles of right embodied in the ancient digests of Christian jurisprudence, when he established the maxim, that "European princes, or their subjects, by coming to occupy the soil of the gentile natives, did not thereby become the owners of their lands, and that if the object of bringing them to Christian civilization gave them some right, this was not that of seizing their lands, but that of buying them first with preference to others."

This is the principle which prevails throughout the code of the *Recopilacion de Leyes de Indias*. For, in the first place, it is obvious that in those laws the rights of the Indians to their lands are clearly respected according to the prescriptions of the code, which direct that the assignment of lands to Spaniards be made without injury to the Indians, and that such as may have been granted to their injury or inconvenience be restored to them to whom they rightfully belong. The same is established by the following law:

"We ordain that the sale, benefice and composition of lands be made in a manner that to the Indians be left in abundance all such as may belong to them, both as their individual and their community lands."

And in order that the Indians might be better protected in their rights to lands, and might not easily lose them by selling them without close reflection, it was prescribed that they could not sell their lands except before a magistrate; and that even after the sale they might rescind the contract within thirty days and retain their lands, if they wished; and that if the lands of the Indians had been occupied by others, even for the space of nine years, they should be restored to them. It is also decreed that the settlers be not allowed to establish themselves near the lands of the Indians, or to have near them cattle which may injure their crops; and should this injury accidentally occur, the Indians must be fully compensated, besides their perfect liberty to kill any cattle doing them any injury.

And although it was deemed necessary for the civilization and welfare of the Indians to induce them to form towns while cultivating their lands, having in them their church and instruction, and their own magistrates, the statutes provide that besides their houses and gardens in the towns, they should retain their right to other lands belonging to them; and that when they would change domicile, and would freely move to other places of their own will, the authorities should not prevent them, but should allow them to live and remain in them, it being at the same time forbidden to force them to move from one place to another. In their towns they were to be induced to practice some trades, business or employment suitable to them, particularly agriculture; and in order that they should not be molested, it was rigorously forbidden to the Spaniards to dwell in their towns; and in a special manner it was also forbidden to sell or give them wine, arms, or anything which might injure them or bring them to trouble.

It is also worth considering what such a code enacts in regard to their wars. Instead of keeping them in subjection with rigor, or punishing them with severity in their rebellious commotion, we find that the Emperor Charles V. enjoins on all viceroys, judges and governors, that if any Indians would rise in rebellion, they ought to strive to reduce them and to attract them to the royal service with mildness and peace, without war, theft or deaths; and that they must observe the laws given by him for the good government of the Indians, and good treatment of the natives, granting them some liberties if necessary, and forgiving them the crimes of rebellion committed by them, even if they were against His Imperial Majesty and royal service. And should they be the aggressors, and being armed, should they commence to make war on the peaceable settlers and their towns, even then the necessary intimations should be made to them once, twice and three times, and more, if necessary, until they be brought to the desired peace.

The same code contains many enactments regarding the good treatment of the Indians; for instance, it recommends to all the authorities, and even to the viceroys, the care of providing for them, and of issuing the necessary orders that they be protected, favored, and overlooked in their failings, in order that they may live unmolested and undisturbed, seeing to the severe punishment of the transgressors molesting them. It especially charges the Attorneys-General to watch particularly over the observance of the laws enacted for their instruction, protection, good treatment and prosperity, while it is provided that they may have in their towns their own mayor and supervisors, elected by themselves, and that an official, high in dignity, should visit, among others, the towns of the Indians at least every three years, and see that they be not ill-treated in anything. Finally, for their greater protection, it was decreed by the king that there be protectors and defenders of the Indians; that these be prudent and competent men, and that they perform their duties with the Christian spirit, disinterestedness and prompt attention with which they are obliged to assist and defend them.

Consequently, there can be no doubt that this precious code of the *Recopilacion* reflects throughout the true spirit of Christian charity to which the Indians are entitled, as the aboriginal owners of their lands, and as men created by the same God who made us, ransomed by the same Redeemer that saved us, and destined, like all others, to the same heaven. But, it may be said that, notwithstanding the spirit of Christian civilization pervading the code, its laws were frequently disregarded, and the Indians had much to suffer from the Spanish settlers. Be that as it may, there can be no doubt that most, if not all, of the Spanish monarchs were sincerely anxious, and took proper measures to see the natives of America protected and attracted to Christian civilization. This is particularly true of Queen Isabella, in whom, Prescott observes, the Indians found an efficient friend and protector. Then, the immense distance intervening between the colonies and the Mother Country must have naturally prevented the vigorous enforcing and perfect observance of the laws; yet the same author tells us that Cardinal Ximenes' eye penetrated to the farthest limits of the monarchy. He sent a commission to Hispañola to inquire into and ameliorate the condition of the natives.

And, when the natives were oppressed, there were not wanting some Las Casas, who bravely espoused the cause of the oppressed, frequently crossed the Atlantic to acquaint the Crown with the real evils, made the halls of kings ring with their loud and eloquent appeals in behalf of the Indians, secured just measures, and obtained visitors and protectors to examine and redress the wrongs.

It was, no doubt, due to such measures and vigilance that the Indians were not only preserved, but frequently advanced to a comparatively good state of civilization. One of the latest writers on Our Continent, Mr. Charles Mackay, observes that "in Mexico and South America they still thrive." "They," says Sothern, "enjoyed for many generations a greater exemption from physical and moral evil than any other inhabitants of the globe." "We were exceedingly struck," says Stephens, on the descendants of the Caribs, "with the great progress made in civilization by these descendants of cannibals, the fiercest of all Indian tribes." Throughout South America, millions of the natives have been preserved and considerably advanced to the knowledge and manners of Christian civilization, under the influence of good laws and Christian instructors, while nine-tenths of the people of Mexico have been similarly benefited.

But to return to our California and our Missions. It is pleasing to find in their fresh records that, within a very short time, many missionary establishments were erected, and thrived, each being directed by two Franciscan Fathers, under whom numerous tribes of Indians were daily instructed in the lessons of Christianity; some easy trades were practiced, large tracts of land were tilled, luxurious orchards and vineyards gladdened the country; and the whole coast, from Sonoma to San Diego, was alive with countless herds of cattle of every description.

There were then no hotels in the country; each Mission was situated some forty miles from the nearest one, and afforded hospitable entertainment to travelers, who could go with perfect safety from one end of the country to the other. The twenty-one Missions were so many patriarchal settlements or communities of Indians, each ranging from 1500 to 2500, each individual working for all, all working for each, and all enjoying peace and plenty. In 1834, the crops of the twenty-one Missions came up to 122,500 bushels of grain, while the head of horned cattle belonging to the same numbered 424,000, all for the exclusive benefit of the inmates of those Missions, which numbered at that date 30,600 souls, truly blessed with plenty, but still more blessed on account of their acquired habits of industry, their daily Christian instruction and the practical lessons of morality constantly inculcated to them.

Well may California be proud of her heroic, disinterested Christian pioneers, who in a short time transformed numberless barbarous tribes into comparatively well-civilized Christian communities; and well may we echo to-day with sweet strains of joyous melody the solemn *Te Deum* intoned here for the first time one hundred years ago.

In conclusion, let me pray that the mission of the Franciscans—the establishing of Christianity in this country—may ever prove successful, and that our prosperous city may ever be favored with God's choicest benedictions, which will be the case if its citizens will be guided by the Christian counsels inaugurated here a century ago.

Christian principles will insure peace and happiness, and good moral Christian lives will keep the state of society in a sound and prosperous condition. The code of the Gospel is the code of the sovereign legislator, who has an absolute right to enforce it, who demands our humble submission to it, and who has declared that on our compliance with its provisions depends our happiness, temporal and eternal. It is obvious that we shall not witness the next Centennial here; but I hope and pray that we may see it from on high, celebrated here again with Christian spirit and becoming solemnity.

At the conclusion of Mr. Dwinelle's oration, at the Pavilion, General Vallejo addressed the assemblage in the Spanish language, of which the subjoined is a translation:

GENERAL M. G. VALLEJO'S ORATION

Honored by the cordial invitation tendered me by the Board of Directors of the present celebration, through the most Reverend Archbishop Alemany, I present myself before you for the purpose of narrating, in a few but significant words, the history of the discovery, occupation and foundation of this Mission of our holy Father, San Francisco de Asis, a name which it has borne with dignity since the time it was so called by the indefatigable missionary, Father-President Junípero Serra and companions, in respect and veneration for the founder of their Seraphic Order.

Would that I were possessed of the necessary ability to do justice to the merits of those men, to whom is due the civilization of so many thousands of souls, and of numberless others that will succeed them. But, if my incapacity is great, my ardent desire to comply with the duty which has been imposed upon me, and which I have gladly accepted, is still greater. I only wish to ask your kind indulgence.

I shall be as brief in my discourse as a subject of such great magnitude as this will permit. Before, however, entering into the particulars of our present subject matter, I may be permitted to give a condensed synopsis of the events by which this port of San Francisco came into the possession of the Crown of Spain.

In the years 1542 and 1543 the navigator Cabrillo sailed up and down the coast, and passed San Francisco without having determined anything but the formation of the coast line.

In 1578, Sir Francis Drake, an English buccaneer, anchored and remained a month, perhaps, in the small bay on the northern extremity of the ocean or open bay of the Farallones, at the same place which was called by us the port of Tomales. Drake gave this latter bay his name, and the surrounding country he called New Albion. There is a bare possibility of Drake's entering the present bay of San Francisco, but the weight of evidence is against him. There is no doubt that it was in the bay of Tomales that the vessel from China, called the "San Agustin," was sunk in the year 1595. It is beyond contradiction that the name of San Francisco was given to the bay at that time, on account of some circumstance unknown to us, perhaps in honor of the Patron Saint of the day on which the vessel arrived.

It is an absurdity to suppose that there can be any connection between Sir Francis Drake and San Francisco, except in the imagination of some visionary geographer. Very little is known concerning the voyage; but the wreck of the "San Agustin" was afterward brought by the currents into the port of San Francisco (the Golden Gate), and as far as Yerba Buena, at Clark's Point, where I was shown fragments of the same about two hundred years after (1830), by the veteran officer Don José Antonio Sanchez.

In 1603, the Admiral Sebastian Vizcaino, having on board of his flag-ship one of the pilots of the "San Agustin," sailed up and down the coast, stopping, without landing in the bay of San Francisco (not the present one), which was that of Tomales, near Point Reyes. Vizcaino took very extensive and correct geographical observations; but the only copy of his chart in existence is made on such a small scale that very little information can be derived from it concerning this portion of the coast.

In subsequent years several vessels from the Philippine Islands came down the coast on their way to Acapulco; no mention, however, is made that any of them ever touched at any point on the coast of California, although it is certain that from the voyages in question we have notes concerning its coast. By some data obtained therefrom, and particularly from the observations of Vizcaino, the first pilot of the Philippines, Don José Gonzales Cabrera Bueno, made several sea charts which, together with a theoretical Treatise on Navigation, was published in Manila in the year 1734. This work gives a description of the coast from Point Reyes to Point Pinos with the same degree of accuracy as can be given in the present day, with the exception of what appertains to the Golden Gate and the unknown interior of the bay of San Francisco. In it there is described perfectly the ancient bay of the same name, near Point Reyes, as the present one was not known at that time, and not discovered until thirty-five years later.

On the 31st of October, 1769, the expedition from San Diego was the first that made explorations in California overland. In it came Portolá, Rivera y Moncada, Fages and Father Crespí. They ascended the hills now called Point San Pedro (county of San Mateo), from whence they saw the bay of the Farallones, which extends from Point San Pedro to Point Reyes; and they also noticed Cabrera Bueno's bay of San Francisco, and the Farallones. On the 1st of November they sent a party to Point Reyes. On the 2d of the same month several hunters of the expedition ascended the high mountains more toward the east; and, although we have no correct information as to the names of those hunters, it is certain that they were the first white inhabitants who saw the large arm of the sea known at present as the bay of San Francisco. The portion that was seen by them was that which lies between the San Bruno mountains and the estuary or creek of San Antonio (Oakland). They discovered the bay, unless the honor is accorded to the exploring party that returned on the 3d of November, who also had discovered the branch of the sea, by which they were prevented from reaching Point Reyes, and the primitive bay of San Francisco. On the 4th of November the whole of the expedition saw the newly-discovered bay, and they tried to go around it by the south; but not being able to do so, they returned to Monterey.

The next exploration had in that direction was made by Pedro Fages and Father Crespí, in the month of March, 1772, from Monterey; and was with the view of going around the arm of the sea reaching Point Reyes, and arriving at the bay of San Francisco of the first navigators. For greater accuracy in the description I am about to make, I ask permission to use the names by which the places through which they passed are known at the present day.

Fages and Father Crespí started escorted by a guard of soldiers of the company of volunteers of Cataluña, and another from that of the "Cuero," or Leather coats. They arrived at Salinas river (to which they gave the name of Santa Delfina), crossed it, and, passing by the site upon which is now located Salinas City, they went over the hills and arrived at the place where the town of San Juan de Castro now stands. They continued their journey through the valley known to-day as the San Felipe, in the immediate vicinity of Hollister. After this they crossed the Carnedero creek (known at present as Gilroy), ascended and crossed the small hills of Linares (Lomita de la Linares) and the dry lake known as the rancho of Juan Alvires; went over the gap of Santa Teresa, and entered the valley of Santa Clara, where are situated the cities of San José and Santa Clara, only separated from each other by the Guadalupe river.

"Here," said Father Crespí, "is a magnificent place to found a Mission, because it possesses all the necessary resources: abundance of good lands, water, and timber, and a great many gentiles to baptize." Thence they continued along the eastern shores of the bay, arrived at Alameda creek (Alvarado City, Vallejo's Mills and Centerville), followed along the bay towards the north, crossed San Lorenzo creek (Haywards), thence to San Leandro, Oakland, San Pablo, El Pinole, Martinez, Pacheco, Suisun bay, and crossed the San Joaquin river at a point not far distant from Antioch. This was on the 30th of March.

As the expedition did not possess the means of surmounting such obstacles as it met and reaching Point Reyes, which was its objective point, it was determined to return to Monterey by a different route—that is, along the foot-hills of Mount Diablo. The President of the Missions having become fully convinced of the impossibility of establishing that of San Francisco immediately at its own port, as he lacked the means of transportation by sea, and in order to proceed by land, additional exploring parties were deemed necessary. He reported the failure of the expedition of Fages to the Viceroy of New Spain. The viceroy gave orders to Captain Don Fernando Rivera y Moncada, who had been appointed successor to Fages in command of the military posts (presidios) of New California, to make a second examination, for the purpose of discovering the most appropriate localities for the foundation of the Missions in project. At the same time, in his letters of the 25th of May, he calls upon Father Junípero to aid and assist the new commander and to occupy and establish Missions in the most convenient and suitable places.

Accordingly, having made the necessary preparations, Captain Rivera started from Monterey on the 23d of November, 1774, accompanied by Father Francisco Palóu, an escort of sixteen soldiers, and some servants. They prosecuted their journey without having encountered any drawback as far as the valley of Santa Clara; but from there they went to the west of the bay between its shores and the adjacent hills.

Following the level plains in the said valley, they passed by Bay View, Mayfield, the Pulgas (Menlo Park), Redwood City, Belmont, San Mateo, San Bruno and Laguna de la Merced, and reached Point Lobos. They crossed the ravines, and ascended the mountain whence they beheld the entrance to the port of San Francisco (the Golden Gate). On the 4th of December they planted the symbol of Christianity on the most elevated point close to where now stands the castle or fortification of the national government, that is, on the southern portion of what forms the mouth of the said harbor; "on account of that being a spot on which no Spaniard or Christian had yet trod," according to the narrative of Father Palóu.

That cross I saw myself, in the year 1829, having come to San Francisco on business pertaining to the military service. No location was at that time made either for a garrison (presidio) or Mission, as the severity of the winter months compelled the expedition to return to winter quarters at Monterey; and they verified it by going over the route that was taken by the expedition of 1769, which was by San Pedro, and Spanishtown (Half Moon bay), in the county of San Mateo, Point New Year, Santa Cruz City, Watsonville in Santa Cruz county, Pajaro City, Castroville, Salinas and Monterey, which had been their starting point.

In the year 1775, during the months of August and September, Captain Ayala entered the bay of San Francisco, on board the packetboat "San Carlos," this being the first historically authenticated vessel that sailed into that bay. He remained forty days and explored it in all directions. Captain Ezeta and Father Palóu came up from Monterey as far as the place where Rivera and the same missionary Father had planted the mentioned cross, but they did not find the crew of the "San Carlos."

The next attempt to found a religious and military establishment at San Francisco proved successful. The Lieutenant-Colonel, Don Juan Bautista de Anza, by orders from the Viceroy, Fra Don Antonio Marie Bucarelli y Ursúa, recruited soldiers and settlers (pobladores) in Sinaloa and gave them all the aid possible to facilitate their journey to their new homes in Upper California. Being all assembled at San Miguel de Orcasitas (Sonora), they started upon their march on the 29th of September, 1775, by way of the Colorado river, which had already been explored by the same Anza in another expedition. The colony was composed of thirty married soldiers and twelve families of settlers, which, together, formed a total of two hundred souls, who were to found and establish the new town. Before the departure of this expedition by land in March, 1775, one ship and two packet-boats sailed for San Blas, taking on board provisions and effects for the Missions and presidios. Providence favored the three vessels, which were successful in their operations. On the 4th of January, 1776, Lieutenant-Colonel Anza arrived at the Mission of San Gabriel with his expedition. Urgent business concerning the security of the establishments in Southern California detained him there. By the 12th of March he had already reached the Mission of El Carmelo, accompanied by the chaplain, Father Pedro Font, and his escort. On the 22nd of March he set out on a journey to examine the region of country of this port of San Francisco, and arrived at the place where Father Palóu, in accord with Captain Rivera, had planted the cross in December, 1774. Having examined the locality well, Anza and the Lieutenant-Colonel Don José Joaquin Moraga decided that a garrison (presidio) should be founded there, and that this subordinate officer should be the one to carry the project into execution.

The expedition continued on their journey; and, according to Father Palóu, upon arriving at the bay, which was called "Las Lloronas" (the primitive name of Mission

Bay), they crossed a creek by which a large lake is drained, which was called "De Los Dolores," and that site appeared to them a suitable place for a Mission, which had to be founded in the vicinity of the new advanced military post (presidio). They continued on their journey, and went further north than the place where Fages and Father Crespí had been, and then returned to Monterey.

On the 17th of June, 1776, the expedition of soldiers and families from Soñora started for Monterey. The Military force was commanded by Lieutenant Don José Joaquin Moraga; it was composed of one sergeant, two corporals and ten or twelve soldiers, with their wives and children. There were also, in the party, seven families of resident settlers, five servants, muleteers and vaqueros (stock herders), who took care of 200 head of cattle belonging to the king and private individuals. This is concerning the new garrison. In what appertains to the Mission, I will say that there were Fathers Francisco Palóu and Pedro Benito Cambon, two servants and three neophyte Indians, one of whom was from the Mission of San Carlos, and the two others from Old California, these having 86 head of cattle in their charge.

The expedition took the same route as that of 1774, and arrived safely on the 27th of the same month at the Lake of Dolores, where it had to wait for the packet boat "San Carlos," to determine upon the location of the garrison and fort. Meantime, it occupied itself in exploring the surrounding country. On the 28th, the Lieutenant ordered an enramada, a hut made of branches of trees, to be made, which might serve as a chapel for the purpose of celebrating mass; and it was in it that the first mass was said on the 29th, which was the feast of the glorious apostles Saints Peter and Paul. The Fathers continued celebrating in the same "Enramada" every day until the garrison (presidio) was established near the landing place, where good water could be obtained and the land was appropriate. I said good water, as subsequent experience proves it to be excellent and possessing some marvelous qualities. In proof of my assertion, I appeal to the testimony of the families of Miramontes, Martinez, Sanchez, Soto, Briones and others, all of whom had wives that bore twins upon several instances; and public opinion attributes, not without reason, these wholesome results to the virtues of the waters of the "Polin," which still exists. The exploration party remained a whole month encamped awaiting the arrival of the ship, during which time the soldiers and settlers were busy cutting timber in order to gain time.

The month having expired without the packet boat making its appearance, the commander, Moraga, determined to make over to the spot which he had in the course of his explorations selected as more appropriate for the new garrison (presidio). This he did on the 26th of July, and all hands went to work and made barracks out of "Tule," which might serve them as places of shelter. The first barrack that was built was dedicated to serve as a chapel, and the first mass was celebrated by Father Palóu on the 28th. But, by order of Lieutenant Moraga, there remained near the lake de los Dolores the two missionary priests and servants, with the stock and everything else appertaining to the Mission—all under the immediate protection of six soldiers. The Fathers occupied themselves in building houses, the soldiers of the guard and one resident settler assisting in the work. This was the reason why the Reverend Father Palóu certified on the first page of the primitive Books of Baptisms, Marriages and Deaths, that the Mission had been founded on the first day of August, 1776.

I beg leave to be permitted here to mention (because it has some connection with part of our history) that during the month of August Father Palóu administered, on the 10th day, the waters of Baptism, *ad instantem mortem,* to a child a few days old, who was the legitimate son of Ygnacio Soto and Maria Barbara Lugo, my mother's aunt, which said child was called Francisco José de Los Dolores; and on the 25th day a little girl fifteen days old, the legitimate daughter of José Antonio Sanchez and Maria de Los Dolores Morales, was baptized and called Juana Maria Lorenza. This child was taken to the baptismal font of the Mission by Don José Cañizares, pilot of the packet boat "San Carlos."

The long looked for "San Carlos" entered the port of San Francisco and anchored at twelve o'clock A. M. on the 18th of August, opposite the encampment where the garrison had to be erected. Captain Quirós, his pilots and the chaplain (Father Nocedal) went immediately on shore. After the customary salutation had passed, they inspected the land selected by Moraga for a garrison, as well as that of the Mission, and it was agreed that both places were suitable for the purposes to which they had been destined. According to the very words used by the Rev. Father Palóu, in his diary of the expedition, which reads: "About the middle of September, 1776, the soldiers had already built their wooden houses, all duly roofed; the Lieutenant had his royal house, and a warehouse made of the same material had been completed of sufficient capacity to contain all the supplies that the vessel had brought. It was immediately decided that the festival should be celebrated with a solemn procession, fixing upon the day as that of the 17th of September, the same on which Our Mother the Church celebrates the memory of the Impression of the Wounds of our Seraphic Father Saint Francis. The day could not have been more appropriate, as it was that of the Patron Saint of the Port, of the new garison (presidio), and of the Mission. And for taking possession of the Mission was fixed the 4th day of October, which is the very day of our Seraphic Father, Saint Francis."

The ceremony of the solemn procession and foundation of the Mission took place on the 4th of October. The Lieutenant, Don José Joaquin Moraga and his soldiers, Don Fernando Quirós, commander of the packet boat, his two pilots, the major part of his crew, and, lastly, the never-forgotten Father Palóu, Thomas de la Peña, Cambon and Nocedal were present. I will quote from Father Palóu again: "A solemn mass was sung by the Fathers; the ceremony of the formal possession was made by the royal officers, and when it had been completed all went into the church and sang a *Te Deum Laudamus,* with the ringing of bells, and, at times, firing salutes with cannon and other fire-arms, the ship responding with its artillery."

It is not only the diary of Father Palóu that serves me as authority to fix upon with exactness the day of the possession and foundation respectively of the garrison and Mission. These data I had obtained a long time before I had seen and read the said diary from the lips of the same military men and settlers who were eye-witnesses to those ceremonies; that is to say, from Lieutenant Moraga, from my father, Don Ygnacio Vallejo, Don Marcos Briones, Galindo, Castro, Pacheco, Bojorques, Bernal, Higuera, Peralta, Amézquita, Franco Flores, Hernandez, Mesa and others whose names I do not here enumerate, as I do not wish to be too lengthy.

The temporary building of the church was situated at a distance of about one thousand varas to the northwest of the spot where the actual temple now stands. The lake of Dolores was at the time located and could be seen to the right of the road coming from the Presidio to the Mission between two hills, one of which still exists, the other one has disappeared before the progressive march of this rich emporium.

On the 8th day of October of the mentioned year, 1776, the erection of the present temple of the Mission of San Francisco was commenced, and we to-day on this centennial anniversary, have met here, not only to honor the memory of those who dedicated it to the service of God, but also to show our admiration of the great principles by which they were impelled, namely, the faith of Him who died nailed to the cross for the redemption of man.

Providence, which is infinitely wise and bountiful, has permitted that our venerable pastor should make mention of my father's being one of those brave men who aided and assisted the missionaries with his sword. Consequently, at the same time that I satisfy your desires, I comply with a duty very satisfactory to myself in being the exponent of events that transpired one hundred years ago, the date upon which commenced the life and existence of San Francisco, which we can with pride style the Queen City of the Pacific. *Justitæ soror fides*—Faith is the sister of Justice. I shall be guided in my remarks by a pure and holy love for these two sisters. The invigorating breath of the gospel, as I said before, was given to us by some Franciscan Friars, who were indeed poor and humble Missionaries of Good, but rich in Faith and Hope in the success of their grand and arduous task. By this means were sown the prolific seeds of Christianity that has given such marvelous results during the one hundred years of its existence, which this rich and populous city counts; having written it to-day the Metropolitan Church, and which, by circumstances and coincidences that would be too lengthy to narrate, bears also the name of San Francisco. The Metropolitan Church, I said. Yes, it is the one over which our worthy Archbishop Alemany so honorably presides.

Let us for a moment transport ourselves from this day to the former century, and let us compare the present gathering here to an assemblage of that epoch. The latter consisted of a handful of men who were brave Christians, armed to the teeth, and of another still smaller party of humble ministers of Christ, but gifted with wonderous fortitude and a firm determination that nothing could change or oppose, as they had come to preach the Word of God and were resigned to take upon themselves the crown of martyrdom. Both of these parties were liable to become at any moment the victims of a rude crowd of naked savage gentiles, some of whom had come to them at first through curiosity, others prompted by a spirit of destruction, and all of them to obtain the presents which were given to them for the purpose of alluring them and inspiring them with confidence and have them hear for the first time the words of the Gospel.

The audience whom I have the honor to address on this occasion is a true representative of the high culture and advanced civilization of the nineteenth century, enjoying all the security and privileges which that state of society guarantees to them.

What a vast difference, gentlemen, between what was, and what we see to-day, in this centennial which we celebrate! Let us bear in mind that in the course only of one hundred years, this privileged place has taken a gigantic stride and fallen into the hands of a society worthy of prosecuting the work that was begun by those true Pioneers. The Mission of San Francisco, which at one time was situated on a desert, yet protected by the hand of Providence, to-day may be seen nearly in the centre of this populous city of the same name.

The foundation of the Mission and military post (Presidio) having been completed, the packet-boat sailed on the 21st, for San Blas. During its stay in the port the commander (Quirós) had lent all the aid possible to the Mission in getting a carpenter and some sailors help in the construction of doors and windows for the church and house of the missionary Fathers, also in the building of the altar, as well as in many other things. Not satisfied with all this, Captain Quirós left four of his crew to work as day laborers on the buildings that were being erected and in the tilling of the ground, which was immediately commenced.

I remember this, together with other things, that I heard in my youth from the eye-witness of these transactions. Among them I should mention the boatswain of the packet-boat known by everybody as Neustramo Pepe. This brave man, who was a Catalonian by birth, had a heart as sensitive as a woman's. He visited my father's house at Monterey a great many times in after years, and in conversation had with our family he often related the fact of the foundation of the Post and Mission of San Francisco, where he had worked with an energy worthy of all praise.

A great many times and on several occasions he said to my father, shedding tears: "Do you remember, Don Ygnacio, our farewell on board the packet-boat when Captain Quirós gave the banquet to the officers and priests? Do you recollect how afterwards the military and naval officers, with the priests, who were assembled at the landing place on the beach, embraced one another and shook hands? Do you remember that from there, after we weighed anchor, all the military men and the priests went towards the strip of land that projects out and forms the southern cape of the Port (where now stands the fortification), and while they were there they waved their handkerchiefs and their hats to us as we passed, kindly bidding us a last adieu? What a solemn day was that, my friend! Do you remember how the currents dragged our vessel towards the opposite shores of the harbor; and how we were there exposed to great danger, until a favorable breeze came up from the northwest, and saved us from being dashed against the cliffs of rocks? Yet, in the midst of that tribulation, and such despair, we left in sorrow for you who remained exposed, and at the mercy of so many barbarians. Why, man, even Quirós shed tears!"

Before leaving our friend, Neustramo Pepe, it is very gratifying to me to mention that his popularity among our people was so great, than no sooner would there be news of the arrival of some ship on the coast—that is, at San Diego or some other inhabited place—than every one would inquire whether Nuestramo Pepe had come; and if he was there he would be received with enthusiastic hurrahs and cries of acclamation by all the people present.

We already have our apostolic men engaged in the great work of the redemption of thousands of gentiles to whom God had opened the way to heaven. It seems to me that I see those intrepid men (ministers of the altar and warriors of shield and sword), in these regions, surrounded by a ferocious and barbarous people whom they had to conquer for God and their sovereign. Combining the two expedients, which affects the human heart most? The main object which both priests and soldiers had in view had to be attained. *"Suaviter in modo fortiter in re."* The mildness of the minister of God upheld by the force of armed men produced the desired effects.

The assiduity of the missionaries never relaxed before the numerous obstacles daily thrown in their way. With the meekness of true Apostles, they succeeded in getting the barbarians to present themselves voluntarily to receive the waters of baptism. By holy abnegation, the example of their virtues, and of their constancy, they gained the confidence of a considerable number of catechumens who gradually began to draw near.

It is a fact known by all the Californians, old as well as new, that whole tribes from the surroundings of the bay came to accept a religious faith, which, till then, had been wholly unknown to them; but, for all that, there were some turbulent, wicked ones who from the commencement had been opposed to the advance or progress of the *foreigners,* as they called the Spaniards in their own dialect. This feeling of animosity was made evident a few days later when the *Buri-buri* from the Indian villages (rancherias) afterwards called San Mateo, attacked one hut situated about three miles from the Laguna de Los Dolores and set it on fire. Such was the terror which this act caused in them, that not even the assurance of protection which was promised them by the garrison was sufficient to prevent their crossing on their tule rafts to the opposite side of the peninsula, which to-day is Marin county, as well to that on the East, which is known at present as Oakland, Alameda, etc. The fugitives kept away for some time; but at last they commenced to visit the Presidio, and, by December, became so courageous, that they considered themselves strong enough to commit depredations on the Mission.

The commanding sergeant of the guard, Juan Pablo Grijalva, caused one of those who had been hostile to be flogged, and this act enraged and alarmed the friends of the culprit. Two of them fired their arrows at the soldiers, but luckily did not do any harm. On the following day the sergeant determined to chastise the audacity of those who had been turbulent, after which an encounter took place with them in which one of the residents was wounded who killed his antagonist with one shot, and his body fell into the estuary. The rest of the Indians fled, but went to some rocks from whence they continued their hostilities.

A shot well aimed by the sergeant struck one of the gentiles in the thigh, the ball going through and lodging in the rocks, from where it was taken by the Indians. The death of one and the wounding of another of the savages discouraged them to such a degree that they asked for peace, which the sergeant granted them. Nevertheless, the two Indians who had been the cause of the encounter were taken prisoners. The sergeant had them chastised severely, giving them to understand that if, in the future, they again manifested hostility they should forfeit their lives. Fhs unfortunate occurrence retarded somewhat the conversion of those gentiles for several months; but about the beginning of 1777 they could be seen about the Mission, and three of them were baptised on the 29th of June of that year.

On the 6th of January, 1777, a party of armed soldiers, under the command of Lieutenant Moraga, with an escort, and Father Tomás Peña, went from San Francisco to the place where the Mission of Santa Clara was founded; and another came later, accompanying Father José Murguía, from San Carlos or the Carmelo, bringing provisions and supplies for that same place. Both priests were to remain in charge of the new establishment. Father Murguía, did not arrive until the 21st, but Father Peña had already celebrated mass there on the 12th.

The work of the missionaries continued without interruption on the part of the Indians. In 1778, the ship " Santiago," *alias* "Nueva Galicia," arrived from San Blas, bringing on board a cargo of provision for the Mission of San Francisco, together with other effects and merchandise for the Presidio.

Nothing worthy of mention occurred until the latter part of June, 1779, on which date the ship "Santiago" entered the port of San Francisco again with supplies and merchandise for the Mission and Presidio. In the year 1780 the vessel "Santiago" did not visit the port of San Francisco, but left at Monterey one hundred fanegas (Spanish bushels) of corn and other merchandise, which it became necessary to transport by land with very great difficulty. Worse was the fate not only of San Francisco, but of all the Missions and garrisons (Presidios) of Northern California in 1781, as no provisions or yearly supplies from the king arrived. This caused great inconvenience, and did considerable damage to the conquest.

Our virtuous missionaries had in that year already reaped such abundant fruits from the vineyard which they were cultivating for our Lord Jesus Christ, that the Reverend Father-President Junípero Serra came to San Francisco, for the first time, and, exercising the powers with which he had been vested by the Holy See, administered the Sacrament of Confirmation to Sixty-nine neophytes.

The following year of 1782 was also unfortunate on account of the great loss suffered by the Missions in the death of the old missionary Father, Friar Juan Crespí. This venerable man and wise apostle had already counted thirty years of missionary life among the Indians, and came to New California in the expedition that founded the first establishment at San Diego, in the year 1769. In the next succeeding year he was present at the foundation of the Mission of San Carlos de Monterey. I have already related the active part which he took with the Commander Fages in trying to find a place suitable for the establishment of another Mission at the port of San Francisco. These eminent and invaluable services which he rendered entitle him to the highest position among the many worthy missionaries of his Seraphic Order.

On the 13th of May, 1783, two vessels entered our ports with supplies and provisions for the presidios and Missions that had already been founded. Friar Pedro Benito Cambon, who had been absent on several occasions, was sent back to this Mission to accompany Father Palóu.

On the mentioned date, two other vessels arrived with more provisions and merchandise, bringing an auxiliary force of missionaries, composed of the Reverend Fathers, Friar Juan Antonio García Rioboo and Friar Diego Noboa. Both of these clergymen remained in the Mission of San Francisco, and took part with the resident ministers in celebrating the feast of *Corpus Christi* with all the solemnity that their means allowed.

After this they were called away by the President and ordered to go to Monterey. The missionary Fathers, at the same time that they worked for the good of the soul, did not neglect material happiness.

When they had a pretty large congregation of converts under subjection, they dedicated them to works of industry. Besides the agricultural pursuits, from which the missionaries as well as the neophytes and catechumens were to receive their subsistence, adobes, bricks, tiles, etc., were made, and the construction of the holy temple was begun; granaries, residences, quarters and a guard-house for the soldiers, and lastly houses for those Indians who had been converted to Christianity, were built. It will be readily seen by this account that the most worthy Fathers were constantly employed in their spiritual as well as temporal labors; although the latter were always subordinate to the former.

In one of my journeys to San Francisco, during the year 1826, I found this Mission in all its splendor and state of preservation, consisting, at that time, of one church, the residence of the Reverend Fathers, granaries, warehouses for merchandise, guard-house for the soldiers, prison, an orchard of fruit trees and vegetable garden, cemetery, the entire rancheria (Indian village) all constructed of adobe houses with tile roofs—the whole laid out with great regularity, forming streets, and a tannery and soap factory—that is to say, on that portion which actually lies between Church, Dolores and Guerrero streets, from north to south, and between Fifteenth and Seventeenth streets, from east to west. I think that the neophytes living in the Mission, in San Mateo, and in San Pedro reached six hundred souls.

In the year 1830, I was directed by my superior officer to continue to serve at the presidios. Everything was in the same state of preservation in which I had left it in 1826.

I recollect, with joy that on the 4th of October, 1830, while the Reverend Father Friar Tomás Estenega was minister of the Mission, and I was acting as adjutant of the garrison (presidio), the military commander was invited to take part with his officers in the celebration; consequently, all the soldiers were present that he who now addresses you had under his orders. Salutes were fired in front of the church and residence of the priests on that day in regular order. There were also present at the celebration of the holy Patron Saint, the Reverend Fathers, Friar José Viader of the Mission of Santa Clara, Friar Buenaventura Fortuni, of that of San Francisco Solano, and Friar Juan Amorós, of that of San Rafael. During the mass the last priest mentioned officiated, while Fathers Viader and Fortuni acted as deacon and sub-deacon—Father Estenega (who was still young) being left in charge of the choir, music, etc.

A sermon was preached by Father Viader, relating to the festivity of the holy Patron, and to the foundation of the place on the 4th of October, 1776.

This was the last celebration at which four Spanish priests, from Spain, assisted with the same object as that had by the meritorious Pioneers, and the ministers Palóu, Cambon, Peña and Nocedal, on the 4th of October, 1776, *one hundred years ago.* What a singular coincidence! I will give a short biography of those apostolic men.

Reverend Friar José Viader was a man of refined manners; tall in stature, somewhat severe in his aspect, open and frank in his conversation. He was as austere in religious matters as he was active in the management of the temporalities of the Mission of Santa Clara, which he always administered. He became remarkable, among other things, because the Rosary, which he carried fastened to the girdle of the Order around his waist, had a large crucifix attached to it.

Friar Fortuni was a holy man who was incessantly praying; he could always be seen in or out of the Mission with the Breviary in his hand, or reciting the Rosary in the church: he was very learned and affable in his intercourse with the people of those times; and was very humble, and, besides, a great apostle.

Friar Tomás Estenega was a young man of medium height, the personification of activity, of jovial disposition, select and varied in his conversation, an excellent and very sincere priest. He had seen a great deal of the war of the revolution in Spain, and was there during the French invasion, when Napoleon I. and his brother Joseph tried to appropriate to themselves that privileged land.

Friar Juan Amorós was sanctity itself; and if I possessed the eloquence of the great orators, I would consume more time in depicting the brilliant qualities which adorned that venerable missionary. But not having those talents I shall limit my remarks, and say that Father Amorós was a model of virtue, charity, humility, and of Christian meekness—a man without a blemish, of a candid heart, and of most exemplary life; he was the admiration of his contemporaries and the astonishment of the tribes of the aborigines.

When I was a child, nearly seventy years ago, I knew him at the Mission of San Carlos of Monterey as chaplain of the garrison of the same name. When he came to celebrate mass in the chapel of the soldiers on Sundays he always brought a few sweet figs, dates and raisins in the sleeves of his habit, which he distributed after mass to the boys of the Sunday school; but this he did after he had given instruction in Christian doctrine for half an hour. On the 14th of July, 1832, this apostolic missionary died at the Mission of San Rafael, at half-past three o'clock in the morning.

The register of his burial says that he was a native of the Province of Catalonia (Spain), born on the 10th of October, 1773; took the habit of Our Seraphic Father San Francisco on the 28th day of April, 1791; was admitted into the Order by making the necessary vows on the 30th of the same month of the following year, and was ordained priest in the month of December, 1797. On the 4th of March, 1803, he left Catalonia to come to the college of San Fernando, in the City of Mexico, where he arrived on the 26th of July.

In 1804, animated by his great zeal for the conversion of the gentiles, with the blessing of his superiors, he came to the Missions of Upper California, where he arrived in the commencement of the year 1804, and was appointed as minister to the Mission of San Carlos, where he lived fifteen years, acting as resident apostolic minister. From there, by permission of his superior, who was the Reverend Father Prefect Friar Mariano Payeras, he went to that of San Rafael, where he worked and labored with astonishing perseverance until his death. He was buried in the Mission church on the 14th of July, at five o'clock in the afternoon.

I must remark that the Mission of San Rafael was for several years a branch of that of San Francisco, and always remained under the jurisdiction of this Presidio. I speak with so much feeling of kindness toward Father Amorós, because I am cognizant of his great virtues, his pure heart and sincere devotion. Moreover, it was with him that I made my first Confession; and from his holy hands I received for the first time the consecrated bread of the Eucharist.

I have already made mention of his moral gifts; it remains now for me only to describe his physical aspect; and I could not give you a more exact idea of him, nor draw a more perfect likeness from the original, than by calling attention to the person of a most esteemed ecclesiastic who is here present; his stature, manners, features, smile and amiable disposition all bring back to my memory the image of that holy man. Neither Rulofson nor any other of our most skilled photographers could produce as perfect a picture of Father Amorós than that which we have before us in the person of our venerable Archbishop, Joseph Sadoc Alemany. And, at the same time, I feel highly pleased to say that it is not only in the physical qualities that I find a great resemblance in the two men.

I must observe here, that during the first years of the foundation, as the Indians of the Buri-buri tribe were not willing to live in this place on account of it being extremely cold, and destitute of those fine groves of trees which the hand of Providence was pleased to plant in the region which they occupied, and as the Indians from San Pedro were enjoying the benefits of their fertile lands, and hence opposed to come and live in a climate so different from that in which they were born, in order to remedy this inconvenience, and at the same time avail themselves of religious instruction, both tribes petitioned the Father ministers, asking to be allowed to live on their lands, obligating themselves to build chapels and to dedicate themselves to agricultural pursuits and other labors, all of which was done with great success.

The priests went every Saturday, accompanied by an escort, said mass, preached, and then returned to the mother church. The ministers maintained for some time a chapel and storehouses for grain amongst the Juchiyunes, Acalnes, Bolgones, and Carquinez Indians, who occupied that portion of Country known as Contra Costa. The chapel was located in what is known to-day as the rancho of San Pablo, where the missionaries went to comply with their ministerial duties, and besides, to direct the works and attend to the administration of their temporalities.

The immense wealth of the Mission of San Francisco, was acquired from those three farms, and from its own lands, which were situated from Rincon Point to Hayes Valley (El Gentil), Divisadero, and the garrison (Presidio) to Point Lobos. These were recognized as its boundaries, from the time of the ancient founders; upon which grazed all its cattle, horses, sheep and hogs, and from which abundant crops of wheat, corn and beans were harvested.

The foundation of San Rafael was made on the 14th of December, 1817. High Mass was celebrated by the Rev. Prefect, Father Vicente Francisco de Sarria, assisted by Fathers Luis Gil, Ramon Abella and Narciso Duran, with sermon and other ceremonies analogous to the occasion. Father Sarria baptised four little Indians, and called them respectively by the names of Rafael, Miguel and Gabriel (in honor of the three Archangels), and the fourth by his own name, Vicente Francisco. Father Luis Gil de Taboda remained as resident priest there.

This Mission was the fourth daughter of that of San Francisco; the first having been that of Santa Clara, as I have already said, the second that of Santa Cruz, which was founded on the 29th of August, 1791, and the third was that of San José, founded on the 11th of June, 1797. The last one was that of San Francisco Solano (Sonoma Valley), founded in 1823; abandoned soon after on account of the incursions of the Indians, and re-established in 1827, under the supervision of the virtuous Father Fortuni; but it was not rebuilt permanently until 1830.

The Spanish successors of the worthy Fathers Palóu and Cambon in this Mission were, if my memory serves me right, Friars Ramon Abella, Juan Lucio, Juan Cabot, José Altimira and Tomás Estenega. I was personally acquainted with all of them, and I can testify to their being worthy ministers of God and indefatigable apostles.

And now, permit me to make a few remarks in defense of the good name of some of the individuals who governed this country during the Mexican Administration, whose reputation has been sometimes wantonly attacked; while nothing has ever been said against the governors, under Spain, who preceded them.

Much has been said, and even more has been written, concerning the Missions and their great wealth. And who are they that figure in that drama? Who are its authors? Are they, perchance, impartial men? or, to say the least, have they an accurate knowledge of the history of the Missions or this Upper California? No, no! gentlemen; they were foreign writers, interested parties, and consequently partial in their style; who, without reflection, hurriedly advanced, as undeniable fact, that which was false, all for the purpose of deluding the ignorant and of profiting by the utterance of base falsehoods, at the same time that they flattered their taste by censuring indirectly and unfairly the acts of the collectors of the Missions, styling them thieves, etc. That the Missions were rich we all know. But what were those riches? This they do not tell us. Nevertheless, these riches consisted in moveable stock and agricultural productions; but they make no mention of pecuniary wealth.

That the Mexican governors robbed the Missions is an absurdity. The first Mexican governor, Don Luis A. Argüello, a native of San Francisco, was decidedly a protector of the Missions and a friend to the missionaries. He died poor, leaving his family no other patrimony than the small rancho of Las Pulgas, with a few head of stock.

The second governor, Don José Maria de Echeandía, exercised his authority in the time of the Republic; and although he was always directly opposed to the Spanish priests because they would not swear to the Mexican constitution, nevertheless, he extended to them his protection as much as it was in his power, and in conformity with the instructions which he had from the new government. From this resulted, necessarily, a misunderstanding between the ancient ministers and the new governor who esteemed them highly; and if he had to act against some of them, it was done for a legal cause, and not because he had any antipathy or hatred towards them.

After having governed the country for five years, Echeandía had great difficulty in collecting and getting together, by the aid of the priests of San Luis Rey and San Juan Capistrano, who were his friends, the sum of three thousand dollars which he needed to return to Mexico. Don Manuel Victoria was the third governor, who, from his coming into power, gained the good will of the missionaries and was always upon the best terms with them. All the steps towards secularization which had been taken by his predecessor were annulled by Victoria, even before he was in possession of the government. His official conduct was despotic, and he forced the Californians to send him out of the country, yet it would be an injustice to accuse him of having robbed either the country or the Missions. The priests aided him pecuniarily, that he might be able to leave.

Don José Figueroa, the fourth Mexican governor, was an educated and upright man. He died poor at Monterey.

Castro, Gutierrez, Chico, Alvarado, Micheltorena, and, lastly, Pio Pico, all had to contend with revolutionary elements. The priests had disappeared, the neophytes had left the Missions and gone away to the villages of the gentiles, and the government, under such circumstances, had to take possession of the lands which were claimed by the Missions, through the power which it possessed, and in order to defend the country against an *invasion with which it was threatened.*

When the old missionaries saw that the political tornado was about to burst upon the Mission system, they commenced to convert into money all their movable property, such as cattle and stock. In the Missions of San Gabriel, San Fernando, San Juan Capistrano and San Luis Rey, they killed by contract with private individuals, during the years 1830, 1831 and 1832, more than sixty thousand head of cattle, from which they only saved the hides. The pecuniary wealth of the Missions in their primitive days, which were more productive, was sent out of the country to Spain, Mexico or Italy. This I know; and presume, and even believe, that all of it arrived safely at its place of destination. Be that as may, neither the governors nor the Californians ever partook of any of that wealth, with the exception of $20,000, which, upon an occasion of imperative necessity, we, the members of the Deputation, together with other prominent citizens, obtained from Father José Sanchez of the Mission of San Gabriel, to facilitate the payment of the expenses of a military force destitute of everything at the time, thus avoiding the commission of greater evils.

During the lengthy period of the war of Independence, and even afterwards, the Missions supplied the troops of the "Cuera" (leather coats) with provisions and other effects, as no more yearly supplies had been sent from Mexico.

But it is necessary to bear in mind that the Spanish flag waved over California, and that the priests did no more than comply with the orders of the king, at the same time that they looked for their own protection and that of the Missions, soldiers being constantly engaged in protecting the Missions, and in continuous campaigns for the purpose of keeping the Indians under subjection. Without those soldiers, the

Indians would have risen immediately against the Missions, and all the white inhabitants would have inevitably perished.

The missionaries from the College of our Lady of Guadalupe, Zacatecas, came from Mexico in the year 1832, and it was the lot of the Mission of San Francisco to have, as missionary Father, José Marie Gutierrez, who continued here for some time. After that, Fathers Lorenzo Quijas and Mercado had charge of it alternately. When this Mission was secularized, it was delivered over to several overseers (mayordomos) who were appointed by the political government, until the Indian priest, Prudencio Santillan, took charge of it. This Reverend Father had been ordained *in sacris* by the first Bishop in California, Friar Don Francisco García Diego.

I have occupied the attention of this intelligent audience so long for the purpose of giving a detailed narration of the primitive history of the Presidio, Mission and Pueblo of San Francisco, which up to the year 1846, did not count a population any greater than that within this fine hall—a weak fortification, one or two officers, a company of soldiers and a handful of resident settlers in twenty-five or thirty houses.

What a change is presented to our view to-day! A great city, which, having absorbed the three points mentioned, has filled the entire peninsula with a population of nearly three hundred thousand inhabitants, dedicated to all the arts known to the highest degree of civilization. The harbor and city, protected by strong fortifications and well-equipped ships of war, situated on the most advantageous position, it is destined to become the grand commercial center of India, China and Japan, at the same time that it will be such for the entire northern coast of the Pacific. What shall be the destiny which the Supreme Benefactor has prepared for this portion of our beautiful native land for the next coming hundred years? I entertain the full conviction that the hand of the Great Creator, by which is guided the progress and happiness of mankind, will carry us to the highest degree of excellence in all the branches of knowledge. Then, it is to be hoped, that those who will celebrate that day taking a retrospective view of the present epoch, will remember with gratitude what this generation, by divine aid, has established for them, to carry on, until they reach moral, intellectual and physical perfection.

And let us from this moment send cordial salutations to our fortunate decendants who will see the brilliant dawn of the second Centennial of the Foundation of the Mission of San Francisco de Asis.

FATHER GONZALEZ'S LETTER ON THE STATE OF THE MISSIONS IN THE 1830-40 DECADE

In the work entitled "Our Centennial Memoir," published by P. J. Thomas, of San Francisco, to which we have alluded elsewhere, is an interesting translation from a letter of the Venerable Father Gonzalez to Father Adam, of Santa Cruz. Describing the condition of the Missions and the losses they sustained through the oppressive acts of the Mexican Government, was written in September, 1864, from the Apostolic College of our Lady of Los Dolores, Santa Barbara. Father Gonzales was the last of the old pioneer missionaries who labored to plant the Cross in these golden regions.

"REV. AND DEAR SIR:—On my landing in this country, which happened on the 15th of January, 1833, there were in existence from San Diego up to San Francisco Solano 21 Missions, which provided for 14,000 or 15,000 Indians. Even the poorest Missions, that of San Rafael and Soledad, provided everything for divine worship, and the maintenance of the Indians. The care of the neophytes was left to the missionary, who, not only a pastor, instructed them in their religion and administered the sacraments to them, but as a householder, provided for them, governed and instructed them in their social life, procuring for them peace and happiness.

"Every Mission, rather than a town, was a large community, in which the missionary was President, distributing equal burdens and benefits. No one worked for himself, and the products of the harvest, cattle and industry in which they were employed was guarded, administered and distributed by the missionary. He was the procurator and defender of his neophytes, and, at the same time, their Chief and Justice of Peace, to settle all their quarrels, since the Mission Indians were not subject to the public authorities, except in grievous and criminal cases.

"This system, though criticized by some politicians, is the very one that made the Missions so flourishing. The richest in population was that of San Luis Rey; in temporal things, that of San Gabriel. Mine was that of San José, and, although I was promised, as it was on the gentile frontier, it would not be secularized, it, too, succumbed in 1836.

"In the inventory made in January, 1837, the result showed that said Mission numbered 1,300 neophytes, a great piece of land, well tilled; the store-houses filled with seeds; two orchards, one with 1,600 fruit trees; two vineyards—one with 6,039 vines, the other with 5,000; tools for husbandry in abundance; shops for carpenters, blacksmiths, shoemakers, and even tanneries, and all the implements for their work.

"The fields were covered with live stock; horned cattle, 20,000 head; sheep, 15,000; horses, 459. For the saddle 600 colts of two years, 1,630 mares, 149 yoke of oxen, thirty mules, eighteen jackasses and seventy-seven hogs.

"Twice a year a new dress was given to the neophytes, amounting in distribution to $6,000. When the Mission was secularized I delivered to the mayor-domo then in charge some $20,000 worth of cloth and other articles which the store-house contained.

"The church of the Mission of San José was neatly adorned, and well provided with vestments and other religious articles. Thirty musicians served in the choir, and they had a very neat dress for feast days.

"Of the Mission of Santa Clara, we can say the same more or less.

"The other Missions, called the 'Northern,' though having been already secularized, were in utter bankruptcy, and the same can be affirmed for the most part of those of the south, down to San Diego; for it was observed that as long as the Missions were in the hands of the missionaries everything was abundant; but as soon as they passed into the hands of laymen everything went wrong, till eventually complete ruin succeeded, and all was gone. Yet, we cannot say that the ambition of those men was the cause, since, though the government in the space of four years, divided seven ranches to private individuals—the smallest of a league and a half—yet in spite of this cutting off of part of my Mission lands, the Misson was every day progressing more and more.

"We have not to attribute the destruction of these establishments to rapacity; for though we can presume that something was taken, this was not the principal agent of destruction; but the blunder was made in their enterprises and the high fees paid to the chief steward and other salaried men, etc.

"The government of Mexico, up to the year 1830, acknowledged a debt in favor of these Missions of over $400,000, without counting other minor debts. Finally, we have to acknowledge that a manifest punishment from God was the cause of the destruction of the Missions, since theft alone could not accomplish it and the subsidy given to the government would not affect them. On the contrary, left to the priests, the Missions would have prospered, and other establishments still more opulent would have been erected in the Tulares, even with out any protection from the government, and deprived of the subsidy of the Pious Fund of $400,000, if the revolution of Spain in the year 1808 and that of Mexico in 1810 had not put an end to the prosperity of the missionaries. If zealous missionaries had been left amongst the savage tribes roaming through this vast territory, from the Sierra Nevada to the Coast Mountains, called then by the priests 'Tulares,' all would have been converted to Christianity, and would not have perished, as we see them now.

"I was able to save only a small relic of these tribes during the pestilence of 1833, in which I collected together some 600 Indians. I would have saved more during the small-pox epidemic of 1839, but my Mission had already been secularized, and I had no resources. I could do nothing for the Indians, who were like boys of one hundred years. It is only with liberality you can draw them towards you; give them plenty to eat and clothes in abundance, and they will soon become your friends, and you can then conduct them to religion, form them to good manners, and teach them civilized habits.

"Do you want to know who were the cause of the ruin of these Missions? As I was not only a witness but a victim of the sad events which caused their destruction, I have tried rather to shut my eyes that I might not see the evil, and close my ears to prevent hearing the innumerable wrongs which these establishments had suffered. My poor neophytes did their part, in their own way, to try and diminish my sorrow and anguish."

PADRE JUNIPERO SERRA'S LETTER OF JULY 3, 1769 TELLING OF HIS ARRIVAL AT SAN DIEGO

On the Feast of our Lady of Mount Carmel, July 16, 1769, was founded at San Diego the first Mission in Upper California. Thomas' MEMOIR (already quoted) contains the translation of an important letter, which throws some light upon the matter. So remarkable is the event that the letter, dated July 3, 1769, addressed by the Father-President of the Franciscan Missionaries to his future biographer, Father Palóu, will without doubt, be read with deep interest:

"My Dear Friend:—Thank God I arrived the day before yesterday, the first of the month, at this port of San Diego, truly a fine one, and not without reason called famous. Here I found those who had set out before me, both by sea and land, except those who have died. The brethren, Fathers Crespí, Vizcaino, Parron and Gomez, are here with myself, and all are quite well, thank God. Here are also the two vessels, but the San Carlos without sailors, all having died of the scurvy, except two. The San Antonio, although she sailed a month and a half later, arrived twenty days before the San Carlos, losing on the voyage eight sailors. In consequence of this loss, it has been resolved that the San Antonio shall return to San Blas, to fetch sailors for herself and for the San Carlos.

"The causes of the delay of the San Carlos were: first, lack of water, owing to the casks being bad, which, together, with bad water obtained on the coast, occasioned sickness among the crew; and secondly, the error which all were in respecting the situation of this port. They supposed it to be thirty-three or thirty-four degrees north latitude, some saying one and some the other, and strict orders were given to Captain Villa and the rest to keep out in the open sea till they arrived at the thirty-fourth degree, and then to make the shore in search of the port. As, however, the port in reality lies in thirty-two degrees thirty-four minutes, according to the observations that have been made, they went much beyond it, thus making the voyage much longer than was necessary. The people got daily worse from the cold and the bad water, and they must all have perished if they had not discovered the port about the time they did. For they were quite unable to launch the boat to procure more water, or to do anything whatever for their preservation. Father Fernando did everything in his power to assist the sick; and although he arrived much reduced in flesh, he did not become ill, and is now well. We have not suffered hunger or other privations, neither have the Indians who came with us; all arrived well and healthy.

"The tract through which we passed is generally very good land, with plenty of water; and there, as well as here, the country is neither rocky nor overrun with brush-wood. There are, however, many hills, but they are composed of earth. The road has been good in some places, but the greater part bad. About half-way, the valleys and banks of rivulets began to be delightful. We found vines of a large size, and in some cases quite loaded with grapes; we also found an abundance of roses, which appeared to be like those of Castile. In fine, it is a good country, and very different from old California.

"We have seen Indians in immense numbers, and all those on this coast of the Pacific contrive to make a good subsistence on various seeds, and by fishing. The latter they carry on by means of rafts or canoes, made of tule (bullrush) with which they go a great way to sea. They are very civil. All the males, old and young, go naked; the women, however, and the female children, are decently covered from their breasts downward. We found on our journey, as well as in the place where we stopped, that they treated us with as much confidence and good-will as if they had known us all their lives. But when we offered them any of our victuals, they always refused them. All they cared for was cloth, and only for something of this sort would they exchange their fish or whatever else they had. During the whole march we found hares, rabbits, some deer, and a multitude of berendos (a kind of a wild goat).

"I pray God may preserve your health and life many years.

"From this port and intended Mission of San Diego, in North California, third July, 1769.

"Fr. Junípero Serra."

STATEMENT OF GEORGE HYDE AND LETTERS IN THE HYDE CONTROVERSY

Inasmuch as the reputation of Mr. Hyde was involved in the charges made against him while he served as alcalde of San Francisco in 1847, and as he, like all gentlemen with a high sense of honor, feels sensitive in the matter, I have granted him the space in these pages to give his own statement concerning the charges and the attending circumstances. It is as follows:

"A ring had been formed which induced Mr. Edwin Bryant, my predecessor in office, to arbitrarily make changes and alterations in the surveys, pending the act of making old surveys rectangular, thereby breaking his own contract with the citizens and injuring some to oblige this ring; all of which was proved when the first charge against me to this effect was before the commission. Immediately after I assumed office, in June, 1847, this party approached me to secure similar results. I was solicited to cause the survey of the 100 vara lots on the south side of Market street, to be moved forty feet further south, in order to make certain lots they desired to procure, south of Howard or Folsom street, more eligible, by lifting them out of the boggy location; and also to make a block of land at the junction of Bush and Battery, or thereabout, more eligible for business purposes. I declined, because it would be an arbitrary act and injure many persons who already had vested rights. I was also asked to change the survey of the water and beach lots, by making the lots into slips of 50 varas wide—streets intervening from the beach out to ship channel. This was also refused, because the survey, as fixed by Mr. Bryant, was nearly completed. I soon after this became the object of frequent anonymous attacks from the *California Star,* which culminated in the charges concocted and preferred, and which, so far as they went, were triumphantly disproved. They were actually turned against my assailants, for the whole matter was well understood in its correct light by the entire community. I was opposed to the sale of the water and beach lots, as granted by General Kearny, and sought to influence the Governor to allow a postponement, but I, being in office by military appointment, had to obey orders, and the lots were sold as surveyed. C. L. Ross, under his name, bought a number of lots for individuals *who were members of the ring* previously referred to. Their first effort was to get rid of paying the customary fees for recording the deeds. Coached as to the objections he was to interpose, Ross urged many silly reasons for refusing to pay, and finally submitted the matter to the Town Council, which body decided in my favor. Ross still persisted in refusing to pay, and I agreed to leave the matter to Hombres Buenos (arbitrators), each selecting one, and these two the third. Mr. Ross, after a few days, informed the alcalde that he had selected Mr. Folsom. On the following day the true state of the case was discovered. Folsom was one of the actual purchasers; and of course no decision was ever reached. Putting all these things together, it is very easily seen who of my assailants had motives for defacing maps, preferring charges, etc., and likewise to perceive *why* the committee bringing the charges refused to appear before the commissioners to continue proceedings. They well knew that a further exposure would consign them to ruin and the contempt of the public.

"GEORGE HYDE"

The annexed letters are literally copied in vindication of Alcalde Hyde:
"To George Hyde, 1-Alcalde:

"SIR: I acknowledge the receipt of your letter of yesterday evening enclosing a copy of a letter purporting to be a letter from the Town Council to the Governor together with his reply thereto, and also your several requests to which I respectfully return the following: I was not present at any meeting of the Town Council sitting as Commissioners to investigate the Charges preferred against you by a Committee of Citizens, nor has there been any such meeting publicly held since December last. Consequently I am not aware of the subject having been entertained; but have heard that the determination you allude to, soliciting the Governor to remove you, was made by the four members whose names you have mentioned, at a secret meeting which I was not invited to attend. I have not been officially called on to sit in my capacity as commissioner to investigate since last December, nor has there been an official meeting of the board. But four of the ten charges have as yet been entertained, and I know that you have repeatedly solicited the board to cause them to be brought to a speedy determination. Throughout the entire proceedings, and up to the present time, the Gentlemen whose names you mentioned have publicly expressed in my hearing that the Committee preferring the Charges have completely failed to prove them and that its proceedings were a perfect humbug; two of the persons preferring the charges have also admitted that fact in my presence, one saying that he wished he had never had anything to do with it, the other that he would not bother himself any more about it. I am very Respectfully, Your Obt. Servant,

"W. S. CLARK."

"San Francisco, March 20, 1848."

"SAN FRANCISCO, July 16, 1855.

"Geo. Hyde, Esq.

"Sir: I rec'd yours of the 25th June, in regard your question when Alcalde in 1847. I was chairman of a committee of the Town Council of San Francisco, to investigate the charges preferred against you, and in respect to the first interrogation, I say that it is not true they were established by proof. To the second, that, by the testimony, you fully and completely exonerated yourself from all responsibility.

"Yours Respect,
"ROBERT A. PARKER."

"SAN MATEO, July 23rd, 1855.

"MY DEAR SIR: I received your note of June 25th requesting an answer to two interrogatories therein contained concerning certain charges preferred against you whilst alcalde. I say that the two charges as examined, were not established by proof. In reply to the second, I say that in my opinion you did clearly exonerate yourself from all culpability, and it was so generally understood at the time.

"Yours truly,
"W. D. M. HOWARD."

"Geo. Hyde, Esq."

"SAN FRANCISCO, August 4, 1855.

"DEAR SIR: Your note dated 25th June last, came to hand a day or two ago; this must be my apology for the delay occasioned. With regard to the charges preferred against you in 1847, I will take the liberty of saying, that it was well understood then, that they were preferred by a few individuals merely for the purpose of gratifying personal animosity. Some nine or ten charges were forwarded to the Council by the Governor, only two of which underwent an examination; and the committee who conducted the prosecution of them had every latitude allowed them, not only by the Council but by you also. The first charge was commenced on the 25th Octo., and concluded on the evening of the first Nov. 1847. Some four or five evenings of a couple of hours each being the time employed. From this last date, until about the third of December following, when the second charge was entertained and concluded at one sitting, no meeting of the Council, as examiners, was held. After that, the whole affair was viewed as a farce by the public; was considered as abandoned, inasmuch as frequent meetings were called at your solicitation, to which the Committee prosecuting the charges invariably failed to attend. It was about the first of March, 1848, when two members of the Council, in a secret manner, on their own responsibility, occasioned by personal feeling (originating in a matter entirely foreign to the matter of the charges,) opened a correspondence with Gov. Mason, alleging that the charges were admitted by you to be true, and hence recommended your removal, which the Gov. refused to do. As a matter of justice to you I will add that I was present at all the meetings and I distinctly declare that you never made any admission of the kind whatever; the character of the testimony was such as clearly exculpated you from all blame. To your interrogatory then, is it true that either one or both of the charges examined before the Council were held to be established by proof?—I declare that it is not true. I distinctly and positively assert that you maintained your innocence, and vindicated your fair fame throughout the whole affair, and that too by all the testimony taken.
I am, sir, with sincere respect,

"Very truly yours, &c.,
"W. S. CLARK."

"To George Hyde, San Francisco."

FIRST SAN FRANCISCO DIRECTORY

Eight or ten years since I prepared a list of the inhabitants of Yerba Buena, Mission Dolores and Presidio in 1846, which comprised the district of San Francisco, and the same was published in the *Morning Call*. Shortly after the article appeared in print I met the late Hall McAllister on Montgomery street one forenoon, and he stopped me to say that he had read the article referred to in the *Call*, and had filed among his legal archives three of the newspapers as part of his large record of legal matters. The same are doubtless now in existence as part of the mass of records, the accumulation of many years of his brilliant and successful practice in the profession that he loved.

The following is a similar list of names in the three villages above named on the 9th day in July, 1846, that the Mexican Eagle was displaced by the Stars and Stripes, by Captain Montgomery of the United States Navy. In the preparation of the names of the early residents at the time the government was changed, I have been very careful to omit none of the people that lived in the district; and I have revised the published list:—

Nathan Spear (retired from business on account of ill health), Mrs. Nathan Spear, two servants.

Mrs. Susanna Martinez Hinckley, and one servant.

William M. Smith, auctioneer.

Captain Eliab Grimes, capitalist.

John Vioget, Maria Montero, his wife, two children and one servant.

José Benavides.

William A. Leidesdorff, merchant and real estate owner, and one servant.

Jack Fuller, Chona Linares, his wife, two daughters, two sons and two servants.

W. D. M. Howard (merchant), and three servants.

Henry Mellus, merchant.

Wm. R. Bassham, clerk to Mellus & Howard.

José Jesus Noe, last Alcalde under the Mexican regime.

Doña Guadalupe, wife of José Jesus Noe, four sons and two daughters (who were all small children) and four servants.

Miguel Noe, son of ex-Alcalde Noe.

Francisco Ramirez (Chilean), trader.

Trinidad Moya (Mexican), trader.

Gregorio Escalante (Manila), baker.

Juana Briones de Miranda, one of the first settlers in Yerba Buena, who is still living (1889) on her large tract of land in Mayfield, Santa Clara County, at the advanced age of four-score and ten years; two sons and three daughters—small children.

Apolinario Miranda (husband of the former), and three servants.

——Seregee (young Russian), clerk to Leidesdorff

THIS FIRST DRAFT OF SAN FRANCISCO'S FIRST DIRECTORY—JULY 10, 1846— is in the handwriting of William Heath Davis. The complete register of the town's inhabitants appears in the appendix.

Presentacion Miranda de Ridley and one servant.
Robert Ridley (husband of the former), Lessee of Vioget's Hotel.
John Evans, wife, three sons and three daughters.
Tomás Miranda.
John Baywood (known by the name of John Cooper), wife and son.
John Sullivan, wood cutter and dealer, and two very young brothers.
Peter Sherreback and wife.
R. M. Sherman.
William Heath Davis, merchant, and two servants.
Josiah Belden.
Henry Neal, clerk to Mellus & Howard.
George Glidding, formerly clerk to bark "Tasso."
Henry Richardson, formerly clerk to bark "Sterling."
Josefa Benavides, daughter of Mrs. Vioget.
Josefa Montero, sister of Mrs. Vioget.
H. F. Teschemacher, clerk to Henry Mellus' bark "Tasso," and afterwards agent for the same vessel.
Joseph P. Thompson, clerk to Mellus & Howard.
Mrs. John C. Davis, wife of John C. Davis.
John C. Davis and one servant, William J. Reynolds (Chino), John Rose, John Finch, tinker, ship-wrights, house-builders and blacksmiths.
Benito Diaz (Custom-House officer), wife, three small children and mother-in-law.
John Thompson, blacksmith.
Mrs. Montgomery; afterwards married Talbot H. Green alias Paul Geddes.
Charles E. Pickett.
George Denecke, baker.
Vicente Miramontes, wife and six children.
Francisca Vidal.
Charles Meyer, clerk to Leidesdorff.
Rafael Vidal.

Francisco el Negro, cook (Peruvian.)
Juan el Negro, pastryman.
Carmel Tadeo, washerwoman.
Blas Tadeo.
Blas Angelino, wood cutter.
Juan Agramon, wood cutter.
Juan Bernal and Chona Soto, his wife.
Victor Prudon and Teodosia Boronda, his wife, Marcella Boronda, sister of Mrs. Prudon.
Antonio Ortega, Chica García, his wife.
Antonio Buhan (Peruvian), gambler.
Mary Bennett, husband and four children.
Daniel Sill, miller and hunter.
Charles Clein, proprietor of saloon.
Alexander Leavett, carpenter.
Juan Lara, shoemaker.
A. A. Andrews, builder, and Rosalia Haro, his wife, two children and one servant.
Thos. Smith (Smith & Co.), proprietor of saloon.
Maria Antonia Valle de Dawson, owner of land near the Blucher Rancho.
Guadalupe Berreyesa, grantee to a large tract of land.
J. H. Brown, saloon-keeper.
William Johnson, owner of schooners in the bay of San Francisco.
John Ackerman, clerk to W. A. Leidesdorff.

Mission Dolores

Padre Real, of the Mission San Francisco de Asis.
Francisco Guerrero, Sub-Prefect of the District of San Francisco.
Josefa de Haro, wife of Francisco Guerrero, two sons and two servants.
Francisco de Haro, Ex-Alcalde.
Miliana Sanchez, wife of Francisco de Haro.
Francisco de Haro, Jun.
Ramon de Haro.
Natividad de Haro.
Prudencio and Alonzo de Haro, small children and two servants of the household.
Tiburcio Vasquez, mayordomo, Mission Dolores.

Alvina Hernandez, wife of Tiburcio Vasquez, eight children and two servants.
Candelario Valencia. (Valencia street is named after him.)
Paula Sanchez, wife of Candelario Valencia, and two servants.
Eustaquio Valencia.
José Ramon Valencia.
Lucia Valencia.
Tomasa Valencia.
Francisco Valencia.
José Jesus Valencia and Julia Sanchez, his wife.
Rosa Valencia.
Amadeo Valencia.
Catalina Valencia, second wife of José Jesus Noe.
Leandro Galindo and Dominga Sotelo, his wife.
Nazario Galindo.
Josefa Galindo.
Seferino Galindo.
Benerito Galindo.
Genaro Galindo.
Maria Galindo.
Antonia Galindo.
Manuela Galindo.
Chino Sanchez and Jesus Alviso, his wife, five small daughters.
Isabel Sanchez.
José Gomez and Eusebia Galindo, his wife.
Guadalupe Gomez, female.
Bernardino García, married to Mrs. Hilaria Read.
Hilaria Sanchez Read, of Read's rancho in Marin County.
John Read, of Read's rancho, Marin County.
Hilarita Read, of Read's rancho, Marin County.
Carmel Cibrian de Bernal.
Bruno Valencia and Bernarda Duarte, his wife, and four children.
Militon Valencia.
Felipe Soto.
José Santa Maria, Secretary to Sub-Prefect Guerrero.
Augustin Davila and Jesus Feliz, his wife, and two children.
Augustin Davila, Junior.
Tutiana Avila. Dolores Avila. Magin Feliz.
Toribio Tanferan (Peruvian) and Maria Valencia, his wife, and seven children.
José Cornelia Bernal, husband of Carmel Cibrian.
José Jesus Bernal.
Angel Alviso and Josefa Sotelo, his wife.
Ysidor Jalapa. Rafaela Jalapa.
Mariano Jalapa.

PRESIDIO

Doña Guadalupe Briones de Miramontes.
Candelario Miramontes, her husband.
Ygnacio Miramontes.
Rodolfo Miramontes.
Arciano Miramontes.
Raimundo Miramontes.
José de los Santos Miramontes.
Juan José Miramontes.
Doña Luz Briones, who is still living at the great age of more than a century; with her sister Doña Juana Briones de Miranda, at Mayfield, Santa Clara County. (1889)
Dolores Miramontes.
Ramona Miramontes.
Manuel Peña (an old soldier of the Mexican army) and Guadalupe, his wife.
Dolores Peña.
Maria de Los Angeles Peña.
Carmel Peña. Maria Peña.
Antonia Peña. Francisco Peña.
Eusebio Soto, (an old artilleryman of the Spanish and Mexican armies, with the rank of Corporal) and Martina Mendoza, his wife and three children.
Marta Soto.
Francisco Soto.
Joaquin Peña (an old soldier of the Spanish and Mexican armies, with the rank of Corporal) and Eustaquia Mojica, his wife.
José de la Cruz Peña.

CHINESE IN CALIFORNIA

In 1881 and 1882 while I was in the capital of the nation I became acquainted with John McDermett, a resident and capitalist of Washington, and I frequented his home, and in those visits I made to him and his family, he and myself would often get into discussions over the unacceptable immigration from China to the State of California. He thought, from a humane standpoint, the people of California were, as a class, too harsh and severe in their treatment of the Mongolians. Of course, during our arguments I opposed all suggestions in behalf of the Chinamen, but I could never convince him that their presence was demoralizing to the youthful people of the young State, and that they had been extracting millions of gold continuously for many years. About three years ago Mr. McDermett came to California for the first time, to visit a married daughter residing in the city, and viewed many points of interest in the State of perpetual flowers. One day I said to him that I would be pleased to devote one or two days in showing him the city. We visited Chinatown, and I took him into basements and cellars which were inhabited by Chinese, and the smell from the filth that surrounded their habitations was so offensive that he and I were glad to retreat to the street above us and into the pure air. From Washington street I called my friend's attention to both sides of Stockton street, which were once the residences of capitalists and merchants of the town, which were now populated by the Mongolians the whole line of the street from California to south side of Broadway. When we crossed the latter street, and got out of the Chinese quarters, northward, Mr. McDermett remarked: "This portion of Stockton street is an American town."

The Eastern tourist became satisfied and convinced that this class of people was injurious to the prosperity of California, morally and commercially.

I have been favored with the following item upon the Chinese influence in San Francisco by Mr. S. P. Leeds, editor of the *Commercial Record*, which is an expression of his observation (written in 1888) of the detrimental effect of the Mongolian upon the morality of our population:

"The influx of the Chinese began before 1838, with a single Mongolian as stated previously by yourself. It has steadily increased, until now there are probably several hundred thousand in the United States. At first, while few in numbers, they were docile, meek and subservient. They would give the entire sidewalk to every man of other nationalities whom they met. They entered into menial services and did the best they could. They were moderately honest and strictly attentive to their industries. But as their numbers increased they began to display their natural dispositions, and they passed from petty pilferings to robberies; from light dissipations to sensualities; from praiseworthy neatness to uncleanliness; from little assaults to murders; from willing workers to arbitrary usurpers of many industries. In this latter case they over-estimated their power, and threatened to quit work in some factories, unless all white employes should be discharged. This action aroused such a storm of resentful indignation that they dropped the subject. They have taken another course and are running factories, in which only Chinese find employment.

"As an illustration the following incident is narrated. A manufacturer of bird cages finding that he could employ Chinese at less wages than he paid white men, took two or three of them into his factory. After a while one of them left, under pretence of going to China; but recommended his cousin as a good steady fellow to fill his place, which was given to him. The same method was adopted by another of them with the same result. This occurred several times, as fast as those employed had learned the art of making bird cages. During this time they had found out where the employer procured his materials and who were his customers. They started a factory in Chinatown and offered their cages to the dealers at a great reduction in price from what they had been paying. The manufacturer finding his sales rapidly falling off, went among his customers to learn the cause, and discovered that his false economy in hiring Chinese had ruined his business, and he had soon after to close it and seek some other occupation. This will be the final result to all trades in which the Chinese are given work, for the same reason.

"They have the control of the manufacture of cigars, shoes and slippers; common clothing; six or eight jewelry establishments, several hardware stores, numerous express wagons; and have recently invaded the higher branches of commerce by becoming exporters of American products to China markets: and soon no flour will be shipped there except by them. This deprives the mill men of a profitable branch of their business, which will be more seriously felt when the Chinese execute their intended purpose of building a large flouring mill. They have also established a Marine Insurance Company, and will, unless they are kept out of the country, in time obtain the control of all branches of business, the same as they have done in Manila.

"Their immorality is of the most iniquitous character. They are regardless of female virtue, and take especial delight in inducing young girls into their premises for the most flagrant purposes. Their brothels are boldly open upon some streets, where boys are ruined for life by visiting those abominable haunts.

"Regardless of human life, they would to-day, if they knew themselves to be powerful enough to escape the vengeance which should follow the deed, murder every white man and boy in the city, and only spare the women and girls for a fate worse than death. They have been a curse to every country where they have gained a foothold."

Note—The above shows the intensity of feeling which was held by many Californians during the period from 1880 to 1900. Reason has now taken the place of prejudice whenever the Chinese are concerned.

ROSTER OF OFFICERS OF STEVENSON'S REGIMENT

Colonel Jonathan D. Stevenson was in command of the New York regiment of one thousand volunteer soldiers, which was sent by the United States Government to California, with the following officials attached thereto, namely:

FIELD OFFICERS.
Colonel, J. D. Stevenson.
Lieutenant-Colonel, Henry S. Burton.
Major, James A. Hardie.

STAFF OFFICERS.
Surgeon, Alexander Perry.
Asst, Surgeon, Robert Murray.
Asst. Surgeon, William C. Parker.
Captain William G. Marcy, Commissary.
Lieutenant J. C. Bonnycastle, Adjutant.
Captain Joseph L. Folsom, Asst. Quartermaster.

NON-COMMISSIONED STAFF
Sergeant-Major, Alexander C. McDonald.
Quarter-master Sergeant, Stephen Harris.
Quarter-master Sergeant, George G. Belt.
Quarter-master Sergeant, James C. Low.

SUTLER'S DEPARTMENT.
Sutler, Samuel W. Haight.
Clerk, James C. L. Wadsworth.

COMPANY A.
Captain, Seymour G. Steele.
Lieutenant, George S. Penrose.
Lieutenant, Charles B. Young.
Lieutenant, George F. Lemon.
Sergeant, Sherman O. Houghton.
Sergeant, Walter Chipman.
Sergeant, Edward Irwin.

COMPANY B.
Captain, ———Turner.
Lieutenant, Henry C. Matsell.
Lieutenant, Thomas E. Ketchum.
Lieutenant, E. Gould Buffum.
Sergeant, James Stayton.
Sergeant, Charles C. Scott.
Sergeant, John Wilt.
Sergeant, Charles Richardson.
Sergeant, James D. Denniston.

COMPANY C.
Captain, J. E. Brackett.
Lieutenant, Theron R. Per Lee.
Lieutenant, Thomas J. Roach.
Lieutenant, Charles C. Anderson.
Lieutenant, Wm R. Tremmels. (Died off Cape Horn.)
Lieutenant, George D. Brewerton.
Sergeant, Edmund P. Crosby.
Sergeant, William Johnson.
Sergeant, George Robinson.

COMPANY D.
Captain, Henry M. Naglee.
Lieutenant, George A. Pendleton.
Lieutenant, Hiram W. Theall.
Lieutenant, Joseph C. Morehead.
Sergeant, Aaron Lyons.
Sergeant, William Roach.
Sergeant, Henry J. Wilson.

COMPANY E.
Captain, Nelson Taylor.
Lieutenant, Edwards Williams.

OFFICERS OF STEPHENSON'S REGIMENT

Lieutenant, William E. Cuttrell.
Lieutenant, Thomas L. Vermeule.
Sergeant, John M. O'Neil.
Sergeant, Henry S. Morton.
Sergeant, James Maneis.
Sergeant, Abraham Van Riper.

COMPANY F.

Captain, Francis J. Lippitt.
Lieutenant, Henry Storrow Carnes.
Lieutenant, William H. Weirick.
Lieutenant, John M. Huddart.
Sergeant, James Queen.
Sergeant, Thomas Hipwood.
Sergeant, James Mulvey.
Sergeant, John C. Pulis.

COMPANY G.

Captain, Matthew R. Stevenson.
Lieutenant, John McH. Hollingsworth.
Lieutenant, Jeremiah Sherwood.
Lieutenant, William H. Smith.
Sergeant, Walter Taylor.
Sergeant, William B. Travers.
Sergeant, James Mehan.
Sergeant, John Connell.
Sergeant, George Jackson.

COMPANY H.

Captain, John B. Frisbie.
Lieutenant, Edward Gilbert.
Lieutenant, John S. Day.
Sergeant, Eleazer Frisbie.
Sergeant, William Grow.
Sergeant, Henry A. Schoolcraft.
Sergeant, James Winne.

COMPANY J.

Captain, William E. Shannon.
Lieutenant, Henry Magee.
Lieutenant, Palmer B. Hewlett.
Sergeant, Joseph Evans.
Sergeant, Joshua S. Vincent.
Sergeant, B. Logan.

COMPANY K.

Captain, Kimball H. Dimmick.
Lieutenant, John S. Norris.
Lieutenant, George C. Hubbard.
Lieutenant, Roderick M. Morrison.
Sergeant, Jackson Sellers.

CHAPLAIN,

Rev. T. M. Leavenworth.

STEVENSON'S REGIMENT COMES TO CALIFORNIA

The regiment sailed from New York on September the 26th, 1846, in three transports of about eight hundred tons burden each, namely: "Thomas H. Perkins," Captain James Arthur, (formerly of the "California," a hide ship); "Loo Choo," Captain Hatch, (formerly of the "Barnstable," also a hide ship), and ship "Susan Drew," Captain————, for San Francisco. The troops were equally divided among the vessels. After leaving New York, the three ships soon parted company and were out of sight of each other until their arrival at Rio Janeiro, where they remained ten days.

On Colonel Stevenson's arrival at Rio Janeiro, he found an American naval squadron in port. While he was preparing to salute the squadron's flag, the captain of the port came on board and asked Col. Stevenson if he was intending to salute the Brazilian flag. The Colonel replied that he was not, but was preparing to salute the flag of the squadron. Then the captain of the port asked if he would exchange salutes, to which the Colonel replied he would do so with pleasure.

After the salute to the American flag was fired, the Colonel sent Captain Folsom to the flag-ship of the squadron to inform the Commodore that he was in command of the New York regiment on its way to California; and also, that he intended to salute the Brazilian flag. The Commodore said that there was no intercourse between the Brazilian government, and the American Minister and himself. That as Colonel Stevenson was in command of his regiment, he could do what seemed best, but the relations were somewhat strained between our representatives and that government. When Captain Folsom returned, Colonel Stevenson sent an officer on shore, to the captain of the port to inform him that he declined to fire the promised salute to the Brazilian government. The justification of declining to salute the Brazilian flag was the severe criticism which had been passed upon certain imprudent remarks of Minister Wise the day before Folsom visited the flag-ship. Wise was the god-father at the christening on board the flag-ship, of a child born in the fleet of transports during their voyage to Rio Janeiro, and spoke of the infant being greater as to nationality than the child-princess, who had been christened but a short time previous at the Palace.

Probably there was unpleasantness between minister and government, anterior to the christening incident. The Imperial Council met and passed a resolution to order the transports, as well as other American vessels, out of port. Colonel Stevenson, after his ships dropped anchor, issued a general order to the regiment that one-third of the men should have liberty on shore one day; and on the next two succeeding days one-third should enjoy a similar privilege. Colonel Stevenson had taken up his quarters on shore and when that resolution was passed, he was informed of the fact by an English merchant.

When he heard this he went back to his fleet to countermand the order, to avoid any collision between the soldiers and the citizens; and he informed the men of the probable difficulty. He instructed the companies to prepare themselves to be ready for the emergency, everything must be in perfect order, and perhaps the next time they went on shore, it would be with fixed bayonets. As he stated this, the men went aloft and manned the yards and cheered him. He visited the other two ships and countermanded his order, giving the same reasons for doing so. He was also cheered from the yards by them; all of the men being eager for a fight. Colonel Stevenson went on shore, and as he landed on the mole he was met by many thousand people and was asked the reason of the cheering on the three ships. He stated the above mentioned facts, and told the citizens if the resolution which was passed should be enforced, he would land one thousand men with fixed bayonets, and they would have one thousand men worse than so many devils turned loose on them, and also have the American naval squadron's batteries opened upon the city under which fire the Emperor's palace would inevitably be destroyed. But the Imperial resolution was never put in force. The Commodore seeing the commotion on the mole went on shore to ascertain its cause and there thanked Colonel Stevenson for his action in the matter.

In leaving Rio Janeiro the "Perkins" sailed directly for her destination, and arrived on the 6th of March, 1847, one hundred and sixty-five days from New York, with the Colonel of the regiment and her pro rata of the soldiers. After departing from Rio Janeiro the "Loo Choo" and "Susan Drew" stopped at Valparaiso. Both vessels reached San Francisco in the same month, but after the arrival of the "Perkins."

The voyage of the fleet from the Atlantic to the Pacific oceans was without any material interruptions to mar the comforts of their loads of humanity. These troops were the first that ever left the Atlantic coast of the United States to go so great a distance to a foreign country.

SOME PARTICULARS REGARDING STEVENSON'S REGIMENT

When Colonel Stevenson reached San Francisco he found orders awaiting him from General Kearny for the distribution of the companies of the regiment, which were as follows: Sonoma one, Presidio two, Monterey two, Santa Barbara three, and Los Angeles two companies. On the arrival of these companies at Los Angeles, they found a battalion of five hundred Mormon soldiers, and the latter were turned over to Colonel Stevenson's command. In July the battalion was disbanded. A new company of Mormons was organized under Captain Davis, and sent to San Diego, and remained there until April or May, 1848, when it was mustered out of service. Colonel Stevenson took command at Monterey where he established his head quarters. Early in June, 1847, he received orders from Washington to take command from Santa Barbara southward, with headquarters at Los Angeles, to the line of the boundary of the Territory newly acquired by conquest, during the pendency of diplomatic discussion over the terms of the Treaty of Guadalupe Hidalgo, which was not ratified until May 30, 1848. In August, September and October, 1848, the entire regiment was mustered out of service, and the soldiers became citizens of the new country, and were living under their own flag.

When Stevenson arrived he found California in a state of tranquility, the result of the good work of Commodore Stockton; a long account of which I have given. There is no doubt whatever that Colonel Stevenson, arriving as he did soon after the battle of the river of San Gabriel, which stamped the naval officer as the conqueror and hero of the war, demonstrated to the Californians the endless power and resources of the United States, to perpetuate its authority over the conquered country.

After the disembarcation of the regiment, the three ships departed for China, for cargoes of Chinese merchandise for New York and other Eastern ports.

The ship "Brutus," Captain Adams, was chartered by the government to transport the stragglers of the regiment, who had been left behind, and also stores for the command at San Francisco. She sailed from New York for her destination and arrived in April, 1847.

The ship "Isabella" sailed from Philadelphia on August 16th, 1847, with a detachment of one hundred soldiers, and arrived at California on February 18th, 1848; at the same time that the ship "Sweden" arrived with another detachment of soldiers.

Before and after war was declared between the United States and Mexico, a journey to California overland was attended with dangers. The person making the journey would feel as if exiled to some foreign land. It took from four to six months to accomplish it.

Colonel Stevenson, during his long residence in California, has invariably won the respect and esteem of his fellow citizens by his manly and upright line of action. All that he has done has been prompted by a fixed principle of honor, probity and integrity. He is still in full possession of his mental faculties and exercises his mind more effectually than do many who have not reached his term of years. He has ever been kind, courteous and obliging to his friends, and even many strangers have cause to be grateful for some benevolent action on his part. It is to be hoped that he may be spared for many years to gladden the hearts of his friends by his presence among them. (1888.)

I may here remark that his son, Captain Matthew R. Stevenson, whom I knew after the arrival of the regiment, was a high-minded, brave young officer of the regular army. He died at the time of our civil war, in 1861, in the service of his country during that eventful period of the nation's life.

In the winter of 1881-82, I was at the capital of the nation. On the morning before Christmas, Mr. James B. Metcalfe and myself made a trip to the tomb of the Father of his country (Mount Vernon) to view the interesting relics, that were preserved for our citizens and those of other nations to look at, as memorials of General Washington. In nearing the wharf that Washington used, or the site on which the old one stood in his days, I observed a tall, stout, well-dressed gentleman looking at me, while at the same time he approached, and said: "Are you a Western man from California?" I replied, "Yes." He then asked my name which I told him. "Oh!" he said, "I was in your store in San Francisco many times in 1847; I was then a lieutenant in Stevenson's regiment and my name is Hollingsworth. I will take pleasure in showing you and your friend the sights of Mount Vernon." Colonel Hollingsworth was the Superintendent of Mount Vernon at that time. He went with us to the general's chamber and showed us the bedstead on which Washington died; then to the room which General Lafayette had occupied, where everything remained just as this noble friend of liberty and comrade of Washington had left it. The apartment in which Mrs. Martha Washington died, was next opened for our inspection, and the original furniture stood as she had used it. From the house we went to the tomb of both the husband and wife. All of these objects interested us very much. Col. Hollingsworth presented us with several relics from trees that were planted by General Washington's own hands; for which we were very grateful and expressed our thanks, as well as for the courteous attentions he had bestowed upon us, because I was an old Californian from the country that he liked, and which as he remarked to me, he hoped to see again.

Many years ago some of the energetic and patriotic women of the nation formed a company for purchasing Mount Vernon and many relics, as permanent mementos of Washington, for the people of the United States. The property was bought for two hundred thousand dollars, by two hundred thousand women of the country.

MISSIONS AND THEIR WEALTH: HACENDADOS AND THEIR PROPERTY

When I was at the port of San Luis Obispo, in the bark "Louisa," in the year 1831, the Mission of that name was wealthy, with sixty thousand head of cattle and thousands of sheep and horses. The great wealth of the Missions, while under Spanish and Mexican control, in cattle, horses and sheep, will be shown by the following enumeration of their live stock, before and after their secularization—before and after the year 1830.

Mission Sonoma: 30,000 cattle and 1,000 horses and mares. The stock on the rancho Suscol before mentioned belonged to the Mission.

Mission of Santa Clara: 65,000 cattle, 30,000 sheep and 4,000 horses and mares.

Mentioning this Mission, recalls to my mind a transaction in hides and tallow, with the Fathers Mercado and Muro, in my earlier dealings with them in September, 1844, which showed that the Missions acted in unison with each other. I received from Father Mercado of the Santa Clara Mission, a letter to Father Muro of Mission of San José, requesting him to deliver to me two hundred hides, which he did, as part payment for some goods I had sold the former. I had not pressed the matter at all; but he said it was the same as if he had paid for them himself.

Mission San Juan Bautista: More than 60,000 cattle, 2,000 horses and mares and 20,000 sheep.

Mission San Antonio: Don José Ábrego, administrator in 1833 and 1834; 10,000 cattle, 500 horses and mares, 10,000 sheep. There were 1,000 Indians at the Mission.

Mission San Miguel: 35,000 cattle, 1,000 horses and mares and 20,000 sheep.

Soledad (Mission): 25,000 cattle, 1,000 horses and mares and 10,000 sheep.

La Purisima Concepcion (Mission): 20,000 cattle, 1,000 horses and mares and 15,000 sheep.

Mission Santa Ynez: 20,000 cattle, 1,500 horses and mares and 10,000 sheep.

Mission San Fernando: 50,000 cattle, 1,500 horses and mares and 20,000 sheep.

Mission San Gabriel: 80,000 cattle, 3,000 horses and mares and 30,000 sheep.

Mission San Luis Rey: 60,000 cattle, 2,000 horses and mares and 20,000 sheep.

Mission San Juan Capistrano: 20,000 cattle, 1,000 horses and mares and 10,000 sheep.

Mission of San Diego: 15,000 cattle, 1,000 horses and mares and 20,000 sheep.

Mission of Santa Barbara: 20,000 cattle, 1,000 horses and mares and 20,000 sheep.

Mission San Buena Ventura: 25,000 cattle, 1,500 horses and mares and 10,000 sheep.

The following is a list of the solid men of the department, anterior to and after the change of government.

Francisco P. Pacheco: Ranchos San Felipe and San Luis Gonzales, about 90,000 acres of land; 14,000 cattle, 500 horses and mares and 15,000 sheep. That rich hacendado was a large buyer of merchandise, and I sold many goods to him in 1844 and 1845. He hauled the hides and tallow from his hacienda, a distance of sixty miles, to the embarcadero of Santa Clara, now the town of Alviso.

David Spence: Rancho Buena Esperanza, 25,000 acres of land; 4,000 head of cattle, 500 horses and mares.

Juan Malarin: Ranchos Zanjones, Guadalupe, Correos and Chualar, 8 leagues of land; 6,000 cattle, 200 horses and mares, and 2,000 sheep.

James Watson: Rancho San Benito, 2 leagues of land; 2,000 cattle, 100 horses and mares, and 1,000 sheep.

Teodoro Gonzales: Rancho San Cenobio or Rincon de la Punta del Monte; 5,000 cattle and 300 horses and mares.

Estevan de la Torre: Rancho Escarpines, two leagues of land; 1,600 cattle and 150 horses and mares.

Estevan Munrás: Rancho Laguna Seca, 3 leagues of land; 3,000 cattle, and 200 horses and mares.

Feliciano Soberanes: Ranchos Ex Mission Soledad and San Lorenzo; 4,000 cattle, 2,000 sheep and 300 horses and mares. This land was the old Mission Soledad and pursuant to the law of secularization was sold by order of the government. After the arrival of a Bishop in California, he called on Señor Soberanes, who was ill at the time, and requested him to give back to the Church the property above named—an advisable act, if he, Soberanes, wanted to save his soul. The old hacendado replied to the Reverend Father, that he had decided to leave the land to his heirs and he must decline his request.

Charles Wolter: Rancho Toro, 4 leagues of land; 3,000 cattle, 2,000 sheep, 150 horses and mares.

Sebastian Rodrigues: Rancho Bolsa del Pajaro, 2 leagues of land; 2,000 cattle, and 100 horses and mares.

José Amesti: Rancho Los Corralitos, 4 leagues of land; 5,000 cattle, 300 horses and mares, and 2,000 sheep.

Juan Antonio Vallejo: Rancho Pajaro, 4 leagues of land; 4,000 cattle and 200 horses and mares.

W. E. P. Hartnell: Rancho Alisal, 2 leagues of land; 2,500 cattle and 200 horses and mares.

James Stokes: Rancho de las Verjeles; 2,200 cattle and 100 horses and mares.

José Rafael Gonzales (Pintito): Rancho San Miguelito de Trinidad, 5 leagues of land; 4,500 cattle, and 200 horses and mares.

Juan Wilson: Rancho Guilicos, 4 leagues of land; 3,000 cattle, and 500 horses and mares.

Government Rancho Nacional: in Monterey Valley; 6 leagues of land; 15,000 cattle, and 200 horses and mares.

Santiago and José Ramon Estrada: Rancho Buenavista, 3 leagues of land; 2,000 cattle, and 200 horses and mares.

Joaquin Estrada: Rancho Santa Margarita, 6 leagues of land; 4,000 cattle and 300 horses and mares and 2,000 sheep.

José Simeon Castro: Rancho Bolsa Nueva y Moro Cojo, 8 leagues of land (the present site of the city of Castroville); 6,000 cattle and 500 horses and mares.

Francisco Rico: Rancho San Bernardo, 3 leagues of land; 3,000 cattle, and 100 horses and mares.

José Ábrego: owner of the following ranchos:—Punta Pinos, 1 league of land, now the present site of "Pacific Grove;" Noche Buena, near the Hotel Del Monte, 2 leagues; Saucito, 1 league and San Francisquito, 3 leagues. Those ranchos contained 4,000 cattle, 200 horses and mares and 2,000 sheep.

Juan Anzar: Rancho Los Aromitas y Agua Caliente, 3 leagues of land; 4,000 cattle, 200 horses and mares and 4,000 sheep.

Charles Wolter: Rancho Tularcito; 1,000 cattle and 50 horses and mares.

William G. Dana, Rancho Nipoma, 32,728 acres of land; 6,000 cattle, 500 horses and mares and 10,000 sheep.

Joaquin and José A. Carrillo: Rancho Lompoc, 38,335 acres; 2,000 cattle, 200 horses and mares and 1,000 sheep.

Salvio Pacheco: Rancho Monte Diablo, 18,000 acres of land; 3,500 cattle, 300 horses and mares and 4,000 sheep.

Henry D. Fitch: Rancho Sotoyomé, 11 leagues of land; 14,000 cattle, 1,000 horses and mares and 10,000 sheep.

John A. Sutter: Rancho New Helvetia, 11 leagues of land; 4,000 cattle, 800 horses and mares and 10,000 sheep.

William A. Richardson: Rancho Saucelito, 19,571 acres of land; 2,800 cattle and 300 horses and mares.

Rafael Garcia: Ranchos Tomales and Baulinas, 2 leagues of land; 5,000 cattle and 150 horses and mares.

Ygnacio Pacheco: Rancho San José, 6,660 acres of land; 3,300 cattle and 400 horses and mares.

John Marsh: Rancho Los Médanos, 4 leagues of land; 5,000 cattle, 500 horses and mares, and 5,000 sheep.

Tomas Pacheco and Agustin Alviso: Rancho Potrero de los Cerritos, 3 leagues of land; 4,000 cattle, 200 horses and mares and 2,000 sheep.

Anastasio Carrillo: Rancho Punta de la Concepcion, 24,992 acres of land; 4,000 cattle and 500 horses and mares.

Ex-Alcalde José Jesus Noe: Rancho San Miguel, 1 league of land; 2,000 cattle and 200 horses and mares.

Hilaria Sanchez Read: Rancho Tamalpais, 2 leagues of land; 2,000 cattle, 200 horses and mares and 1,000 sheep.

Juan Temple: Rancho Los Cerritos, 5 leagues of land; 14,000 cattle, 5,000 sheep and 1,000 horses and mares.

Ricardo Vejar: Rancho San José, 22,720 acres of land; 8,000 cattle and 600 horses and mares.

Abel Stearns: Rancho Alamitos, 6 leagues of land, and other ranchos, amounting to many thousand acres; 30,000 cattle, 2,000 horses and mares, and 10,000 sheep.

Juan Ávila: rancho El Nigüil, 4 leagues of land; 9,000 cattle and 500 horses and mares.

Pio Pico and Andres Pico: Rancho Los Coyotes, 56,980 acres of land; in Los Angeles county; 10,000 cattle, 1,500 horses and mares, and 5,000 sheep; also ranchos Santa Margarita, Los Flores and San Mateo, in San Diego county, with many thousand acres of land; 10,000 cattle, 2,000 horses and mares and 15,000 sheep.

Carlos Antonio Carrillo: Rancho Sespe, 6 leagues of land; 5,000 cattle, 1,000 horses and mares and 5,000 sheep.

Ygnacio del Valle: Rancho Camulos, 22 leagues of land; 5,000 cattle, 1,000 horses and mares and 5,000 sheep.

HACENDADOS AND THEIR PROPERTY

Manuel Dominguez: Rancho San Pedro, 10 leagues of land; 8,000 cattle, 1,500 horses and mares and 5,000 sheep.

Bernardo Yorba: Ranchos Santiago de Santa Ana, 11 leagues of land; La Sierra, 4 leagues: El Rincon, 1 league; those ranchos in all contained 11,000 cattle, 1,500 horses and mares and 8,000 sheep.

Agustin Machado: Rancho La Ballona, 13,920 acres of land; 10,000 cattle and 600 horses and mares.

Julio Verdugo: Rancho Los Verdugos, 8 leagues of land; 5,000 cattle and 500 horses and mares.

John Roland and William Workman; Rancho La Puente, 48,790 acres of land; 5,000 cattle, 500 horses and mares and 5,000 sheep.

José Sepúlveda: Rancho San Joaquin, 11 leagues of land; 14,000 cattle and 3,000 horses and mares.

José Antonio Aguirre: Rancho San Pedro, 2 leagues of land; 3,700 cattle.

José Loreto and Juan Sepúlveda: Rancho Los Palos Verdes, 31,600 acres of land; 5,000 cattle, 1,000 horses and mares and 5,000 sheep.

Nasario Dominguez: Rancho San Pedro, 2 leagues of land; 5,000 cattle and 300 horses and mares.

Ygnacio Machado: Rancho Ballona, 13,920 acres of land; 3,600 cattle and 200 horses and mares.

Antonio Maria Lugo: Rancho San Antonio, 11 leagues; and Chino, 6 leagues of land; 30,000 cattle and 1,500 horses and mares.

José Maria Lugo: Rancho San Antonio; 3,000 cattle and 500 horses and mares.

Vicente Lugo: Rancho San Antonio; 4,000 cattle and 400 horses and mares.

Tomás Yorba: Rancho Santiago de Santa Ana, 8 leagues of land; 6,000 cattle, 400 horses and mares and 4,000 sheep.

Teodosio Yorba: Rancho Santiago de Santa Ana, 7 leagues of land; 4,800 cattle and 500 horses and mares.

Tomás A. Sanchez: Rancho La Ciénega; 2,000 cattle, 1,000 horses and mares and 15,000 sheep. This hacendado was Sheriff of Los Angeles county from 1860 to 1868.

José Noriega and Robert Livermore: Rancho Los Pozitos, 2 leagues of land; 2,000 cattle, 200 horses and mares and 2,000 sheep.

Fulgencio and Mariano Higuera: Rancho Agua Caliente, 2 leagues of land; 3,500 cattle, 350 horses and mares and 4,000 sheep.

Antonio Suñol: Rancho El Valle de San José, 51,573 acres of land; 6,600 cattle, 500 horses and mares and 5,000 sheep.

Agustin Bernal: Rancho El Valle de San José, 4,000 cattle, 400 horses and mares and 4,000 sheep.

Juan Bernal: Rancho El Valle de San José; 2,300 cattle, 200 horses and mares and 2,000 sheep.

Tiburcio Vasquez: Rancho Corral de Tierra, 1 league of land; 2,100 cattle and 200 horses and mares; in San Mateo county.

Francisco Sanchez: Rancho San Pedro, 2 leagues of land; in San Mateo county; 2,000 cattle and 200 horses and mares.

Joaquin Ruiz: Rancho La Bolsa Chica, 2 leagues of land; 2,400 cattle and 500 horses and mares.

José Antonio Yorba: Rancho Santiago de Santa Ana, 2 leagues of land; 3,200 cattle and 300 horses and mares.

Ramon Yorba: Rancho Santiago de Santa Ana, 2 leagues of land; 2,500 cattle and 400 horses and mares.

Macedonio Aguilar: Rancho La Ballona, 2 leagues of land; 4,800 cattle, 400 horses and mares and 2,000 sheep.

Diego Sepúlveda: Rancho Los Palos Verdes, 2 leagues of land; 2,300 cattle and 300 horses and mares.

Francisco Sepúlveda: Rancho San Vicente, 38,000 acres of land; 5,000 cattle and 500 horses and mares.

Francisco Ocampo: Rancho San Bartolo, in Los Angeles Valley; 8 leagues of land; 7,000 cattle and 350 horses and mares.

John B. R. Cooper: Rancho Molino, 3 leagues of land; 6,000 cattle and 200 horses and mares; also Ranchos Sur, 2 leagues of land, and Bolsaó de Potrero y Moro Cojo, or La Sagrada Familia, 2 leagues of land; 3,000 cattle and 200 hundred horses and mares.

Juan María Anzar and Manuel Larios: Ranchos Santa Ana, 1 league, and Quien Sabe, 6 leagues of land; in San Juan Bautista Valley; 4,000 cattle, 300 horses and mares and 4,000 sheep.

Ygnacio Palomares: Rancho San José (Pomona), 2 leagues of land; 3,000 cattle and 500 horses and mares.

Pedro Ávila: Rancho El Nigüil, 2 leagues of land, in Los Angeles Valley; 3,400 cattle and 300 horses and mares.

Henrique Ávila: Rancho Los Cuervos, 2 leagues of land; 2,200 cattle, 300 horses and mares and 2,000 sheep.

José Maria Ávila: Rancho Los Cuervos, 2 leagues of land; 2,000 cattle and 200 horses and mares.

Antonio Ygnacio Ávila: Rancho Sauzal Redondo, 5 leagues of land; 4,500 cattle and 500 horses.

Andres Pico: Ex-Mission San Fernando, 11 leagues of land; 5,000 cattle, and 500 horses and mares. Some years after the secularization of the Mission of San Fernando, it became impoverished, and 121,620 acres of its lands were granted to Eulogio de Célis; probably Pico became a joint owner with him in the large tract.

To enumerate all the ranchos in the department, with the live stock on them, would take too many pages. I have only mentioned, comparatively, a few or some of the more important haciendas, to illustrate their great wealth.

After their downfall, the Missions became destitute and the lands were granted by the authorities of the department to citizens of the young country. Those men became stock-raisers, and through the experience gained by their observations of management by the Fathers, they succeeded in reinstating the lost riches of California, which were taken from the missionaries; and they even accumulated more than twofold the former wealth of the primitive land. They became extensive hacendados, and were inspired by the numerous evidences around them, which remained only as monuments that were fast crumbling away, of the energy, perseverance and industry of the good Fathers, in their days of plenty and their acquisition of property.

I may have alluded before to the facts contained in the statement, which leads me to make the assertion, without fear of a successful contradiction, that the Department of California previous to and after the ruin of the Missions, in proportion to the population, was the richest of any country under Spanish dominion and inhabited by citizens of Castillian extraction.

There were one thousand and forty-five grants of ranchos of all sizes made by the governors; deducting from that number two hundred and forty-five (which it is presumed were not stocked with animals) will leave eight hundred ranchos, which were probably all stocked; averaging 1,500 head of cattle to each rancho, and making a total of 1,200,000; this was after the Missions became poor. There are eighty-seven haciendas above mentioned, with an average of 5,310 cattle to each. When, in addition, the horses and sheep are considered, surely no stronger proof of the assertion as to the wealth of the Department of California at that period, could be either required or produced.

RECORD OF SHIPS ARRIVING FROM 1774 TO 1847

I am indebted to Mr. James Alexander Forbes, for the following list of arrivals and vessels at California ports from 1774 to 1847. Mr. Forbes for years occupied the post of official government translator and keeper of the Spanish and Mexican Archives in the United States Surveyor General's office, for the District of California; without his aid I could not have obtained any data concerning the earlier shipping.

He was the son of the well known pioneer, James A. Forbes, who, during his lifetime, was esteemed and respected by all who had social and business relations with him. J. A. Forbes, Jr. was educated in Santa Clara College, and being a master of several languages, obtained the position of Official Translator of the laws of California, in the years 1867, 1868, 1869, 1870; he had the reputation of being the most accurate translator and fluent interpreter in the State. His father came to California in the year 1829; he was British Vice-Consul for many years. He married a native California lady of Castillian descent; he was a highly educated gentleman speaking the English, Spanish and French languages with great accuracy and fluency; it was very entertaining and instructive to listen to his conversation. During his consulate, his official acts gave satisfaction to his government, and his private life was irreproachable. His death occurred in 1881, at the ripe age of 79 years; leaving a family of ten children.

1774.
San Carlos.
Principe, July, 24.

1776.
San Carlos.
San Antonio, June 6th.
Principe.

1778.
San Carlos arrives on the coast July 22.
Order for vessels that bring supplies to take back salt, March 8th.

1779.
San Carlos arrives at San Diego Feb. 15.
Princesa and Favorita anchored in the Bay or Port of San Francisco on the 15th of September, 1779. The vessels belonged to His Majesty King of Spain and came on an exploring expedition under command of Don Ygnacio Ortega. They reached up to 65° and some minutes north latitude and did not go to 70° north latitude as ordered because the coast turned to the south. Garland (Spanish brig) captured by an English man of war, June 7th, 1779.

1783.
San Carlos, June, 2.
Favorita, July 27.

1784
Favorita, Spanish man of war, Oct. 25th.

1786.

Spanish Frigate Aranzazu, Feb. 11th, Santa Lucia, June 7th, Favorita, Sept. 29th, Princesa, Sept. 21st, Spanish war ships, with materials for Presidio buildings. Order prohibiting passengers on board vessels to carry more than 2 pounds of tobacco, October 5th.

1787.

Astrolabe and Boussole, anchored at Monterey, with La Pérouse, the explorer, April 12th.
Princesa, at Monterey, Feb. 27th.
Aranzazu, January 6th.
Boussole, Jan. 6th Astrolabe, Jan. 6th, French vessels.
San Carlos, Sept. 29th.

1788.

San Carlos, Sept. 7th.
Princesa, at Santa Barbara, Oct. 8th.
Frigate Aranzazu, Dec. 21st, came into port and Mateo Rubio, a soldier, was wounded by the firing of a cannon.

1789.

Frigate Aranzazu at Santa Barbara, Oct. 2.

1791.

Aranzazu, August 22d.
Princesa, October 24th; saw unknown vessel in distress in Pichilingue Bay.
Princesa (Spanish Frigate) arrived at Loreto with Naturalist José Longinos Martinez and Jaime Senseve, Botanist, to make collections for the Museum of Natural History, October 25th.
Aranzazu (Spanish Frigate), Juan Bautista Matute, Captain. He says to the Governor of the Department: "By last advices from the Court of Madrid, which I delivered at Nootka, it appears that the King does not wish that port to be abandoned." Monterey, June 12th.
Aranzazu, Juan Hendrick, Captain; January 25th.
Frigate Concepcion at anchor in Nootka harbor with Ramon Antonio Saavedra, March 7th.

1794.

Princesa, January 17th.
Sutil, February 28th.
Mexicana, February 28th.
Arrival of Vancouver expedition on the same date, Feby 28th.
Frigate Concepcion, April 26th.
Mexicana at San Francisco, June 10th.
The Frigate Concepcion wrecked off Pichilingue Bay, Lower Cal., July 5th.
Saturnina, August 5th.
Sloop Horcasitas, August 29th.
Concepcion in San Diego, Dec. 17th.
Chatham, at Monterey, Nov. 2nd.
Discovery, at Monterey, Nov. 5th.
Aranzazu, Oct. 22nd, at Santa Barbara; at Monterey Nov. 14.
Unknown English vessel at Santa Cruz, November 30th.
English launches arrived at Santa Cruz and precautions were taken to prevent men from landing November 30th. The English launches depart and cause no disorder; December 1st.
Frigate Aranzazu, bound for Nootka from Monterey, July 12.
Discovery, (Eng. ship) with Vancouver on board. Expedition under Vancouver arrived the second time on November 6th.
Chatham, (Am. ship) Peter Puget master.

1795.

Resolution, (Eng.) Feb. 6th.
Achilles, (Eng.) May 22nd.
Phœnix, (Eng.) Sept. 10th.
Aranzazu, September 23rd.
Resolution, (Eng.) at San Diego. Oct 1st.
Active, (Eng. war vessel) with an English Commissioner on board, March 3rd.
Resolution, (Eng. man of war) Captain Juan Loche, seeking supplies that were furnished September 6th.

1796.

Spanish Frigate Concepcion from Manila, anchored at Santa Barbara, July 25th.
Sloop Loreto, July 25th.

RECORD OF SHIPS ARRIVING FROM 1774 TO 1847

Sutil, arrived July 11th.
Providence, (British man of war) W. Broughton, Commander, at Monterey.

1797.

American ship ———, Captain Dows forcibly put on shore eleven foreigners from his vessel, Oct. 6th.
Paquebot S. Carlos, wrecked and lost in the harbor of San Francisco, March 23rd.
Concepcion and Princesa, (Spanish frigates) have come to guard the ports of California, March 7th, and April 13th.
Magallanes, Spanish vessel at Santa Barbara, Dec. 5th.
Goycochea, commander of Santa Barbara (Spanish war vessel) keeps guard up and down the coast, to see if they can discover the "Fama," but see nothing.
San Carlos, April 14th.
Unknown large vessel seen off the coast, May 23rd.
Three more large vessels seen off the coast, May 11th.
Spanish Frigate Princesa, at Santa Barbara, May 27.
Several vessels sighted off the coast, July 4th.
Frigate Princesa seen off the coast of San Diego, July 22; and the same vessel at San Diego, October 20th.

1798.

Fama, (Am. ship) January 7th.
Brig Active, March 31st.
Magallanes, March 31st.
Otter, Captain Ebenezer Dow.
Concepcion, October 19th.

1799.

Eliza, Captain James Rowan, June 12th.
Eliza, (Eng. ship) Jas. Rowan, captain, writes to Pedro Alberin, Comandante of San Francisco, about getting wood and water, Nov. 10th.
Mercedes, (Eng. sloop of war) at San Diego, July 6th.

1800.

Betsy, (Am. vessel) at San Diego Aug. 11th.
Nuestra Señora de la Concepcion, Spanish frigate, Aug. 25th.
Princesa (Spanish frigate,) Aug. 25th.

1801.

Enterprise, (Am. vessel) at San Diego, July 3rd.

1803.

Alexander (Am. vessel) John Brown capt., at San Diego, Mar. 13th.
Mexican schooner San Joaquin, and Lelia Byrd, (Am. vessel,) in San Diego June 20th.
Santa Ana, (Mex. schooner.)
Catalina, 12 guns and 62 men was ordered off the coast, but did not go Oct. 15th.
Alexander, (Am.) Captain Brown, Feb-7th.
Lelia Byrd, (Am.) Captain W. Shater, at San Diego Feb. 15th.

1804.

O'Cain, (Am. vessel) 60 men, 15 canoes, 5 boats, and 16 guns, went into San Quentin for repairs and provisions, when ready was ordered off the coast, but stayed until she had killed all the otter from Rosario to Santo Domingo. Mar. 24th, O'Cain, captain.
Hazard, Sept. 6th.
Active, (Eng. man-of-war) Sept. 13th.
Racer, (Am.) lands soldiers at Ensenada.

1806.

O'Cain, (Am.) José O'Cain, master, in San Luis Obispo Jan. 2nd.
Racer, (Am.) at San Diego July 16th.
Juno, (Russian ship) Resanoff, captain and agent of Russian-American Fur Company, at San Francisco Apr. 16th.
Peacock. (Am.) the captain captured three Spanish soldiers that were rescued by giving up four American prisoners. Monterey, July 15th.

1807.

Racer, (Am.) at San Diego, July 25th.
Alert, Captain Caleb Winship.

1813.

Mercurio, June 19th, captured by Nicolás Noé, captain of the Flora, (Spanish war vessel) detained at Santa Barbara until Sept. 3rd, following. Jorge, captain of the Mercurio.

1814.

Isaac Todd, Captain Frazer Smith, Feb'y 21st.

Raccoon, (Eng.) Captain W. Black, March 29th.

1815.

Columbia, July 18th.

1816.

Rurick, (Russian ship) Kotzebue, captain, Colonel, (Eng. ship) October 10th.

Extraordinary proceedings of the Lydiá (Am. ship.) She was taken, off the Refugio Rancho near Santa Barbara, by Californians, who sailed with her to Monterey, with Captain Henry Gyzelaar, her master, on board, February 5th.

The Governor of the Department sets the Lydia free; she was an American smuggler, March 9th.

Ship Albatross, smuggler, Captain W. Smith, January 25th.

Rubio, Kalzule, Rurick, Russian, October 15th.

Suvárof Chiríkof, Ermenia, Russian ships, at San Francisco, Sept. 16th.

Eagle, (Am. ship) at Refugio, Wm. Heath Davis, owner and captain.

1817.

Caminante, Captain W. Smith Wilcox, Mar. 13th.

La Cazadora, (Spanish frigate) September 30th, at Monterey.

Padushkin, a Russian officer, came to San Francisco with small boats with a letter from St. Petersburg to the Governor, April 10th.

1818.

San Ruperto, (Spanish ship) with all the crew sick with the scurvy, arrived at Monterey, February 14th.

Argentina, Santa Rosa, Hypolite Bouchard, captain, insurgent vessels or privateers, Nov. 22nd.

1819.

Cossack, (ship) brings Captain Pablo de la Portilla, with troops from Mazatlan, August 17th.

San Carlos, (Spanish ship) with munitions of war, etc., to Monterey, Aug. 25th.

Nueva Reina de los Angeles, Aug. 10th.

Nueva Reina de los Angeles, at San Diego, September 6th.

1821.

Frigate Rita.

Brig San Francisco Javier, Oct. 8th.

British frigate————May 30th.

1822.

Eagle, (Am. schooner) seized by the Government for smuggling, August 1st, and sold at auction at Santa Barbara, Nov. 8th.

San Carlos, March 10th.

Apollo, Dec. 19th.

1823.

Apollo, Jan. 20.

Am. ship Eagle, Captain William Heath Davis.

Tartar, July 24th.

Buldákof, (Russian) Aug. 31st.

Apolonia, Sept. 25th.

Am. ship Massachusetts, Oct. 6th.

Mentor, Nov. 12th.

1824.

Buldákof, Jan. 8th.

John Begg, John Lincoln, master, Sept. 25th.

Buldákof, Aug. 12th.

Rosanio, Sept. 25th.

Predpriate, Oct. 8th.

French man of war Creiser, Dec. 2nd.

Reina, Dec. 10th.

1825.

Eng. brig Eliza.

Am. brig Arab.

Spanish man of war Aquiles, P. Angulo, commander.

Morelos, formerly San Carlos, Flaminio Agazini, commander.

Pizarro, Eng. brig.
Am. schooner Rover, J. B. R. Cooper, master.
Espeleta.
Juan Battey, John Burton, master.
Russian Brig Elena, Moraviof, master.
Am. Whaler, Ploughboy, Chadwick, master.
Sachem, (Am.) W. A. Gale, master.
Maria Ester, (Mex. brig) Davis, master.
Eng. ship Bengal.
Apollo, whaler, at Santa Cruz.
Merope, (Eng. ship) supposed to be the Espeleta.
Kiahkta, (Russian brig).
Junius, (Eng. brig) Carter, master.
Asia, Spanish man of war, 70 guns, 400 men, José Martinez, commander, surrendered at Monterey to the Mexican authorities.
Constante, Spanish man of war, surrendered with the above, and re-named Apolonia.
Factor, (Am. whaler) John Alexis, master.
Spy, (Am. schooner) George Smith, master.
Nile, (Am. brig) Robert Forbes, master.
Recovery, (Eng. whaler) W. Fisher, master.
Tartar, (Am. schooner) Benj. Morrell, master.
Santa Rosa.
Snow.
Tamaahmaaha, (Am. brig) John Michi, master.
Washington, (Am. schooner) Robert Elwell, master, A. B. Thompson, supercargo.
Huascar, (Peruvian brig) J. M. Oyagüe, master, W. E. P. Hartnell, passenger.
Whaleman whaler.
Tomasa.
Triton, Jean Opham, master.
Thomas, W. Clark, master.

1826.

Sirena brought money to California.

Solitude, (Am. ship) Chas. Anderson, master.
Blossom, (Eng. exploring) Beechey, commander.
Gen. Bravo, (Mex. brig) Melendez captain.
Washington, whaler, Wm Kelley, master.
Argony, (Russian brig) Inestrumo, master.
Paragon, (Am. whaler) David Edwards, master.
Olive Branch, (Eng. brig) W. Henderson, master.
Santa Apolonia, (Mex. Schooner) Manuel Bates, master, Sanchez Ramar, supercargo.
Timorelan, (Haw. brig) seal and otter hunter at Santa Barbara.
Peruvian, (Am. whaler) Alex. Macy, master.
Mero C. (Am. ship) Barcelo Juan, master.
Mercury, (Am. whaler) W. Austin, master.
Baikal, (Russian brig) Benseman, master.
Waverly, (Haw. brig) W. G. Dana, master.
Harbinger, (Am. brig) J. Steel, master.
Charles, Aw. whaler.
Adams, (Am. ship) Danl. Fallon, master.
Speedy, Eng. Ship).
Courier, (Am. ship) W. Cunningham, master.
Inore, (Haw. brig).
Thomas Nowlan, (Eng. ship) W. Clark, master.
Cyrus, (Am. schooner) David Hariens, master.
Theresa Maria, (Am. ship) W. Gulnac, master.
Alliance, (Am. ship).

1827.

Blossom, (exploring expedition) Beechey, commander.
Harbinger, (Am.) J. Steele, master.
Olive Branch, (Eng.) W. Henderson, master.
Andes, Seth Rodgers, master.
Paraiso.

Solitude, J. Anderson, master.
Thomas Nowlan, J. Wilson, master
Carimaca.
Magdalena.
Tenieya.
Oliphant.
Maria Ester, David J. Holmes, master.
Huascar, J. M. Oyagüe, master.
Waverly, T. Robbins, master.
Sachem, W. A. Gale, master.
Okhotsh, D. Zarambo, master.
Massachusetts.
Isabella.
Héros, A. Duhaut-Cilly, master.
Spy, George Smith, master.
Griffon.
Young Tartar.
Golovnin.
Tamaahmaaha, J. Michi, master.
Favorite.
Baikal, Etholin, master.
Franklin, J. Bradshaw, master.
Cadboro.
Concrete.
Tomasa.
Courier, W. Cunningham, master.
Fulham, H. Virmond, master.
Washington, R. Ewell, master.

1828.

Phoenix, W. Ratiguende, master.
Franklin, J. Bradshaw, master.
Clio, W. Williams, master.
Vulture, Richard Barry, master
Funchal, S. Anderson, master.
Sucre, Melendez, master.
Griffon, C. Pitnack, master.
Andes, Seth Rodgers, master.
Verale, W. Deny, master.
Fulham, H. Virmond, master.
Kiakhlā.
Laperin.
Rascow, W. Fisher, master.
Guibale, T. Robbins, master.
Harbinger, J. Steele, master.
Courier, W. Cunningham, master.
Arab.
Héros, A. Duhaut-Cilly, master.
Baikal, Etholin, master.
Minerva, D. Cornelio, master.
Huascar, J. M. Oyagüe, master.
Karimoko.
Thomas Nowlan, J. Wilson, master.
Telemachus, J. Gillespie, master.
Emily Marsham, master.
Washington, R. Elwell, master.
Times, W. Ross, master.
Brillante, Waverly T. Robbins, master.
Maria Ester, Dav. J. Holmes, master.
Pocahontas, J. Bradshaw, master.
Okhotsk, D. Zarembo, master.
Solitude, J. Anderson, master.
Wilmantic, J. Bois, master.

1829.

Franklin, J. Bradshaw, master.
Andes, Seth Rodgers, master.
James Coleman, Hennet, master.
Maria Ester, H. D. Fitch, master.
Volunteer, W. S. Hinckley, master.
Susana, Swain, master.
Rosalia, Bruna Colespedriguez, master.
Ann, Burnie, master.
American.
Indian.
Vulture, Rich. Barry, master.
Funchal, Stephen Anderson, master.
Dolly, W. Warden, master.
Planet, G. Rutter, master.
Joven Angustias.
Baikal, Benseman, master.
Alvino.
Kiahktā.
Wilmington, John Bon, master.
Thomas Nowlan, J. Wilson, master.
Warren, W. Rice, master.
Santa Barbara.
Okhotsh, D. Zarembo, master.
Washington, W. Kelly, master.
Trident, Felix Esterlin, master.
Brookline, W. A. Gale, master.
Tamaahmaaha, J. Michi, master.
Waverly, T. Robbins, master.

1830.

Leonor, H. D. Fitch, master.
Thomas Nowlan, J. Wilson, master.

Maria Ester, J. A. C. Holmes, master.
Ayacucho, Joseph Snook, master.
Cyrus, David Harriens, master.
Seringapatam, grounded on Blossom Rock.
Whaleman, Joseph Ruddock, master.
Globe, Moore, master.
Catalina, C. Christen, Eulogio de Célis, supercargo.
Pocahontas, John Bradshaw, master.
Danube, Sam Cook, master.
Planet, John Rutter, master.
Washington, R. Elwell, master, carried horses to the Sandwich Islands.
Chalcedony, Joe Steel, master.
Emily, took prisoners to Santa Barbara.
Volunteer, W. S. Hinckley, master; carried Joaquin Solis and his suite as prisoners to San Blas (banished.)
Brookline, Jas. O. Locke, master.
Convoy, (Am. brig) Perkins, master.
Funchal, Stephen Anderson, master.
Jura.
Dryad, from Columbia river.

1831.

Louisa, (Am. bark) Geo. Wood, master.
Phoebe Ann, trades on the coast.
Ayacucho, John Wilson, master.
California, W. A. Gale, supercargo.
Leonor, H. D. Fitch, master.
Guadalupe, California built schooner by Joseph Chapman at San Pedro.
Wm. Little, Harry Carter, master.
Marcus, N. S. Bassett, master.
Baikal, Livovich, master.
Globe, Moore, master.
Whalehound, whaler.
Pocahontas, Bradshaw, master.
Catalina, Holmes, master brought Government stores, and also Governor José Figueroa, in 1833.
Whaleman, whaler.
Convoy, (Am. brig) Pickens, master.
Urup, D. Zarembo, master.
Margarita, carried J. M. Padres from Monterey.
Volunteer, Jos. O. Carter, master
Dryad, brought Doctor David Douglas, botanist.

Fanny, whaler.
Harriet, whaler.

1832.

Chalcedony, J. Steel, master.
Don Quixote, (Am. bark) J. Meek, master.
New Castle, Stephen Hersey, master.
Balance, Ed. Daggett, master.
Planet, sailed from Boston with the California.
California, W. A. Gale, master.
Spy.
Urup, D. Zarembo, master.
Crusader, (Am. brig) Thos. Hinckley, master.
Josephine, W. A. Richardson, master; lost at Santa Catalina Island.
Polifemia, Bradshaw, master.
Tranquilina, Geo. Prince, master.
American, whaler, Nov.
Victoria, Brewer, master.
Bolivar, Nye, master; all men sick with the scurvy; carried horses to the Sandwich Islands.
Ayacucho, John Wilson, master; the fastest vessel on the coast up to the time she was beaten by the Volunteer, in 1833.
Jóven Victoriano, September.
Pocahontas, Bradshaw, master.
Waverly, W. Sumner, master.
Roxana, Frank Thompson, master.
Wm. Thompson, Stephen Potter, master.
Anchorite, whaler.
Phoebe, whaler.
Friend, L. B. Blindenberg, master.

1833.

Catalina, (Mex. brig) J. C. Holmes, master.
Friend, L. B. Blindenberg, master.
Loriot, Gorham H. Nye, master.
North America, N. Richards, master.
Roxana, F. Thompson, master.
Polifemia.
Isabel, J. C. Albert, master.

Helvetius, (Am. whaler).
Dryad, (Eng. brig).
Bolivar, Dominis, master.
Lagoda, J. Bradshaw, master.
Facio, Santiago Johnson, master.
Crusader, Thos. Hinckley, master.
Enriqueta, Lewis Young.
Kitty, (Am. whaler).
Leonidas, formerly U. S. Dolphin, J. Malarin, master.
General Jackson, (Am. whaler).
Alert, Faucon, master.
Harriet, Blanchard Carter, master.
Don Quixote, John Meek, master, W. S. Hinckley, supercargo.
Leonor, H. D. Fitch, master.
Fakeja, R. Smith, master.
Ayacucho, Stephen Anderson, master.
Margarita, (Mex. schooner).
Volunteer, Shaw, master.
Charles Eyes, (Eng.) B. T. Chapman, master.
Santa Barbara, (Mex.) T. M. Robbins, master.
California, (Am. ship) Jas. Arthur, master.
Baikal, Livovich, master.

1834.

Facio Santo, Johnson, master.
Lagoda, J. Bradshaw, master.
Clarita, (Mex. bark).
Avon, (Am. brig) W. S. Hinckley, master.
Morelos, (Mex. sloop of war) Lieut. L. F. Manso, commander.
By Chance, Hiram Covell, master.
Pacifico, consigned to J. A. Aguirre.
Jóven Dorotea, Benito Machado, master.
Crusader, W. A. Richardson, master.
Leonor, H. D. Fitch, master.
Ayacucho, J. Wilson, master.
Europe, properly called Urup, D. Zarembo, master.
Loriot, Gorham H. Nye, master.
California, (Am. ship) Jas. Arthur, master.
Natalia, (Mex.) Juan Gomez, master. This was the brig Napoleon Bonaparte escaped on from Elba Feb. 28, 1815.

Polifemia, N. Rosenburg, master.
Llama, W. M. Neill, master.
Don Quixote, J. Meek, master.
Magruder, W. Taylor, master.
Refugio, (Mex.) built at San Pedro.
Bonanza, (Eng. schooner).
Margarita, (Mex.)
South Carolina, Joe Steel, master.
Peor es Nada, (Better than Nothing) Ch. Hubbard, master.
Feighton.
Pulga.
Steriton, Whaler.
Tansuero, L. Amist, master.
Wm. Sye, D. A. Riddle, master.
Marta, Tim W. Ridley, master.
Rosa, (Sardinian ship) Nic Bianchi, master.

1835.

Gange, H. Chaudiere, master.
Iolani, Jas. Rogers, master.
Catalina, R. Marshall, master.
Mariguita, Ag. Poncabaré, master.
Pilgrim, Ed. H. Faucon, master.
Loriot, Gorham H. Nye, master.
Facio, James Johnson, master; grounded at San Pedro, and was saved by the Pilgrim.
Ayacucho, James Scott, master.
Matador, consigned to John Parrott, Leon Bonnett, master.
Framner.
Alert, (Am. ship) Faucon, master.
Lagoda, Bradshaw, master.
Peor es Nada, built at Monterey, by Joaquin Gomez.
Garrafilia.
Clementine (Eng. brig) Jas. Hanley, master.
Liverpool packet, (Eng. whaler).
Diana, (Am. brig).
California, (Am. ship) Jas. Arthur, master.
Avon, (Am. brig) W. S. Hinckley, master.
Juan José, (Peru. brig) consigned to Miguel Pedrorena.
Bolivar, (Am. brig) Dominis, master.

Leonor, H. D. Fitch, master.
Margarita.
Polifemia, N. Rosenberg, master.
Washington, whaler.
Sitka, Basilio Wacodzy, master.
Maria Teresa, (Mex. brig).
Trinidad, (Mex. brig).
Rosa, Nic. Bianchi.
Primavera, (Mex. brig) Carlos Bane owner and master.

1836.

Hector, (Am.) Norton, master.
Leonidas, (Mex.) Gomez, master.
Loriot, (Am.) J. Bancroft, master.
Isabella (Haw.) N. Spear, owner.
Peor es Nada, Gerald Kuppertz, master.
Pilgrim, Faucon, master.
Convoy, otter hunter, (Am. brig) Bancroft, master.
Sitka, (Russian) Basil Wacoocky, master.
Peacock, (U. S. sloop of war) Stribling, commander; flag-ship of Commodore Kennedy.
Brixon, (Eng.)
California, (Am. ship) Arthur, master.
Rasselas, (Am. ship), Carter, master.
Europa, (Am. ship) Winkworth, master.
Ayacucho, (Eng. brig) Wilson, master.
Rosa.
Catalina, (Mex. brig) Snook, master.

1837.

City of Genoa, (Chilian) at Monterey in December.
Catalina, (Mex. brig) Snook, master.
Baikal, (Russian) Stephen Vouks, master.
Alciope, (Am. ship) Curtis Clap, captain.
Harvest, (Am.) A. Cash, master.
Loriot, otter hunter, (Am. brig) Bancroft, captain.
Diana, (Am. brig) W. S. Hinckley, captain.
Clementine, (Eng. brig) Handley, captain.
Indian, (Eng. whaler) Freeman, captain.
Nancy, (brig) Fautrel, captain.
Llama, (Eng.) W. Brotchie, captain.
Sarah, (Am. brig) Joseph Steel, captain.

Veloz Asturiano, (Ecuador) C. V. Gafan, captain.
Venus, (French corvette) Petit Thonars, captain.
Starling, (Eng. war vessel) Lieut. Kellert, commander.
Sulphur, (Eng. war vessel) Edward Belcher, commander.
Bolivar, (Am. brig) G. H. Nye, master.
Iolani (Haw. schooner) Paty, master.
Toward Castle, (Eng.) Emmett, master.
Pilgrim, (Am. brig) Faucon, master.
Crusader (Columbian) came from Callao.
Leonor, (Mex.) Chas. Wolter, captain.
Cadboro, (Eng.) W. Brotchie, captain.
California, (Mex. schooner) H. Paty, captain.
Kent, (Am. bark) Stickney, captain.
True Blue, (Haw.) Ragsdale, captain.
Delmira, (Ecuador) Vioget, captain, M. Pedrorena, supercargo.

1838.

Fearnaught, (Eng. brig) R. Dare, captain and owner.
Nereid, (Eng.) W. Brotchie, captain.
Kamamalu, (Am. brig) formerly Diana, W. S. Hinckley, captain.
Alert, (Am. ship) Penhallow, master.
Cadboro (Eng.)
Plymouth, (Am. bark) Paty, master.
Index, (Eng. bark) Scott, master.
Kent, (Am. bark) Stickney, master.
Ayacucho, (Eng. brig) Wilson, master.
Leonidas, (Mex. brig) Juan Malarin, master.
Bolivar, (Am. brig) Nye, master.
Flibberty Gibbett, (Eng. schooner) Rodgers, master.
Daniel O'Connell, (Columbian) Andrés Murcilla, master.
Sitka, (Russian) Wacoocky, master.
California, (Am. ship) Arthur, master.
Rasselas, (Am. ship) Barker, master.
Catalina, (Mex. brig) Snook, master.
Clarita, (Mex. bark) Chas. Wolter, master.
Vénus, (French man of war) October.
Commodore Rodgers, wrecked Nov. 19th.

Sulphur, (Eng. man of war) Belcher, commander, December.

1839.

Monsoon, (Am. ship) Vincent, master. Shaw, supercargo, June 2nd.
Ayacucho, (Eng. brig).
Corsair, (Am. brig) Wm. S. Hinckley, captain and supercargo, with full cargo of merchandise; brought the first gristmill for Spear, from Callao.
Index, (Eng. bark) Scott, master.
Clarita, (Mex. bark) Wolter, master.
Catalina, (Mex. bark) Snook, master.
Baikal, (Russian).
California, (Am. ship) Arther, master.
Bolivar, (Am. brig) Nye, master.
Clementine, (Eng. brig) Blinn, master. John A. Sutter arrived on this ship as passenger from Hawaiian Islands.
Artémise, (French frigate).
Maria, (whaler).
Elvantes, (Peruvian).
California, (Mex. schooner).
Sulphur, (Eng. man-of-war) Belcher, commander.
Juan José (Colombian brig) Duncan, master, Pedrorena, supercargo.

1840.

Daniel O'Connell, (Colombian).
U. S. sloop of war St. Louis, Forrest commander.
Alciope, (Am. ship) Clap, master.
Nikolai, (Russian) Kuprianof, master.
Joseph Peabody, (Am. brig) Dominis, master.
Union, (Am. schooner).
Lausanne, (Am.) Spalding, captain.
Juan José, (Colombian brig) Thos. Duncan, master.
Index, (Eng bark) Scott, master.
Ayacucho, (Eng. brig) Wilson, master.
California, (Mex.) T. M. Robbins, master.
Monsoon, (Am. ship) Geo. Vincent, master.
Elena, (Russian) S. Vallivade, captain.
Angelina, (French ship) N. Jena, captain.
Morse, (Am. schooner) Henry Paty, captain.
Bolivar, (Am. brig) Nye, captain.
Forager, (Eng.)
Alert, (Am. ship) Phelps, captain.
Don Quixote, (Am. bark) Paty, captain.

1841.

Jóven Carolina, Colombian brig) from Guayquil, Captain Miguelon, March—
Maryland, (Am. schooner).
Ayacucho, (Eng. brig) Wilson, master.
Juan Diego, (Mex. schooner).
Llama, (Am.) Jones, captain.
Orizaba. (Mex. transport).
Hamilton, (Am.) Hand, captain.
Cowlitz, (Eng. bark) Brotchie, captain.
Lausanne. (Am.) Steel, captain.
Yorktown, U. S. man-of-war, Aulick, commander.
Bolina, (Mex. schooner) trading on the coast.
Flying Fish, (Am.) Knox, master.
Lahaina, (Eng. whaler).
U. S. ship Vincennes, flag-ship of Commodore Wilkes exploring expedition.
U. S. brig Porpoise, Ringgold, commander, attached to the "Vincennes" (exploring expedition.) The sloop of war Peacock of the same expedition was lost on the Columbia River bar, and her officers and crew were rescued by the other vessels before mentioned.
Columbia, (Eng. bark) Humphries, master.
Julia Ann, (Am. schooner) from New York, Wm. A. Leidesdorff, master.
George Henry, (Am. bark) Stephen Smith, owner and master.
Eliza, French whaler, Malherbe, master.
Index, (Eng. bark) Scott, master.
Catalina, (Mex. brig) Chris. Hansen, master.
Chato, (Mex. brig) Machado, master.
Tasso, (Am. bark) Hastings, master.
Bolivar, (Am. brig) G. H. Nye, master.
California, (Mex. Government schooner) Cooper, master.

Don Quixote, (Am. bark) Paty, master.
Clarita, (Mex. bark) Wolter, master.
Alert, (Am. ship) Phelps, master.
Leonidas, (Mex. brig) Stokes, master.

1842.

California, (Mex. Government schooner) Cooper, master.
Primavera, (Mex. brig) A. Chienes, master.
Llama, (Am.) Jones, master.
Index, (Eng. bark) Wilson, master.
Esmeralda, (Mex. brig) Hugo Reid, master.
Fama, (Am. ship) Hoyer, master.
Constante, (Chilian ship) F. Unamano, master.
Bolivar, (Am. brig) G. H. Nye, master.
United States, Commodore Jones' flag-ship, Captain Armstrong commander.
Cyane, (U. S. ship of war) Stribling, commander.
Palatina, (Mex.) came from the Mexican Coast.
Relief, (U. S. store ship) J. Sterrett, commander.
Tasso, (Am. bark) Hastings, master.
Catalina, (Mex. brig) Hansen, master.
Alert, (Am. ship) Phelps, master.
Jenny, (Hamburg ship) John Mein, master.
Republicano, (Mex, brig) Machado, master.
Jóven Fanita, (Mex. schooner) Limantour, master.
Jóven Guipuzcoana, (Mex. bark) Snook, master.
Fernando, (Mex. brig).
Don Quixote, (Am. bark) Paty, master.
Clarita, (Mex. bark) Wolter, master.
Chato, (Mex. ship) brought General Micheltorena and landed him and his troops at San Diego.
Julia Ann, (Am. schooner) Leidesdorff, master.
Maryland, (Am. brig) Blinn, master.
Alex. Barclay, (German whaler).
Barnstable, (Am. ship) Hatch, master.
California, (Am. ship) Arthur, master.

1843.

George Henry, (Am. bark) from Peru, with Mrs. Smith, her mother and Manuel Torres, as passengers, Stephen Smith, master.
Fanny, Feby. 1st.
Don Quixote, (Am. bark) John Paty, master.
Vandalia, (Am. ship) Everett, master.

1844.

Vandalia, (Am. ship) Everett, master.
Constantine, (Chilian ship) Feb. 27th.
California, (Mex. Government schooner) Cooper, master.
Sterling, (Am. ship) Vincent, master, March 29th.
Julia, Dalton, master.
Juanita, (Eng. schooner) Wilson, Oct. 11.
Fama, (Am. ship) G. H. Nye, master.
Trinidad, Oct. 11.
Clarita, (Mex. bark) J. Vioget, master, Sept. 5th.
California, (Am. ship) Arther, master.

1845.

California, (Am. ship) Arther, master.
Jóven Guipuzcoana, (Mex. bark) Orbell, master.
Tasso, (Am. bark) Hastings, master.
Maria, Dec. 19th, F. W. Holstein, master.
Matador, Natchin, master, Oct. 30th.
Cowlitz, (Eng. bark) Brotchie, master.
Primavera, (Mex. brig) Chienes, master, May 23rd.
Julia, Dalton, master, Sept. 29th.
Star of the West, lost off Monterey Bay (already mentioned).
Argo. Whaler, Oct. 23rd.
Fama, (Am. ship) G. H. Nye, master, May 28th.
Vandalia, (Am. ship) Everett, master.
Juanita, (Eng. schooner) Wilson, master.
Clarita, (Mex. bark) J. Vioget, master.
Catalina, (Mex. brig).
Farisco, Yndarte, master, Oct. 2nd.

1846.

Don Quixote, (Haw. bark) John Paty, master, March 10th.

Euphemia, (Haw. brig) Thos. Russom, master, March 31st.
Moscow, (Am. bark) W. D. Phelps, master, March 10th.
Alfredo, March 2nd.
Angola, (Am. bark) S. Varney, master June 17th.
Fanny, whaler, Feby. 3rd.
Hannah, (Am. brig) March 25th. John F. Schander, master.
Maria Teresa, May 11th.
California, (Mex. Government schooner) Cooper, master.

1847.

Commodore Shubrick, (Am. schooner) July 6th.
T. H. Benton, (Am.) July 21st.
Anäis, (French) July 21st.
Providence, (Am. schooner) July 24th.
Euphemia, (Haw. brig) Russom, master, November.
Jóven Guipuzcoana, Mex. bark).
Barnstable, (Am. ship) Hall, master.
Mathilde, (Danish).
Mary Ann, (Haw. schooner).
Laura Ann, (Eng. schooner).
William, (Am. brig).
Eveline, (Am. brig).
Primavera, (Mex. schooner).
Malek Adhel, (Am. brig).
Maria Helena, (Chilian vessel).
Commodore Shubrick, (Am. schooner) November 13th.
Anita. (Am. bark).
Tonica, (Am. schooner).
Henry, (Am. brig).
Currency Lass, (French schooner).
Elizabeth, (Am. brig) Cheevers, master.
Angolo, (Am. bark) S. Varney, master.

1848.

Laura Ann, (Eng brig).
Euphemia, (Haw. brig) Russom, master.
Malek Adhel, (Am. brig).
Charles, (Am. ship) David Carter, supercargo.
Natalia, (Chilian bark) Juan Manuel Luco, supercargo and owner.
S. S. (Haw. schooner).
Lady Adams, (Am. brig) Coffin, supercargo. James Lick came in her as a passenger from Callao, Peru.
Eveline, (Am. brig).
Starling, (Haw.)
Anita, (Am. bark) Quarter-master's vessel.
Louisa, (Haw.)
La Flecha, (Spanish).
Adeaida, (Chilian).
Providence. (Am. schooner).
Mary, (Haw. schooner).

After the receipt of the list of arrivals of vessels from Mr. Forbes, it reminded me of revising my former estimate of the exports of hides and tallow from 1828 to 1847, a period of twenty years, of thirty-three vessels with cargoes in the aggregate of 1,068,000 hides. I have taken the year 1800, the time the missions were fairly started in the raising of live stock, down to their impoverishment; but the enterprise was continued by the haciendados in the only wealth of the department as already mentioned. I find in the list before me, that the vessels were numerous, which visited California in those primitive days. I have taken the years 1800 to 1847, and I find the arrivals were six hundred vessels of all sizes and nationalities. In my conjecture I take only two hundred of them, which is certainly a liberal deduction, and allow to each one thousand hides exported yearly. This will give a total of 9,400,000 hides for two hundred vessels for forty-seven years. The tallow that was exported during the same period would be two arrobas for each hide, giving a total of 18,800,000 arrobas of tallow. I think it perfectly accurate to estimate the exportation of hides and tallow for forty-seven years at 5,000,000 hides and 10,000,000 arrobas of tallow, a deduction of nearly one-half from the first calculation, but not the increase of cattle on 600,000, 900,000 and 1,200,000 head at different periods of the forty-seven years as will be observed. In other words, the cattle which were killed yearly as an income to the department, kept those animals from over-running the immense territory of over seven hundred miles of coast. Probably my first figures are the more correct of the two estimates.

The readers can judge for themselves which of the two will give the most knowledge concerning those articles which constituted the leading commerce in the primitive days of the Department of California.

Anterior to the year 1800 there were many cattle slaughtered by the missions; surely the hides and tallow as articles of commerce from time immemorial, were not thrown to the wild beasts of the forest to feed on, but were bought by merchants and traders and shipped to different parts of the world, as the memorandum of shipping on my table, will fully attest.

END.

BIBLIOGRAPHY

BIBLIOGRAPHY

FOR those wishing to acquire a more detailed knowledge of early California days the following books are recommended. Many have appeared in reprint, although the original edition is preferable. The dates given indicate the first edition.

    BANCROFT, HUBERT H., *History of the Pacific States.* 1882-91.

    BARRY AND PATTEN'S, *Men and Memories of San Francisco.* 1873.

    BRYANT, EDWIN, *What I saw in California.* 1848.

    CENTURY MAGAZINE, *Vols. XVII and XIX.*

    COLTON, WALTER, *Three Years in California.* 1850.

    COLTON, WALTER, *Deck and Port.* 1850.

    DANA, RICHARD H. JR., *Two Years before the Mast.* 1840.

    ELDREDGE, ZOETH, *The Beginnings of San Francisco.* 1912.

    FRÉMONT, JOHN C., *Memoir of my Life.* 1887.

    KOTZEBUE, OTTO VON, *New Voyage Around the World.* 1821.

    PALÓU, *Life of Junípero Serra.* 1787.

    REVERE, JOSEPH WARREN, *A Tour of Duty.* 1849

    ROBINSON, ALFRED, *Life in California.* 1846.

    SHERMAN, WM. T., *Memoirs.* 1875.

    SOULÉ, FRANK ET AL., *Annals of San Francisco.* 1855.

    TAYLOR, BAYARD, *El Dorado.* 1850.

    WISE, LIEUT. HENRY A., *Los Gringos.* 1849.

    The Life of Junípero Serra may be read in the English translation by George Wharton James.

INDEX

INDEX

A

Ábrego, José, 17.
Abell, Alex. G., 293.
"Admittance" American Ship, 106
Aguardiente, 121.
Aguirre, José Antonio, 3, 47, 71, 248.
Alameda County Seats, 330.
Alcaldes, 84, 86, 299.
"Alciope" American Ship, 172.
"Alert" American Ship, 3, 17.
Alta California, newspaper, 217.
Alvarado, Doña Guadalupe, 170.
Alvarado, Gov. Juan B., 16, 28, 85, 114, 117, 126, 127, 128, 133, 149, 158, 172, 175.
Amador, José M., 33.
Alviso, Ygnacio, 33.
American Flag raised, 267.
American leanings of Californians, 47.
American Occupation of 1842, 111.
American Occupation of 1846, 212.
Ameste, José, 17.
Amusements, see California Amusements.
Annexation to United States, 141.
de Anza, Juan B., xx
Argüello, Don Luis, 181.
Argüello, Santiago, 34.
Argüello, Don Santiaguito E., 251, 279.
Arrellanes, Don Teodoro, 124.
Arrest of Americans, 46, 51, 139.
Arther, Captain James, 3.
Asaderas, 36.
"Ayacucho" British Brig, 3, 12, 17, 27.

B

Baker, Colonel, 34.
Bale, Dr. Edward T., 16, 137.
Bancroft, Captain James, 102, 103.
Bandini, Juan, 34, 172, 278.
Barry & Patten's, 222.
Bartlett, Lieutenant Washington A., 75, 268, 275, 299.
Barter trade, 5.
Battle of Los Angeles 1838, 16. See also Alvarado and Carrillo.
Battle of San Fernando 1838, 129.
Battle of San Gabriel River, 282.
Battle of San Pasqual, 280.
Bay of San Francisco, 26, 54, 100.
Beach Grants at Yerba Buena, 175.
Beale, Lieutenant, 279, 281.

Bears, 224, 303-4. See also Grizzly Bears.
Beaver skins, 5, 164.
Beef supplies for ships, 257.
Belden, Josiah, 265, 292.
Bell, Alexander, 128.
Belmont, 33.
Benicia, 316.
Bennett, Mrs., 195.
Benton, Senator Thomas H., xxiv.
Berry, James, 172.
Bibliography, 411.
Biddle, Commodore, 212.
Bidwell, John, 133.
Bigler, John, 205, 231.
Black, James, 4.
"Blossom" H. M. S., 181.
Blucher Rancho, 109.
Bodega, 22.
"Bolivar Liberator" American Brig, 3.
Bonnycastle affair, 244.
Boston Ships, 105, 107, 153.
Branch, Francis, 51, 123.
Brannan, Samuel, 213, 214-5-6-7, 307, 311.
Briones, Doña Encarnacion, 196.
Briones, Felipe, 32, 63.
Briones, Doña Guadalupe de Miramonte, 42.
Briones, Juana, 12.
British Men-of-war, supplies for, 98.
"Brooklyn" American Ship, 307.
Bryant, Edward R., 276.
Bryant and Sturgis, 17, 244, 248.
Buckalew Point, 257.
Buri-buri Rancho, 6, 223, 299.
Burke, Michael, 123.
Burnett, Peter H., 230.
Burton, Lewis T., 51, 123.

C

Cabestros, 39.
"California" American Ship, 3, 17, 24, 27.
California Amusements, 76, 79, 80, 92-3, 195.
California Battalion, 276.
California, Characteristics, 67, 189.
California Customs, 60, 61, 64, 65, 66-7-8-9, 72-3-4-5, 83, 143, 182-3, 195, 206, 208, 295.
California Diet, 41, 42.
"California" Mexican Schooner, 17, 102, 188.
California Missions, 204, 232, See also Missions.
California Pioneers, Society of, 227.

417

California Revolt, 270.
California Star (newspaper) 216.
"California" Steamer, 309.
California, The name, xix-xx.
California Wine, 6, 117, 120-1-2, 287, 298.
California Women, 61.
Californian, The (newspaper), 216.
Calistoga, 216.
Camilo, Indian Chief, 135.
Campbell, Alex. Sr., 214.
Caponeras, 35.
Carrillo, Carlos, 16, 88.
Carrillo, Francisca Benicia, 4.
Carrillo, José Antonio, 16, 128.
Carrillo, José Ramon, 302, 303.
Carrillo, Maria Ygnacia, 32.
Carson, "Kit," xxvi.
Carter, Captain Joseph O., 8.
Castle Point, 4.
Castro family, 32.
Castro, General José, 16, 46, 47, 87, 126, 130, 142.
Castro, Manuel, 17, 46, 134, 275, 320.
Castro, Guillermo, 33.
Castro, Victor, 218.
"Catalina" Mexican Brig, 17.
Cattle Raising, 31-2, 74, 135, 138, 158, 241, 322-3-4.
Célis, Eulogio de, 17.
Central Wharf 1849, 231.
Chinese in California, 338, See also Appendix.
Choate, Rufus, 227.
Cibrian, Doña Carmel, 299.
"Clarion" American Schooner, 188.
"Clarita" Mexican Bark, 17.
Clark, William S., 28.
Claxton, Commodore, 47.
Clay, Henry, 277.
"Clementine" British Brigantine, 18.
"Collingwood" H. M. S., 267-8.
Communicating through U. S. Consuls, 296.
Condition of San Francisco Streets, 316.
"Congress" U. S. S., 112, 269.
Conquest of California, 279, 284.
"Conroy" American Brig, 102.
Constitutional Convention 1849, 88-9, 230, 250.
Cooper, Captain John B. R., 2, 16, 18, 51, 163.
Cordua, Theodore, 189.
"Corsair," 24, 150, 176.
Cortéz, Hernando, xix.
Council of War, Monterey 1846, 267.
"Courier" American Ship, 242.
"Cowlitz" Hudson's Bay Co's vessel, 91.
Culverwell's Account of American Occupation 1842, 111.
Custom House built by Davis, 315.
"Cyane" U. S. S., 111.
"Cybele" American Brig, 324.

D

Dana, William G., 51, 123.
"Daniel O'Connell" British Ship, 176.
Davis, Robert G., 18, 104.
Davis, Captain William H., 199.
Davis, William Heath, viii, 15, 16, 18, 20, 104, 110, 117, 128, 132, 156, 178, 185, 189, 210, 225, 232, 242, 250, 261, 268, 272, 274, 284-5, 288, 289, 293-4, 309, 314, 333-4-5.
"Delmira" Ecuadorian Brig, 17.
Den, Dr. Nicholas A., 123.
"Diamond" Ship, 29.
Diaz, Benito, 156.
Diaz, Manuel, 17.
Diego, Bishop García, 223.
Diezmo, 35.
Dominguez, Manuel, 271.
"Don Quixote" American Bark, 3, 16, 17, 71, 73, 104-5, 109, 112, 131, 133, 145, 148, 191, 202, 260, 296-7.
Donohue, Kelly & Co., 214.
Douglas, Dr., 206-7.
Drought of 1831, 56.
Dupont, Captain Samuel F., 267.
Dye, Job, 133.

E

"Eagle" American Brig, 199, 338.
Early American Settlers, 123.
Earthquake of 1838, 16, 18.
Eating Contest, 258.
Elk, 31, 324.
Elwell, Robert, 123.
English designs on California, 99.
Esplandián, Las Sergas de, xix.
Esquimaux hunters, 22.
Estrada, Don José Ramon, 46.
Estudillo, José Joaquin, 12, 33, 71, 113, 224, 292.
Estudillo, Señorita Maria de Jesus, 75, 113.
"Euphemia" British Brig, 240, 260, 262-3, 265, 273, 284, 293, 305-6.
Exploring Expedition (Brit.) 1839, 103.

F

Faucon, Captain E. F., 243.
"Fama" American Ship, 24, 184.
Fanega (definition), 136.
Fear of British, 268.
"Fearnaught" Brig, 174.
Fire of 1851, 227.
Fire Company Organized, 228.
First California Bridge, 150.
First U. S. Customs House, 153.
First Steamer on Bay of San Francisco, 180.
First Gold Dust in Trade, 308.
First Military Company, 225.
First multi-storied brick building, 315.
First Steamer from U. S. reaches San Francisco, 308.
Fish industry, 77, 162.
Fitch, Henry D., 33, 109.
Flood of 1839-40 in Sacramento Valley, 55.
Flour industry, 136.
Flower Gardens, 213.
Flugge, Charles W., 130, 189.
Forbes, James Alexander, 80, 236, 268.
Forced Military Service, 161.
Foreigners at Monterey 1838, 16.

Fortifications at Black Point, 181.
Fort Ross, 22.
Fourth of July Celebrations, 23, 27.
Franciscan Order, 57. See also under Missions.
Frémont, Captain John Charles, xxv, 14, 230, 276-7, 284, 291.
Fresada, 41.
Fresh water spring at Yerba Buena, 154.
Fuller, John Casimiro, 185.

G

Gafia, Doña Luisa Avila de, 208.
Gale, William G., 27, 252.
"George Henry" American Bark, 109.
Gillespie, Lieutenant Archibald H., xxvii.
Gillespie, Mr. and Mrs. C. V., 311.
Goat Island, 184.
Gold, 159, 165-6, 222, 308-9, 320, 328.
Gomez, Captain Manuel, 118.
Gonzalez, Father José Maria de Jesus, 58.
Gonzalez, Rafael, 17, 141.
Government of California, 84.
Graham, Isaac, xxiv, 47.
Green, Talbot H., 211, 226.
Grimes, Captain Eliab, 118, 156, 157, 158, 185, 264.
Grimes, E. & H., 260, 289.
Grist Mills, 137, 176.
Grizzly Bears, 80.
de la Guerra, Don José, 88, 239.
de la Guerra, Pablo, 17, 88, 262.
Guerrero, Francisco, 23, 50, 151-2, 188.
Gulnac, William, 176.

H

Hacendados, 221. Also see Appendix.
Halleck, Captain Henry W., 29.
de Haro, Francisco, 23, 50.
de Haro, Doña Josefa, 50.
"Harriet Blanchard" American Schooner, 8.
Hartnell, William E. P., 2, 16, 88.
Hawes, Horace, 311.
Hensley, Major Samuel J., 251, 279.
Hepburn, H. P., 226.
"Hibernia" whaleship, 156.
Hides and Tallow, 8, 31, 35, 153-4, 204, 246, 255, 332.
Hill, Daniel, 51, 123.
Hinckley, William Sturgis, 3, 16, 26, 146, 149-50-1, 176.
Hoeppner, Andres, 258.
Holidays observed in California, 197.
Holmes, Oliver Wendall, 101.
Honesty, 83.
Honolulu, 104, 294.
Horsemanship, 82.
Horse raising, 43-4-5, 135, 143.
"Hortensia" American Bark, 15, 320.
Howard, W. D. M., 24, 186, 187, 210-1-2, 213, 225, 228, 229, 265, 306.
"Hounds" The, 310-1.
Household arrangements, 60.
Hunting deer in Yerba Buena, 177.
Huntington, Hopkins, Crocker, Stanford, 216.

Hudson's Bay Company, 28, 80, 91.
Hyde, George, 299-300-1-2.

I

Illegitimate Children, 143.
Indians, 6, 7, 63, 169, 172, 208, 237.
Immigration of Women, 160.
Injustice of U. S. toward Californians, 190.
Intermarriage, 125.
"Isabel" Mexican Schooner, 18.

J

Jimeno, Manuel, 89.
Jimeno, Dona Augusta, 89.
Jones, U. S. Consul J. C., 1, 2.
Jones, Commodore Thomas Ap Catesby, 71, 111-2-3, 115-6, 118-9, 316, 333.
"Jóven Carolina" Columbian Schooner, 178.
"Jóven Guipuzcoana" Mexican Bark, 47, 112-3, 306-7.
Juarez, Cayetano, 32.
"Julia Ann" American Schooner, 102, 104.
Junta Departmental, 84.
Jurupa Rancho, 172, See also under Ranchos.

K

Kearny, General Stephen Watts, 75, 230, 279, 281, 285, 290, 302.
"Kent" American Bark, 175.
"Kent Hall," 175, 211.
Kinlock, George, 2, 16.
King, Thomas Butler, 317.
Kostromitinoff, Pedro, 22.

L

"Lagoda" American Ship, 27.
Laguna Salada, 150.
Land Otter and Beaver, 164, 205, 222.
Larkin, Thomas Oliver, 7, 16, 28, 29, 47, 114, 117, 141, 229, 275.
Lassen, Peter, 178.
Leavenworth, T. M., 302.
Leese, Jacob Primer, 12, 16, 23, 25-6, 28, 29, 30, 91, 299-300.
Leese, Spear and Hinckley, 26.
Leidesdorff Estate, 225.
Leidesdorff, William A., 213.
"Leon" French Ship, 143.
"Leonidas" Mexican Brig, 3.
Limantour, José, Y., 144-5.
Lippitt, F. J., 29.
List of Ships at Yerba Buena July 4, 1837, 27.
Livermore, Obadiah, 218.
Livermore, Robert, 33.
Los Angeles, 11, 25, 120, 127, 146, 284.
"Louisa" American Bark, 154.
Lugo Antonio Maria, 146.

M

McAllister, Hall, 311.
McDougal, John, 230.
McKinley, James, 109, 130.
McLane, Louis, 292.

McLoughlin, Governor of Hudson's Bay Co., 91.
"Magnolia" whaleship, 156.
Malarin, Captain Juan, 3, 17.
Manteca, 35.
Mare Island, 31.
Marsh, Dr. John, xxiii, 128, 133.
Martinez, José, 63, 66, 68, 70, 75, 304.
Martinez, Maria Antonia, 10.
Martinez, Doña Rafaela, 68.
Martinez, Captain Ygnacio, 4, 9, 20, 32, 63, 201.
Mason, Colonel Richard B., 230, 301.
Matanza, 40, 64.
Maxwell, Dr. R. F., 285.
Mellus, Frank, 245, 247.
Mellus, George, 247.
Mellus, Henry, 24, 72, 106, 159, 226, 227, 243-4.
Mellus & Howard, 211, 245.
Meek, Captain John, 3, 201.
Menlo Park, 33.
Mercado, Father, 165.
"Merienda," 139, 187.
Merritt, Ezekiel, xxviii.
Mervine, Captain William, 267, 269, 271.
Mesa, Juan Prado, 64, 233.
Metate, 177.
Mexican Customs Duties, 105, 107, 263.
Mexican Customs House, 153-4.
Mexican Jealousy of U. S., 47.
Mexican Laws, 28, 230.
Mexican neglect of California, 291.
Mexican Priests, 57.
Mexican Revenue Cutter Service, 102.
Mexican torture, 171.
Micheltorena, Governor Manuel, 34, 85, 120, 126, 130, 132-3-4.
E. Mickle & Company, 214.
Military Exemptions, 160.
Miramontes, Candelario, 7.
Mission activities, 252.
Mission blankets, 7.
Mission Dolores, 6, 80, 232.
Mission Indians, 19, 253.
Mission Life, 200.
Mission San Francisco de Asis, 6.
Mission San Gabriel, 11, 25.
Mission San José, 6, 33, 43.
Mission San Juan Capistrano, 134.
Mission San Luis Rey, 147.
Mission San Rafael, 4, 31.
Mission Santa Clara, 6, 7, 33, 56.
Mission Street, 213.
Missions, 58.
de Mofras, Eugene Duflot, 52, 98.
Money in California, 159.
Monica, Richardson's Indian, 54, 100.
"Monsoon" American Ship, 18.
Monterey, 2, 16, 112, 114-5.
Montgomery, Captain John B., 268, 272-3.
Moraga, Joaquin, 32.
Munras, Estevan, 17.
Muro, Father, 165.
Murphy, Timothy, 4, 155.

N

Nacional Rancho Suscol, 32.
Native Californians, 146.
Natoma Street, 227.
"Nicholas" Mexican schooner, 18, 242.
Noriega y de la Guerra, Captain, 239, 240.
Norris, Samuel, 29.
Norris Ranch, 158.
Norton, Charles E., 215.
Norton, Myron, 311.
Nye, Captain, G. H., 3.
"Nymph" American schooner, 24.

O

Oakland, 325.
Occupation of Monterey by Sloat, 266.
O'Farrell, Jasper, 155. See also Appendix.
"Ohio" U. S. S., 309-10.
Olompali Rancho, 135.
Orange Culture, 121.
Orejanos, 40.
"Orion" British whaleship, 9.
Osborn and Brannan, 214.
Osio, Antonio M., 17.
Otter Hunting, 5, 123, 200, 203, 205-6, 252.
Ox-Carts, 10.

P

Pacheco, Dolores, 33.
Pacheco, Francisco, 17.
Pacheco, Governor, 255.
Pacheco, Mariano, 89.
Pacheco, Doña Ramona, 89.
Padilla, Juan, 150.
Padre Quijas, 6, 7.
Palmer, Cook & Co., 317.
Palo Alto, The, 223.
Palos Verdes Rancho, 224.
Panoche, 174.
Parada, 39.
Park, Thomas B., 17, 243.
Paty, Henry, 254.
Paty, Captain John, 109, 188, 191-2-3.
Paty, John Henry, 194.
Paty, McKinley & Co., 72, 109, 144, 156.
Pratt, O. C., 214.
Parrott, John, 162-3, 312.
"Peacock" U. S. sloop-of-war, 95.
Peck, Sherman, 2, 204.
de Pedrorena, Miguel, 17, 250, 279.
Penhallow, Captain D. P., 17.
Peralta, Domingo, 44, 55, 178.
Peralta, Doña Encarnacion, 304.
Peralta, Luis, 32.
Peralta, Vicente, 82, 325, 326.
Peralta, Ygnacio, 68.
Perry, John, 174-5.
Phelps, Captain William D., 197-8.
Pickett, C. E., 275.
Pico, Andres, 127, 279-80.
Pico, Jesus "Totoi," 291.
Pico, Pio, 127, 131, 230.
Pinto, Rafael, 17.

INDEX

Poett, Dr., 312.
"Polin" spring, 55.
Polk, President James K., xxv.
Population of California, 52, 230.
Population of San Francisco, 74.
"Porpoise" U. S. S., 95.
Portsmouth Square, 7.
"Portsmouth" U. S. S., 212.
Powers of Governor, 85.
Powers and duties of Prefect, 84.
Presidio of San Francisco, 4.
Prudon, Victor, 141.
Pursers' Bills, 269.

R

Rae, William G., 28, 91-2, 94, 157.
Rancho Agua Caliente, 125.
Rancho El Chino, 219.
Rancho Huichica, 28.
Rancho Jesus Maria, 169.
Rancho Jurupa, 279.
Rancho Nacional Suscol, 138.
Rancho Nipomo, 292.
Rancho Petaluma, 135.
Rancho Pinole, 32.
Rancho Boca de la Cañada del Pinole, 32.
Rancho Las Pulgas, 33.
Rancho San Antonio, 32.
Rancho San Jacinto Nuevo, 249.
Rancho San Joaquin, 323.
Rancho San Leandro, 32, 327.
Rancho San Lorenzo Bajo, 33.
Rancho San Miguel, 299.
Rancho Santa Ana, 172, 286.
Rancho Santa Anita, 143.
Rancho Santa Margarita, 285.
Rancho Santa Rosa, 32, 135.
Rancho Sotoyome, 33.
Rancho Temblec, 135.
Rancho Tia Juana, 168.
Rancho rodeos, 38.
Ranchos, owners, etc., see Appendix.
Read, John, 4.
Reading, P. B., 128, 133, 205.
Reata, 238.
Redwood City, 33, 233.
Refugio, 203.
"Rhone" American Ship, 318.
Reid, Hugo, 144.
Revolt of Californians, 224.
Revolution against Governor Chico, 134.
Revolution of 1844, 126-7-8-9, 130.
Reynolds, Stephen, 2, 260.
Richardson, Captain William A., 4, 9, 12, 13, 14, 15, 42, 101, 140, 173, 269, 274.
Richardson, Mariana, 10, 14.
Ridley, Robert, 93, 212, 265, 300.
Riley, General Bennet, 230.
Robbins, Thomas W., 123-4.
Robinson, Alfred, 3, 24, 27, 89, 243-44, 310.
"Rochelle," American Bark, 319.
Rodriguez, Jacinto, 17.
Rotcheff, Alexander, 22, 53, 96.
"Rover," American schooner, 18.
Royce, Professor Josiah, xxvii.
Russell, Colonel William H., 270, 276, 288.
Russian American Fur Company, 22, 31.
Russian hunters, 22.
Russom, Captain Thomas, 260.

S

Sacramento, 19, 216.
Sacramento River, 5.
Sacramento Valley, 166.
Saddles, 65-6.
Salmon fishery, 162.
Sandwich Islands, 2.
Santa Barbara, 2.
Santa Barbara Channel Islands, 109.
San Diego, 2, 15, 34, 146, 170, 272, 333-4.
San Francisco, 3, 11, 75.
San Francisco Streets, 270.
San Joaquin River, 5.
San José, 230.
San Leandro, 71.
San Luis Obispo, 2.
San Nicolas Island, 109.
San Pasqual, 279.
San Pedro, 2, 119.
Sanchez, José, 6.
Sanchez, Don José de la Cruz, 146.
Sanchez, Don Juan, 133.
Saunders, John H., 122.
Saucelito Ranch, 4, 12.
"Savannah" U. S. S., 271.
Saw Mill, 109.
Scott, James (Diego), 3, 27.
Sea Otter, 4, 22, 102.
Sebo, 35, See also Hides and Tallow.
Sectionalism, 128.
"Senator," Sacramento River steamer, 313.
Sepúlveda, Don Dolores, 42.
Sepúlveda family, 146.
"Seringapatam," East India Company's Ship, 181.
Serra, Junípero, xx.
Seymour, Admiral, 268.
Shakespearean performance, 226.
Shaw, Captain Thomas, 2, 27, 232, 242.
Sheep, 135.
Ship Arrivals Monterey 1839, 24.
Ship Arrivals at Yerba Buena and Monterey before 1847, Appendix.
Ship building, 10.
Ship Captains 1838, 17.
Shipping, San Francisco Bay 1849, 231.
Shoemaking, 257.
Sill, Daniel, 176-7.
Silva, Don Mariano, 115.
Simmons, Hutchinson & Co., 156.
Sitka, Alaska, 1, 11.
Sloat, Commodore John Drake, 230, 266.
Smuggling, 156, 176.
Smith, Charles, 1.
Smith, Captain James, 156.
Smith, Jedediah, xxii.
Smith, William M., 180.
Snook, Captain Joseph, 17, 47, 279.

Soap and Candles, 257.
Soberanes, Mariano, 17.
Sola, Governor Pablo Vicente de, 9, 118.
Solano, Francisco, Chief, 135.
Soto, Francisco, 33.
South American Insurgents, 118.
Southworth, Eli, 253-4.
Spanish Priests, 57.
Sparks, Isaac J., 51, 205.
Spear, Nathan, 2, 12, 16, 18, 26, 50, 52, 76, 87, 96, 97, 135, 136-7, 157, 162, 175, 249, 265.
Spence, David, 2, 16, 114.
Squatters, 237, 326, 328.
Stanford, Leland, 216.
Stanislaus, Chief, 233, 236.
Starkey, Janion & Co., 260.
Star Spangled Banner at Los Angeles, 284.
"Star of the West," British Brig, 162.
Steam ferry San Francisco Bay, 218.
Stearns, Abel, 34, 50, 130, 218, 221, 287.
Steel, Captain, 257.
Stetson, Edward L., 178.
Stevenson, Colonel Jonathan Drake, 317. See also Appendix.
"St. Louis," U. S. S., 47.
Stock raising, 17, 28.
Stockton, Commodore Robert F., 212, 230, 251, 269-70, 272, 278, 280-81, 282, 283-4, 289.
Stokes, James, 16.
Strawberries (wild), 187.
Sub-prefects, 84.
Sugar Cane, 285.
Supercargoes, 58.
Survey of San Francisco by O'Farrell, 155.
Sutter, Captain John A., 19, 20, 22, 53, 109, 128, 131, 166, 221-22.
Sutter's Mill, Gold at, 166.
Swasey, William F., 263. See also inside back cover.

T

Tallow, 35. See also under Hides and Tallow.
"Tasso," American Bark, 145.
"Tava," Mexican Schooner, 253.
Teal, Hiram, 163-4.
Tennent, Dr. Samuel J., 69.
Temescals, 34, 80.
Teschemacher, H. F., 244.
Thompson, Captain A. B., 3, 24, 123, 172, 253.
Thompson's Cove, 257.
Titcomb, Rufus, 163.
de la Torres, Joaquin, 275.
Torres, Manuel, 10.
Trading Ships in 1838, 17.
Traveling in California, 59.
Turkey shooting, 199.
"Two Years before the Mast," 17.

U

United States and California, 53.
"United States," U. S. S., 111, 118.
United States vessels San Francisco February 1849, 309.

V

Vallejo, José Antonio, 17.
Vallejo, José Jesus, 33, 233.
Vallejo, General Mariano Guadalupe, 4, 31, 47, 53, 87-8, 95, 128, 135-6, 138, 140-1, 234, 336-7.
Vallejo, Salvador, 32, 236.
Vallejo, Rosalia, 30.
Valley of Hunger, 20.
Vaqueros, 38.
Vassault, Ferdinand, 215.
Vegetables for whaleships, 154.
Venture in Chinese goods, 318.
Venture in flour, 306.
Vigilantes of 1856, 338.
Vignes, Louis or Luis, 120, 122.
"Vincennes," U. S. S., 95, 101.
Vincent, George, 242.
Vioget, John J. (Jean Jacques), 17, 92, 250, 258-9.
"Volunteer," American Bark, 2, 154, 177.

W

War vessels at San Diego in 1846, 272.
Ward, J. C., 308-9.
Warner's Ranch, 125.
Warner, John J., 125.
Warren, Major William, 16, 18.
Watchman's Point, Yerba Buena, 212.
Watson, Captain Harry B., 212, 268.
Watson, James, 2, 16.
Weed, John, 104.
Westgate, Frank, 178.
West, Marcus, 32.
Whaleships, 154, 156.
Wheat, 22, 136.
Wheeled Vehicles, 60.
Wilkes, Commodore Charles, 95, 99.
Wild game, 77.
Wild horses, 35.
Wild Indians, 34.
Williams, (Don Julian), Isaac, 220.
Wilson, Captain John, 3, 12, 90.
Wine industry, 6, 120-1-2.
Wise, Lieutenant Henry Augustus, 10.
Wolter, Captain, 17.
Wood, Captain George, 1.
Wolfskill, William, 194.
Workman and Rowland, xxiv.

Y

Yale, Gregory, 29.
Ybarra massacre, 166-7, 170.
Yerba Buena Cove, 3, 12.
Yerba Buena, 75, 172.
Yerba Buena (Goat) Island, 76.
Yorba, Doña Vicenta, 286.
Yoscolo, 233, 235.
Yount, George, 205.

Z

Zalvidea, Father José Maria, 147.
Zapaje, Chief, 321.

www.ingramcontent.com/pod-product-compliance
Lightning Source LLC
Chambersburg PA
CBHW081201170426
43197CB00018B/2888